MOON HANDBOOKS

JAMAICA

OLIVER HILL

JAMAICA

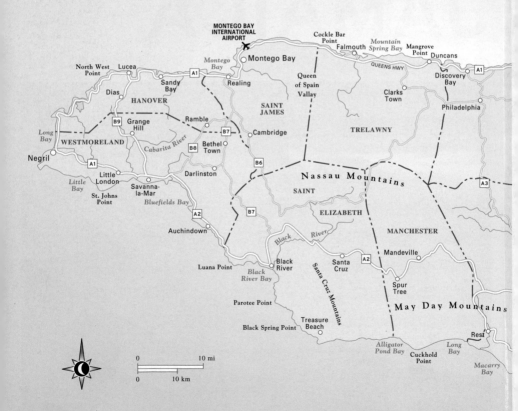

Caribbean Sea

MONTEGO BAY
INTERNATIONAL
AIRPORT

Montego Bay
Bay

Montego Bay

North West
Point
Lucea

Sandy
Bay

Dias

Realing

HANOVER

Ramble

B9
Grange
Hill

Long
Bay

WESTMORELAND

Cabarita River

B8
Bethel
Town

Negril

A1

Little
London

Darlinston

Little
Bay

Savanna-
la-Mar

St. Johns
Point

Bluefields Bay

A2

Auchindown

Luana Point

Parotee Point

Black Spring Point

Cockle Bar
Point
Falmouth

Mountain
Spring Bay
Mangrove
Point
Duncans

QUEENS HWY

A1

Queen
of Spain
Valley

Discovery
Bay

Clarks
Town

SAINT
JAMES

TRELAWNY

Philadelphia

Cambridge

B7

B6

Nassau Mountains

A3

SAINT

B7

ELIZABETH

MANCHESTER

Black

River

Santa
Cruz

A2

Mandeville

Black
River

Black
River Bay

Santa Cruz Mountains

Spur
Tree

May Day Mountains

Treasure
Beach

Rest

Alligator
Pond Bay
Cuckhold
Point

Long
Bay

Macarry
Bay

0   10 mi

0   10 km

© AVALON TRAVEL

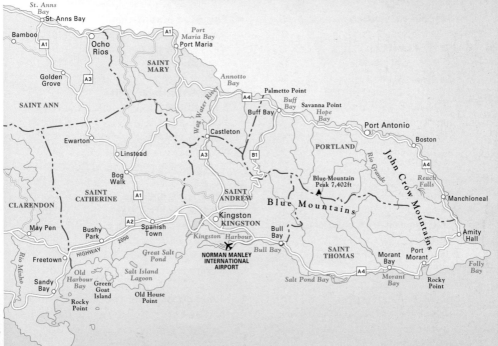

Contents

Discover Jamaica

It's hard to argue with the assertion Jamaicans make that theirs is a blessed island. Little beats simple luxuries like picking a fresh mango from a tree for breakfast, bathing in a crystal clear waterfall, or sitting in the shade to watch the sun climb the sky while hummingbirds flit about on a gentle breeze heavy with the scent of tropical flowers. It's no wonder that for more than a century visitors have come to Jamaica to escape cold northern winters and luxuriate in the island's tropical climate and calm Caribbean waters. Its lush forests and varied topography are dotted with spectacular natural features – caves, white-sand beaches, swimming holes, waterfalls, and majestic mountain peaks – with plenty for adventure seekers to explore. Quaint villages sprinkle the countryside, and Kingston, the country's bustling urban center, is the heart of Jamaica's vibrant culture and spirit.

Stay at one of Jamaica's many luxury resorts and you're sure to be pampered and indulged to no end. Hot stone massages, candlelit gourmet dinners, soft reggae music, and lapping waves are just the beginning. In fact, many of the island's resorts have perfected the art of luxury to such a degree that it's entirely possible to miss the depth and color of the country's culture beyond the resort walls. Outside the hotel gates is where you will find the ongoing evolution of a nation barely 50

years old, where preachers – religious, musical, and political – lend vibrancy to everyday life.

Ironically, it wasn't the tropical climate or endless natural beauty that brought worldwide attention to Jamaica in the 20th century. It was a young man growing up with the odds stacked against him in the ghetto of Trench Town, who managed to make his truthful message heard above the din of political violence and clashing Cold War ideologies of the 1970s. Robert Nesta Marley, along with band members Peter McIntosh and Bunny Livingston, became a beacon of hope, not just for disenfranchised Jamaicans, but for sufferers the world over. Today, countless singers keep Marley's legacy alive and fuel Jamaica's music industry, the most prolific on the planet.

Whether you're seeking to explore the country's rich history, soak in the sunshine and the clear, warm waters of the Caribbean, or savor the prized Blue Mountain Coffee, you'll come to understand what makes this island so exceptional. Most importantly, you'll find the Jamaican people are warm and charismatic, eager to share the best their island has to offer.

Planning Your Trip

► WHERE TO GO

KINGSTON

Metropolitan Kingston is an energetic city with remarkable restaurants, a pulsating nightlife, and many of Jamaica's cultural and historical treasures. There's no sugarcoating the juxtaposition of poverty and wealth, but their coexistence inspires a prolific music industry and vibrant visual arts scene. Beaches, waterfalls, and cool mountains are just a short drive away. In neighboring St. Catherine, fishing villages in Hellshire and Old Harbour Bay make great day-trip destinations and offer some of Jamaica's freshest seafood.

THE BLUE MOUNTAINS

Straddling the parishes of St. Andrew, St. Mary, Portland, and St. Thomas, the Blue Mountains produce some of the world's finest coffee and afford visitors spectacular views, cool air, and the best hiking and bird-watching in Jamaica. There are two main routes up the southern slopes leading to either Buff Bay on the North Coast via Irish Town, or Blue Mountain Peak via Mavis Bank.

PORT ANTONIO AND THE EAST COAST

Port Antonio, Portland's parish capital and the biggest town in the east, has an old-world charm that lingers in luxurious villas and hilltop resorts. Despite Portland's claim as the first Caribbean tourist destination, it has, for better or worse, been excluded from the massive development projects of the past 50 years, and the area's natural beauty remains its principal draw. Hiking trips to lush forests, waterfalls, and challenging peaks

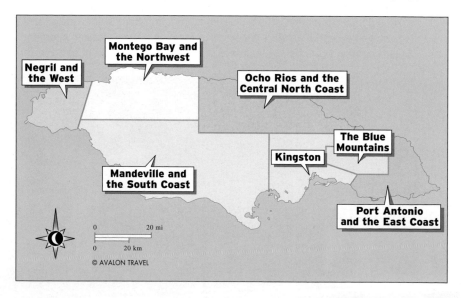

Chukka Caribbean operates zip line tours over Y.S. Falls along the South Coast.

in the interior can complement lazy beach days along the coast.

OCHO RIOS AND THE CENTRAL NORTH COAST

Throngs of tourists disembark cruise ships each day in Ocho Rios, and many head to Jamaica's most popular tourist destination, Dunn's River Falls. A maze of duty-free stores and other shops vie for customers on the western side of town, while world-class hotels and villas stretch along the water's edge. Contrasting the hustle and bustle of Ocho Rios, St. Mary is laid back, with several plantation tours offered among its hills, mountains, and quiet fishing villages.

MONTEGO BAY AND THE NORTHWEST

Montego Bay (known as Mobay) is Jamaica's Vibes City, famous for its rebellious past and vibrant present. Beaches and plantation tours are popular attractions, and hotels book up several times throughout the year for lively festivals and events. Rivers along the eastern and western borders offer rafting, and Mobay has an active yacht club with a lively social calendar. Neighboring Trelawny encompasses a rugged inland terrain known as Cockpit Country, riddled with caves and underground rivers.

NEGRIL AND THE WEST

Jamaica's westernmost parish has the country's most popular beach resort town, Negril. Once a quiet fishing village, Negril is known as the capital of casual, where recreational activities like water sports and cliff jumping complement the inactivity of relaxing in the sun. A wetlands area inland from the beach is backed by gentle hills suitable for hiking and bird-watching.

MANDEVILLE AND THE SOUTH COAST

The South Coast comprises Jamaica's off-the-beaten-track region, where waterfalls, crocodile-infested wetlands, and seafood are the main attractions. Treasure Beach, a string of bays and fishing villages, is Jamaica's community tourism heartland. Mandeville offers cool highland air and the western hemisphere's oldest golf course, as well as several fine restaurants. Clarendon, farther east, is a small parish with swaths of unexplored coastline and a unique ethnic heritage.

▶ WHEN TO GO

Jamaica has typically been marketed as a destination for escaping the winter blues, but it can be just as good, or better, in the heart of the northern summer, when temperatures are comparable or even cooler than in places as far north as New York.

Jamaica's hurricane season with regular low pressure systems accompanied by rain, runs from June through October. In the absence of a large front, however, rainfall usually lasts only a few minutes and shouldn't be cause for concern in planning a trip.

The high and low season should be more of a factor in planning a trip, as many establishments set rates according to the typical demand for rooms in any given month. High season runs December 15–April 15, when accommodations can be twice as high as during the low season. Some establishments set their own specific dates, and others vary pricing throughout the year, whether for Easter, Thanksgiving, or the week between Christmas and New Year's. If escaping the winter blues is not your first priority, visiting during the low season can be much more cost-effective. Check with each establishment when planning a trip to see how prices vary seasonally.

The Jamaican calendar is filled with annual events, many of which are worth considering in planning a trip. A music festival like Rebel Salute, Jazz & Blues, Follow Di Arrow, or Sumfest is one of the best ways to jump out of the tourist box and appreciate Jamaica's culture alongside Jamaicans from all walks of life. If music isn't your thing, there are several other annual events, like the Calabash Literary Festival, food festivals, and fishing tournaments.

IF YOU HAVE...

- **ONE WEEK:** Visit Negril, Kingston, and the Blue Mountains.
- **TWO WEEKS:** Add Ocho Rios and Port Antonio.
- **THREE WEEKS:** Add Montego Bay and Treasure Beach.

one of many gazebos at Sandals Montego Bay

▶ BEFORE YOU GO

Passports and Visas

Jamaica now requires passports for all visitors, including those from the United States and United Kingdom. A tourist visa is required for many nationalities. A complete listing of visa requirements can be found on the website of the Consulate General in New York (www.congenjamaica-ny.org/visas). Visitors must also be able to demonstrate sufficient funds to cover their stay and be in possession of an onward or return ticket or itinerary. It helps to know where you will be staying on arrival, as immigration officials tend to detain visitors on entry until they can provide an address.

What to Take

Most Jamaican ATMs will accept foreign debit cards to dispense cash. The best exchange rates are found at foreign exchange traders like Scotia DBG and FX Trader. Banks accept travelers checks, but typically have long lines and offer poor rates.

Jamaicans dress to impress when going out to nightclubs like Cristal Night Club in Port Antonio.

Where clothing is concerned, what to take depends entirely on the nature of your trip. Most all-inclusive hotels have semi-formal dress codes (a collared shirt, dress shoes) for their fine dining restaurants; if church or a business meeting is in order, formal attire is a must.

If nobody needs to be impressed, however, Jamaica can be the most casual place on earth, where certain esteemed members of society refuse to wear shoes for greater proximity to Mother Earth, and nude beaches abound at hotels like Couples, Breezes, and Hedonism. However, outside the beach resort towns like Negril, entering a place of business without a shirt will be frowned upon.

Cool, light-colored cotton clothes are best for the heat and humidity. Obviously, so is your favorite bathing suit. For cool evenings, pack a long-sleeved shirt and long pants.

Many travelers to Jamaica are surprised to find that Jamaicans rarely wear shorts on a normal day, while jeans and full suits are common everyday attire. It is not necessary to buy an entire wardrobe of Hawaiian shirts before your trip, and in a pinch plenty are sold in gift shops across the island with the requisite "Jamaica, no problem" printed across the front.

You'll definitely want to bring your most flashy getup if you're planning a night on the town. In nightclubs such as Fiction and Privilege in Kingston, women are remarkably dressed up; men will come dressed in their shiniest shoes and most "criss" jacket to "flex" in the corner till the dance floor heats up.

For hiking and overnights in the higher elevations of the Blue Mountains, you'll want a sweatshirt, parka, boots, and warm socks.

Explore Jamaica

▶ THE BEST OF JAMAICA

Two weeks is a good length for a trip to Jamaica and provides enough time to relax on the beach while also venturing beyond the sun and sand for a mix of adventure and culture. Highlights include Negril's West End, a few days in quiet Belmont, Kingston's culture and nightlife, and Portland's aristocratic history and lush natural beauty.

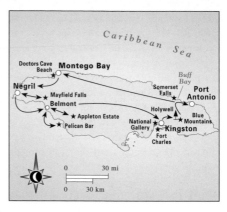

Day 1

Arrive at the airport in Montego Bay, check-in for two nights, and dine at the HouseBoat Grill or the more casual and every-bit-as-good Scotchie's. Hit up a bar for an evening drink to gauge the scene along the Hip Strip.

Day 2

Take tours of Rose Hall and Greenwood Great House in the morning. Then visit Doctors Cave Beach in the afternoon. Have dinner at Day-O Plantation followed by a play at Fairfield Theatre.

Day 3

Drive west to Negril for cliff jumping by late morning. Visit Royal Palm Reserve in the afternoon to fish and check out the waterfowl, then visit Bongo's Farm for sunset.

Day 4

In the morning, drive southeast to Savanna-la-Mar and then turn inland to Mayfield Falls. Spend the morning exploring the falls and gardens. On the return back to Negril, take the northern route stopping to visit Alexander Bustamante's birthplace at Blenheim before enjoying grilled lobster at Half Moon Beach in Hanover.

Day 5

Check out of your hotel and drive east toward Belmont, stopping at Blue Hole Garden and Roaring River along the way. Settle into a beachside cottage at Horizon Cottages and dine on fresh seafood or fried chicken across the road.

Day 6

Drive south to Parotee Point and head to Pelican Bar, a one-of-a-kind watering hole and ramshackle fried fish joint located a mile offshore on a sandbar. Go snorkeling and enjoy fried fish and a cold beer. On your way back to Belmont, stop in Black River for a boat trip into the morass.

Day 7

Drive inland and take a tour of Appleton Estate in the morning, followed by a stop on Bamboo Avenue for jelly coconut and a visit to Y.S. Falls in the afternoon. Pull over in Middle Quarters for fresh shrimp on the way back to Belmont, where you will spend another night.

Winnifred Beach in Port Antonio

Day 8

In Belmont, visit Peter Tosh Memorial Garden in the morning followed by a nature hike with Rasta Bryan. Depart in the afternoon for Kingston, arriving in time for dinner.

Day 9

Downtown sights in the morning could include the National Gallery, a stroll along Ocean Boulevard, and a visit to Liberty Hall. Visit Legend Café at the Bob Marley Museum for lunch and take a tour in the early afternoon. Stop by Hope Botanical Gardens for a juice at Ashanti Garden before heading back down to Devon House for ice cream and shopping. Go out on the town at night in New Kingston.

Day 10

Visit the Mutual Gallery and then head out to Fort Charles in Port Royal by mid-morning, followed by lunch at Gloria's. Take a boat to Lime Cay for a swim in the afternoon. Dine at Fisherman's Cabin before returning to Kingston to go out on the town and hit the hay.

Days 11 and 12

Drive northeast from Kingston into the Blue Mountains for hiking in Holywell and two nights at Woodside. Stop at Strawberry Hill and splurge on a beer to check out the view—it's well worth it.

Start the next day with early-morning coffee and birding at Twyman's Estate, fueled by a fresh roasted pea-bean blend, the connoisseur's choice. Have lunch at The Gap Cafe, followed by an afternoon swim in the spring-fed pool at Woodside and then a home-cooked dinner.

Day 13

Leave for Port Antonio via Buff Bay immediately after breakfast. Check in to your hotel, take a swim and then a nap. Wake up for lunch at Cynthia's and a swim on Winnifred Beach. Hit Roof Club, La Best, or Cristal Night Club in the evening to scope out the local scene.

Day 14

Get up early to head west towards Montego Bay for departure with time to stop by Somerset Falls along the way.

LOCAL SPAS AND HOT SPRINGS

LAIDBACK SPAS

Jamaica has world-class spas based predominantly at the high-end resorts. These facilities are not for those traveling on a tight budget or those seeking an authentic Jamaican vibe. There are several inexpensive local spas that tend to be rough around the edges but can make for entertaining and relaxing visits.

Kiyara Ocean Spa

Located at the luxurious Jamaica Inn in **Ocho Rios,** Kiyara prides itself on offering natural herbal remedies at the water's edge. Many of the ingredients used for facials and infusions are grown on property.

Jake's Driftwood Spa

Based at the Bedouin-inspired rustic chic Island Outpost property in **Treasure Beach,** Driftwood Spa features seaside cabanas facing the water where the surf lulls visitors into a trance as they receive treatments that merge holistic techniques and philosophies from around the globe into a potent blend of Caribbean treatments developed by wellness guru Sally Henzell.

views from Strawberry Hill

Strawberry Hill

Home of the "Strawberry Hill Living" concept, which marries Aveda treatments and Ayurvedic healing philosophies, this spa features five treatment rooms that include hydrotherapy, a sauna, yoga deck, and plunge pool. It has one of the best panoramic views in Jamaica, high up in the cloud forests of the **Blue Mountains** where lush vegetation and cool mountain air promote health and tranquility.

The Caves

Nowhere else in Jamaica can you get a massage inside a cave filled with candles and flower petals. Soaking in the Jacuzzi located in a private chamber carved into the cliffs in **Negril,** with a window overlooking the sea, you'll realize this is the perfect spot for relaxation.

NATURAL SPRINGS

Several natural springs in Jamaica are reputed to have healing powers and have been developed to varying degrees as treatment centers.

Bath Hot Springs

The best of Jamaica's old-school treatment centers, Bath Hot Springs in **Port Antonio** has Turkish-style tiled basins as well as more modern Jacuzzi tubs. The mineral-heavy water at Bath exits the hillside piping hot, with curative properties that give it its reputed healing powers.

Milk River Baths

The water at Milk River in Clarendon along the **South Coast** exits its source lukewarm, but what it lacks in heat it makes up for in curative properties. A minimum of three baths is recommended, but it is not advisable to stay in the water for longer than an hour because the water is highly radioactive – more so even than the springs at Vichy in France.

Bubbling Spring

Located in Middle Quarters along the **South Coast,** this informal spring facility is visited mostly by locals looking to ease muscle and joint pain. The spring water is cool and refreshing, and there's a bar and restaurant on the property.

► ROOTS AND CULTURE

These are the must-see historical sites and must-do events for those travelers wishing to delve into the pulsating cultural milieu that shapes and defines Jamaican society. Keep tabs on the weekly events calendars in Kingston and Negril to plan your time in these areas. The roots of Jamaican popular music will become vivid with this tour, which touches on the island's evolving music industry.

Day 1

Arrive in Montego Bay for one night at Richmond Hill. If you arrive in the morning, visit Greenwood Great House or Bellefield Great House for a step back in time with a stop at Scotchie's for jerk either before or after the tour. Visit the Gallery of West Indian Art for some inspiration before dinner at Mobay Proper or The HouseBoat Grill. Hit Margaritaville to catch the pinnacle of Mobay nightlife if you still have energy before bed.

Day 2

Hit Doctors Cave Beach in the morning and then head to Negril in the afternoon to catch sunset and dinner on the Cliffs at LTU or Pushcart Grill & Rum Bar. Check out the night's live reggae band on the beach or at Negril Escape on Tuesdays.

Day 3

Make a loop from Negril to Roaring River and Blue Hole Garden or Mayfield Falls before descending to Half Moon Beach along the Hanover coast. Head back to Negril for dinner at Whistling Bird, Kuyaba or Chill Awhile.

Day 4

Leave for Kingston in the morning, stopping

sunset washes over Kingston

Tuff Gong Studios

in Belmont to pay your respects to a reggae legend at Peter Tosh Memorial Garden. Make a pit stop in Middle Quarters for "swimps" and then in Scott's Pass, Clarendon, to meet the Rasta elders at the headquarters of the Nyabinghi House of Rastafari.

Day 5

Hit Kingston's cultural sights, or any combination of the Bob Marley Museum, Tuff Gong Studios, Culture Yard, and the National Gallery. Call Rita at Vynil Records to arrange a stop to buy the latest 45s. Have dinner at Hellshire Beach or at Gloria's in Port Royal before a night out on the town at Quad or Fiction followed by a street dance.

Day 6

Leave in the morning for Jamnesia Surf Club in Bull Bay. Spend the day surfing and hanging with Billy Mystic and family.

Day 7

Spend the morning sampling the ritualized Rasta life at Bobo Hill if you're in the mood

for some serious worship. Visit Reggae Falls in the afternoon before heading back to Kingston in the evening for dinner and another night out.

Day 8

Leave in the morning for Port Antonio, checking in at Great Huts, Drapers San or Goblin Hill. Spend the afternoon at Reach Falls or on the beach with a quick visit to Folly Ruins.

Day 9

Depart first thing for Ocho Rios stopping in Charles Town to meet the maroon coronel to take in some history and vision. In Ocho Rios, visit Reggae Xplosion at Island Village before dinner at Tropical Vibes on Fisherman's Beach.

Day 10

Visit Blue Hole Falls in the morning before a transfer to Montego Bay for an evening departure. Stop by Time 'N' Place or Culture Restaurant in Falmouth for a bite.

THE ADRENALINE JUNKIE'S FIX

For adventure travelers looking to jump from one adrenaline rush to the next, Jamaica can satisfy almost any craving.

SKYDIVING
Based at the Boscobel Aerodrome just outside **Ocho Rios** in the parish of St. Mary, **Skydive Jamaica** offers the ultimate adrenaline rush.

KITE SURFING
Burwood Beach, located 20 minutes east of **Montego Bay,** is home to **Brian's Windsurfing and Kitesurfing.** Lessons are offered for those uninitiated in this thrilling sport, while experienced kite surfers can simply rent gear.

WINDSURFING
Tropical Beach Water Sports, located next to the airport in **Montego Bay,** has the best windsurfing equipment for rent in Jamaica. Chaka Brown, who runs the rental operation, also rents Jet Skis and other motorized watercraft.

skydiving in Boscobel, St. Mary, with Skydive Jamaica

SURFING
Jamnesia Surf Club, located in **Bull Bay,** east of Kingston, has professional surfing equipment and respectable surf on a good day. A skateboard park entertains when the seas are flat.

WHITEWATER RAFTING
While dependent on rainfall conditions, whitewater rafting is possible throughout most of the year on the Great River with **Caliche Rainforest Whitewater Rafting,** 30 minutes west of **Montego Bay** in the parish of Hanover.

CLIFF JUMPING
The cheapest adrenaline fix in Jamaica, cliff jumping on **Negril's West End** is one thrill you won't have to pay for. There are several locations suitable for jumping into the azure waters, with **Rick's Cafe** being the most famous for the highest cliffs around at some 60 feet above the water. Other good jump spots at restaurants in Negril include **The Sands, LTU Pub & Restaurant, Pushcart Restaurant and Rum Bar,** and **3 Dives Jerk Centre.** Hotels on the cliffs good for jumping include **Xtabi, Rockhouse,** and **Tensing Pen.** Beyond the lighthouse, the waters tend to be less calm as the waves meet the cliffs.

MOUNTAIN BIKING
While few may be cut out for the ultimate rush of biking down from **Blue Mountain Peak,** Jamaica offers world class single-track riding the island over. In **Ocho Rios,** the St. Mary Off-Road Bicycling Association (SMORBA) hosts the annual **Fatta Tyre Festival,** drawing enthusiasts locally and from abroad. SMORBA is the best resource for those looking to link up with other riders.

► HIDDEN BEACHES AND HILLSIDE HIKES

Hikes, bird-watching, secluded beaches, and mangrove tours are indispensable to a greater appreciation of Jamaica's natural wonders. Jamaica is a relatively small island, and can be traversed in about five hours without stopping, but the diversity and ruggedness of the island's landscape makes it exhausting to try to fit in too much.

Transportation is an important consideration when planning an eco-vacation, as many of the less-visited sights are remote and require a rental car or driver. Excursions into remote parts of Cockpit Country and the Blue Mountains require a four-wheel-drive vehicle, but for most places SUVs are not necessary and the expense is not justified. Barrett Adventures operates island-wide, and is the best charter outfit for helping to coordinate transportation for part of or an entire trip.

Day 1

Arrive in Montego Bay and head directly to Good Hope Plantation in Trelawny. Spend a few hours on the beach at Silver Sands or Harmony Cove before a relaxing dinner in the great house.

Day 2

Explore Cockpit Country on horseback in the morning, with lunch back at the Great House. Head to Burwood Beach in the afternoon for windsurfing or kite surfing, before a casual dinner at Time 'N' Place nearby.

Day 3

Depart in the morning for Negril, stopping at Half Moon Beach for lunch and a dip. Continue on to Tensing Pen to spend the afternoon jumping off the cliffs and relaxing by the pool.

Day 4

Depart for Belmont stopping at Bongo's

Tensing Pen is a sophisticated assortment of comfortable, unpretentious cabanas atop the cliffs.

VITAL VITTLES: JAMAICA'S BEST FOOD

JAMMIN' JERK
Scotchies Tree in Kingston
Jo Jo's Jerk Pit and More in Half Way Tree, Kingston
Scotch on the Rocks in Ocho Rios
Scotchie's in Montego Bay
Aunt Gloria's in Falmouth, Montego Bay
Father Bull Bar, Jerk Centre and Restaurant in Montego Bay
All Seasons Restaurant Bar and Jerk Centre in Spur Tree Hill, South Coast

POWERFUL PATTIES
Yatte Man in Redlight, Blue Mountains
Niah's Patties in Negril

INCREDIBLE CURRY GOAT
Soldier's Camp in Port Antonio
Claudette's Top Class in Spur Tree Hill, South Coast

Howie's HQ in Middle Quarters, South Coast

SUMPTUOUS SEAFOOD
Gloria's Seafood Restaurant in Port Royal on the Palisadoes, Kingston
Cynthia's at Winnifred Beach, Port Antonio
Dragon Lounge in Whitehouse, Montego Bay
Far Out Fish Hut and Beer Joint in Greenwood, Montego Bay
Erica's Cafe in Negril
Dervy's Lobster Trap in Hopewell, Negril
Marcia Williams' Rasta-Colored Roadside Shop in Middle Quarters, South Coast
Little Ochie, South Coast

DESTINATION DINING
Belcour Lodge in the Blue Mountains
Mille Fleurs in Port Antonio
Day-O Plantation in Fairfield, Montego Bay
HouseBoat Grill in Montego Bay

Whether pork, chicken, or both, Scotchie's never disappoints when you're craving jerk.

Coyaba Gardens

Day 5

Depart for the Blue Mountains, stopping in Black River for a morning kayak or pontoon boat safari to see the crocs, then stop by Y.S. Falls for an early afternoon dip, before hitting the road. Overnight at Forres Park in Mavis Bank, Lime Tree Farm, or Whitfield Hall.

Day 6

Rise early for a hike up Blue Mountain Peak. Descend by early afternoon and head to Woodside for your last two nights.

Day 7

Hike the trails of Holywell, or visit Cinchona Botanical Gardens in the morning, then visit the Twyman's Old Tavern Coffee Estate for a tour and to pick up some beans to take home. Have dinner at The Gap Café, Strawberry Hill, or back at Woodside.

Day 8

Farm for a jelly coconut, hike up the hill, and eat lunch at the Black Star Line before heading to Roaring River and Blue Hole Garden. Spend the night at Horizon or Culloden Cove in Belmont or Whitehouse, and squeeze in some snorkeling before sunset.

Rise early for the drive back to Montego Bay, stopping in Ocho Rios for a dip at the Blue Hole on the White River or at One Love Trail on the seaside, followed by a garden tour at Coyaba Gardens. Leave Ochi in time for an evening departure from Mobay's Sangster International.

KINGSTON

Kingston is the heartbeat of Jamaica; it drives the island's cultural and economic pulse. While Jamaica's major tourist centers of Montego Bay, Ocho Rios, and Negril are a surreal world straddling a party paradise inside walled all-inclusive resorts and a meager existence outside, where locals hustle just to get by, Kingston is refreshing for its raw, real character. The capital city is Jamaica's proud center of business and government and an important transshipment port for Caribbean commerce. The tourist economy, on which the country as a whole is overwhelmingly dependent, takes a back seat in Town, Kingston's island-wide nickname. This is the Jamaica where the daily hustle to make ends meet gives fodder to an ever-growing cadre of young artists following in the footsteps of reggae legend Bob Marley.

As such, Kingston is an essential stop for understanding the cultural richness of this small island. Jamaica's diverse cultural mosaic is nowhere more boldly revealed than through the country's art, music, dance, and theater, all of which are concentrated here. Kingston's vibrant nightlife is a world unto itself with clubs, parties, and stage shows that entertain well into the morning almost any night of the week.

But like any urban setting, Kingston is not without problems, and a negative reputation has plagued the city for decades. Downtown Kingston is at first sight a case study in urban decay. Blocks upon blocks of buildings haven't seen a paintbrush in years, and many are crumbling and abandoned. The city became known as a breeding ground for political violence in the late 1970s, when neighborhood "dons"

© OLIVER HILL

HIGHLIGHTS

◖ **Tuff Gong Recording Studio:** Bob Marley's production base offers a "Making of Music" tour, including a visit to the studio, record printing shop, gallery, and herb garden (page 32).

◖ **National Gallery:** The National Gallery is the crown jewel of the Institute of Jamaica, where visitors can view Jamaican art from its roots to the present day (page 36).

◖ **Liberty Hall:** The building where Marcus Garvey based his United Negro Improvement Association today houses a multimedia gallery and reference library on all things Garvey, Jamaica's first national hero and one of the most influential men of the 20th century (page 36).

◖ **National Heroes Park:** The one-stop shop to learn about the people whose contributions are paramount to the Jamaican experience, from slavery to independence (page 37).

◖ **Emancipation Park:** The most judicious starting point for a walk around New Kingston, the park has an impressive statue sculpted by Laura Facey evoking emancipation (page 38).

◖ **Devon House:** The former house of self-made Jamaican millionaire George Steibel, the museum fronts an array of great shops and restaurants (page 41).

◖ **Bob Marley Museum:** Jamaica's most revered son is alive and stronger each day thanks to the music and unstoppable legacy featured at 56 Hope Road (page 42).

◖ **Mutual Gallery:** This is an essential gallery for art enthusiasts keen to get a preview of the up-and-coming artists in Jamaica's dynamic arts scene (page 44).

◖ **Hellshire:** An assortment of fried fish and lobster shacks crowd this popular weekend spot where Kingstonians relish the rustic chic (page 87).

◖ **Lime Cay:** Once a haven for buccaneers, this sleepy outpost comes alive on weekends with sound systems, fried fish, and an idyllic beach (page 95).

LOOK FOR ◖ TO FIND RECOMMENDED SIGHTS, ACTIVITIES, DINING, AND LODGING.

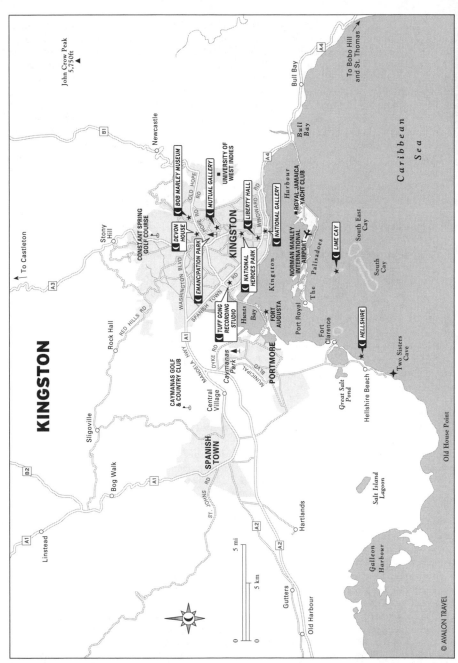

KINGSTON

John Crow Peak
5,750ft ▲

To Castleton

To Bobo Hill
and St. Thomas

Bull Bay

Caribbean Sea

Newcastle

BOB MARLEY MUSEUM
MUTUAL GALLERY
UNIVERSITY OF
WEST INDIES
LIBERTY HALL
NATIONAL GALLERY
DEVON HOUSE
ROYAL JAMAICA
YACHT CLUB

Stony
Hill

CONSTANT SPRING
GOLF COURSE

EMANCIPATION PARK

KINGSTON

NATIONAL
HEROES PARK

LIME CAY

South East
Cay

South Cay

TUFF GONG
RECORDING STUDIO

Hunts
Bay

FORT
AUGUSTA

Kingston
Harbour

NORMAN MANLEY
INTERNATIONAL
AIRPORT

The Palisadoes

Port Royal

Rock Hall

RED HILLS RD

Fort
Clarence

HELLSHIRE

Two Sisters
Cave

CAYMANAS GOLF
& COUNTRY CLUB

Caymanas
Park

PORTMORE

Great Salt
Pond

Hellshire Beach

Old House Point

Sligoville

Central
Village

SPANISH
TOWN

Salt Island
Lagoon

Bog Walk

Hartlands

Galleon
Harbour

Linstead

Gutters

Old Harbour

5 mi

5 km

© AVALON TRAVEL

were put on the payroll of competing political forces to ensure mass support at election time. Downtown neighborhoods like Allman Town, Arnette Gardens, Rima, Tivoli, Rose Town, and Greenwich Town are still explosive, politicized communities where gunshots are hardly out of the ordinary. Other communities farther out have also gained notoriety, like Riverton City, next to the dump, and Harbour View, at the base of the Palisadoes.

Despite the severity of crime and violence in these areas, Kingston is not to be feared, as even many Jamaican countryfolk might suggest. With a good dose of common sense and respect, and a feel for the Jamaican runnings, or street smarts, there is little chance of having an altercation of any kind.

St. Andrew parish surrounding Kingston was at one time a rural area dominated by a handful of estates. Since becoming the nation's capital, however, Kingston has spilled over and engulfed much of the relatively flat land of the parish, its residential neighborhoods creeping ever farther up the sides of the Blue Mountain foothills. At the heart of St. Andrew is the bustling commercial center of Half Way Tree, where shopping plazas butt up against one another, competing for space and customers. There are still unpaved patches of St. Andrew, however, like the expansive Hope Botanical Gardens, the Mona campus of the University of the West Indies, and countless well-laid-out properties where it's easy to imagine the days when the parish was completely rural.

Twenty minutes due west of Kingston is Spanish Town, still seemingly sore about losing its preeminence as Jamaica's capital and business center. Seldom visited by outsiders from Jamaica or abroad, Spanish Town played a central role in the island's early history as a major population center, first for the Tainos, then for the Spanish, and finally for the British. Each group left its mark, a fact recognized by the United Nations, which has considered the city for World Heritage Site status. The city lies at the heart of St. Catherine, a parish whose moment of glory has sadly passed in a very tangible sense. Neglect and urban blight permeate Spanish Town.

Nevertheless, it's littered with fascinating heritage sites and has a beautiful square, a few notable churches, memorials, and glimpses of bygone glory. It is a convenient stop on most routes out of Kingston to destinations across the island.

Together the parishes surrounding the greater metropolitan area are home to about 43 percent of the island's 2.8 million residents. Perhaps to a greater extent than in some other developing countries, poverty and wealth share an abrasive coexistence in Jamaica, especially in Kingston. This inevitably leads to widespread begging and insistent windshield-washers at stoplights. Apart from these regular encounters, Kingston is relatively hassle-free compared with other urban centers on the island, where hustlers tend to be more focused on the tourist trade and are visibly aggressive in their search for a dollar. Kingston is one of the few places in Jamaica where visitors with a light complexion can seemingly blend into the normal fabric of society. Kingstonians have other things occupying their attention, and visitors go almost unnoticed.

PLANNING YOUR TIME

Kingston has a tendency to consume time, so it's perfect for those who like to idle about and soak up local culture. Skylarking, or idling, is in fact one of Jamaica's favorite pastimes. For visitors looking to hit all the important historical and cultural sites in a rush, at least two nights in a two-week visit to Jamaica should be dedicated to Kingston, and certainly more during a longer stay in order to adopt the local pace and enjoy the sights, food, and nightlife. Most of the historical sights downtown can be seen in one day. Uptown attractions tend to be conveniently concentrated in the Half Way Tree/Hope Road area and will consume another day if you wish to fit in **Devon House, The Bob Marley Museum,** and **Hope Gardens,** with a little shopping and eating in between. The noteworthy attractions in Spanish Town can all be seen in half a day.

As a place of business, Kingston's inevitable bureaucratic red tape can be frustrating at worst and a challenge to negotiate at best. Most of the island's music studios and production houses are located in Kingston, which makes it *the* base for those looking to engage in the entertainment industry. Kingston's nightlife heats up on the weekends with stage shows and parties held almost weekly at one venue or another, but there are worthwhile events almost every night of the week, and the most popular regular street dances are all held on weeknights. Theater performances are held several nights a week. It is worth calling ahead when planning a visit if you would like to catch a theater or dance performance.

If you can, plan to spend a Sunday at **Lime Cay.** Kingston's most popular beach, just off the coast of Port Royal, has become a hub for the city's young and hip.

Kingston is hardly inexpensive in terms of accommodations, and a meal out for two can match New York City prices if you want to flirt with high society. Still, a night on the town doesn't need to cost more than US$20, and there's always a way to get by regardless of budgetary constraints.

HISTORY

Kingston didn't become an important city, or a city at all for that matter, until well after the British captured Jamaica from Spain in 1655. It wasn't until the great earthquake of 1692 left the nearby boomtown of Port Royal almost entirely underwater that Kingston's population grew to any size—thanks to the survivors fleeing from across the harbor. A subsequent disaster, a devastating fire in 1703, left Port Royal virtually abandoned and sealed the town's fate as a literal backwater. Prior to this, Kingston's Downtown area was dominated by a fishing and pig-farming village known as Colonel Beeston's Hog Crawle.

The well-organized city was built to take advantage of the outstanding natural harbor that had put Port Royal on the map in the first place, and it was named in honor of William of Orange, who ruled England from 1689 to 1702. Before long, Kingston became an immigration point for merchants from around the Caribbean seeking fortune in the slave trade and associated commerce. When slavery

was abolished in 1834, Kingston's population swelled as many former slaves rejected the rural life that reminded them of a not-so-distant past. Country folk began migrating to Kinston in great numbers in search of a fresh start.

Thanks to brisk trade that continued along Kingston Harbor, the city soon challenged the capital of Spanish Town in economic importance. In 1872, after what proved to be years of futile resistance, the disgruntled bureaucrats in Spanish Town finally ceded power. Uptown Kingston remained predominantly rural well into the mid-1800s, when wealthier Kingstonians began seeking refuge from the swelling shantytowns that sprang up around Downtown. Most areas of Uptown today still include "manor" or "pen" in reference to the parcels of land that contained the farming estates of yesteryear.

In 1907, a massive earthquake destroyed the majority of buildings along the waterfront, further exacerbating the flight to Uptown of those with means. By the 1930s, prices plunged for the commodities that still formed the base of Jamaica's economy, causing widespread riots around Kingston. This was a time of social and political unrest throughout the African Diaspora, catalyzing the Jamaican labor movement and bringing leaders Marcus Garvey, William Gordon, and Alexander Bustamante to the fore. By the time Jamaica was granted its independence on August 1, 1962 (it technically remains a protectorate of the British crown), redevelopment along the harbor was slated as a priority. Unfortunately for the waterfront area, most of the economic development that ensued took place along the city's new hip strip, Knutsford Boulevard, in New Kingston, and farther uptown in Half Way Tree and along Hope Road.

Violent political campaigns in the 1970s and 1980s gave Kingston international notoriety, but visitors today rarely find themselves subject to or even observers of violent crime.

ORIENTATION

The parish of Kingston encompasses what is today referred to as Downtown, as well as the

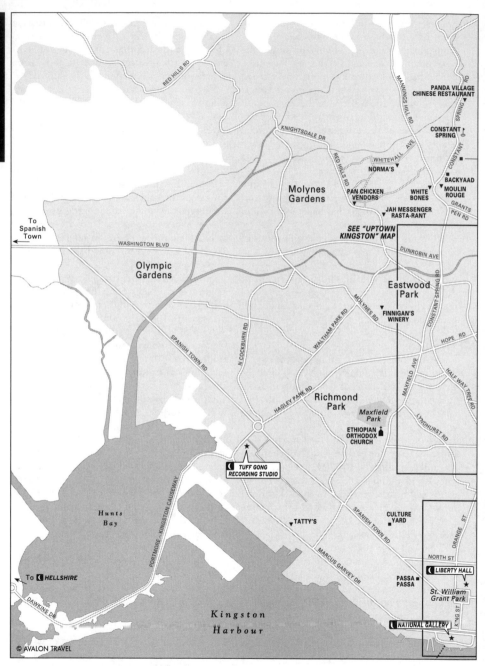

To
Spanish
Town

RED HILLS RD

MANNINGS HILL RD

KNIGHTSDALE DR

RED HILLS RD

SPRING RD

PANDA VILLAGE
CHINESE RESTAURANT

CONSTANT
SPRING

WHITEHALL AVE

NORMA'S

Molynes
Gardens

PAN CHICKEN
VENDORS

WHITE
BONES

BACKYAAD

MOULIN
ROUGE

CONSTANT

GRANTS
PEN RD

JAH MESSENGER
RASTA-RANT

SEE "UPTOWN
KINGSTON" MAP

WASHINGTON BLVD

DUNROBIN AVE

Olympic
Gardens

Eastwood
Park

CONSTANT SPRING RD

MOLYNES RD

FINNIGAN'S
WINERY

SPANISH TOWN RD

N COCKBURN RD

WALTHAM PARK RD

HOPE RD

MAXFIELD AVE

HALF WAY TREE RD

HAGLEY PARK RD

Richmond
Park

Maxfield
Park

LYNDHURST RD

ETHIOPIAN
ORTHODOX
CHURCH

PORTMORE–KINGSTON CAUSEWAY

★
☾ TUFF GONG
RECORDING STUDIO

Hunts
Bay

TATTY'S

CULTURE
YARD

SPANISH TOWN RD

ORANGE ST

NORTH ST

To ☾ HELLSHIRE

DAWKINS DR

MARCUS GARVEY DR

PASSA
PASSA

☾ LIBERTY HALL
★

St. William
Grant Park
★

KING ST

Kingston
Harbour

☾ NATIONAL GALLERY
★

© AVALON TRAVEL

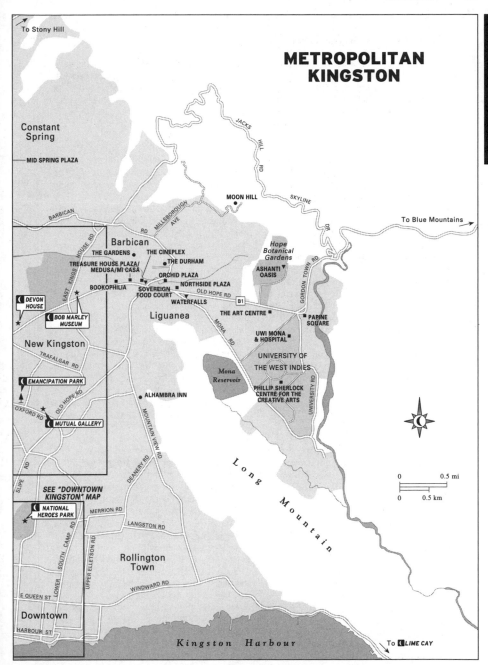

METROPOLITAN KINGSTON

To Stony Hill

Constant Spring

MID SPRING PLAZA

BARBICAN

JACKS HILL RD

SKYLINE

MOON HILL

To Blue Mountains

MILLSBOROUGH AVE

RD

Barbican

Hope Botanical Gardens

THE GARDENS
THE CINEPLEX
THE DURHAM
TREASURE HOUSE PLAZA/ MEDUSA/MI CASA
ORCHID PLAZA
ASHANTI OASIS
BOOKOPHILIA
NORTHSIDE PLAZA
SOVEREIGN FOOD COURT
OLD HOPE RD
WATERFALLS

EAST KINGS HOUSE RD

DEVON HOUSE

BOB MARLEY MUSEUM

Liguanea

THE ART CENTRE

B1

PAPINE SQUARE

GORDON TOWN RD

New Kingston

TRAFALGAR RD

EMANCIPATION PARK

OLD HOPE RD

OXFORD RD

MUTUAL GALLERY

MONA RD

UWI MONA & HOSPITAL

UNIVERSITY OF THE WEST INDIES

Mona Reservoir

PHILLIP SHERLOCK CENTRE FOR THE CREATIVE ARTS

UNIVERSITY RD

ALHAMBRA INN

MOUNTAIN VIEW RD

SLIPE RD

SEE "DOWNTOWN KINGSTON" MAP

NATIONAL HEROES PARK

MERRION RD

DEANERY RD

LANGSTON RD

LOWER SOUTH CAMP RD

UPPER ELLETSON RD

Rollington Town

WINDWARD RD

E QUEEN ST

Downtown

HARBOUR ST

Kingston Harbour

Long Mountain

To LIME CAY

0   0.5 mi

0   0.5 km

DOWNTOWN AND UPTOWN

Uptown and Downtown are used to describe geographical regions in metropolitan Kingston, but the names are also used locally to describe the social classes that live within each general area. In a socioeconomic sense, Downtown refers to Kingston's "have-nots," while Uptown refers to the "haves."

The bulk of the city's poor population is concentrated in tenement yards and shantytowns, most of which are found in and around Downtown. In recent years, squatter settlements have sprung up throughout the city, however, usually on marginal land around the drainage gullies.

Kingston's wealthy tend to live Uptown where some of the island's most excessive concrete mansions boast spectacular views and cool breeze, even in the dead of summer. The slums of Downtown Kingston stand in stark contrast to the concrete mansions that dot areas like Beverly Hills, Jacks Hill, Norbrook, Cherry Gardens, Red Hills, and Stony Hill. Many of these grand homes lay empty, however, while still others were never completed before being abandoned. It is said that many of these unfinished residences belong to "druggists" (narcotics traffickers) who either fled the country after drawing too much attention with their conspicuous displays of wealth or were nabbed by the authorities.

Downtown

Downtown Kingston hugs the northern shores of the world's seventh largest natural harbor, which helped the city become one of the most important export centers for Europe-bound goods, as well as a major transshipment port for Caribbean cargo. As the nature of trade and commerce changed over the years, the Downtown area has seen less and less direct economic benefit from shipping, which is today focused between the wharves west of Downtown along Marcus Garvey Drive and the causeway leading to Portmore. The modern wharves are unmistakable, with massive cranes servicing an endless stream of container ships that make Kingston Harbour one of the busiest ports in the world.

Development since independence has been focused almost exclusively above Cross Roads, leaving the Downtown area neglected. In 2009 the government established a tax incentive for companies to relocate their corporate headquarters Downtown, with the mobile phone provider Digicel the first to announce it would take up the offer. Digicel Group CEO Colm Delves said the move reflects an optimism for the area and that immediately following the announcement, property values began to rise in the area. Downtown sees a lot of activity during the day, with many government offices still located there, including the Survey Department, the Urban Development Corporation, the Jamaican Parliament, the Supreme Court, the Institute of Jamaica, and most ministry buildings.

The Bank of Jamaica, with its Coin and Notes Museum, and Scotia Bank both have their headquarters along the waterfront. It's not the best place for a lonely stroll at night, as the business area becomes a bit desolate and the Parade area tends to attract a few vagrants.

A new wave of Chinese and Indian immigrants have set up a slew of retail outlets along King and Orange streets, somewhat reviving what was once Kingston's Chinatown.

Jubilee and Coronation Markets more or less fuse together into a seemingly endless array of stalls west of **the Parade** along West Queen Street, marking the heart of Downtown. As the name suggests, the Parade was once used as a marching ground for British troops. Today it is a poorly maintained park where domino games abound. The adjacent market has a distinct buzz and thick air that fluctuates with little warning between the aroma of fresh produce and wafting herbs to an unpleasant stench. It takes some courage to stroll through the market and navigate the cacophony, but it's worth doing at least once, as it's an experience unto Downtown Kingston alone. The bus terminal just south of the heart of the market is the principal departure point for routes around the country. Expect overpacked and cramped seats and blasting R&B and dancehall music for the duration of your ride, no matter the destination.

Uptown

Until well into the 1800s, St. Andrew parish consisted of a handful of large private estates covering the rolling Blue Mountain foothills. When Downtown Kingston began to overcrowd, the land was parceled off and sold to accommodate the overflowing city with new residential neighborhoods, subdivisions, and gated townhouse communities. Many areas of greater Kingston still retain the name of the farming estates on which development took place. Constant Spring, Hope, Mona, and Papine were all rural estates that are now Uptown neighborhoods.

New Kingston is a hub of business activity and nightlife, and has been the focal point for urban development since independence. Some of the busiest nightclubs, bars, and restaurants are found along or just off of Knutsford Boulevard, as are many hotels catering to business travelers and tourists. New Kingston is a small area bound by Trafalgar Road and Oxford Road, which run parallel to each other at the northern and southern ends respectively.

North of Trafalgar Road, the residential neighborhood of **Trafalgar Park** extends to Hope Road, and from there **Liguanea** extends west and north to the boarder of Barbican. **Barbican** is a predominantly residential neighborhood that extends up the slopes toward Jacks Hill.

Directly west of New Kingston is **Half Way Tree** (often pronounced "Half-a-Tree"), the capital of St. Andrew parish and the city's commercial core. Shopping plazas abound, with the **clock tower,** Half Way Tree's most notable landmark, located at the main intersection, and the Transport Center in between northbound Eastwood Park Road and southbound Constant Spring Road. The Transport Center is a departure point for public transportation around the city and for major points around the island. Route taxis also leave from Half Way Tree. A few steps west of the heart of Half Way Tree stands the historic St. Andrew Parish Church.

The name Half Way Tree apparently refers to a large cotton tree that at one point before the British takeover of 1655 provided shade for resting soldiers traveling between a base in Greenwich, St. Andrew, and a fort in Spanish Town. The tree no longer stands. Plenty of shopping, several restaurants, and a few notable hotels are found in the general area.

Along Hope Road

Running from Half Way Tree in the heart of St. Andrew northeast to Papine Square, Hope Road was for a time the quintessential Uptown address, one which marked Bob Marley's rise to fame and fortune when he moved there from the ghetto of Trench Town in the early 1970s. Several noteworthy attractions, a few restaurants, and plenty of shopping line the busy thoroughfare.

Must-see sights including **Devon House,** the **Bob Marley Museum,** and **Hope Gardens** are found along Hope Road. The University of Technology (UTECH) is also located here, and Mona, the main campus of the University of the West Indies (UWI), is a stone's throw away just southeast of Papine. On Saturdays, **Papine Square** comes alive with drumming and singing when Rastafarians from His Imperial Majesty's School of Bible Study and Sabbath Service, based in a squatter settlement in the hills above Irish Town, descend for their weekly Nyabinghi Sabbath service. Barbican Road winds off Hope Road at Sovereign Centre with a few notable restaurants in Orchid Village plaza.

The clock tower in Half Way Tree is at Kingston's busiest intersection and the hub of its principal commercial district.

© LANCE WATSON

Palisadoes, a 16-kilometer-long, thin strip of land that runs from the roundabout at Harbour View to the tip of Port Royal.

Originally laid out in a grid bound by Harbour, North, East, and West Streets, the old city of Kingston soon overstepped these boundaries with ramshackle residential neighborhoods springing up on every side. Over the years, some of these areas have seen simple zinc shacks replaced by homes of slightly better stature. Most of the buildings in the area below the central square, or **Parade,** as it is known, are commercial, with limited middle-income housing in high-rise buildings near the waterfront.

Most of the more bustling areas of Town are actually located in St. Andrew parish. The two most developed areas are the hubs of **New Kingston,** immediately north of Cross Roads, and **Half Way Tree,** immediately to the east of New Kingston. **Hope Road,** where several businesses and sites of interest are located, runs northeast from Half Way Tree Square all the way to **Papine** on the northern edge of town. From there, Highway B1, which is little more than a narrow, winding road that often becomes impassable on the descent due to landslides, leads into and over the Blue Mountains. Half Way Tree Road is also a major thoroughfare; it starts at Cross Roads, turning into Constant Spring Road north of the Clock Tower in Half Way Tree, and runs to the northernmost edge of town, where it becomes Stony Hill Road, and later turns into Highway A3, leading to St. Mary parish and the North Coast via Junction.

Metropolitan Kingston is often referred to as the Corporate Area and is divided into two regions referred to by Kingstonians as **Uptown** and **Downtown.** In a spatial sense, Downtown Kingston is the old city, laid out in a well-organized grid, whereas Uptown encompasses an urban and suburban sprawl with little order, the result of more recent economic development. The junction at **Cross Roads** forms a dividing line between Downtown and Uptown.

The Blue Mountain foothills flank the entire city, forming a constant backdrop. Along with a handful of high-rises in New Kingston, the hills provide the best natural landmarks for spatial orientation when moving about the city. Kingston's most affluent residential neighborhoods hug the hills from Long Hill in the southeast at the foot of the Dallas Mountains, wrapping around to Beverly Hills, Mona, Hope Pastures, Barbican, Jack's Hill, Graham Heights, Norbrook, Stony Hill, and Red Hills, from east to west.

SAFETY

Kingston is a city of nearly one million people, the vast majority of whom know poverty. It is important to keep in mind that people will say and do just about anything that gives them the opportunity to eat, or "*nyam* food." While some may use physical intimidation to get what they want, a more common occurrence is for someone to pretend to know you or yell aggressively from across the street, "Come here!" When you get the feeling that an advance of this sort may lead to an uncomfortable situation, go with that inclination. It helps to keep petty cash on hand to ease tensions when strategically necessary. If you're driving, there's almost always someone nearby to help direct your parking and then volunteer to watch your car while you go about your business. When you return to the car the helpful volunteer will certainly expect a tip. While you don't need to be intimidated by these everyday occurrences, a bit of change or a small bill will put you in good stead for the next time.

For women travelers unaccustomed to aggressive men, Jamaica will most certainly be an eye-opener. Shyness is not a strong part of the Jamaican way, and Jamaican men will put on all kinds of charm to seduce women with creative and tactful words. While most of these approaches are harmless, it's important to never let down your guard and to maintain a certain degree of aloofness, taking everything with a grain of salt. Standards for what is considered acceptable language are very different in Jamaica from most North American and European countries, and language commonly used for flirtation in Jamaica might be considered sexual harassment in other places.

In club settings, dancing can be very sexual and intimate, with "whining and grinding" a part of normal conduct. Jamaican women are a tough lot, however, and generally run things, or have control over the situation. When a man displeases them, they have no problem making it known. You should feel perfectly comfortable doing the same—with a degree of diplomacy to avoid offending the suitor's pride.

Crime and violence certainly exist in Kingston, although visitors are unlikely to encounter it. In fact, it would take real effort for a foreigner to be a victim of gun violence in Kingston, perhaps only by making the mistake of wearing an orange People's National Party (PNP) T-shirt while walking through Tivoli Gardens, one of the city's most notorious ghettos and a stronghold for the Jamaica Labor Party (JLP). Political situations linked to sensitive constituencies like Tivoli Gardens can cause these garrison communities to flare up with tension and violence, usually demonstrated by residents barricading the streets in one of the only displays of power they can muster. Should you be unfortunate enough to be caught in Kingston under these circumstances, avoid going Downtown and keep abreast of the news and discuss safety with locals. The U.S. embassy is typically the first to sound an alarm issuing prompt travel advisories anytime such a situation exists. Jamaica has a history of liaisons between politicians and dons, the strongmen who rule many of the impoverished areas of Kingston and Spanish Town, and it's best to avoid getting involved in any way as a visitor.

Generally speaking, the only time foreigners are in the press associated with crime is in cases where they have tried to exit the country carrying drugs. Sticking by the right set of locals and hanging in the right places, Kingston is no more dangerous a place than any other big city in the developing world where wealth and poverty coexist.

Sights

Kingston's main draws relate to Jamaica's history, heritage, and culture as opposed to the natural features that form the basis of the tourism economy concentrated on the north and west coasts. Given the progression of development in uptown Kingston over the past several decades, most of the historical sites of interest, as well as those associated with the Institute of Jamaica, are located Downtown. The more popular hangouts, as well as most restaurants, bars, clubs, and shopping plazas, are located Uptown. As Jamaica's music scene has decentralized over the past decades, thanks in large part to technological advances, the Downtown production studios of yesteryear that gave birth to and controlled the industry, like Sir Clement "Coxsone" Dodd's World Disc, or his even more successful Studio One, have been replaced by scores of modern studios scattered around the residential suburbs, often based at the homes of the artists and producers who run them.

DOWNTOWN

Jamaican art pioneer Edna Manley was honored with a re-creation of her sculpture *Negro Aroused* on Ocean Boulevard along the waterfront at the end of King Street. It's as good as any a place to begin a tour of Downtown.

Along Ocean Boulevard, anglers casually reel in their lines and children jump off big concrete blocks into the choppy waters of Kingston Harbour. It's a great place for an afternoon stroll or to watch sunsets over the Hellshire Hills.

The free **Coin and Notes Museum** (Bank of Jamaica, Nethersole Place, between East and Duke Sts., tel. 876/922-0750, ext. 2108, 9 A.M.–4 P.M. Mon.–Fri.) provides a history of money in Jamaica from the time when goods were bartered to the present. The in-between period saw the circulation of coins from many countries, including Spain and Mexico. Curators Sandra Moody and Elan Edwards have a wealth of knowledge to share with visitors.

For souvenirs, the **Crafts Market** (7 A.M.–6 P.M. Mon.–Sat.) at the junction of Ocean Boulevard and Port Royal Street, features some authentic Jamaican crafts, as well as an ever-increasing slew of Jamaican-flag-covered trinkets, T-shirts, and towels imported from China.

◖ Tuff Gong Recording Studio

Tuff Gong Recording Studio (220 Marcus Garvey Dr., tel. 876/937-4216 or 876/923-9383, www.tuffgong.com) operates as living proof that a recording artist can own his music and be in control of his product and legacy. Bob Marley started as a struggling artist much

like the one depicted by Jimmy Cliff in Perry Henzell's film *The Harder They Come*. He was subject to the same producer-artist relationship that made voicing the next tune an economic imperative rather than a carefully planned and executed project. When Marley built Tuff Gong Recording Studio he seeded an empire that continues to earn millions of dollars per year. Today the studio operates as Marley's legacy, with his wife Rita and children Ziggy and Cedella in charge. The studio offers a guided tour, where visitors can see the entire music production process. The studio can be booked for recording for about US $40 per hour. A small record shop on-site sells CDs and other Tuff Gong paraphernalia.

Culture Yard

Culture Yard (6–8 1st St., off Collie Smith Dr., contact property manager Clifford "Ferdie" Bent, tel. 876/572-4085, 8 A.M.–6 P.M. daily, US$10) is a project developed by the Trench Town Development Association and offers a museum tour based

© OLIVER HILL

Founded by Bob Marley, Tuff Gong remains one of Kingston's most active recording studios.

KINGSTON

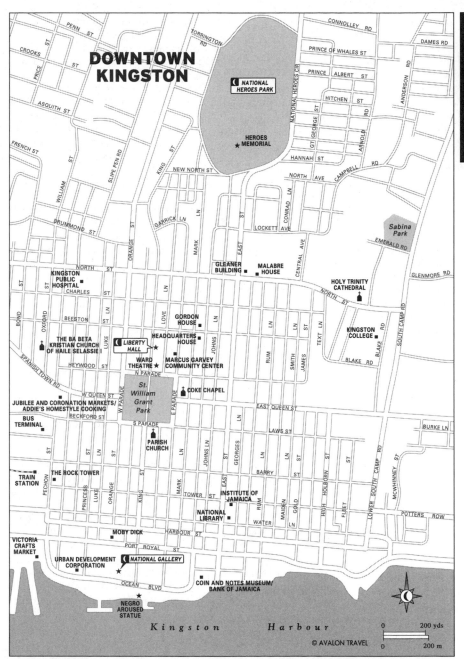

DOWNTOWN KINGSTON

around Bob Marley's former home in the ghetto of Rima. It has been deemed a historical site. Visiting Culture Yard is a decent excuse to see the slums of **Trench Town,** which have retained the dire conditions that gave birth to songs like "Concrete Jungle" and "No Woman No Cry," even if the cost for a look-around feels more like charity than value. The area is marked by a large mural of Marley, visible from Spanish Town Road. Visiting Culture Yard is safe, but the communities in and around Trench Town remain explosive, so it's not a good idea to go wandering on your own. Colin Smikle (tel. 876/370-8243 or 876/978-5833, colinsmikle@yahoo.com) can arrange community tours around Kingston, including Culture Yard.

A few years ago the Trench Town Development Association was established to carry out projects to benefit the community. Another success has been the **Trenchtown Reading Centre** (Lower 1st St., contact Christopher Stone, tel. 876/546-1559, stonec@kasnet.com, www.trenchtownreadingcentre.com), which moved into a new building in 2000 and was refurbished in 2005. The reading center welcomes book donations.

St. William Grant Park

The Parade, also known as St. William Grant Park, was a popular congregation ground for a host of labor leaders, including William Grant, Marcus Garvey, and Alexander Bustamante, who spoke regularly before large audiences in the decades preceding independence. Originally a parade ground for British soldiers, as the name implies, the park divides King Street into upper and lower regions. The park itself was recently refurbished in an Urban Development Corporation bid to rid it of a sullied reputation after years of neglect, and it is certainly more pleasant today than just a few years ago. Once called Victoria Park, it was renamed in 1977 to honor William Grant for his role in Jamaica's labor movement. Grant was a follower of Marcus Garvey and joined forces with Alexander Bustamante in championing workers' rights.

In 1938, both he and Bustamante were arrested for fomenting upheavals among the early trade unions. In the early 1940s, Grant broke with Bustamante's Industrial Trade Union and drifted into poverty and obscurity. Nevertheless he was given the Honor of Distinction in 1974 for his contribution to the labor movement, which paved the way for Jamaica's independence. Three years later Grant died. The St. preceding his name is understood to abbreviate "sergeant," attributable to his service in the military or as a militant member of the United Negro Improvement Association.

Kingston Parish Church (tel. 876/922-6888) stands on the corner of South Parade and King Street. It was consecrated in 1911 after having been rebuilt following the earthquake of 1907, which virtually flattened all of downtown. The church was constructed as a replica of the original, with the addition of a clock tower. The original church had stood from when the city was planned and built following the earthquake of 1692. Inside there are several pieces of Jamaican art and a few statues gifted by the Chinese (Our Lady at the High Altar) and Lebanese (St. Thomas) governments.

Coke Church (tel. 876/922-2224), the most prominent building on East Parade, stands on the site of the first Methodist chapel in Jamaica. The present structure was rebuilt after the 1907 earthquake, replacing the original built in 1840 and named after Thomas Coke, who founded the Methodist missions in the British Caribbean. It is one of the few buildings of brick construction in Kingston.

For a guided tour lasting about half an hour, call Juliet Gordon (tel. 876/925-8798 or cell tel. 876/362-9319, oldejamaica@yahoo.com, www.oldejamaicatours.com, US$5 for adults US$2 for children) who runs **We Jamaica Tours.** Mrs. Gordon can arrange transportation from anywhere in Kingston and specializes in historical churches around the Corporate Area, like Holy Trinity, the Jewish Synagogue, St. Andrew Parish Church, East Queen's Street Baptist, Coke Methodist, Cots

Kirk, and Spanish Town Cathedral, as well as other historical sites island wide. She's been leading tours since 2005 with a JTB-licensed operation.

The **Ward Theatre** (tel. 876/922-0453 or 876/922-3213, wardtheatre@wardtheatrefoundation.com, www.wardtheatrefoundation.com, visitors welcome 9 A.M.–5 P.M. Mon.–Fri. or for scheduled events) facing the park on North Parade was also a regular venue for Garvey speeches. The theater, like many buildings in town, has gone through many incarnations, the latest being a gift from Colonel Charles Ward, who became wealthy as the "Nephew" in the rum company Wray and Nephew. The rum manufacturer, still among the biggest in Jamaica, started in the Shakespeare Tavern, which once stood beside the theater. Ward Theatre hosts occasional events, including its famous pantomime performances, some of which are posted on the theatre foundation's website. Renovations have been ongoing at the theater since early 2009, with no established

completion date. Call or check the website for an update.

Institute of Jamaica

The Institute of Jamaica (IOJ) (Main Bldg., 14–16 East St., tel. 876/922-0620 or 876/922-0626, ioj.jam@mail.infochan.com, www.instituteofjamaica.org.jm) was founded in 1879 by Governor General Anthony Musgrave to encourage "Literature, Science and Art," as the letters on the main building's facade read. The institute has several divisions: Natural History, National Gallery, National Library, Museum of History and Ethnography, African-Caribbean Institute, and Liberty Hall. It is directed by Vivian Crawford, a multifaceted man who claims Maroon heritage, and chaired by UWI professor Barry Chevannes. The IOJ publishes an excellent series called *Jamaica Journal,* which delves into a range of contemporary topics from dancehall music to sea sponges off Port Royal to national heroes. It's a great way to

© OLIVER HILL

The Ward Theatre on North Parade has provided an important stage for leaders and artists, from Marcus Garvey to Alexander Bustamante to Louise Bennett.

get a glimpse at the introspective side of the Jamaican people.

NATIONAL GALLERY

The National Gallery (12 Ocean Boulevard, tel. 876/922-1561, http://about.galleryjamaica.org, 10 A.M.–4:30 P.M. Tues.–Thurs., 10 A.M.–4 P.M. Fri., 10 A.M.–3 P.M. Sat., closed Sun. and Mon., US$1.15 adults, US$0.55 students and persons 65 and over) is the go-to place for a concise overview of Jamaican art, from Taino artifacts and colonial art dating to Spanish and English rule, to pieces charting the development of Jamaican intuitive and mainstream expressions. The works at the National Gallery reflect Jamaica's landscapes and its people, and their history, religion, spirituality, and folklore. Artists whose work is part of the gallery's permanent collection include Mallica "Kapo" Reynolds, Barrington Watson, Albert Huie, Carl Abrahams, John Dunkley, and Edna Manley.

THE NATURAL HISTORY DIVISION AND THE MUSEUM OF HISTORY AND ETHNOGRAPHY

The Natural History Division is the oldest division of the IOJ and is housed adjacent to the Institute's main building on the ground floor. The Museum of History and Ethnography (10 East St., 8:30 A.M.–5 P.M. Mon.–Thurs., 8:30 A.M.–4 P.M. Fri., US$4 adults, US$3 for students with ID, US$1 children 12 and under) features temporary exhibits at its headquarters ranging from colorful examples of contemporary Jamaican life to historical commemorations of events and movements in Jamaican history.

The permanent exhibits at the satellite museums include the Hanover Museum, parish museum located at the old prison in Lucea, The Museum of St. James at the Civic Centre in Montego Bay, the Fort Charles Museum in Port Royal, and the People's Museum of Craft and Technology in Spanish Town Square.

THE JAMAICA MILITARY MUSEUM

The Jamaica Military Museum (Up Park Camp, contact Michael Anglin, cell tel. 876/818-4725, US$1 adults, US$0.50 children, 10 A.M.–4 P.M. Wed.–Sun.) is a collaborative effort between the Jamaica Defense Force (JDF) in consultation with the staff of the Museum of History and Ethnography showcasing Jamaica's military past, starting with the Taino and the Spanish-Taino encounter, with a few old tanks and uniforms on display from the British period, to the present JDF uniforms and medals. No reservations needed.

The **Museum of Jamaican Music** is a new development envisioned as part of the IOJ's museum network and dedicated to conserving Jamaica's musical history. Presided over by the IOJ's Museum of Ethnography under the leadership of director and curator Herbie Miller (tel. 876/922-0620), the museum supports research into and documentation of all aspects of Jamaican musical history. A temporary exhibit in the ethnography division of the Institute features a display containing musical memorabilia.

LIBERTY HALL

Liberty Hall (76 King St., tel. 876/948-8639, libertyhall@cwjamaica.com, www.garveylibertyhall.com, museum 10 A.M.– 4 P.M. Mon.–Fri., US$1 adults, US$0.50 children) is the latest addition to the IOJ. The rehabilitated building was Marcus Garvey's base of operations in the 1920s and today has a small reference library with a wealth of knowledge related to the man and his teachings. Liberty Hall houses a multimedia museum and resource center as well as continuing Garvey's vision with programs for local youth. Garvey's influence on the Jamaican psyche is profound. Liberty Hall is the best place to grasp his importance as a founder of pan-Africanism, just a few blocks up from St. William Grant Park and the Ward Theatre, a hotbed of Jamaica's labor movement.

AFRICAN-CARIBBEAN INSTITUTE OF JAMAICA (ACIJ)

The African-Caribbean Institute of Jamaica

(ACIJ, 12 Ocean Blvd., tel. 876/922-4793 or 876/922-7415, acij@anngel.com.jm, 8 A.M.–4:30 P.M. Mon.–Thurs., 8 A.M.–3:30 P.M. Fri.) has been run under the direction of Bernard Jankee since 1995. The Institute's mandate is to "collect, research, document, analyze and preserve information on Jamaica's cultural heritage, through the exploitation of oral and scribal sources." The ACIJ has a memory-bank program in which oral histories are recorded around the country and then transcribed, as well as an active publications program featuring the ACIJ Research Review. There is a small library at the office where the Institute's top-notch academic publications can be browsed and purchased. The ACIJ also runs an outreach program in schools and does presentations in universities in Jamaica and abroad. The ACIJ has a tradition of collaboration with individual researchers and institutions. Projects have included studies of traditional religions like Kumina and Revival, and research on the Maroons.

National Heroes Park

National Heroes Park, which encompasses **Heroes Memorial,** occupies 30 hectares below Cross Roads on Marescaux Road within the large roundabout known as **Heroes Circle.** The roundabout surrounds what was once the city's main sporting ground, later becoming the Kingston Race Course. The park was also the site of several important historical events, including Emancipation Day celebrations on August 1, 1938; the jubilee celebrating Queen Victoria's reign in 1887; and the free Smile Jamaica concert where a wounded Bob Marley offered the people of Kingston a 90-minute performance in defiance of his would-be assassins in 1976. Heroes Park is also said to have been the battleground where warring factions from East and West Kingston would face off in organized skirmishes.

The memorial, located at the southern end of the park, commemorates Jamaica's most important historical figures and events. Black Nationalist Marcus Garvey rests here, as does labor leader Alexander Bustamante, who formed the Jamaica Labor Party, and his cousin Norman Manley, who founded the opposition People's National Party. Norman's son Michael Manley, who gave the country its biggest communist scare for his closeness with Cuba's Fidel Castro, is also interred here. Paul Bogle and George William Gordon are also honored for their role in the Morant Bay Rebellion, which was at the vanguard of Jamaica's civil rights movement in the post-emancipation period. The most recent icon to be laid to rest at Heroes Memorial is the cultural legend Louise Bennett, referred to lovingly by all Jamaicans as "Miss Lou," who died in June 2006.

Other Sights

Headquarters House (79 Duke St., tel. 876/922-1287, 8:30 A.M.–4:30 P.M. Mon.–Fri., free admission) is home of the Jamaica National Heritage Trust, which oversees the country's heritage sites; it dates from 1755 and is a good example of Georgian architecture. Merchant Thomas Hibbert built the house in a contest to see who could construct the most ornate edifice with which to impress a local girl. There's a nice gallery on the ground floor with antiquities. It is also called Hibbert House. The Jamaican Parliament was housed at Headquarters House until it outgrew the small confines of the main chamber.

Gordon House (81 Duke St., tel. 876/922-0202) was built in 1960 to replace Headquarters House as the meeting place for Jamaica's House of Representatives. There's not much to see, but visitors can drop in and experience Jamaican political wrangling at its most civil in a House of Commons or Senate session.

The building is named after labor leader George William Gordon (1815–1865), born to Scottish planter Joseph Gordon, who owned Cherry Gardens Estate, and a quadroon slave. Young Gordon taught himself to read and write and became a successful businessman while still in his teens before going into politics. A champion of the underdog, Gordon was not popular with his peers in politics who represented the landed elite. After being elected to the Assembly in 1944, he failed to regain a seat until 19 years later when he was elected to represent St. Thomas-in-the-East, where he owned substantial landholdings. Gordon was a vocal opponent of the Custos, as well as the Governor General Edward Eyre. At the same time, he allied himself with Paul Bogle, another champion of the poor, both in politics and in religion. (They were both Native Baptists, seen at the time as a lower-class religion.) When unrest in St. Thomas culminated in the Morant Bay Rebellion, Gordon was held responsible and swiftly court-martialed and hanged. Bogle was hanged shortly thereafter. Both were made national heroes when the Order was established in 1969.

The *Jamaica Gleaner* building (7 North St., tel. 876/922-3400), home to the country's longest-running newspaper, is on North Street, with the cricket grounds of **Sabina Park** a few blocks to the east. Also nearby, on Duke Street, is Jamaica's only synagogue, the **United Congregation of Israelites,** which dates from 1912.

The Ba Beta Kristian Church of Haile Selassie I, led by the Abuna Ascento Foxe, is located on Oxford Street in front of Coronation Market and is worth a visit for its colorful service on Sunday afternoons. Women must cover their heads, wear dresses, and sit on the right side of the aisle. Men should not cover their heads. The church sponsors community initiatives as well as the Amha Selassie basic school located next door.

Jubilee and Coronation Markets sort of fuse together starting at West Parade and running along West Queen Street and Spanish Town Road to Darling Street. It's certainly worth a visit to mosey around and browse through the stalls, renowned for touting the best bargains in town on produce and just about anything else. Not the place for high-end gear, but the experience is gritty Jamaica at its best—with all its accompanying smells. While it's most comfortably enjoyed accompanied by a local, there is no danger to going

unaccompanied as long as you can handle unsolicited attention from hagglers seeking a sale. If you're a woman, it's guaranteed the market men will display a typical lack of shyness in approaching you with romantic interest.

Marcus Garvey Community Center (69½ Church St.) is the present-day venue for meetings of the Marcus Garvey People's Political Party (MGPPP) (6 P.M.–8 P.M. every Thurs.) which certainly had a stronger following when its iconic leader still attended. A fish fry is held on the last Friday of every other month (Oct., Dec., Feb., etc.), accompanied by a sound system, of course.

Trinity Cathedral (1–3 George Edly Dr., tel. 876/922-3335, 8:30 A.M. Sun. service, weekday mass at 5:30 P.M.), presided over by Father Kenneth Richards, replaced the old cathedral on Duke and Sutton, which was destroyed in the earthquake of 1907. Trinity has been center stage for several important national events. Archbishop Samuel Carter is buried on the site, and Michael Manley's funeral—attended by Fidel Castro and Louis Farrakhan, among a host of other dignitaries—was held there. A relatively small-scale earthquake destroyed the stained glass on the cathedral's south face in 1951; it was subsequently replaced with clear glass. In the years since, mischievous children have broken many of the panes by throwing stones. The original mosaic tile on the north wall has been uncovered, and a Spanish restoration team is set to restore the rest of the mosaic walls, which were at some point painted over with white. Caretaker Craig Frazer leads tours of the building and points out interesting details. A generous tip is sure to make the pious young man even more devout.

UPTOWN
◖ Emancipation Park
At the corner of Knutsford Boulevard and Oxford Road (tel. 876/926-6312 or 876/968-9292, emanpark@cwjamaica.com) two figures stand resolute, cast in bronze, their bodies thick and steadfast. A strong black

© OLIVER HILL

Trinity Cathedral is one of the most impressive structures Downtown, even while Jamaica's Catholic faith holds little sway in the country.

man faces a voluptuous woman, their heads proudly lifted to the sky as if at once acknowledging the rectitude of their long struggle for freedom and silently praying for guidance in a new era. The work, titled *Redemption Song,* was the winner of a blind competition commissioned to give the newly constructed Emancipation Park a meaningful headpiece. It was controversial for several reasons. First, its creator, Jamaican sculptor Laura Facey (www.laurafacey.com), has a very fair complexion. Second, the figures are naked, and the man could be considered well endowed. Some people wanted the sculpture immediately removed, and Facey was the talk of the island for weeks. In the end, artistic freedom prevailed and the sculpture was kept in place, much to its opponents' chagrin.

In late 2006, Facey opened an exhibit at the gallery in the natural history building of the Institute of Jamaica, where the central work was an homage to *Redemption Song:* a multitude of scaled-downed figures—identical to those on the corner of Emancipation Park—packed into a canoe reminiscent of the way they were brought through the Middle Passage. For Facey, the piece was part of a continuum consistent with the earlier work, which sets those captive souls on a new course to freedom. David Boxer, curator of the National Gallery, opened the exhibit by paying tribute to *Redemption Song* with the following words:

> . . . *their heads are raised heavenwards in prayer...yes, this is a prayer—the work is a silent hymn of communion with, and thanksgiving to, the almighty...Their nudity is part of their potency*

Redemption Song and the controversy that surrounded it reflect the deep wounds slavery left on Jamaica and the world at large. Emancipation Park is among the best-maintained public spaces in all of Kingston, perfect for reflecting on the past, relaxing on one of the many benches, or just taking a stroll. Events are held frequently on a stage set up at the center

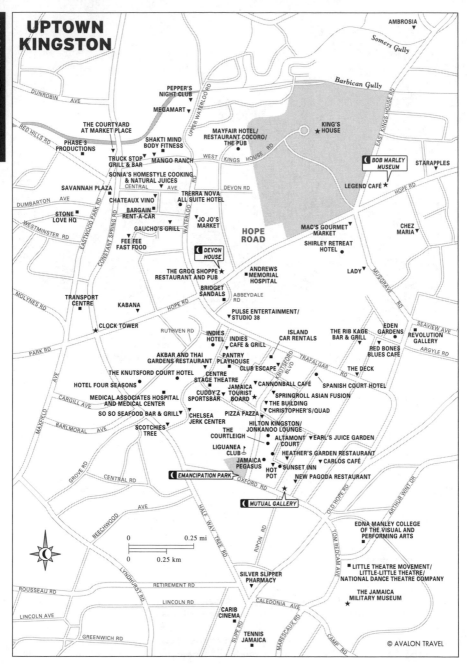

UPTOWN KINGSTON

of the park and next door at the Liguanea Club or on top of the NHT building.

Half Way Tree

Half Way Tree is the capital of St. Andrew, the parish that envelops Kingston. The bustling commercial area seen today is a far cry from its rural days when it was a popular rest stop for travelers between Kingston and Spanish Town. Several historical sites are wedged between the acres and acres of the concrete, strip mall-covered jungle.

The **clock tower** at the junction of Half Way Tree, Hope, Constant Spring, and Hagley Park Roads, was erected in 1913 as a monument to King Edward VII of England. It's the classic symbol of Half Way Tree.

St. Andrew Parish Church (free) also referred to as Half Way Tree Church, is one of the oldest Anglican churches on the island. The present church has a foundation that dates from 1692, when the earthquake destroyed the previous structure (which had stood only for a decade). One of the first U.S. Consuls to Jamaica, Robert Monroe Harrison, brother of U.S. President Benjamin Harrison, is buried there, along with his wife. Philip Livingston, a Jamaica-based merchant and son of one of the founding fathers of the United States, was married in the church. Outside there's an old, poorly maintained cemetery.

The **Half Way Tree Courthouse** adjacent to the Parish Church is a good example of Georgian architecture, dating from 1807. The front of the building is covered with latticework, presumably to keep out the heat as a form of early air conditioning. The building has been repaired and altered several times to fix storm damage, while it miraculously escaped damage during the 1907 earthquake.

The courthouse has seen many uses, from ex-slaves obtaining their certificates of freedom to agricultural society meetings. After the construction of the Resident Magistrates Court on nearby Maxfield Avenue in 1920, court sessions were no longer held at Half Way Tree Courthouse. Up until the mid-1980s, the building was used as a branch of the Institute of Jamaica called the Junior Centre, which held skills-training courses. In 2002, the center reopened and for a time hosted dance classes of the National Dance Theatre Company under the direction of late UWI professor Rex Nettleford. The courthouse was listed as a Jamaica National Heritage Trust (JNHT) site in 1957, and in 1985 the *Jamaica Gazette* declared it a National Monument. Meanwhile the structure suffered neglect and decay.

One important trial held at the Half Way Tree Courthouse was that of Alexander Bedward, a popular folk hero and founder of a Native Free Baptist sect known as Bedwardism. Bedward was an early Black Nationalist who spoke out against the religious and government authorities of the day. For this he was committed to Bellevue asylum until his death in 1930.

The **Ethiopian Orthodox Church** (McDonald Lane) was founded in Jamaica in 1972. This is the original state church of Ethiopia to which Haile Selassie I belonged. The church has an awkward relationship with Rastafarians in Jamaica; many of them have been baptized as Ethiopian Orthodox, including Bob Marley's children. To this day, the construction remains incomplete with little more than a foundation in place. Its construction has been held up by a lack of cosmic alignment and a lack of togetherness in the Rasta community, according to Rasta elder Kojo and many others who share his view. Meanwhile, many inside the Ethiopian Church scorn Rastas for considering Haile Selassie a God.

Kingston's **Hindu Temple** (139 Maxfield Ave.) holds events for all the major Hindu holidays including Ganesh Puja and Diwali. Local Hindus attend in heavy numbers on Sunday mornings.

◖ Devon House

Still one of Kingston's finest homes (26 Hope Rd., Great House, tel. 876/929-6602,

876/929-0815, or 876/926-0829, devonhousejamaica@cw.com, www.devonhouse-jamaica.com, guided tours 9:30 A.M.–5 P.M. Mon.–Sat., last tour at 4:30 P.M., US$5 for adults, US$1.50 for children under 12), Devon House is a source of pride for the City. The mansion was constructed in 1881 by Jamaica's first black millionaire, George Stiebel, who made his fortune in Venezuelan gold. Some of the city's predominantly white elite of the day were less than happy to be outdone by a black man; it is said that Lady Musgrave—wife of Governor General Lord Musgrave, who founded the Institute of Jamaica—actually had a road built (Lady Musgrave Road) so she wouldn't have to bear the humiliation of passing the spectacular mansion that humbled even her husband's residence. For many years Devon House was home to the National Gallery, before it relocated to Ocean Boulevard in 1983. Today the inside is furnished and decorated with a range of English, French, and Caribbean antiques, as well as some reproductions. The courtyard behind Devon House is full of boutique shops.

🔳 Bob Marley Museum

Located in Bob Marley's former residence at 56 Hope Road, just north of New Kingston, the house and museum (tel. 876/927-9152, US$20 adults, US$10 children 4–12, www.bobmarley-foundation.com/museum.html) has been turned into a shrine to the man and his music, with rooms full of newspaper clippings and personal effects. One-hour tours run Monday–Saturday; tours start at 9:30 A.M. and the last tour leaves at 4 P.M. Around back, there's a gift shop and a gallery has transient exhibitions. A comfortable, cozy theater is a great place to catch a movie. A presentation on Marley is available as part of the tour, and the theater is also used for occasional touring international film festivals.

Legend Café, on one side of the main gate, has great steamed fish and fresh juices. Marley's Land Rover sits under a protective carport in the other corner of the yard in front of a wall

plastered with Wailers photos. Photos are not allowed inside or behind the main building that houses the museum.

Along Hope Road

King's House (Hope Rd. at Lady Musgrave Rd., tel. 876/927-6424, fax 876/978-6025, visits scheduled by written request) has been the home of the Governor General since the capital was moved from Spanish Town in 1872. Jamaica's official head of state is appointed by the Queen of England for six-year terms. King's House was formerly the residence of Jamaica's Anglican Bishop. The original building was destroyed in the 1907 earthquake and rebuilt in 1909. The grounds have nice gardens that can be toured. Jamaica House, just south of King's House on the same grounds, is now the location for the Prime Minister's offices and is closed to the public.

Hope Botanical Gardens (just below University of Technology on western side of Hope Rd., 6 A.M.–6:30 P.M. daily, free admission), managed by the Nature Preservation Foundation (tel. 876/970-3505 hopegardens.zoo@gmail.com), is more pleasant and impressive than the Hope Zoo (tel. 876/970-2459, 10 A.M.–4 P.M. daily, adults US$2, children 3–11 US$1.10), located in the same large park. The zoo is more of a nursing home for a few lost and found animals: sheep, a monkey, a handful of flamingos, and several iguanas. You won't find leopards or elephants.

The **University of the West Indies** (Mona Rd. and University Rd., www.mona.uwi.edu), in the quiet residential neighborhood of Mona, is worth a visit as the campus sits at the base of the Blue Mountains and has extensive rolling lawns with interesting ruins of the old Mona Estate aqueduct and a beautiful mural created by Belgian artist Claude Rahir with the help of UWI students.

The cut-stone University Chapel by the main entrance is an excellent example of Georgian architecture. It was transported block by block from Gales Valley Estate in Trelawny at the bidding of Princess Alice, first chancellor of the University. The former sugar warehouse was given a new life at UWI, its interior decorated with materials from all the countries the university has served. The coats of arms of these countries are inlaid in the chapel ceiling.

Cherry Gardens Great House

Cherry Gardens Great House (46 Upper Russell Heights) was built by Scottish Planter Joseph Gordon, father of national hero George William Gordon, who was born to a quadroon slave in humble quarters next to the main house. George William Gordon went on to become a successful mulatto businessman who agitated for civil rights until he was executed for taking a stand. A drive up through Cherry Gardens gives a glimpse into Uptown, with concrete mansions covering the landscape. Cherry Gardens Great House is a breath of fresh air amongst monstrosities seemingly built with no regard for the surrounding environment. The great house itself is an architectural masterpiece, where louvered windows keep the inside dark and cool while allowing the breeze to move freely through. Though the house is not open to the public, the owners, Oliver Jones and family, are friendly enough and don't mind people stopping by for a look at the outside.

ART STUDIOS AND GALLERIES

The Rock Tower (8 Pechon St. at Tower St., 876/922 9229, 876/509-0480, or Fidel Sutherland at 876/377-1381, melinda@rocktower.org, www.rocktower.org, 9 A.M.–5 P.M. Mon.–Fri.) also known as ROKTOWA by the artists, is an inner-city gallery that helps develop local talent by encouraging linkages between practical art and export markets. Creative Director Melinda Brown brought the concept from her pioneering studio in New York City's Meatpacking district to Downtown Kingston, where she continues her crusade for urban renewal through community art. ROKTOWA artists work in oil, clay, and alabaster, among other materials.

© OLIVER HILL

Cherry Gardens Great House

The Easel (134 Old Hope Rd., Liguanea Plaza by Wendy's, just above Sovereign Centre adjacent to Mothers restaurant, tel. 876/977-2067, 9 A.M.–5 P.M. Mon.–Wed., 10 A.M.–6 P.M. Thurs.–Sat.) sells painting supplies and has a gallery with Jamaican abstract, realist, and expressionist artists represented, among them Eugene Campbell, David Pottinger, Richard Hall, and Gonzalez Barnes. The average painting sells for US$450, but prices range from US$100–2,500. The gallery is managed by Abigail Smith and Managing Director Yvonne Roach.

Revolution Gallery (44 Lady Musgrave Rd., tel. 876/946-0053, 10 A.M.–6 P.M. Mon.–Fri., 10:30 A.M.–3 P.M. Sat.) has some exceptional crafts as well as excellent work by Jamaican painter Natalie Barnes, among many more.

Island Art & Framing (Orchid Village, 20 Barbican Road, tel. 876/977-0318, islandart@cwjamaica.com, www.islandartandframing.com) sells a wide variety of local and imported arts and crafts and can frame just about anything.

Sanaa Studios (25 Barbican Rd., behind Burger King, tel. 876/977-4792 or 876/822-7528, info@sanaastudios.com, www.sanaastudios.com, 10 A.M.–5 P.M. Mon.–Fri., 10 A.M.–2 P.M. Sat.) offers classes in ceramics, drawing, painting, art photography, and jewelry making. A small gallery has a steady flow of exhibits by students and others. Drop-in rates are US$20–35 for three-hour sessions.

Amai Craft (Shop #27, Red Hills Trade Centre, 30 Red Hills Rd., tel. 876/920-9134, ashbrook@anngel.com, 10 A.M.–5 P.M. Mon.–Fri., 10 A.M.–2 P.M. Sat.) sells paintings specializing in Jamaican intuitive, or self-taught, artists. Belgium-born Herman van Asbroeck, the proprietor, founded the gallery in 2000 but has been living in Jamaica for more than three decades. The gallery is located upstairs from the unassuming framing shop Herman runs on the ground floor.

Grosvenor Gallery (1 Grosvenor Terrace, Manor Park, tel. 876/924-6684, grosvenorgallery@cwjamaica.com) has contemporary art exhibits and occasional crafts fairs that brings artists and craftspeople from around Jamaica. Call for upcoming events.

The Art Centre (202 Hope Rd., across from the University of Technology, tel. 876/927-1608, artcentre.ja@gmail.com, 9 A.M.–5 P.M. Mon.–Fri., 10 A.M.–4 P.M. Sat., free admission) is housed in a uniquely designed apartment building commissioned by A. D. Scott in the 1960s. Inside, colorful murals adorn the walls and art is displayed on the upper two levels as part of the building's permanent collection. The gallery uses the ground floor space for its transitory exhibits. Rosemarie Thwaites is the gallery director. Paintings start around US$100. On the same compound there is an art supply and framing shop.

(Mutual Gallery

The Mutual Gallery (2 Oxford Rd., New Kingston, tel. 876/929-4302, 10 A.M.–6 P.M. Mon.–Fri., 10 A.M.–3 P.M. Sat., free admission), run by curator/director Gilou Bauer, is Kingston's most dynamic venue for new artists. The Mutual Gallery holds a yearly competition looking for trends and upcoming talent; new artists are invited to compete by submitting a catalog of works and a proposal for what they plan to do in the competition. From the initial submissions, 10 artists are then asked to submit two original pieces created for the competition. Then five or six finalists are asked to submit a minimum of three additional works, from which the winner is determined. Contestants must be Jamaican or have lived in Jamaica for at least two years. The first-prize winner receives US$1,500 and the People's Prize winner receives US$750. The five judges on the selection committee tend to be members of Jamaica's artistic and academic community. The Gallery sells many artists' work, which can be viewed in a storage/viewing room at the back, taking 30 percent gallery commission. Uptown Jamaicans and collectors are the most frequent buyers. Exhibitions are sponsored by local corporations.

Entertainment and Events

Many Jamaicans love a good party or "session" as they call it, and Kingston has the most consistent and varied nightlife to support partygoers and dance enthusiasts. Don't be alarmed should someone approach to within intimate distance for what is known as a slow "whine" in a club or at a street dance. But it's not just "whining" that Kingston offers. While still less than cosmopolitan in terms of its entertainment offering (you won't find an opera house), the city does support a wide array of cultural and artistic forms from modern dance to art and theater. Of course music touches everybody, and Kingston's nightclubs deliver a raw celebration of music on dance floors and in the streets.

There's no need to hurry in Jamaica, as everything inevitably starts late—certainly true for nightlife. Family-oriented and cultural entertainment generally starts earlier in the evenings, between 7 and 10 P.M. Few people go out to a nightclub before midnight, and clubs don't typically fill up until 2 or 3 A.M. Street dances start particularly late and can be quite boring until a sizeable crowd gathers and people start showing off their moves amidst pan-chicken vendors, enormous speakers, wafting ganja smoke, and a rising sun. Expensive all-inclusive parties maintain an exclusive crowd with ticket prices in the range of US$100. These parties have become quite popular, with the Frenchman's parties at the vanguard of Kingston high society chic for its food and select crowd. UWI and University of Technology campuses host parties somewhat regularly.

LIVE MUSIC

Live music and stage show performances in Kingston are not as frequent or varied as some would expect given the prominent role music plays in Jamaican life. Nonetheless, there are a handful of venues that feature somewhat regular acts. Stage shows are held routinely and there are large events at least once a month at **Mas Camp Village,** located on Oxford Road at the southern boundary of New Kingston.

Jokers Wild and other promoters use the popular venue regularly. Mas Camp is a massive venue that holds occasional stage shows and has been the site for Bacchanal, Kingston's version of carnival, with parties every Friday from February to April. In 2009, Sandals boss Gordon "Butch" Stewart's *Jamaica Observer* newspaper announced the hotel chain would build a Sandals City on the site. The announcement was followed a few months later with news a Marriott would be brought to New Kingston, but a timeline for these developments was not defined. Neighbors don't appreciate the noise and have challenged use of the area as a concert venue, which could bode well for it being put to an alternate use. But if partygoers get their way, Mas Camp will be around for some time to come.

Village Café (20 Barbican Rd., tel. 876/970-4861) features live music at least once a week, typically on Tuesday. Usually the acts are of the obscure up-and-coming variety and draw a young crowd.

Jamaica Association of Vintage Artistes and Affiliates (JAVAA) (7–9 Hagley Park Rd., Half Way Tree Entertainment Complex next to York Plaza, tel. 876/908-4464, www.javaa.com.jm) holds occasional shows at the Pegasus Hotel or smaller productions at other venues (admission typically US$15–20). JAVAA carries the torch for Jamaica's early music from the 1950s to the 1980s, from lovers' rock to rocksteady, ska, and roots reggae. The organization was formed to bring recognition and financial support to these artists, many of whom participated in the formation of Jamaican popular music, as they reach their golden years. Tickets are available from JAVAA members and at the JAVAA office.

Backyaad (126 Constant Spring Rd., call Chris Daley for info, tel. 876/456-5556, linkjohnnydaley@yahoo.com) is a spacious outdoor venue that hosts occasional concerts and comedy sessions. Comedy jams are held inconsistently on the last Wednesday of the month.

Jam World is a large venue in Portmore that hosts Sting, an annual Boxing Day event.

FESTIVALS AND EVENTS

Several annual events are worth being in Kingston for, including **Bacchanal,** which runs February to April; the **Reggae Film Festival,** held the last week in February; the **Observer Food Awards** held in late May; **Caribbean Fashion Week** in early June; and **Restaurant Week,** typically held the third week in November when participating restaurants slash prices and feature culinary novelties. The **Strawberry Hill High Stakes Backgammon Tournament,** held in the nearby Blue Mountains, is a must for dedicated fans of the game with an appetite for competition.

The Excellence in Music and Entertainment Awards, more popularly known as the **EME Awards,** celebrate the best in Jamaican entertainment, with a ceremony staged each year in early February. The brainchild of renowned 102 FM radio personality Richard "Richie B" Burgess, the awards ceremony is filled with pageantry and grandeur a la Jamaicana, with women sporting the latest hairstyles, and the biggest deejays of the day passing through with entourages 20-plus strong.

Jamaica's Girls and Boys Championships, better known as Champs, is an annual track and field meet held in late March that sees Kingston's hotels booked with fans from home and abroad who come out in hoards to watch the competition. The energy at the National Stadium is palpable, with fans screaming and waving for their schools.

Moving Mountains (www.movingmtns.posterous.com) is a three-day house music festival held each year in on the third weekend in March at Strawberry Hill. Held the week before the Winter Music Conference in Miami, Moving Mountains brings house DJs from abroad who ascend to Strawberry Hill for a one-of-a-kind party weekend with a spectacular backdrop of Kingston.

The *Jamaica Observer* Food Awards, the brainchild of larger-than-life fashionista, food critic, and *Jamaica Observer* lifestyle editor, Novia McDonald-Whyte, was established in 1998 to celebrate excellence in culinary presentation. It affords patrons an opportunity to taste what's new and different in Jamaica's food industry, with over 60 booths showcasing the country's scrumptious offerings, from the tried-and-true jerk sauces, rum, and Blue Mountain Coffee, to more exotic offerings. Top winners are awarded two full scholarships each year to the Hospitality Department at the University of Technology with 20-odd awards presented to establishments that have excelled. Dubbed "The Caribbean's Oscar Night of Food", the event is held on the east lawns of Devon House in late May each year. Contact Novia (tel. 876/511-2479) for further details and tickets, which usually run about US$100.

Kingston Restaurant Week, staged the second or third week in November by *The Jamaica Gleaner* in association with Stephanie Scott's SSCO Event Management (tel. 876/978-6245 or cell tel. 876/564-1700) is one of the best times to be in Kingston for those who love to sample restaurants. Prices are slashed by up to 50 percent, and participating venues offer patrons new creations in an attempt to develop loyal customers who will return throughout the year. The week-long program has extended to other towns across Jamaica over the years, with participating restaurants now spanning the island, especially in Ocho Rios and Montego.

NIGHTCLUBS

Quad (20–22 Trinidad Terrace, tel. 876/754-7823, quadnightclub@gmail.com, US$12) is Kingston's longest-standing Uptown nightclub, with three levels. Christopher's Bar and Lounge is on the ground level, with Oxygen Nightclub on the second floor, and Voodoo Lounge on the top level. Patrons frequently go from one floor to the next throughout the night depending on the genre of music and vibe on each level.

Club Privilege (14–16 Trinidad Terrace, tel. 876/622-6532, vip@clubprivilegeja.com, www.clubprivilegeja.com, open Thurs., Fri., and Sun., admission US$12) is a slick club located above

Treasure Hunt gaming lounge that prides itself on being the most exclusive venue in town. Bottles of champagne and Moet adorn two bars, with lounge furniture in the cordoned-off VIP area overlooking a large dance floor. Privilege is the only club in Jamaica that stocks Ace of Spades champagne, Black Hennessey, and Patrón tequilas. The club features U.S. alternative music on Alternative Thursdays (10 P.M.–4 A.M.), club night on Fridays featuring reggae and hip hop, and oldies on Retro Sundays (9 P.M.–2 A.M.). On the first Saturday of every month, Reboot features funky house with visiting DJs from all over the world. Drinks range from US$5 for a beer to US$785 for a bottle of Ace of Spades champagne.

The Building (69 Knutsford Blvd., tel. 876/906-1828 or 876/906-1829), formerly known as the Asylum nightclub, was renamed and transformed in 2009 from a New Kingston landmark nightclub into a ready-to-go rental venue with sound system, lighting, and bars. The venue features regular promotions like ladies' night on Tuesdays and Street Vybz Thursdays, hosted by Vybz Kartel. The continuity of such events cannot be guaranteed, so call ahead. The admission cost is based on the specific function, typically ranging from US$4 to US$12.

Limelight (Half Way Tree Entertainment Complex, 5–7 Hagley Park, tel. 876/908-0841) is a popular bar that hosts several promoters each week for independent parties which typically run from midnight to 5 A.M. Bounty Sundays is promoted by veteran dancehall master Bounty Killer, Hot Mondays is hosted by Fire Links, Boasy Tuesdays, a.k.a. Blazey Blazey, is hosted by dance master Blazey, and Expression Thursdays is hosted by the Dance Expressions troupe.

Fiction (Unit #6, Marketplace, 67 Constant Spring Road, tel. 876/631-8038, fictionloungeja@gmail.com, www.fictionloungeja. com, 6 P.M.–4 A.M. Mon.–Sat., cover typically US$12) is the newest Uptown nightclub in Kingston, with a popular ladies' night on Thursdays. Call or go online for actual event schedules. Fiction quickly became a magnet for Jamaica's young elite partygoers after opening in early 2009. It offers a varied bar menu and a wide selection of local and imported liquors, with a Johnny Walker whiskey bar, a cordoned off VIP section, and elegant styling that would be just as at home in the trendiest Miami or New York hot spot.

BARS
New Kingston
Christopher's (20–22 Trinidad Terrace, tel. 876/754-7823) bar and lounge, located on the ground floor of Quad, has a busy, pleasant, upscale atmosphere with free Wi-Fi and good bar food. Battered jumbo shrimp, crab cakes, and two beers go for US$25. Christopher's is a favorite after-work spot for Kingston's corporate set.

Club Escape (24 Knutsford Blvd., tel. 876/960-1856, open 24/7, US$6 for men, US$5 for ladies after 9 P.M. Fri. and Sat.) is an outdoor bar and nightclub that often has heated dominoes games in the early evenings, plus a mix of music that includes hip hop and reggae. Lunch is served 11 A.M.–4 P.M. daily except Sunday, with items like chicken, oxtail, curry goat, and pepper steak (US$3.50–5). Light items like kebabs and grilled and jerk chicken are served in the evenings until 3 A.M.

The Deck (14 Trafalgar Rd., tel. 876/978-1582, richard@thedeck.biz, open daily from 4:30 P.M. until the last person leaves) is a large venue with a boat motif. Fishing nets hang from what was once the roof of an auto garage. There are a few billiards tables and a decent bar food menu (US$4–15). Friday's after-work jam is popular, and weekend nights are generally busy when music blares and patrons are occasionally inspired to dance.

Studio 38 (38-A Trafalgar Rd., tel. 876/906-6465) is an open air bar at the Pulse Entertainment complex catering to an older crowd, but rejuvenated frequently when Pulse models are on hand for one of their many annual events and after parties.

Half Way Tree
Bin 26 Wine Bar (876/908-1322, bin26winebar@gmail.com) has a few tables offering indoor/outdoor seating and wine by the glass

SOUND SYSTEMS AND STREET DANCES

Sound systems fostered the development of Jamaican music. Starting out as little more than a set of speaker boxes on wheels, the sounds would set up at different points around town or arrive in rural areas to feed a thirst created by the advent of radio in the country in 1939, which brought American popular music, whetting Jamaica's appetite for new sounds. Jamaica's musicians responded by bringing traditional mento and calypso rhythms to the R&B and pop tunes the people were demanding, ultimately giving birth to the ska, rocksteady, reggae, and dancehall genres. Jamaican sound systems have grown in conjunction with reggae music and dancehall, one giving voice in the street to the other's lyrical prowess and social commentary from inside the studio. While a number of different sounds vie for the top ranking at clubs and stage shows, historically they were the voice of the street dance, having replaced the African drums of yesteryear.

A sound generally comprises a few individual selectors who form a team to blast the latest dancehall tunes, using equipment that ranges from a home stereo system at max output for those just starting out, to the most sophisticated equipment operated by the more established names. Street dances like Passa Passa foster the development of DJ artistry, providing a venue for the different sound systems to flex and clash, like the ever-popular Stone Love, Renaissance, Black Chiney, or Razz and Biggy. These sounds grew on the coattails of King Tubby, among the biggest sound system personalities of all time. Sound clashes are held often, during which each sound attempts to outperform the other, with the ultimate judge being the crowd, which expresses approval with hands raised in the air as if firing a pistol, accompanied by the requisite shouts of "braap, braap, braap, braap!" or "pam, pam, pam!"

Street dances fill an important role in providing entertainment and an expressive outlet for Kingston's poorest. Dances are held for special occasions, including birthdays, funerals, and holidays. Many started as one-off parties but were so popular they became established as regular weekly events. Typically a section of street is blocked off to traffic and huge towers of speakers are set up. Sometimes the street is not blocked off at all, but the early-morning hours when these dances are held see little traffic, and what does flow is accommodated by the dancers – who sometimes use the passing vehicles to prop up their dance partner for a more dramatic "whine."

While clubs across Uptown Kingston assess an admission fee, which varies depending on the crowd they are looking to attract, the street is a public venue where all are welcome. Uptown people might have traditionally preferred a bar setting, but Downtown people have resorted to creating the party on their doorstep. Increasingly, Uptown folks venture down to the poor areas on nights when dances are held to partake in a scene that doesn't exist anywhere else and has come to be acknowledged as an invaluable cultural phenomenon where DJs flex their skills to discriminating crowds.

In the past, noise ordinances became the favorite justification for police raids to "lock off di dance," but today the dances are for the most part tolerated by the authorities as harmless entertainment effective in pacifying the city's poor. Intellectuals like Jamaican poet Mutabaruka, who claims "the more dance is the less crime," have come to endorse and encourage these dances as healthy community events. Even though they are often held in areas obviously scarred with urban blight and associated with violence, like Tivoli Gardens and Rae Town, violence is not a part of the street dance. Rather, it is a place where people come to enjoy, decked out in their flashiest clothes (jackets and fancy shoes for men, skimpy skirts and tops for women) to drink a Guinness, smoke a spliff, perhaps, and catch up on the latest dances.

Regular patrons at these events welcome visitors from Uptown and abroad, but care should be taken to show respect and concede that you are clearly not on your turf. Plenty a "bad man" frequent these dances, and even if they are not wanted by the authorities, they tend to like creating the impression that they are and accordingly don't appreciate being photographed without granting their approval first. Parts of Downtown, especially along parts of Spanish Town Road, can be desolate and a bit dodgy at night, and many drivers use that as an excuse to proceed with caution at red lights rather than coming to a stop.

Any intended regularity to street dances struggles under the constant threat from police who have a mandate to lock off music in public spaces at midnight during the week and at 2 A.M. on weekends. Promoters complain that this doesn't allow them to recoup their investment in venue and liquor, and that street dances reduce crime by giving the youth a free venue for enjoyment, but such claims have fallen on deaf ears. Despite the challenges, dedicated party promoters keep at it and struggle through, even if they have to change venue or even move out of town and take their dance on the road, as was the case with "Dutty Fridaze." Other dances that began on the street were forced into the club by regular disruptions by the police. Some of the more regular dances around town include:

- **Uptown Mondays,** put on by Whitfield "Witty" Henry (Savannah Plaza, Half Way Tree, cell. 876/468-1742)

- **Boasy Tuesdays** (Limelight, Half Way Tree Entertainment Complex), run by dancer and promoter extraordinaire, Blazey (cell tel. 876/507-7254 or 876/354-0130)

- **Weddy Weddy Wednesdays** (Stone Love HQ, Half Way Tree)

- **Giveaway Wednesdays** (Russell Road off Beechwood Avenue) hosted by dancer Mumsel

- **Passa Passa** (Spanish Town Rd. and Beeston St., Wednesdays starting around 2 A.M.)

- **Street Vybz Thursdays** (The Building) put on by Vybz Kartel in a club setting, but one that sufficiently evokes the street dance vibe

- **Expression Thursdays** (Limelight) hosted by Dance Expressions troupe

- **Port Royal Fridays** (Port Royal) can heat up in the evenings after the fish fry shops cool down

- **Something Fishy** (Rae St., Rae Town) on Fridays and Sundays; a regular oldies session is kept by the Capricorn Inn bar

- **Wet Sundaze** (Auto Vision car wash at 8 Hillview Ave.)

- **Passion Sundays** (Kno Limit Sports Bar, 1 Hillview Ave., Half Way Tree)

- **Bounty Sundays** (Limelight, Half Way Tree Entertainment Complex) is hosted by dancehall icon Bounty Killer

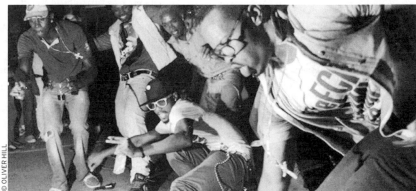

© OLIVER HILL

Boasy Tuesdays is one of the hottest weekly street dances in Kingston.

CARIBBEAN FASHION WEEK

Jamaica's contribution has been central to a bourgeoning Caribbean fashion industry. **Pulse Entertainment** (38-A Trafalgar Rd., tel. 876/960-0049, www.pulsemodels.com, www.caribbeanfashionweek.com), founded by Kingsley Cooper and Hillary Phillips in 1980, started holding Caribbean Fashion Week (CFW) in 2001. CFW has become a wildly successful annual event, described by British *Vogue* as one of the most important fashion trends on the planet. Held during the first half of June, the week is filled with fashion shows, parties, more parties, and some of the world's most striking women clad in creative attire designed by a young cadre of imaginative talent. It's definitely one of the best times of year to be in Kingston.

Pulse Entertainment has found great success in supporting an ever-swelling corps of young model hopefuls, mostly from Jamaica, and giving them a chance on the world stage. Some of the most successful Pulse models have been featured in the world's foremost magazines, like *Sports Illustrated* and *Esquire* (Carla Campbell), *Vogue* (Nadine Willis and Jaunel McKenzie), and *Cosmopolitan* (Sunna Gottshalk). At the same time, CFW has provided a forum for established Caribbean designers like Cooyah's Homer Bair, as well as others like Uzuri, Mutamba, and Biggy. Bob's daughter Cedella Marley never fails to create a splash with her proud and tasteful Catch a Fire line.

CFW events are held at numerous venues around the capital, centered on the National Indoor Sports Centre. These typically include Studio 38 at the Pulse Entertainment Complex and the stately Villa Ronai in Kingston's uptown suburb of Stony Hill. Fashion Week attendees descend on Kingston amidst a tangible buzz created by an invasion of models, fashion media, and increasingly, designers from the United States and Europe coming to catch a glimpse of the latest unabashed creation with the potential to spur a trend reaching far beyond the little rock of Jamaica.

or bottle and appetizers. Wines are imported from most major wine-producing regions, including Spain, France, Italy, Chile, Argentina, California, Australia, and New Zealand.

The Experience (7 Merrick Ave., contact Darren Neita, cell tel. 876/429-0235, 5 P.M.–midnight Wed.–Thurs., 5 P.M.–2 A.M. Fri.–Sat., 3–10 P.M. Sun.) is a hip bar located at the back of a garden behind Angela's Fabulous Fashions. Some of the best curried goat around is served on Fridays and Saturdays, and patrons come to play dominoes on Sundays, with live jazz performances on a good Sunday.

Chateaux Vino (9 Merrick Ave., between South and Central, contact Terry-Ann Arnold, cell tel. 876/376-2874, chateauxvino@gmail.com) is a cozy and well-appointed wine and martini bar that opened in late 2009.

The Pub (Mayfair Hotel, tel. 876/926-1610 or 876/926-1612, 9 A.M.–1 A.M. weekdays, till 2 A.M. Fri.–Sat.) has a nice ambience by the pool.

Kno Limit Sports Bar (8 Hillview Ave., tel. 876/285-7775, kitchen open 11:30 A.M.–9 P.M., bar open until you say when Mon.–Sat.) has a nice outdoor courtyard space with a flat panel TV behind the bar. Kno Limit is perhaps best known for Passion Sunday (midnight Sun.–3:30 A.M. Mon.), a popular street party held weekly. The kitchen serves traditional Jamaican fare, including fried, baked, and roast chicken, plus tripe and beans, shrimp, conch, lobster, and cooked food (ground provisions, or tubers). The bar was opened in October 2006 by entrepreneur Junior Cox right before the start of World Cup Cricket in 2007, with Donna Hibbert managing.

Moulin Rouge (120-A Constant Spring Rd., 4 P.M.–you say when Tues.–Sun., admission US$4 Thurs.–Fri.) is a rooftop billiards hall. Thursday night is oil wrestling, Coyote Friday sees waitresses dress up in Western-inspired outfits, with young talent showcased on Sundays (9–12). Contact supervisor Lilly Labarr (cell tel. 876/866-3393) for upcoming events. A kitchen is open during the day (9 A.M.–6 P.M.).

Liguanea

Medusa (96 Hope, behind Treasure Hut shopping plaza, tel. 876/978-3741 or 876/381-4466, 4 P.M. until last person leaves Mon.–Sat.) located on a second-story wood deck built by proprietor Jason Lee in 2005, is the perfect spot for an evening drink. Patrons dance the night away for Latin Night, held every other Saturday. The Wednesday evening (6 P.M.–1 A.M.) all-you-can-drink special is very popular (US$12).

Waterfalls (160 Hope Rd., tel. 876/977-0652) is a banqueting facility that does functions and is open to the public as a nightclub on Thursdays (9 P.M.–4 A.M., US$6) for oldies featuring Merritone Disco sound, and a mixture of reggae, Calypso, and hip hop from the 1960s, 1970s, and 1980s. It's one of the few places in Kingston that catches the vibe of an old dancehall straight out of the 1960s, with the crowd skanking to ska, rocksteady, R&B, and reggae classics well into the night. The cover charge includes complimentary soup. Known for its older crowd, Waterfalls also offers an all-inclusive Sunday brunch (US$20/person, 10:30 A.M.–3 P.M.) featuring live Jamaican-flavored jazz.

PERFORMING ARTS
Theater

Jamaica has a vibrant tradition in theater, pantomime, and spoken word performances, with annual shows and competitions sponsored by the **Jamaica Cultural Development Commission** (www.jcdc.org.jm). Events are held throughout the year but come to a head during the weeks around Emancipation and Independence in early August.

Little Theatre Movement, the **Little-Little Theatre,** and the **National Dance Theatre Company** (4 Tom Redcam Ave., tel. 876/926-6129, www.ltmpantomime.com) share a property on the edge of Downtown. The Xaymaca Dance Theatre also performs here in late October. Plays run throughout the year; call for details on performances. Pantomime performances run December 26–early May, with school plays after that. The National Dance Theatre performs July–August. Henry Fowler, Rex Nettleford, Barbara Gloudon, Louise

"Miss Lou" Bennett, Oliver Samuels, and Ken Hill are some of the founding members of the Little Theatre Movement.

Centre Stage Theatre (70 Dominica Dr., beside New Kingston Shopping Centre, tel. 876/960-3585, annual performance series info 876/968-7529) is a small venue where productions tend to be family-oriented musicals in a mixture of English and Patois. Centre Stage usually holds two annual performance series, August–November, and December 26–late April/early May. For further information contact Rosie Williams at Jambiz International (876/754-3877, www.jambizonline.com). The cast usually includes renowned Jamaican comedians Oliver Samuels and Glen "Titus" Campbell.

Green Gables Theatre (6 Cargill Ave., off Half Way Tree Rd., 876/926-4966 or 876/929-5315, www.jamaicastages.com) is the venue for Stages Production plays, which typically run at 8 P.M. Wednesday–Saturday and with two shows at 5 P.M. and 8 P.M. on Sunday.

The **Louise Bennett Garden Theatre** and the Ranny Williams Entertainment Centre (36 Hope Rd., tel. 876/926-5726, hrd@jcdc.org.jm, www.jcdc.org.jm) host occasional plays and concerts as well as bingo, book launches, and barbecues a couple of times a month.

Phillip Sherlock Centre for the Creative Arts (UWI Mona, tel. 876/927-1047) puts on UWI productions, including those of the student dance society. The building that houses the arts center is architecturally impressive.

The Theatre Place (8 Haining Road, 876/908-0040) is Kingston's newest theatrical venue, opened in late 2009 and run by Pablo Hoilett (cell tel. 876/364-4752, themediaplanet@gmail.com). The theater typically puts on comedies and other plays (admission US$12).

Ward Theatre (North Parade, Downtown, tel. 876/922-0360 or 876/922-0453) holds occasional plays, pantomimes, and special events.

Pantry Playhouse (2 Dumfries Rd., tel. 876/960-9845, admission US$12–15) features comical productions throughout the year in a quaint outdoor setting in the heart of New Kingston. Plays usually run for three months, and performances are generally held

KINGSTON'S WEEKLY NIGHTLIFE

Most bars have happy hours after work on Friday. Street dances are subject to change based on police activity. Other regular events fall out of fashion and are discontinued with little notice.

MONDAY

Games Night at Cuddy'z (Shops #4-6, New Kingston Shopping Center, Dominica Dr.) starting at 6 P.M.

Uptown Mondays Street Dance in Savannah Plaza (Constant Spring Road, Half Way Tree, 11 P.M.-2 A.M.) Contact promoter Whitfield "Witty" Henry (cell. 876/468-1742) for details. Admission is typically around US$2.

Hot Mondays at Limelight (Half Way Tree Entertainment Complex, midnight-4 A.M.)

Martini Mondays at Carlos Café (22 Belmont Rd., New Kingston) with free martinis for the ladies 6-9 P.M.

TUESDAY

Oldies Night at The Deck (14 Trafalgar Rd., 7:30 P.M.-midnight)

Live Music at Village Café (Orchid Plaza, Liguanea, 10 P.M.-2 A.M. select Tuesdays)

Ladies Night at The Building (69 Knutsford Boulevard, New Kingston 10 P.M.-4 A.M.)

Boasy Tuesdays at Limelight (Half Way Tree Entertainment Complex, midnight-4 A.M.) Contact promoter Blazey (cell. 876/507-7254) for details.

WEDNESDAY

Jazz Night at The Deck (14 Trafalgar Rd.), with occasional live jazz

Weddy Wednesday at Stone Love HQs (Half Way Tree, 10 P.M.-2 A.M.)

Passa Passa Street Dance (Spanish Town Road, Downtown 2-6 A.M.)

Brand New Machine at Fiction Lounge (Unit #6, Marketplace, Half Way Tree), with guest DJs, fashion shows, and art exhibits with an indie vibe

THURSDAY

Soca Night at The Deck during Bacchannal season, February 4-April 8 (14 Trafalgar Rd., 7 P.M.-midnight)

Latin Night at Jonkanoo Lounge in the Hilton (77 Knutsford Boulevard, New Kingston, classes starting at 7 P.M., club till 3 A.M.)

Street Vybz at The Building (69 Knutsford Boulevard, New Kingston, 10 P.M.-4 A.M.)

Alternative Thursdays at Club Privilege (14-16 Trinidad Terrace, New Kingston, 10 P.M.-3 A.M.)

Wednesday–Sunday. Me and Mi Chapsie, a play about older women going with younger men, was a popular play performed in 2009 and a good example of the comical lean to most of these productions.

The outdoor amphitheatre at **Edna Manley College of the Visual and Performing Arts** (1 Arthur Winter Dr., tel. 876/929-2350) hosts poetry readings on the last Tuesday of every month starting at 7:30 P.M.; regular dance performances are held in the indoor theatre next door.

Dance

Ashe Caribbean Performing Art Ensemble & Academy (call executive director Conroy Wilson for performance dates and location, tel. 876/960-2985 or 876/997-5935, www.

asheperforms.com, asheperforms@gmail.com) has regular performances throughout the year. Ashe is a full-time dance company that travels frequently and does "edutainment" projects in schools across the island.

Movements Dance Company (Liguanea, contact director Monica Campbell, tel. 876/929-7797 or 876/999-7953, maccsl@cwjamaica.com) was founded in 1981 by Monica Campbell McFarlane, Pat Grant-Heron, Michelle Tappin-Lee, and Denise Desnoes and has since grown into one of Jamaica's most dynamic and versatile dance companies. Both traditional Jamaican and Caribbean rhythms inform the company's repertoire. The schedule of performances climaxes each year with the annual Season of Dance in November. The company also travels

Ladies' Night at Fiction (Unit #6, Marketplace, Half Way Tree, 11 P.M.-4 A.M.)
Oldies Night with Merritone Disco Sound at Waterfalls (160 Hope Rd., Liguanea, 10 P.M.-3 A.M.)

FRIDAY
After Work Jam at The Deck (14 Trafalgar Rd., 7 P.M. until the last person leaves)
Fish Fry Lyme in the square at Port Royal, 9 P.M.-midnight
Krazy Karaoke Night at Carlos Café (22 Belmont Rd., New Kingston, 10 P.M.-2 A.M.)
Karaoke Night at Morgan's Harbour in Port Royal
Club Night at Fiction (Unit #6, Market Place, 67 Constant Spring Rd., 11 P.M.-4 A.M.)
Club Night at Club Privilege (14-16 Trinidad Terrace, New Kingston, 10 P.M.-2 A.M.)
Vintage Live Music at JAVAA (select weeks, or last Friday of the month), at alternating venues (tel. 876/908-4464), starting at 9 P.M.
Something Fishy session at the Capricorn Inn, 10 P.M.-4 A.M.
The Jamaican German Society (33 Seymour Ave., tel. 876/946-1409) weekly drinking session for friends of Germany, 6 -11 P.M. or later

SATURDAY
Color Me Single at Carlos Café (22 Belmont Rd., New Kingston, 9 P.M.-3 A.M.), hosted by Dancehall Queen Carlene with games and prizes
Latin Night at Pepper's (Upper Waterloo Rd., Half Way Tree) or in the bar at the Courtleigh Hotel (85 Knutsford Blvd., New Kingston) on alternating weeks, from 10 P.M.-3 A.M. (admission US$7). Contact selector Tony Pryce (cell. 876/294-8074) for details.
Live Music at Jo Jo's Jerk Pit and More (12 Waterloo Rd., Half Way Tree, 10 P.M.-midnight)
Lounge and Club Night at Fiction (Unit #6, Market Place, 67 Constant Spring Rd., Half Way Tree), with occasional guest DJs

SUNDAY
Oldies Street Dance in Rae Town (10 P.M.-2 A.M.)
Wet Sundaze at Auto Vision (8 Hillview Ave. 6 P.M.-12 A.M.)
Retro Sundays at Club Privilege (14-16 Trinidad Terrace, New Kingston, 9 P.M.-2 A.M.)
Bounty Sundays at Limelight (Half Way Tree Entertainment Complex, midnight-4 A.M.)
Passion Sundays at Kno Limit Sports Bar (1 Hillview Ave., midnight-4 or 5 A.M.)

to perform in the United States, the United Kingdom, Canada, and neighboring Caribbean islands.

CINEMAS
Carib Cinema plays Hollywood films (Cross Roads, box office tel. 876/926-6106, movie times tel. 876/906-1090, www.palaceamusement.com, typical show times 5 P.M. and 8 P.M. daily, admission US$6).

The **Cineplex** (shop 47a Sovereign Center, tel. 876/978-3522, movie times tel. 876/978-8286, admission US$6) is also owned by Palace Amusement and has more of the same Hollywood films.

If you'd prefer to stay in and watch a movie, **Movie Shac** (inside Loshusan supermarket in Barbican Centre, tel. 876/978-SHAC, 10 A.M.–9 P.M. Mon.–Sat., 10 A.M.–7 P.M. Sun.) has a mix of classics and new releases on DVD.

BETTING AND GAMBLING
Gambling was, until recently, illegal in Jamaica, while "gaming" was not, so long as you are 18 and over. Off-track betting (OTB) is supported by nearby Caymanas Park racetrack with OTB outlets across the island carrying local as well as overseas races. Video Gaming Machines are found throughout the island thanks to Supreme Ventures, with a few locations in Kingston to play the odds against a machine. Popular gaming lounges include **Acropolis** (Loshusan Plaza, 29 East Kings House Rd., tel. 876/978-1299, 1 P.M.–1 A.M.

THE LIFE AND LEGACY OF "MISS LOU"

The life of Louise Bennett Coverley (September 7, 1919–July 26, 2006) spanned an evolution in the identity of the Jamaican people. Born in Downtown Kingston at 40 North Street, she was raised during a tumultuous time alongside the growth of Jamaica's Labour Movement, whose leaders were agitating for racial equality. Miss Lou became an outspoken poet, social commentator, and performer at an early age, converting thick Patois – considered at the time the language of the illiterate underclass – into a national art form and a source of pride. Miss Lou began publishing books in Jamaican Creole in the early 1940s, before pursuing opportunities in London to further her performance career. She brought Jamaican folk culture to media and stages around the world, giving presence to a nation yearning for independence. Jamaican folk culture is based overwhelmingly on African traditions, and in bringing her stories and poems into performance and literary forms, Miss Lou validated an integral part of the country's heritage that had for centuries been scorned. While there are still plenty of examples in contemporary Jamaica of shame of an African past, Miss Lou dispelled the taboo associated with this rich heritage with her warmth and lyrical genius. When Jamaica gained its independence in 1962, Miss Lou's popularity was further cemented as a proven ambassador for the Jamaican identity in the birth of a new era. Miss Lou was a founding member of the Little Theatre Movement.

Mon.–Thurs., 1 P.M.–3 A.M. Fri.–Sat. 10 A.M.–1 A.M. Sun.), **Monte Carlo Gaming** (Terra Nova Hotel, 17 Waterloo Rd., Terra Nova Hotel switchboard: tel. 876/926-2211, 11 A.M.–4 A.M. Mon.–Fri., 11 A.M.–6 A.M. Sat.–Sun.), and **Treasure Hunt Gaming** (14–15 Trinidad Terrace, tel. 876/929-2938, 24 hours a day, 7 days a week).

Caymanas Park horse track (racing@cwjamaica.com, www.caymanasracetrack.com) is recognized as one of the best horse-racing tracks in the Caribbean. Regular races are held on select Wednesdays and Saturdays, with the occasional Monday race, and are usually well attended. In 2009, a proposal to start regular Sunday races met strong opposition from Christian groups, which objected to gambling on a holy day. Admission ranges US$0.50–4, depending on seating. Caymanas Track Ltd. (CTL) supports a large network of OTB sites around the corporate area, which offer simulcast races from around the world when races aren't being broadcast from Caymanas.

Shopping

Kingston is full of shopping plazas and strip malls. Half Way Tree has the highest concentration of shopping plazas in Jamaica, which include: Lane Plaza, on the eastern side of Hope Road; Pavilion, Central, Twin Gates, and Savannah Plazas, on the block between Eastwood Park and Constant Spring Roads; and Mall, Tropical, 7th Avenue, Premiere, and Village Plazas on the north side of Constant Spring Road.

DEVON HOUSE SHOPS

The courtyard at Devon House Shops (26 Hope Rd., at the corner of Trafalgar) is home to some of the nicest boutique shops in Kingston, in addition to offering tantalizing treats to stimulate your palate.

Starfish Oils (tel. 876/908-4763, www.starfishoils.com) is one of Jamaica's best cottage industries, which makes soaps, oils, and candles perfect for compact gift items and everyday use. These products come standard in the bathrooms at many of Jamaica's best hotels. Starfish also has an outlet in Manor Park Plaza.

The Pottery Store (Shop #2, tel. 876/906-5016, potterystore@gmail.com, www.wassiart.com, Mon.–Sat. 10 A.M.–6 P.M.) features pieces by Wassi Art Pottery Works located in Ocho Rios, which showcases the finest in Jamaican pottery. Every last Saturday of the month The Pottery Store offers discounts of up to 15 percent on select items. Items range significantly in price (US$4–480).

T's and Treasures (Shops #3 and 4, tel. 876/968-0750, 10 A.M.–8 P.M. Mon.–Sat., 1:30 P.M.–7 P.M. Sun.) sells books on travel and culture, cultural DVDs, souvenirs, apparel, and trinkets.

Things Jamaican (Shops #12–14, tel. 876/926-1961, www.thingsmadeinjamaica.com, 9 A.M.–8 P.M. Mon.–Fri., 10 A.M.–8 P.M. Sat., noon–8 P.M. Sun.) sells a wide array of crafts, books, and creative gift items.

Molasses Taste of Jamaica (shops 6 and 7, tel. 876/908-1322, 11 A.M.–6 P.M. Mon. , 11 A.M.–11 P.M. Tues.–Sat.) retails Jamaican spirits, including rums, rum creams, and liquors, as well as a collection of Jamaican and Cuban cigars.

Elaine's Elegance (Shop #8, tel. 876/920-0357, eelegance@anngel.com.jm) sells cut-work embroidery dresses, skirts, blouses, and jackets for fashionable women—all handmade by Elaine. Craft items like woodwork, fruit bowls, and fridge magnets are also sold at Elaine's.

TREASURE HOUSE PLAZA

Located at 96 Hope Road, this plaza has a variety of shops open 10 A.M.–6 P.M. Monday–Saturday.

SoHo (tel. 876/978-9256) sells evening and casual wear for women and attracts a primarily Jamaican clientele; the products vary from gaudy to semi-formal and elegant.

La Pluma Negra (tel. 876/946-1672) mainly sells casual, going-out wear, mostly T-shirts and accessories.

The **Cooyah** store located at the plaza, as well as others found around Jamaica, sell knockoff

Cooyah clothing and are best avoided. The founder of Cooyah, Homer Bair, started a new line true to the roots of the Cooyah brand, CY (www.cyevolution.com), which is considered the official reggae brand, worn by some of the most popular reggae and dancehall artists. CY gear is screenprinted in Hollywood, Florida, and retails online. CY can be found in the Kingston area at **Ammar's** (Village Mall, Half Way Tree, tel. 876/926-4667 9:30 A.M.–6 P.M., until 7 P.M. Fri.–Sat.), **Collectibles** (Shop #10, Mall Plaza, tel. 876/926-4439; Shop #18 Village Plaza, tel. 876/926-2596), and **Carby's Souvenir Discount Centre and Craft Village** (Shop #4, Twin Gates Plaza, tel. 876/926-4065, 9:30 A.M.–6:30 Mon.–Thurs., till 7:30 P.M. Fri.–Sat.).

CLOTHING AND ACCESSORIES

Sarai Clothing (Harbour View, by appt. only, contact Sister May, cell tel. 876/372-6265) has Rasta gear, Ethiopian sharmas, dresses, and men's and children's clothing.

Mutamba (tel. 876/387-4112 (Muta) or 876/320-1209 (Amber), by appt. only), a clothing line developed by outspoken Jamaican Pan-Africanist dub poet Mutabaruka and his wife, Amber, is very popular for its minimalist chic aesthetic.

J'adore (Shop #33, tel. 876/754-8386, 10:30 A.M.–6:30 P.M. Mon.–Thurs., 10:30 A.M.–8 P.M. Fri.–Sat.), has clothes imported from Europe, fit for clubbing or going out.

Flirt (Shop #12, Manor Park Plaza, tel. 876/931-9332, flirtboutiqueja@gmail.com) has women's apparel for the nightclub or a dinner out.

Bling Bling (Shop #5, Mid Spring Plaza, 134 Constant Spring Rd., tel. 876/925-3855, 10 A.M.–8 P.M. Mon.–Sat.) has all the bling you'll need to flex big at the club or a street dance. Prices range considerably (US$1.50–357). Sharon Beckford is the friendly proprietor.

Bridget Sandals (1 Abbeydale Rd., opposite the Hope Road entrance to Devon House, tel. 876/968-1913, www.bridgetsandals.com, 9 A.M.–6 P.M. Mon.–Sat., US$65–120) sells unique and tasteful handcrafted leather footwear for women. Manufacturing flaws are repaired free of charge. Founder Bridget Brown and son Jonathan Buchanan run the shop.

Lee's Fifth Avenue (Tropical Plaza, Half Way Tree, tel. 876/926-8280, www.leesfifthavenue.com, 10 A.M.–7 P.M. Mon.–Sat., 11 A.M.–4 P.M. Sun.) sells quality, trendy, brand-name clothes like Levi's, Puma, and Tommy Hilfiger.

Loran-V Boutique (Shop #2, Northside Plaza, 26 Northside Dr., off Hope Rd., tel. 876/977-6450, loran_v_swimwear@yahoo.com, 9 A.M.–5 P.M. Mon.–Fri., 10 A.M.–2 P.M. Sat.) makes swimwear and light apparel for men and women on-site with a handful of women at sewing machines churning out well-designed bikinis and trunks.

Stanley & Empress (Starapples courtyard, 94 Hope Rd., noon–8 P.M. Wed.–Sat., tel. 876/577-3625 or 876/359-3634, stanleyandempress@gmail.com, www.stanleyandempress.com) has a collection of Jamaican-designed and -inspired apparel and accessories for men and women.

Like Dat (Mid-Spring Plaza, 134 Constant Spring Rd., cell tel. 876/818-0760) sells a range of Jamaica-inspired roots wear attire.

Swiss Stores (Shop #2, Mall Plaza, tel. 876/926-4861) sells a wide selection of watches, duty-free for foreign residents and tourists.

BOOKSTORES

Bookland (53 Knutsford Blvd., New Kingston, tel. 876/926-4035, 9 A.M.–6 P.M. Mon.–Fri., 10 A.M.–5 P.M. Sat.) has the best selection of Carribean and Jamaican books, and magazines as well as souvenirs.

Kingston Bookshop has several locations around town (70-B King St., tel. 876/922-4056; 74 King St., tel. 876/922-7016; Pavilion Mall, 13 Constant Spring Rd.; Boulevard Shopping Ctr. Shop #6,; The Springs, 17 Constant Spring Rd., Shop #2; Liguanea Post Mall). Kingston carries Jamaican and Caribbean titles, as well as imports from the United States and Europe covering all kinds of subject matter; in addition, it's a major force in Jamaica's textbook market. Downtown stores operate 9 A.M.–5 P.M., Uptown stores run until 6 P.M.

Sangster's Book Stores is another major chain with several locations around town (97 Harbour St., tel. 876/922-3819; 33 King St., tel. 876/967-1930; Shop #6, 17 Constant Spring Rd., tel. 876/926-1800; 20 Constant Spring Rd., tel. 876/926-0710; 28 Barbados Ave., tel. 876/960-2488; Shop #20, 106 Hope Rd., tel. 876/978-3518; 137 Mountain View Ave., tel. 876/928-3893).

Bookophilia (92 Hope Rd., tel. 876/978-5248, 11 A.M.–8 P.M. Mon.–Thurs., 11 A.M.–9 P.M. Fri., 10 A.M.–7 P.M. Sat., noon–5 P.M. Sun.) opened in April 2008 with a great selection of books and magazines. There's a small kiosk in the corner of the cozy shop serving Blue Mountain coffee, tea, cookies, and muffins (US$1–3). The signature drink is the Gingerbread Chai Latte (US$3). A worldbeat night is held every last Friday of the month (6–9 P.M.). Bookophilia lures first-time customers with a free cup of coffee.

Bolivar Bookshop & Gallery (1-D Grove Rd., tel. 876/926-8799) is a nice boutique with a small art gallery and more rare books than can be found at the other bookstores in town.

Headstar Books and Crafts (54 Church St., tel. 876/922-3915, headstarp@hotmail.com) is an Afrocentric bookshop run by Brother Miguel.

RECORD SHOPS

Techniques Records (99 Orange St., in front of Jamaica Lifestock, contact shop owner Winston Riley, tel. 876/967-4367 or 876/858-6407, 9 A.M.–7 P.M. Mon.–Sat.) has what is perhaps Kingston's best selection for all kinds of traditional music and oldies, with LPs, 33s, and 45s, as well as the latest singles and CDs.

Derrick Harriott's One Stop Record Shop (Shop #36, Twin Gates Plaza, Constant Spring, tel. 876/926-8027, derrickchariotharriott@hotmail.com, 10 A.M.–6:30 P.M. Mon.–Sat.) has a good selection of oldies as well as the latest LPs and 45 singles.

Rockers International Records (135 Orange St., tel. 876/922-8015, 9 A.M.–4 P.M. Mon.–Sat.) specializes in reggae, and has CDs and LPs, 33s, and 45s, with the latest domestic singles and imports.

Tad's International Records (Shop #21, 78¾ Hagley Park Rd., tel. 876/929-2563 or 876/845-3195) has an extensive catalog of reggae from the early days of Gregory Isaacs, Dennis Brown, and John Holt, to more contemporary Terry Linen, Cecile, Teflon, and Anthony B.

Best Buds (11 Fairway Ave., off Lady Musgrave Ave., tel. 876/946-1400, 9 A.M.–6 P.M. Mon.–Sat.) must be one of the few stores on the planet to sell plants, floral arrangements, and all kinds of domestic and imported CDs, but no vinyl.

Rock 'N' Groove Muzik (Shop #9, Northside Plaza, tel. 876/977-3538, 9 A.M.–6 P.M. Mon.–Sat.) has a great selection of reggae, gospel, R&B, rap and soca on CD.

Sonic Sounds Record Manufacturing Company (25 Retirement Rd., tel. 876/926-1204), run by Jason Lee, sells vintage reggae on vinyl, including 33s and 45s. Customers must buy a minimum of three of each item. Sonic no longer distributes. It was founded in 1978 by Jason's father, Neville Lee, brother of Byron Lee, who was front man for Byron Lee and the Dragonaires until his death in 2008. Byron Lee and the Dragonaires were ambassadors of Jamaican Music from 1964, when their first producer and former prime minister of Jamaica Edward Seaga selected the band to back a showcase of talent at the World's Fair. Eventually the group earned a listing in the *Guinness Book of World Records* as the longest-running band. Neville managed Dynamic Sounds, the studio Byron Lee bought from Seaga, changing the name from West Indies Records Limited. Neville later left Dynamic to found Sonic.

Vynil Records (16 Keesing Ave., off Hagley Park Rd., tel. 876/757-4765, contact proprietor Rita Armandi, tel. 876/849-8404, oj36rec@ cwjamaica.com, www.oj36records.com, 9 A.M.–3 P.M. Mon.–Thurs., 9 A.M.–1 P.M.

Fri.) is a retailer of reggae 33s and 45s. The shop is oriented toward the export market, as most Jamaican selectors use digital formats these days.

Dynamic Sounds (15 Bell Rd., tel. 876/923-9138, 9 A.M.–5 P.M. Mon.–Fri.) is a studio full of history, founded by former prime minister Edward Seaga before the ambitious young man left the music industry for politics. It became a seminal recording studio, documenting the birth of Jamaica's music industry out of the thirst and excitement generated by the explosion of American popular music on the local airwaves, and the yearning for a national identity around the time of independence.

Today Dynamic Sounds retails vintage records and contemporary CDs (US$9–15), singles, rhythm tracks on 45s (US$.75), and complete albums on 33s (US$3.50). Dynamic Sounds is owned by Byron Lee, son of the legendary late Byron Lee. You must buy at least two of each item.

All Access Entertainment (Shop #24, Central Plaza, 13 Constant Spring Rd., contact Kumi, tel. 876/908-4949, 9:30 A.M.–5:30 P.M. Mon.–Fri.) is a wholesaler of both vinyl and CDs, with vintage and new artists represented on singles and rhythm tracks on 45s. Customers must purchase a minimum of three of each item.

ELECTRONICS

Innovative Systems (downstairs in Sovereign Centre, tel. 876/978-3512) sells all kinds of electronics goods, from USB cables to headsets.

Photo Express (Shop #36, Premier Plaza, Half Way Tree, tel. 876/929-6221, 8:30 A.M.–5:30 P.M. Mon.–Sat.) does film developing within 24 hours and sells compact flash cards, SD cards, cameras, batteries, bags, and accessories.

Electro-World, at Mall Plaza in Half Way Tree (tel. 876/926-5851 or 876/922-4516) has a good selection of electronics, including FireWire cables and earphones.

Watts New has outlets at Tropical Plaza in Half Way Tree (Shop #9, tel. 876/906-4174) and next to Waterfalls (160 Old Hope Rd. in Liguanea, tel. 876/970-0192).

Speaker Doc (St. Andrew Plaza, tel. 876/931-2627) can fix most any problem with speakers.

Should you need to get a computer part or accessory or need a repair, try **Royale Computers & Accessories** (Shop #31, Pavilion Mall, 13 Constant Spring Rd., tel. 876/906-1067, www.royalecomputers.com) or **Logic Microsystems** (32 Hagley Park Rd., tel. 876/920-3791, 9 A.M.–5 P.M. Mon.–Fri., 10 A.M.–3 P.M. Sat., info@logicmicrosystems.com, www.logicmicrosystems.com).

ARTS, CRAFTS, AND GIFTS

Craft Cottage (Village Plaza, 24 Constant Spring Rd., tel. 876/926-0719, 9:30A.M.–5:30 P.M. Mon.–Thurs., 9:30 A.M.–6 P.M. Fri.–Sat.) is a good place for authentic Jamaican arts and crafts.

Jamaica Herb & Spice (53 Westminster Rd., tel. 876/754-3587, 876/868-3777 or 876/861-3460, bluejamaica@kasnet.com) wholesales soaps and oils made by Blue Mountain Aromatics, one of the best cottage industry producers of personal care products in Jamaica. It's best to call ahead to schedule a visit.

Market at the Lawn is held the last Sunday every other month 10 A.M.–5 P.M. at Truck Stop (18 West King's House Road). The open-air market features farmers who bring fresh produce to sell alongside arts and crafts vendors. Contact Kaili McDonnough (tel. 876/585-7233, thelawnkingston@gmail.com, www.marketatthelawn.com) for more information.

Original Bamboo Factory (Caymans Estate, Spanish Town, tel. 876/746-9906 or 876/869-6675, hamilton1@cwjamaica.com or bamboojamaica@gmail.com, www.originalbamboofactory.com) has what you need if you're in the market for bamboo furniture or just want to see how it's put together.

Faith D'Aguilar (26 Gore Terrace, tel. 876/925-8192 or 876/475-7832) sells and refurbishes antique furniture and other oddities.

Books Plus and **The Piano House** (43 Constant Spring Rd., tel. 876/926-8268, 9:30 A.M.–6 P.M. Mon.–Sat.), at the same location and both run by Owen Brown, features a used bookstore in which Brown also sells renovated pianos. Brown runs a humble music school out of the shop, offering piano, flute, and guitar lessons. Call to inquire about any upcoming performances.

Sports and Recreation

Kingston is not known for its outdoor recreational opportunities. Nevertheless, there are plenty of options, including diving, hiking, golf, tennis, and even surfing, within the greater area.

The **National Stadium** hosts most important sporting events on the island, including the home games of the national soccer team Reggae Boyz (www.thereggaeboyz.com) and track and field events. Next door at the **National Arena** and the **Indoor Sports Centre,** several trade shows and events are held, including Caribbean Fashion Week. For more information contact the Jamaica Football Federation (20 St. Lucia Crescent, tel. 876/929-0484, 876/929-8036, or 876/926-1182, soccer@thereggaeboyz.com or

jamff@hotmail.com) and ask for press officer Garth Williams.

Sabina Park, located Downtown on South Camp Road, hosts some home games for the West Indies cricket team (www.windiescricket.com). The **Jamaica Cricket Association** (tel. 876/967-0322 or 987/922-8423, jcacricket@hotmail.com, www.jamaicacricket.org) based at Sabina, controls the sport on the island.

We Jamaica Tours, run by sole operator Juliet Gordon (tel. 876/925-8798 or cell tel. 876/362-9319, oldejamaica@yahoo.com, www.oldejamaicatours.com, US$2 for children, US$5 for adults) arranges sports tourism tours to cricket matches, athletics meets, and training sessions, or to venues like Sabina Park stadium.

GOLF

Kingston's most reputable golf course is **Caymanas Golf & Country Club** (Mandela Hwy., tel. 876/746-9772, 876/746-9773, or 876/746-9774, play@caymanasgolfclub.com, www.caymanasgolfclub.com), west of Town. Designed by Canadian architect Howard Watson in 1958, the course features elevated greens with lush fairways cut through limestone hills. The views from the tees are excellent, with Guango trees providing natural obstacles and occasional shade. Nonmembers pay greens fees of US$50 weekdays, US$55.50 weekends and holidays, plus US$22.50 for a cart. The Hilton offers a US$198-per-night golf package inclusive of green fees and cart. A restaurant and bar on-site is open to the public.

Constant Spring Golf Club (152 Constant Spring Rd., tel. 876/924-1610, csgc@cwjamaica.com) has a more humble course located in the middle of Uptown Kingston. Built by Scottish architect Stanley Thompson in 1920, the short, tight course is challenging, with an excellent view at the 13th hole. Carts go for US$20 for nonmembers, green fees are US$45 on weekdays, US$50 on weekends. Clubs are available from the pro shop (tel. 876/924-5170) for US$35, and a caddy will cost you US$13.50. The course is a par 70 (Blue tees 9,197 yards; White tees 5,866 yards; Red tees 5,205 yards). Canadian National Railways built a magnificent hotel just below the course, parallel to the 18th hole fairway, which was long ago converted into the Immaculate Conception High School, one of Kingston's most prestigious.

Putt n' Play Amusement Park (Emancipation Park, 78 Knutsford Blvd., New Kingston, tel. 876/906-4814, www.puttnplayja.com) has a miniature golf course and a number of low-adrenaline rides suitable for children, like bumper cars, merry-go-rounds, and flight simulators.

RACKET SPORTS

Liguanea Club (80 Knutsford Blvd., tel. 876/926-8144, liguaneaclub@cwjamaica.com), across from the Courtleigh Hotel, has squash, billiards, and tennis, plus an outdoor swimming pool. Membership is required to use the facilities. Visitor membership is available for US$78 per month.

Tennis Jamaica (2A Piccadilly Rd., book a court at tel. 876/929-5878 or 876/906-5700, ask for Sheron Quest, 280 Piccadilly Rd., www.tennisjamaica.com, 6 A.M.–6 P.M. daily), formerly the Jamaica Lawn Tennis Association (JLTA), has courts and can set up partners. Nonmembers pay US$4.50 per hour 6 A.M.–4 P.M., US$6.70 per hour 4–6 P.M. Members (US$22.50/year) pay US$3.35 per hour 6 A.M.–4 P.M., US$5 per hour 4–6 P.M. The organization sometimes holds tournaments. Heading toward Cross Roads on Half Way Tree Road or Old Hope Road, turn onto Caledonia Avenue at the light and then take a right onto Marescaux Road. After you pass the National Water Commission on the left, take the next right at the front entrance of L. P. Azar, a textile store that serves as a good landmark. The courts are at the end of the road.

The **Jamaica Pegasus** (81 Knutsford Blvd., tel. 876/926-3690, ext. 3023, or ask for the tennis court) has well-maintained, lit courts. Peter Berry and Kevin Riley are the tennis pro coaches, and Thilbert Palmer is director of tennis. Court fees are US$14 per hour during the day, US$19 per hour at night, which covers a lesson for a single player or the court for you and your partner. Tennis rackets are available and included in the lesson fee; otherwise there is a US$10 charge per racket if you're playing on your own.

POLO

The **Kingston Polo Club** (contact Lesley Masterton-Fong Yee, tel. 876/381-4660 or 876/922 8060, or Shane Chin, tel. 876/952-4370, chinrcpolo@yahoo.com) is located on the Caymanas Estate west of town off Mandela Highway. It can be reached by taking the same exit as for the Caymanas Golf

& Country Club, about 100 meters west of the turnoff for Portmore. The Kingston Polo Club season runs early January–August 7 and is host to some of the highest-handicap polo played on the island, starting with the ICWI international women's team, ICWI 18 goal, and the NCB High International 15 goal tournament in May. Matches are held at 4 P.M. on Wednesdays and 10 A.M. on Sunday mornings.

PAINTBALL

Sun Coast Adventure Park (12 Mile, sales office cell tel. 876/485-0015 or park manager James Worton tel. 876/564-6999 or 876/995-9450, info@suncoastadventurepark.com, www. suncoastadventurepark.com, 9 A.M.–5:30 P.M. Sat.–Sun., admission US$8), located about 30 minutes east of Kingston in the neighboring parish of St. Thomas, offers paintball (US$30 per person, US$40 with upgrade and US$8 for an additional 100 paintballs), a ropes course, maze, and hiking trails.

WATER SPORTS

Even though Kingston has a lot of waterfront acreage, it's not put to great use: there are no cafés, restaurants, or bars on Ocean Boulevard, as one might hope or expect. Nevertheless, there are plenty of places around to have a dip, including Rockfort mineral baths, the pool at the Mayfair Hotel, Cane River Falls east of Town, and beaches on Lime Cay and west of town at Hellshire and Fort Clarence. Lime Cay and Sugarman's Beach, to the right just before entering Hellshire Beach, are probably the most inviting in the greater Kingston area.

Surfing

If you're looking to catch some waves, don't miss **Jamnesia Surf Camp** in Bull Bay, where the most active members of the Jamaica Surfing Association's (tel. 876/750.0103, www. jamsurfas.webs.com) tight-knit family congregate. The association has raised the profile of Jamaican surfing in a commendable fashion, organizing events and contests at home and competing overseas with a national team.

Diving

Port Royal Divers (Morgan's Harbour, tel. 876/382-6767, paul@portroyaldivers.com, www.portroyaldivers.com), led by Paul Shoucair aboard his 8.5-meter boat, will take experienced divers to the reefs off Lime Cay to some recent wrecks (US$50 per person for two dives including tanks and weights; gear is an additional US$30). Paul also does PADI certification courses for multiple persons: US$450 for Open Water certification, US$350 for Advanced, US$500 for Rescue Diver, and US$500 for Divemaster certification. It is illegal for tourists to dive without a Jamaica Tourist Board–licensed diver like Paul. Diving sites around Kingston include the sunken ship *Edena*, Black Tip, Texas, Winward Edge, and Cayman Trader close to Lime Cay. If you're lucky you may see eagle rays, nurse sharks, and turtles.

Boating

The **Royal Jamaica Yacht Club** (Palisadoes Park, Norman Manley Blvd., tel. 876/924-8685 or 876/924-8686, fax 876/924-8773, rjyc@kasnet.com, www.rjyc.org.jm), located on the eastern side of Kingston Harbor next to Norman Manley International Airport beside the Caribbean Maritime Institute, holds regular regattas: Spring Regatta around the second week in February, RJYC Globe Fishing tournament in March, and Independence Regatta at the end of July or early August. Yachters arriving to Jamaica from overseas should clear customs in Port Royal before seeking a slip at the yacht club. You can also come directly to the club, which can contact customs and immigration. Slips can accommodate vessels up to 50 feet, while the visitors' dock can accommodate larger vessels. Fees are US$1.50 per foot for the first six days and US$1 thereafter; electricity, water, and fuel are also offered. Visitors are welcome to use the restaurant, bar, and pool. Patricia Yap-Chung is the secretary/manager. If you want to sign on as crew, make your interest known at the club and there's a good chance one of the boats will take you on. Yearly membership costs US$385.

Sail Jamaica (contact instructor Marisa

Shea, cell tel. 876/881-7569, sailjamaica@ gmail.com, www.sailjamaica.com.jm) offers sailing lessons and courses for children and adults, both long-term after-school programs (US$250) and weekend learn-to-sail courses (US$120). Tailored lessons and courses can also be arranged for short-term visitors.

Bikini Sundayz (contact Maurice Johnson, cell tel. 876/381-1281, marjohno@hotmail. com, US$15, half price for women wearing bikinis) is a bi-weekly (call to find out which Sunday) cruise aboard the *Fun N Frolic* party yacht that leaves Morgan's Harbour in Port Royal for Lime Cay at 3 P.M. and returns at 9 P.M. The cruise attracts mostly young adults and has a sound system and selectors, two bars, and a restaurant on board.

Retro on the Seas, also aboard *Fun N Frolic,* leaves from Morgan's Harbour at 9 P.M. on the last Saturday of each month with groovy selections as the soundtrack for a four-hour cruise around Kingston Harbour.

Fishing

Local anglers go out to the California Banks about 16 kilometers offshore from Port Royal. Nigel Black operates **Why Not Fishing Charters** (tel. 876/995-1142) out of Morgan's Harbour Marina.

Other fishing expeditions can be arranged by inquiring with Anthony DuCasse at **DuRae's Boat Sales** (18 Rosewell Terrace, tel. 876/905-1713, duraes@cwjamaica.com), the best powerboat parts supplier on the island, in business since 1966, or at **E & S Fishing Supplies** (Harbour View Shopping Centre, tel. 876/928-7910, 9 A.M.–6 P.M. Mon.–Sat.), which sells lines, rods, tackle, and bait.

Running

Jamaica Hash House Harriers (www.jamaicahash.org) is a running group better known as "a drinking club with a running problem" or "the world's largest disorganization." The club welcomes visiting runners and drinkers to join the pack. Contact Emile Finlay (cell tel. 876/997-4700, efinlay@cwjamaica. com, emile@finlayestates.com). Hash runs take place approximately every two weeks, usually on a Sunday, with occasional holiday hikes and runs scheduled as well.

Jamdammers Running Club (info@jamdammers.com, www.jamdammers.com) is a formal organization that celebrates Jamaica's "out of many, one people" motto. Its founding members are Jamaicans from all walks of life who ran regularly at the Mona Reservoir, or "The Dam."

SPAS AND FITNESS CENTERS

The Jamaican hospitality industry is making a concerted effort to brand Jamaica as a premier health and spa tourism destination. In Kingston there are a few good options when it comes to affordable pampering.

Nirvana Day Spa (39 Lady Musgrave Rd., tel. 876/978-1723, 7 A.M.–7 P.M. Mon.–Fri., 8 A.M.–6 P.M. Sat., 10 A.M.–3 P.M. Sun.), owned by Gaudia Aquart, is located at the Eden Gardens complex and offers manicures and pedicures (US$29–41), massages (US$36–56), facials (US$50–71), mud and herb body wraps (US$57–79), body scrubs (US$36–53), and hair removal (US$6–36). Prices do not include tax. Nirvana also offers services at the Jamaica Pegasus Hotel (7 A.M.–11 P.M. Mon.–Sat., 10 A.M.–6 P.M. Sun.).

Jencare Skin Farm (82 Hope Rd., tel. 876/946-3494 or 876/946-3497, jencarejender@yahoo.com) is a slightly more upscale day spa that offers complete bodywork from nails (US$31) to facials (US$43) to massage (US$50). You can also get a haircut (US$7).

Shakti Mind Body Fitness (5 Bedford Park Ave., turn left before Megamart heading Uptown off Upper Waterloo, tel. 876/906-8403 or 876/920-5868, info@shaktimindbodyfitness.com, www.shaktimindbodyfitness. com, open daily) is a full-service fitness center offering cutting-edge classes for body and mind, as well as a spa and fitness-lifestyle store. Choose from over 50 classes, including indoor cycling, yoga, body sculpt, Pilates, and Zumba. Shakti often has guest instructors from the United States. Nonmembers are welcome for drop-in classes (US$11). Regular classes run 8:30 A.M.–6:30 P.M. Monday–Thursday, 8:30–10:30 A.M. Saturday, and 10 A.M.–noon Sunday. Call ahead for spinning, as the classes are often booked. Appointments can also be made for spa treatments such as deep tissue, Swedish, and Thai massage, as well as eyelash tinting and body waxing with qualified therapists. Shakti is owned and operated by certified yoga teacher and aromatherapist Sharon McConnell (sharon@shaktimindbodyfitness. com). Essential oil scents fill the air and set a relaxing mood. See the website for a full schedule of classes and offerings. Great, healthy food is available, too, including the signature Shakti Granola Bars.

Island Massage Therapy and Yoga (tel. 876/924-5503 or cell tel. 876/818-4771, namaste_ja@hotmail.com, US$20) holds intimate regular classes, typically with fewer than 10 people (6 P.M. Mon.–Thurs., 10:45 A.M. Tues.–Thurs.) led by American expat Barbara Gingrich in an informal home studio setting. Barbara will also hold sessions at other locations by special request. Massage is by appointment only. Call for directions.

Daling Chinese Acupuncture & Moxibustion (39 Lady Musgrave Rd., tel. 876/978-3838) offers acupuncture service for a variety of ailments.

Rockfort Mineral Spa (Windward Rd., between the Shell gas station and the Carib Cement factory, tel. 876/938-6551, 7 A.M.–5:30 P.M. Tues.–Sun., US$2.50 adults, US$1.50 children) has one of Kingston's few public swimming pools adjoined by a bathhouse. Sitting on the remains of a British Fort from whence it gets its name, the baths are fed by mineral water from the Dallas Mountains. A large swimming pool outside is complemented by enclosed whirlpool tubs that come in different configurations and are available for 45-minute sessions: two-seater (US$14), four-seater (US$17), eight-seater (US$26), or 12-seater (US$31). The tubs are heated with electric heaters; by 10 A.M., they're hot and ready for use. Additionally, the spa has a stress-management center offering 45-minute massages (US$35) and reflexology sessions (US$25).

Body Fusion (61 Constant Spring Rd., tel. 876/968-1999, 5:30 A.M.–9 P.M. daily, US$7 per day for nonmembers, one-month membership costs US$50) has good equipment, including free weights, treadmills, stairclimbers, stationary bikes, and NordicTracks. Aerobics classes are also offered (6 A.M. and hourly 5:30–7:30 P.M. Mon.–Fri., 7:30 A.M. on Sat.).

Accommodations

Kingston is not known for its luxury rental villas or five-star hotels. Nonetheless, comfortable and affordable options abound. Most business travelers tend to stay in New Kingston or Half Way Tree for easy access to the corporate district. Spanish Court, The Courtleigh, and Terra Nova are business traveler favorites. For those with more down time, it may make sense to seek quieter options in residential neighborhoods or on the edge of town. Alhambra Inn, The Gardens, Moon Hill, or Neita's Nest in Stony Hill are favorites for those seeking a quiet and refreshing respite from the city. Don't expect a lot in the way of amenities for less than

US$100, with the higher end of the spectrum pushing US$300 for suites at a few hotels.

The outlying communities of the corporate area in St. Catherine don't have much in the way of inviting accommodations, with a strip of pay-by-the hour dives along Port Henderson Road, commonly known as Back Road, in Portmore, and a few similar establishments in Spanish Town.

NEW KINGSTON
Under US$100
Indies Hotel (5 Holborn Rd., tel. 876/926-2952, indieshotel@hotmail.com, www.

indieshotel.com, US$39 s with fan and TV, US$47 with air-conditioning, US$61 with phone; US$64 d, US$81 t) is a no-frills hotel with basic rooms in a very convenient central location. There is a restaurant and bar in the inner courtyard where meals are served. Continental breakfast is US$2.50 and up and dinner is from US$6.

Sunset Inn (1-A Altamont Crescent, tel. 876/929-7283, sunsetinn@mindspring.com, US$74 d, US$84 king, US$93 for two doubles, US$85 with kitchenette) is basic but has all the essentials. Amenities include hot water, cable, air-conditioning, and dressers in all the rooms.

US$100-250

◖ Spanish Court Hotel (1 St. Lucia Avenue, Kingston 5, 876/926-0000, info@spanishcourthotel.com, www.spanishcourthotel.com) is the newest hotel in New Kingston, opening in 2009 with competitive rates, a chic, Miami-esque design, and excellent service. Rooms are well appointed with flat-panel TVs, warm and cozy decor and comfortable bedding. It has quickly become a favorite home-away-from-home for visiting businesspeople. The Spanish Court Café serves lunch and dinner and is open to nonguests.

◖ Altamont Court (1 Altamont Terrace, tel. 876/929-4497, altamontcourt@cwjamaica.com, www.altamontcourt.com, US$115) is a great value relative to other options in the area, and its location in a quiet little corner of New Kingston makes it convenient without being on highly-trafficked Knutsford Boulevard, the corporate district's main thoroughfare. However, many of the city's restaurants and much of its nightlife is centered on Knutsford Boulevard, which is only a five-minute walk away. The Altamont has 57 standard rooms and one large suite. Standards come with two doubles or one king. For US$140 you get a loft with the bedroom upstairs and a living area and pullout sofa, microwave, and fridge. The Alexander Suite is a spacious and luxurious room with an expansive bathroom that has a tub and a separate shower. Wireless Internet is included in all the rooms, and there is a computer in the business center. Three meeting rooms are also available. A restaurant by the pool serves breakfast, lunch, and dinner.

The Knutsford Court Hotel (16 Chelsea Ave., tel. 876/929-1000, sales@knutsfordcourt.com, www.knutsfordcourt.com, US$142) is well situated within easy walking distance to the restaurants, bars, and nightclubs on Knutsford Boulevard. The hotel is owned by the Hendricksons, who also operate the Courtleigh and Sunset Resorts on the North and West Coasts. The Knutsford is their most downscale property, but it offers amenities like a 24-hour business center, gym, meeting rooms, two restaurants, and a bar. The rooms are decent with wooden furniture, and all the standard amenities like phone and cable TV. Two townhouses in the courtyard have the property's best suites.

The Courtleigh Hotel & Suites (85 Knutsford Blvd., tel. 876/929-9000, fax 876/926-7744, courtleigh@cwjamaica.com, www.courtleigh.com, US$207 standard, US$550 presidential suite) is a popular business rest located between the Jamaica Pegasus and the Hilton. Rooms are modern, and guests have free wireless Internet throughout the property. Continental breakfast is included, and there are mini-fridges in rooms, cable TV, air-conditioning, and a 24-hour gym.

Jamaica Pegasus (81 Knutsford Blvd., tel. 876/926-3690, US$171 s/d, US$215 jr. suite, rates include breakfast) is a government favorite. It's the choice hotel for visiting and local officials, given its status as a joint venture between John Issa's SuperClubs and the Urban Development Corporation (UDC). The Pegasus is a popular venue for local government and private sector functions, as it has some of the largest conference facilities and ballrooms in town. A beautiful pool, 24-hour deli, and tennis courts round out this premier New Kingston property.

◖ Alhambra Inn (1 Tucker Ave., tel. 876/978-9072, 876/978-9073, or 876/978-4333, alhambrainn@cwjamaica.com, US$110 for two double beds, US$120 for king, US$20 per extra person) is a nice boutique hotel with a country feel across Mountain View Road from the National Indoor Stadium and a five-minute drive from New Kingston and Downtown. Twenty spacious rooms with comfortable sheets and a lush courtyard make the inn a cool option where the air-conditioning is barely necessary, even in the summer. Bring soap and shampoo, as the soap provided is not high-end. Wi-Fi is available in the courtyard. The Inn started as a reception center and began offering accommodations in 1996. It is owned by the amicable Sonia Gray-Clarke and her husband Trevor Clarke, an antiques collector whose hobby has helped bestow the Alhambra with its distinct character.

Eden Gardens (39 Lady Musgrave Rd., tel. 876/946-9981, US$120) wellness and business centre has large, comfortable suites with broad, functional desks and kitchenettes. Wireless Internet is included, and the property has conference facilities, a pool, and a restaurant. While the decor in the rooms is far from fancy, the place is functional and conveniently located in a quiet, well-laid-out compound. Eden Gardens is located in Liguanea, one of Kingston's most highly regarded residential neighborhoods, with ample greenery surrounding the duplex condos that provides an ideal setting for independent travelers.

The **Hilton Kingston** (77 Knutsford Blvd., tel. 876/926-5430, US$186–282) has a total of 300 rooms, 180 in a 18-story tower and 120 garden rooms in four buildings surrounding the central courtyard and pool area. The bar by the pool is one of the most popular congregating areas in New Kingston for an evening drink, with poolside buffet dinners (US$30) served daily, accompanied by Jazz on Thursday evenings. The lobby features beautiful brass-molded sculptures depicting faces of Jamaica in the reception area, and a giant painting of Bob Marley holding a meditation with his signature spliff graces the upper walls. A 24-hour cafe serves coffee, sandwiches, and excellent pastries on one side of the lobby where plush couches and coffee tables afford guests a another area for congregating. Rooms have either king-size beds or two doubles, air-conditioning and cable TV, and while not the most modern in town, linens are soft and clean, bathrooms have shower tubs with Crabtree & Evelyn toiletries, and the balconies on the upper floors boast nice views of town and the surrounding hills. The **Jonkanoo Lounge,** a low-key club off the courtyard, holds a Latin Night on Thursdays with salsa classes at 7 P.M. followed by dancing into the early morning hours (US$7 cover). DSL is available in the rooms, with Wi-Fi in the lobby and poolside for US$17.50 per day. The hotel also offers conference rooms, a business center, and private meeting rooms. General Manager Frank Rosheuvel ensures the Hilton Kingston offers excellent service in all areas and gives back to the community through a number of initiatives, including an annual youth golf tournament benefiting area schools.

Hotel Four Seasons (18 Ruthven Rd., tel. 876/929-7655, hfsres@cwjamaica.com, www.hotelfourseasonsjm.com) owned by Ms. Helga Stoeckert, offers single or deluxe rooms (US$100) with either two single or two queen beds, and 27 deluxe poolside rooms with two queen or one king bed (US$110). The hotel complex is large with a total of 76 rooms. The newer rooms are by the pool in the back.

HALF WAY TREE
Under US$100

Shirley Retreat Hotel (7 Maeven Ave., tel. 876/946-2679, srhospitality@yahoo.com, US$80–90 s/d, US$10 per extra person) has 13 rooms with either two twins or two double beds. The rate includes continental breakfast, and a kitchen on-site does meals to order (US$7–10 for lunch/dinner). There's cable TV, telephones, and refrigerators in the more expensive rooms. The hotel is owned and operated by the United Church in Jamaica and Grand Cayman and managed by executive director Shernette Smith.

The **Durham** (4 Durham Ave., contact Oliver Magnus, cell tel. 876/368-1036, oliver-magnusja@hotmail.com, US$30 per person) is a five-bedroom house that can be rented in its entirety or by the room. Three rooms have king beds, one of which has air-conditioning, while the others have fans. Two smaller rooms have double beds. All rooms have TV and private bath. Guests can use the kitchen and common areas, which include an expansive lawn around back suitable for entertaining.

US$100-250

Terra Nova All Suite Hotel (17 Waterloo Rd., tel. 876/926-2211, info@terranovajamaica.com, www.terranovajamaica.com) has comfortable rooms with two double beds (US$207), junior suites with minibar included (US$261), executive suites with whirlpool tubs and a bit more space (US$331), and three royalty suites with balconies (US$686 Blue Mountain and Darby suites, Terra Nova suite). Internet is included. Terra Nova has a great lunch buffet (US$22) throughout the week with a different theme each day, and it offers one of the best Sunday brunch buffet (US$28) selections in town with a mix of international and local food.

Mayfair Hotel (4 Kings House Close, tel. 876/926-1610 or 876/926-1612, mayfairhotel@cwjamaica.com, US$72–150 for 2 single beds or 1 double) located next to King's House, the home of the Governor General, has eight houses, each with five medium-size bedrooms with air-conditioning, hot water, and cable TV. Quilted blankets adorn the beds and recent renovations have added new bathroom tile and split air-conditioned units. On the large lawn there's a decent-sized swimming pool, restaurant, and snack shop. There's also a bar in the style of an English pub. Nonguests are welcome to use the pool (US$3.50) and dine at the restaurant. An independently run, excellent Japanese-Jamaican fusion restaurant, Cocoro, is located on the hotel grounds.

The Gardens (23 Liguanea Ave., tel. 876/927-8275, 876/977-8141, or 876/927-5957, mlyn@cwjamaica.com, US$75–90 for 1 bedroom, US$120 exclusive, US$165 for 2 bedrooms) has seven two-bedroom townhouses in a quiet and green setting. The townhouses have spacious living/dining rooms and full kitchens on the ground floor with a master and second bedroom upstairs, each with private bath. Guests can rent out a single bedroom of the two-bedroom units for the lower rate. Wireless Internet reaches most of the property. Air-conditioning and cable TV are in all bedrooms. Owner and manager Jennifer Lyn also operates Forres Park Guest House in Mavis Bank.

Over US$250

Moon Hill (5 Roedeen Close, tel. 876/620-8259, reservations@moonjamaica.com, www.moonjamaica.com, US$100 per person or US$500 per night for exclusive rental, US$3,000 per week for up to eight guests) is a staffed, private, four-bedroom villa in the foothills of the Blue Mountains, where cool breezes keep temperatures a good five degrees cooler than on the plains below. Removed from the hustle and bustle of the city, the villa is only 10 minutes away from the heart of New Kingston and Half Way Tree business districts, attractions, restaurants, and nightlife. The one-acre property is surrounded by lush hills affording complete privacy. On the grounds there's a swimming pool shaded by fruit trees and an organic garden producing many of the ingredients used in the kitchen. The menu is tailored and priced specifically to the palate of guests, who can decide on what and when they wish to dine. Bedrooms have king- and queen-size beds, cable TV, fans, and private baths with hot water. An entertainment room features a projection screen, and a component stereo feeds surround sound throughout the villa. Wi-Fi covers the property. A 24-hour concierge attends to any need and helps guests create tailored tours to explore Kingston and other destinations of interest, coordinating stays at other exclusive villas and boutique hotels across the island.

Food

If there's anything to demonstrate that Kingston has a bona fide cosmopolitan side, it's the food. The city's offerings reflect the country's motto, "Out of Many, One People," with Indian, Chinese, and African influences deeply entrenched. Recent Mexican, Cuban, Lebanese, and Japanese immigrants have also made their mark at a few recommendable restaurants. Of course Jamaica's traditional fare, including jerked meats and seafood specialties, can also be found in abundance in Kingston. The price for a filling meal varies according to the venue, with traditional Jamaican staples available for as little as US$5, and Wednesday's lobster and steak buffet dinner at the Terra Nova going for about US$43.

DOWNTOWN

(Moby Dick Restaurant (3 Orange St. at the corner of Port Royal and Harbour Streets, Downtown, tel. 876/922-4468, 9 A.M.–7 P.M. Mon.–Sat.) is a landmark establishment owned by the McBeans since 1985 and the best place to grab lunch Downtown. The restaurant dates from the early 1900s, when it was opened by a Mr. Masterton to service his workers at the port. Moby Dick specializes in curry dishes accompanied by roti, with an ambience reminiscent of India: The cashier sits on a raised structure by the entrance with an overseer's view of the dining area. Some of the best curried dishes anywhere in Jamaica are offered, both seafood, like shrimp and conch for US$14, and landed staples like goat and oxtail for US$8.50–11.50) with good fresh fruit juices (US$1.50).

Addie's Homestyle Cooking (Coronation market, Downtown, tel. 876/366-4727, 6 A.M.–6 P.M. Thurs.–Sat.), opened by Adelina Wellington in 2009, serves up typical Jamaican fare like fried or brown stew chicken, curry goat, and oxtail (US$2.50–3.50).

Tatty's (29 4th St., Greenwich Farm, no phone) is open for lunch only. Tatty's makes a trip into one of Kingston's most notorious shantytowns worth it for the peanut juice (US$3 for a bottle) and delicious steamed fish (US$4.50–7).

NEW KINGSTON
Jerk

Sweetwood Jerk Joint (located beside Putt n' Play Amusement Park on Knutsford Blvd., tel. 876/906-4854, sweetwoodja@yahoo.com, 11:30 A.M.–10 P.M. daily) serves jerk pork, sausage, chicken, lamb, conch, and roast fish, prepared on a coal-fired pit smoked with sweetwood and seasoned with Scotch Bonnet peppers.

(Scotchies Tree (2 Chelsea Ave., contact manager Jeremy McConnell, cell tel. 876/382-3789, 11 A.M.–11 P.M. Mon.–Sat., 11 A.M.–9 P.M. Sun., US$4–11) serves the award-winning jerk pork and chicken made famous at the first location in Montego Bay, accompanied by festival, roasted bread fruit, sweet potato, and yam. The Mobay branch's success begot a second location in Drax Hall, St. Ann, just west of Ochi, which led to the establishment of a Kingston location in mid-2010 to the delight of jerk lovers from the corporate area.

Chelsea Jerk Center (7 Chelsea Ave., tel. 876/926-6322, 7–10 P.M. Mon.–Thurs., 7 P.M.–1 A.M. Fri.–Sat., 11 A.M.–10 P.M. Sun.) has decent fast-food-style jerk at affordable prices (US$3.50–6).

Jamaican

Yaad Vybz (downstairs courtyard, New Kingston Shopping Centre, tel. 876/435-1594, 7 A.M.–5 P.M. Mon.–Fri.) is a small cook shop run by Gregory McFarlane that serves Jamaican staples, like fried or brown stew chicken, curry goat, and oxtail accompanied by rice and peas and natural juices (US$3–5).

Cuddy'z Sportsbar (Shops #4–6, New Kingston Shopping Center, Dominica Dr., tel. 876/920-8019, 11:30 A.M.–11:30 P.M. Mon.–Fri., 11:30 A.M.–1 A.M. Sat., 1–11 P.M. Sun.) is owned by Jamaica's favorite cricket star, Courtney "Cuddy" Walsh, the first cricket bowler to take 500 wickets in test cricket. He is also a recipient of the UNESCO award for good sportsmanship—this comes through in his demeanor off the field as proprietor as well. Cuddy'z is flush with TVs at every table and large flat-panels around the bar, making it the best place in town to catch a big game in the presence of a guaranteed raucous crowd. Typical sports-bar fare of burgers and fries (US$6–7) is complemented by Jamaican staples like curry goat and stewed chicken (US$6.50) or ribs, tenderloin, and shrimp (US$17). Flip Fridays offers two-for-one drinks from 6 P.M. until close.

The Pantry (2 Dumphries Rd., tel. 876/929-6804 or 876/929-4149, thepantry52@yahoo.com) is a roadside cook shop (noon–3 P.M. Mon.–Fri.) that's a popular lunch spot, serving Jamaican staples like fried chicken, brown stew fish, and curry goat (US$3.50).

Indies Cafe & Grill (8 Holborn Rd., tel. 876/920-5913, 12:30 P.M.–1 A.M. Mon.–Sat., 3 P.M.–midnight Sun.) is a popular local hangout with decent food. Entrées range from roast chicken (US$7) to steamed fish (US$16). The menu also includes pita pockets (US$8.50 chicken or US$10 veg) and pizzas (US$6–9.50 plain, plus US$2–3 for toppings). Indies hosts events most nights of the week. Call for a schedule.

Carlos Café (22 Belmont Rd., tel. 876/926-4186) is a Cuban-inspired bar with Martini Mondays (two for one 6–9 P.M.) and karaoke on Fridays (9:30 P.M.–1 A.M.). Prices range from US$1.50 for garlic bread to US$18.50 for lobster or filet mignon.

Hot Pot Restaurant (2 Altamont Terrace, tel. 876/929-3906, 7 A.M.–6 P.M. daily) serves items like red pea soup (US$1.50–3), stew peas and pigs' tail (US$5), ackee and saltfish (US$5), pigs' feet (US$4.50), and tripe and beans (US$5), as well as whole fish (US$18).

Le Barons Restaurant & Lounge (13 Barbados Ave., tel. 876/929-3872, 11 A.M.–6 P.M. Mon.–Thurs., till midnight Fri.) is a nice spot upstairs in the First Union Financial building with affordable food and an inviting, inconspicuous ambience. A balcony fills up with dominos players, especially on Lyming Fridays. Dishes include lobster, shrimp, pork chops, and steaks (US$4–8).

Red Bones Blues Café (1 Argyle Rd., tel. 876/978-8262, redbones@mail.infochan.com, www.redbonesbluescafe.com, noon–11 P.M. Mon.–Fri., 6–11 P.M. Sat., bar menu continues till the last customer leaves) has great albeit pricey food (ranging from US$17 for linguine to US$50 for grilled lobster) and a nice ambience with regular low-key events like fashion shows, poetry readings, and cabaret performances on a cozy stage in the garden. There's live music on Fridays, a world music selector on Thursdays, and poetry on the last Wednesday of every month. A gallery on the property features Jamaican painting, sculpture, ceramics, and textiles.

The Bird's Nest Restaurant & Bar (2a Chelsea Ave., cell tel. 876/491-1133, bar: 10–midnight Mon.–Sat., kitchen: 10 A.M.–10 P.M., US$4–20) serves an alternating menu of Jamaican dishes like curry mutton, brown stew chicken, steamed or escoveitch fish. The place used to be called Lime Cay, but patrons new to the restaurant and bar kept ending up on the little island off the Palisadoes of the same name, so management was compelled to change the name.

Meat and Seafood

❰ So So Seafood Bar & Grill (4 Chelsea Ave., tel. 876/906-1085, 10:30 A.M.–1 A.M. Mon.–Sat., 3 P.M.–midnight Sun.) is a nice seafood joint owned by Michael Forrest. It serves excellent steamed or fried fish (US$9–11/lb.), various shrimp dishes (US$11), curry or stewed conch (US$10), and lobster in season (US$20–23). Finger food is also served, including crab back, bammy, fries, fish tea, and mannish water, a broth made of all sorts of animal parts said to promote virility. The pleasant ambience with Christmas lights and a little waterfall, reggae in the speakers, and good food make So So a definite misnomer.

Heather's Garden Restaurant (9 Haining Rd., tel. 876/926-2826, 11:30 A.M.–11 P.M. Mon.–Fri., 5–11 P.M. Sat.) is owned by Meleta Touzalin, who bought the business when Heather went off to fly airplanes. Heather's serves items like sweet and sour, brown stew, or kebab chicken; brown stew, sweet and sour, or grilled fish; grilled, curry, or garlic shrimp;

garlic or curry lobster; sweet and sour pork and pork chops, accompanied by mashed potatoes, French fries, egg fried rice, or rice and peas (US$10.50–22).

Indian and Chinese

Gwong Wo (12 Trinidad Terrace, tel. 876/906-1288 or 876/906-1388, 11 A.M.–9 P.M. Mon.–Sat., noon–9 P.M. Sun.) has excellent fried fricassee chicken and rice (US$3.50–7).

Springroll Asian Fusion (73 Knutsford Blvd., tel. 876/908-4376 or 876/908-4377, US$10–30) serves Chinese, Japanese, and Thai specialties.

Akbar and Thai Gardens Restaurant (11 Holborn Rd., tel. 876/906-3237, noon–3:30 P.M. and 6–10:30 P.M. daily) has decent Indian and Thai food with staples like chicken or shrimp pad Thai (US$10 and US$17, respectively), and items ranging from chicken tikka masala (US$11) to lobster bhuna (US$24) from the Indian repertoire.

New Pagoda Restaurant (5 Belmont Rd., tel. 876/926-2561) serves decent Chinese food for US$4–17.

Cafés, Delis, and Juice Bars

Pizza Pazza (77 Knutsford Blvd., tel. 876/929-9636 or 876/968-4095, 10 A.M.–10 P.M. Mon.–Thurs., 10 A.M.–6 P.M. Fri., noon–6 P.M. Sat., closed Sun.) serves pizza, wraps, burgers, wings and fries, and fried, baked, and jerk chicken. There are also more hearty dishes like curried goat, fried fish, stew pork, oxtail, stew peas, chicken and conch soup, ackee and saltfish, mannish water, and escovitch fish. Outdoor seating available.

Cannonball Café (20–24 Barbados Ave. behind Pan Caribbean Bank, tel. 876/754-4486, 7 A.M.–6 P.M. Mon.–Sat.) serves sandwiches (US$4.50), lasagna (US$9), quiche (US$9), and salads (US$7), in addition to coffee (US$3), pastries, scones (US$3.50), and juices. The atmosphere is relaxing and cozy; wireless Internet is offered free for customers at all three locations: New Kingston, Barbican, and Manor Park.

Earl's Juice Garden (28 Haining Rd., tel.

876/920-1677; 6 Red Hills Rd., tel. 876/754-2425; earlsgarden@hotmail.com) makes excellent juices and baked goods (US$2–5). Owners Earl and Cheryl Chong offer free seminars on the last Saturday of each month (22 Westminster Rd., tel. 876/920-7009, 10 A.M.–1 P.M.) and have a culinary academy (at the Red Hills Rd. location, 2–6 P.M. on the last Sunday of the month) where the Chongs teach students how to prepare 11 raw dishes and one cooked.

Vegetarian

❬ Mother Earth (13 Oxford Terrace, off Old Hope Road just below the intersection with Oxford Road, tel. 876/926-2575, 8 A.M.–4 P.M. Mon.–Sat., US$4.50–5.50) is an excellent veggie and fish joint owned by Georgia Adams serving pepper pot, fish, red pea, and gungo pea soups and entrees like tofu creole, Chinese veggie steak, veggie mince balls, two-bean stew, ackee and saltfish, and tofu or fish chop suey. Meals are accompanied by roti or rice and peas, pumpkin rice, and calalloo rice. Fresh natural juices (US$2–2.25) include beet root, cane, calalloo, June plum, orange, and papaya. Mother Earth serves dishes exemplary of Jamaica's colorful vegetarian, or *ital*, culinary repertoire, in a down-to-earth, no-frills setting.

Seven Basics & More run by the **Country Farmhouse** (3 Vinery Road, Vineyard Town, tel. 876/930-1244 or 876/930-1245) is a vegetarian restaurant and deli, retailing among other things Blessed Delights baked products made by Ngozi (tel. 876/899-6332), many of which are vegan. Ngozi supplies Legend Café at the Bob Marley Museum and other outlets around Town.

Healthy Bites (48 Lords Rd., across from JAMPRO, or Jamaica Trade & Invest, tel. 876/817-0938 or 876/582-1853, healthy-bitesjs@yahoo.com, noon–3 P.M. Mon.–Fri.) prepares raw foods (J$6) and juices (US$2.50). Joy Smith is the creative chef behind the enterprise.

HALF WAY TREE
Jerk

❬ Jo Jo's Jerk Pit and More (12 Waterloo Rd., tel. 876/906-1509, 876/906-1612, or 876/906-2804) does regular Jamaican breakfast starting at 8 A.M. It also does lunch Monday to Wednesday with Jamaican staples, a grill day on Thursdays featuring barbecued ribs, homemade burgers, steaks, lamb and chicken (noon–10 P.M.), and the Jerk Pit on Fridays and Saturdays (noon–10 P.M.) serving jerk chicken, pork, lamb, and conch in addition to the complete menu including soups, and Philly cheese steak sandwiches. The bar is open during regular business hours. Jamaican breakfast is served on Sundays as well, starting at 8 A.M. and featuring mackerel rundown.

Truck Stop Grill & Bar (18 West Kings House Rd., 5 P.M.–midnight Sun.–Thurs., 5 P.M.–2 A.M. Fri.–Sat., tel. 876/631-0841, the-experience@truckstopjamaica.com, www.truck-stopjamaica.com) is a popular bar and informal jerk joint with outdoor seating on barrel stools serving jerk chicken or pork (US$4–7); steamed, fried, or roasted fish; and jerk or garlic lobster (US$16/lb.). A beer costs around US$3.

Jamaican

The Grog Shoppe Restaurant and Pub (Devon House, 26 Hope Rd., tel. 876/926-3512, noon–midnight Mon.–Thurs.; noon until you say when on Fri. and Sat., 11 A.M.–midnight Sun.) serves Jamaican staples like stewed oxtail, curry goat, and ackee and saltfish. Prices range from US$7 for curried chicken to US$29 for steak.

Kabana (12 Hope Rd., tel. 876/908-4005, noon–11 P.M. Mon.–Thurs., noon–midnight Fri. and Sat., 10 A.M.–11 P.M. Sun., US$10–34) serves mostly Jamaican food ranging from curry goat to lobster, as well as shrimp, ribs, salmon, and steak. Appetizers include fritters, spring rolls, and spicy shrimp. It serves Jamaican brunch (US$14) on Sundays, which includes dishes like ackee and saltfish, mackerel rundown, steamed callaloo, roast breadfruit, boiled banana, yam, jerk chicken, and rice and peas.

❮ Sonia's Homestyle Cooking & Natural Juices (17 Central Ave., tel. 876/968-6267, 7 A.M.–5:30 P.M. Mon.–Fri., 7:30 A.M.–5 P.M.

© OLIVER HILL

Sonia's Homestyle Cooking & Natural Juices in Half Way Tree is one of the best places for authentic, affordable eats.

NYAMMINGS: FOOD ON THE GO

While it is sometimes said that Jamaica's national dish is fried chicken from KFC, there are a host of authentically Jamaican fast-food joints to compete for that title, like Tastee Patties, Juici Patties, Island Grill, and Captain's Bakery, serving ackee and saltfish. In fact, only select international franchises have been able to survive in Jamaica; notably, both McDonald's and Taco Bell were unable to do enough business to stay viable and closed shop. Others, like Domino's Pizza, Pizza Hut, Popeye's, and Subway, do relatively well in a few locations scattered around town. Pan chicken, patties, and loaves have traditionally been the food of choice for Jamaicans on the go.

Pan chicken vendors set up all over town from evening until the early morning. Some of the best spots in town for real, hot-off-the-grill pan chicken include the line of vendors next to one another on Red Hills Road just beyond Red Hills Plaza heading towards Meadowbrook and Red Hills.

You can also whiff the pan chicken as you approach Manor Plaza in Manor Park on the upper reaches of Constant Spring Road in the evenings.

A few dependable **jerk vendors** hawk their fare in the evenings on the corner of Northside Drive and Hope Road by Pizza Hut, and they have a devoted following. Jerk pork (US$8.50/lb.) is sold on one side of the plaza and jerk chicken (US$3.50/quarter) on the other.

Sat., 8 A.M.–5 P.M. Sun., US$5–7.50) is Half Way Tree's best and most authentic sit-down eatery for Jamaican dishes like fried chicken, curry goat, and oxtail. Natural juices (US$1–2) like guava, cucumber, June plum, Otaheite apple, and soursop vary based on seasonal availability. The menu changes daily. Tamra is the assistant manager, and owner Sonia's daughter. **Mango Ranch** (16½ West Kings House Rd., manager Orasha "Dex" Bailey cell tel. 876/470-1591, tel. 876/906-5230, 10 A.M.–midnight Mon.–Sat., bar open 6 P.M.–midnight Sun.) is a restaurant and pool bar next to a car wash that opened in early 2009. The kitchen serves different items every day, with dishes like curried goat, stew peas, oxtail, escovitch fish, jerk chicken or pork, and fried or stew chicken.

Pepper's Night Club (Upper Waterloo Rd., tel. 876/969-2421 or 876/905-3831), set in a big open-air compound next to Megamart, has very good food (US$4–14), the pepper shrimp being the highlight. The bar can be lively and has plenty of billiard tables.

The Cove (3 Winchester Rd., contact owner/manager Lez 'Zaza' Lindo, cell tel. 876/480-9883 or 876/884-6578, thecove@gmail.com, 7 A.M.–3:30 P.M. Mon.–Fri., 6–11 P.M.

Wed.–Sat., US$5–20) is a jerk and fried-fish joint serving typical Jamaican dishes for breakfast and lunch like ackee and salt fish, steamed vegetables, fried chicken, and curry goat in a casual outdoor setting.

Caribbean and International Fusion

Norma's on the Terrace (Devon House, 26 Hope Rd., tel. 876/968-5488, normasjamaica@kasnet.com, 10 A.M.–10 P.M. Mon.–Sat.) is the first restaurant started by Norma Shirley, one of the Caribbean's most revered chefs for her innovative cuisine based on the island's culinary heritage. Norma's is in a beautiful setting overlooking the courtyard at Devon House. The food is on the pricey side, with entrées like stuffed chicken breast (US$14), lamb chops (US$40) and lobster (US$43). Appetizers include ackee with saltfish (US$11), marlin salad (US$13), and crab back (US$14).

Habibi Latino Restaurant (Shop #35, The Courtyard at Market Place, tel. 876/968-9296, 11 A.M.–11 P.M. Mon.–Sat., 3–11 P.M. Sun.) is easily one of Kingston's finest eats. Co-owners Abdul El Khalili and Yani Machado, of Lebanese and Cuban origin respectively, bring together their native cuisines as if they were created for each other, delivering tasty combinations of hummus appetizers, rosemary-seasoned steak, and *tostones* (fried plantains). A meal for two costs around US$50.

Café Aubergine (tel. 876/754-1865, cafe_aubergine@mail.infochan.com, www.cafeaubergine.com, noon–10:30 P.M. daily) opened a branch in the Courtyard at Market Place in July 2006, giving Kingston-based fans of the original location in Moneague, St. Ann, a closer alternative. The restaurant was founded by partners Neville Anderson and the late Rudolf Gschloessl, and features a mix of Caribbean and Mediterranean cuisine. Entrées range from pork tenderloin (US$12) to lamb chops (US$32) and grilled loup de mer (US$40).

❰ Susie's Bakery & Coffee Bar (Shop #1, Southdale Plaza, behind Popeye's on Constant Spring Rd., tel. 876/968-5030, 8 A.M.–10 P.M. Mon.–Sat., 9 A.M.–7:30 P.M. Sun.) is an excellent spot for dinner with outdoor seating and items like seafood penne, steak, ribs, fish, and lamb chops (US$20–29). Dinner is served starting at 6:30 P.M.

Susie's well-prepared entrées, natural juices, and homemade pastries, while not inexpensive, are worth every penny. Indoor seating by the deli and fresh salad bar complement the elegant courtyard seating next to the outdoor bar with a lively schedule of theme nights throughout the week.

Japanese, Chinese, and Indian

Just west of the Junction of West Kings House Road and Constant Spring Road, the **Courtyard at Market Place** (67 Constant Spring Rd.) has become the premier international food court in Kingston.

Taka's East Japanese Restaurant (Shops #50 & 51, tel. 876/960-3962, noon–10 P.M. Wed.–Sun., 5–10 P.M. Tues., closed Mon.) has the best sushi in Jamaica at competitive prices (US$25 per person for a full meal) and a very convincing ambience. Taka Utoguchi opened the restaurant in 2005.

Jewel of India (Shop #37, tel. 876/906-

3983, noon–10 P.M. daily, reservations recommended) serves North Indian cuisine in an upscale South Beach contemporary atmosphere with Indian Buddha bar music. Dishes range from chicken shorba and tomato soup (US$5) to lamb (US$13), lobster (US$30), tandoori filet mignon (US$28), and masala lamb chops (US$23). The bar has a nice range of liquor and an extensive cocktail menu, including house items Kama Sutra, Indian Sunrise, Indian Smooch, and Vindaloo Margarita. The food can be hit or miss and the expense quickly adds up.

China Express (Shop #53, Market Place, tel. 876/906-9158 or 876/906-9159, noon–9:30 P.M. Sun.–Thurs., noon–10 P.M. Fri.–Sat.) has decent Chinese food in a nice setting. Items on the menu range from wonton soup to Cantonese lobster (US$34). It's a popular lunch location.

❰ Restaurant Cocoro (Mayfair Hotel, 4 West Kings House Close, tel. 876/929-0970, noon–10 P.M. Tues.–Sun.) is a Japanese restaurant opened in late 2006 by Takahiro Sawada. The restaurant offers some of the most attentive service in all of Kingston, with traditional Japanese dishes like shrimp shumai (US$6), edamame (US$3), and seaweed salad (US$4), as well as creative dishes that incorporate typical Jamaican cuisine like the Cocoroll, a deep fried pork and tomato roll, or the Pirates Roll with jerk chicken and tomato (US$7). While Taka's East Japanese Restaurant takes the prize for most authentic Japanese cuisine, Cocoro is an excellent option in a nice quiet setting on the veranda of the Mayfair.

Fee Fee Fast Food (Shop #7, Lane Plaza, Half Way Tree, tel. 876/929-5465, 7 A.M.–6 P.M. Mon.–Sat., US$3.50–7) has Indian-Caribbean dishes like roti, curry chicken, and curry goat, with red pea soup with beef on Wednesdays and Saturdays, chicken or beef soup with pumpkin on other days. Oxtail and other chicken dishes are also available. Fee Fee delivers all over Kingston (US$1.15–2), down to Cross Roads and up to Manor Park. The breakfast menu changes

KINGSTON

daily, with porridge and hearty Jamaican dishes like ackee and saltfish, callaloo and cabbage, and stew chicken. **Dragon Court** (6 South Ave., tel. 876/920-8506, 11:30 A.M.–9:30 P.M., till 10 P.M. for takeout daily) serves decent Chinese food ranging from chicken dishes (US$7) to lobster (US$29).

Little Tokyo (7th Avenue Plaza, 876/908-0721, 10:30 A.M.–9 P.M. Mon.–Thurs., 10:30 A.M.–10 P.M. Fri.–Sat., noon–7 P.M. Sun.) is a Chinese/Japanese greasy fast-food joint that claims to serve "the best food in town." Best or not, it's relatively affordable (US$5–10).

Tropical Chinese (Mid Spring Plaza, 134 Constant Spring Rd., tel. 876/941-0520, noon–10 P.M. daily, closed only on Christmas and Good Friday) serves entrées like chicken (US$8.50), shrimp with cashew nuts (US$16), steamed whole fish (US$28.50), lobster dishes (US$23.50), eggplant (US$7), seafood (US$17), and stewed duck (US$14). Brothers Chris and Fred Chai run the place.

Panda Village Chinese Restaurant (Shop #21, Manor Park Plaza, 184 Constant Spring Rd., tel. 876/941-0833, 11:30 A.M.–9 P.M. Mon.–Thurs., 11:30 A.M.–10 P.M. Fri. and Sat., US$5–8) has dependable Chinese food with chicken, fish, and shrimp dishes.

Meat and Seafood

Gaucho's Grill (20-A South Ave., tel. 876/754-1380) serves a blend of Jamaican and American food with an alleged Italian touch. The ambience is relaxing with open-air seating by a reflecting pool. The bar makes a decent margarita. Prices range from inexpensive for a quarter chicken (US$6.50) to a bit pricey for steak or lobster (US$26).

The Terra Nova Hotel & Suites (17 Waterloo Rd., tel. 876/926-2211) has an excellent restaurant that does the best regular buffets in town. The Sunday brunch buffet is exceptional (11 A.M.–4 P.M., US$30), and daily lunch buffets (noon–3 P.M., US$23) have a different theme each day of the week: Tuesday is Caribbean; Wednesday Italian; Thursday Jamaican; and Friday is seafood. The steak and lobster buffet

dinner on Wednesdays (6:30–10 P.M., US$41) will surely satisfy the most demanding date.

Prendy's On The Beach (7 South Avenue, tel. 876/906-9058 or cell tel. 876/575-6063., prendysonthebeach@yahoo.com, 11 A.M.–midnight Mon.–Sat., 9 A.M.–midnight Sun.) is a favorite Hellshire Beach fish joint that opened a location in the heart of Half Way Tree in 2009. It's one of the best places to get fried, roast, and steamed fish in town, accompanied of course by festival and bammy. Fish runs US$12 per pound for fried fish, US$15/lb. for steamed or brown stew, while shrimp goes for US$15 per serving and lobster costs US$16 per pound.

White Bones (1 Mannings Hill Rd., at the junction with Constant Spring Rd., tel. 876/925-9502, 11:30 A.M.–11 P.M. Mon.–Sat., 2–10 P.M. Sun.) has a great setting with fish tanks, nets, and Christmas lights, and excellent seafood to match. Appetizers start at US$8.50 and include raw or grilled oysters, soup du jour, and salads. Entrées include snapper fillet (US$20) and grilled snapper burger (US$11.50). The popular all-you-can-eat crab buffet (US$20) is on Thursdays.

The Rib Kage Bar & Grill (12 Braemar Ave., tel. 876/978-6272, 11 A.M.–10:30 P.M. Mon.–Thurs., 11 A.M.–11:30 P.M. Fri. and Sat., 1–9 P.M. Sun., US$6–30) is the best place in town for ribs: fingers, tips, spare, and baby back. Chicken, fish, and lobster dishes are also served. The outdoor setting is pleasant for downing a beer with friends. Takeout and delivery are also offered.

Cafés and Delis

Rituals Coffee Roasters (Shop #5, Village Plaza, tel. 876/754-1992, www.ritualscoffeehouse.com, 8 A.M.–7 P.M., Mon.–Thurs., 8 A.M.–8 P.M. Fri., 8 A.M.–9 P.M. Sat., 9 A.M.–6 P.M. Sun.) is a coffee shop serving espresso, lattes, cappuccinos, tea, pastries, pastas, salads, and sandwiches. The Village Plaza shop is the first Jamaican franchise outlet of the Trinidad-based chain.

Susie's Bakery & Coffee Bar (Shop #1, Southdale Plaza, behind Popeye's on Constant

Spring Rd., tel. 876/968-5030, 8 A.M.–10 P.M. Mon.–Sat., 9 A.M.–7:30 P.M. Sun.) has prepared foods like lasagna and made-to-order sandwiches, as well as excellent natural juices. The pastries sold at Susie's are all homemade, ranging from mouth-watering whipped cream–filled eclairs to tiramisu and passion-fruit cake (US$4–8). Dinner is served starting at 6:30 P.M. with items like pork chops, steaks, ribs, and fish (US$6.50–33.50).

Café Concheta (Shop #1, Mid Spring Plaza, 134 Constant Spring Rd., tel. 755-3608, 8 A.M.–8 P.M. Mon.–Fri., 10 A.M.–9 P.M. Sat.) serves Blue Mountain Coffee, smoothies, beer and wine, pastries, wraps, sandwiches, salads, soups, and other light foods like stuffed crab backs with garlic bread in a cozy parlor with a living room vibe. Wi-Fi is available to customers free of charge.

Cannonball Café (Manor Centre, Manor Park, tel. 876/969-3399, 7 A.M.–7 P.M. Mon.–Fri., 9 A.M.–5 P.M. Sat.–Sun.) prepares sandwiches (US$5), beef lasagna (US$9), quiches (US$9), and salad (US$7), in addition to coffee (US$3), pastries, scones (US$3.50), and juices. The atmosphere is relaxing and cozy; wireless Internet is offered free for customers at all locations.

HOPE ROAD
Jamaican
Legend Café (56 Hope Rd., at the Bob Marley Museum) is open during museum hours (9 A.M.–5 P.M. daily), serving Jamaican staples as well as escovitch fish (US$17) and fresh juices (US$2).

Starapples (94 Hope Rd., tel. 876/927-9019, starapples@cwjamaica. com, 11:30 A.M.–9 P.M. Mon.–Thurs., 11:30 A.M.–10 P.M. Fri., 9 A.M.–10 P.M. Sat., 9 A.M.–6 P.M. Sun.) serves excellent dishes, from appetizers (US$2–4) like saltfish fritters, pepper shrimp, and crab cakes to entrées (US$5–16) like escovitch fish, curried shrimp, and reggae lobster in coconut curry. More typical Jamaican fare is also served, including roast yam and saltfish, jerk chicken, and curry goat, as well as creative vegetarian dishes like vegetable lasagna and callaloo quiche. The setting is nice, with indoor and outdoor seating with a view of busy Hope Road.

African Entertainment & Restaurant (94-N Old Hope Rd., between Commissioners office and Texaco station, tel. 876/303-5181 or 876/459-9198, 7:30 A.M.–9 P.M. daily) serves Jamaican staples like rice and peas, pot roast or jerk pork, steamed or brown stew fish, curry goat, and saltfish with okra, ackee, or callaloo, plus many different preparations of chicken: barbecued, sweet and sour, jerk, brown stew, and fried. Sides include dumpling, banana, yam, green and ripe fried plantain (US$2.50 small, US$3.25 large), as well as peanut porridge for breakfast (US$1). African dishes are prepared on select Mondays and Wednesday or done to order on weekends for special events. Dances and cultural events are sometimes held.

Caribbean and International Fusion
Chez Maria (7 Hillcrest Ave., tel. 876/927-8078 or 876/978-7833, chezmaria@cwjamaica.com, www.chezmaria.webs. com, 11:30 A.M.–3 P.M. Mon.–Sat., 6–10 P.M. Sun.) is a Lebanese restaurant that makes its own pita bread and scrumptious pizzas. All the typical Lebanese favorites are covered on the menu, from tabouleh salad to hummus to grape leaf mehsheh, as well as good-value main dishes (US$9–18) like kafta kabob, shawarma, filet mignon, shrimp, and lobster. The pizza is the best in town, and other Italian dishes, like the notable shrimp linguine, are also excellent.

Chilitos (64 Hope Road, tel. 876/978-0537, noon–10 P.M. Mon.–Sat., 5–9 P.M. Sun.) is a self-described Jamexican restaurant serving quesadillas, tacos, and burritos, as well as mixed drinks. A 2-for-1 happy hour is 5–7 P.M. Wednesday.

Mi Casa (96 Hope Rd., next to Medusa, tel. 876/978-3741, 8 A.M.–2 A.M. Mon.–Sat., US$4–17) is a Cuban *paladar,* or home cooking–style eatery, serving typical Cuban fare as well as Jamaican staples. Cuban-style food includes dishes like pork strip steaks, accompanied by *congris,* the Cuban-style rice and peas, and *tostones* (fried green plantains). The Jamaican menu (US$4–11) features items like roast pork and fried, grilled, jerk, or Chinese roasted chicken.

☖ Guilt Trip (20 Barbican Rd., tel. 876/977-5130, 10 A.M.–11 P.M. Tues.–Sat., 6–10 P.M. Sun.) is well known for its desserts, and it serves up an innovative and well-executed dinner menu that includes portobello mushrooms over mashed sweet potatoes, beef tenderloin, shrimp, soups, and salads. It's reasonably priced, with most entrées in the US$11–21 range. Head chef and owner Colin Hylton is one of Kingston's top chefs, whose simultaneous work as a caterer pushes him to refine his art, to the benefit of Guilt Trip's dynamic menu.

Habibi Latino Express (Shop #6, Liguanea Plaza, cell tel. 876/321-4572, 9 A.M.–9 P.M. daily) opened a new location in Liguanea geared toward takeaway customers. The menu is the same as the Market Place location, specializing in Lebanese food with items like falafel, hummus, tabbouleh, and kabobs (US$10–20).

Lillian's Restaurant (237 Old Hope Rd., tel. 876/970-2224, 11:30 A.M.–6 P.M. Mon., 11:30 A.M.–3 P.M. Tues.–Fri., US$5–10) is a training facility at the School of Hospitality and Tourism Management at the University of Technology. It serves dependable food at affordable prices like chicken, pork, lamb, shrimp, pasta dishes, and desserts. An international cuisine series is held during two semesters of the year during which Friday evening dinners are served.

Chinese and Indian

Tamarind (Shop #28, Orchid Village, 20 Barbican Road, tel. 876/977-0695 or 876/702-3486, 11 A.M.–10 P.M. Tues.–Sun.) is a North Indian-Chinese fusion restaurant with smart, modern decor and a delectable menu prepared

SWEET SPOTS

Kingston has several shops to satisfy cravings for sweets, ice cream, and pastries.

Sub Zero (Emancipation Park, New Kingston, cell. 876/424-9715, 10 A.M.–10 P.M. Mon.-Thurs., 2-11 P.M. Fri.-Sun.) is an ice cream shop that serves softies and scoops in cups and cones, as well as sandwiches, french fries, and gyros.

Cafecino (Hilton lobby, tel. 876/926-5430, ext. 4702) is a 24-hour pastry, sandwich, and coffee shop.

Scoops Unlimited (Devon House, 26 Hope Rd., tel. 876/929-7028 or 876/926-0888, 11 A.M.–10 P.M. daily, cones US$2-5, containers US$3.50-10), serves Devon House I Scream, which most Jamaicans rate as the country's best. It gets quite busy on Sundays, with a long line pouring out the door into the courtyard.

Chocolate Dreams (Devon House, 26 Hope Rd., Shop #2, tel. 876/927-9574, michelle@chocolatedreams.com.jm, www.chocolatedreams.com.jm, 10 A.M.-7 P.M. Mon.-Thurs., 11 A.M.-9 P.M. Fri.-Sat., 2-8 P.M. Sun.) retails delectable chocolate treats on par with any Godiva creation. All the chocolate treats are produced at the 9 Roosevelt Avenue (better known as Herb McKinley Avenue) location, where there's also a retail location.

Brick Oven (next to Scoops Unlimited, Devon House, 26 Hope Rd., tel. 876/968-2153, 9:30 A.M.–6 P.M. Mon.-Thurs., 9:30 A.M.-8 P.M. Fri.-Sat., 11:30 A.M.-8 P.M. Sun.) sells cakes, pastries, and taffies.

Häagen Dazs (Shop #1-D, Barbican Centre, next to Loshusan, 29 East Kings House Rd., tel. 876/927-8660, 11A.M.-11 P.M. daily, US$3.50-9.50) serves cups and cones.

Patta Kake Bakery (Shop #10, Lane Plaza, Liguanea, tel. 876/702-2958, 10 A.M.-7 P.M. Mon.-Sat.) serves cakes, veggie and meat loaves, and other pastries.

Guilt Trip (20 Barbican Rd., tel. 876/977-5130, 10 A.M.-11 P.M. Tues.-Sat., 6-10 P.M. Sun.) makes some of the best cakes and desserts in town.

by chefs straight from Delhi. The offerings include items like Mutton biryani, spring rolls, fish Szechuan, prawns nest, noodles, fried rice, Afghani, sweet garlic and Thai chicken, chicken tikka, and the Tamarind tandoori platter of assorted kabobs.

China Max (Shop #27, Orchid Village, 18–20 Barbican Rd., tel. 876/927-1888 or 876/927-1388, 11 A.M.–9:30 P.M. Mon.–Sat., 12:30–9:30 P.M. Sun.) is a Chinese restaurant under the same ownership as Gwong Wo, with a menu typical of most Chinese restaurants including wontons, soups, shrimp, chicken, pork, fish, and lobster dishes (US$3–25).

❰ Pushpa's (Northside Plaza, tel. 876/977-5454 or 876/977-5858, 11 A.M.– 10 P.M. daily, US$4–6.50) is by far the best restaurant in the complex and among the best Indian restaurants on the island, serving a mix of North and South Indian dishes, including dosas and idli on Sundays. Lunch specials include chicken dishes like moghlai, vindaloo, and kurma; vegetarian dishes like aloo mutter, paneer mutter, and eggplant curry; and mutton, shrimp, and fish served either curried, fried, or vindaloo.

There are three Chinese restaurants right next to one another in Northside plaza, creating Uptown Kingston's closest approximation to a Chinatown: **Golden State** (tel. 876/977-9213), **Dragon City** (tel. 876/927-0939), and **Dragon Heights.** All three keep similar hours (11:30 A.M.–9 P.M. Mon.–Sat., 2–9 P.M. Sun.), though Dragon Heights opens earlier (10 A.M.) on Sundays. Of the lot, Golden State has especially good service and decent food.

Cafés and Delis

Daily Bread (Orchid Village, 20 Barbican Rd., tel. 876/970-4571, 9 A.M.–10 P.M. Mon.–Sat.) is a branch outlet of Susie's and offers a great hot lunch buffet (US$10–24) with items like fried or barbecued chicken, shrimp, rice, soups, natural juices and pastries.

Cannonball Café (Barbican Centre, 29 East Kings House Rd., next to Loshusan supermarket, tel. 876/946-0983, 7 A.M.–7 P.M. Mon.– Thurs., Sat.–Sun., 7 A.M.–9 P.M. Fri.) has

sandwiches (US$4.50), beef lasagna (US$9), quiches (US$9), and Greek salad (US$7), in addition to coffee (US$3), pastries, scones (US$3.50), and juices. The atmosphere is relaxing and cozy; wireless Internet is offered free for customers.

Bookophilia (92 Hope Rd., tel. 876/978-5248, 11 A.M.–8 P.M. Mon.–Thurs., 11 A.M.–9 P.M. Fri., 10 A.M.–7 P.M. Sat., noon–5 P.M. Sun.) is a cozy bookstore that serves Blue Mountain coffee, tea cookies, and muffins (US$1–3), as well as a signature Gingerbread Chai Latte (US$3).

Meat and Seafood

❰ Cynthia's for Quantity and Quality (Phoenix Ave., tel. 876/960-1612 or 876/920-4740, Mon.–Sat. breakfast 8–10:30 A.M., takeout only, lunch noon–4 P.M.) serves steamed, escoveitch, and brown stew fish, curry goat, curry chicken, and baked or fried fish or pork (US$7–10). The natural juices are among the best in town (US$2).

Ambrosia (29 East Kings House Rd., tel. 876/978-1299, 11:30 A.M.–midnight daily, US$5.50–24), inside the gaming lounge of Acropolis, specializes in Jamaican dishes like oxtail, peppered shrimp, and fish and bammy. International food is also served, including rack of lamb, ribs, eight- and 16-ounce steaks, burgers, and club sandwiches. Ambrosia has a casino vibe, with gaming machines ringing loudly in the arcade next door adding to the din of the restaurant and bar.

Vegetarian

❰ Ashanti Oasis (Hope Botanical Gardens, Hope Rd., tel. 876/970-2079, noon–6 P.M. Mon.–Sat. dining in, takeout until 6:30 P.M., 12:30–5:30 P.M. Sun.), owned by Yvonne Hope, has some of the best and most reasonably priced vegetarian food in Kingston—in what must be the most natural setting on the manicured grounds of Hope Gardens. Combo meals are the best value, giving a taste of everything for US$4, or US$3.50 per single serving of any one dish. The menu changes daily and includes items like chile tofu in smoked

© OLIVER HILL

Ashanti Oasis at Hope Botanical Gardens cooks up some of Kingston's best vegetarian fare with excellent natural juices.

sauce. Juices (US$1.50) are the best in town. Call to find out what will be on the menu the following day.

Food for Life (Cedar Valley Rd. and Old Hope Rd., cell tel. 876/848-9592, 6 A.M.–10 P.M. Mon.–Sat.) is run by Ista Masters, who dishes up turned cornmeal, nut rundown, seafood, and Irish moss, honey moss, naseberry, and soursop juices.

Vihope (Orchid Village, tel. 876/977-1378, 8 A.M.–5 P.M. Mon.–Thurs., 8 A.M.–4 P.M. Fri.) is a vegetarian restaurant serving a palatable rotating takeout menu with items like veggie chunks and pea soup as well as natural juices. The proprietor also operates the **Healthy Diet** eatery at the University of the West Indies Mona Student Union, where meat items are also served.

Sovereign Food Court
Downstairs at Sovereign Centre (106 Hope Road at Barbican Rd., tel. 876/978-3463), the food court has several options for a quick bite. A US$3.50 purchase at any of the participating shops gets you a half hour of wireless Internet access.

Ice Cream Man (tel. 876/978-3842, 11 A.M.–10 P.M.) serves ice cream as well as pizza by the slice (US$2.25–3.50) or whole (US$8) and pastries.

Nick & Allis (tel. 876/978-3463, 10 A.M.–8:30 P.M. Mon.–Thurs., 10 A.M.–9 P.M. Fri.–Sat.) serves fruit salads, wraps, sandwiches (US$2.25–4.50) and fruit juices (US$1.50–2).

Little Tokyo (tel. 876/946-0388, 11 A.M.–10 P.M. Mon.–Thurs., 11 A.M.–11 P.M. Fri.–Sat.) serves Japanese-Chinese fast food.

OK Sushi & Noodles (tel. 876/946-0838) also serves Chinese and Japanese fast food.

Pastry Passions (tel. 876/927-9105, pastrypassionshome@gmail.com, 10 A.M.–9 P.M. Mon.–Sat., 2–9 P.M. Sun.) serves excellent pastries and coffee.

Kibby Korner (Shop #10, Sovereign Mall, tel. 876/978-3762, US$2.75–6.50) has affordable Lebanese food, including falafel, kibby, and kebabs. A grape leaf combo gives you a mix of dishes, and an assortment of sides is also available.

Jamaica Juice (Shop #14, tel. 876/978-9756, 10 A.M.–9 P.M. Mon.–Thurs., 10 A.M.–9:30 P.M. Fri.–Sat., noon–8 P.M. Sun., US$3–5) is perhaps the best shop in Sovereign's food court, with fresh juices, smoothies, as well as food items, most notably chicken or chickpea roti. The mango smoothie is highly recommended.

Other Sovereign food court restaurants include **Kowloon** (tel. 876/978-3472, 11 A.M.–9 P.M. Mon.–Thurs., 11 A.M.–9:30 P.M. Fri. and Sat., 12:30–7 P.M. Sun.), serving passable Chinese fast food, and **Deli Works** (Shop #1-A, tel. 876/927-4706, 10 A.M.–7 P.M. Mon.–Thurs., 10 A.M.–8 P.M. Fri., 10 A.M.–9 P.M. Sat., 9 A.M.–3 P.M. Sun.). Deli Works is a bit steep and intermittently appetizing, with a hot food line dishing out entrées like fried chicken, oxtail, and shrimp (US$7–10) accompanied by ground provisions, rice, and natural juices (US$2.25). The food is pricier than average for the typical Jamaican fare and at times, not the most appetizing. An adjoining café serves coffee and pastries and offers customers free Wi-Fi.

WASHINGTON BOULEVARD AND RED HILLS ROAD AREA
Jamaican

C **Norma's** (31 Whitehall Ave., tel. 876/931-0064, 8:30 A.M.–4:30 P.M. Mon.–Sat.) takeout is the best home cooking in town for Jamaican staples like curry goat, oxtail, and stewed chicken—and you won't find better value; at times fish and shrimp are also available. Call in advance to find out what's on the menu and to make sure it "nah sell-off" yet. Ask Norma if you can view the kitchen around back with its industrial-sized pots and flurry of activity. Lunches come in small (US$3) or large (US$3.50). Oxtail is US$6.50, and juices are US$1.50.

Ital and Vegetarian

Jah Messenger Rasta-rant (Shop #17, St. Andrew Plaza, 90-B Red Hills Rd., contact Jah T, cell tel. 876/310-6819, 7 A.M.–7 P.M.

Mon.–Fri.), owned by reggae great Luciano, a.k.a. Jah Messenger, serves Ital fare like curried veggies (US$5) and brown stew fish (US$6.50).

Mi Hungry Whol'-Some-Food (80 Horwood Drive, Washington Garden, off Washington Blvd., contact I-Wara, tel. 876/454-4766, closed Saturday) serves vegetarian raw food renditions of pizza, patties or "happies," sweet and savory fruit and vegetable pies, and burgers (US$5–6.50) as well as fresh natural juices (US$3–5). Take a left onto Weymouth Drive off Washington Boulevard coming from Half Way Tree and take the second left and continue the junction at the top of the road and take a right on Horwood.

SPECIALTY FOOD STORES

The best place to buy produce, at least where price and freshness is concerned, is **Coronation Market** Downtown, just west of St. William Grant Park. For everything else, go Uptown.

Jo Jo's Market (12 Waterloo Rd., in front of junction with South Ave., tel. 876/906-1509 or 876/906-1612, 7 A.M.–6 P.M. Mon.–Fri., 8 A.M.–6 P.M. Sat., 8 A.M.–4 P.M. Sun.) is the best place Uptown for fresh produce, including fruits and juices.

Finnigan's Winery (5 Cranbourne Ave., tel. 876/960-7799 or cell tel. 876/816-3375, 10 A.M.–5 P.M. Tues.–Fri., 11 A.M.–6 P.M. Sat.) has a great selection of imported cheeses, meats, and wines. Tom Finnigan sees his business as a "supplier of necessities, not luxury goods." Excellent sandwiches are prepared on the spot, and a pizza oven was installed in late 2009, paving the way for a seated dining experience. A courtyard in the back hosts occasional film showings and parties.

Mac's Gourmet Market (49-A Hope Rd., in same parking lot as T.G.I. Friday's, tel. 876/927-3354, 10 A.M.–7 P.M. Mon.–Sat., 10 A.M.–5 P.M. Sun.) retails a mix of imported meats, wines, cheeses, produce, and locally produced cottage-industry products including sauces, salad dressings, and desserts. A prepared-foods section has wraps and lobster and potato salads, while a hot section at the back serves rotisserie chicken and ribs.

The Lannaman family owns a small chain of health-food and nutritional products stores throughout the Kingston area. They include **Health & Nutrition** (Sovereign Centre, tel. 876/978-3529) and **Fit for Life** (King's Plaza, tel. 876/926-4207), where you can find Tom's of Maine products, Knudsen's Spritzers, hemp shampoo, and other granola-lovers' fare.

Natural Health Whole Food Store (Shop #1, Orchid Village Plaza, 20 Barbican Road, 876/977-1192; Shop #14 Mid Spring Plaza, 134 Constant Spring Road, 876/755-4587 or 876/925-1037; 10 A.M.–6 P.M. Mon.–Thurs., 10 A.M.–7 P.M. Fri.–Sat.) sells natural and organic food products, nutritional supplements, herbal supplements and teas, health and beauty products, and books and magazines.

SUPERMARKETS

Empire Supermarket (1 Retirement Rd., tel. 876/960-1309, 8:30 A.M.–8:30 P.M. Mon.–Thurs., 8:30 A.M.–9:30 P.M. Fri.–Sat., 9 A.M.–2 P.M. Sun.; Lane Plaza, Liguanea, tel. 876/970-2496, 8:30 A.M.–9 P.M. Mon.–Thurs., 8:30 A.M.–10 P.M. Fri., 10:30 A.M.–10 P.M. Sat., 9 A.M.–4 P.M. Sun.) has good prices, but you won't find much in the way of exotic foods.

John R. Wong Supermarket (1 Tobago Avenue, tel. 876/926-4811), which has a lot of ethnic foods, is the most central supermarket in New Kingston.

Sovereign Supermarket (1 Barbican Rd., tel. 876/927-5955; Sovereign Manor, 184 Constant Spring Rd., tel. 876/969-5792) is a bit pricey but has a good variety of foodstuffs and basic kitchen wares.

Loshusan (Barbican Centre, 29 East Kings House Road, tel. 876/978-8101) has a wide selection of imported products and a good produce section. It makes nice pastries and a decent whole grain baguette. There's also a sushi bar making rolls to order and a video rental outlet.

Michi Supercentre (2–4 Savannah Ave., off of Washington Boulevard, tel. 876/969-3333) is full-service supermarket with a household section and a deli with Jamaican cooked food and pastries.

Megamart (29 Upper Waterloo Rd., tel. 876/969-3899; Portmore Mall, tel. 876/988-1172) is one of the bigger supermarkets in town.

Hi-Lo Food Stores (13 Old Hope Rd., tel. 876/926-6123; ¾ Barbican Rd., tel. 876/946-3400; Cross Roads Plaza, tel. 876/926-7171; Manor Park Plaza, tel. 876/924-1411) is another basic supermarket.

Lee's Food Fair & Lee's Family Pharmacy is at 86-B Red Hills Road (tel. 876/931-1560).

PriceSmart (111 Red Hills Rd., tel. 876/969-1242) is a wholesale membership supermarket. It can be well worth signing up if you're in town for awhile and feeding a large group.

STONY HILL
Accommodations and Food

Boon Hall Oasis (4 River Rd., Stony Hill, tel. 876/942-3064, lunch noon–5 P.M. Thurs.–Sat., brunch 10 A.M.–3 P.M. Sun., and dinner by reservation) is a beautiful rainforest-like garden venue in the Stony Hill area of St. Andrew. The all-inclusive brunch buffet (US$22) is excellent, with typical Jamaican fare like ackee and saltfish, liver, mackerel, boiled banana, and dumpling. Lunch (US$15) dishes include fish, chicken, and curry goat, while shrimp, chicken, and lobster dishes are served for dinner (US$25 and up). Steven Jones owns the place. Take a right on Eerie Castle road in Stony Hill square and a left at Roti Bar onto River Road. A steep decline leads off River Road to the parking area on the left.

Country Style Restaurant (Stony Hill Square, tel. 876/942-2506, 7:30 A.M.–9 P.M. daily) serves typical Jamaican and Chinese dishes ranging from curry mutton, stew pork, or escovitch fish (US$4) to curried shrimp (US$10.50). Georgianna's, based at the same location, offers catering.

Neita's Nest (tel. 876/469-3005, neitasnest@ neitasnest.com, www.neitasnest.com, US$50/

person) is a bed-and-breakfast with clean rooms and terrific views. It's a bit remote at 15 minutes from Kingston and can be a bit awkward for those without their own transportation. **Villa Ronai** (Old Stony Hill Rd., tel. 876/960-0049) in the upscale Stony Hill area is a beautiful mansion owned by Pulse Entertainment that hosts periodic events, including private parties for Fashion Week. The villa is slated for development into a destination resort and spa with an entertainment lifestyle lean, restaurants and shops.

Information and Services

GOVERNMENT INFORMATION OFFICES

The **Jamaica Tourist Board** (64 Knutsford Blvd., tel. 876/929-9200, fax 876/929-9375, info@visitjamaica.com, www.visitjamaica.com, 8:30 A.M.–4:30 P.M. Mon.–Fri.) has a small library with staffers available to assist visitors with information on Jamaica's more popular attractions.

The **Jamaica National Heritage Trust** (79 Duke St., tel. 876/922-1287, www.jnht.com) is located Downtown in the historic Headquarters House. The Trust can provide information on Heritage sights across the island.

The **Survey Department** (23½ Charles St., tel. 876/922-6630 or 876/922-6635, ext. 264, patricia.davis@nla.gov.jm) sells all kinds of maps. Contact Patricia Davis in the business office. The Survey Department is a division of the National Land Agency, based on Ardenne Road.

SPECIALIZED TRAVEL SERVICES

Doctor Bird Expat Services (contact director Adrien Lemaire, drbird.ja@gmail.com, tel. 876/376-1426) is a concierge service offering just about anything an expat or visiting heads of state, celebrities, and business executives could want while in Jamaica, from private security and armored cars to shipping and customs clearing, chartered aircraft and boats, party planning, villa rentals, and sourcing of domestic help and tutoring.

Countrystyle International (62 Ward Avenue, Mandeville, tel. 876/488-7207 or 876/962-7758, diana@countrystylejamaica.com, www.countrystylejamaica.com) led by Diana McIntyre-Pike, is an organization that promotes community tourism under the slogan, "where the beaches end, our countrylife begins." The organization leads culinary, cultural, and study tours, arranging itineraries, transportation, and accommodation.

DaVinci Jamaica Vacations (info@davincijamaica.com, www.davincijamaica.com) is a Kingston-based travel company that specializes in intimate, off-the-beaten-track roaming tours of the island. DaVinci sells all things Jamaican, all places in Jamaica, and the full cast of Jamaican people; if it is safe, legal, and their clients want to experience it, they'll do it. Preset packages or customized vacations are offered, emphasizing Jamaica's cuisine with a unique food tour of the island and "The Bohemian West and East" food mini-tour weekend packages. Accommodations are arranged based on the budget and taste of clients.

POLICE AND IMMIGRATION

Police stations are located at Half Way Tree (142 Maxfield Ave., tel. 876/926-8184), Downtown Kingston Central (East Queen St., tel. 876/922-0308), and Constant Spring (2–3 Casava Piece Rd., tel. 876/924-1421).

Immigration (25 Constant Spring Rd., tel. 876/906-4402, tel. 876/906-1304) is responsible for granting extensions of stay or processing the paperwork for visas.

HOSPITALS AND MEDICAL FACILITIES

UWI's **University Hospital** (Papine Rd., Mona, tel. 876/927-1620) has a good reputation and is probably the best public hospital in Jamaica. Tony

Thwaites is UWI's private facility (University Hospital, Mona, tel. 876/977-2607).

Andrews Memorial Hospital is located at 27 Hope Road (tel. 876/926-7401, emergency tel. 876/926-7403).

Medical Associates Hospital and Medical Center (18 Tangerine Place, tel. 876/926-1400) is a private clinic with a good reputation. It also has a pharmacy at the same location.

Eye Q Optical (Shop #10, Lower Manor Park Plaza, tel. 876/925-9298; Courtleigh Corporate Center, 8 St. Lucia Avenue, New Kingston, tel. 876/906-1493) is the best spot in town to get your eyes tested or pick up a pair of prescription glasses.

Pharmacies

Andrews Memorial Hospital Pharmacy (27 Hope Rd., tel. 876/926-7401) is open 8 A.M.– 10 P.M. Monday–Thursday, 8 A.M.–3:30 P.M. Friday, closed Saturday, 9:30 A.M.–3:30 P.M. Sunday.

Liguanea Drugs and Garden (134 Old Hope Rd., tel. 876/977-0066) and **Lee's Family Pharmacy** (86-B Red Hills Rd., tel. 876/931-1877) are two other local pharmacies.

COMMUNICATIONS AND MEDIA

Jamaica Information Service (58-A Half Way Tree Rd., tel. 876/926-3590; TV Div. 37 Arnold Rd., tel. 876/922-3317) accumulates all kinds of data and statistics, as well as archival television footage.

The **Public Library** (Main Branch, 2 Tom Redcam Rd., tel. 876/928-7975 or 876/926-3315, ksapl@cwjamaica.com, jamlib.org.jm) has a decent collection and allows visitors to check out books by leaving a deposit. Internet is available free of charge at a handful of computer terminals.

Hot Off The Press (New Kingston Shopping Centre, tel. 876/968-4547, 8:30 A.M.–5 P.M. Mon.–Fri., 10:30 A.M.–3 P.M. Sat.) can satisfy most printing and imaging needs.

Music and Production Studios

Tuff Gong (220 Marcus Garvey Dr., tel. 876/923-9380, 876/923-9381, 876/923-9382, or 876/923-9383, www.tuffgong.com), the recording studio founded by Bob Marley, can be booked for recording sessions, mixing, and mastering (US$35/hour during the week, US$40/hour on weekends, inclusive of one engineer). Tuff Gong has welcomed numerous international artists, among them Senegal's Youssou N'Dour, who came to Jamaica in 2009 to record a Bob Marley tribute album at the legendary studio.

Caveman Studio (4 Halibut Close, Doncaster, cell tel. 876/774-5217, caveman.international@yahoo.com) has a Mackie 24-track together with Nuendo and access to numerous contemporary artists and live studio musicians. Bargain rates for recording (US$215/hour) and mixing (US$70/mix) make Caveman a top choice in Kingston for streamlined production. Dub plates vary in price depending on the artists, but generally for a big name like Richie Spice or Warrior King it'll run around US$500, with bigger artists like Sizzla charging at least double that.

Big Ship (8 East Riverside Drive, Havendale, US$35/hour, tel. 876/925-2409 or 876/655-0141, bigshipmusic@gmail.com) is led by reggae great Freddie McGregor and run by his son, Stephen, a.k.a. "The Genius" (stephen.mcgregor@gmail.com). The studio can be booked when not in use by Big Ship artists.

Flames Production (56 Ken Hill Drive, tel. 876/934-0827 or 876/765-2518) is a production company led by reggae icon Tony Rebel (www.tonyrebel.com). The location is home to Tony's studio, where dub plates are recorded and CDs and DVDs of Flames recording artists can be purchased, among them of course recordings by Tony Rebel and his wildly successful relative, Queen Ifrica, whose Montego Bay album released in 2009 received great critical acclaim. Flames is responsible for producing the annual **Rebel Salute** roots reggae and dancehall festival staged in St. Elizabeth every January.

Anchor Studios (7 Windsor Ave., tel. 876/978-2711, www.anchorstudios.com), run by Gussie Clarke, has reel-to-reel as well as Pro Tools. Rates are US$215 and US$260 per hour, respectively.

Exodus Nuclear Studio (Shop #12, 90½ Red Hills Rd., tel. 876/361-0333, garyexodus@ hotmail.com), run by Ryan "Gary Exodus" Braithwaite, is a popular venue for recording dub plates (US$12) and singles (US$30/hour inclusive of engineer).

The Mixing Lab Recording Studio (58 Dumbarton Ave., tel., 876/929-7362) has recorded many reggae greats and continues to churn out occasional hits.

Penthouse Recording Studio (6 Ballater Ave., Pembroke Hall, tel. 876/929-7446) distributes and retails Penthouse label records as well as Flames Production (Tony Rebel), HMG (Morgan Heritage), Gargamel (Buju Banton), and Ghetto Vibes (Errol Dunkley). Artists on the Penthouse label include Nadine Sutherland, Daville, Chaka Demus, Tiger, Cutty Ranks, Richie Stephens, Sanchez, Wayne Wonder, Beres Hammond, Marcia Griffiths, and Freddie McGregor, among others. Donovan Germain is CEO of Penthouse. Both CDs and records, 45s and 33s, are sold.

Phase 3 Productions (Unit #35, Winchester Business Center, 15 Hope Rd., tel. 876/929-5975, contact@phase3prod.com, www. phase3prod.com) has the best video production and multimedia equipment for rent, from tripods to cameras to flat-screen TVs. Phase 3 also produces music videos and events.

Newspapers
Kingston is home to two daily newspapers, the *Jamaica Gleaner* (www.jamaica-gleaner.com) and the *Jamaica Observer* (www.jamaicaobserver. com), and a weekly, the *Sunday Herald* (www. sunheraldja,com), all of which are distributed island-wide. The *Gleaner* was the island's first daily and is considered the paper of record; it also publishes *Jamaica Star*, the entertainment daily where you'll find the latest gossip on feuds between recording artists. The *Star* also publishes the advice column, "Dear Pastor," and photos of partygoers from Kingston's happening nightlife scene, as well as the occasional candid camera shots of people caught off guard for laughs. The *Observer* was established by Sandals chairman Gordon "Butch" Stewart to counter the overwhelming media force behind Oliver Clarke's

Gleaner, which rarely smiles on the Sandals boss in its copy. The *Observer* has its version of the *Star,* the entertainment tabloid, *Chat!.*

Local Societies and Organizations
The **Jamaica Orchid Society** (contact president Jeremy Whyte, tel. 876/927-2148, jeremy.whyte@ uwimona.edu.jm, www.hamlynorchids.com/jaos. htm) holds its impressive annual Spring Show the last weekend in March (9:30 A.M.–6 P.M.) at the orchid house at Hope Gardens or the grounds of the Jamaica Horticultural Society (intersection of Gibson Drive and Gibson Close in Hope Pastures). The society meets on the first Saturday of each month at the Joint Trades Unions Research and Development Centre (1 Hope Blvd.) at 4 P.M.; visitors are welcome. Members bring plants to discuss and hold short lectures and a judging session, where members learn about orchids and how to judge shows.

Claude Hamilton, an accredited judge of the **American Orchid Society** (tel. 876/927-6713) is the largest commercial grower in Kingston and the number one expert in Jamaica. He has a large nursery, **Hamlyn Orchids** (31 Kings House Ave., www.hamlynorchids.com, 8:30 A.M.–5 P.M. daily), which can be toured by calling ahead to set up a visit.

The **Georgian Society of Jamaica** (Richmond Park Great House, 58 Half Way Tree Rd., contact honorary secretary Pauline Simmonds, tel. 876/754-5261, www.georgian-jamaica.org) is a private society dedicated to the appreciation of Jamaica's architectural heritage from the Georgian period, and to the restoration and preservation of Georgian buildings. Geoffrey Pinto is the society's founder. The society has a list of public and private buildings its members tour on their outings, scheduled every few months. Richmond Park Great House is now headquarters for Xerox Jamaica.

The **Natural History Society of Jamaica** (contact Eric Garraway, tel. 876/927-1202, eric. garraway@uwimon.edu.jm, naturalhistory@ hotmail.com) holds regular meetings, typically once a month, to discuss and explore the country's natural environment. Call or email for information about trips or exact meeting times and location.

Post Offices and Parcel Services

Post Offices are located Downtown at 13 King Street (tel. 876/858-2414, www.jamaica-post.gov.jm/contactus.htm), Cross Roads (tel. 876/364-6316), and Half Way Tree (118 Hagley Park Rd., tel. 876/364-6119).

Shipping services are available through **DHL** (19 Haining Rd., tel. 876/920-0010) and **FedEx** (40 Half Way Tree Rd. and 75 Knutsford Blvd, 1 888/GO-FEDEX).

Telephone, Internet, and Fax

Several locations around Kingston offer free Wi-Fi access to customers with laptops. These include: **Jo Jo's Jerk Pit and More** (12 Waterloo Rd., in front of Junction with South Ave., tel. 876/906-1509 or 876/906-1612, 7 A.M.–6 P.M. Mon.–Fri., 8 A.M.–6 P.M. Sat., 8 A.M.–4 P.M. Sun.), **Cannonball Café** (20–24 Barbados Ave. behind Pan Caribbean Bank in New Kingston, tel. 876/754-4486; Manor Centre, Manor Park, tel. 876/969-3399; 7 A.M.–7 P.M. Mon.–Fri., Sat.–Sun. 9 A.M.–5 P.M.; Barbican Centre, 29 East Kings House Rd. next to Loshusan supermarket, tel. 876/946-0983; 7 A.M.–7 P.M. Mon.–Thurs. and Sat.–Sun., 7 A.M.–9 P.M. Fri., **Christopher's** (20–22 Trinidad Terrace, tel. 876/754-7823), **Daily Bread** (Orchid Village, 20 Barbican Rd., tel. 876/970-4571, 9 A.M.–10 P.M. Mon.–Sat.), **Indies Cafe & Grill** (8 Holborn Rd., tel. 876/920-5913, 12:30 P.M.–1 A.M. Mon.–Sat., 3 P.M.–midnight Sun.), and **Susie's** (Shop #1, Southdale Plaza, behind Popeye's on Constant Spring Rd., tel. 876/968-5030, 8 A.M.–10 P.M. Mon.–Sat., 9 A.M.–7:30 P.M. Sun.).

The **Jamaica Library Service** offers Internet access free of charge at all branches.

All the mobile carriers, meanwhile, offer wireless USB modems on post-pay or prepaid plans.

Surf Café (Shop #29, Lane Plaza, 106 Hope Rd., tel. 876/298-6799, 9 A.M.–5 P.M.) offers Internet access on several computers by the 15-minute interval (US$.55).

Digicel (10 Grenada Way, tel. 876/511-5000) offers island-wide wireless cards for laptops on both prepaid and post-pay plans. GSM chips can be bought at the Digicel outlet on Knutsford Boulevard and across the street behind the Tourist Board at Digicel headquarters. Digicel's USB modem costs US$41, with prepaid and post-pay customers paying the same rate of US$0.45 per MB.

Claro (30–36 Knutsford Boulevard, www.claro.com.jm, tel. 876/621-1000) offers a similar USB modem for US$68.

Cable & Wireless (1-888/225-5295 or 876/926-9700), which operates in Jamaica as LIME, has a similar 3G USB modem that it sells for US$65. LIME offers unlimited prepaid plans by intervals of 24 hours (US$5), weekly (US$15), or monthly (US$45), and post-paid plans for US$10 per month for 50MB, US$15 for 100MB, or US$25 for 1GB. If you have a Huawei E1756 or E166 USB modem, it should work with LIME's pre-paid or post-paid SIM cards, you'd just have to purchase a card (US$8) and buy credit, or make a deposit for the post-paid plan.

MONEY

Scotia DBG (7 Holborn Rd., tel. 876/960-6699 or 888/225-5324 (CALL DBG), info@scotiadbg.com, 8:30 A.M.–3 P.M. Mon.–Thurs., 8:30 A.M.–4 P.M. Fri.) and **FX Traders** (1-888/398-7233) offer the best exchange rates. FX Traders has *cambios* at: Cross Roads FSC, 13 Old Hope Rd. (9 A.M.–5 P.M. Mon.–Sat.); Shop 7, Boulevard Super Centre, 45 Elma Crescent (9:30 A.M.–5:30 P.M. Mon.–Sat.); King Street FSC, Woolworth Building, 83 King St. (9 A.M.–5 P.M. Mon., Tues., Thurs.–Sat., 9 A.M.–3:30 P.M. Wed.); K's Pharmacy, Shop 17, Duhaney Park Plaza (10 A.M.–6 P.M. Mon.–Fri., 10 A.M.–5 P.M. Sat.); Central Office FSC, 20 Tobago Ave. (9 A.M.–5 P.M. Mon.–Sat.); Pavilion FSC, Shop 30 Pavilion Mall, Constant Spring Rd. (9 A.M.–5 P.M. Mon.–Sat.); Park View Supermarket, 7 Chandos Place, Papine (8:30 A.M.–7 P.M. Mon.–Thurs., 8 A.M.–8 P.M. Fri.–Sat.).

ATM withdrawals are usually the most convenient way to get cash, but foreign charges and poor exchange rates are drawbacks. Depending on the amount you are changing, a few lost dollars in fees and rates can be worth the convenience. All the major banks will cash travelers checks, but lines are typically long, slow-moving, and overwhelmingly frustrating.

Western Union (main office at 2 Trafford Place, tel. 876/926-2454) has offices all over the island, including in Kingston at Cross Roads; 20 Tobago in New Kingston; Hi-Lo in Liguanea Plaza; at BluMenthal in Lower Manor Park Plaza; and in Pavilion Mall on Constant Spring in Half Way Tree (Shop #30 upstairs, and Super Plus downstairs).

Banks

Scotiabank has branches with ATMs at the following locations: Downtown (35–45 King St., tel. 876/922-1420), Cross Roads (86 Slipe Rd., tel. 876/926-1530 or 876/926-1532), Liguanea (125–127 Old Hope Rd., tel. 876/970-4371), New Kingston (2 Knutsford Blvd., tel. 876/926-8034), Portmore (Lot 2, Cookson Pen, tel. 876/989-4226), Bushy Park (tel. 876/949-4837), and UWI (tel. 876/702-2518 or 876/702-2519). Some Scotiabank ATMs, namely at Barbican Centre and in New Kingston, allow you to withdraw US dollars in addition to local currency.

First Caribbean has branches with ATMs in New Kingston (23–27 Knutsford Blvd., tel. 876/929-9310), Downtown (1 King St., 876/922-6120), two in Half Way Tree (78 Half Way Tree Rd., tel. 876/926-7400; Twin Gates Shopping Centre, tel. 876/926-1313), in Liguanea (129½ Hope Rd., tel. 876/977-2595),

and in Manor Park (Manor Park Plaza, tel. 876/969-2708).

RBTT has branches with ATMs at the following locations: Downtown (134 Tower St., tel. 876/922-8195), New Kingston (17 Dominica Dr., tel. 876/960-2340), Half Way Tree (6-C Constant Spring Rd., tel. 876/968-4193; Tropical Plaza, 12½ Constant Spring Rd., tel. 876/968-6155), and Liguanea (Sovereign Centre, 106 Hope Rd., tel. 876/928-7524).

NCB has branches with ATMs at the following locations: Downtown (37 Duke St., tel. 876/922-6710), Cross Roads (90–94 Slipe Rd., tel. 876/926-7420), New Kingston (32 Trafalgar Rd., tel. 876/929-9050), and Half Way Tree (Half Way Tree Rd., tel. 876/920-8313).

LAUNDRY

Bogues Brothers runs three laundry facilities in Kingston: **Spic 'n' Span** (26 Lady Musgrave Rd., on corner of Trafalgar, tel. 876/978-7711, 7 A.M.–6 P.M. Mon.–Sat., 9 A.M.–4 P.M. Sun.), **Molynes Fabricare** (55 Molynes, tel. 876/923-4234), and **Liguanea Fabricare** (144 Old Hope Rd., tel. 876/977-4900). All have dry cleaning, drop-off laundry service, and self-service.

Supercleaners Dry Cleaners & Launderers (25 Connolley Ave., tel. 876/922-6075, 7 A.M.–5 P.M. Mon.–Sat.) has a plant Downtown behind Sabina Cricket Grounds, where the drop-off service can get your clothes back the same day.

Getting There and Around

GETTING THERE
By Air
Norman Manley International Airport (tel. 876/924-8546 for arrival and departure information) is located on the Palisadoes heading towards Port Royal east of Downtown. Domestic flights leave from a small terminal by the cargo area, reached by taking a left off the boulevard leading to the main terminal before reaching the roundabout.

Skylan Airways (tel. 876/932-7102, reservations@skylanjamaica.com, www.skylanjamaica.com, office hours 8:30 A.M.–4:30 P.M. Mon.–Fri.) is the only commercial domestic carrier operating out of Norman Manley, with six weekly flights (Mon., Wed., Fri.) with morning and afternoon departures. The morning flights depart Kingston at 7:30 A.M., with the return departing Montego Bay at 8:30 A.M., while the afternoon flights depart

Kingston at 4 P.M., with the return leaving Montego Bay at 5 P.M. The trip lasts about half an hour and costs US$70 each leg. Skylan also offers charters when its aircraft is not in use on regularly scheduled flights. Skylan operates a Jetstream 32 19-seater aircraft with a pressurized cabin.

Jamaica Air Shuttle (tel. 876/906-9025, 876/906-9026, or 876/906-9027, www.jamaicaairshuttle.com) is an affiliate of air cargo and courier companies Airways International and Airpak Express, which began offering regular flights between Kingston and Montego Bay in late 2009. It departs from Tinson Pen Aerodrome with three Beach 99 Turbo Props seating 12 and one Queen Air with a five-person capacity. The carrier has 62 flights weekly scheduled Monday to Saturday (US$120 each way) and also offers charters.

Historically, most domestic flights in small aircraft departed from Tinson Pen, but there has been little continuity of service among carriers with a slew of different domestic airlines coming and going over the years.

Ground Transportation

The **Knutsford Express** (18 Dominica Drive, tel. 876/960-5499 or 876/971-1822, www.knutsfordexpress.com) is popular with Jamaicans and tourists alike, offering the most comfortable coach service between Kingston, Ocho Rios, and Montego Bay with two or three daily departures from each city. New Kingston–Montego Bay departs at 6 A.M., 9:30 A.M., 2 P.M., and 5 P.M. Mon.–Fri., 6 A.M., 9:30 A.M., and 4:30 P.M. on Saturdays, 8:30 A.M. and 4:30 P.M. on Sundays. Buses run between the parking lot behind New Kingston Shopping Centre and Pier 1 in Montego Bay. The trip lasts four hours depending on traffic and costs US$20 prepaid, US$23 on the day of travel.

Buses ply routes around town and between Kinston and major points on the eastern side of the island. The main bus terminals for routes out of Kingston are the Transport Centre hub in the heart of Half Way Tree (tel. 876/754-2610) and the Urban Transport Centre below Coronation Market on Port Royal Street and Water Lane (876/754-2584). Buses depart throughout the day to Port Royal (US$0.50), Spanish Town (US$1), Bull Bay (US$0.50), Morant Bay (US$1.50), Mandeville (US$3), Port Antonio (US$3), Ocho Rios (US$3), Savanna-la-Mar (US$7), Montego Bay (US$6), and Negril (US$8) .

Route taxis and **mini buses** depart from Cross Roads, Half Way Tree, by the roundabout on upper Constant Spring Road in Manor Park for destinations due north and at the roundabout in Papine for destinations in the Blue Mountains. Route taxis or minibuses depart for Kingston from virtually every city or town in the surrounding parishes and from parish capitals across the island. Route taxi fares are typically slightly higher than buses on the overlapping routes, but don't typically connect faraway points.

GETTING AROUND
On Foot

Jamaicans who walk around Kingston generally don't do so by choice, day or night, and are ridiculed as "walk foots" by their fellow citizens. It's mainly due to the prestige of driving, and more importantly, the heat that pedestrians suffer; the safety concerns around Town are generally exaggerated and vehicles stopped at lights offer little protection, anyway. There is really no better way to get to know the layout of some of the more congested areas like Downtown around the Parade, Knutsford Boulevard's Hip Strip, and around the center of Half Way Tree than to go on foot. Beyond that, route taxis and public buses are the best way to move about for those without a car.

By Bus

Jamaica Urban Transit Company (www.jutc.com, flat fare US$0.75) operates buses in and around the Corporate Area. Routes are extensive, but service and schedules can by daunting. Covered street-side bus stops are scattered along all the major thoroughfares throughout the city, and the more people gathered there, the sooner you're likely to see a bus. This is definitely the most economical way to move about.

By Taxi

Taxis are relatively safe off the street, but it's always best to call a dispatch to ensure accountability. Fares are assessed by distance rather than with a meter, and you may want to haggle if it seems too high. Downtown to New Kingston should cost around US$4.25, New Kingston to Half Way Tree around US$3.50, Half Way Tree to Papine about US$4.25. **City Guide Taxi** (tel. 876/969-5458) is a decent and dependable service, as are **Safe Travel Taxi Service** (tel. 876/901-5510) and **El-Shaddai** (tel. 876/969-7633). All the taxis in Jamaica tend to use white Toyota Corolla station wagons, and when you see one of these, chances are it's a taxi and can be waved down.

By Car

Rental cars tend to be very expensive across the island, but unfortunately indispensable when it comes to independently moving about and exploring remote areas. For the upper reaches of the Blue and John Crow Mountains, a four-wheel-drive vehicle is indispensable. Pervasive potholes in town don't really warrant a 4x4. Check with your credit card company to see if it covers insurance.

Unlicensed rental operators abound. While they may be cheaper (US$50/day) than more reputable agencies, there is less accountability in the event that anything should go worse than planned. These private rentals don't take credit cards, often want a wad of cash up front, and usually don't offer insurance. These informal agencies are best avoided.

Listed rates do not include insurance or the 16.5 percent GCT. Insurance is typically US$15–40, depending on coverage. A deposit is taken for a deductible when customers opt for anything less than full coverage. The use of select gold and platinum credit cards obviates the need to purchase insurance from the rental agency. Check with each individual establishment for their particular policies.

Compact Car Rentals (178 Mountainview Ave., tel. 876/978-4914, compactcarrental@yahoo.com, www.compactcarjamaica.com) rents Toyota Yaris (US$50), Corolla (US$65), and Camry (US$80) sedans, as well as Honda Civics (US$75), Accords (US$100), and CR-Vs (US$100) of varying years with a three-day minimum. Compact offers free pickups and delivery from Norman Manley International Airport.

Island Car Rentals (17 Antigua Ave., tel. 876/926-5991 or Norman Manley tel. 876/924-8075, icar@cwjamaica.com, www.islandcarrentals.com) has a wide range of vehicles from the Toyota Yaris (US$44 low season/$55 high season) and Camry (US$99 low/$109 high) to Honda Civic (US$58 low/$59 high) and Accord (US$78 low/$87 high), Suzuki Grand Vitara (US$99 low/$109 high), and Space Wagon (US$83 low/$90 high).

Fiesta Car Rental (14 Waterloo Rd., tel. 876/926-0133, fiesta@kasnet.com, www.fiestacarrentals.com) has fairly new Japanese vehicles, including Hyundai Accents (US$89) and one Honda Accord (US$170) and Suzuki Gran Vitara (US$146).

Budget (53 South Camp Rd., tel. 876/759-1793, Norman Manley tel. 876/924-8762, US tel. 877/825-2953, UK tel. 800/731-0125, budget@jamweb.net, www.budgetjamaica.com, 8 A.M.–4:30 P.M. Mon.–Fri., 8 A.M.–10 P.M. daily) has a range of vehicles from Toyota Yaris (US$60 low season/$75 high season) and Daihatsu Terios (US$75 low/$100 high) to VW Passats (US$95 low/$120 high).

Bargain Rent-A-Car (1 Merrick Ave., tel. 876/926-1909; Norman Manley Airport, tel. 876/924-8293; info@avis.com.jm, www.avis.com.jm) is the Avis franchise in Jamaica, with a range of vehicles including Hyundai Accent, Mitsubishi Lancer, Subaru Forrester, and Toyota Yaris, Corolla, and Camry, as well as vans. Prices range from the Yaris (US$74 low season/$114 high season) to the Nissan Urvan minibus (US$125 low/$166 high).

Ideal Car Rentals (43 Burlington Ave., tel.

876/926-2980) has a decent selection of Japanese models including a few four-wheel-drives.

Bowla's Car Rental (50 Dumbarton Ave., tel. 876/960-0067, bowlasrentacar@cwjamaica.com) offers a wide range of cars, unlimited mileage, short-term and long-term rentals starting at US$75 per day, and free rides to and from the airport. Bowla's fleet includes: Toyota Fortuner and Toyota Camrys, Mistusbishi Grandis, Hyundais, Mazdas, and Nissans.

Spanish Town and St. Catherine

With over a million people, the parish of St. Catherine has the largest share of Jamaica's population. Spanish Town, the sedate parish capital, was Jamaica's center of government until the British bureaucrats relocated to Kingston in 1872. Known simply as Spain or St. Jago in street lingo, the city has a rich heritage but has been largely left to decay. Its central square is more a bend along the road than a center of activity. Still, it has impressive facades and is home to Jamaica's national archives. The oldest Anglican Church outside of England is within a five-minute walk.

Spanish Town and surrounding communities like Old Harbour and Freetown have grown rapidly with housing schemes that respond to a demand for low-income housing from first-time home buyers. Most activity in Spanish Town today revolves around the two malls and bus park along Burke Road. Mandela Highway has heavy traffic into Kingston from Spanish Town during weekday rush hours (between 7 A.M. and 9:30 A.M. and back out in the evenings between 4 P.M. and 7:30 P.M.).

PORTMORE VICINITY

Immediately west of Kingston, past the wharves and across the causeway is Portmore, a bedroom community supporting the overflow from the burgeoning corporate area. As the causeway meets land on the St. Catherine side of the water, **Fort Augusta** sits on a point overlooking the harbor.

Portmore consists mainly of private and government-sponsored housing developments, with **Jamworld Entertainment Centre** and **Caymanas Park** horse-racing track on its northern side, reached by taking a right on the Portmore Parkway when coming off the bridge. Jamworld is the site for **Reggae Sting,** an annual show held on Boxing Day that never ceases to cause a stir. Accommodations in Portmore consist exclusively of hourly-rate joints, some of them dodgier than others.

Fort Augusta

Named after the mother of King George III, the fort was completed in the 1750s after an arduous construction process during which many workers suffered sickness and fevers. The area on which it was built was known as Mosquito Point. The fort was the sentinel on the harbor during a time when Spanish reprisals were still a tangible fear, and it served as a well-stocked arsenal. Ships coming into Kingston Harbour would unload their ammunition at the fort as a safety measure, but fewer precautions were taken at the fort itself; in 1782 the magazine containing 300 barrels of gunpowder was struck by lightning. The resulting explosion destroyed the building, killing 300 people, and broke windows as far as 27 kilometers away. Today the Fort is the site of Jamaica's only female prison. The St. Catherine Parish Council has made overtures toward demolishing the prison to allow for restoration of the fort, but the issue has gained little traction.

Port Henderson

Once a busy entry port for new arrivals to Spanish Town, Port Henderson today is little more than an extension of Portmore. There are several budget hotels like **Casablanca** (2–4 Port Henderson Rd., tel. 876/939-6999, US$44–51), which has air-conditioning, cable, and hot water, and even includes complimentary breakfast for two, but it sees very few tourists.

Fort Clarence (admission US$1.50) is the nicest beach in the greater Kingston area. It is usually well maintained, but it can accumulate seaweed and trash the farther away you go from the main area where the admission fee is charged. It is just east around the bend from Hellshire.

(Hellshire

Once a quiet anglers' beach, Hellshire has become the quintessential rustic chic weekend hangout, with prices varying widely depending on the appearance of customers at many of the beach shack restaurants. There are a handful of dependable and honest shacks including Shorty's, the most highly recommended, Aunt May's, Aunt Merl's, and **Prendy's** (876/575-6057, 876/881-9689 or 876/589-7926), where you can get a good fried fish with accompanying *festival*. There are several other beach shack restaurant besides these, many of which will have your wallet if you're not careful. Be sure to come to an agreement as to what you'll be charged when selecting a fish from the cooler, and don't allow any generous add-ons, as these will certainly not come as a gift. A snapper large enough for one person shouldn't cost more than the Jamaican dollar equivalent of US$15.

Hellshire Beach itself can be a bit littered, but the water is generally clean enough to swim in spite of the fishermen scaling snapper along the shoreline. The sand gets a bit cleaner as you walk east along the beach past the multitude of fried fish stands. There are peddlers and hustlers of all kinds at Hellshire, and it can be a bit dodgy at night. Horseback rides are offered by Damian (tel. 876/479-3250, US$14/hr). Don't be alarmed by constant solicitations from vendors and beggars; it's the basis of their livelihood and can be considered part of Hellshire's color.

Two Sisters Cave

Managed by the Urban Development Corporation (tel. 876/999-2283 or 876/953-9238, 9 A.M.–6 P.M. Wed.–Sun., admission US$3 for adults, US$2 for children), Two Sisters Cave was a regular hangout for the

© OLIVER HILL

Fishermen clean snapper on Hellshire Beach.

first Jamaicans centuries ago. Two cavernous caves, one with a deep pool suitable for swimming, lie about 100 meters apart down a series of steps. Security personnel no longer allow swimming.

For a less-developed cave option, where there are no security guards posted, another cave about 100 meters back toward Hellshire from Two Sisters Cave, can be reached by a footpath descending from the road.

SPANISH TOWN

Originally founded as Villa de la Vega or Santiago de la Vega by the Spanish, the city was named Spanish Town after the British takeover in 1655. The old part of the city is well organized in a grid with Spanish Town Square at its center. There is little activity in the historic part of the city today, however, with most of the hustle and bustle centered on the commercial plazas along Burke Road.

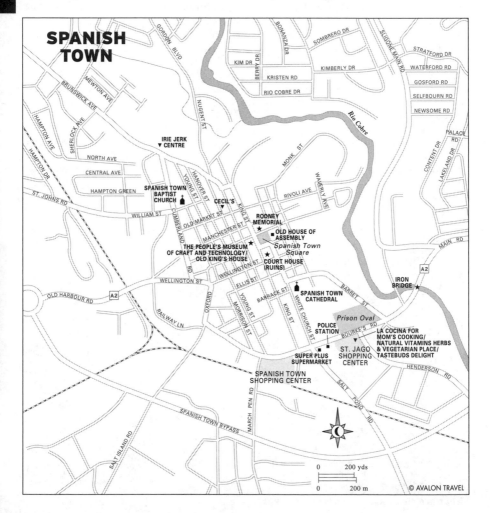

The Rodney Memorial gives an allure to Spanish Town Square despite its general dilapidation.

Sights

Spanish Town Square was laid out by Jamaica's first colonial rulers as their Plaza Mayor. It is surrounded by the burnt remains of the old courthouse on its southern side, Old King's House on the west, the Rodney Memorial, and behind it the National Archives on the north side; the Old House of Assembly, now parish administration offices, on its eastern side, is the only building facing the square that's still in use.

The People's Museum of Craft and Technology (call caretaker Tyrone "Arab" Barnett to schedule a visit, cell tel. 876/384-2803, tel. 876/907-0322, 9 A.M. to 4 P.M. Mon.–Thurs., till 3 P.M. Fri., admission US$1.50 adults, US$0.50 children), located in the Old King's House complex on Spanish Town Square, began as a Folk Museum in 1961 and was refurbished in 1997 when Emancipation Day was declared a national holiday. The exhibit has indoor and outdoor sections with carriages, early sugar and coffee processing machinery, and a variety of other colonial-period implements.

The **Rodney Memorial,** on the northern side of Spanish Town Square, was erected in homage to Admiral George Rodney, a British naval officer who prevented what was seen as imminent conquest by an invading French and Spanish naval fleet led by Admiral de Grasse in 1782. The memorial is housed in a spectacular structure for its European palatial look and gives a nice facade to the National Archives housed just behind. The statue of Rodney was contracted to one of the most respected sculptors of the day, Englishman John Bacon (1740–1799), who reportedly made two trips to Italy before finding the right block of marble for the job. A panel inside Rodney's octagonal "temple" tells in Latin of Rodney's victorious sea battle, which restored some dignity to Britain, badly defeated by the French-American allies in the American War of Independence. Rodney was duly lauded as a national hero and £1,000 was allocated for the monument, which would eventually cost nearly £31,000. The two brass cannons displayed just outside the statue enclosure were taken from defeated Admiral de Grasse's flagship, *Ville de Paris.*

Spanish Town Cathedral, or the Anglican Cathedral Church of St. James, stands on the site of the Roman Catholic Red Cross Spanish Chapel, originally built in 1525 and run by Franciscans. Cromwell's Puritan soldiers destroyed the Spanish chapel along with another on the northern end of town known as White Cross, run by Dominicans. The church has been destroyed and rebuilt several times through a series of earthquakes and hurricanes. It became the first Anglican cathedral outside England in 1843, representing the Jamaican diocese. It's also the oldest English-built foundation on the island, after Fort Charles in Port Royal. Several monuments of historical figures are found inside and in the walled churchyard.

Spanish Town Baptist Church, or Phillippo Baptist Church as it is better known (at the junction of Cumberland Rd. and Williams St.), is located a few blocks northwest of the square. The church was built in 1827 on an old artillery ground and later went on to play an active role in the abolition movement. Abolitionist Reverend James Murcell Phillippo arrived in Jamaica in 1823 and later established the church with help from freed slaves. On the night of emancipation in 1838, when local authorities granted Jamaica's slave population full freedom, 2000 freed slaves were baptized in the church. There is a tablet in the churchyard commemorating the act of emancipation, which was celebrated there after the proclamation was read in front of Old King's House.

The **Iron Bridge** over the Rio Cobre on the eastern edge of Spanish Town was erected in 1801 and shipped in prefabricated segments from where it was cast in England by Walker of Rotherham. Today it is used as a pedestrian crossing and is in a poor state of preservation. Designed by English engineer Thomas Wilson, it was the first prefab cast-iron bridge erected in the Western Hemisphere.

White Marl Taino Museum (call curator Tyrone "Arab" Barnett to schedule a visit, cell tel. 876/384-2803) was being relocated as this book went to press. The museum was said to be sited on a former Taino settlement, the largest in Jamaica pre-discovery. The museum had to be moved due to sketchy security in the area. It features artifacts and displays pinpointing Taino archeological sites across the island and providing information on the lifestyle and practices of these first Jamaicans.

Mountain River Cave (caretaker Monica Wright, tel. 876/705-2790), with its Taino wall paintings first uncovered in 1897, is located 21 kilometers due northwest from the roundabout at the beginning of St. John's Road on the western edge of Spanish Town. After leaving an Uptown suburb area, St. John's becomes Cudjoe's Hill Road as you pass through red earth hills on the way to Kitson and then Guanaboa Vale, the stomping ground of Juan de Bolas. A few kilometers beyond a beautiful old church, pull over at Joan's Bar & Grocery Shop, marked by a painted facade reading Cudjoe's Cavern. Monica will indicate the trailhead that leads down a steep hill across the meandering Thompson's River and up the facing bank through cacao and passion-fruit stands to where the small cave is caged in against vandals. The cave itself is shallow and unspectacular, but its paintings are interesting; it's easy to make out a man with a spear, a turtle, some fish, and a few women. The paintings are said to be authentic, given the ash and bat guano mix used, supposedly a typical medium for the earliest Jamaican artists. The highlight of this attraction, apart from the well-preserved petroglyphs, is the beautiful walk through lush forests and Thompson's River, which has a large pool upstream and a waterfall downstream from the crossing, fitting for a cool dip.

Accommodations

Spanish Town is by no means a tourist mecca, and the few accommodation options available are more frequently used by lovers seeking privacy than anybody else. Perhaps the only real reason to overnight in Spanish Town is if your car breaks down and you're too tired to hop in a taxi to Kingston.

Rajmaville Hotel (Lot 30–32 Brunswick

Ave., tel. 876/749-5636, rajmaville@cwjamaica.com) could be the ideal place to stay in such a scenario, with a bar and gaming lounge (tel. 876/749-2802) downstairs that could very well help you realize a change of fortune. The hotel offers basic rooms for US$34 with cold water. Hot water, a queen-size bed, and larger room runs US$56, while the suites with two queen-size beds and a kitchenette run US$95.

Food

Spanish Town Shopping Centre (Burke Road) has a food court with several quick eating options. **Jamanda's Flava of Jamaica** (tel. 876/984-9498, 7 A.M.–9 P.M. Mon.–Thurs., 7 A.M.–10 P.M. Fri.–Sat., 2–9 P.M. Sun.) offers Jamaican staple dishes and sells Devon House ice cream.

Shadow On The Roof (19 Burke Rd., cell tel. 876/874-8196, Mon.–Sat. 7 A.M.–9 P.M.) is a cool bar and restaurant with a pool table and stage area.

Irie Jerk Centre (21 Brunswick Ave., tel. 876/749-5375, 9 A.M.–midnight daily) serves fried and jerk chicken (US$2/piece, a quarter chicken for US$4, whole US$15) and pork (US$9/lb.) and beer to wash it down (US$2). Irie also cooks curry goat, porridge, and soup.

At **St. Jago Shopping Centre,** the small food court has some good options. **La Cocina for Mom's Cooking** (Shop #31, tel. 876/943-9355) serves Spanish-inspired Jamaican fare like brown stew chicken and fish, fried fish and chicken, curry mutton, stew pork, stew peas, and chicken soup (US$2.50–3.50). **Tastebuds Delight** (Shop #32, tel. 876/907-5024, 7 A.M.–8 P.M. daily, closing at 10 P.M. on Sundays, US$2–4) also has Jamaican dishes ranging from chicken to oxtail. **Natural Vitamins Herbs & Vegetarian Place** (tel. 876/984-1305) is the best place around to get vegetarian dishes and urban Ital cuisine.

Cecil's (35 Martin St., tel. 876/984-2986 or 876/984-2404, 10 A.M.–10 P.M. Mon.–Sat., US$3–11) is easily Spanish Town's most-lauded restaurant. Cecil Reid was a chef at a number of other restaurants for years before opening his own place in 1983. Menu items have a decidedly Asian lean, with more sueys than you've

ever heard of, including chop suey, chow mein, fried rice, choy fan, ham choy, suey mein, as well as more typical curry dishes, beef, chicken, and lobster. A beer costs US$1.50 and fresh juices are US$1.

Services

St. Catherine Parish Library (tel. 876/984-2356, 9 A.M.–6 P.M. Mon.–Fri., 10 A.M.–5 P.M. Sat.), located across from Spanish Town Cathedral, offers free Internet access on a few computers.

Getting There and Around

Spanish Town is served by Kingston's JUTC with buses from Half Way Tree Transport Centre and the Downtown bus terminals departing every 10 minutes on the 21 and 22 series routes.

Private Coaster buses arrive and depart from bus stops a few paces down Molynes Road across Eastwood Park Road from the Transport Centre. They charge just over US$1 one-way fare. Route taxis ply all major roads in Spanish Town and can be flagged down if need be, charging anywhere from US$.75 to US$1.75 around town.

If you're driving, the most direct route to Spanish Town is along Spanish Town Road or Washington Boulevard to Mandela Highway. Stay to the right at the first roundabout. You will see the Old Iron Bridge on your right just after crossing the Rio Cobre as you enter town. Take a right at the stoplight at the gas station immediately thereafter to reach the historical sites surrounding Spanish Town Square or to pass through town for Linstead, Moneague Walkerswood, and Ocho Rios. Heading straight at the stoplight leads to the commercial district and Prison Oval.

WEST OF SPANISH TOWN

Heading west out of Spanish Town along the bypass, take a left following well-marked signs at the second roundabout along Old Harbour Road, which leads southwestward through vast tracts of sugarcane fields toward the town of Old Harbour.

Old Harbour

Continuing on Old Harbour Road 18 kilometers southwest of Spanish Town, you arrive at the town of Old Harbour, a congested little backwater full of storefronts and food vendors next to the square. A clock tower dating from the 17th century is the town's centerpiece.

Old Harbour was the disembarkation point for the first Indian indentured laborers arriving in 1845, who were brought to Jamaica following emancipation by plantation owners who suddenly found themselves lacking willing workers. A century later the bay was used as a U.S. Naval anchorage during World War II, with bases set up on Little Goat Island and at Salt Creek and Sandy Gully nearby on the mainland. The Americans didn't depart until 1949.

Old Harbour Bay, 4.8 kilometers south of town, is historically significant as the place where Columbus met with the preeminent Taino leader referred to as the Cacique of Xamayca in 1494. It was an important port serving Spanish Town under Spanish rule and later under the British it was the principal port for the area, until Port Royal and later Kingston took over in imports and import. Originally called Puerto de Vaca (Cow Bay) by Columbus in reference to the manatees, or sea cows, that once flourished there, today the town is little more than a fishing village. Fish stalls along the waterfront peddle fried fish, conch soup, and lobster. **Cheryl's** (cell tel. 876/410-3299, 10:30 A.M.–10 P.M. Tues.–Sun.), serving fried fish, bammy, and veggies right on the water with a sea breeze, is highly recommended.

Old Harbour Bay has a few islands, including Little Goat Island and Great Goat Island. A trip to the islands for a picnic can be arranged with local fishermen, some of whom live in ramshackle huts there.

Colbeck Castle, or the ruins where it once stood, can be found about three kilometers northwest of Old Harbour near the Clarendon border. To get to the abandoned ruins, head inland at the clock tower and keep straight ahead rather than right at the Y intersection. After passing a large farm with five buildings perpendicular to the road, you will soon cross

© OLIVER HILL

the ornate clock tower in Old Harbour Square

a bridge over a small river. Take the first left after the bridge. Within 1.5 kilometers you will arrive at the ruins.

Built by Colonel John Colbeck, who came with the English to take Jamaica from the Spanish in 1655, the castle and its past are shrouded in mystery; its date of construction is thought to have been somewhere around 1680. In its day, it was the biggest great-house structure of its kind, obviously built with defense from the Spanish and Maroon insurgents in mind. Its present appearance suggests it fell victim to fire in slave revolts. Designed in the style of a 17th-century Italian mansion, with ornate arches and a 12-meter-high tower in each corner, Colbeck Castle was the epicenter of a strategically located immense landholding in close vicinity to Spanish Town and Old Harbour.

NORTH OF SPANISH TOWN

The first free village for ex-slaves was established at **Sligoville,** just north of Spanish Town, when Jamaica's pro-abolition transition period governor Howe Peter Browne, known as the Marquis of Sligo, granted land to Baptist missionary James Phillippo. Browne's former summer residence, **Highgate House,** now a JNHT site, can be reached by taking a left heading east off the main road to the north coast from Spanish Town (A1).

Nearby, the father of the Rastafarian movement, Leonard Howell, fled persecution on the North Coast to establish the Rasta commune of **Pinnacle.** Eventually, Pinnacle was smothered and Howell committed to a mental institution by the authorities, who would have none of his reverence for Ethiopian Emperor Haile Selassie I.

Bog Walk, derived from Boca de Agua in Spanish, is a gorge prone to flooding, entered by traversing **Flat Bridge.** Horrendous traffic tends to accumulate on either side of the old stone single-lane bridge, especially as the weekend begins and comes to a close. Midway through the gorge on the west flank you can see the Pum Pum Rock, named as such because it bears a remarkable resemblance to part of a woman's anatomy.

Linstead, celebrated in the folk song *Linstead Market,* still has a busy market on Saturday. The island's public records were kept under guard at the Anglican Church in this small inland town when the French threatened invasion in 1805. The church has been destroyed and rebuilt several times.

On the border with St. Ann, **Ewarton** is noticeable from kilometers away by the stench created by aluminum processing if the bauxite plant is in operation. There's little to see in Ewarton, and it's not likely to be a place you'll want to spend too much time.

East of Kingston

The areas along the coast east of Kingston include the communities of Harbour View, Seven Mile, Palm Beach, and Bull Bay. The Palisadoes, a 16-kilometer-long stretch that runs from the roundabout at Harbour View to the tip of Port Royal, is home to the Kingston Yacht Club and Marina, the Marine Research Institute, Norman Manley International Airport, Plumb Point Lighthouse, Port Royal, and just offshore, the Kingston area's most popular beach on the small island of Lime Cay.

The community of **Harbour View** surrounding the roundabout at the base of the Palisadoes

was built on the site of **Fort Nugent,** originally constructed by a Spanish slave, James Castillo, and later fortified by Governor Nugent in 1806 to protect the eastern approach to Kingston Harbour. Today all that remains of the fort is the Martello tower, which takes its name from the first such tower, built in Corsica and popularized throughout England.

PORT ROYAL AND THE PALISADOES

Part of Kingston parish, the Palisadoes is a thin stretch of barren sand, brush, and mangroves; it acts as a natural barrier protecting Kingston Harbour, with Port Royal at its western point. History has not smiled on this corner of Jamaica, perhaps due to some divine justice aimed at washing clean the sins and abuses that made Port Royal Britain's first commercial stronghold in Jamaica. After Lord Cromwell seized Jamaica for Britain from the Spanish in 1655, Port Royal grew in importance, as the town's strategic location brought prosperity to merchants who based themselves there. The merchants were joined by pirates and buccaneers, who together through their commerce, pillaging, and looting created one of the busiest and most successful trading posts in the New World. Imports included slaves, silks, silver, gold, wine, and salmon, while exports consisted mostly of rum, sugar, and wood. The British collaborated with the pirates as an insurance policy against the Spanish, who were thought to be seeking revenge on the island's new colonial masters. Port Royal flourished, with a local service economy growing alongside its bustling maritime commerce until June 7, 1692, when a massive earthquake left 60 percent of Port Royal underwater, immediately killing 2,000 people. Eight hectares supporting the principal public buildings, wharves, merchant shops, and two of the town's four forts disappeared into the sea. Aftershocks rocked the rattled city for months. In 1703 a fire devastated what little remained of Port Royal, sending most survivors across the harbor to what soon grew into the city of Kingston. The town also sustained significant damage in the earthquake of 1907, and then again during Hurricane Charlie in 1951.

Sleepy Port Royal is well worth a visit. The village is hassle-free and small enough to stroll leisurely around in a few hours. Scuba trips can be arranged through Port Royal Divers, based out of Morgan's Harbour Marina. On weekends the square comes alive with a sound system and an invasion of Kingstonians, who come for the fish and beach just offshore at Lime Cay.

Plumb Point Lighthouse

Protecting the approach to Kingston Harbour, Plumb Point Lighthouse was built in 1853 and has gone out only once since, during the earthquake of 1907. Sitting on a point named Cayo de los Icacos, or Plumb Tree Cay (a reference to the coco plum by the Spanish), it is constructed of stone and cast iron and stands 21 meters high. Its light is visible from 40 kilometers out at sea. The beach immediately to the west is known for its occasional good surf, as is the shoreline between Plumb Point and Little Plumb Point. The area is also known for its strong currents, however, and surfers should use caution.

Fort Charles

Fort Charles (tel. 876/967-8438, 9 A.M.–4:45 P.M. daily, US$3 admission/tour) is the most prominent historical attraction in town and the most impressive, well-restored fort in Jamaica. Built in 1656 immediately following the British takeover, it is the oldest fort on the island from the British colonial period, and one of the oldest in the New World. Originally it was named Fort Cromwell on Cagway after Lord Protector of England Oliver Cromwell (ruled 1653–1658), who was responsible for designing the strategic takeover of the island meant to give Britain control over the Caribbean basin. The fort was renamed in 1662 when the monarchy was reinstated in England with Charles II as King. Fort Charles sank a meter during the earthquake of 1692.

Admiral Horatio Nelson (1758–1805), lauded as Britain's all-time greatest naval hero for his victorious role in the Battle of Trafalgar, spent 30 months in Jamaica, much of it at Fort Charles. Nelson was given charge of the Fort while the island was caught in fear of a French invasion; he spent the tense period pacing and nervously scanning the horizon from what's now referred to as Nelson's Quarterdeck, a raised platform along the southern battlement. On the inside wall of the fort there is a plaque commanding those who tread Nelson's footprints to remember his glory.

© OLIVER HILL

inside the walls of Fort Charles

Also within Fort Charles walls, there is the grogge shop and a very nice little museum managed by the Museum of History and Ethnography, with period artifacts, old maps, and information about Port Royal and its glorious and notorious inhabitants.

Other Attractions

St. Peter's Church, built in 1725, replaced earlier churches on the site destroyed by the 1692 earthquake and then the 1703 fire that again ravaged Port Royal. Inside there are several period items on display. In the churchyard is the tomb of Lewis Galdy. One of the founders of St. Peter's, Galdy miraculously survived the 1692 earthquake after being swallowed by the earth and spit out by the sea, where he was rescued. The tomb is inscribed with the complete legend of Galdy, who went on to become a local hero.

McFarlene's Bar is the oldest tavern in Port Royal, constructed in the 1800s, and one of the few buildings to withstand Hurricane Charlie in 1951. Unfortunately the pub no longer serves pints.

The **Old Gaol** (jail, Gaol Street) was once a women's prison.

Giddy House sits half-submerged at an awkward angle in the earth behind Fort Charles. It was built in 1888 as an artillery store by the British Navy, but the earthquake of 1907 left the building skewed as a reminder that dramatic seismic events can humble vicious buccaneers as much as the world's foremost navy.

The **Old Naval Hospital** is the oldest prefabricated cast-iron structure in the Western Hemisphere. The hospital was built in 1818 on the foundation of another hospital destroyed by fire a few years prior, using slave labor under the direction of the Royal Engineers of the British Army. The hospital went out of use in 1905 before getting a new lease on life as the Port Royal Centre for Archaeological and Conservation Research in 1968. Seventeen hurricanes have not fazed the structure, nor did the earthquake of 1907 do it any harm.

◖ Lime Cay

Lime Cay is a paradisiacal islet, just barely big enough to sustain some vegetation. The beach gets crowded on weekends, especially on Sunday, and is worth a visit to take in the local scene. Launches leave for Lime Cay on weekends from Y-Knot Bar or at Morgan's Harbour (US$10 per person round-trip); you can also get there on any other day, for a slightly higher price when the boats don't fill up. At times there are launches from the old Ferry Dock area that will do the trip for a bit less, especially for small groups.

Accommodations

Morgan's Harbour Hotel (1 Port Royal Rd., tel. 876/967-8040, info@morgansharbour. com, www.morgansharbour.com, US$141 including continental breakfast, US$178 all-inclusive) is the only option in Port Royal and has acceptable rooms with air-conditioning and cable.

Slip fees at the hotel marina are very reasonable at US$1 per foot per day, plus tax, similar to rates found across the island. Water, electricity, and laundry services are available. Morgan's Harbour was built on the former naval shipyard (US$7 adults, US$3.50 children for the launch to Lime Cay).

Food

Gloria's Seafood Restaurant has two locations ("Bottom," 1 High St., tel. 876/967-8066, managed by Cecil; and "Top," on the beach side, 15 Foreshore Rd., tel. 876/967-8220, managed by Angela) and is a must for anyone who appreciates seafood (US$10 for a fried fish and bammy). Gloria died a few years ago, but her legacy lives on with her children now running the business. Service can be slow owing to the crowds that swarm in, especially on Friday evenings and after church on Sundays. Gloria's does some of the most dependable and delicious fried escoveitch fish with Jamaican marinade, a local twist of Spanish "escabeche," which uses onion, carrot, cho-cho (pear squash or chayote), scotch bonnet pepper, pimento, and vinegar. Both Gloria's locations have a laidback setting good for unhurried meals with a view of the water.

Y-Knot (tel. 876/967-8448 or 876/967-8449, 9 A.M.–7 P.M., daily, 9 A.M. till you say when Fri.–Sun.), at Port Royal Slip Way, is an excellent bar that serves food (chicken, fish, pork, shrimp, and ribs; US$4–14) on weekends. Y-Knot is the home of Lime Cay Tours, where launches leave daily for Lime Cay (US$12).

Fisherman's Cabin (tel. 876/967-8800, 4 P.M.–midnight Mon.–Wed., 10 A.M.–2 A.M. Thurs.–Sun., US$7–14) has tables right on a dock overlooking the harbor down in a corner by Port Royal Square.

The whole of Port Royal is a popular weekend outing destination for Kingstonians who come seeking the fish, lobster, and seafood platters.

Getting There

JUTC buses leave from the downtown bus terminal (Route #98, US$1) or hire a taxi (US$25). Route taxis between Downtown and Port Royal run sporadically, leaving once filled with passengers.

The ferry service, which once brought passengers between downtown Kingston and Port Royal, has unfortunately been discontinued.

BULL BAY

Bull Bay is a quiet fishing community along the A3, 15 minutes east of Kingston. It has a long beach that lacks fine sand but also lacks crowds. It is a nice place for a dip, and the surf is decent for sport at times. The community is perhaps best known for reggae artist and Jamaican surfing champion Billy "Mystic" Wilmot, who runs an irie surfing guest house on the beach, and as home to the Bobo Shanti (Ashanti) House of Ras Tafari, which has its base at nearby Bobo Hill.

Sights

About 1.5 kilometers before reaching Bull Bay, a sign for **Cane River Falls** marks a left off the main road onto Greendale Road by Nine Mile Square. The attraction is on the right just before a bridge and cannot be missed. The "falls" are nothing to write home about compared to other falls across Jamaica and hardly justify the US$3 entrance fee. Nevertheless, it's a nice place to relax and get some food to the sound of the passing water, which varies from a bubble to a roar depending on recent rainfall.

Cane River meets the sea just before Bull Bay at Seven Mile, on the main road east of Kingston heading toward St. Thomas. The river is formed by the Barbeque and Mammee rivers, among smaller tributaries that run down the northern slopes of the Dallas Mountains. The falls were once the stomping ground of Three Finger Jack, a legendary Robin Hood–like cult figure who terrorized the planter class with kidnappings for ransom and murder. Almost 200 years later, the falls became a favorite cool-off spot for Bob Marley, who sang " . . . uppa Cane River to wash my dread, upon a rock I rest my head . . . " in the song, "Trench Town."

Bobo Hill (at top of Weisse Rd., call the Bobo Congress at 876/578-6798) is home to the Bobo Shanti, or Bobo Ashanti, House of Ras Tafari. Known for their peaceably militant interpretation of Marcus Garvey's teachings, the Bobo have been popularized by many dancehall artists who proclaim an affiliation. Paramount to Bobo philosophy and lifestyle are the ever-present themes of self-confidence, self-reliance, and self-respect. The Bobo can often be seen around Kingston, their locks carefully wrapped with a turban, peddling natural-fiber brooms, one of their signature crafts. At the center of the Bobo philosophy is the holy trinity between Bobo Shanti founder Prince Emmanuel Charles Edwards, who is said to have carried the spirit of Christ; Marcus Garvey, the prophet of the Rastafari Movement; and Haile Selassie I, the Ethiopian emperor who is their King of Kings.

Leonard Howell, recognized as the first Jamaican to proclaim the divinity of Haile Selassie I, founded a commune at the inception of the movement in Pinnacle, St. Catherine, similar to the community found today at Bobo Hill. Despite popular belief to the contrary, the Bobo are among the most open and welcoming of the various Houses of Ras Tafari. While it might not be appreciated should you just turn up unannounced to sightsee at their commune, sincere interest is well received, and they routinely open their home and hearth to visitors from around the world. Some visitors stay several days with them to share food and partake in their ritualized lifestyle. While there is no fee assessed to enter their commune, it is customary to bring a contribution, which should be offered based on your means and the degree of hospitality you have enjoyed at their cost. To reach the camp, turn left on Weisse Road right after a bridge about 1.5 kilometers past Shenique's Hair Salon in the center of Bull Bay. It's best to clarify your interest in visiting by calling ahead so that someone is there to receive you.

Entertainment

Little Copa (Nine Mile, along the main road between Kingston and Yallahs, no phone) has karaoke on Thursdays and ladies' night on Fridays. The club has a large indoor dance floor that gets packed for the occasional live performance.

Bamboo Club (Greendale Rd.) keeps sessions dubbed More Girl on Fridays and Sizzling Wednesdays starting around 9 or 10 P.M.

Surfing

Jamnesia Surf Club, located in the community of Eight Mile, just before reaching Bull Bay (look for the surfboard sign right after the driveway beside AB&C Groceries, next to Cave Hut Beach, tel. 876/750-0103, cell tel. 876/545-4591, jamnesiasurf@yahoo.com, www.jamsurfas.webs.com) is Jamaica's number-one surfing destination. It's run by Billy "Mystic" Wilmot, of Mystic Revealers fame, his wife Maggie, sons Icah, Inilek, Ivah, and Ishack, and daughter Imani. They are great hosts for a surf vacation and offer the widest variety of boards for rental, as well as complete surf vacation packages. Rates vary from US$10 per person to camp with your own tent, to US$15 for use of their tents with linens, sleeping mat, and pillow, to US$25 in the sole camp room, or US$30 for two.

Bungalows rent for US$40 s or US$60 d. Nearby apartments can be rented for US$40. Very affordable weeklong packages include a tent and two meals daily. Breakfast (US$3.50), lunch (US$5), and dinner (US$7.50) are also offered.

There are two good surf seasons, one during the summer (June–Sept.), the other in winter (Dec.–March). The fall and spring seasons are more of a gamble as far as surf is concerned, but the accommodation rates are lower off-season and open to negotiation. The property also features a skateboard bowl for when the water is flat.

Every other Saturday starting around 9 P.M., Jamnesia Sessions are held with live music. Jamnesia also offers a **surf shuttle** (US$30 per person), taking surfers to spots along the Palisadoes, like near the lighthouse, as well as surfing excursions farther afield. The shuttle also provides tailored tour guide services for those looking to be accompanied on excursions around town, up to Blue Mountain Peak or to Bobo Hill.

THE BLUE MOUNTAINS

The highest mountain range in Jamaica, the Blue Mountains harbor a rich history, having provided refuge for runaway slaves, transplanted French-Haitian coffee farmers, and even Bob Marley, when he sought safety and seclusion at Strawberry Hill following the attempt on his life in 1976. Today the area attracts visitors principally for its lush nature, colorful birdlife, delicious coffee, and fresh air.

Blue Mountain Peak, the highest point in Jamaica at 2,256 meters, offers a stunning view of five parishes: Kingston, St. Andrew, St. Thomas, Portland, and St. Mary. The Blue Mountain range forms a physical barrier to the northeasterly weather fronts that frequently descend on the island, giving Portland and St. Thomas especially copious amounts of rainfall compared to the southern coastal plains of Jamaica, where drought is common.

During the rainy season (October and November), the mountain peaks often cloud over by mid-morning. Skies are clearest June–August and December–March.

Within an hour's drive from Kingston, Irish Town, Hardwar Gap, and Mavis Bank are great destinations for a quick escape from the urban jungle. This is where rural Jamaica is at its coolest. The elevation and lush greenery are a welcome retreat from the heat on the plains and foothills around Town. The road up and the rugged terrain are not for the faint of heart, but the prized Blue Mountain coffee, breathtaking views, diverse vegetation, and abundance of native birds are more than

© OLIVER HILL

THE BLUE MOUNTAINS

HIGHLIGHTS

((Belcour Lodge: This colonial-era home offers a culinary garden tour not to be missed by foodies and horticulturalists (page 102).

((Strawberry Hill: One of Island Outpost's gems, this boutique hotel boasts spectacular views and a fascinating history (page 103).

((Alex Twyman's Old Tavern Coffee Estate: This stands out as one of the most spectacular coffee estates in Jamaica for its location and the quality of its beans (page 104).

((Holywell National Park: Less strenuous to reach than Blue Mountain Peak, Holywell is a pleasant park at Hardwar gap with amazing views and meandering trails great for exercise and birding (page 106).

((Blue Mountain Peak: Blue Mountain Peak offers Jamaica's top view: Hikers typically set out early to be at the top for sunrise, when skies tend to be clear (page 111).

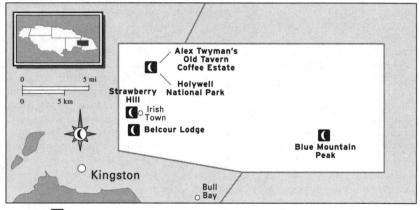

LOOK FOR **((** TO FIND RECOMMENDED SIGHTS, ACTIVITIES, DINING, AND LODGING.

adequate rewards, and few are sorry for making the effort.

PLANNING YOUR TIME

A few days in Kingston perfectly sets the stage for a nice break into the Blue Mountains. Most of the guesthouses in the mountains can arrange transportation to and from Town; once here, hiking trails abound, and local transport can be found easily with a little patience. Anywhere from two nights to a week should be allowed for a trip into the Blue Mountains, especially for those planning to do some serious hiking or birding. The main draws are relaxation, sipping coffee, and enjoying nature, and your length of stay should therefore depend on how much time you want to dedicate to these essential pastimes.

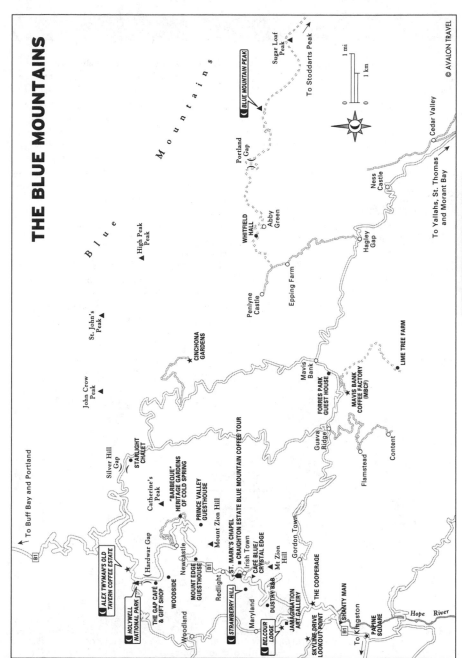

THE BLUE MOUNTAINS

To Buff Bay and Portland

B1

HOLYWELL NATIONAL PARK

THE GAP CAFÉ & GIFT SHOP

WOODSIDE

ALEX TWYMAN'S OLD TAVERN COFFEE ESTATE

Hardwar Gap

Silver Hill Gap

STARLIGHT CHALET

Catherine's Peak

"BARBEQUE" HERITAGE GARDENS OF COLD SPRING

PRINCE VALLEY GUESTHOUSE

Mount Zion Hill

Newcastle

Redlight

MOUNT EDGE GUESTHOUSE

Woodland

Maryland

STRAWBERRY HILL

BELCOUR LODGE

ST. MARK'S CHAPEL

CRAIGHTON ESTATE BLUE MOUNTAIN COFFEE TOUR

Irish Town

CAFÉ BLUE/ CRYSTAL EDGE

B1

DUSTRY B&B

JAMAICAN IMAGINATION ART GALLERY

SKYLINE DRIVE LOOKOUT POINT

Mt Zion Hill

Gordon Town

THE COOPERAGE

SHANTY MAN

B1

To Kingston

PAPINE SQUARE

Hope River

John Crow Peak

St. John's Peak

Blue

Mountains

High Peak Peak

CINCHONA GARDENS

Penlyne Castle

Epping Farm

Mavis Bank

FORRES PARK GUEST HOUSE

MAVIS BANK COFFEE FACTORY (MBCF)

Guava Ridge

Flamstead

Content

LIME TREE FARM

Sugar Loaf Peak

BLUE MOUNTAIN PEAK

To Stoddarts Peak

Portland Gap

WHITFIELD HALL

Abby Green

Hagley Gap

Ness Castle

Cedar Valley

To Yallahs, St. Thomas and Morant Bay

N

0   1 mi

0   1 km

© AVALON TRAVEL

Maryland to Hardwar Gap

Turning left at the Cooperage onto the B3 leads up a series of some 360-plus hairpin turns that can leave unaccustomed passengers a bit nauseated. The windy road first passes through the lower hills and valleys of Maryland before reaching the principal hamlet along the route, Irish Town. **Irish Town** has as its centerpiece St. Mark's Chapel, a quaint little church reached by a 15-minute walk along a footpath.

SIGHTS
☾ Belcour Lodge

Belcour Lodge (left at a white milestone marker below Maryland and 10 minutes from Papine, call Robin Lumsden at least 24 hours in advance to schedule a visit, tel. 876/927-2448, limlums@cwjamaica.com) is a beautiful private, colonial-era home set in a lovely, little river valley amid expansive gardens. Robin and Michael Lumsden offer Culinary Tours that include a stroll around the yard. Visitors will find an apiary with around 100 colonies, a citrus orchard, and other fruit trees. Robin markets Belcour Blue Mountain Honey, as well as Belcour fruit preserves, chutneys, and hot sauces, produced on a cottage-industry scale from all natural, local ingredients. The garden tour is accompanied by a gourmet brunch, lunch, or high tea (US$25 per person). Orchids and a host of other flowers attract a wide variety of birds, most notably beautiful hummingbirds. You'll want to take home some honey and sauces—they're outstanding.

Art Galleries

The Jamagination Art Gallery (3 Belcour Lodge, contact Wayne Gallimore, cell tel. 876/849-4189, tel. 876/476-4417, wayne@jamagination.com.jm, www.jamagination.com.jm), a short walk from Belcour Lodge on

Belcour Lodge is a beautifully preserved colonial-era house on well-maintained grounds. Culinary garden tours are offered among the orchids and bees.

© OLIVER HILL

the same estate, has a varied collection including works from intuitive and trained painters, plus sculpture, masks, and eccentric furniture pieces in the home gallery throughout the house. Most of the works are for sale. There is no charge for viewing, but an appointment is required. The gallery also sells Giclées, or state-of-the art reproductions on canvas at a fraction of the cost of originals.

Andy Jefferson (tel. 876/944-8206, cell tel. 876/367-5976 or 876/824-2586, andyj@flowja.com, www.andyjefferson.com) is a prominent expat artist who can be found by taking the first right after the 18-mile post heading toward Newcastle. Andy welcomes visitors to his home studio and gallery by appointment.

St. Mark's Chapel
A beautiful old church that sits up on a hilltop in Irish Town, St. Mark's is a great destination for a short hike. As you arrive at the junction in Irish Town where the driveway to Strawberry Hill leads up to the left, the chapel looms up ahead.

Mount Zion Hill
This Rastafarian farming community is based in a squatter settlement known as Mt. Zion Hill (call Priest Dermot Fagan to request a visit, cell tel. 876/868-9636). The carefully maintained trail and fence along the path up the hill demonstrates the respect given to Priest Dermot Fagan, referred to simply as "the priest" by his followers, who rank in the range of 50-odd adults and children living at Zion Hill. Fagan has established His Imperial Majesty School of Bible Study and Sabbath Service, with a small yurt-like structure at the entrance to the community serving as its chapel. The small community follows primarily an agrarian life, growing food and herbs and selling roots wine around town to bring in a little cash. There are several people who espouse the school's teaching but live in town rather than on Zion Hill. It becomes evident when the group descends on Papine Square every Saturday for a Nyabinghi Sabbath Service of singing and drumming that the following is

significant indeed. Fagan advocates a total rejection of and distancing from the Babylonian system that has separated humankind from direct reliance on our labor and the food we can provide for ourselves. He warns of an even greater divide between man and his sustenance through the impending mass implantation of micro-biochips. He sees the use of implantable homing devices in soldiers in Iraq or in medical patients, or their common use in wildlife management, as a precursor to more universal implantations, which he says will result in the consolidation of the global labor force and a new kind of slavery. The Mt. Zion Hill community has established itself as one of the more colorful, albeit apocalyptic, Houses of Rastafari.

◖ Strawberry Hill
Strawberry Hill (tel. 876/944-8400, www.islandoutpost.com) is an exclusive hotel owned by Chris Blackwell's Island Outpost. It has an assortment of guest cottages that hug steep hillsides with a restaurant and bar as the property's centerpiece at its highest point. The property welcomes nonguests to enjoy the view, food and drinks, spa treatments, and the gift shop. It's well worth a visit for a luxurious afternoon or evening.

The **Strawberry Hill High Stakes Backgammon Weekend** (held annually one long weekend in April, contact Alistair Macbeath, alistairmacbeath@yahoo.com, tel. 876/942-2311 or 876/999-0741, US$550 to enter) is billed as the coolest backgammon tournament on Inaugurated in 2006, the entrance fee includes food and drink. A maximum of 32 competitors are admitted. The winner receives around US$6,000, while positions 1–6 earn back their entry fee or more. There's a consolation event for the losers. The tournament is organized as a round robin with the top two players of each group moving on to the next round. The weekend is filled with activities, from a cocktail reception hosted by Strawberry Hill owner and the world's most acclaimed reggae producer, Chris Blackwell, to kick it off on Friday, with an Ibiza-style pool party on Saturday afternoon, and typically a reggae dinner show with one of the coolest crooners from Jamaica's bountiful repertoire of artists old and new in the evening. A prize-giving ceremony is held on the lawn on Sunday. The event is billed as the coolest backgammon tournament on earth.

The hotel boasts an Aveda concept **spa and wellness center** with a holistic approach to rejuvenation, dubbed Strawberry Hill Living.

Craighton Estate Blue Mountain Coffee Tour

Craighton Estate Blue Mountain Coffee Tour (farm tel. 876/944-8653, or call Kingston office for tour bookings, 876/929-8490, www.craightonestate.com, 8 A.M.–4 P.M. daily, US$15 adults, US$7 children), owned by Japan-based Ueshima Coffee Company, offers a one-hour tour featuring a walk around the working coffee farm. Ueshima is one of the foremost exporters of Jamaican Blue Mountain Coffee to Japan, the leading foreign market for the prized product.

🍘 Alex Twyman's Old Tavern Coffee Estate

The Twymans (contact David Twyman in Kingston office to arrange a visit, tel. 876/924-2785, cell tel. 876/865-2978, farm cell tel. 876/399-1222, dtwyman@colis.com, www.exportjamaica.org/oldtavern, www.old taverncoffee.com) grow some of the best Blue Mountain Coffee. The estate is being run by David, son of owners Dorothy and the late, great coffee farmer Alex Twyman.

The Twymans bought their property in 1968 and persevered through extreme challenges in

---

JAMAICAN COFFEE: CULTIVATING AN INDUSTRY

Coffee is one of 600 species in the *Rubiaceae* family, understood to have its center of origin in what is today Ethiopia. The plant's beans and leaves are believed to have been chewed by the earliest inhabitants and later brewed by ancient Abyssinians and Arabs, the latter credited with originating the global coffee trade. Jamaica's relationship with the revered bean dates to 1728 when a former governor, Nicholas Lawes, introduced coffee of the Typica variety to his Temple Hall estate just past Stony Hill in upper St. Andrew. Its cultivation was formalized in earnest with large plantations covering hundreds of acres established in the nearby Blue Mountains by an influx of planters fleeing Haiti in the years leading up to the neighboring country's 1804 independence. By 1800, there were 686 coffee plantations in Jamaica, with exports totaling 15,199 tons, according to Jamaica's Coffee Industry Board (CIB). These early planters discovered that the intact plantation economy and the cloud forest climatic conditions were conducive to lucrative coffee production. The misty climate allowed the coffee berries to ripen slowly, a process said to grant the end product its smooth, full-bodied flavor, free of bitterness. The bumper earnings of these early plantations were short-lived, however, deteriorating when global demand subsided and competition from other colonies imposing a smaller coffee tax increased. The abolition of slavery and emancipation further challenged Jamaica's large-scale coffee plantations; when labor became scarce, the country's production deteriorated and the bean's cultivation was soon dominated by smallholders. By 1850 there were only 186 plantations left in Jamaica, with exports falling to 1,486 tons, according to CIB records.

Jamaica's Coffee Industry Board, established in 1950, was set up to control the quality of Jamaica's coffee product and participate directly in the production process. Two government-owned processing plants, Mavis Bank Coffee Factory and Wallenford Coffee Company, operate under its wing. The beans are supplied by their own farms and by thousands of small-scale growers. The CIB also regulates the coveted Blue Mountain Coffee registered trademark, allowing only farms certified by the board in the parishes of St. Andrew, St. Thomas, Portland, and St. Mary, all located at

obtaining a Coffee Board License, which allows them to sell directly to their customers and market their beans as "Blue Mountain Coffee," a coveted trademark belonging to Jamaica, just as Champagne belongs to France. The Twymans take a natural approach on the farm, limiting use of chemical fertilizers and pesticides while employing traditional fermentation and sun-drying processes. The unique climatic conditions found at the Twymans' Estate requires a longer maturation period—the berries remain on the trees for 10 months due to the near-constant cloudy mist blanketing the mountains around Hardwar Gap.

Three different roasts are produced from the Twymans' beans: medium, medium dark (Proprietors' Choice), and dark roast. Peaberry beans produce an additional variety. Peaberry is an unusual bean, where one side of the normally paired beans does not develop. As a result, a smaller bean with a unique mild flavor develops. It is not fully understood what causes peaberry beans to grow this way. The peaberry beans are carefully separated and sold as a distinct variety prized by many coffee connoisseurs.

The Twymans' choice beans are served at Norma's on the Terrace, Suzie's, Cannonball Café, and at Strawberry Hill. Kraft Cottage in Village Plaza retails Twyman's coffee, and it is sold directly on the farm, at the Kingston office, and online for best value at US$30 per pound plus shipping (for orders write to oldtaverncoffee@kasnet.com).

"Never put coffee in the freezer, because it will take on the flavor of anything that's in there," advised Alex Twyman, who had a wealth of information on anything to do with

THE BLUE MOUNTAINS

an elevation between 2,000 and 5,000 feet, to use the name. Wallenford and Mavis Bank Coffee Factory produce a large portion of Jamaica's export crop, around 80 percent of which is sent to Japan. Mavis Bank Coffee Factory commercializes a line of finished products under the JABLUM brand. Government equity in both entities is understood to have been on the block for years, even while some private coffee estates, most notably Craighton, have changed hands.

Obtaining a certification by the CIB as a producer of Blue Mountain Coffee is a challenge, especially for small farmers trying to earn a living off their farms. It can take several years, as certification demands scrupulous adherence to and implantation of the farming practices and production processes sanctioned by the CIB.

Jamaican coffee produced at lower elevations can also be of high quality, even it doesn't attract the same attention or price as Blue Mountain Coffee. Jamaica Prime, Premium Washed, and High Mountain Supreme are some of the names Jamaican coffee has sold under when not originating from the Blue Mountains. There are notable coffee producers in several parishes around Jamaica, among them farms in Bog Walk and St. Catherine, at Key Park Estate in Westmoreland, at Aenon Park along the Clarendon/St. Ann border, at Clarendon Park, and in Maggoty, in St. Elizabeth.

Jamaica's climate is at once a blessing and a curse for the country's coffee farmers. It's the high altitude mist cover that nurtures the bean to give it its distinct character, but the country's highest peaks are also most exposed and vulnerable to hurricanes and tropical storms, which can destroy several years' work in one night. The lack of insurance for the industry since Hurricane Ivan in 2004 has made production at many small farms a real gamble. Combating disease is also a constant struggle for Jamaica's coffee farmers. Nonetheless, today's coffee industry employees some 50,000 Jamaicans and brings in around US$35 million in foreign exchange each year. Retailing at around US$30 per pound in Jamaica and around US$50 per pound in North America and Europe, Jamaica Blue Mountain Coffee continues to fetch a high price, which is one of the few reasons Jamaica's coffee industry, as a whole, remains viable.

the precious bean. There is no charge for a guided tour of the gorgeous estate; instead, guests are encouraged to show their appreciation by buying a pound or two of coffee before departing.

HIKING AND BIRD-WATCHING

Catherine's Peak quickly becomes visible rising to the right as you drive up to Newcastle from Red Light, easily distinguishable by the clutter of communications antennas at the summit. The peak is a one-hour hike from the Parade ground at Newcastle, where there is plenty of parking. A rough road goes all the way up, but it becomes impassable to anything but a four-wheel-drive vehicle. Jamaica Defense Force soldiers stationed at Newcastle restrict access to all vehicles except those carrying the most trustworthy-looking visitors. It's best to hoof it from Newcastle rather than drive part of the way.

◖ Holywell National Park

Holywell National Park (entry US$5, or US$1.50 for residents) sits atop Hardwar Gap, affording a view of St. Andrew Parish to the south and St. Mary and Portland to the north. The birding is excellent in the 50-hectare park, which borders Twyman's Old Tavern Coffee Estate on the north side and is a haven for migratory birds in the winter months. Hiking trails lead to a few peaks, and there's also a loop trail.

The **Oatley Mountain Loop Trail** is paved with gravel and about 1.2 kilometers long, with a steep ascent to Oatley Mountain Peak at 1,400 meters. Three lookout points along the way offer great views of St. Andrew, St. Mary, and Portland.

The **Waterfall Trail** is also about 1.2 kilometers long, meandering along the mountain edge and then following a stream with a small waterfall at the end.

Shorter and less strenuous trails include the **Shelter Trail** (600 meters), the **Blue Mahoe Trail** (350 meters), and the **Wag Water/Dick's Pond Trail** (630 meters).

Rustic accommodations in cabins at the park are available through the **Jamaica Conservation and Development Trust**

© OLIVER HILL

The Blue Mountains present plenty of opportunities for bird-watching.

(JCDT) (29 Dumbarton Ave., Half Way Tree, tel. 876/920-8278 or 876/920-8279, jamaica-conservation@gmail.com, www.greenjamaica.org.jm).

ACCOMMODATIONS
Under US$100

Dustry Bed & Breakfast (off Dustry Rd., between Newcastle Rd. and Maryland, tel. 876/944-8394 or 702/727-0752, US$150 for two) offers rustic accommodation at the home of expats Andrew and Lisa Gordon, self-described hippies who have been living in the Blue Mountains since the 1970s. The rustic homestead cannot be seen from the road and is best suited for the fit and adventurous, as it requires a 10-minute walk uphill to reach.

Mount Edge Guesthouse (just before the 17-mile marker approaching Newcastle, call Michael Fox, tel. 876/944-8151 or 876/351-5083, mfox80@yahoo.co.uk, jamaicaeu@kas-net.com, www.jamaicaeu.com, US$20–40 per person) has three simple cottages hanging on the edge of a cliff with double beds and private baths, plus a main building containing two private rooms with a shared bathroom and living and dining room. A third building has bunk beds for four with an adjoining bathroom. Amenities include hot water, Internet, a small roadside bar, and a trail to the river. Mountain bikes are available.

Prince Valley Guesthouse (contact Jackie or Bobby Williams, cell tel. 876/892-2365 or U.S. tel. 845/679-5736, jaqdes@netstep.net, design@jackieoster.com, US$30 per night, US$200 per week) is located on a small coffee farm in Middleton Settlement in the Blue Mountains with one rental unit consisting of two spacious bedrooms, with two queen beds in one and a single bed in the other, and a shared bathroom. Two air mattresses are at hand for extras, with linens and towels provided. Amenities include a microwave, refrigerator, TV, coffee maker, and toaster. The lodging is ideal for backpackers. Reservations require a money wire via Western Union. Credit cards are not accepted. The guesthouse offers airport pickups from Norman Manley International for US$50, or you can take a route taxi from Papine for about US$3. To get there, take the first right after Mount Edge Guesthouse at Bubbles Bar, followed by your first right, and then a left after crossing a little ramp.

Starlight Chalet & Health Spa (Silver Hill Gap, tel. 876/969-3070 or 876/924-3075, Kensworth Nairne cell tel. 876/414-8570, sales@starlightchalet.com, www. starlightchalet.com, US$80) is a quaint retreat past Hardwar Gap. Reach Starlight Chalet by heading north from Hardwar Gap. Where the road forks, keep to your right and go straight ahead until you reach Section. Turn right at Section and travel until you reach Starlight Chalet & Health Spa at Silver Hill Gap.

Cabins and camping are available at **Holywell National Park** through the Jamaica Conservation and Development Trust (JCDT) (29 Dumbarton Ave., Half Way Tree, tel. 876/920-8278 or 876/920-8279, jamaicaconservation@gmail.com, www.greenjamaica.org.

jm). Book at least two weeks in advance for a weekend stay in one of three self-contained cabins (two one-bedroom units with open layout for US$50, one two-bedroom unit for US$70; resident rate US$34 for one-bedroom, US$45 for two-bedroom). Camping (US$10 nonresident, US$2.25 resident) is also available with shower stall, toilets, and barbecue pits on-site (US$5 nonresidents or US$1.10 residents).

US$100-250

"Barbeque" Heritage Gardens of Cold Spring (located just below Newcastle, contact proprietor Eleanor Jones, tel. 876/960-0794, 876/960-8627, or 876/978-4438 on weekends and after 5 P.M., b.eleanor@gmail.com, www. heritagegardensjamaica.com, US$100 for two, US$20 for each additional person) is an old coffee estate with large barbecues, the flat areas where coffee is laid out to dry, hinting at the property's illustrious past as an important coffee processing estate. Irish naval officer and botanist Mathew Wallen established the coffee farm when he came to Jamaica in 1747. Wallen is credited with bringing several exotic plant species to Jamaica, including watercress, dandelion, nasturtiums, and bamboo. The cottage on the property sleeps up to six and has a rustic but comfortable feel with hot water and a cool breeze. The gardens are well cared for, and the entire property boasts spectacular views. The cottage makes a good base for hiking in the western section of the Blue Mountains and is a short walk to Newcastle, where the road up St. Catherine's Peak begins.

The Gap Café & Gift Shoppe (cell tel. 876/539-1771 or 876/579-9526) runs as a bed-and-breakfast inn with a one-bedroom apartment (US$100) containing two twin beds, a private bath, kitchen, and TV room.

Over US$250

Strawberry Hill (tel. 876/944-8400, www.islandoutpost.com) was once the site of a British naval hospital and remains a place where people seek health and refuge from the heat and dusty air on the plains below. Chris Blackwell, founder of Island Records and Bob Marley's first international producer, bought the property in 1972. Shortly thereafter, Marley took a retreat here after an attempt on his life during a spell of particularly heated political violence in 1976. Strawberry Hill is the highest of St. Andrew's limited high-end market, both in ambience and elevation (945 meters). Rates start at US$385 for a deluxe one-bedroom villa and climb to US$515 for a studio with a veranda overlooking Kingston.

The hotel boasts an Aveda concept spa and wellness center with a holistic approach to rejuvenation dubbed Strawberry Hill Living. Views from the well-appointed villas are spectacular. The restaurant serves some of the best food around and is a popular spot among high-society locals, many of whom make a habit of driving up for Sunday brunch. The smoked marlin eggs Benedict should not be missed. The winding ride up that takes guests to Irish Town is not for the weak of heart. A helicopter pad is located on-site, adjacent to Blackwell's private cottage, and transfers can be arranged from Norman Manley (US$600) or from any other part of the island.

⟨ Woodside (contact Robin Lumsden, tel. 876/927-2448, cell tel. 876/383-8942, limlums@cwjamaica.com, US$300 for three bedrooms, US$400 for four bedrooms, US$500 for five bedrooms, minimum two-night stay) is a beautiful, staffed, colonial house on a 12-hectare coffee farm located about 1.5 kilometers past Newcastle just below Hardwar Gap and Holywell National Park. Woodside is a stylish base for hiking in the park, birdwatching, and exploring the western reaches of the Blue Mountains. The house is impeccable in its old-Jamaica feel and boasts spectacular views, gardens, and a spring-fed pool. There is no better place for a cool escape during Jamaica's hottest months or for a relaxing retreat with friends and family any time of year.

FOOD
Shanty Man (Gordon Town Rd., cell tel. 876/533-3513, 9 A.M.–10 P.M. Sun.–Fri.,

Woodside has one of the best vantage points in the Blue Mountains on a 12-hectare coffee farm.

US$2–5) serves ital food out of a little Rasta-colored restaurant along the road between Papine and the Cooperage, just before the turnoff up to Skyline Drive. The menu features items like tofu, pumpkin soup, rice 'n' peas, and sautéed ackee with potato and carrot.

Café Blue (tel. 876/944-8918) serves Blue Mountain Coffee and pastries and retails local sauces, candles, and soaps. Café Blue is owned by the Sharps, who own Coffee Traders and offer tours on their farm, Clifton Mount.

⟨ Crystal Edge (Winsome Hall, tel. 876/944-8053), located next door, serves good Jamaican dishes at Jamaican prices. The restaurants are located just before Irish Town where the road starts to level out and the sharp curves become less pronounced.

Strawberry Hill (tel. 876/944-8400, www.islandoutpost.com, appetizers US$13–20, US$30–50 for entrées) has a varied menu of Jamaican and international cuisine and spectacular views from the wraparound porch. While it is by no means a budget eatery, the ambience will leave you with no regrets for having splurged. It's best to make reservations in advance.

The Gap Café & Gift Shoppe (cell tel. 876/539-1771 or 876/579-9526, 10 A.M.–5 P.M. Wed.–Sun.) is a restaurant with indoor and outdoor seating serving a rotating home-style menu with items like curried goat, oxtail and beans, crab backs, and callaloo-stuffed chicken breast (US$10.50–16). The restaurant boasts the most spectacular views over Kingston and St. Andrew at 4,200 feet above sea level. Located two miles past the Jamaica Defense Force hill station at Newcastle, the restaurant will open on off-days by reservation. It is said Ian Fleming wrote his first James Bond book, *Dr. No,* at the Gap.

Starlight Chalet (Silver Hill Gap, tel. 876/969-3070, 7 A.M.–5 P.M., later with reservations) serves Jamaican dishes at reasonable prices (US$10–25), bakes cakes and pastries from scratch, and prepares natural juices with whatever fruit is in season.

In Redlight, a series of stalls line the road where residents can usually be seen hanging out with speakers blaring from one of the small rum bars.

Yatte Man, or Blane "Smaker" Walker (cell tel. 876/285-8025, 10 A.M.–8 P.M. Sun.–Fri.), a once up-and-coming boxer, sells delicious homemade fish, chicken, and ital (vegetarian) patties (US$1) from one of the stalls about three quarters of the way through the main drag on the left, before the road begins to rise again toward Newcastle. Look out for the Star of David painted on the stall and a display case filled with patties.

Bubbles Bar (contact proprietor Reid, cell tel. 876/349-3484 or 876/773-1134), about halfway between Redlight and Newcastle, is the only watering hole around, selling basic supplies in addition to beer and rum. The bar marks the turnoff to Middleton down a poor road that falls sharply. The first hairpin to the right descends further toward the valley floor. Another hairpin turn to the left, 200 meters past a rise in the road over a landslide, leads down toward Prince Valley Guesthouse, run by Bobby "Scorcha" Williams and his wife Jackie, on the opposite side of the hill. A four-wheel drive, or at least a car with good clearance and decent traction, is critical to get much beyond the landslide.

Karen's One Stop (cell tel. 876/429-2551, US$5–10), located just past the hairpin turn to the left, is the only place around to get Jamaican staples like fried or BBQ chicken, fish, calalloo, and rice 'n' peas cooked to order any time of day. Karen also sells basic foodstuffs to area residents.

Mavis Bank and Blue Mountain Peak

Mavis Bank is a sleepy village nestled in a river valley in the shadow of Blue Mountain Peak. Its principal economic foundation for the past century has been the Mavis Bank Coffee Factory, which keeps many of the area's residents employed. The area is a good base for exploring the upper reaches of the Blue Mountains and for birding.

A few homey accommodation options around Mavis Bank offer visitors a chance to prepare in relative comfort for the trek up Blue Mountain Peak, which requires a somewhat grueling four-wheel-drive journey to the trailhead at Abbey Green, or alternatively, a two-hour hike.

MAVIS BANK

Sights

Mavis Bank Coffee Factory (MBCF) (right off the Main Road as you reach Mavis Bank from Gordon Town, tel. 876/977-8005, 876/977-8013, or 876/977-8015, admin@mbcfcoffee.com, 8:30 A.M.–noon and 1–3:30 P.M. Mon.–Fri., tour reservations recommended, US$8 adults, US$3.50 children) was established in 1923 by an English planter, Victor Munn. As the biggest coffee factory in Jamaica, it has been the economic foundation for the area since. The company is currently owned by the National Investment Bank of Jamaica (NIJB) and the founding Munn family, who share 70/30-percent stakes. Today, operations at the 327-worker factory are overseen by local PNP politician Senator Norman Grant, who holds the position of managing director.

Mavis Bank Coffee Factory is supplied by six of its own plantations, including Abbey, St. Thomas, and Orchard Rest, and around 5,000 independent farms. Most of the picking is done by local women, who receive about US$50 per box full of berries. Of this, the vast majority goes to the farm owner where the berries were picked. The coffee is then left outside to dry for 5–7 days, weather permitting, or dried in a giant tumbler for two days if it's too rainy outside. Once dry, the coffee is aged in big sacks for 4–6 weeks before the outer parchment, or hull, is removed and the beans are cleaned and roasted. The whole process takes 3–4 months from bush to mug. Four grades (peaberry, 1, 2, and 3) are produced at MBCF, around 75–80 percent of which is consumed in Japan, with 5

percent going to the United States and 4 percent to Europe and the rest of the world. The remainder goes to local markets. MBCF processes 1.4 million pounds of green beans per year from 6,000 farmers.

The best tours of the factory are led by Doreen "Barbara" Johnson (tel. 876/895-3437), who has worked at MBCF since 1987.

Cinchona Gardens, while not the best-maintained botanical gardens, have a spectacular variety of plants, including many orchid species, making it a magical place with an incredible view. Cinchona Gardens can be reached by turning left at the Anglican church in Mavis Bank, and then descending to cross the Yallahs River at Robertsfield. Once you cross the river, either keep left at the fork to Cinchona via Hall's Delight, or take the right at the fork to reach Cinchona via Westphalia. Both roads are impassable for anything but 4x4 vehicles, or vehicles with good clearance. The bumpy journey takes about an hour from Mavis Bank. The caretaker at Cinchona is Lloyd Stamp (cell. 876/459-8582), known by everyone simply as "Stamp" or "Stampy." He lives in a little house at the bottom of the gardens. There's no admission cost, but given the gardeners' poor government salaries, it's advisable for visitors to "leave a ting" when presented with the visitors' book for signing. Tips should be in the range of US$5–10 per person. The garden is open to visitors and tended from 7:30 A.M. to around 6 P.M. daily. Call Stamp prior to your visit to check on the weather and the best route to take, as road conditions are in a constant flux and one may be better than the other at any given time.

Another route to Cinchona descends from Section above Hardwar Gap. Turn right at section and descend to St. Peters. In St. Peters turn off the main road to the left toward Chestervale and Clydesdale rather than continuing the decent toward Guava Ridge. At Clydesdale, you'll see barbeques used to dry coffee beans, a water wheel, and an old great house now in ruins that hints of its more glorious past as a coffee plantation. It's a fitting place for camping for those with their own tent. From Clydesdale, an

© OLIVER HILL

Coffee cures for months in the store room at the Mavis Bank Coffee Factory in the Blue Mountains.

old road leads to Cinchona that takes about 1.5 hours to walk, or a bit quicker for intrepid drivers with a four-wheel-drive vehicle. The views hold more natural beauty on the route down from Section, but it takes quite a while longer to reach Cinchona. **Jill Byles** (tel. 876/977-8007 or cell tel. 876/487-5962, paraisoj@cwjamaica.com), a retired horticultural enthusiast who lives at Guava Ridge near Mavis Bank, offers tour guide services (US$50 per day regardless of group size) on hiking trails in the area. Jill can guide visits to **Cinchona, Flamstead,** and **Governor's Bench,** a footpath named after Governor Alexander Swettenham, who lived at Bellevue, a great house in the hills now owned by the University of the West Indies that's used for retreats and visitor accommodations.

The only remains of the great house at Flamstead is an old chimney. Flamstead was used as a lookout point as far back as the Taino period and during the Napoleonic Wars, served as a residence for Admiral Rodney, and was used as a base for the British army. Former Jamaican trade ambassador Peter King built a house on the site before being murdered in 2006. A plaque on the house he built notes that the site helped prove the usefulness of longitude as first measured by John Harrison's marine chronometer in 1761 by Harrison's son William. The Harrisons would eventually take the 20,000-pound sterling prize offered by the British crown for a solution to the problem of measuring longitude in the age of sail.

THE BLUE AND JOHN CROW MOUNTAINS NATIONAL PARK

Consisting of nearly 81,000 hectares in the parishes of St. Andrew, St. Mary, St. Thomas, and Portland, the Blue and John Crow Mountains National Park (BJCMNP, tel. 876/920-8278, jcdt@cybervale.com, www.greenjamaica.org.jm) covers the highest and steepest terrain in Jamaica. This alpine terrain is the last-known habitat for the endangered Giant Swallowtail butterfly, the second-largest butterfly in the world, which makes its home especially on the northern flanks of the range. Several endemic plant and bird species reside in the park as well, and many migratory birds from northern regions winter there. Among the most impressive of the native birds are the streamertail hummingbirds—known locally as doctor birds—and the Jamaican tody, the Jamaican blackbird, and the yellow-billed parrot. The Blue Mountains generally are the source of water for the greater Kingston area and for this reason, among others, it is important to tread lightly and disturb the environment as little as possible. The BJCMNP has the largest unaltered swath of natural forest in Jamaica, with upper montane rainforest and elfin woodland at its upper reaches.

◖ Blue Mountain Peak

The centerpiece of the Blue and John Crow Mountains National Park, Blue Mountain Peak can be reached by a variety of means depending on the level of exhaustion you are willing to endure. Generally, people leave from Whitfield Hall at Penlyne, St. Thomas, after having arrived there by four-wheel-drive vehicle. For ambitious hikers, however, there's also a 4.5-kilometer trail from Mavis Bank to Penlyne Castle, which is pleasant and covers several farms and streams. This option also obviates the need to send for a four-wheel-drive vehicle. From Penlyne Castle, you follow the road to Abbey Green (3.2 km) and then from there to Portland Gap (3.7 km). At Portland Gap there is a ranger station, sometimes unmanned, with bunks, toilets, showers, and campsites. These facilities can be used for US$5 by contacting the JCDT, which asks that visitors register at the ranger station. From Portland Gap to the peak is the most arduous leg, covering 5.6 kilometers. Warm clothes, light rain gear, and comfortable, supportive footwear are recommended.

Blue Mountain Peak is a mildly challenging four-hour hike from **Whitfield Hall,** a rustic farmhouse with a great fireplace. Trips to overnight at the farm and climb Blue Mountain by sunrise can be arranged through **Barrett Adventures** (contact Carolyn Barrett, tel. 876/382-6384, info@barrettadventures.com, www.barrettadventures.com).

From Portland Gap westward along the Blue Mountain range there are several other important peaks along the ridge, which are hiked to a far lesser extent. These include Sir John's Peak, John Crow Peak, and Catherine's Peak. Get your hands on a copy of *Guide to the Blue and John Crow Mountains* by Margaret Hodges; it has the most thorough coverage of hiking trails throughout the national park. Otherwise locals are the best resource.

ACCOMMODATIONS

Forres Park Guest House (reservations office tel. 876/927-8275, in Mavis Bank tel. 876/977-8141, mlyn@cwjamaica.com, www.forrespark.com, US$75–200) is the best option for birdwatchers and hikers, especially for groups. A two-story main house and four cabins are surrounded by a small coffee farm that attracts many endemic and migratory bird species. The large veranda is a great vantage point, as all three of Jamaica's hummingbirds—vervain, Jamaica mango, and streamertail—frequent the bushes all around the chalet-style main house. Rooms range from basic to more well-appointed, with a true mountain cabin feel. You won't miss the lack of air-conditioning, as nights are pleasantly cool. Hot water, on the other hand, comes well appreciated. Two additional superior deluxe rooms were added in 2007, including a suite with a whirlpool tub and a 90-degree view of the mountains, and another large room below, also with a king-size four-poster bed and a private balcony, opening out onto a semi-private garden (US$200). Forres Park is a great launch pad for excursions into the Blue Mountains and Cinchona gardens. The Lyn family owners have one of the largest coffee farming and processing operations on the island.

❦ Lime Tree Farm (Tower Hill, cell tel. 876/881-8788, hello@limetreefarm.com, www.limetreefarm.com, US$130 per person per night, inclusive of three meals per day including wine with dinner; other alcoholic beverages served at additional cost) overlooking Mavis Bank, and with a spectacular view of Portland Gap, Blue Mountain Peak, and the Yallahs River Valley, is a small coffee farm with tastefully decorated concrete cabins owned by partners Charles Burberry and Rodger Bolton. The property is run as an all-inclusive lodging, and the hosts prepare excellent meals that make Lime Tree Farm one of the best values in Jamaica. Meals are shared in the open-air communal kitchen/lounge/dining area, which gives the place a warm, family vibe. Charlie's heritage is quite distinguished indeed; his grandfather, Hugh Foot, was colonial secretary of Jamaica from 1945 to 1947. He later became governor general from 1951 to 1957, during which time he oversaw moves leading up to independence in 1962. Foot, also known as Lord Caradon, marveled in the "the charm and strength of Jamaica in her variety," a commentary brought to life by his heirs at Lime Tree Farm. A four-wheel-drive vehicle is needed to reach the property and can be obtained in Kingston or Mavis Bank.

Whitfield Hall (Penlyne, St. Thomas, tel. 876/927-0986 or 876/878-0514, bookings@ whitfieldhall.com, www.whitfieldhall.com, dorm bunks US$20, Coronel Whitfield room in main house US$50) a few kilometers Past Hagley Gap, lies just over the border in the parish of St. Thomas. It is a beautiful old house and coffee farm that offers rustic accommodation in a grand setting with a well-appreciated fireplace to fend off the night chill. Whitfield is the most common starting point for expeditions up to Blue Mountain Peak via Portland Gap, which generally start in the early morning hours to arrive at the summit for sunrise, when hikers have the best chance at taking in a crisp view. As the morning progresses, clouds tend to roll in, often obscuring the peaks and valleys. A guide to the peak is facilitated from Whitfield Hall for US$36 per party. Penlyne is only accessible by four-wheel-drive from Mavis Bank. Transportation can be arranged from any point in Kingston or Mavis Bank, with the cost depending on distance (US$40 from Mavis Bank, US$65 from Papine Square, US$100 from Kingston).

At **Portland Gap** (29 Dumbarton Ave., Half Way Tree off Eastwood Park Rd., tel. 876/920-8278 or 876/920-8279, jamaicaconservation@

gmail.com, www.greenjamaica.org.jm) there are six wooden cabins. Cabin one has six bunks sleeping 12, at US$27/night; the second cabin has nine bunks, sleeping 18, for US$40/night; Cabins 3–6 are unclosed with no beds but with space for up to 15 people to sleep on the floor. Foam sleeping mats can be rented for US$0.60 per night, but hikers should carry their own sleeping bags. Pit toilets and fire pits are available. A US$1.15 user fee is assessed at the ranger station or when booking the cabins through the JCDT.

FOOD AND SERVICES

Mavis Bank is not the place to go for culinary delights or nightlife of any kind. Nonetheless, **Karen's Container Bar** around the corner from Forres Park is open whenever there are customers to serve.

In Mavis Bank square, **By-Way Bar** is a livelier local hangout. Also in the square is the post office and police station (tel. 876/977-8004).

To venture farther into the mountains, a four-wheel-drive vehicle is necessary. If you're heading up to Blue Mountain Peak you can call Whitfield Hall (tel. 876/364-0722) for a vehicle to meet you at the constabulary, which is a good place to leave your two-wheel-drive car if you have one.

GETTING THERE AND AROUND

The Blue Mountains are accessible from three points of entry: from Kingston via Papine; from Yallahs, St. Thomas, via Cedar Valley; and from Buff Bay, St. Mary, on the North Coast via the B1, which runs alongside the Buff Bay River. The last route is subject to landslides and has been impassable to all but four-wheel-drive vehicles for several years.

There are two main routes to access the south-facing slopes of the Blue Mountain range. The first, accessed by taking a left onto the B1 at the Cooperage, leads through Maryland to Irish Town, Redlight, Newcastle, and Hardwar Gap before the Buff Bay River Valley opens up overlooking Portland and St. Mary on the other side of the range.

The second route, straight ahead at the Cooperage along Gordon Town Road, leads to Gordon Town, and then taking a right in the town square over the bridge, to Mavis Bank. Continuing beyond Mavis Bank requires a four-wheel-drive vehicle and can either take you left at Hagley Gap to Penlyne or straight down to Cedar Valley and along the Yallahs River to the town of Yallahs.

Getting to and around the Blue Mountains can be a challenge, even if keeping lunch down on the way isn't. Only for the upper reaches, namely beyond Mavis Bank, is it really necessary to have a 4x4; otherwise the abundant potholes and washed-out road is only mildly more challenging to navigate than any other part of Jamaica because of its sharp turns.

A hired taxi into the Blue Mountains will cost from US$25 for a drop-off at Strawberry Hill, to US$100 for the day to be chauffeured around. Route taxis travel between Papine Square and Gordon Town throughout the day (US$2), as well as to Irish Town (US$3.50), but you must wait for the car to fill up with passengers before heading out.

To reach Whitfield Hall, the most common starting point for hiking Blue Mountain, four-wheel-drive taxis can be arranged through Whitfield Hall.

Many travelers find letting a tour operator take care of the driving is the easiest, most hassle-free way to get around the island. One of the most dependable and versatile tour companies on the island is Barrett Adventures (contact Carolyn Barrett, cell tel. 876/382-6384). Barrett can pick you up from any point on the island, getting off the beaten path more often than any other tour company in Jamaica. Barrett also books many of the best budget accommodation options across the island, including a few spots in the Blue Mountains.

Colin Smikle (cell tel. 876/370-8243 or 876/978-5833, colinsmikle@yahoo.com) offers a tour he dubs "Blue Mountain in a Hurry" ($150 for one or two persons with their own vehicle), where he'll guide hikers up and down in a day.

THE BLUE MOUNTAINS

PORT ANTONIO AND THE EAST COAST

The parishes of Portland and St. Thomas form Jamaica's easternmost region and contain the island's least exploited natural treasures. A quiet town in the center of Portland's coast affectionately known as "Portie," Port Antonio boasts some of Jamaica's most secluded beaches among a handful of other stunning natural wonders. The world-famous Blue Hole, or Blue Lagoon, where ice-cold spring water mixes with the warm waves lapping in from the sea, is surreal beyond measure and reason in itself to visit the region.

Navy Island, an abandoned little paradise in the middle of Port Antonio's twin harbors, is surrounded by coral reefs and sand bars. Steep, lush hills rise from a coastline dotted with beaches, inlets, and mangroves. Reach Falls is a nature lover's paradise, where local guides take visitors by the hand along trails that only they can see through the middle of the river. In Bath, natural hot springs have a mineral composition that is said to cure almost any ailment. When one of these destinations occupies top priority on your daily agenda, life just seems to flow at the right speed. Perhaps the languid pace of this side of the island is just meant to be, and as a visitor you won't be sorry for the lack of crowds.

Located about 65 kilometers from Morant Bay around the eastern flank of the John Crow Mountains and about 95 kilometers east of Port Maria, Port Antonio is the largest town in Portland, and the parish capital. The fact that the area attracts only a minute fraction of the three million or so visitors Jamaica gets each year is either the way it should be or a crying shame, depending on whom you ask. Those

HIGHLIGHTS

◖ **Errol Flynn Marina:** This world-class facility in the heart of Port Antonio has a sea wall lined with flowers and benches (page 121).

◖ **Bonnie View:** No degree of dilapidation to the remains of one of Errol Flynn's grand hotels can take away its view (page 121).

◖ **Winnifred Beach:** One of Portland's finest beaches also has great seafood at Cynthia's. Winnifred is a popular gathering place for locals and is especially crowded on Sundays (page 122).

◖ **Folly Mansion:** A perfect metaphor for the state of Portland's boom-to-bust tradition, Folly is still impressive even as it lies in ruins (page 123).

◖ **Blue Hole:** Popularly known as the Blue Lagoon, a 55-meter-deep freshwater spring wells up in a protected cove to mix with the warm tide (page 124).

◖ **Reach Falls:** Dotted with caves and crystal-clear pools, the island's most exciting waterfalls carve through a lush valley (page 124).

◖ **Upper Rio Grande Valley:** Home base for the Windward Maroons, the wide river valley has a rich history and some of the island's most unspoiled wilderness (page 139).

◖ **Bath Hot Springs:** Said to cure all manner of diseases, the hot springs and baths are

never crowded and provide rejuvenating relaxation (page 148).

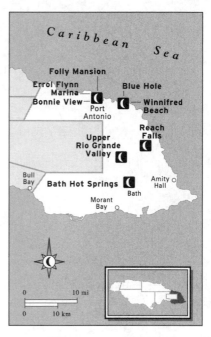

LOOK FOR ◖ TO FIND RECOMMENDED SIGHTS, ACTIVITIES, DINING, AND LODGING.

who depend on the tourist trade complain the area is not marketed to its potential, while it is said those who own the area's most extravagant private homes prefer it just the way it is.

PLANNING YOUR TIME

Some say Port Antonio is a place time forgot. What's clear is it's an easy place to fall in love with, and despite the languid pace, it's impossible to get bored. You'll want to give the area no less than three days to get in all the main sights without feeling rushed, but if you go there at the

beginning of a trip to Jamaica, it's possible you won't want to see anything else, unless of course you're unlucky enough to be there for an extended period of rain, which is not uncommon.

Port Antonio is small enough to fit in two main activities in a day. Folly Mansion is a good morning activity, when the sun lights up the side facing the sea, and is nicely complemented with an afternoon at the beach. The dusk hours are best spent on a bench at the marina with a Devon House I Scream ice-cream cone in hand.

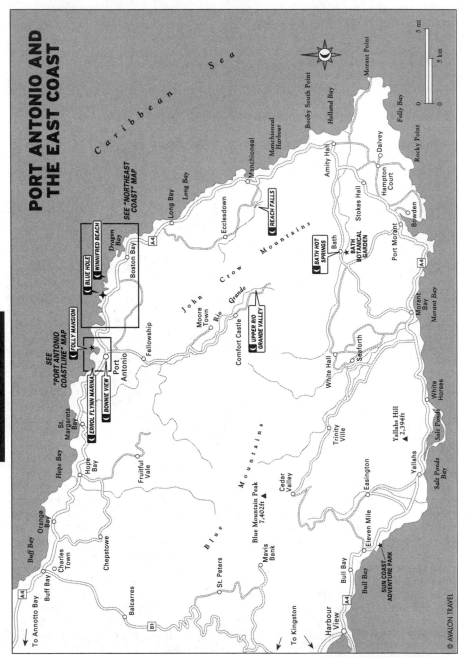

PORT ANTONIO AND THE EAST COAST

SEE "NORTHEAST COAST" MAP

SEE "PORT ANTONIO COASTLINE" MAP

BLUE HOLE
WINNIFRED BEACH
FOLLY MANSION
ERROL FLYNN MARINA
BONNIE VIEW
REACH FALLS
BATH HOT SPRINGS
BATH BOTANICAL GARDEN
UPPER RIO GRANDE VALLEY

Caribbean Sea

Morant Point
Booby South Point
Holland Bay
Fidly Bay
Rocky Point
Dalvey
Manchioneal
Manchioneal Harbour
Amity Hall
Hampton Court
Bowden
Stokes Hall
Port Morant
Ecclesdown
Bath
Long Bay
Long Bay

John Crow Mountains

Dragon Bay
Boston Bay
Fellowship
Moore Town
Rio Grande
Comfort Castle

Port Antonio

St. Margarets Bay
Hope Bay
Hope Bay
Fruitful Vale

Morant Bay
Morant Bay
White Horses
Seaforth
White Hall
Trinity Ville
Salt Ponds
Yallahs Hill ▲ 2,394ft
Salt Ponds Bay
Yallahs

Buff Bay
Orange Bay
Charles Town
Chepstowe
St. Peters
Balcarres
Mavis Bank
Cedar Valley
Blue Mountain Peak ▲ 7,402ft

Blue Mountains

Easington
Eleven Mile
Bull Bay
Bull Bay
SUN COAST ADVENTURE PARK
Harbour View

A4
To Annotto Bay
Buff Bay
B1
To Kingston

5 mi
5 km

© AVALON TRAVEL

If you're planning on heading into the higher reaches of the Rio Grande Valley, it will take up at least a day there and back if you're to fit in a hike to the falls and at least three days round-trip to hike with Maroon guides to the site of Nanny Town, higher up in the Blue Mountains.

HISTORY

Port Antonio did not develop until Portland was established as a parish in 1723. Originally called Titchfield, the town was concentrated on the peninsular hill dividing the twin harbors that still retain the town's original name. Port Antonio, like much of the eastern side of the island, was not developed in the early colonial period thanks to the rough terrain not suitable for sugar, the principal cash crop during the slavery period. To further dissuade European settlers, the Maroons had their eastern stronghold inland from Port Antonio up the Rio Grande Valley.

Port Antonio was completely transformed, starting in 1876, by the banana trade, which turned the hills into lucrative plantations in a way sugar never could; the area grew further in recognition when the empty banana steamers returned with New Englanders who'd heard about paradise in Portland, Jamaica. Steamer captains George Busch and later Lorenzo Dow Baker basically invented the lucrative banana trade by encouraging local farmers to plant the "green gold" as they fed an exploding, almost accidental demand in the northeastern United States. Jamaica dominated world banana production until 1929, when Honduras took over as top producer after blight destroyed Jamaica's crop. But this was not before Baker was able to invent a new trade in tourism, building the Titchfield Hotel, one of the most extravagant hotels in the Caribbean, which enticed the world's early steam-set to discover Port Antonio. Tourism dropped off during the Great Depression, but the area experienced a brief resurgence in the 1950s and 1960s when it became a chic destination for Hollywood stars, with the likes of Errol Flynn and Ian Fleming making it their preferred stomping ground.

PORTLAND'S BANANA BOOM

The global banana trade, currently a multibillion dollar industry, has its roots in Portland and St. Thomas. The originators of the banana trade were American sea captains George Busch and later Lorenzo Dow Baker of the 85-ton *Telegraph,* who arrived in 1870. These two established a lucrative two-way trade, bringing saltfish (cod), shoes, and textiles from New England, where they found the bananas sold at a handsome profit. Baker was the most successful of the early banana shippers; he eventually formed the Boston Fruit Company in 1899, which later became the United Fruit Company of New Jersey and went on to control much of the fruit's production in the Americas. As refrigerated ships came into operation in the early 1900s, England slowly took over from the United States as the primary destination, thanks to tariff protection that was only recently phased out. With the establishment of the Jamaica Banana Producers' Association in 1929, smallholder production was organized, a cooperative shipping line established, and the virtual monopoly held by United Fruit was somewhat broken. In 1936 the association became a shareholder-based company rather than a cooperative due to near-bankruptcy and pressure from United Fruit. It was perhaps this example of organized labor that gave Marcus Garvey the inspiration for a shipping line to serve the black population in the diaspora and bring commerce into its hands. In the 1930s, Panama disease virtually wiped out the Jamaican banana crop, hitting small producers especially hard. Banana carriers and dockworkers were at the fore of the labor movements of 1937-1938, which led to trade unions and eventually the establishment of Jamaica's political parties.

Some of the world's wealthiest people visited and bought property in the area. Since then Portland has been somewhat overshadowed in promotional efforts by tourism developments in Ocho Rios, Montego Bay, and Negril.

ORIENTATION

The town of Port Antonio is easy to get around on foot or bicycle, with the farthest-flung attractions being no more than a few kilometers apart. For all nature attractions you will need a ride. While the main road (A4) along the north coast passes through Port Antonio, it follows many different streets before coming out again on the other side of town. Approaching from the east, the A4 first becomes West Palm Avenue, then West Street going through the center of town, before joining Harbour Street in front of the Royal Mall, which later becomes Folly Road and then finally once again simply the main road (A4). Harbour Street and William Street together form a one-way roundabout circling the Court House and the Parish Council.

Titchfield Hill, the old part of town, sits on a protrusion next to Navy Island, which divides the East and West Harbours. Titchfield has several interesting gingerbread-style buildings and a few guesthouses, with Fort George Street, King Street, and Queen Street running the length of the peninsula parallel to one another. In town itself, most of the action is on Harbour and West Streets, where the banks, a few restaurants, two nightclubs, and Musgrave Market are located. From Harbour Road, West Avenue starts up again, wrapping around a residential district and becoming East Avenue before reuniting with the Main Road, at this point called Allen. Red Hassell Road, which is the delineator between East and West Palm avenues, is the route to the Rio Grande Valley.

East of Port Antonio along the coast are a series of hills dropping gently down to coves and bays, which help delineate the districts of Anchovy, Drapers, San San, and Fairy Hill. Farther east lies Boston and then Long Bay. The main beaches including San San, Frenchman's Cove, Dragon Bay, and Winnifred are all located on this stretch of coast east of town, as is the Blue Hole and Reach Falls just past Manchioneel.

Port Antonio

Sheer wealth is readily apparent everywhere east of Port Antonio along the coast, sometimes to an astonishing degree; however, the town's over-the-top grandeur has been fading for decades, leaving in its place potholed roads, dilapidated historical sites, and an increasingly desperate dependence on a barely trickling tourism trade. Some of the most beautiful real estate in Jamaica—and perhaps in the entire world—can be found in the vicinity, much of it overgrown and conspicuously neglected. The restaurant and bar on Navy Island, a two-hectare piece of land that protects Port Antonio's West Harbour, has trees growing up through the rotting floorboards with little remaining to remind visitors of the parish's more glamorous days. Efforts to return Navy Island to its former glory have apparently lost steam. Similarly, the restaurant at Blue Hole, or Blue Lagoon, as it was popularized in the movie of the same name, was closed from 2003 to 2007. Michael Lee Chin, one of Jamaica's wealthiest businessmen, recently took control of the land on the western shores of the Lagoon, in addition to buying Trident Castle and the Trident Hotel from Earl Levy, but planned refurbishments at both properties have yet to materialize.

Many residents ask themselves why this unique and marketable natural treasure has been so poorly managed. Some blame the area's remoteness, exacerbated by winding, potholed roads, and say the new North Coast Highway, which incidentally stops at Port Antonio's town limits, is key to turning the area around.

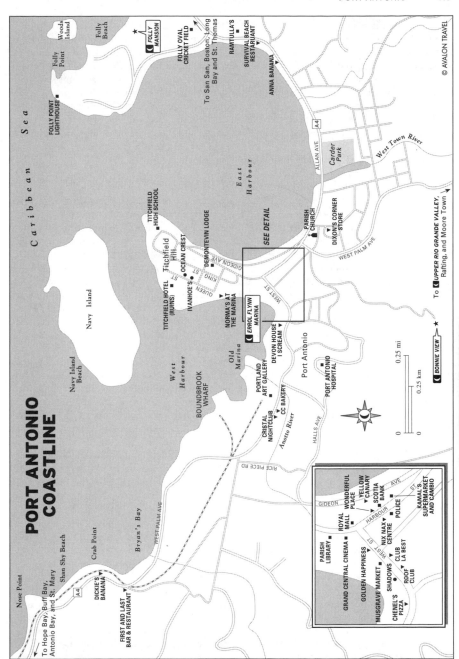

© AVALON TRAVEL

PORT ANTONIO

PORT ANTONIO COASTLINE

Nose Point

To Hope Bay, Buff Bay,
Antonio Bay, and St. Mary

A4

DICKIE'S BANANA

FIRST AND LAST BAR & RESTAURANT

Shan Shy Beach

Crab Point

Bryan's Bay

WEST PALM AVE

RICE PIECE RD

Caribbean Sea

Woods Island

Folly Beach

★ FOLLY MANSION

Folly Point

FOLLY OVAL CRICKET FIELD

RAMTULLA'S

SURVIVAL BEACH RESTAURANT

To San San, Boston, Long Bay and St. Thomas

ANNA BANANA

FOLLY POINT LIGHTHOUSE

East Harbour

A4

ALLAN AVE

Carder Park

West Town River

Navy Island

Navy Island Beach

West Harbour

BOUNDBROOK WHARF

Old Marina

TITCHFIELD HIGH SCHOOL

Titchfield Hill

OCEAN CREST

DEMONTEVIN LODGE

KING ST

QUEEN ST

GIDEON AVE

TITCHFIELD HOTEL (RUINS)

IVANHOE'S

NORMA'S AT THE MARINA

ERROL FLYNN MARINA

DEVON HOUSE I SCREAM

PORTLAND ART GALLERY

CC BAKERY

CRISTAL NIGHTCLUB

Anotto River

SEE DETAIL

WEST ST

Port Antonio

PORT ANTONIO HOSPITAL

PARISH CHURCH

DIXON'S CORNER STORE

WEST PALM AVE

To ◖UPPER RIO GRANDE VALLEY, Rafting, and Moore Town

HALLS AVE

0   0.25 mi

0   0.25 km

◖ BONNIE VIEW ─→ ★

Detail inset:

GIDEON

WONDERFUL PLACE

YELLOW CANARY

SCOTIA BANK

AVE

ROYAL MALL

HARBOUR ST

NIX NAX CENTRE

POLICE

KAMAL'S SUPERMARKET AND CAMBIO

PARISH LIBRARY

WEST ST

CLUB LA BEST

GRAND CENTRAL CINEMA

GOLDEN HAPPINESS

MUSGRAVE MARKET

SHADOWS

ROOF CLUB

CLUB

CHENEL'S PIZZA

Some blame Jamaica's promotional institutions like the Jamaica Tourism Board or the Urban Development Corporation for mishandling resources and retarding the development process; still others blame the elite villa owners, many of them absent much of the year to return for brief spells when they prefer the quiet, old world character of the land, free from masses of transient tourists and preserved in time as a result.

Despite the seemingly stagnant pace of development, efforts have been made and are under way to return Port Antonio to its former glory and jump-start the economy of what should be one of the Caribbean's most popular, exclusive tourist destinations. The new Errol Flynn Marina on the West Harbour in the heart of Port Antonio was inaugurated in 2004 and has world-class facilities, low docking fees, as well as a new Russian-Eurasian restaurant. Never mind that the aforementioned Navy Island development was slated for inclusion in the Marina project before funds disappeared. Other recent developments have seen Butch Stewart, who owns the Sandals and Beaches all-inclusive resorts, buy Dragon Bay, formerly one of the area's top resorts (made famous as a set for the movie *Cocktail).* Stewart is apparently waiting on the government, or some sign from God, to reopen the property as an ultra-luxury all-inclusive.

What is certain is that the present trickle of visitors who come through Port Antonio do not constitute a strong enough driving force to support a healthy economy, leaving crumbling Folly Mansion, its enormous structure built in the Roaring Twenties with a cement-salt water mix, an ironic symbol of stagnation. But few who visit can help but comment on the area's tremendous natural beauty. Secluded white-sand beaches, extravagant villas, plentiful rivers, and strikingly unique topography where the hills fall gently to the sea make Port Antonio and the northeast coast an immediate favorite.

The reality is that any hope of a new economic boom may have faded, despite the memory of Portland as the Caribbean's first tourist destination as a result of the banana trade in the early 19th century. Port Antonio saw a brief comeback in the 1960s and 1970s when it became the playground of choice for the rich and famous from around the world, many of whom left grand mansions seemingly transplanted from old world Europe to the lush green hills of Portland. These past luminaries include the film star Errol Flynn, who left an important legacy in Port Antonio when he died in 1959. Many of Flynn's former properties lie in ruins today.

SIGHTS

The heart of historic Port Antonio, known as **Titchfield Hill,** is best visited by strolling around the peninsula, consuming little more than an hour at a leisurely pace. Titchfield Hill is today a run-down neighborhood dotted with several buildings that hint at more prosperous times with decorative latticework and wide front steps leading up to wraparound verandas. The **Demontevin Lodge** (21 Fort George St., tel. 876/993-2604) is a case in point. It was once the private home of David Gideon, who became Custos of Port Antonio in 1923. Today it is a tired hotel operated under unenthusiastic management and not recommended for lodging, but its decorative gingerbread house ironwork reminiscent of old sea captains' homes on the Massachusetts coast is striking and worth a look. Demontevin hosts a popular karaoke night on Fridays.

The foundation and scattered ruins of the **Titchfield Hotel,** built by banana boat captain Lorenzo Dow Baker of the Boston Fruit Company, stand across Queen Street from Ocean Crest Guest House and are now occupied by the Jamaica Defense Force, which patrols Navy Island across the water. At its peak the Titchfield was the favored watering hole for luminaries like Bette Davis, J. P. Morgan, and Errol Flynn, who ended up buying the place in addition to Navy Island and the Bonnie View Hotel, overlooking the town from the best perch around. The Titchfield was destroyed and rebuilt several times before it was gutted and abandoned after Flynn's death.

At the tip of the Titchfield peninsula stands **Titchfield School,** constructed on the ruins of **Fort George.** Built by the English to defend against Spanish reprisals that never came, Fort George never really saw any action but operated nonetheless until World War I. It had walls three meters thick and embrasures for 22 cannons, a few of which are still present. Nobody manages this historic site, making it free and accessible anytime.

(Errol Flynn Marina

Errol Flynn Marina (tel. 876/993-3209 or 876/715-6044, fax 876/715-6033, info@errolflynnmarina.com, www.errolflynnmarina.com, 8 A.M.–5 P.M. daily) has slips for 32 boats. Vessels under 50 feet are charged US$0.75 per foot per day, over 50 feet US$1.25 per foot per day; electricity and water are also available at metered rates (US$0.24/kWhr for electricity and US$0.09/gallon of water). A well-laid-out and planted promenade along the waterfront has benches. Wireless Internet is included for marina guests, and there is an Internet café open to nonguests (US$4/hour). **Devon House I Scream** and **Norma's at the Marina** are both located within the gated complex, and the scenic waterfront makes a romantic spot to let evening drift into night. A private beach faces Navy Island just beyond Norma's. The park along the waterfront is open to the public (7 A.M.–11 P.M. Mon.–Fri., 7 A.M.–midnight Sat. and Sun.), as is the beach, marina and restaurant; the docks and pool are reserved for marina guests. The beach is open to customers of Norma's. The Errol Flynn Marina is owned by the Port Authority of Jamaica and managed by Westrec Marina. The marina opened in September 2002 and was renamed the Errol Flynn Marina in 2006.

Port Antonio Marina, also under the control of the Port Authority of Jamaica, also offers docking ($0.35/foot) with water, electricity, and showers, but no security after 4 P.M. By car, access the Port Antonio Marina down the road next to the old train station across from CC Bakery. The difference between them comes down to security, proximity to the bar

and restaurant, and complimentary wireless Internet.

Navy Island

Navy Island, originally called Lynch's Island, is a landmass slightly larger than Titchfield Hill, about 0.75 kilometer long with an area of about two hectares. It protects Port Antonio's West Harbour with a large sandbar extending off its western side. The island was at one point sited for construction of the town, but the British Navy acquired it instead as a place to beach ships for cleaning and repairs. A naval station was eventually built there, and later Errol Flynn bought the island and turned it into an exclusive resort. Today Navy Island is owned by the Port Authority; it's meant to be developed at some undetermined future time. A private bid for the land put together by a consortium of local landowners was blocked by the Authority, which seems wary of ceding control in spite of doing nothing with the land for the moment, to the dismay of many local residents.

The island is not serviced by any official tourist operation, but it's a great place to tromp around and explore, and the Jamaica Defense Force Officers there on patrol are friendly enough to visitors. Dennis Butler (cell tel. 876/809-6276) will take visitors to the island (US$10 per person, US$20 with lunch) from Shan Shy Beach just west of Port Antonio, adjacent to his father's restaurant, Dickie's Banana.

(Bonnie View

The Bonnie View Hotel (Bonnie View Rd.) is another dilapidated former Errol Flynn property, no longer in operation as a hotel. The view is the best in town. To get there, take the washed-out Richmond Hill Road directly across from the Anglican Church on the corner of West Palm and Bridge streets. Bonnie View is not an organized attraction and there is no cost to have a look around as long as no one is around to make reference to the sign on property that states all sightseers must pay US$3 (J$150), which doesn't compute for today's exchange rate and dates the effort. Bonnie View makes a good early-morning walk from town for some aerobic exercise, and if someone asks for money to look at the view, perhaps offering to buy a drink from the nonexistent bar would provide adequate incentive for someone to establish a legitimate business there once again. The hill is passable by car if you drive at a snail's pace up the steep, potholed road.

Other Sights

Musgrave Market (6 A.M.–6 P.M. Mon.–Sat.) is located across from the square in the heart of Port Antonio. The market sells fresh produce toward the front and down a lane on one side. The deeper in you go toward the waterfront, the more the market tends towards crafts, "Jamaica no problem" T-shirts, and Bob Marley plaques. The most authentic artistry can be found at the very back where **Rockbottom** (cell tel. 876/844-9946), a woodcarver since 1980, has his setup. His nickname comes from his sales pricing, he says. For jewelry, clothing, and other Rasta-inspired crafts, check out Sister Dawn's (Shop #21, cell tel. 876/486-7516, portlandcraftproducers@yahoo.com).

Boundbrook Wharf is the old banana-loading wharf just west of town, behind the old railway station that now serves as the Portland Art Gallery. While not as busy as in the banana-boom days, the wharf continues to be used on occasion. The wharf makes a good 20-minute walk from town. Just north from the entrance to the wharf, a sandy lane leads off the main road to the beach, where fishing boats are tethered in front of the small fishermen's community.

◖ Winnifred Beach

Winnifred, known as the people's beach, lies in a wide, shallow, white-sand cove. It is a beautiful, free public beach in the Fairy Hill district just east of San San and the Blue Lagoon. It's also the best place for conch soup and fried fish. Food and beverages are sold by a slew of vendors, and there's a nice restaurant.

Named after the daughter of Quaker minister F. B. Brown as a rest place for missionaries,

teachers, and the respectable poor, Winnifred has remained decidedly local, thanks perhaps to the trust that once managed the area and had provisions ensuring that locals could access and enjoy the beach. The Urban Development Corporation now controls the land, but local resistance to its being developed has ensured that it remains a local hot spot.

Cynthia's, on the western end of the beach serves excellent fried fish with rice and peas (US$10). Undoubtedly someone will ask for a "contribution," but it's not necessary. Instead, support the vendors. The rocky road down to the beach has two access points from the main road. The best route goes through the housing development on the ocean side of the road less than 0.75 kilometer east of Dragon Bay. A turn into a housing development across the road from Jamaica Crest, followed by a quick right in front of the Neighborhood Watch sign, allows you avoid the worst part of the road that descends off the main next to the former Mikuzi.

Other Beaches

Shan Shy Beach on Bryan's Bay charges no entry fee and is home to a beach complex run by Donovan "Atto" Tracey (tel. 876/394-1312). An open, covered building has a billiards room with two tables.

One of the less-frequented beaches in Port Antonio, Shan Shy is a good place to take off on snorkeling or fishing excursions, which can be arranged through Atto or Dennis Butler (cell tel. 876/854-4763, US$20–50 depending on number of passengers and distance; Dennis can also be contacted via his mother, Marjorie, cell tel. 876/869-4391) of Dickie's Banana. The beach is located five minutes west of town at a sharp curve in the main road.

Around the bend in White River, Lucky Star Cookshop and Bar overlooks a another angler's beach. It's a favorite cool-out spot for local men, who are often found in the evenings playing poker and dominos.

Errol Flynn Marina has a well-maintained, private beach for guests of the Marina and patrons of Norma's at the Marina.

Directly in front of the crumbling Folly

© OLIVER HILL

Frenchman's Cove is a romantic inlet with a wide sandy beach and a river meandering down to meet the sea on one side.

Mansion, **Folly Beach** is a small beach with a narrow strip of sand. It has coral and a rough floor and sees few visitors.

Frenchman's Cove (entrance fee US$5) is one of the most picturesque coves in Jamaica. The beach here is well protected and drops off steeply after the first 20 meters.

Dragon Bay is a private beach protected by guards. In the near future, however, visitors may be able to gain access to Dragon Bay Resort.

Boston Beach, in a protected cove a few minutes east of Winnifred, consistently gets the best swells in the area and has a surf shop.

San San Beach (10 A.M.–4 P.M. daily, US$5) is the most exclusive beach in Port Antonio. It's located at the base of San San Hill, where many of the area's nicer villas are. The fine-sand beach hugs a cove next to Alligator Head and overlooks Pellew Island, from where a protective reef extends eastward to the mouth of Blue Hole.

◖ Folly Mansion

Just east of Port Antonio along Alan Avenue,

a left onto a dirt road before the cricket pitch follows the edge of East Harbour out to Folly Point Lighthouse. A right turn after the cricket pitch along a grassy vehicle track through low-lying scrub forest leads to Folly Mansion, which is an unmanaged attraction (free and always accessible) on government-owned land. Folly was for a few years after its construction the most ostentatious building in Jamaica, before it started to crumble. Built by Connecticut millionaire Alfred Mitchell in 1905, the mansion had 60 rooms and an indoor swimming pool and was made almost entirely of cement. Apparently the cement was mixed with salt-water, which proved a bad combination. The salt not only weakened the cement but rusted the steel framework, causing almost immediate deterioration. Nonetheless, Mitchell lived in the mansion with his wife, a Tiffany heiress, and their family on and off until his death in 1912, and it wasn't until 1936 that the house was abandoned. On the waterfront in front of the pillared mansion is the humble little **Folly Beach,** which faces small Wood Island, where

Mitchell is said to have kept monkeys and other exotic animals. The beach isn't bad for a swim, but care should be taken as the sea floor is not even and parts are covered with sharp reef. The area is known to have a strong current at times.

The name "Folly" predates Mitchell and his ill-fated mansion, as made clear by **Folly Point Lighthouse,** which was built and named in 1888. Apparently the name refers to Baptist minister James Service, who once owned the property, having acquired it piece by piece. For this he was lauded with a playful expression extolling his frugal ways, which were *not,* in fact, based in folly. Many legends surround the mansion, the most popular story being that the mansion was built as a wedding gift, but the bride ran off in tears when her dream home began to crumble as soon as she was carried across the threshold.

Folly Point Lighthouse stands on a point extending along the windward shore of East Harbour. The lighthouse is not generally open to the public, but the property manager is known to let visitors in on occasion. A track usually too rutted and muddy for a vehicle runs along the water's edge between the lighthouse and the mansion.

(Blue Hole

Blue Hole is also commonly known as the **Blue Lagoon** thanks to a 1980 Randal Kleiser adventure film of the same name starring a teenage Brooke Shields. This Blue Lagoon has no relation to the film, though locals will make the connection erroneously. Portland's Blue Hole is Jamaica's largest underground spring-fed lagoon, of which there are many smaller ones scattered across the island. The Blue Lagoon is made all the more unique by its location in a 55-meter-deep protected cove along the coast, where warm tidal waters gently mix with fresh water welling up from the depths. Some claim Blue Hole has no bottom. At one time, Robin Moore, the author of *The French Connection,* owned much of the land surrounding the lagoon; today his cottages lie in ruins. A restaurant and bar with a deck overhanging the lagoon has

been closed for several years. In 2006 Michael Lee Chin, National Commercial Bank (NCB) chairman and one of Jamaica's richest men, took over the lease for the land bordering the western edge of the lagoon. A handful of craft vendors line the beach waiting patiently to make a sale. The restaurant was dilapidated and falling into the water, but chatter could be heard about the possibility that Island Outpost would take over management of the attraction.

Blue Hole is located east of San San Beach and Pellew Island, just past the well-marked turnoff for Goblin Hill heading east. Turn onto the lane off the main road along the Blue Lagoon Villas and continue down to a small parking area along the beach.

(Reach Falls

Reach Falls (tel. 876/993-6606 or 876/993-6683, www.reachfalls.com, 8:30 A.M.–4:30 P.M. Wed.–Sun., US$10 adults, US$5 children under 12, US$4.25 residents), or Reich Falls, as it's sometimes spelled, is located in a beautiful river valley among the lower northeast foothills of the John Crow Mountains. The river cascades down a long series of falls that can be climbed from the base far below the main pool where the attraction, which is managed by Jamaica's Urban Development Corporation (UDC), is based. You will want to start at the bottom and continue far above the main pool to get the full exhilarating experience. To climb the full length of the cataracts requires about two hours, but if you stop to enjoy each little pool it could easily consume all day. Before reaching the dedicated parking area there is a dirt road just before a wooden shack that leads down to the base of the falls.

To get to Reach Falls, head inland by a set of shacks just east of Manchioneel up a picturesque winding road. The turnoff is marked by a large sign for Reach Falls. Unofficial guides made their services mandatory for years when the falls were officially closed as a managed attraction. These guides often congregate at a fork in the road where you turn left to get to the falls. The guides still offer their services on days when the UDC-managed sight

© OLIVER HILL

Climbers take a brief pause before proceeding up Reach Falls.

is closed. The guides are in fact indispensable when it comes to climbing the falls, as they know every rock along the riverbed, which is very slippery in certain places. As always, get a sense of what your guide will expect for the service up front (US$5–10 is reasonable) to avoid the discomfort associated with unmet expectations when you leave. Leonard Welsh ("Sendon") and Byron Shaw (tel. 876/891-1061 or 876/871-3745) are recommended guides on Monday and Tuesday, when the UDC-managed sight is closed; contact Rugy ("Taliban") at the Look In Lookout bar (cell tel. 876/538-6667) to arrange for a guided visit. A few craftsmen have stands along the road selling wood carvings, and Rene is a charismatic local craftsman who makes lung exercisers, which he claims enhance breathing ability and lung capacity.

Two local guides/lifeguards have been employed by the UDC since it opened the attraction officially in early 2007. The UDC's lease on the property extends from a little below the main pool to a little above it, and unofficial guides will be turned away from the main

waterfalls area on either side of the leased land. **Mandingo Cave,** which is found further up the river, is not currently part of the official tour offered but can be reached by going with the local guides.

Arts and Crafts

The **Portland Art Gallery** (9 A.M.–6 P.M. Mon.–Sat.) is located inside the old Railway Station by the Banana Docks on West Street, about a 10 minutes' walk from the Main Square. Hopeton Cargill (cell tel. 876/882-7732 or 876/913-3418), whose work includes landscape paintings, portraits, and commercial signs, is the gallery director.

At the **Jamaica Palace Hotel** (tel. 876/993-7720, 7 A.M.–9 P.M. daily), the late Sigi Fahmi established a large collection of Ken Abendana Spencer paintings for sale. A Portland native, the late Ken Spencer was one of the most prolific artists in the country's history. He captured scenes from Jamaican life with quick, effortless strokes that allowed him to sell his paintings very cheaply and distribute them widely, becoming well recognized. The hotel lobby, while far from inviting, is filled with kitsch art by the late owner. Other artists whose work is represented at the hotel include John Campbell and Ann-Marie Korti. A walk around the hotel is a real trip.

Philip Henry (tel. 876/993-3162, philartambokle@hotmail.com) is a talented artist who has prints, portraits, and sculpture for sale in his small home studio. Call or email to set up an appointment.

Michael Layne (19 Sommers Town Rd., tel. 876/993-3813, cell tel. 876/784-0288, miclayne@cw.jamaica.com) is considered by many the top ceramist in the parish and has exhibited at galleries in Kingston countless times. Layne was born and raised in Portland, studying at Titchfield High School and then going on to Edna Manley College in Kingston to concentrate in ceramics. Today Layne teaches art at Titchfield High School and works out of his home studio (open by appointment), where he creates works that include large bottles, bowls, and vases assembled with clay slabs, decorated with oxides, and single fired.

Marcia Henry (Lot #5, Red Hassell Lane, tel. 876/993-3162) is a talented local artist with a home studio.

Carriacou Gallery (in Hotel Mocking Bird Hill, tel. 876/993-7134, 9 A.M.–5 P.M. daily) features work of co-owner Barbara Walker, in addition to many other local artists.

ENTERTAINMENT AND EVENTS

Port Antonio is not a haven for club-goers by any means, but there are a few good venues that hold regular theme nights throughout the week, as well as occasional live performances. Several times a year, stage shows are set up around the area, Somerset Falls being a favorite venue for concerts and Boston and Long Bay also hosting occasional events. Many of the area's upscale villa owners and visitors prefer to entertain with dinner parties, which can be quite lavish.

Nightclubs
Cristal Night Club (19½ West Palm Ave.,

contact Peter Hall, cell tel. 876/288-7657, cristalniteclub@yahoo.com, open 5 P.M.–close Wed. and Sat.) is Port Antonio's newest club, reopening in March 2009 after years of dormancy. The club features Ladies' Night 11 P.M.–2 A.M. Wednesday with free drinks all night for the ladies, and the Portland Day Rave starting at 5 P.M. on Saturday, morphing into the club sessions that go through the night.

Club La Best (5 West St., contact club manager/owner Chris, cell tel. 876/896-9024) does Ladies' Night on Wednesdays (US$2, ladies free) with a disco, R&B, and reggae mix; after-work jams that stretch into long club hours on Fridays (free) with mostly dancehall music; and Smart Casual Sundays (US$2), with reggae and R&B vintage music. Wednesday is a slower night. Live shows, when they happen, are held on Saturday nights. Club La Best opens at 9:30 P.M. and closes when the last person leaves. The club holds around 800 people, who crowd in for occasional radio DJs and performers. Club La Best opened in April 2006.

Roof Club (11 West St., managed by Shawn "Blue" Rankine, cell tel. 876/449-0852, 10 P.M. until the last person leaves, US$3) is open for Ladies' Night on Thursdays, Crazy Saturdays, and occasional special events on Fridays. It's the longest-standing nightclub in Port Antonio, open for the past 33 years. It generally plays dancehall, reggae, and R&B—in other words the perfect mix for bumping and grinding, or "whining," in local parlance. It's an earthy, at times seedy, place with old wooden floors, a DJ booth on one side, and the bar opposite with neon lights and a disco ball hanging from the ceiling. Don't be surprised if a patron approaches and uses a forward introduction by commanding, "buy mi a drink nuh."

Bars
Marybelle's Pub on the Pier (Errol Flynn Marina, tel. 876/413-9731, bellmar_bell92@yahoo.com, noon–11 P.M. daily) serves drinks and finger food like burgers, pizza, salads, and fruit by the pool. The bar offers customers complimentary Wi-Fi.

⟨ Irie Vibes (Shop #10, West Harbour Plaza, by KFC, run by William Saunders, cell tel. 876/375-4495, noon–close Mon.–Sat., 4:30 P.M.–close Sun. and holidays) bar, pool hall, and gaming lounge is a popular hangout overlooking the West Harbour. Drinks run US$1–5.

Eye Candy (Royal Mall, no phone, noon–11 P.M. weekdays, noon–1 A.M. weekends) has a pool table and dominos.

Festivals and Events

Fi Wi Sinting (contact founder Sister P, cell tel. 876/426-1957, www.fiwisinting.com)

FI WI SINTING

Translated into English as "something for us," Fi Wi Sinting (contact Pauline Petinaud, a.k.a. "Sista P," cell tel. 876/426-1957, www.fiwisinting.com) is an Afro-centric family fun day held on the third Sunday in February, which is Presidents' Day weekend in the United States. The event began in 1991 as a fundraiser for a local school and has grown in popularity each year as more and more Jamaicans and foreign visitors arrive in Portland to celebrate Jamaica's African heritage. African dance and drumming, Mento sessions, Kumina and Jonkunnu performances, crafts, and food are the main draws. The event is a draw for Rastafarians who maintain African heritage as a central pillar of their philosophy and lifestyle, and Rasta dub poet Mutabaruka is a regular selector.

Most Jamaicans find the idea of Black History Month absurd, seeing black history as something people should live with and recall every day, week, and month of the year. Nonetheless, February is chock full of events celebrating the country's African heritage, and Fi Wi Sinting is the largest grassroots event of its kind; here it's evident that the country's heritage and traditions haven't disappeared. The event is held at Somerset Falls and begins at 10 A.M.

© LANCE WATSON

Nyabinghi elder and master drum maker Roy "Ras Carter" Bent keeps the heartbeat with his *bredren* and *sistren*.

is a must-see festival celebrating Jamaica's African heritage. It's held the third Sunday in February.

Portland All Fest (contact Somerset Falls, tel. 876/913-0046, info@somersetfallsjamaica. com, www.somersetfallsjamaica, held mid-March) is a family fun day with food, swimming, and concerts at the open-air venue at the base of Somerset Falls.

Bling Dawg Summer Jam (info@somersetfallsjamaica.com, www.visitjamaica.com, held in July) is one of several annual events held at Somerset Falls. Bling Dawg is a well-recognized promoter who brings together an array of dancehall artists for the event. Contact Somerset Falls for more information.

Portland Jerk Festival (Jerk Festival office, Shop #33, Royal Mall, 2–4 Fort George St., contact the kind and helpful secretary Dahlia Minott, tel. 876/715-6553, or chair person Sybil Rendle, cell tel. 876/389-1601, or vice-chair and regional manager for Jamaica Tourism Board, www.visitjamaica.com) is held on the first Sunday in July and admission tends to be around US$10. Local arts, crafts, and concerts complement every kind of jerk food imaginable. The venue was once in Boston but was relocated to Folly Oval in 2007.

The **International Blue Marlin Tournament** (contact Ron DuQuesnay, chair of the Sir Henry Morgan Angling Association, cell tel. 876/909-8818, rondq@mail.infochan.com, US$170 registration) is held out of the Port Antonio Marina each October. The event draws anglers from far and wide and also runs a concurrent 35-canoe folk fishing tournament for local anglers who fight the billfish with hand-held lines and usually bring in a better catch than the expensive big boats.

One of the highlights of the annual event calendar is the **Flynn Flim Festival** (no, that's not a typo, it's a play on words) (contact the Errol Flynn marina, cell tel. 876/715-6044) held during the third week in June and featuring Errol Flynn movie screenings, a rafting race down the Rio Grande, a Flynn look-alike contest where patrons dress as Errol or one of his ladies in their favorite Flynn movie. Jazz on

the pier in the evenings serves as a continuation of the Ocho Rios Jazz Festival.

SHOPPING

Things Jamaican (Errol Flynn Marina, tel. 876/715-5247, 10 A.M.–8 P.M. daily) is a great little outlet for Jamaican products, arts and crafts, clothing and accessories, aromatherapy, books, and DVDs.

Royal Mall is a surreal building with a mosaic of facades built by the late Sigi Fahmi, who's also responsible for one of the area's most atrocious buildings, the Jamaica Palace Hotel. Its construction evokes an assortment of European styles, with several shops inside, a few of them worth checking out.

Sportsman's Toy Box (Shop #28, tel. 876/715-4542, 9 A.M.–5 P.M. Mon.–Fri.) sells diving and fishing equipment.

Portland Jerk Festival Office offers fax and photocopy services when it is in operation, typically the six months prior to the festival.

Hamilton's Bookstore (24 West St., contact co-owner Avarine Moore, tel. 876/993-9634, 9 A.M.–7 P.M. Mon.–Sat.) has a small but decent selection of Jamaican folk books and cookbooks.

A&G Record Mart (4 Blake St., contact Janet cell tel. 876/488-1593 or 876/427-8766, 10 A.M.–9 P.M. Mon.–Sat.) has a great selection of CDs, DVDs, LP singles and complete albums, 45s, and 33s. Gospel, R&B, dancehall, reggae, soul, soca, and calypso are well represented.

SPORTS AND RECREATION

Carder Park is the community football field across the road from East Harbour that comes alive for several family-fun events throughout the year, like the dominos championship.

Folly Oval is the town's cricket pitch and where the schools practice sports; it extends along the edge of East Harbour. The large field hosts the annual Portland Jerk Festival.

Island Massage Therapy & Yoga (cell tel. 876/818-4771, Portland tel. 876/993-7605, Kingston tel. 876/924-5503, namaste_ja@ hotmail.com, US$90/per hour for massage) is led by Barbara Gingerich, who is both a certified massage therapist and yoga instructor. Barbara holds sessions in a studio at her house and on her large veranda, which has a stunning view of the sea and gardens. You can also have Barbara come to you for an additional charge if you're staying in the area. She works between Kingston and Port Antonio; yoga classes are priced based on group size.

Water Sports

Pellew Island is a private island, given, as the legend has it, by industrial magnate and famed art collector Baron Von Thyssen to supermodel Nina Dyer, one of his many brides, as a wedding gift in 1957. Nina Dyer committed suicide some five years later, and Von Thyssen himself died in 2002. The island is now slated for development of four villas, which are up for sale. While there are no organized tours of the private island, fishermen from the small beach adjacent to Blue Hole can take visitors over for excellent snorkeling along the reefs around the island.

Lady G'Diver (Errol Flynn Marina, contact Steve or Jan Lee Widner, office tel. 876/715-5957, cell tel. 876/995-0246 or 876/452-8241, ladygdiver@cwjamaica.com, www.ladygdiver.com) runs diving excursions from the Marina. Port Antonio's waters are quieter than those off Ocho Rios or Montego Bay and are less over-fished. Wall diving is especially popular. Lady G'Diver offers a wide range of packages and programs, from basic PADI certification to Master courses. The most basic is the two-dive package (US$84 plus US$7 per person for equipment rental).

Barrett Adventures by Lark Cruises (contact Captain Carolyn Barrett, cell tel. 876/382-6384, info@barrettadventures.com, www.barrettadventures.com) operates two cruises out of Port Antonio, a round-trip to Cuba, and a Pirates of the Caribbean cruise to Port Royal (US$1,000 per person per week for 2–6 persons, US$900 for 7–8 persons). Other destinations are also possible to arrange. If the 40-foot *Jeanneau* is in the area, day cruises can be arranged (US$125 per person for 2–6 persons, US$100 per person for 7–10 persons).

Otherwise, day cruises are generally based out of Montego Bay. Provisioning is at the passenger's expense, while the captain and cook are included. Shorter charters for less than a week are also offered (US$150 per person per day).

Bicycling

Pro Bicycles (3 Love Lane, contact Rohan who runs the shop, cell tel. 876/838-2399 or 876/993-2341, 9 A.M.–5:30 P.M. daily) has a few basic, all-terrain, 18-speed bicycles (US$10/day). They're not in the best shape, but you can't beat the price.

Blue Mountain Bicycle Tours (121 Main St., Ocho Rios, tel. 876/974-7075, info@bmtoursja.com, www.bmtoursja.com) runs a popular downhill biking tour that has been somewhat truncated over the past few years due to landslides that blocked the upper reaches of the route. While the operation is based in Ocho Rios, people staying in Portland can link up with the bus in Buff Bay before it leaves the coast to ascend the B1 into the Blue Mountains to where the lazy downhill ride starts.

Horseback Riding

Riding is offered by **Gold Course** Delroy Course (cell tel. 876/383-1588, Winston (brother) cell tel. 876/485-1773), who hangs out by the driveway to Frenchman's Cove across from San San Golf waiting on potential customers. Delroy takes groups of up to four persons on a 1.5-hour trip around to San San Beach, or 4–5 hour trip to Nonesuch Caves, starting at US$20 per person and going up to US$30 for longer trips. A small sign with red letters hangs across from the gate at Frenchman's Cove, marking Delroy's outdoor "office."

Golf and Tennis

The **San San Golf & Country Club** (tel. 876/993-7644) located across the street from Frenchman's Cove, gets very little use nowadays and is officially closed, but people with their own clubs often sneak in to use the driving range or play a few holes—to the chagrin of owner Ernie Smatt.

Goblin Hill (San San, tel. 876/993-7537) allows nonguests to use the hotel's hardtop **tennis courts** (US$15/hour, US$12 for a pair of rackets). Goblin Hill was recently wired with state-of-the art Digicel broadband wireless internet, affording the hotel the most reliable and fast service available in Port Antonio.

ACCOMMODATIONS

Port Antonio has a wide range of accommodation options with a notable concentration of high-end villas. Nonetheless, budget hotels and guesthouses dot the coast from town all the way to Long Bay. As in many parts of Jamaica, there are no street numbers, and roads are often referred to as the "main." Refer to the maps in this book for exact locations.

Under US$100

There are two recommended, well-maintained guesthouses among the general dilapidation on Titchfield Hill. Both are owner-managed.
Ivanhoe's (9 Queen St., tel. 876/993-3043, ivanhoesja@hotmail.com, lornacamburke@hotmail.com, US$30–60) is a classic Jamaican wooden house with a red painted zinc roof surrounded by a white picket fence. In the center of the compound is a small courtyard with vines and flowers all about. The rooms are comfortable and airy, and the better ones have good views over the East Harbour. Rooms with a combination of queen-size and single beds all have TV and private baths with hot water. Breakfast and dinner are available to order.

Ocean Crest (7 Queen St., tel. 876/993-4024, lydia.j@cwjamaica.com) is located next door to Ivanhoe's and owned by Lydia Jones, a friendly and warm woman who takes pride in being attentive to her guests. The building is a more typical concrete construction, with tiled floors in the rooms. Ocean Crest rooms range from basic interior (US$35) to two top-floor balcony rooms (US$50 with fan, US$60 with fan/air-conditioning) with a view over the East Harbour. There is an open kitchen (with stove, refrigerator, pots, and utensils) for use by the guests, and Ms.

Jones can also prepare breakfast on request (US$5). Ocean Crest is near all the useful conveniences such as ATMs, banks, supermarkets, craft market, restaurants, nightclubs, and public transportation. All the rooms have private bathroom, ceiling fan, hot water, and cable TV. There's a living and dining room and an open porch. The living room can be used for small conferences or meetings of up to 20 people.

Shadows (West St., cell tel. 876/828-2285, US$40) is a guesthouse and restaurant/bar in the heart of town owned and managed by the amicable Barrington Hamilton. The five small rooms have double beds, cable TV, air-conditioning, and private baths with hot water.

Drapers San Guest House (Drapers, tel. 876/993-7118, carla-51@cwjamaica.com) sits oceanside toward the easternmost end of Drapers district; it's an excellent budget option. A few rooms have shared baths (US$50, incl. breakfast and GCT) and a few have private baths (US$60). Two newer rooms offer a step up: Rasta Cottage (US$70) is self-contained with a private bath and veranda; the other "high-end" room is in the main building with its own bath and shared veranda (US$60). Drapers San owner Carla Gullotta is an avid reggae fan and can help arrange trips to stage shows and cultural heritage sights and events. She is also a good contact for travelers interested in visiting Culture Yard in Trench Town, Kingston.

Wright's Guest House (Tipperaire Rd., cell tel. 876/838-2399, US$40) managed by Rohan Lawrance (nephew of the Wrights) has five basic double-occupancy rooms with full-size beds, fans, hot water, and TV. To get there head east of Blue Lagoon 1.2 kilometers, and take the next left after Dragon Bay into the development signed Lower Zion Hill Fairy Hill Gardens; go left again, and you'll see two apartment buildings in one lot. Winnifred Beach is 20 minutes away on foot.

Search Me Heart (Drapers, cell tel. 876/453-7779 or 876/452-7177, info@searchmeheart.com, www.searchmeheart.com, US$60 per room, including breakfast) is a comfortable and clean two-bedroom cottage run as a guesthouse by Culture and his wife Roseanna. Amenities include hot water in private bathrooms and standing fans. The cottage is about a 10-15 minute walk to Frenchman's Cove, one of Port Antonio's best beaches. Culture offers tours for guests and nonguests to area attractions.

US$100-250

The Fan (contact Nino Sciuto, tel. 876/993-7259 or cell tel. 876/390-0118, info@villaswithclass.com, nino@villaswithclass.com, www.villaswithclass.com, US$160–180) is a private villa in the hills above Drapers with a breathtaking view of Dolphin Bay, Trident Castle, and Blue Mountain Peak. The villa rents two guest apartments. The grand suite, located on the top level, has a king bed, a large living room, kitchen, and balcony. The junior suite, on the ground level, has a double bed and a couch that can be turned into an extra bed if needed. Meals are prepared to order at an additional cost by the housekeeper, who would expect a tip equivalent to 10 percent of the rental cost for your stay, as is the norm. The Fan's owner, Gloria Palomino, also runs The Gap Café, a small bed-and-breakfast near Hardwar Gap in the Blue Mountains, and offers mountain and seaside packages for guests interested in experiencing both Port Antonio and the Blue Mountains.

Bay View Villas (Anchovy, tel. 876/993-3118, info@bayviewvillas-ja.com, www.bayviewvillas-ja.com, US$90) has 21 rooms in a large building with a variety of room arrangements. The hotel sits above Turtle Crawle Bay just east of Trident Castle. B&B (US$102) as well as all-inclusive (US$126) packages are offered. Rooms are comfortable and airy with TV, air-conditioning, balconies, and private bathrooms with hot water.

San San Tropez (San San, tel. 876/993-7213, info@sansantropez.com, www.sansantropez.com, US$75–250) is an Italian restaurant and five-bedroom accommodation just east of the San San police station. Rooms are comfortable with cable TV, air-conditioning, ceiling fans, and private bathrooms with hot water. There is a swimming pool on the property. Fabio Federico Favalli is the owner and managing director. The restaurant has eastern Jamaica's most authentic Italian cuisine, serving freshly prepared pizza and spaghetti, as well as fish, lobster, and meat dishes (US$10–30).

Fern Hill Club (tel. 876/993-7374 or 876/993-7375, fernhill@cwjamaica.com, www.fernhillclubhotel.com, US$95–182) began as a 31-unit timeshare complex. Owners Carol and Vincent Holgate have been consolidating the rooms over the past decade. There are a handful of villas separate from the main building—some one-bedroom, some two-bedroom—which are a good value, while not by any means state of the art. The property itself covers a hillside and has great views at every elevation level, especially from the open-air dining room and bar area.

Frenchman's Cove (tel. 876/993-7270, fax 876/993-7404, flawrence@cwjamaica.com, www.frenchmans-cove-resort.com, US$95–295, inclusive of tax and continental breakfast) remains one of Jamaica's prime properties, considered by some to have the best beach on the island. The cove itself is small with a short, wide beach and fine white sand. Fifteen villas are scattered about a large property. The three villas in use and the 12 rooms in the main house are not sparkling by any means and could certainly use more attention than they get, but for its proximity to an excellent beach, Frenchman's is still a good accommodation option, especially for a family that is more interested in affordability and convenience than shiny shower rods.

Jerk lunch is cooked every afternoon on the beach, which is open to nonguests as well (9 A.M.–5 P.M. daily, admission US$5). Manager Frank Lawrence has worked on the property since 1959, when he started on the construction work and then worked as a waiter during the height of Port Antonio's glamorous tourism boom. After its opening in 1961, Frenchman's Cove quickly became one of the most exclusive resorts around. Formerly a part of Cold Harbour Estate—which encompassed all of San San, Frenchman's, and Drapers Harbour—Frenchman's Cove is today owned by the Weston family, which runs several international business ventures. Frenchman's Cove Villas have suffered repeated hurricane damage, especially during Gilbert in 1988, but according to Mr. Lawrence, the main house has remained in operation since opening.

Moon San Villa (tel. 876/993-7777, Sansan1999@hotmail.com, www.moonsanvilla.com) is run as a bed-and-breakfast and is the most affordable way to stay next to the Blue Lagoon. The villa has four double-occupancy rooms (US$125–165 low season, US$135–175 high season) that rent individually. While not directly on the water, Moon San overlooks the Blue Lagoon strip of villas that are among the most luxurious in Jamaica. Guests have easy water access, as well as access to the beach at Frenchman's Cove. Breakfasts are communal, with a view out to sea. It's not a place for exclusive privacy, but Moon San makes a good base for excursions and frequent dips in Blue Hole. Owner Greg Naldrett also operates Blue Mountain Bicycle Tours. Complimentary use of the African Star water taxi is included to deliver guests to San San Beach, Blue Hole, and Frenchman's Cove.

C Goblin Hill (tel. 876/993-7537, reservations office tel. 876/925-8108, reservations@goblinhill.com, www.goblinhillvillas.com), farther up the hill in the San San district, is an excellent option for families or couples. The spacious rooms and self-contained duplex suites (US$115–195 low season to US$125–265 high) are a great value, especially for a family. The two-bedroom duplex suites have large master rooms with a second bedroom on the opposite end upstairs, and a living area and kitchen downstairs. The living rooms have sliding doors that open onto a beautiful lawn rolling down and exposing a view of San San Bay, also visible from the master bedroom. Goblin Hill is well situated for all the best attractions on one of Port Antonio's grandest hillsides. While its interiors may be less extravagant than at some of its neighboring villa properties, Port Antonio is much more than art on the walls, and Goblin Hill boasts a large swimming pool, tennis courts, and comfortable digs within easy walking distance of San San Beach and the Blue Lagoon. Guests get complimentary use of the beach at Frenchman's Cove.

Jamaica Palace Hotel (tel. 876/993-7720, pal.hotel@cwjamaica.com, www.jamaicapalace.com, US$170–190), just across Turtle Crawle Bay from Trident, is an enormous concrete compound with giant checkerboard-tiled courtyards, a gallery that defines kitsch in the lobby, a swimming pool in the shape of Jamaica surrounded by hot black surface, and stale bedrooms that are shocking for their total lack of regard for the verdant surroundings outside.

Jamaica Palace was built by the late Sigi Fahmi, a baroness who began building Trident Castle before running out of funds and selling it to the architect Earl Levy. Now run by Sigi's husband Nazar Fahmi, Jamaica Palace was obviously constructed in an attempt to one-up Trident with enormous columns out front that boast of excess. Clearly Fahmi was a dear customer of Carib Cement, as the hotel's construction gave the company plenty of business. Definitely not an ecotourism lodge, rooms at the Palace are cavernous with old air-conditioning units, private baths with hot water, and TV. It's the only place in Jamaica that offers a room with a round bed in the middle. The ceilings are very high; the walls are whitewashed concrete and covered in art. Several large caged birds are on the property, and it's a great place to get a Ken Spencer painting and catch a glimpse of the bold creations of the Baroness herself.

Over US$250

Trident Castle (www.tridentcastle.com) next door to Jamaica Palace, built by Earl Levy, is also available for rent (US$5,500 nightly low season, US$7,500 high season) and sleeps

16–18 people. The castle has a full-time staff of three housekeepers, three waiters, one bartender, one chef, and three gardeners. Many celebrities and nobility have found Trident Castle adequately grandiose for their time in Jamaica.

◖ Hotel Mocking Bird Hill (Drapers, tel. 876/993-7134, 876/993-7267, 876/619-1215, or 876/619-1216, info@hotelmockingbirdhill.com, www.hotelmockingbirdhill.com) has pleasantly decorated garden view (US$195/255 low/high season) and sea view (US$235/295 low/high season) rooms with ceiling fans and mosquito nets. Wireless Internet is available in the lounge, where a computer is set up for guest use. Solar hot-water systems, locally minded purchasing practices, and minimal-waste policies have earned Mocking Bird Hill an ecofriendly reputation. With stunning views of both the Blue Mountains and Portland's coast, it's hard not to love the place. The owners, Barbara Walker and Shireen Aga, keep several large dogs that can often be seen tagging along behind the innkeepers. The hotel is closed every year in September for maintenance. To get to the hotel, take a right immediately after Jamaica Palace and climb for about 200 meters. The entrance will be on your left.

Geejam (San San, tel. 876/993-7000, 876/618-8000, or 876/383-7921, reservations@geejam.com, www.geejam.com, US$595–705 low season, US$2,035–2,125 high season) is a recording artists' paradise where the likes of Les Nubians, No Doubt, India Arie, Amy Winehouse, and Tom Cruise have chosen to take their working vacations. Sitting on a low hill overlooking San San Bay, the property consists of the main house with three bedrooms, three cabins dispersed across the property, and a one-bedroom suite below the recording studio. Inside the huts, more than the basic amenities are covered: TV, Apple home theater systems with DVD, iPod docks, and minibar are included. Wi-Fi covers the entire property. More importantly, the mattresses are comfortable, linens soft and clean, and there's hot water in the showers.

Two cabins and the suite have steam rooms as well. The main house, more of a bona-fide villa, is decorated with contemporary Jamaican art and has a stylish pool out front. The recording studio is located at the lower reaches of the property, a deck with whirlpool tub crowning its roof. The studio has all the latest gear and oversized windows overlooking the water. While the property is specifically designed as the ideal recording retreat for a band-sized group locking down the entire property (US$5,795/6,500 daily low/high season), it is also ideal for couples or other kinds of retreats. The property is located a 10-minute walk from San San Beach, with the Blue Lagoon also a stone's throw away. Rates include a full staff.

Kanopi House (contact Michael Fox, tel. 876/993-8509, cell tel. 876/351-5083, info@kanopihouse.com, www.kanopihouse.com, US$600–1000 all-inclusive) is the latest addition to Port Antonio's high-end market. Four

a bedroom at Kanopi House, an assortment of jungle cottages on the eastern bank of Blue Lagoon

© OLIVER HILL

self-contained wooden cottages stand on stilts along the jungle-covered slope rising from the eastern bank of the Blue Lagoon. For a Medicine Man rush or even a spoiled-Tarzan kind of feel, there's no place like Kanopi, and it's the only accommodation option that actually sits on the lagoon. The most tasteful and simple decor adorns the cottages' exposed wood interiors. The cottages are naturally cool in the shade of the forest, with ceiling fans rather than air-conditioning, and do not have TV. The bathrooms are well laid out, and each cottage has a wide veranda with an outdoor grill. Elaine Williams Galimore is the friendly housekeeper and cook. Kanopi's entrance branches off the driveway to Dragon Bay. When the project is complete, Kanopi is slated to have 14 one- and two-bedroom cottages with king-size beds.

Villas

Port Antonio's villas are definitely some of the nicest in Jamaica, and far less pricey than those in Ocho Rios and Montego Bay. Typically these villas either have breathtaking hilltop views over mountains and out to sea, or are directly on the water, like the famous Blue Lagoon Villas—the most coveted real estate in Jamaica, perfectly placed between San San Bay and the Blue Lagoon. Blue Marlin, Nautilus, San Bar, San Cove, and Bonne Amie are among the crème de la crème. A full staff and all the amenities of home come standard in all these villas; the main difference in prices reflect principally the level of opulence you should expect.

Many of the area's villas book through **Villa Vacation** (2 West St., tel. 876/993-2668, cell tel. 876/778-3241 or 876/420-9376, yvonne. blakey@cwjamaica.com, www.villavacation. net), run by Yvonne Blakey. Yvonne lives in Port Antonio, represents many of the area owners, and can perfectly tailor your interests with a villa to put you in paradise. Most of the villas are also members of the Jamaica Association of Villas and Apartments (JAVA).

◀ **Wilk's Bay** (contact owners Jim & Mary Lowe, tel. 876/993-7400, cell tel. 876/471-9622, reservations@wilksbay.com, www.wilksbay.

© OLIVER HILL

Nautilus is among the premiere waterfront villas in the San San district east of Port Antonio.

com, US$225–450 low season, US$275–600 high season) has one-, two- and three-bedroom villas, each staffed with its own cook/housekeeper. The recently refurbished property, situated on Wilk's Bay between Frenchman's Cove and Alligator Head, is ideal for couples, small groups, or families. Wilk's boasts a white-sand private beach, a dock, and a swimming pool. Bedrooms have air-conditioning, high ceilings, mahogany woodwork, and louvered windows. Last minute bookings can stay on a B&B plan with no minimum time, based on availability. Plans are afoot to add six stand-alone units and a reception area.

Lolivya (tel. 876/993-7400, cell tel. 876/471-9622, reservations@wilksbay.com, US$500–750) is a beautiful four-bedroom villa overlooking Pelew Island, Alligator Head, and San San's most prized stretch of oceanfront. The villa is owned by Jim and Mary Lowe, thus the name Lo-liv-ya.

Ocean Shell (contact Desmond Gouldbourne, tel. 876/993-2144, cell tel.

876/878-4816, desmondgouldbourne@yahoo.com, US$500/550 low/high season) shares a corner of Wilk's Bay with the Lowes' property. The four-bedroom villa has king-size beds in three rooms and two twins in the fourth. There's a private swimming pool, all rooms have air-conditioning, and there's cable TV in all four bedrooms and the living room. The villa is staffed with a cook, housekeeper, butler, and gardener.

Nautilus (contact owner Xavier Chin, cell tel. 876/383-2446, reservations@nautilusvillas.com, xavierchin@hotmail.com, www.nautilusvilla.com, US$800/night, or US$5,000 weekly) is a beautiful three-bedroom villa with a large deck extending over the water between Pellew Island and Blue Hole. Perfect for small families or a group of three couples, the villa boasts a modern gas grill, a three-person staff, kayaks, and a comfortable living room upstairs with broadband Internet access, a stereo system with speakers inside and out, and cable TV.

(San Bar (tel. 876/929-2378 or 876/926-0931, dianas@cwjamaica.com or bookings@windjammerjamaica.com, www.sanbarjamaica.com, US$10,500/12,000 weekly low/high season) is a six-bedroom villa sleeping a maximum of eight adults and six children, ideally situated among the Blue Lagoon Villas with a clear view of Pellew Island and Alligator Head. Easily one of the best villas around, San Bar boasts an oversized hot tub on the deck, impeccable furnishings, and more balconies than you'll want to count. Cable TV, broadband Internet, iPod docks and a stereo keep guests well plugged in.

San Cove (www.sancovejamaica.com, US$7,000/8,000 weekly low/high season) is a sister property to San Bar that also books directly through the Stewart family, which owns the properties. San Cove can be annexed with San Bar to expand the accommodation capacity for larger groups who want to remain close. The highlight of this four-bedroom, three-story luxury villa is its exceptionally large deck with grill and picturesque gazebo, fit for relaxing in the shade or enjoying a fine meal at the water's edge. Amenities are the same as at San Bar.

Gremlin Hill (contact owner Gaia Budhai, tel. 305/534-9807, gaiamylove@yahoo.com, www.gremlinhill.com, US$2,500/3,400 weekly low/high season, two-night minimum stay) has a great vantage point over Pellew Island. The artfully decorated villa has accommodations for eight. Master Chef Linette Bernard's reputation precedes her. The villa is a popular venue for intimate yoga and other retreats. Bookings can be made either through the owner or locally through Yvonne Blakey's Villa Vacation.

(Norse Hill (www.norsevillas.com, US$3,500/4,000 weekly low/high season) was built by Iris and Reidar Johanssen as their winter home. The Johanssens lived amazing lives, jumping across the globe before their time in Hong Kong during the 1930s. The Norwegian-style chalet is accordingly grand and filled with art and antiques from China. Norse Hill is a steadfast, gorgeous, stately structure, with an industrial-size kitchen, three bedrooms, and a loving and dedicated staff. The master bedroom and the slightly less opulent room on the other end of the chateau both have large tiled bathrooms and oversized mirrors. Verandas look out over the pool and gardens and, beyond that, the wide-open sea. All the amenities are there, including DSL. The property itself is arguably the best endowed in Port Antonio. Hectares of botanical gardens sit on top of a hill looking over San San Bay. An enormous ficus tree shades the best seat in town, a real contender against Henry Morgan's Lookout, which later became Noel Coward's Firefly. The gardens have extensive pathways through lush flowerbeds.

Norse Point (US$1,400/1,750 low/high season weekly) is the only one-bedroom villa in Port Antonio. The little-sister property to Norse Hill, this quaint cottage lies directly across a short stretch of water from Pellew Island, between San San Beach and Blue Hole.

Alligator Head (contact manager, David Lee, tel. 876/993-7453, or cell tel. 876/298-5675, david@alligatorhead.net, www.alligatorhead.net, US$2,500 daily for up to eight) rents two villas, one three-bedroom and one four-bedroom, sleeping six and eight respectively, with some 17 staff attending to the peninsular estate, two beaches, several pools, two jet skis, and Wi-Fi across the property included.

Villas with Class (info@villaswithclass.com, www.villaswithclass.com), run by Nino Sciuto, offers booking services for many of the area's villas and runs a community-oriented site featuring the attractions and services.

Chateau En Exotica (contact Henri and Joyce Verne, tel. 561/793-7257 or 561-793-7257, exotica@webtv.net, www.jamaicadreamvillas.com, US$645/745 low/high nightly for up to six) is a spectacular four-bedroom villa perched atop a hill in the San San district. Amenities include a Jacuzzi, pool, and stunning views.

FOOD
Continental and Jamaican

First and Last Bar & Restaurant serves up authentic Jamaican dishes including curry goat, oxtail, brown stew fish, chicken, pork, tripe and bean, ackee and saltfish, mackerel, rundown, and callaloo. Howard "Howie" Cover (cell tel. 876/367-7700) owns the bar, and Clement Chambers (cell tel. 876/450-5143) runs the restaurant, with his wife Anna doing the cooking.

Green Palm Restaurant & Bar (19½ West Palm Ave., tel. 876/715-4482, 8 A.M.–5 P.M. Mon.–Sat.) serves Jamaican staples during the week and seafood dishes like fish, conch, and lobster (US$10–20) for Seafood Fridays (4 P.M.–midnight).

Chenel's Pizza (28-A West St., tel. 876/440-0968, 9 A.M.–11 P.M. Mon.–Sat., US$2–30) is run by Michael "Mikey" Badarie (cell tel. 876/364-5833), who serves fresh natural juices, hot dogs, burgers, sandwiches, and of course pizza—by the slice or whole 10" and 16" pies with 15 different toppings available.

Yellow Canary (1 Harbour St., contact Crissie, cell tel. 876/404-8161,

8 A.M.–5 P.M. daily, US$2–4.50), also known as Bramwell's Restaurant, serves typical Jamaican fare for breakfast and lunch: ackee and saltfish, liver, corned beef, stew peas, cow foot, curry goat, stewed pork, brown stew fish, and fried chicken.

Nix Nax Centre (16 Harbour St., across from Texaco, tel. 876/993-2081 or cell tel. 876/329-4414, 8 A.M.– 7 P.M. Mon.–Thurs., 8 A.M.–8 P.M. Fri.–Sat., 2–8 P.M. Sun., US$3–5) serves Jamaican favorites like fried chicken, curry goat, and stewed pork. Ackee with saltfish and stewed chicken are served for breakfast daily.

Wonderful Palace Fast Food (9 Harbour St., tel. 876/993-2169, 9 A.M.–9 P.M. Mon.–Sat., 3–9 P.M. Sun., US$3–8) has decent Chinese and Jamaican staples.

Dixon's Corner Store (12 Bridge St., tel. 876/993-3840, 8:30 A.M.–6:30 P.M. Mon.–Fri.) is an Ital restaurant serving excellent vegetarian dishes (US$3) like veggie chunks, veggie steak, fried whole-wheat dumplings, steamed cabbage, and saltfish. Delicious fresh juices (US$1) like sorrel and ginger are also served. Mr. and Mrs. Dixon run the place.

Anna Banana Restaurant (7 Folly Rd., tel. 876/715-6533 or contact manager Daniela Trowers, cell tel. 876/483-3672, 11 A.M.–11 P.M. daily) serves seafood and meat items. Fish costs about US$12/pound, with the pepper shrimp (highly recommended) at US$16/pound. There's a happy hour 6–7 P.M. on Fridays, offering a 25 percent discount on all drinks and a selector playing music to keep patrons entertained till closing.

Survival Beach Restaurant (Allan Ave., Oliver Weir cell tel. 876/384-4730, son Everton cell tel. 876/442-5181) is an Ital shack on the beachfront marked by a yellow picket fence on East Harbour. Vegetarian food, jelly coconut, and Ital juices are served at reasonable prices (US$5–10).

Golden Happiness (2 West, tel. 876/993-2329, 10:30 A.M.–10 P.M. Mon.–Sat., 2–9 P.M. Sun.) is the best Chinese food in town, but the place lacks ambience and is best for takeout. The food is good value (US$4–7).

Cynthia's (Winnifred Beach, tel. 876/347-7085 or 876/562-4860, 9 A.M.–6 P.M. daily), run by Cynthia Miller, serves the best fish, lobster, and chicken accompanied by vegetables, rice and peas, roast breadfruit, and festival at the best value (US$7–15). Painter, Cynthia's business partner and chef, can be found out back in the kitchen.

Woody's Low Bridge Place (Drapers, tel. 876/993-7888, 10 A.M.–10 P.M. daily), run by Charles "Woody" Cousins and his charismatic wife Cherry, is definitively the coolest snack bar and restaurant in Port Antonio; it serves what is quite possibly the best burger (US$2.50) in Jamaica. Woody's Low Bridge Place opened in 1986 but Woody has been in the tourism business since 1963.

Sir P's Cook Shop (cell tel. 876/787-5514) serves up local dishes like jerk chicken, roast fish and bammy, conch, and natural juices. Peanut porridge and pastries are served in the morning.

Soldier's Camp (83 Red Hassell Rd., tel. 876/715-2083 or cell tel. 876/351-4821, 6 P.M.– you say when), better known as Soldji's, draws a healthy cross-section of locals on Wednesday and especially Friday nights for deliciously seasoned *janga,* or crayfish, as well as jerk chicken, pork, and curry goat. Special order can be arranged on any other night. The bar is open daily 10 A.M.–9 P.M. Everold "Soldji" Daley, a former soldier with the U.S. Army, opened the joint in 2003 after returning to Jamaica in 1998 from the United States.

Devon House I Scream (Errol Flynn Marina, tel. 876/993-3825) serves the best ice cream for kilometers around, but avoid the tubs that have thawed and refrozen.

Caribbean Fusion and International

Dickie's Banana (Bryan's Bay, about 1.5 km west of town center, cell tel. 876/809-6276, reservations required, hours based on demand, US$25 per person) is also known as "Best Kept Secret" since it was the winner of the *Jamaica Observer's* Best Kept Secret award in 2002. It has wonderful food at a great value and even

better service. Five courses are served up based on Dickie's creative culinary magic, with no ordering necessary. Just let him know if there's something you'd prefer or something you don't eat and he'll take care of the rest. For the main course there's a choice of fish, chicken, goat, lobster, or vegetarian. Dickie Alvin Butler is assisted by his wife Marjorie Edwards (cell tel. 876/869-4391) and their son Dennis (cell tel. 876/809-6276).

Rusalka Restaurant & Bar (upstairs at the Errol Flynn Marina, cell tel. 876/715-5756 or 876/298-8773, 11 A.M.–11 P.M. daily) specializes in Central Asian and Russian cuisine; the menu changes every few weeks but the most popular dishes are served consistently. Appetizers include grilled feta cheese and beetroot salad served with warm crostinis (US$5), rice pilaf with chicken and raisins (US$15), stroganoff served with olive oil mash and buttered vegetables (US$15), and pelmeni, pork and beef minced and wrapped in dough and served in a clear chicken broth accompanied by olive bread, sour cream and salad, or mayonnaise and grated cheese (US$20). Rusalka also serves veggie dishes like seasonal vegetable stir-fry (US$10). Jamaican classics on offer include steamed yellow snapper in a butter sauce served with parsley white rice (US$15–25), chicken curry served with seasonal steamed mixed vegetables, rice and peas (US$9.50), and jerk chicken supreme (US$11). Live entertainment on Fridays and Saturdays features local groups from Portland and musicians from Kingston and Montego Bay.

Norma's at the Marina (tel. 876/993-9510, www.normasatthemarina.com, 10 A.M.– 10 P.M. Tues.–Sun., US$10–27) is the latest of Norma Shirley's reputable establishments. This is Port Antonio's only bona fide high-end restaurant, serving dishes like lamb, steak, lobster, pork chops, shrimp, chicken, and pan-seared fish. The food at Norma's is dependably good, smoked marlin being the famous specialty appetizer.

Mille Fleurs (at Hotel Mockingbird Hill, tel. 876/993-7134, 876/993-7267,

876/619-1215, or 876/619-1216, entrées run US$25–40) is open daily for breakfast (8–10:30 A.M.), lunch (noon–2:30 P.M.), and dinner (7–9:30 P.M.). Mille Fleur changes its menu on a daily basis, serving creative dishes that emphasize the use of local, fresh ingredients, like jerk meat with papaya salsa or a pimento-roasted steak with rum-honey glaze served alongside grilled banana or pineapple. Reservations strongly recommended. Local jack fruit is also infused into salads and pesto dishes served with cassava flour pasta. One of the best restaurants around, Mille Fleurs features creative dishes fusing elements of Asian, European, and Jamaican cuisine.

Groceries
Chucky's Wholesale (21-A West St., tel. 876/715-4769, 7:30 A.M.–8 P.M. Mon.–Sat.) has groceries.

Ramtulla's Supercenter (Folly Rd., tel. 876/715-5132) is the most modern supermarket in Port Antonio, with the largest selection of groceries.

For groceries, you can also head to **Kamlyn's Supermarket and Cambio** (19 Harbour St., tel. 876/993-2140; 12 West St., tel. 876/993-4292; cambio 8:30 A.M.–5 P.M. Mon.–Thurs., 8:30 A.M.–6 P.M. Fri., 8:30 A.M.–5 P.M. Sat., closed Sun.; supermarket 8:30 A.M.–7 P.M. Mon.–Thurs., 8:30 A.M.–8:30 P.M. Fri., 8:30 A.M.–9 P.M. Sat.).

Kamal's (12 West St., tel. 876/993-4292, 8:30 A.M.–8 P.M. Mon.–Sat., 9 A.M.–4 P.M. Sun.) is a grocery and cambio owned by Mr. Sinclair, who also owns Kamlyn's.

CC Bakery is at 1 West Palm Avenue (tel. 876/993-2528).

INFORMATION AND SERVICES
Portland Parish Library (1 Fort George St., tel. 876/993-2793) offers free Internet access on a set of computers in the junior library and at the computer lab in the adult section.

Don J's Computer Centre (Shop #10, Royal Mall, tel. 876/715-5559, 9 A.M.–7 P.M. Mon.–Sat.) has Internet access (US$1/hr).

Faxing and VoIP calling services are also offered.

Banks, Laundry, and Shipping
Scotiabank is located at 3 Harbour Street (tel. 876/993-2523).

Firstcaribbean has a branch on Harbour Street (tel. 876/993-2708).

Ever-Brite Cleaners and Laundromat (17 West Palm, tel. 876/993-4071, 9 A.M.–8 P.M. daily.) can take care of your dirty clothes for US$5 per load.

For shipping services, **DHL** operates through local agent **Port Antonio Company** (City Centre Plaza, tel. 876/993-9401 or 876/993-3617, 9 A.M.–5 P.M. Mon.–Sat.).

Police and Medical Emergencies
Port Antonio Police is located at 10 Harbor Street (tel. 876/993-2546), whereas **San San Police** is at the base of San San Hill (tel. 876/993-7315).

Police advice in Port Antonio includes all the typical warnings: Don't sleep with the door wide open, watch your belongings on the beach, don't use drugs in public, and be wary of thieving prostitutes. Petty theft incidents are reported regularly, but on the whole Port Antonio is relatively crime-free compared to other areas of the island. Constable Brown and Superintendent Bowen are in charge at the Port Antonio constabulary.

Port Antonio Hospital (Naylor's Hill, tel. 876/993-2426) is run by doctors Terry Hall and Jeremy Knight, who have a very good reputation.

Eric Hudecek at **Modern Dentistry** (9 West Harbour St., tel. 876/715-5896, cell tel. 876/860-3860 or 876/371-2068, info@modern-dentistry.de) is a highly regarded dentist with a smart, well-equipped office overlooking Navy Island. He is sought out by patients from across Jamaica and abroad.

Dr. Lynvale Bloomfield (32 Harbour St., tel. 876/993-2338) has a private practice in town and also owns **City Plaza Pharmacy** (City Center Plaza, Harbour St., tel. 876/993-2620).

GETTING THERE

Port Antonio is served by route taxis from Buff Bay (US$1.50) from the west and Boston (US$1.50) and Morant Bay (US$4.50) from the east. Minibuses leave twice daily for these areas from Market Square. Taxis gather in Market Square and in front of the Texaco station on Harbour Street. Most guesthouses and hotels arrange transportation from Kingston or Montego Bay airports, Kingston being the closer international airport at about 2.5 hours away.

Driving from Kingston, the shortest route (B1) passes over Hardwar Gap in the Blue Mountains before descending to the coast in Buff Bay. From Buff Bay, head east along the coast until you reach Port Antonio. The road over Hardwar Gap is regularly blocked by landslides and is at times impassible for years on end. This route takes about two hours.

The alternate route from Kingston (A3) passes over Stony Hill and then through Castleton, St. Mary, and Junction before hitting the coast around Annotto Bay. When the road through the Blue Mountains is blocked, this is the quickest route between Kingston and Port Antonio, taking about 2.5 hours.

A third route (A4), every bit as scenic, follows the coast east of Kingston along the southern flanks of the Blue Mountains through Morant Bay, turning west at Hector's River. This route takes 2–3 hours on decent roads.

The Ken Jones Aerodrome, 10 minutes west of Port Antonio, receives flights from Kingston, Oracabessa, Montego Bay, and Negril with charter operators International Airlink (tel. 876/940-6660, res@intlairlink.com, www.intlairlink.com) and Jamaica Air Shuttle.

GETTING AROUND

The town of Port Antonio is compact enough to get around comfortably on foot. For any of the attractions east, west, and south of town, however, it is necessary to jump in a route taxi or hire a private charter. If you're feeling energetic, traveling along the coast between town and Winnifred Beach or even Boston by bicycle

is very feasible. Route taxis congregate by the Texaco station on Harbour Street for points east, and in Market Square for points west and south. It's easy to flag down route taxis along the main road. Expect to pay around US$1.50 for a ride a few kilometers down the coast as far as Boston.

Richard Dixon (cell tel. 876/312-4743) is a dependable taxi man for charters, as are Indian (cell tel. 876/866-6920); William Reid, a.k.a. Busout (cell tel. 876/849-0867); and Aldwyne (cell tel. 876/358-8086).

Fisher Tours (cell tel. 876/852-0177) can give you a lift around for reasonable rates. Driver Andre Thomson will take you from Kingston airport to Port Antonio for US$120, or on excursions to places like Reach Falls from Port Antonio for US$20/person. Andre's van has a capacity of eight.

Eastern Rent-A-Car (16 West St., manager Kevin Sudeall tel. 876/993-4364 or cell tel. 876/850-2449, eastcar@cwjamaica.com, www.lugan.com/east.html) has a Toyota Yaris (US$85/day) or Corolla (US$75), Honda Accord (US$120), Toyota RAV4 (US$120), and Mitsubishi Gallant (US$120), Lancer (US$90), or Space Wagon (US$120). Longerterm rentals will be discounted.

◖ UPPER RIO GRANDE VALLEY

Nestled between the Blue Mountains and the John Crow Mountains are the culturally rich communities of the Upper Rio Grande Valley. These include the farming communities of Millbank and Bowden Pen and the Maroon community of Moore Town. Trails, including Cunha Cunha Pass, lead into the lush rain forest of the park and provide an opportunity to see the endangered Giant Swallowtail, the largest butterfly in the Western Hemisphere. The best way to get to know this area is by contacting the Maroon Council to learn from the people who have staked out this land as their own for centuries.

Rio Grande Rafting (tel. 876/993-5778, 9 A.M.–4 P.M. daily, US$72/raft) is a much-

© OLIVER HILL

The Upper Rio Grande Valley is home to the Winward Maroons, the Giant Swallowtail Butterfly, and most of the island's endemic birds.

touted attraction controlled by the Tourism Product Development Corporation, operating along the banks of the wide and gentle Rio Grande River. Eighty-three raft captains compete fiercely for clients, who enjoy the sedate relaxation of a 2.5-hour ride down the river on long bamboo rafts. To reach the start of the ride, take Breastworks Road from Port Antonio, keep right on Wayne Road in Breastworks past Fellowship, and keep right following the signs to Berridale. The raft ride ends in St. Margaret's Bay by the mouth of the river at Rafter's Rest. Transporation is not included in the cost of rafting. For Moore Town, take a left over the bridge at Fellowship Crossing.

MOORE TOWN

The stronghold of Jamaica's Windward Maroons, led by Colonel Wallace Sterling since 1995, Moore Town is a quiet community located along the banks of the Rio Grande, about an hour's drive south of Port Antonio. Prior to the election of Colonel

Sterling, the Moore Town Maroons were led by Colonel C. L. G. Harris (from 1964), and before him, it was Colonel Ernest Downer (from 1952).

Colonel Wallace Sterling can organize B&B-style homestays (cell tel. 876/898-5714, US$30/person) in the community, as well as hikes to Nanny Town farther up into the mountains. It's a two- to three-day hike round-trip that will cost US$100 per person for guides, food, and shelter. If you don't bring your own tent, guides will use materials from the bush to make shelter at night. Along the way you're likely to pick up a few basic Maroon words like *medysie* (thank you). If you are unable to reach Colonel Sterling, Moore Town Maroon Council Secretary Charmaine Shackleford (cell tel. 876/867-6939) can also help arrange homestay visits and guides.

The Maroons have maintained their customs throughout the years, as well as their language, a mix of West African tongues brought by captured slaves who belonged to the Ahanti,

Fanti, Akan, Ibo, Yoruba, and Congo peoples, among others.

Sights

Bump Grave (admission by donation) is the final resting place of Nanny, the legendary Maroon leader and Jamaica's first national heroine. It's the principal attraction in Moore Town; a plaque and monument recall her glorious leadership and victory over British forces that tried unsuccessfully to conquer the Maroons. Bump Grave is fenced off, but the gate can be opened by the caretaker of the school located across the road. Call to alert the Colonel (cell tel. 876/898-5714) or Maroon Council Secretary Charmaine Shackleford (cell tel. 876/867-6939) of your arrival to ensure someone is around to open the gate.

Nanny Falls is a small waterfall within an easy hour's walk from Moore Town. Ask any local to indicate where the trail starts, just above Nanny's grave. There is also an alternate, longer route, about three hours round-trip, if you're looking for more of a workout. The Colonel can help arrange a guide (US$10).

The **Moore Town Maroon Cultural Center** is at time of writing still in the conceptual stages, but there is adequate momentum from the Maroon Council and the Institute of Jamaica to guarantee that the project will develop over the coming years. The concept is to establish a museum and cultural center for the exhibition and preservation of Maroon heritage. Young people will be taught to make and play drums and the *abeng,* a traditional Maroon horn used to communicate over great distances. The *abeng* is said to have struck fear into the hearts of the British, who were never able to conquer the Maroons. Craft items, toys, and a whole range of items considered the basis of the Maroon culture are also to be produced, and the center will have an adjoining gift shop and restaurant to accommodate visitors. "We are looking at a living thing rather than strictly an exhibition of the past," Colonel Sterling said about the project. The

Maroon Council is currently working with UNESCO and the IOJ in developing the plans and securing funding.

Accommodations

Ambassabeth Cabins (Bowden Pen, Lennette Wilks, cell tel. 876/395-5351 or 876/381-1528, US$50 per cabin, sleeps 2–4; US$25 for a tent that can sleep eight) is the most remote accommodation option in the Rio Grande Valley, located above Millbank at the uppermost reaches. The famous Cunha Cunha Pass Trail leaves from there, as does the White River Trail, leading to a series of cascades. There is an unmanned ranger station maintained by Ms. Wilks in Millbank, just over the border into St. Thomas two miles before reaching Bowden Pen. The Quack River and White River Falls are both nearby. Ms. Wilks can arrange trail guides and meals, as well as cultural entertainment. There are a total of eight cabins, which can house up to 20 people in all. Cabins have beds with sheets and blankets; towels and bug dope should be brought along. One cabin has a private bath with shower; the others share common facilities. There's also an indoor dining and recreation area. Cabins come with breakfast, rundung (a coconut sauce) with fish or vegetables.

Millbank is 17 miles up the river valley from Port Antonio; as an alternative to the route from the Rio Grande Valley, there is a well-established 5.5-mile trail from Hayfield, St. Thomas. Trained guides at Ambassabeth are knowledgeable in biodiversity and local cultural history. The Cunha Cunha Pass Trail connects Portland and St. Thomas over the Blue Mountains, where a lookout point at Cunha Cunha gives spectacular views.

Getting There and Around

Barrett Adventures (contact Carolyn Barrett, cell tel. 876/382-6384, info@barrettadventures. com, www.barrettadventures.com) offers transportation to and from the Blue and John Crow Mountains, as well as a hiking expedition from the Portland side or from Kingston.

East of Port Antonio

The region east of Port Antonio is dominated by the John Crow Mountains, which run northwest to southeast and butt up against the Blue Mountains, where they meet with steep slopes falling down to the sea near Hector's River. The John Crow Mountains are some of the less-traversed territory on the island, and even the coast in the area, which varies from fine sandy beaches to windswept bluffs, sees few visitors. A few minutes' drive east of Port Antonio, Boston is a quiet community that is said to be the original home of jerk. Long Bay is the area's predominant tourist strip, though it only has a handful of budget accommodations serving a trickle of backpackers and adventurous travelers.

BOSTON

Boston was bustling in the early years of the banana trade, when it took the name of the North American city that made it prosperous for a brief period. Boston is the alleged origin of jerk seasoning, but the **Boston Jerk Center** that claims this fame has become overrun with hustlers unmindful of the fact that their harassment has damaged the area's reputation. The jerk center is easily recognizable on the western edge of the community of Boston Bay just before crossing a bridge and going over a rise in the road heading toward Port Antonio. Max (cell tel. 876/435-3013) operates one of the newer stalls and may just be a good bet where integrity is concerned. Many vendors will insist you buy their "noni juice," said to have aphrodisiacal properties and to improve overall performance; others will simply beg for money. Beyond the annoyance, there are also serious inconsistencies in the quality and pricing of food at Boston Jerk Center. Weekends,

Boston Bay has a quiet, thin strip of sandy beach and crystal clear turquoise waters. Waves big enough for surfing come in frequently enough to support a small crew of die-hards who congregate around the surf shack.

© OLIVER HILL

PORT ANTONIO

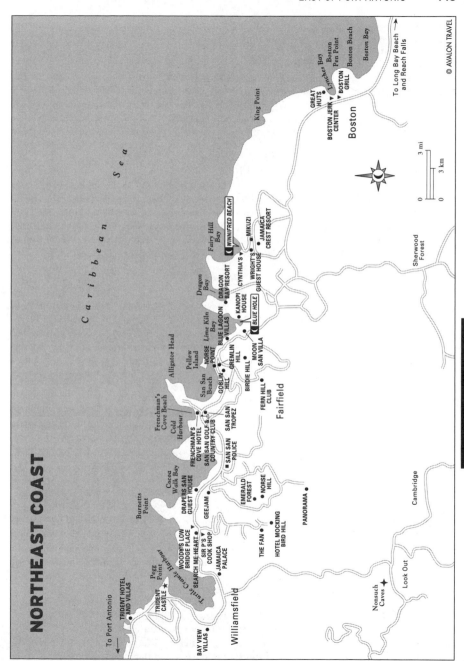

NORTHEAST COAST

To Port Antonio

TRIDENT HOTEL AND VILLAS

Pegg Point

TRIDENT CASTLE ★

BAY VIEW VILLAS

Turtle Crawle Harbour

Cocoa Walk Bay

Burnetts Point

WOODY'S LOW BRIDGE PLACE

SIR P'S ▼ COOK SHOP
SEARCH ME HEART

JAMAICA PALACE

Williamsfield

DRAPERS SAN GUEST HOUSE

GEEJAM

THE FAN

HOTEL MOCKING BIRD HILL

EMERALD FOREST

NORSE HILL

PANORAMA

Frenchman's Cove Beach

Cold Harbour

FRENCHMAN'S COVE HOTEL

SAN SAN GOLF & COUNTRY CLUB

SAN SAN POLICE

Alligator Head

Pellew Island

San San Beach

GOBLIN HILL

SAN SAN TROPEZ

BIRDIE HILL

FERN HILL CLUB

Fairfield

NORSE POINT

GREMLIN HILL

MOON SAN VILLA

Lime Kiln Bay

BLUE LAGOON VILLAS

Dragon Bay

DRAGON BAY RESORT

KANOPI HOUSE

BLUE HOLE

CYNTHIA'S

WRIGHT'S GUEST HOUSE

Fairy Hill Bay

WINNIFRED BEACH

MIKUZI

JAMAICA CREST RESORT

Sherwood Forest

Cambridge

Look Out

Nonsuch Caves ✦

King Point

Caribbean   Sea

GREAT HUTS

BOSTON JERK CENTER

BOSTON GRILL

Boston

Boston Pen Point

Lynches Bay

Boston Beach

Boston Bay

To Long Bay Beach and Reach Falls

0   3 mi
0   3 km

© AVALON TRAVEL

PORT ANTONIO

when it gets busier, are the best time to take a stab if you must eat where jerk is said to have originated, as during the week the meat can sit on the grill until it goes cold before someone comes along to eat it. Fish is also served, but this is not the best place for it. If you do order fish, size it and understand what you will pay before it gets cooked. The best time to eat jerk is during the annual Portland Jerk Festival (July) when the multitudes don't let the meat sit around for long before eating it up. Based in Boston in years past, the festival relocated recently to Port Antonio's Folly Oval.

Boston Beach (free) is on a picturesque cove with turquoise waters that sees more local than foreign visitors, especially on weekends. Boston Bay can have a decent swell suitable for surfing and is the only place around where you can rent boogie-boards and surfboards.

Accommodations and Food

Great Huts (overlooking the water near the Jerk Center, cell tel. 876/353-3388 or 876/993-8888, drpaulshalom@yahoo.com, www.greathuts.com, US$60–400) is a stylishly rustic accommodation in the heart of Boston, offering Bedouin-style tents and tree houses with meals served to order. The place was developed by Paul Rhodes, an American doctor who has practiced extensively in Jamaica. Charles Town Maroons led by Frank Lumsden are known to make an appearance on select Friday evenings for drumming sessions.

Boston Jerk Grill (cell tel. 876/878-5015 or 876/993-8093, garnetk13@hotmail.com, open 10 A.M.–late Mon.–Sat., restaurant closed on Sun.) may be a better option than the neighboring Jerk Center. It's also a good place for local dishes, with friendly management under Garnet King. King can arrange catering as well. Fried chicken, brown stew pork (US$5), and grilled lobster (US$10) represent the range of items on the menu. The bar is open daily.

LONG BAY

Long Bay is a sleepy fishing village with one of the most picturesque and unspoiled beaches in Jamaica. A few low-key accommodation spots

have sprung up over the past decade, serving a trickle of off-the-beaten-track travelers. Long Bay's beach is also known for having a decent swell on occasion and draws surfers from nearby Boston Bay, as well as the diehard Mystic crew from Jamnesia in Bull Bay, St. Andrew. At times the current can be quite strong; precaution is always advised.

One of the most curious attractions, if it can be called that, in Long Bay is the home of the late Ken Abendana Spencer, one of Jamaica's most prolific and noted painters of the 20th century. The building, located on Pen Lane a few hundred meters inland from Fisherman's Park, resembles a science fiction scene from *Batman* or *Mad Max,* with a 10-meter-high wall—built to keep out thieves, according to Spencer's common-law wife, Charming (cell tel. 876/412-4116). Charming resides in the first floor of the immense structure built in the vein of a castle but never completed. Charming's two sons, Ken Abendana Spencer Jr. ("Jr.," cell tel. 876/448-7374) and Kensington Spencer ("Hopie," cell tel. 876/429-7380) also live on the property and receive guests, who can tour the surreal building and purchase Spencer paintings by both father and son Jr., also an artist who works in his father's style.

Accommodations

Blue Heaven Resort (cell tel. 876/420-5970, info@blueheavenjamaica.com, www.blueheavenjamaica.com) has two very basic cottages for a total of three rooms on a private cove just west of Long Bay Beach. The two adjoining rooms rent for US$45 per night, while the stand-alone "Sunrise Cottage," which sits closest to the water's edge, goes for US$80 (all are double occupancy). A kitchen and bathroom adjoin the rooms. Owner/manager Natasha Duncan includes hot breakfast in the nightly rate, and longer stays are open to some price negotiation.

Seadream Villa (contact manager David Escoe, tel. 876/890-7661, vwaterhous@aol.com, www.jamaican-escape.com, US$80–200) offers basic accommodations right in the middle of Long Bay Beach. The villa has three bedrooms—two downstairs with two double and two single beds, and one upstairs with two single beds—accommodating up to eight total. Three full baths have hot water. There's cable TV and a CD player. The library with Internet access is less than five minutes away by foot.

Likkle Paradise (tel. 876/913-7702, US$40), marked by a small sign across the road from Blazer on the Bay, is owned by Ms. Herlette and run by her family members. Two rooms are available for rent, one with a queen-size bed, kitchen, TV, and adjoining bath, the other a double with a separate bath dedicated for guest use.

Morgan's Glass House Guest House (across from the Texaco gas station on the beach, contact Letecia Cunningham, a.k.a. Mama Lue, cell tel. 876/891-0516, US$40–50) is a basic guest house with two rooms downstairs, each with two twin beds and a shared bath and a big kitchen and living room, and three rooms upstairs, two with one double bed each, and one with two twin beds. There is a kitchen upstairs with living room and shared bath. The bigger rooms go for the higher rate.

Food

The **Glass House Restaurant** (10 A.M.– 10 P.M. Mon.–Sat.), owned by Morgan's Glass House Guest House and managed by Mama Lue, is located next door and marked with a sign that reads **Sweet Daddy.** It's the best place for typical Jamaican dishes at local rates (US$3–5).

Chill Out Beach Bar & Restaurant (tel. 876/913-7171, contact Maria cell tel. 876/508-1521, 10 A.M.–10 P.M. daily, US$5–30) is a popular spot on Long Bay Beach for a bite or a drink. Chill Out hosts dances on special occasions. Local dishes and excellent seafood are served.

Blazer on the Bay Restaurant & Bar (located where Yahimba used to be, contact Paula, cell tel. 876/421-0646 or 876/407-4416, 8 A.M.–10 P.M. daily, US$5–30) serves Jamaican staples like fried and curried chicken, pizza,

© OLIVER HILL

Chill Out Beach Bar & Restaurant on the eastern end of Long Bay is the best spot around for a drink or a meal.

and shrimp, conch, fish, and lobster. It is located toward the eastern end of Long Bay Beach, just west of Chill Out Beach Bar.

Fisherman's Park (corner of Pen Lane and the main road, contact manager Wayne, cell tel. 876/350-4815, 7 A.M.–9 P.M. daily, US$3–8.50) is an open-air bar and restaurant on the west side of town that serves fish when available, in addition to Jamaican staples.

MANCHIONEEL

Portland's most quintessentially authentic seaside village, Manchioneel sees few visitors; a small anglers' beach known as Sandshore, at the east end of the community, is the main attraction.

Accommodations and Food

Hotel Jamaican Colors (Ross Craig district, cell tel. 876/893-5185 or 876/407-4412, hoteljamaicancolors@hotmail.com, www.hoteljamaicancolors.com, US$70) is run by a nice French couple, Martine and Robert Bourseguin, who live on property with their son Romain. Rooms are basic but comfortable in five bungalows and a larger cottage, with private baths and hot water, fans, and TV. Air-conditioning is available in a few rooms.

A nice pool and hot tub are located in front of the dining area. Bungalows sleep three (US$100) or four (US$125), and the larger cottage sleeps six (US$135).

Zion Country (Muirton Pen, just east of Manchioneel, contact Free-I, cell tel. 876/451-1737 or 876/871-3623, info@zioncountry.com, www.zioncountry.com, US$55 including breakfast) has four basic rooms that share a sea-view balcony, with standing fans. Each room has two single beds with shared bathrooms. To get there keep straight at the sharp bend in the main road following the signs on the eastern end of Manchioneel.

Uncle Lenny's (Castle, tel. 876/913-1680, 8:30 A.M.–9 P.M. Mon.–Fri., US$2.50–3) serves tasty local dishes like stewed beef, stewed peas, and fried chicken.

Getting There and Around

Route taxis are the most affordable way to get between Port Antonio and points east along the coast. Route taxis depart Port Antonio from the square and can always be stopped along the road provided they aren't overflowing with passengers. Otherwise, for day trips to Reach Falls, which is a few kilometers off the main road, it's best to hire a driver.

Morant Bay

St. Thomas parish holds an important place in Jamaican history. In the early colonial period, its mountainous terrain played an important role in providing sanctuary to the runaway slaves who formed the Maroon settlements of eastern Jamaica. Later, it became an important sugar- and banana-producing region under British rule. And finally, with the slaves freed but not being permitted advancement in society, the parish erupted in a rebellion that gave birth to Jamaica's labor rights movement.

At the center of what was once some of Jamaica's prime sugarcane land, Morant Bay is a laid-back town with little action beyond the central market. Between Morant Bay and

Port Morant, 11 kilometers to the east, there are a couple of basic accommodation options that make a convenient base for exploring the rivers and valleys that cut across the southern slopes of the Blue Mountains, as well as the isolated beaches and Great Morass on Jamaica's easternmost tip.

SIGHTS

The burning **Morant Bay Courthouse** played a central role in spurring the Morant Bay Rebellion of 1865, in which disenfranchised poor led by Paul Bogle revolted against the local government and the white planters, sending tremors through the British Empire. A **statue of Paul Bogle** created by Jamaican art pioneer Edna Manley, wife of Peoples National Party founder Norman Manley, stands in front of the courthouse. The building was in use until early 2007 as the St. Thomas Parish Council offices before it was, once again, gutted by fire. A historic marker by the statue honors the many patriots buried behind the building, "whose sacrifice paved the way for the independence of Jamaica."

The **Morant Bay Market** on the main road has an excellent stock of produce and a fish market in the back that rivals that of Downtown Kingston. It is a great place to stop for a stroll around to take in a bustling market.

Lorna's Crafts (cell tel. 876/396-9337) has some nice Jamaican crafts, jewelry, and Rastafarian motif goods in the Old Arcade.

East Fest (Goodyear Oval, Springfield, St. Thomas) is held annually on Boxing Day (December 24). The event is organized and hosted by the cultural reggae group Morgan Heritage (www.morganheritagemusic.com).

PRACTICALITIES

Dave's Place (cell tel. 876/461-3103) just past Scotia serves good chicken.

Scotiabank is located at 23 Queen Street (tel. 876/982-2310), and **NCB** is at 39 Queen Street (tel. 876/982-2225).

The Morant Bay **police station** (7 South St., guard office tel. 876/982-2233, crime office tel. 876/734-7111) is located just off the main road through town.

EAST OF MORANT BAY

In **Stony Gut,** eight kilometers north of Morant Bay, a marker placed by the JNHT indicates Paul Bogle's birthplace and the place where his Revival Baptist church once stood. To get there, head inland at the center of town to Morant, where a right turn leads to the nondescript hamlet of Stony Gut.

Heading straight in Morant leads to Seaforth, a small community along the Morant River. North of the main intersection you soon come to a bridge across the river where the road forks. A right leads farther up the river to **Sunny Hill,** an important

Rastafarian center in St. Thomas where occasional Groundations are held. It is said one of the first Rasta communes was formed in Trinity Ville, near Sunny Hill, as early as 1934. For info on upcoming Rasta-related events, contact St. Thomas native Karl Wilson (cell tel. 876/439-1471). Alternatively, for Rasta events island-wide, including those at Sunny Hill, contact Paul Reid, known as Iyatolah (cell tel. 876/850-3469) or Charlena McKenzie, known as Daughter Dunan (cell tel. 876/843-3227) at Jamaica's Nyabinghi headquarters in Scott's Pass, Clarendon.

Reggae Falls, located near Seaforth, is a popular spot for locals to come splash around by an old dam on the Morant River and jump off the large rocks along the river. There is a hut nearby where drinks and food are served.

A left across the bridge at the intersection in Seaforth leads to Mt. Lebanus, a picturesque district with fruit trees growing along the river, which has lots of pools suitable for swimming.

Port Morant

Overgrown and noticeably forgotten today, Port Morant was at one time busy exporting barrels of sugar, rum, and bananas. Today there is an oyster operation on the eastern side of the harbor bordering the mangroves that reaches down to Bowden across the bay. The oyster-growing zone is protected from fishing and serves as a spawning area as well. Several fishermen keep their boats on the waterfront and can be contracted to tour the mangroves and visit the lighthouse on Point Morant. Karl Wilson (cell tel. 876/439-1471), a director of the St. Thomas Environmental Protection Agency, has been working with fishermen and other local groups to encourage sustainable use of the vast mangrove reserve, one of Jamaica's last untouched marine wilderness areas. Karl can arrange marine and mountain tours to the best sights in the area.

The **Morant Point Lighthouse** sits on Jamaica's easternmost point. Cast of iron in London, the 30-meter-tall lighthouse was erected in 1841 by Kru people, indentured

PAUL BOGLE AND THE MORANT BAY REBELLION

Paul Bogle was the founding deacon at the Native Baptist Church in Stony Gut, St. Thomas, a village at the base of the Blue Mountains about eight kilometers inland from Morant Bay. Bogle founded a church where African elements similar to those found in Revival were strong and a black pride ethos was a central doctrine. Baptist churches throughout Jamaica provided an alternate philosophy to the Anglican church, which had descended from the Church of England and for the most part represented the suppressive mandate of the white planter class and government. Bogle used the church as a base to gather support for a militant resistance movement, similar to that envisioned by Sam Sharpe in the Christmas rebellion 34 years earlier in that violence was not the intended means.

Bogle lived in the post-emancipation period, during which the vast majority of his fellow men were denied suffrage, justice, and equal rights, while he, a mulatto landowner, was one of 106 persons in the parish allowed a vote. The five years leading up to the Morant Bay Rebellion coincided with the American Civil War (1861-1865), which complicated the economy of Jamaica. Local food shortages owing to floods and drought, combined with a slump in imports from the fragmented United States, created a mood in Jamaica rife with discontent. While the white ruling class controlled both the legislature and the economy, the poor

felt subjugated and left to fend for themselves in difficult times. Petty crimes rooted in widespread poverty and social decay were severely punished by local authorities responding to the landowners.

Governor Edward Eyre blamed the condition of the poor on laziness and apathy, while Baptist Missionary Society secretary Edward Underhill sent a letter to the British Secretary of State for the Colonies outlining concerns about poverty and distress among the poor black population. The so-called Underhill Letter spurred a series of civic meetings known as the Underhill Meetings, which provided a public forum for the poor to voice their discontent. Mulatto legislator George William Gordon, Bogle's comrade both in the church and in politics, led several such well-attended meetings in Kingston and elsewhere, in which he criticized the colonial government.

On October 7, 1865, Bogle and some followers staged a protest at the Morant Bay courthouse, disputing severe judgments made on that particular day. When a standoff with the police came to blows, arrest warrants were issued against 28 of the protesters, including Paul Bogle. After the police were deterred from arresting Bogle by a large crowd of his followers in Stony Gut, they returned to Morant Bay and told the chief magistrate (*custos rotulorum*) of Bogle's plans to disrupt a meeting of the Ves-

Africans brought to Jamaica in the post-emancipation period. There is a beautiful, desolate beach along Holland Bay just north of Morant Point. To get there, head east from the village of Golden Grove through the Duckenfield Sugar Plantation. Four-wheel-drive is essential in the rainy season, but otherwise it is possible to get through without it.

Stokes Hall Great House, located in the parish of St. Thomas near Golden Grove, was built by Luke Stokes. A former governor of the island of Nevis, he came to Jamaica shortly after the conquest of the island by the British. Like many of the early houses it was built in a strategic location and was securely fortified.

Stokes Hall Great House was destroyed by the 1907 earthquake and today stands in ruin. The house is currently owned by the Jamaica National Heritage Trust but not managed by anyone.

◖ Bath Hot Springs

The town of Bath was erected using government resources and had a brief glamorous history as a fashionable second-home community for the island's elite. The splendor was short-lived, however, and the town quickly declined to become a backwater—as it remains today.

Bath Mineral Spring or "The Bath of St.

try on October 11. The *custos* sent an appeal to the governor for assistance and called out the local volunteer militia. The next day Bogle and 400 followers confronted the militia in Morant Bay; during the ensuing violence, the courthouse was burned and the *custos* was killed, along with 18 deputies and militiamen. Seven of Bogle's men were also killed in the fighting, which quickly spread throughout the parish. Several white planters were killed, kidnapped, or hurt, and, as the news spread throughout the island, fear of a more generalized uprising and race war grew, prompting Governor Eyre to declare martial law and dispatch soldiers from Kingston and Newcastle. The Windward Maroons were also armed after offering their services, and it was they who ultimately captured Bogle, bringing him to a swift trial and death sentence in Morant Bay. George William Gordon was also implicated in the Rebellion, taken to Morant Bay, and hanged. Martial law lasted for over a month following the rebellion, during which time hundreds were killed by soldiers or executed by court martial, while over 1,000 houses were burned by government forces. Little regard was taken for differentiating innocent from guilty, augmenting a general sense of fear in St. Thomas and around the island.

The Morant Bay Rebellion pushed Britain to discuss the blatant injustices in its colony asset in the West Indies. Governor Eyre was ultimately removed from his post for excessive use of force while English Parliament debated whether he was a murderer or hero. Many sought to indict him on murder charges for the execution of George William Gordon, but others, including the Anglican clergy, supported his actions as a necessary means to uphold the control of the Crown.

Meanwhile, the Jamaica House of Assembly, which had operated as an independent legislative body since 1655, was dissolved and Jamaica became a Crown Colony under the direct rule of England. In the following years, the colonial power ushered in more egalitarian measures that lessened the power that had been exerted by the landed elite for centuries.

Paul Bogle and George William Gordon were considered troublemakers and virtually expelled from the national psyche through the remainder of the colonial period. At independence their memory was rekindled as Jamaica began to come to terms with its past and contemplate its identity and future. At the 100th anniversary of the Morant Bay Rebellion, Bogle and Gordon were featured prominently and were declared national heroes in 1969, when the order was created. Today the rebellion is remembered during National Heritage Week and Heroes Weekend, which coincides with the anniversary of the uprising, the second week in October.

PORT ANTONIO

Thomas the Apostle" as it is properly called, was discovered by the runaway slave Jacob in 1695 on the estate of his master, Colonel Stanton. Jacob found that the warm waters of the spring healed leg ulcers that had plagued him for years; he braved possible punishment to return to the plantation to relate his discovery to Stanton. In 1699 the spring and surrounding land was sold to the government for £400. In 1731 the government allocated £500 to develop the bath and a road to the spring, and a small town was built.

The hot springs are located 50 meters north of the **Bath Hotel and Spa,** itself located about three kilometers on a precariously narrow, winding road north of the town of Bath. An easy-to-follow path leads to the source, where water comes out from the rocks piping hot on one side and cold on the other. There are massage therapists on hand who use wet towels to give an exhilarating treatment, albeit exorbitantly priced (typically around US$14). These masseurs are either lauded or despised by visitors and can be quite aggressive in offering their services from below the gate of the hotel. Some visitors swear by their technique, however, which involves slopping hot towels over the backs of their subjects.

The Bath Hotel and Spa has traditional Turkish-style tiled tubs, as well as more modern whirlpool tubs. There are three rates for a dip, depending on how many are enjoying the tub: US$6 for one person, US$8.50 for two, or US$11 for three. The water at Bath is mineral-heavy. It is suggested that bathers stay in the water for 15–20 minutes to derive full benefit.

Basic rooms in the hotel have either private bath or shared bath (tel. 876/703-4345, US$50 private bath, US$33 shared bath). Meals (US$8.50–10) are served throughout the day and range from rotisserie chicken to curried shrimp.

Bath Botanical Garden

Bath Botanical Garden was established by the government in 1779 and is the second-oldest garden of its kind in the Western Hemisphere (one in St. Vincent dates from 1765). The garden retains little of its former glory as a propagation site for many of Jamaica's most important introduced plants, including jackfruit, breadfruit, cinnamon, bougainvillea, and croton. A stand of royal palms lines the road by its entrance, and a two-century-old Barringtonia graces the derelict grounds.

From the western side of Bath, a road runs north to Hayfield, where a well-maintained 8.8-kilometer trail provides an alternate route over the John Crow to the Rio Grande Valley. If you're heading to Portland, head east along the Plantain Garden River to where the main road east of Bath hits the A4 a few miles west of Amity Hall.

Accommodations

Whispering Bamboo Cove Resort (105 Crystal Dr. Retreat, just east of Morant Bay, tel. 876/982-2912 or 876/982-1788, whispering@cwjamaica.com, US$75/80 mountain view/ocean view) is a decent accommodations option with 15 rooms run by Marcia Bennet. Rooms have TV, private bathrooms with hot water, and air-conditioning, except two mountain-view rooms with fans only (US$60). DSL is available in the lobby, and a restaurant prepares food to order.

Brown's Guesthouse (tel. 876/982-6205, US$35–40) is a basic rest with nine rooms with

cable, air-conditioning, hot water, and either double or queen-size beds owned by Neason Brown. Some rooms have kitchenettes, or food can be prepared to order. To get there, follow the main road toward Prospect and look for a sign just east of Whispering Bamboo on the ocean side of the road.

WEST OF MORANT BAY

The road west of Morant Bay toward Kingston hugs the coast, passing through dusty communities where jerk vendors and a few shops mark the centers of the action. This is an area most people just pass through. There are a few notable stops, however, but few accommodation options (beyond a few quickie joints) before reaching Bull Bay in St. Andrew.

White Horses

Just east of White Horses you arrive at **Rozelle Falls,** where locals often congregate to wash or cool off. The falls are visible from the main road (A4).

The **Ethiopian Zion Coptic Church** (service on Sat.) has its headquarters at Crighton Hall in White Horses just before reaching Yallahs, where it sits on more than 600 hectares of land. To get there, turn inland off the main road (A4) by a set of fruit vendors in the middle of White Horses. Coptic Road is on the left, marked with a sign. Said to be 20 million strong, the Ethiopian Zion Coptic Church in Jamaica is led by Everton Shand, chief elder, and spiritual leader Brother Shine. Niah Keith and Brother Love were the founders of the original Coptic Church in Jamaica, while the institution originates in Ethiopia, where it was the official Imperial church for ages from ancient Egypt. A large tablet that dates from 1738 written in Old English was found during excavations and is on display. Many of Jamaica's roots reggae artists have attended the Ethiopian Zion Coptic Church. The White Horses Kumina Group, Upliftment, hosts cultural and sports events in the community on a regular basis.

Yallahs

Sixteen kilometers west of Morant Bay, large

salt ponds can be seen along the coast marking the approach to Yallahs. These ponds were once used as a source for salt and are home to brine shrimp and yellow butterflies. The name Yallahs is derived from the surname of a Spanish family that settled there to raise cattle on a ranch known as **Hato de Ayala.** The road inland from the center of Yallahs leads up along the river to Bethel Gap and from there deeper into the mountains, ultimately reaching Hagley Gap on a poor road traversable only by four-wheel-drive vehicles. Eleven kilometers north of Yallahs across the river from Easington is Judgment Cliff, which collapsed during the earthquake of 1692—burying an entire valley, it is said, in judgment of the Dutchman who maltreated slaves on his plantation. In any case, judgment was not justice, and most of his slaves died alongside him under the weight of a small mountain.

About 1.5 kilometers west of Yallahs, the broad, washed-out **Yallahs River** overflows during periods of heavy rain and dries completely for much of the year near its mouth due to dry, pebbly soil along its bed. At 37 kilometers from its source to the sea, it's one of Jamaica's longest rivers, starting 1,371 meters up and running down the principal trough along the base of the southern slopes of the Blue Mountains. Along the way, it is fed by several tributaries. Bridges built across the Yallahs have a tendency to disappear during hurricanes and are replaced routinely. For most of the year the riverbed near its mouth can be forded with no sign of water. The Yallahs River feeds the Mona Reservoir next to UWI via an aboveground pipe. Along with the Hope River, it is a major water source for the metropolitan area. There are decent beaches around Yallahs: Bailey's Beach to the east and Flemarie Beach just west of town.

Links Seafood Restaurant & Lounge (cell tel. 876/703-3927, 10 A.M.–10 P.M. Mon.–Sat.) on Fleming Beach is a nice chill-out spot to get some grub on the waterfront.

West of Yallahs just shy of the St. Andrew border, Eleven Mile is a small community known as the old stomping ground of legendary Jack Mansong, a.k.a. "Three-Finger Jack." A runaway slave, Three-Finger Jack became a bandit who took justice into his own hands in the vein of a Jamaican Robin Hood. He wreaked terror on the plantocracy and tried to kill a slave trader before ultimately being captured by Maroon leader Quashie, who carried his head to Spanish Town to collect the £300 reward.

Sun Coast Adventure Park

Located about 15 minutes east of the Harbour View Roundabout in 12 Mile, Sun Coast Adventure Park (sales office cell tel. 876/485-0015, park manager James Worton tel. 876/564-6999 or 876/995-9450, info@suncoastadventurepark.com, www.suncoastadventurepark.com, 9 A.M.–5:30 P.M. Sun., admission US$8) offers paintball (US$30 per person, US$40 with upgrade and US$8 for an additional 100 paintballs), nature trails, a ropes course, and the Anansi Maze. Bookings can be made during the week for groups of 10 or more with a deposit.

Getting There and Around

Points between Kingston and Morant Bay along the coast are served by JUTC buses departing from the Transport Centre in Half Way Tree for around US$1. For points farther east or around the coast, a private driver or route taxis are necessary. Taxis and small buses depart from the square in Morant Bay for Bath and Manchioneel as they fill up, costing less than US$5.

PORT ANTONIO

West of Port Antonio

The road west of Port Antonio runs along the coast, cutting inland occasionally through several small towns including St. Margaret's Bay, Hope Bay, and Buff Bay before reaching the border with St. Mary just east of Annotto Bay. The region is characteristically lush with fruit vendors and roadside shops intermittently along the road. Apart from Somerset Falls on the eastern edge of Hope Bay, the area is void of developed tourist attractions, but the sparsely populated coastline is in itself enticing; for the adventurous looking for secluded beaches, there are great opportunities for exploring around Orange Bay.

From Buff Bay, the B1 heads inland, climbing past Charles Town into the Blue Mountains and affording great views. This is the route on which Blue Mountain Bicycle Tours operates.

ST. MARGARET'S BAY

The quiet seaside village of St. Margaret's Bay is notable principally as the end point for the rafts coming down the Rio Grande. There are a few accommodation options and a notable craft shop, **Jah Tobs Crafts** (tel. 876/913-3242) making Rasta-style knits and other craft items including tams, belts, swimsuits, bags, chains, calabash purses, and much more.

Accommodations and Food

◖ **Rio Vista Resort Villas** (on the eastern banks of the Rio Grande, tel. 876/993-5444, fax 876/993-5445, riovistavillaja@jamweb. net, www.riovistajamaica.com, US$75–250) has two-bedroom cottages, a one-bedroom honeymoon cottage with a spectacular view up the Rio Grande (US$155), and four single rooms between the main house and two suites. The one-bedroom cottage is suitable for a couple, the two-bedroom cottages can sleep up to four, and the three-bedroom villa sleeps up to six on two king-size and two full-size beds. To get there, turn right up the hill

just around the corner after crossing the Rio Grande heading east. The "room with a view" is perhaps the nicest cottage, with a private balcony overlooking the river—the view can be appreciated from the inviting king-size bed. The property is run by Sharon, her son Chris and his wife Cyndi, who live on-property.

Paradise Inn (tel. 876/993-5169, paradiseinn295@hotmail.com, US$35–60) is a dive located along the main road (A4) with nine rooms lacking charm, each with one or two double beds. Rooms have cable TV, ceiling fans, and hot water come standard. Four rooms have kitchenettes.

Rafter's Rest (tel. 876/993-5778) is where the bamboo rafts pull in at the end of the 2.5-hour journey down the Rio Grande. There is a restaurant serving Jamaican staples (US$5–15) and a bar overlooking the river. The river is fit for swimming, and there is a beach where the river meets the sea.

HOPE BAY

Sights

Somerset Falls (about 3 km east of Hope Bay, tel. 876/913-0046, info@somersetfallsjamaica.com, www.somersetfallsjamaica.com, 9 A.M.–5 P.M. daily, US$12 adults, US$6 children, free under age 9) is a great place to stop for a dip. The falls are reached by rowboat through cavernous cliffs surrounding a narrow inlet. A bar and restaurant serves beer, rum, fruit juice, jerk chicken and pork, fish, lobster, shrimp, burgers, hot dogs, and fries (US$7–25). A games area has billiards, table tennis, and foosball, with water volleyball in the pool. Occasionally, large events are staged at the venue section next door. The park has a number of caged birds and some deer, recaptured after they escaped in a hurricane years ago.

Likkle Porti, located across the street by the mouth of the Danny River, is owned by the same management as Somerset, with a seafood grill serving roast, steamed, and fried fish, accompanied by bammy and festival in the style of Little Ochie, a South Coast favorite. There's bathing access to the river and sea, with rafting and boat rides offered.

Pauline Petinaud, a.k.a. "Sista P" (cell tel. 876/426-1957), recently moved her African-Jamaican **crafts shop** and guest house from Port Antonio to Hope Bay, where she rents two basic rooms with common kitchen and bath for budget-minded travelers (US$30). Sista P, not to be confused with PNP politician Portia Simpson-Miller of the same pet name, is an important figure behind the movement to celebrate the African heritage inherent in Jamaican culture. Her craft shop sells African-inspired Jamaican items as well as a variety of African imports. She is best known for her founding role in the annual African-heritage festival, Fi Wi Sinting, which translates as "something for us."

J&J Natural Food Restaurant (contact Juba, cell tel. 876/851-8927) in the heart of Hope Bay on the seaside facing the road, serves Jamaican staples.

I-tal Village (cell tel. 876/898-5323, info@italvillage.com, www.italvillage.com, US$30/40 low/high season) is a mellow, simplistic, Rasta-inspired living retreat about three kilometers off the main road near Orange Bay. The retreat is near 6.5 kilometers of volcanic beaches that see virtually no outside visitors. Ital (natural) food is served to order.

BUFF BAY

Buff Bay is a dusty coastal town along the route between Port Antonio and points west. There is little to keep visitors in the area and few accommodation options. In the hills a few minutes inland along the B1, Charles Town is a Maroon community where a cultural heritage tour with the local Maroon Colonel Frank Lumsden makes a detour away from the coast—worthwhile for a few hours' visit.

The most impressive structures in Buff Bay are the **courthouse** and the **St. George**

© OLIVER HILL

PORT ANTONIO

St. George Anglican Church is one of the most impressive structures in the seaside town of Buff Bay.

Anglican Church located across the street. St. George was the official church for the parish of St. George before it became part of Portland in 1867. The present cut-stone structure dates from 1814, but the foundation is much older. Both the church and the courthouse, which is still in use, can be accessed during business hours, and service is held on Sundays.

CHARLES TOWN

Some five kilometers above Buff Bay along what used to be an old Maroon Bridle path up the Buff Bay River (now known as the B1) is the Maroon community of Charles Town.

The **Maroon Museum** (free admission) located at **Asafu Yard** has artifacts and crafts of Maroon heritage. There's an adjoining commercial kitchen producing Jamaican cassava cakes, a gluten-free staple starch dating to the Taino and known locally as bammy.

Charles Town Maroon Colonel Frank Lumsden (cell tel. 876/445-2861) leads visitors on community tours and hikes (US$20/person) to Sambo Hill, the ruins of an 18th-century coffee plantation, Grandy Hole Cave, or Old Crawford Town, an old Maroon Village where Quao settled his people after the first Maroon War in 1739. The Colonel has a group of drummers who perform Koromanti drumming and dance.

A traditional country-style lunch (US$12/person) can be arranged at **Quao's Village** a bit farther upstream, where Frank's brother Keith Lumsden (cell tel. 876/440-2200) manages a swimming hole and rustic restaurant attraction. The spot is named after Maroon warrior Captain Quao (The Invisible Hunter), who, alongside Jamaica's first national hero, Nanny of the Maroons, fought off the British to assert his people's autonomy from the colonists.

A local chef treats visitors to traditional dishes like crayfish rundown (not to be missed) and saltfish rundown accompanied by boiled green banana and ground provisions (yam, coco, dasheen, pumpkin). There is an area where you can pitch a tent to overnight in Charles Town.

Practicalities

Blueberry Hill Guest House (Kildare district, near the Digicel phone tower, contact Devon or Doris Williams, cell tel. 876/913-6814, US$25–35) has seven rooms with private baths and standing fans. Some rooms have TV with a few channels. Some rooms have a nice view overlooking the sea; otherwise, the common veranda is suitable for enjoying the breeze.

B&G Jerk Centre (contact owner Glen Ford, cell tel. 876/859-5107) on the east side of town is the best spot for a roadside bite of jerk pork or chicken (US$4/quarter pound).

Hibiscus Restaurant (adjacent to courthouse, cell tel. 876/466-0946, 9 A.M.–11 P.M. Mon.–Sat., 5–11 P.M. Sun., US$2–3) serves Jamaican staples like fried chicken, curry goat, and stewed peas.

Buff Bay police station (9 First Ave., tel. 876/996-1497) is located opposite the Adventist Church.

Getting There and Around

Points between Port Antonio and Annotto Bay can be reached via route taxi or microbus for under US$5. Route taxis typically run between the closest population centers, and you will have to string together several legs for longer distances. Most route taxis also offer charter service, where rates are not regulated and have to be negotiated. A chartered car between Port Antonio and Hope Bay shouldn't cost more than US$20, with a chartered trip from Port Antonio to Buff Bay or Charles Town costing around US$50 for a couple of people.

OCHO RIOS AND THE CENTRAL NORTH COAST

St. Ann is full of rivers and gardens, thus its well-deserved nickname, "the garden parish." Locals will pronounce Ocho Rios as any incarnation from oh-cho ree-os to oh-cho ryhas or, most commonly, simply "Ochi." Ochi is the biggest town in St. Ann; its name is a creative derivation of the Spanish name for the area, Las Chorreras (Cascades), in reference to the abundance of waterfalls. Before the Spanish conquest, the area was known as Maguana by the Tainos. There are indeed several rivers in the vicinity, but not necessarily eight as the name suggests. Four major waterways flow through the town area of Ocho Rios: Turtle River, Milford River, Russell Hall River, and Dairy Spring River. Just east of town are Salt River and White River, forming the border with St. Mary, and to the west is the famous Dunn's River.

Tourism became important in Ocho Rios in the late 1970s, taking over for bauxite as the area's chief earner. The old Reynolds Pier just west of town is now used to export limestone aggregates, sharing a small bay with the town's cruise ship terminal. The cruise ship industry has been a key component of the city's tourism boom, bringing mixed results. The steady income is appreciated by many businesses, especially those concentrated around the terminal, but the enormous volume of passengers flowing through each day creates a huge demand for services that has not been met with adequate housing for the thousands who have arrived to work in the tourism sector over the past few decades. Many of these arrivals are professionals who have been given little choice but

HIGHLIGHTS

◖ **Coyaba Gardens and Mahoe Falls:** The best-maintained waterfalls and garden combo in Ocho Rios handsomely exemplifies St. Ann's motto of "The Garden Parish" (page 164).

◖ **Wassi Art:** Jamaica's most commercially successful ceramics studio uses local terra cotta and imported white clay to create exceptional works (page 164).

◖ **Bob Marley Mausoleum:** Seeing the humble roots of Jamaica's greatest prodigal son goes miles towards cultivating *overstanding* (page 198).

◖ **James Bond Beach:** Jutting out from the mainland near Goldeneye, this beach park holds popular events, and visitors can swim at Stingray City (page 203).

◖ **Firefly:** Noel Coward's "room with a view" is easily one of the best in Jamaica, if not the Caribbean (page 205).

◖ **Green Castle Estate:** There is no better way to immerse yourself in Jamaica's languid country life than with the orchid tour and high tea in Robin's Bay (page 210).

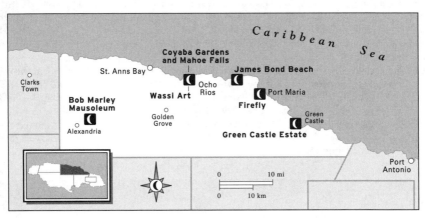

LOOK FOR ◖ TO FIND RECOMMENDED SIGHTS, ACTIVITIES, DINING, AND LODGING.

OCHO RIOS

to resort to living in squatter settlements. Still others come to Ochi with few credentials and earn their living hustling any way they can, making harassment of tourists a widespread problem.

Just west of Ocho Rios is St. Ann's Bay, on the outskirts of which the first Spanish capital was established at Sevilla la Nueva (New Seville). Today Seville is an archeological site and Great House complex where several heritage events are held throughout the year. Farther west along the coast are the communities of Runaway Bay and Discovery

Bay. Runaway Bay is a small town with a golf course, a few resorts, and a small commercial strip along the highway, whereas Discovery Bay is likely Jamaica's most exclusive villa enclave—where rentals go for upwards of US$10,000 per week.

Neighboring St. Mary has in recent years gained the reputation of Jamaica's best-kept secret, a place where hustlers are few and far between and the vast majority carry on with their lives oblivious to the tourism trade. The parish has a beautiful rocky coastline punctuated with beaches of all kinds, with forested hills dropping down rapidly to the sea in places like Oracabessa and the wilderness area between Robin's Bay and Port Maria. Boscobel, 15 minutes east of Ochi, has a small aerodrome with somewhat regular flights. The town is a bedroom community for many workers in Ochi and, as a result of overflow, has developed to the point where several destination resorts and villas line the coast between Ochi and Oracabessa. Oracabessa has become known as an artists' community and produces some of Jamaica's unique crafts (items you won't find at the markets in Ocho Rios or Kingston). Farther east past Galina Point is Port Maria, a sleepy fishing and market town whose days of glory are long gone. Nonetheless it's worth a stop to stroll around a picturesque port town far removed from the country's mainstay tourism economy. St. Mary lacks a tourism hub, which is perhaps central to its charm. Instead, its principal town of Port Maria caters to the parish's predominantly rural population with a few banks and markets. Still farther east is Robin's Bay, an off-the-beaten-track destination populated by fisherfolk and a strong Rastafarian community. The port town of Annotto Bay is quieter yet but still an active transportation hub. The St. Mary interior is some of the prettiest countryside in Jamaica, with areas like Islington covered in rolling hills with spectacular views of the coastline. West of Annotto Bay, the main road splits, continuing eastward toward Portland along the coast (A4) and heading south toward Kingston via Junction and Castleton (A3).

PLANNING YOUR TIME

Unless your goal is to simply loaf on the beach, or you happen to be staying in a destination resort or villa that's too comfortable to leave, Ocho Rios is not a place to spend more than a few days if you're trying to see other parts of the island in a short period of time. It's the most practical base, however, for a number of key attractions, including Dunn's River Falls, Dolphin Cove, Nine Mile, Walkerswood,

Seville Great House, White River Valley, Prospect Plantation, and the Rio Nuevo battle site. Oracabessa is only a half hour away, and there are a couple of good farm tours in that vicinity, in addition to James Bond Beach and Stingray City, which are popular attractions themselves.

Most of these sights are serviced by organized tours that generally consume the better part of a day. If you're driving yourself or have chartered a taxi, however, there's far more flexibility to fit in a string of activities in a day, and there's no reason you can't spend the morning horseback riding at Seville Heritage park and then stop by Dunn's River to cool off and climb the falls on the way back to Ochi. Most developed attractions have factored transportation into their formula, and while they certainly profit by it, it's often worth letting someone else do the driving given the potholed roads and the lack of clear signage. Car rentals in Jamaica are typically very expensive, as is fuel.

Several annual events make a stay in Ocho Rios all the more worthwhile. During Easter, Jamaica's carnival season is in full force with events east and west of Ocho Rios along the coast.

HISTORY

St. Ann figures strongly in Jamaica's early colonial history. Italian explorer Christopher Columbus landed on the shore near Discovery Bay in 1492 while under contract from the Spanish Crown to find a shorter passage to the Far East. Within a few years, the Spanish began to inhabit the island as they systematically wiped out the native Taino population, establishing their capital at Sevilla la Nueva, or New Seville, just west of St. Ann's Bay. Later, after the British seized the island in a carefully executed attack on Santiago de la Vega, or what's now known as Spanish Town, most of the Spaniards who were determined to stay in Jamaica fled to the North Coast, where they regrouped and continued to carry out guerrilla reprisal attacks on the British with the help of Maroon loyalists.

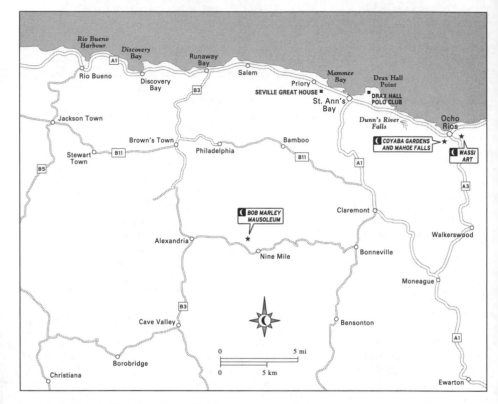

But the British had exploited a disorganization that had its roots in a lack of commitment on the part of the Spanish to develop the island as it had done in many other colonies, a neglect many scholars attribute to the absence of gold in Jamaica. The decisive battle that ended any lingering doubt about the fate of Jamaica occurred at the mouth of the Rio Nuevo, just east of present day Ocho Rios. The town was later at the center of Jamaica's slave economy and sugar boom, with vast plantations around the area. Later, Ocho Rios played an important role in the development of Jamaica's chief mineral export, bauxite, and remains an import shipment point today. When tourism grew to overtake bauxite as the country's chief earner of foreign currency, Ocho Rios was again at the center of this transformation, building the cruise ship terminal to attract the massive flows of capital that continue to play a vital role in the local economy.

SAFETY

Corporal Roger Williams of the Ocho Rios Police Department gives sound advice regarding delinquency in Ocho Rios. According to Williams, harassment in Ocho Rios is higher than in other places due to the large squatter settlements around town that support thousands of people from neighboring parishes. St. Ann is the poorest parish, even though you wouldn't necessarily notice because it is well developed, and many come to Ochi in search of opportunity that doesn't always surface in the formal economy.

Hustlers tend to be more aggressive here than in other parishes, and Williams

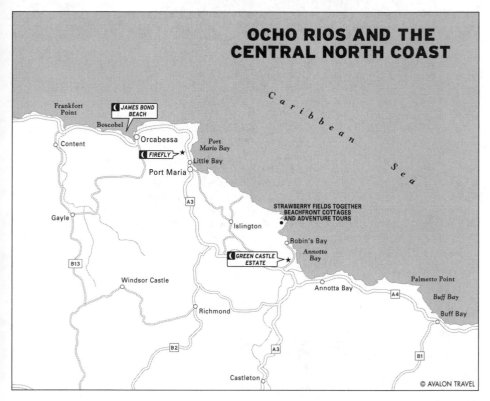

OCHO RIOS AND THE CENTRAL NORTH COAST

Frankfort Point

(JAMES BOND BEACH

Boscobel

Content

Orcabessa

(FIREFLY ★

Port Maria

Little Bay

Port Maria Bay

C a r i b b e a n   S e a

A3

Gayle

Islington

STRAWBERRY FIELDS TOGETHER
BEACHFRONT COTTAGES
AND ADVENTURE TOURS

Robin's Bay

Annotto Bay

(GREEN CASTLE ESTATE ★

B13

Windsor Castle

Richmond

Annotta Bay

A4

Palmetto Point

Buff Bay

Buff Bay

B2

A3

B1

Castleton

© AVALON TRAVEL

recommends greeting advances with a smile, followed by clear communication demonstrating your lack of interest. Ignoring advances is not wise, he says, as it can make the hustler upset. It is not uncommon for people to follow tourists, touting any and every kind of service, tour, or drug. According to Williams, crack use is generally confined to street people, while tourists are often offered cocaine and, most frequently, marijuana. Williams reminds that all drugs are illegal in Jamaica. Prostitution is very apparent in Ocho Rios, and it's not uncommon for women to solicit cruise ship passengers in full view of the police. Williams noted that while prostitution is illegal in Jamaica, it is rarely prosecuted. Many parts of Ocho Rios can feel unsafe at night, and it is indeed best not to go out alone—parts of downtown, like James

Avenue, can be desolate late at night. Petty theft is common, and it's not unheard of for tourists to feel threatened. Women especially should be accompanied walking around town at night.

Behind the inevitable theatrics used by hustlers to get the attention of unassuming visitors, there is a down-to-earth Jamaican sincerity that will often surface by entertaining advances with a "No, thank you," or "I'm all set, thanks, *bredren* . . . " Should undesired suitors not be placated with that, or should they react in a less-than-honorable manner, it's important to remember they are not representative of the majority of Jamaicans, who understand the value of hospitality as a cultural and economic virtue central to the Jamaican idiosyncrasy and the tourism industry alike.

OCHO RIOS

Ocho Rios

Hustling and bustling Ocho Rios can feel stifling at times, with the incessant solicitations and persistent attempts by hopeful locals to sell you something or take you somewhere. But seasoned visitors are hardly troubled once they learn to walk with confidence like they know where they're going and take the attention with a grain of salt. In spite of the chaos and confusion that has become a permanent fixture in the central square by the clock tower, there are still places within a 15-minute walk or five-minute cab ride where natural beauty reigns. Natura Falls, Shaw Park Botanical Garden, White River Valley, and Reggae Beach are a few examples.

The rivers in and around Ochi are also an important draw for the beautiful gardens they sustain and the recreation they provide for swimming and cooling off in the shade. The town of Ocho Rios spills over into the bordering parish of St. Mary, just across the White River.

Much of the North Coast is within easy reach of Ocho Rios, as are several attractions in the interior. Bob Marley's birthplace and mausoleum at Nine Mile is about an hour's drive into the hills, and the birthplace of one of Jamaica's foremost national heroes, Marcus Garvey, is located in nearby St. Ann's Bay, marked by a statue in front of the parish library; it's worth stopping to ponder. Several great beaches dot the coast to the east and west.

The nicest part of Ocho Rios proper, and perhaps one of the nicest developed waterfront areas in all of Jamaica, is the stretch of coastline between Mahogany Beach and the White River, which separates St. Ann from St. Mary. Here, along what could be considered St. Ann's Riviera, Royal Plantation and

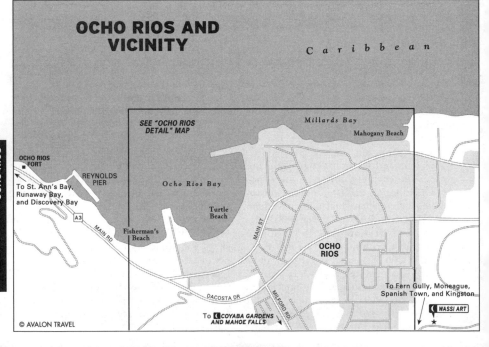

Jamaica Inn share a stretch of spectacular ledged coral shoreline interspersed with small, private beaches. One of Jamaica's finest villas, Scotch on the Rocks, is nestled between the two upmarket hotels.

SIGHTS
Beaches and Waterfalls

Most of the resorts in town and along the coast have cordoned off their seafront areas. Despite the fact that all beaches in Jamaica fall under the public domain, private landowners along the coast can apply for exclusivity permits, a clause in the law most hotels take advantage of.

One Love Trail, about one kilometer west of Island Village Shopping center heading out of town, leads down to a beautiful waterfall spilling down on a small beach protected by a reef just offshore. Caretaker Goshford Dorrington "Histry" Miller (cell tel. 876/893-1867) takes tips for keeping the place clean and sells artwork and natural jewelry.

Turtle Beach (admission US$3) in the heart of Ochi is popular among tourists; several hotels claim large pieces on either side of the public area at the center of the bay.

Mahogany Beach (free) is the most popular beach among locals and heats up on weekends with music blasting and youth playing soccer and splashing around. The beach is located east of the town center off Main Street just past Bibibip's. It's the best place to soak up the local scene and is also the departure point for Five Star Watersports' cruises on their flagship Cool Runnings catamarans. The Mahogany Beach Restaurant & Bar (tel. 876/974-0833, Mitsue Small cell tel. 876/562-9422, Ryon Small cell tel. 876/379-2663, 10 A.M.–3 P.M. Mon.–Sat., US$5.50–22.50) accommodates groups and serves jerk and pork, daily specials, and seafood.

Fisherman's Beach (free), adjacent to Island Village, is one of the best spots around to get fresh seafood—at Tropical Vibes restaurant

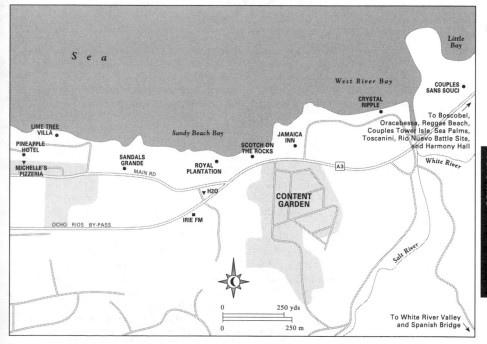

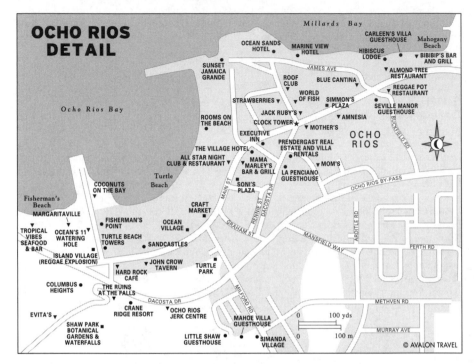

OCHO RIOS DETAIL

or the other fish shacks set up there. This is not a beach for swimming, but rather for chilling out with some food and a beer.

Irie Beach (cell tel. 876/404-8825, thlee4000@hotmail.com, US$12) is small beach on the banks of the White River east of Ochi where locals go to cool off and enjoy picnics. The beach hosts occasional events. A bar and restaurant serves Jamaican dishes. To get there head east out of town, taking a right off the highway opposite the entrance to Jamaica Inn just past the Texaco gas station, following the White River inland until you reach the beach.

Reggae Beach (contact Kavona, cell tel. 876/473-7077, 8 A.M.–6 P.M., 9 A.M.–midnight on Fri.–Sun., admission US$9.50) is a picturesque stretch of sand on an unspoiled cove a few minutes' drive east of Ocho Rios. The beach hosts excellent annual events like Luau and Frenchman's Parties, and an occasional stage show. A bar and restaurant on the property serves a variety of seafood dishes, including lobster, shrimp, fried fish, and chicken (US$12–25).

Laughing Waters (free), probably the nicest beach in Jamaica and the original beach from the James Bond movie *Dr. No,* is located in Mammee Bay, just east of Dunn's River Falls. The property facing the beach is a residence reserved for the prime minister. To get there, park along the seaward side of the highway on the broad shoulder just east of a JPS electrical substation that sits adjacent to the dirt road entrance. The road leads down to the seaside, where a breathtaking waterfall meets the sea. The beach sees few visitors and remains almost a state secret. At times, guards are posted along the road by the path down to the beach and don't allow visitors to pass, in which case the only way to get to the beach is by sea.

Blue Hole River is one of the area's best-kept secrets, consisting of a series of waterfalls along the White River accessed by a trail known

© OLIVER HILL

Irie Beach is a great spot for a refreshing dip in the White River.

locally as Breadfruit Walk. The area is not organized as an attraction, but local men keep the banks clean and will ask for a contribution—US$5–10 is reasonable for a small group. To get there, follow the road up the White River Valley, turning left at the first major intersection, and then make a right along a dirt track adjacent to a JPS pump station. Park and cross the footbridge, continuing along the trail up the hill. The first large pool is found on the left with several other pools, some of them suitable for jumping into from considerable heights as you continue upstream.

River Parks and Gardens

Ocho Rios is known for its lush gardens, though some are far better maintained than others. One of the nicest free waterfalls in Ochi, known as **Nature Falls,** is frequented mostly by locals who come for picnics and to wash off their vehicles in the shade. The river and falls are located just off Shaw Park Road, along a dirt road that branches off the road to Perry Town just past the Y where it splits from Shaw Park Road.

Shaw Park Botanical Garden and Waterfalls (DaCosta Dr., tel. 876/974-2723, 8 A.M.–5 P.M. daily, US$10) is a nice river garden full of ginger lilies and little cascades. There is a rear entrance accessible from Shaw Park Road when the front entrance is closed. This is a great shady and scenic place to get some natural air conditioning when it's hot. The back entrance to the park can be accessed from the end of Shaw Park Road where a little bridge leads from a parking lot by some abandoned apartment buildings into the park.

Turtle River Park (contact Ms. Newman, park supervisor, tel. 876/795-0078, 7 A.M.–8 P.M. Mon.–Fri., 8 A.M.–9 P.M. Sat. and Sun., free) borders the bypass, located straight ahead as you descend from Fern Gully at the junction of Milford, Main Street, and DaCosta Drive. Turtle Park was inaugurated on June 18, 2004. Koi fish, butterfly koi, tilapia, and some turtles in a cage populate the small park.

Fern Gully is a former underground riverbed that was planted with ferns in the 1880s and later paved over to create the main highway (A1) between Spanish Town and the North

Coast. Arts-and-crafts stands line a few of the less precarious curves along the steep, lush, and shady road.

◖ Coyaba Gardens and Mahoe Falls

Coyaba Gardens and Mahoe Falls (Shaw Park Rd., tel. 876/974-6235, coyaba@hotmail.com, www.coyabagardens.com, 8 A.M.–5 P.M. daily, admission US$10 for waterfalls and gardens, US$5 for gardens alone) are the best-maintained gardens in Ochi, with a small waterfall fit for swimming and climbing and a nice museum featuring a history of Jamaica's earliest inhabitants and a display covering the local watershed. Ysassi's Lookout Point, named after the last Spanish governor of Jamaica, boasts spectacular views over Ocho Rios and the bay. There is a snack bar on-site and a Romanesque pavilion above the falls used for events and weddings. Mahoe Falls is on the Milford River, which flows through Coyaba Gardens before descending through town and out the storm gulley by Sunset Jamaica Grande. Owner Simon Stuart's grandmother built the first resort in Ochi at Shaw Park Gardens farther down the hill in 1923. Coyaba was a banana walk, or gully, on Shaw Park Estate until the gardens and waterfall were developed in the early 1990s. To get to Coyaba, turn right opposite the Anglican church heading up toward Fern Gully on Milford Road (A3) and follow the signs off of Shaw Park Road.

Coyaba Gardens and Mahoe Falls

© OLIVER HILL

◖ Wassi Art

Wassi Art (tel. 876/974-5044, info@wassiart. com, www.wassiart.com, 9 A.M.–5 P.M. Mon.–Sat., 10 A.M.–4 P.M. Sun. and holidays) is easily the highest commercial quality and most productive ceramics studio and gallery in Jamaica. A complimentary tour of the ceramics studio is offered, showing visitors the complete cycle of creativity, from processing of clay to the throwing and firing. The raw, red terra-cotta clay used in much of the work is brought from Castleton, St. Mary, before being processed at Wassi. The studio also works with imported white clay.

There are 20 full-time artists on salary, many self-taught who started at Wassi through an apprenticeship program where they developed their skills. The name Wassi is from Jamaican slang, meaning anything terrific, or something sharp like the sting of a wasp that would create an impression. General manager Sylvie Henry oversees the day-to-day operations; the company is owned by Robert and Teresa Lee. Wassi Art began as a hobby of Mrs. Lee's in 1982. The company gets a volume discount with FedEx, savings it passes on to customers who wish to ship pieces abroad. There is a wide range of pottery on display and for sale at Wassi Art, from small souvenir items to huge display pieces (US$5–5,000).

Get there by taking the A3 in the direction of Fern Gully; take a left on Great Pond, and then another left on Bougainvillea Drive.

Museums and Galleries

Reggae Xplosion (Island Village Plaza, tel. 876/675-8895, 9 A.M.–5 P.M. Mon.–Fri., 10 A.M.–5 P.M. Sat., US$7 or US$3.50 for locals) is a museum offering an interactive history of reggae music; push a button to listen to tracks at each booth. Along with the shopping center itself, Reggae Xplosion is owned by Island Jamaica, Chris Blackwell's Jamaican venture.

Harmony Hall (Tower Isle, tel. 876/975-4222, 10 A.M.–6 P.M. Tues.–Sun.) is a beautiful old great house with a gallery on the second floor run by Peter and Anabella Proudlock. It features works by the likes of Susan Shirley and Graham Davis and several other contemporary painters. There is also a nice bookshop in the gallery with cookbooks and works by local authors. A crafts fair is held on Easter weekend in the yard out front, with regular exhibitions during the winter season. Downstairs is Toscanini, the area's best Italian restaurant. The colonial-era building is located five minutes' east of Ochi along the main road.

Historical Sights

Rio Nuevo Battle Site, just east of Harmony Hall, is the location of the decisive battle that left Jamaica in English hands. After three years of guerrilla warfare and harassment of the British, the last Spanish governor, Don Cristobal de Ysassi, finally received reinforcements from Cuba to help retake the island. The first set of troops arriving from Spain landed at Ocho Rios, where they were soon discovered by the British and quickly defeated. The second detail of 557 men was sent from Cuba and landed at the mouth of the Rio Nuevo. They too were soon discovered by British warships, and the battle that ensued left 300 Spanish soldiers dead for Britain's 50. Ysassi miraculously escaped and continued to wage guerilla attacks with a few remaining loyal bands of Maroons on his side until the treaty of Madrid was signed, officially conceding defeat and leaving Jamaica in British hands. Ysassi finally fled the island in handmade dugout canoes from Don Christopher's Point in Robin's Bay. A plaque mounted by the JNHT at the Rio Nuevo battle site reads: "The stockade that once stood here was captured on the 17th June 1658 by Colonel Edward D'oyley and the English forces under his command after a gallant defense by Don Cristobal de Ysassi the last Spanish governor of Jamaica."

Ocho Rios Fort is located beside the Reynolds bauxite installation and the helicopter pad for Island Hoppers. The fort was built in the late 17th century. Like many other forts on the island, it was strengthened in 1780 when a French attack was feared imminent. In 1795, an enemy vessel appeared off Ocho Rios harbor but, fearing the guns there, it made an attack at Mammee Bay. The Ocho Rios Fort was rebuilt by Reynolds Jamaica and contains two of the original guns from Ocho Rios and two of the guns that defended the town of Mammee Bay. The fort is not a managed attraction but is worth a quick stop to have a look around.

East of Ochi

White River Valley runs along the St. Ann–St. Mary border, where the White River was an important feature for the Spaniards, who built the first thoroughfare from the South to North Coasts along its banks. The oldest **Spanish bridge** on the island can still be seen at the river's upper reaches, just above Chukka Caribbean's kayaking and tubing site.

Prospect Plantation (contact property operator Dolphin Cove, tel. 876/994-1058, 8 A.M.–4 P.M. Mon.–Sat.) is a 405-hectare working plantation bought by Sir Harold Mitchell in 1936. Mitchell entertained all manner of dignitaries in his vast property, which beyond the great house has some of the area's most luxurious villas. A tradition was established whereby all his guests would plant a tree on the grounds to mark their visit. The most notable of these tokens of remembrance is the giant mahogany planted by Winston Churchill in 1953 that stands in the driveway behind the great house.

Prospect Plantation offers rides on camel, horse, or jitney with a tour of the great house included. The basic plantation tour (US$32 per adult, free for children under 7) includes a jitney ride, a great house tour, and a stop to pet the camels and see the ostriches. The tour can be upgraded (US$89) to include a 20-minute camel trek. The plantation tour can also be done on horseback (US$58). Nestled among the groves of tropical hardwoods below the great house is a beautiful nondenominational chapel built by Mitchell to mark the passing of his wife, Mary Jane Mitchell Greene, known as Lady Mitchell. The chapel was constructed completely with hardwoods and stone found on the plantation.

ENTERTAINMENT AND EVENTS

Bars and Nightclubs

H2O (Shop #22, Coconut Grove Shopping Centre, tel. 876/795-1728 or 876/332-0035, 12 P.M.–4 A.M. daily), the brainchild of reggae songstress Tanya Stephens, opened in December 2008 as a cozy bar, restaurant, and music venue. The space is well appointed with wooden pub chairs and tables painted with game boards, an aquarium, and a snake terrarium round out the vibe of the place, which fittingly features live music performances on Thursdays, live band karaoke on Fridays, H2O Flow on Saturdays, featuring local and international artists, and oldies/mento/ska night on Sundays. Live music can also be heard during

the week (10 A.M.–4 P.M. Mon. and Wed.) by the H2O Flow house band. The restaurant (serves till 2 A.M.) specializes in local seafood and veggie dishes (US$4–13). Tanya is regularly around and frequently takes to the stage when not performing elsewhere.

Margaritaville (Island Village, tel. 876/675-8800, 9 A.M.–4 A.M. on club nights Mon., Wed., and Sat. and 9 A.M.–10 P.M. on Sun., Tues., Thurs., and Fri.) is Ochi's most popular club with the tourist crowd. This is one of Jimmy Buffet's chains, and it sees a lot of debauchery—the pool party on Wednesdays attracts a large crowd.

Amnesia (70 Main St., tel. 876/974-2633, US$3–7) is Ochi's most authentic Jamaican nightclub. Thursday is Ladies' Night and gets quite busy, with a regular after-work jam and occasional deejay performances on Fridays.

Blitz Nightclub (4 DaCosta Drive, aka Main St., tel. 876/974-4407 or cell tel. 876/899-5540, 10 P.M.–6 A.M. Tues. and Fri., admission US$7) is open only on Tuesdays for

OCHO RIOS

© OLIVER HILL

Fame FM's DJ Nicco gets the crowd moving at Margaritaville, one stop along the station's annual road party across the island.

OCHO RIOS WEEKLY NIGHTLIFE SCHEDULE

TUESDAY
Ocean's 11 Karaoke Night at **Ocean's 11 Watering Hole** (Cruise Ship Pier, tel. 876/974-8444, 8 P.M.-1 A.M.)
Karaoke Night After Party at **Blitz Nightclub** (4 DaCosta Dr., a.k.a. Main St., tel. 876/974-4407, 1-6 A.M.)

WEDNESDAY
Pool Party at **Margaritaville** (Island Village, tel. 876/675-8800, complimentary drinks till 1 A.M., patrons in swimwear pay US$6 cover charge instead of the normal US$12). The place is hopping till 4 A.M.

THURSDAY
Ladies Night at **Amnesia** (70 Main St., tel. 876/974-2633, US$3-7)
Live Music Thursdays at **H2O** (Shop 22, Coconut Grove Shopping Centre, tel. 876/795-1728, 332-0035, noon-4 A.M. daily)

FRIDAY
After Work Jam at **Ocean's 11 Watering Hole** (Cruise Ship Pier, tel. 876/974-8444, 6 P.M.-you say when)
Girls Gone Wild at **Blitz Nightclub** (4 Da-

Costa Dr., a.k.a. Main St., tel. 876/974-4407, US$6, ladies free, 10 P.M.-6 A.M.), sponsored by Magnum Tonic Wine

SATURDAY
Big Sound Night at **Margaritaville** (Island Village, tel. 876/675-8800), featuring guest selectors and occasional dancehall artists
H2O Flow at **H2O** (Shop #22, Coconut Grove Shopping Centre, tel. 876/795-1728 or 876/332-0035) features local and international artists

SUNDAY
Live Band Night with house band Reggae Oceans at **Ocean's 11 Watering Hole** (Cruise Ship Pier, tel. 876/974-8444, 8 P.M.-1 A.M., US$5)
Sunday River Party at **Coyaba Heaven** (New Seville, just below Seville Great House, 9 P.M. until the last person leaves)
Family Fun Day at **Priory Beach** (early evening-early morning) has a waterslide and sound system
Oldies, Mento, and Ska Night at **H2O** (Shop #22, Coconut Grove Shopping Centre, tel. 876/795-1728 or 876/332-0035)

an after party following Ocean 11's karaoke night, and Fridays for ladies night, dubbed Girls Gone Wild, where women pay no cover.

Roof Club (James Ave., no phone) is another typical Jamaican club with a bar and plenty of whining to go around. The club gets busy on weekends.

Spinning Wheel Club (James Ave., no phone) is a local hangout where men gather any time of day for dominoes. There is no bar; it's basically just a hangout spot where you may be able to get in on a game.

Strawberries Night Club (James Ave., no phone) is another earthy Jamaican club where blasting music competes with Roof Club across the street.

Nicky's Bar & Games (Old Buckfield Rd., sign says Swingers on the outside) offers cards

and dominoes, and domestic beers and rums at local prices (US$1–5.50).

Coyaba Heaven (New Seville, just below Seville Great House) hosts a free weekly Sunday River Party just past the water wheel at Seville Heritage Park. Greig "Andy" Anderson (tel. 876/386-1401), Ryan "Ralph" Miller and Stuart "Suck Breast" Murdoch hold a lease on the piece of land with a small river running through, where they've built a thatch-roofed kitchen and tables with steps leading down to the water. Jerk and booze are sold on Sundays from 9 P.M. until the party's over, with local selectors and radio personalities entertaining the crowd.

Priory Beach, a bit farther west, holds a popular dance party on Sunday evenings that last until about 2 A.M. on a good night.

OCHO RIOS

Festivals and Events

Jamaica can be a tough place when it comes to continuity, and some of the more obscure annual events wane with the passing of years, while others regroup and come back stronger than ever. St. Mary hosts a few notable music festivals that are not to be missed should they coincide with a sojourn in the area.

Follow di Arrow is an annual dancehall stage show held at James Bond Beach on the last Saturday in February.

St. Mary Mi Come From is held at James Bond Beach on the first Saturday in August and hosted by conscious reggae icon Capleton, born a short distance away from the venue in Islington. The event showcases some of Jamaica's most popular dancehall artists, many of them inspired Rastas like the fire man himself.

Ocho Rios Jazz Festival (www.ochoriosjazz.com, US tel. 323/857-5358 or 866/649-2137) is held at various venues, from Kingston to Ocho Rios to Port Antonio over the course of seven days, starting around the second week in June. The festival features a few dozen local and international jazz acts.

The **Fatta Tyre Festival** (contact Jonothan Gosse, www.smorba.com, tel. 876/975-3393, smorbaja@hotmail.com) held each year around the second week in February, was created for mountain biking enthusiasts and showcases much of the talent and hard-core guts of the St. Mary Off-Road Bicycling Association. The festival features a Bicycle Bash kickoff at James Bond Beach, with BMX races, stunts, and displays of unusual and pimped-out bikes, followed by several days of competitive and sometimes grueling rides, mostly along single track through the hills of St. Mary.

Ocho Rios sees its share of excitement during carnival season in April with **Bacchanal Jamaica** (info@bacchanaljamaica.com, www.bacchanaljamaica.com, tel. 876/754-5396) hosting a mad soca bashment at Chukka Cove. Bacchanal hosts a series of events during Jamaica's carnival season, which runs from mid-January through Easter. Bacchanal Jamaica is composed of three Mas bands in the Trinidadian tradition—Oakridge, Revelers, and Raiders—which

have promoted parties since carnival festivities began in Jamaica in 1989. While soca music is not Jamaica's most popular, being more indigenous to Trinidad and Tobago or even Barbados, during Jamaica's carnival season it takes center stage at events produced by the group.

Luau is an annual dance session held at Reggae Beach, also around Easter. **Beach J'ouvert,** part of the carnival season's festivities, is held at James Bond Beach in Oracabessa in early April, where revelers whine out to soca and throw paint on each other, with after-parties spilling into Ocho Rios.

Farther inland in St. Ann parish, the Marley family hosts an annual concert on the weekend before or after Bob's February 6 birthday, and nearby the **Claremont Kite Festival** is held on Easter weekend a few months later in a big field, with a stage show in the evening.

Seville Heritage Park hosts a number of excellent events throughout the year, including a **Kite Festival** on Easter Monday and, the main event of the year, the **Emancipation Jubilee** held on July 31.

Once a popular annual festival, **Reggae Sunsplash** has been on ice for several seasons after it was poorly executed and lost money in 2006. Keep your ear to the ground for a potential comeback in the future.

Kampai (baycrestlimited@gmail.com, admission US$50) is one of the best all-inclusive parties held in Ocho Rios over the Easter Weekend put on by BayCrest, a promotions company led by Andrew-David Campbell and Dominic Azan. Held at Enchanted Gardens, or a similar exotic venue, on Easter Sunday, the party features an assortment of food from ribs and beef to pasta and seafood, catered by many of the best Kingston- and Ochi-based restaurants. Bars are plentiful, with sponsoring beverage companies doing their best to impress with creative concoctions, and top-class selectors spinning a mix of soca, dancehall, reggae and hip-hop.

Daydreams (Wright Image Entertainment, US$30) is another popular all-inclusive party, a bit less upscale than Kampai, held on Easter Sunday at an open air venue like the beach at Drax Hall.

SHOPPING

Neville Dread International Boutique (Shop #4, Chuck's Plaza, 78 Main St., cell tel. 876/403-2875) sells mix tapes, Rasta-inspired apparel, dress shirts, Rasta-colored tam hats, and name-brand gentlemen's dress shoes, socks, and boxer shorts. The shop is a long-standing institution; it was established in 1980 by proprietor Neville George Ellis.

Ahead of Time (77 Main St., tel. 876/974-2358) sells Indonesian furnishings and trinkets like carved chests, moon mirrors, handbags, and ceramics and is worth a visit.

David Simpson's Fine Art Gallery (11 Old Buckfield Rd., tel. 876/840-1152) sells canvas wood carvings and ceramics. Viewing by appointment only at Simpson's home.

For the best deals on Jewelry, try **Jewels in Paradise** (tel. 876/974-6929, avi@jewelsinparadise.com, www.jewelsinparadise.com, Mon.–Sat 9 A.M.–5 A.M.) owned by the affable Avi Doshi who will give you the best deals around on brands like Audemars Piguet, Jaeger le Coultre, Corum, and IWC, duty free. **Margaritaville** shares the complex with several duty-free, but nonetheless overpriced, jewelry and gift shops. **Reggae Xplosion** and the **Blue Mountain Cafe** are also located here and accept dollars exclusively. Nevertheless, it's a decent place to get some real Blue Mountain coffee. **Shade Shack** (shop #K-4, tel. 876/675-8965) is one of the best places in Ochi to get brand-name sunglasses; it's staffed by owner Jackie Dodson.

Poco Loco Gifts & Souvenirs (4-A Taj Mahal Shopping Centre, tel. 876/974-3429) and **Coco-Joe's** (12 Burger King Plaza) sell authentic CY Clothing gear, in addition to other brands of T-shirts, clothes, and accessories.

Countless smaller shopping centers vie for the cruise ship dollars farther into the heart of Ochi, most notably in the Taj Mahal complex behind Hard Rock Café. The crafts market on Main Street across from Scotia Bank is definitely worth a visit. There's also another crafts center at Pineapple Place, and a third in Coconut Grove at the eastern junction of Main Street and the Ocho Rios Bypass, across from Royal Plantation, where the best deals can be found.

For clothes and shoes, there are several stores in the downtown area; haute couture will not be featured anywhere. **Deals,** in Soni's Plaza, is the best place for tight-fitting clothes for clubbing in Jamaican style.

Classic Footwear (20 Main St., tel. 876/974-4815) has shoes for both men and women.

The Shoe Works (Shop #6, Ocean Village Plaza, tel. 876/974-5415, 9 A.M.–7 P.M. Mon.–Sat.) has the best service in town for fairly priced name-brand footwear.

Scent of Incense & Things (79 Main St., tel. 876/795-0047), run by Janet Gallimore, is a nice shop selling incense, oils, herbs, spiritual products, and a variety of small gift items.

SPORTS AND RECREATION

Golf

Sandals Golf and Country Club (tel. 876/975-0119, www.sandals.com, 7 A.M.–5 P.M. daily, US$100 green fees, US$45 for locals) is a *Golf Digest* 3.5-star-rated course in the hills above Ochi. The course is compact and very walkable, but carts are also available (US$40). Clubs are also rented (US$30 Wilson/US$45 Calloway), and players are obliged to use a caddy (US$17, plus minimum tip of US$10/person).

A patio restaurant and bar serves burgers, hot dogs, and chicken sandwiches (US$7). The driving range offers baskets of 40 balls for US$4. Sandals guests don't pay greens fees, and special rates apply for guests of several other area accommodations.

Skydiving

Skydive Jamaica (Boscobel Aerodrome, tel. 876/467-6626, toll-free for U.S. or JA 877/348-3688, or U.S. tel. 262/886-3480, info@skydive-jamaica.com, www.skydive-jamaica.com, open daily 8 A.M.–sunset) is the Jamaican branch of a skydiving outfit based in Michigan, Skydive Midwest. Climbs originate from the aerodrome in Boscobel, St. Mary, 15

OCHO RIOS

minutes east of Ocho Rios. Divers climb to 14,500 feet in a King Air dual prop with a 14-person capacity before jumping out of the aircraft for a free dive lasting about a minute and reaching around 150 mph, followed by a seven- to nine-minute canopy ride with the parachute. Jumps cost US$250, US$169 for residents. Video/photo packages cost an additional US$125, or US$99 for residents. The video package consists of a seven- to eight-minute DVD of the jump and a CD with between 75 and 125 digital still photos.

Water Sports

From the Marina at Fisherman's Point there are several outfits that offer sailing, snorkeling, and water sports.

Margarita (contact Paul Dadd, cell tel. 876/381-4357, pdadd@cwjamaica.com) is a 12-meter sloop that can be rented for sailboat charters ranging from day sails to multiple-night trips around the island or to neighboring islands. The boat is chartered with a captain and can accommodate up to 15 people for day sails (US$50/person or US$400 for half day, US$800 full day). For overnight charters (US$1,000/day), the boat can sleep eight passengers.

Fantasea Divers (contact Paul Dadd, cell tel. 876/381-4357, pdadd@cwjamaica.com) caters to hotel and especially villa guests along the North Coast. PADI instructors offer lessons and certification. Certifications range from bubble watching for children (US$65) in the swimming pool to PADI dive master (US$680) to assistant instructor certification (US$1,000).

Resort Divers (Salem Beach, contact Laura or Everett Heron, tel. 876/973-6131 or cell tel. 876/881-5760, heron@resortdivers.com, www.resortdivers.com) is a five-star PADI dive facility, opened in 2007. Resort Divers also operates out of Royal Decameron in Runaway Bay, offering snorkeling, glass-bottom-boat tours, banana boat rides, water skiing, drop-line and deep sea fishing, and parasailing, in addition to its core dive services. Runaway Bay dive highlights include canyons, crevices, and flats, with popular sites being Ricky's Reef, Pocket's Reef, a Spanish Anchor, and wreckages like *Reggae*

Queen, a 100-foot freighter, two airplanes, and a Mercedes Benz car.

From its base in Runaway Bay, Resort Divers will coordinate traditional drop-line fishing excursions with local fishermen. Resort Divers also operates Sharkies Seafood Restaurant at Salem Beach. Resort Divers has been in operation since 1986 with a five-star PADI rating since 1992. Call or visit the website for pricing specific to each activity.

Five Star Watersports (Shop #14, Santa Maria Plaza, 121 Main St., tel. 876/974-2446, toll-free from Jamaica from JA 888/386-7245, toll-free from U.S. and Canada 877/316-6257, redstripecruises@cwjamaica.com or sales@fivestarwatersports.com, www.fivestarwatersports.com) operates three catamarans and a trimaran named some rendition of *Cool Runnings*. Cruises operate Monday–Saturday to Dunn's River Falls (US$72 plus transfer, 12:30–4 P.M.) and include an open bar, snorkeling gear, and the entrance fee to the falls. A **Taste of Jamaica** evening cruise (US $59/person, 5–8 P.M. Fridays only) offers an open bar and Jamaican food like jerk pork, chicken, steak, rice and peas, festival, and bammy. Other cruises offered are the **Wet and Wild** clothing-optional cruise (US$59, 2:30–5 P.M. Thurs., min. 15 persons). The boats depart and return to Mahogany Beach. Drinks at the open bar include Red Stripe, rum punch, rum and Coke, fruit punch, Pepsi, and water.

Organized Tours

Blue Mountain Bicycle Tours (121 Main St., tel. 876/974-7075, info@bmtoursja.com, www.bmtoursja.com, US$93 from Ocho Rios area) runs a popular downhill biking tour which has been somewhat truncated over the past few years due to landslides that blocked the upper reaches of the route. The tour takes passengers to Cascade, above Buff Bay in the Blue Mountains, from where bikers descend for about an hour, have lunch, then descend for another hour to the Fish Dunn waterfall above Charles Town. Brunch is included at a restaurant along with orientation in Spring Hill before starting the ride. The entire excursion lasts 8 A.M.–4:30 P.M.

Chukka Caribbean Adventures (tel. 876/972-2506, ochorios@chukkacaribbean. com, www.chukkacaribbean.com) offers a host of organized tours, from horseback riding to ATV tours, canopy tours with ziplines through the forest, tubing and kayaking on the White River, the Irie Bus Ride to Nine Mile, and Stingray City at James Bond Beach. This is one of the island's most successful operations; it sees almost as many cruise ship passengers as Dunn's River. Chukka Cove, 15 minutes west of Ocho Rios, is the original flagship base for Chukka Caribbean Adventures, which now has operations all over the Caribbean basin.

H'Evans Scent (Free Hill, cell tel. 876/847-5592 or 876/427-4866, info@hevansscent. com, www.mrmotivator.com, www.hevansscent.com, www.paintsplatjm.com, US$85/ person) is an ecotourism outfit run by Derrick Evans, a.k.a. Mr. Motivator, offering ziplines, paintball, ATV tours, nature tours, and an experience where visitors get to mingle with locals 610 meters up in the hills of St. Ann. To get to H'Evans Scent, turn inland along the Bamboo Road in Priory for seven kilometers up the hill. The operation offers transportation from nearby accommodations in Ocho Rios, Runaway Bay, and Discovery Bay.

Strawberry Fields Adventure Tours (tel. 876/610-8658, cell tel. 876/999-7169 or 876/337-6127, kim@strawberryfieldstogether. com, www.strawberryfieldstogether.com) offers a variety of nature excursions based out of Strawberry Fields Together Beachfront Cottages in Robin's Bay, St. Mary. ATV tours (US$125 per person) last three hours, taking visitors through the bush to waterfalls; mountain biking tours lead to any number of places, among them a volcanic black sand beach (US$75), with guided hikes to the same black sand beach and Kwamen Falls (US$20). Snorkeling trips go to Long Reef (US$50), and Land Rover tours with Everton in one of his many rebuilt classic Rovers can also be arranged. Picnic lunches can be added to any of the tours for US$12 per person. Transportation can be arranged at an additional cost.

Lee's Elite Travel and Tours (85 Main St., tel. 876/974-6234, cell tel. 876/487-6793, sales@leestours.com, www.leestours.com) is focused on airport transfers, accommodations bookings, and wedding planning, but Lee's also sells day cruise tours to Nine Mile, Dunn's River Falls, Dolphin Cove, H'Evans Scent, Hooves, and Green Grotto Caves. Lee's arranges transportation and entrance fees at discounted rates for families and groups and offers customized packages that include an airport transfer. Airport transfers to Kingston (US$140 for 1–4 people) and Montego Bay (US$80 per couple) are available. Leroy Villiers and Norma Lee-Villiers run the travel and tours operation.

Spas

The best spas in town are the **Kiyara Ocean Spa** at the Jamaica Inn (tel. 876/974-2514 or U.S. tel. 800/837-4608, reservations@jamaicainn.com, www.kiyaraspa.com) and the **Red Lane Spa** at Royal Plantation (tel. 876/974-5601 or U.S. tel. 305/284-1300, rpres@jm.royalplantation.com, www.royalplantation.com). In Tower Isle, **Couples** (tel. 876/975-4271, www.couples.com) opened a beautiful spa in 2008. All three spas are open to nonguests.

Veronica's Day Spa (54–56 Main St. at the Village Hotel, tel. 876/795-3425) offers aromatherapy massages, reflexology, manicures, pedicures, and waxing.

ACCOMMODATIONS

Ocho Rios has developed a wide array of accommodation options thanks to its place as one of the original resort towns in Jamaica. Nevertheless, at the lower end, conditions tend to be consistently on the shabby side with few exceptions, while there are several good midrange and high-end options.

Under US$100

Simanda Villa (1 Shaw Park Rd., tel. 876/974-0708, simi@cwjamaica.com) may just have the cheapest rooms in Ochi. The accommodations are basic with air-conditioning (US$25) or fan (US$20). Sun Flower

Restaurant on the property serves local dishes like chicken with rice and peas (US$5).

Mahoe Villa Guest House (11 Shaw Park Rd., tel. 876/974-6613) is a cozy and private guesthouse run by Michael Riley. There are seven basic rooms (US$25–30 depending on size) with two single beds, fan, TV, and shared bath; plus two slightly larger rooms (US$40) with private bath and private entrance; as well as a master suite (US$75) with standing fan, a component stereo, TV, a whirlpool bath, two walk-in closets, and a private balcony with a sea view.

La Penciano Guest House (3 Short Lane, tel. 876/974-5472), run by Kenneth Thomas, is a relatively decent dive right in the center of town. The rooms are clean with fans, twin beds, TV, and hot water. The more expensive rooms (US$35) have private baths. Meals can be prepared to order. Longer stays can be negotiated. It should be noted La Penciano also gets its share of short-term guests.

C Carleen's Villa Guest House (85-A Main St., tel. 876/974-5431) is well situated, with a common balcony overlooking the water. It has seven no-frills rooms (US$40) equipped with ceiling fans, two twin beds, TV, and hot water in private baths. There's no pool on the property, and no food, but it's located five minutes away from Mahogany Beach, Ochi's most popular with locals. It has a convenient location between downtown Ochi and Mahogany Beach and is reasonably priced for what you get.

Seville Manor Guest House (84 Main St., tel. 876/795-2900) is a basic but comfortable guesthouse with queen-size beds in double-occupancy rooms (US$55), as well as triple rooms (US$64) that have a queen and a twin. Amenities include air-conditioning and hot water.

Marine View Hotel (9 James Ave., tel. 876/974-5753) has rooms with either king-size or two double beds with air-conditioning and TV (US$65), one double with air-conditioning (US$45, with TV US$50), and one double bed with ceiling fan (US$35). There is a pool and restaurant at this ocean-view accommodation. Credit cards are accepted.

Little Shaw Park Guest House (21 Shaw Park Rd., tel. 876/974-2177, littleshawpark@ yahoo.com, www.littleshawparkguesthouse. com) is the only place in Ochi to offer camping (US$20) in addition to its 22 basic rooms (US$55 fan, US$65 a/c). Rooms range from standard with cable TV and private bath to studio apartments with kitchenette and living area. The property has been owned and managed since 1977 by Deborah and Trevor Mitchell, who have maintained a laid-back, quiet garden setting in spite of the development boom outside the compound walls. The furnishings inside the rooms have apparently changed little since the guesthouse was opened. There is one triple-occupancy room (US$75). The property is a 10-minute walk to the beach and town.

Pineapple Hotel (Pineapple Place, Main St., tel. 876/974-2727, fax 876/974-1706, US$60) has 18 basic rooms with hot water, air-conditioning, housekeeping, security, and pool access. Pineapple is one of the closest hotels to Mahogany Beach, a favorite local hangout.

Carib Resort (tel. 876/970-0305, caribochorios@hotmail.com, www.caribochoriosresort. com) has one- (US$80/90) and two-bedroom (US$140/150) apartments, all with hot water and cable TV.

Crystal Ripple (Shaw Park Beach, tel. 876/974-6132, info@crystalripple.com, www. crystalripplebeachlodge.com, US$80–120) is located on a beautiful beach along White River Bay, adjacent to the Shaw Park Beach Hotel (which is run-down and definitely not recommended). Rooms have cable TV, air-conditioning, and private bathrooms with hot water. Rates include continental breakfast.

The Village Hotel (54–56 Main St., tel. 876/974-9193, villagehtl@cwjamaica.com, www.villagehoteljamaica.com, US$90 includes breakfast) has standard, deluxe, and suite rooms. All rooms have air-conditioning, kitchenette, cable TV, and ceiling fans. The Village Hotel has a swimming pool on property, and The Village Grill serves a mix of international and Jamaican cuisine (US$10–25).

Turtle Beach Towers (Main St., tel. 876/974-2381, turtlebeachtowers@cwjamaica.

com, www.turtlebeachvacations.com, US$65–160) is one of the original and less-attractive apartment-style accommodation options, with its cluster of gray towers at the base of Fisherman's Point resembling government housing projects. Do not book here without first seeing the room in person, as individual owners appoint the apartments according to taste (or neglect, as the case may be), and the decor and amenities vary greatly from unit to unit. Reduced rates can be negotiated for longer stays.

Executive Inn (60 Main St., tel. 876/795-4070, US$100/person) has 20 rooms with one, two, or three beds, and TV, air-conditioning, and private baths with hot water. It includes continental breakfast in its nightly rate. The Executive Inn also runs Carlito's Cafe, located around back on DaCosta serving typical Jamaican dishes.

US$100-250

Columbus Heights Apartments (tel. 876/974-9057 or 876/974-2940, columbushgts@cwjamaica.com, www.columbusheights.com), managed by Jennifer Llewellyn, is a large condo complex on a hill overlooking Ocho Rios, affording great views. Studios and one- and two-bedroom apartments with air-conditioning and hot water range US$100–200, with a US$20 difference between low and high season. Longer stays afford reduced rates.

⟨ Fisherman's Point (Cruise Ship Wharf, contact Charmaine Annikey for bookings, from the US/Canada tel. 877/211-6313, cell tel. 876/798-7647, accounts@selfcateringapartmentsjm.com, www.fishermanspoint.net or www.selfcateringapartmentsjm.com, US$100/125 low/high season) is run as a strata with individual apartment owners pooling their units. These are some of the nicer self-contained units available in Ocho Rios, and while decor and furnishings vary considerably between apartments, there is much better oversight of the conditions than at neighboring Turtle Towers. All units are fully furnished, with hot water, living rooms, equipped kitchens, TV, air-conditioning, and telephones. There is a nice pool at the center of the complex, with Turtle Beach access two minutes away.

Rooms on the Beach (Turtle Beach, Main St., tel. 876/974-6632, toll-free from U.S. or Jamaica 877/467-8737, info@superclubs.com, www.roomsresort.com, www.superclubs.com, US$105–141) is SuperClubs' answer to the demand for a dependable European-plan option on the beachfront in Ochi. Located in the heart of town, ROOMS is a beachfront property with a pool and all the fixtures of an all-inclusive—without the all-inclusive. The rooms are clean, with TV, air-conditioning, telephones, and hot water. The property is a short walk from all the restaurants and nightlife in downtown Ocho Rios.

Crane Ridge Resort (17 DaCosta Dr., tel. 876/974-8051, craneridge@craneridge.net, www.craneridge.net) has 90 units perched on a hill overlooking Ocho Rios off the bypass above Ruins at the Falls. Standard (US$80/133 low/high season) and one-bedroom rooms (US$99/157 low/high season) have private bathrooms with hot water and shared balcony. The two-bedroom suites (US$157/191 low/high season) have a private balcony, whirlpool tub, kitchenette, and living room. The nine three-story buildings surround a large pool with a swim-up bar. Complimentary Wi-Fi is accessible from the lobby and dining room area.

Hibiscus Lodge (83 Main St., tel. 876/974-2676, info@hibiscusjamaica.com, www.hibiscusjamaica.com) has comfortable rooms with air-conditioning, TV, and private baths with hot water. Rooms are either garden (US$135/147 low/high season) or ocean view (US$147/159 low/high season), and come with two twins or one queen-size bed. Rates include breakfast. The hotel is within easy walking distance of the heart of Ochi and Mahogany Beach.

Over US$250

⟨ Jamaica Inn (tel. 876/974-2514 or U.S. tel. 800/837-4608, reservations@jamaicainn.com) is one of the classiest hotels on the island, and it's little wonder it maintains a high rate of repeat guests (60 percent), among them many national and foreign dignitaries. Winston

Churchill stayed in the signature White Suite years ago, and Marilyn Monroe was also a guest. Since these luminaries were at the hotel, the amenities have only improved.

You won't find clocks, TVs, or Internet access in your room at the Jamaica Inn; these items are seen as distractions from what is designed to be the primary activity at this stately accommodation: relaxation. For those who need to stay connected, however, there is wireless Internet in the library and a computer for guest use. What you will find in the rooms is the classiest and most tastefully soothing color scheme and decor anywhere, with open living rooms just off the bedrooms—literally on the beach, and complete with a foot pan to wash off the sand before stepping inside.

Three room categories are differentiated principally by their proximity to the beach and the size of the room: second-floor balcony suites (US$290/550 low/high season), deluxe suites (US$340/670 low/high season), and premier suites (US$420/825 low/high season). The Jamaica Inn sits on one of the nicest private beaches in Jamaica, on Ocho Rios' equivalent of the Italian Riviera.

More exclusive rooms include the White Suite (US$820/1,760 low/high season), and the Cowdray Suite (US$435/860 low/high season), a more humble high-end room. Two spectacular one-bedroom cottages, Cottages 3 and 4 (US$820/1,760 low/high season), have private plunge pools, decks, and outside showers. The six Jamaica Inn cottages were refurbished in 2006 and come in one-bedroom (US$630/1,170 low/high season) and two-bedroom (US$740/1,340 low/high season) options.

The **Kiyara Ocean Spa** (www.kiyaraspa.com) run by Carolyn Jobson, sits beside the cottages along the waterfront and specializes in freshly mixed treatments using all-natural ingredients, many of which are grown on the premises.

Royal Plantation (tel. 876/974-5601 or U.S. tel. 305/284-1300, rpres@jm.royalplantation. com, www.royalplantation.com, US$1,548/1,636 d low season/high season European plan, US$1,978/2,066 d all-inclusive Royal Plan low/

© OLIVER HILL

The Jamaica Inn offers first-class service.

high season, stays of three nights or more receive a 65 percent discount) is an upscale property owned by the Sandals group. It's basically a Sandals resort on champagne and caviar, the extra amenities well appreciated by its guests. Royal Plantation gives guests the opportunity to get off the premises and taste a bit of local cuisine, if they so choose, on the European plan. Royal Plantation has three restaurants: One features "Nouveau Caribbean Fusion," Le Papillon is a French restaurant, and La Terrazza serves Mediterranean cuisine.

Royal Plantation has six room categories: deluxe; premium oceanfront junior suite; luxury oceanfront junior suite, with whirlpool tub and French balcony; the honeymoon grand luxe, with a walkout balcony and larger whirlpool bath with separate shower; the honeymoon plantation one-bedroom suite with living and a whirlpool area with separate standing shower; and the one-bedroom suites have two walkout balconies with lounge chairs and a huge living room area with 1.5 baths. Royal Plan guests have greens fees and transportation to the Sandals Golf Course included.

In addition to the rooms in the main building, there's a three-bedroom villa with a private pool. The top of the villa has two bedrooms sleeping 2–4 persons with a third bedroom downstairs that can be added. All bedrooms have king-size beds.

Red Lane Spa (876/670-9015, www.redlanespa.com) is one of the most comprehensive spas on the island, with 14 full-time employees and eight full-time therapists specializing in different treatments. The spa offers a wide variety of services, from hot stone massage to nails and facials. Specially built for the grand opening of Royal Plantation Inn, the European-inspired spa is open to nonguests as well.

Eden Sands (16 James Ave., cell tel. 876/865-2366, nathanbless@hotmail.com, www.ochoriosbeachvilla.com, US$350 nightly) is a quaint two-bedroom house that sleeps up to eight. The house features cable TV, air-conditioning in the bedrooms, a live-in handyman, security, and a housekeeper. The distinguishing feature is a private beach on Ochi's Riviera, the finest stretch of coast around.

Villas

Scotch on the Rocks (Pineapple Grove, just east of the junction of Main St. and the Ocho Rios bypass, contact Alan Marlor, SunVillas, U.S. tel. 888/625-6007, alan@sunvillas.com, www.sunvillas.com; or rent locally through the owner, tel. 876/871-1312, www.scotchontherocksja.com) is one of Jamaica's top five villas in terms of elegance, luxury, and an all-permeating sense of class, while still remaining unpretentious and full of vibes. The five-bedroom house (US$5,500/7,500 low/high season per week) is well laid out for privacy but still spacious enough for the whole family. Each bedroom has a private bath and a large balcony overlooking the sea. You won't find more soothing rooms anywhere, with soft linens and delicate white curtains that catch the evening breeze to blur the line between heaven and earth. A large pool deck out front

overlooks the sea at the top of a staircase down to the picture-perfect dock with a gazebo on its tip. The exquisite meals are taken either in the large indoor dining room, or more often outside. Scotchie, as the villa is known by those who have become its intimate guests, is situated on Sandy Bay, the equivalent of Ocho Rios' Riviera. The neighbors on either side are the most upscale hotels in town, Jamaica Inn and Royal Plantation, where tennis courts and spa facilities are within a few minutes' walk. The staff at Scotchie is top-notch, including Bryan the Rasta butler, Henry the gardener, Elvis the caretaker, Cherry the cook, and Pauline the housekeeper. By the end of a stay, these exemplary Jamaicans will be family, and if you're so lucky as to taste Cherry's Piña Colada cheesecake, you'll make every effort to take her with you when you leave. A minimum four-night stay is required.

SunVillas (contact Alan Marlor, SunVillas, U.S. tel. 888/625-6007, alan@sunvillas.com, www.sunvillas.com) rents a nice assortment of villas across Jamaica varying considerably in price while all having much more than the basic amenities. Scotch on the Rocks in Ocho Rios and Golden Clouds in Oracabessa are definite highlights on the North Coast.

Prendergast Real Estate and Villa Rentals (7 DaCosta Dr., tel. 876/974-2670, pren@cwjamaica.com), run by Clinece Prendergast and her daughter Jacky, books a large selection of villas, some in the hills overlooking Ochi and others directly on the water in and around town and from Oracabessa to Montego Bay along the North Coast. One of the nicer waterfront properties is **Lime Tree,** an expansive five-bedroom villa in the heart of Ocho Rios along a choice stretch of coastline just off Main Street. Other highlights include Seven Seas, a four-bedroom property on the beach in Mammee Bay, Four Winds, a five-bedroom villa on the beach in Old Fort Bay, and Golden Clouds, a nine-bedroom villa on a two-acre property seafront in Oracabessa.

Prospect Villas (tel. 876/994-1373, ian@prospect-villas.com, www.prospect-villas.com) rents five villas in addition to the

Prospect Plantation great house. The villas (US$2,500–14,000 low season, US$3,500–16,500 high season for a weeklong stay) have three or four bedrooms, with a minimum two-night stay (from US$360/500 low/high per night). Part of the Prospect Plantation Estate, formerly owned by Sir Harold Mitchell, Prospect Villas hosted some of the most important political and entertainment figures of the 20th century, including Charlie Chaplin and Henry Kissinger, to name a few. The villas have every amenity imaginable, from DSL to iPod docks to satellite TV, not to mention the private waterfront and full staff.

Jamaica Association of Villas and Apartments (JAVA) has its local headquarters at the Pompano Commercial Complex in Tower Isle (tel. 876/975-5504 or 876/975-5643, from the US tel. 773/463-6688 or 800/845-5276, javavillas@aol.com, java-jam-villas@cwjamaica.com, www.villasinjamaica.com) and offers booking services for member villas across the island.

Garden House (Shaw Park, across from Coyaba Gardens, tel. 876/974-4481, U.K. tel. for booking +44 1296/614-451, enquiries@gardenhouse-jamaica.com, gardenhouse-jamaica@hotmail.com, www.gardenhouse-jamaica.com, US$4,500/6500 low/high season for up to 19 guests) is a beautiful villa located on a 4.5-acre estate in the hills above Ochi, commanding spectacular views of the city and north coast. The main house has eight guest rooms with air-conditioning and en suite bathrooms, balconies, and walk-in closets. There's a freshwater pool in the garden.

All-Inclusive Resorts

Sunset Jamaica Grande (tel. 876/974-2200, reservations@sunsetochorios.com www.sunsetjamaicagrande.com, from US$325/370 low/high season) is the most prominent hotel on Turtle Beach, occupying the prime piece of real estate on the point of the bay. Refurbished in 2004, Sunset Jamaica Grande boasts the biggest conference facilities in Jamaica, with 3,066 square meters of meeting room space. The hotel has a total of five

restaurants, five swimming pools, and the longest private beach in Ochi. The rooms are clean and well appointed, with full amenities. The Cabana Beachfront rooms on the two-story wing are especially nice, overlooking the lawn and beach area from their low balconies. Free wireless Internet is available to guests in the lobby. Food and beverages at the Sunset are not luxurious by any means, the hotel catering to more of a budget all-inclusive tourist focused on family fun rather than classy meals. Nonetheless, the specialty restaurants, which include Ginger Lily and LaDiva, are markedly better than the buffets and serve high-quality dishes. Liquor is not premium brand. The average stay is four nights. It's one of the most cost-effective places to get married (US$700), with a constant stream of newlyweds.

Sandals Grande Ocho Rios Beach and Villa Resort (Main St., tel. 876/974-5691, www.sandals.com, US$880 weekly) is a 529-room property covering land on both sides of the bypass. Sandals properties are exclusively for couples. Sandals Grande Ocho Rios features three resorts in one, set amid a 100-plus acre seaside estate. The Ciboney Villas are nestled among lush, tropical foliage, and come with private pools. A small white sand beach hugged by a wraparound pier dotted with gazebos dubbed the Grande Promenade, is the prominent feature at The Riviera. The Manor House is set among sprawling lawns and gardens on the opposite side of the road from The Riviera. All three Sandals Jamaica resorts boast rooms with amenities like four-poster king beds, flat panel TVs, CD players, stocked fridge, en suite bathrooms, and air-conditioning. Internet is available for an additional charge. Guests can choose from 11 restaurants, seven pools, and 22 whirlpools, and are offered complimentary access to the Sandals Ocho Rios Golf Club.

ClubHotel Riu Ocho Rios (tel. 876/972-2200, US tel. 888/RIU-4990, clubhotel.ochorios@riu.com, www.riu.com), located in Mamee Bay, is a massive 865-room resort facing the sea. Rooms are clean and well

© OLIVER HILL

Couples Tower Isle is among the finest all-inclusive resorts in Jamaica, especially after it was refurbished in 2008.

appointed in replica furniture and either one king, a king and a double, or two double beds. Riu is among the least expensive of the all-inclusive hotels, but it's hard to see the value when reservations in one of the three "premier dining" restaurants requires standing in a long line 10 A.M.–noon to secure a reservation, and after all that the cuisine tends to disappoint. In the buffet dining room, where no reservations are required, the food quality is decent, albeit overwhelmingly imported. There is little inside the purple-painted buildings to remind guests that they are in Jamaica. Internet access is offered in the café off the lobby for a whopping US$18 per hour.

☾ Couples (www.couples.com, from US$507/551 low/high season) has two all-inclusive resorts just east of town across the border in Tower Isle, St. Mary: **Couples San Souci** (White River, tel. 876/994-1353) and **Couples Tower Isle** (Tower Isle, tel. 876/975-4271), reborn in 2008 after a US$30 million renovation gave the property a sleek South Beach feel.

Couples Resorts are easily at the top of the all-inclusive ranking, first for the quality of the food with a lot of local fruit and produce, a delicious mix of local and international cuisine, details like black pepper grinders at each table, and premium drinks and liquor.

The rooms at Sans Souci, which means "worry-free" in French, are tasteful with simple decor and balconies overlooking a private beach. Couples Tower Isle boasts a private island within swimming distance from the beach, reserved for nudists to hang loose.

FOOD
Seafood
Spring Garden Café and Seafood Grill (tel. 876/795-3149, 11 A.M.–11 P.M.) serves seafood, steak, and chicken (US$8–30). It's located on the bypass near Irie FM.

☾ Tropical Vibes Seafood and Bar (contact Garwin Davis, tel. 876/392-8287 or 876/386-0858, 8 A.M.–11 P.M. daily, US$6.50–21) is a great breezy bar serving the best fresh escovitch fish and bammy in town, as well as lobster, conch, and shrimp.

OCHO RIOS

A host of other fish shacks, grub shops, and craft vendors line the fishermen's beach area. It's possible to set up informal arrangements to charter one of the fishing boats, known as canoes, but bear in mind shady characters and hustlers tend to congregate in the area as well.

Jack Ruby's (1 James Ave., contact Peter Turner, cell tel. 876/381-3794 or 876/974-7289, 11 A.M.–11 P.M. daily, US$5–13) serves local fare, such as fried chicken with rice and peas, as well as seafood.

World of Fish (3 James Ave., no phone, 8 A.M.–1 A.M. daily) serves fish, chicken (US$3.50), rice and peas, curry goat (US$5), stew chicken, and fried, roast, or steamed fish with bammy or festival.

Jerk

⟨ Scotchie's Too (Drax Hall, beside the Epping gas station, tel. 876/794-9457, 11 A.M.–11 P.M. Mon.–Sat., 11 A.M.–9 P.M. Sun., US$4–11) is Jamaica's most respected jerk center, consistently grilling up the best jerk the country has to offer, with pork, chicken, and roast fish accompanied by breadfruit, yam, and festival.

Ocho Rios Jerk Centre (16 DaCosta Drive, tel. 876/974-2549, 10 A.M.–11 P.M. daily, US$5–13) serves pork, whole and half chicken, ribs and fish by the pound, as well as conch, accompanied by breadfruit, sweet potato, bammy, and festival. It's located between Crane Ridge and the stop light at the junction of DaCosta and the road to Fern Gulley.

John Crow's Tavern (10 Main St., tel. 876/974-5895, 9:30 A.M.–12:30 A.M. daily, later on Fri. and Sat., US$8–14) is a small restaurant and bar on Ochi's main drag, a few steps from the Hard Rock Café. Dishes include club sandwiches, oxtail, escovitch fish, curry conch, curry chicken, jerk chicken, and pasta Alfredo and marinara. The mixed vegetables and dip is very popular, as is the coconut jumbo shrimp. Friday is jerk night, with a sound system and a mixed crowd of locals and tourists, with a little band on Saturday nights as well. There are three 42-inch flat-screen TVs generally showing some kind of

sporting event, and free Wi-Fi. Ravi Chatani owns the joint.

International

The Ruins at the Falls (17 DaCosta Dr., tel. 876/974-8888, www.ruinsjamaica.com, noon–10 P.M. daily) has an extensive menu with buffet lunch (US$15) that includes jerk chicken or pork and escovitch fish. Dinner items include Chinese roasted chicken (US$14), grilled lamb chops (US$28), Jamaican-style oxtail, curry goat (US$20), Jamaican Red Stripe butterfly shrimp (US$28), and grilled lobster thermidor (US$35).

An American doctor, Robert Page, created The Ruins in 1960s with bricks brought from a great house in Trelawny. The restaurant is one of the most scenic in Ocho Rios, with its dining room overlooking a natural 12-meter waterfall. The Ruins was once part of a larger property called Eden Bower, which covered much of the hill behind the restaurant, including the plot on which Evita's Italian restaurant sits today. Eden Bower was owned by the Geddes family, one of the founding partners of Red Stripe beer. In 1907 the property was parceled off and sold.

⟨ Blue Cantina (81 Main St., tel. 876/974-2430, 9 A.M.–8 P.M. daily, US$4–6) is a little Jamexican joint located around a sharp corner where James Avenue meets main street on the eastern edge of town. Cecile Henry makes the cantina's specialty tacos from scratch, regarded by some as the best on the island. Ms. Henry bought the business from a man who bought the business from its original Mexican owner, and the culinary knowledge was thus passed down.

Almond Tree Restaurant (83 Main St., tel. 876/974-2676, 7:30 A.M.–10:30 A.M., noon–2:30 P.M., 6–9:30 P.M. daily) serves a mix of Jamaican and international dishes like lobster (US$24), a variety of chicken (US$14), and fish (US$21), pork chops (US$15), lamb chops (US$17), and butterfly shrimp (US$30). A full bar in the restaurant serves the typical Heineken, Guinness, and Red Stripe (US$2.50), as well as mixed drinks. Indoor and outdoor dining areas overlook the water.

Michelle's Pizzeria (tel. 876/974-4322 or 876/974-9484, 11 A.M.–11 P.M. daily) is located at the Pineapple Hotel and has a nice outdoor dining area. Four specialty pizzas are served (10- or 16-inch, US$6–25): Hawaiian delight, seafood sensation, meat lovers, and conscious decision. Other dishes (US$7–8) include lasagna, spaghetti Bolognese, and vegetarian Rasta penne with traditional Jamaican ingredients. Subs are also prepared with smoked ham, jerk pork, fish, or plain cheese.

Evita's (Eden Bower Rd, reached by turning up the hill next to The Ruins, tel. 876/974-2333, 11 A.M.–10 P.M. Mon.–Sat., till 4 A.M. Sun. morning, US$11–30) is an Italian restaurant serving seafood, including lobster, steak, and pasta dishes. While Evita's might lack the upscale edge of Toscanini, the view is excellent and worth a trip.

Passage to India Restaurant & Bar (Sonis Plaza, 50 Main St., tel. 876/795-3182, 10 A.M.–10 P.M. Tues.–Sun., Mon till 3 P.M., US$11–26) serves very authentic North Indian cuisine with dishes like palak paneer, mala costa, chicken vindaloo, lamb, lobster, and shrimp.

Hong Kong International Restaurant (Soni Plaza, 50 Main St., tel. 876/974-0588, 10 A.M.–10 P.M. daily, later on the weekend, from US$8.50) is one of the better places for Chinese food in Ochi, serving chicken, beef, shrimp, seafood, and pork, with noodles and rice. Hong Kong is a bit dodgy in its ambience, making takeout a good option.

Irish Rover (Greenwich Park, Drax Hall, tel. 876/972-9352, cell tel. 876/573-4933, info@irishroverjamaica.com, 10 A.M.–10 P.M. Mon.–Fri., open later on weekends, starting at US$8.50) lays claim to being Jamaica's first Irish pub. Jamaican Winston Samuels and Irish wife Angela opened the place in 2008. The kitchen offers garlic bread ciabatta, garlic mushrooms, chicken wings, coconut shrimp, soups and salads, sandwiches, burgers, baked potatoes, steaks, shepherd's pie, crab cakes, salmon, and snapper, in addition to more typical Jamaican dishes. Reggae night features a live band on Fridays, Latin night brings out Latin dance enthusiasts on select Saturdays, and there's jazz on Sundays (6–9 P.M.). The bar offers a wide selection of liquor, with bottled domestic brews and Red Stripe on tap.

Bibibip's Bar & Grill (93 Main St., tel. 876/974-7438, 9 A.M.–1 A.M. daily, US$7–34) is a nice spot overlooking the water near Mahogany Beach. It features a wide range of seafood, as well as Jamaican and international dishes.

Food at **Coconuts** (Fisherman's Point, opposite Cruise Ship Pier, tel. 876/795-0064, 8 A.M.–10 P.M. daily, US$7–25) ranges from the ménage à trois appetizer (coconut shrimp, chicken samosa, and conch fritters) to jerk chicken quesadillas and wings to a medley of shrimp, conch, and chicken to grilled sirloin strip steak. Coconuts has an all-you-can-drink special (9 A.M.–4 P.M., US$20) that includes house-brand vodka, gin, and Appleton Special rum.

Toscanini Italian Restaurant & Bar (Harmony Hall, Tower Isle, tel. 876/975-4785, US$10.50–24) is the most high-end and best-quality Italian restaurant in town, with tables on the ground floor of a beautifully renovated great house and outside on the patio. Dishes include appetizers like marinated marlin, prosciutto and papaya, and yellowfin tuna tartare and entrées like spaghetti cioppino di mare; the menu changes daily. The food is excellent, but be prepared to pay for it. Toscanini is run by congenial Lella, who is always around the place chatting with customers. Toscanini has been in operation since 1998.

Hard Rock Café (4 Main St., tel. 876/974-3333, hrsales@cwjamaica.com, 11 A.M.–11 P.M. Sun.–Thurs., 11 A.M.–midnight Fri.–Sat., US$10–30) opened in November 2006 in Ocho Rios, bringing the world's greatest tourist trap to one of the Caribbean's foremost tourist towns. Dishes are typical Hard Rock fare, from club sandwiches to burgers and steak. Local memorabilia adorning the walls includes Junior Murvin's guitar, used by Bob Marley for recording of the *Kaya* album, as well as the original handwritten lyrics to "Jammin'." Also on display are a suede jacket worn by Jimi Hendrix and a cap worn by John Lennon.

Ocean's 11 Watering Hole (Cruise Ship Pier, tel. 876/974-8444, manbowen@cwjamaica.com, open when ship in town, closes at midnight at Tues. and Fri.) is a bar and restaurant opened in 2004 on the wharf that services cruise ship passengers primarily. Hours are determined by when the ship is in port (8 A.M.–1 A.M., 4 P.M.–1 A.M. when it's not in port). Much business in Ochi resolves around cruise ship schedules, which tend to change. Call ahead if you're not within sight of the pier to be sure. You can get Red Stripe (US$3) at the bar downstairs; upstairs there's a snack bar, coffee shop, and seafood restaurant with some nice antique coffee equipment that was at one time part of the small coffee museum on-site. Coffee is sold by the cup and by the pound (US$18–26/lb.).

Three Star Restaurant (Rexo Plaza, tel. 876/795-1320, 10 A.M.–9 P.M. Mon.–Sat., US$2–20) serves Chinese food, with dishes like chop suey, sweet and sour chicken, shrimp fried rice, stir fry, and Cantonese lobster.

Jamaican

My Favorite Place Restaurant (Shop #7, Ocean Village, tel. 876/795-0480, 8 A.M.–5 P.M. Mon.–Sat., breakfast only on Sun., US$2–6) serves typical Jamaican dishes like fried chicken, curry goat, escovitch fish, brown stew, and baked chicken; the menu changes daily, apart from the Jamaican staples. Paulette Garvey is the helpful proprietor and manager.

Nice-and-Nuff (Shop #8, Simmon's Plaza, 73 Main St., contact Lesreen Goulbourne, tel. 876/489-2190, 7 A.M.–7 P.M. Mon.–Sat., US$3–4) serves typical Jamaican food for breakfast, lunch, and dinner with items like ackee and saltfish, oxtail, curry goat, and fried chicken. Food is served in foam clamshell lunch boxes ready for takeout.

San-Mar Cafe (Shop #8, Ocean Village Shopping Centre, tel. 876/795-1024, US$2–6) serves local staples and Chinese dishes.

Mom's (7 Evenly St., tel. 876/974-2811, 8 A.M.–10 P.M. Mon.–Sat., US$4–20), not to be confused with Mother's on Main Street, is located in a blue building across from the police station toward the clock tower. It's a local favorite, with oxtail, brown stew fish, baked or fried chicken, curry goat, stewed peas, and stewed beef.

Mama Marley's Bar & Grill (50 Main St., tel. 876/795-4803) serves mediocre Jamaican and international dishes. The restaurant was owned by the late Cedella Marley, Bob's mother, known as Mama B.

Lion's Den (2.4 km west of cruise ship terminal, contact supervisor Joseph Morrison, cell tel. 876/896-1352, US$4–8.50) serves some of the best Jamaican home cooking in the Ocho Rios area, with dishes like fried chicken, curry goat, and stewed pork. It makes a great stop for lunch on the way in or out of Ochi.

Vegetarian

Reggae Pot Restaurant (86 Main St., contact Donovan "Boom Don" Slythe, cell tel. 876/422-4696, or Ras Deano Wynter, cell tel. 876/296-3591, 8:30 A.M.–9 P.M. Mon.–Sat., 10 A.M.–8 P.M. Sun.) serves vegetarian Ital food on a rotating menu with dishes (US$3 small/US$5 large) like brown stew, curried, or stir fry tofu and split peas with veggie chunks. Natural juices are prepared based on seasonal availability. Iyah Steve Boutcher is the third chef and a guitarist trained by the legendary Ernie Ranglin.

One Stop Veggie Shop (Shop #9, Simmon's Plaza, 73 Main St., cell tel. 876/877-1315, US$3–5) sells vegetarian food, porridge, soup, pastries, and natural juice.

Healthy Way Vegetarian Kitchen (Shop #54 Ocean Village, tel. 876/974-9229, 8 A.M.–6 P.M. Mon.–Sat., US$1.50–5) serves escovitch tofu, hominy, or peanut, plus plantain carrot, bulgur porridge, steamed cabbage with banana, and fried dumplings.

Mi Hungry Whol'-Some-Food (Contact Melak Selassie, tel. 876/875-1188) occasionally sets up shop at Coyaba Gardens, serving vegetarian raw food items like pizza and burgers (US$3.50–5.50) and fresh, natural juices (US$3–3.50).

Bakeries, Sweets, and Ice Cream

Golden Loaf Baking Company (72 Main St., tel. 876/974-2635 or tel. 876/974-5417 for the pizzeria, 8 A.M.–8:30 P.M. Mon.–Sat.) makes bread, pastries, and pizzas, and baked chicken.

Tropical Oven (Shop #2, Ocean Village, tel. 876/795-4970) is a bakery selling pastries and breads.

Scoops Unlimited (Island Village, tel. 876/675-8776, 9 A.M.–8:30 P.M. Mon.–Fri., 10 A.M.–10 P.M. Sat and Sun.) is one of the local Devon House I Scream franchises.

Groceries

Coconut Grove Supermarket and Wholesale (188 Main St., tel. 876/974-3049) is the best wholesale liquor store in Ochi, also selling a limited range of grocery items.

Liu's Rexo Supermarket is located at New Ocho Rios Plaza (tel. 876/974-2328).

DJ Supermarket & Wholesale (80-A Main St., tel. 876/974-3462, 9 A.M.–9 P.M. Mon.–Sat.) sells groceries and liquor.

Money's Worth Meat Mart (128 Main, tel. 876/974-2917) is the best place for fresh meat and imported frozen fish if you have trouble finding the local, fresh variety. Beef, chicken, local pork, snapper, Cornish hens, and imported turkey are sold.

Willy's Variety (130 Main St., tel. 876/974-5175, 9 A.M.–8 P.M. Mon.–Sat.) sells groceries, liquor, and hardware.

Park 'N' Shop Wholesale Supermarket is at 20 Main Street (tel. 876/795-4718).

INFORMATION AND SERVICES

The **St. Ann Chamber of Commerce** (tel. 876/974-2629) has tourist booklets that advertise the area's tourism businesses and attractions.

Car Rentals

Freehill Car Rental (Coconut Grove beside Petcom gas station, manager Cecil Subaran, cell tel. 876/865-3704 or tel. 876/795-4966, www.freehillcarrental.com, 8 A.M.–8 P.M. Mon.–Sat., till 5 P.M. Sun.,) rents Toyota

© OLIVER HILL

You won't find meat in any of the sumptuous dishes prepared at Reggae Pot Restaurant.

Corollas, RAV-4s, and the Nissan Cube or March (US$60–110/day, US$500–650/week), as well as scooters. The company also offers airport transfers and tours.

Villa Car Rentals (Shop #7, Coconut Grove Shopping Centre, tel. 876/974-2474, villacarrentalscoltd@msn.com, 8 A.M.–5 P.M. Mon.–Sat., 9 A.M.–2 P.M. Sun.) has the 2006 Toyota Corolla (US$420/week) and 2005 Yaris (US$320/week) plus tax and optional insurance ($50). Linda Mash and Harry Chung are co-owners.

Sunshine Car Rentals (154 Main St., Pineapple Place, tel. 876/974-2980 or 876/974-5025, 8 A.M.–5 P.M. Mon.–Fri., 9 A.M.–2 P.M. Sat.) has 2004 Suzuki Grand Vitaras (US$125/day, US$582/week) and Mitsubishi Lancers (US$149/day, US$700/week).

SunSpree Car Rental (tel. 876/974-6258, cell tel. 876/378-5682, fax 876/974-2652) rents Lancers and Corollas (US$70/day, US$378/week).

Caribbean Car Rentals (99-A Main St., tel. 876/974-2513, 8:30 A.M.–5 P.M. Mon.–Fri.,

9 A.M.–2 P.M. Sat., 9 A.M.–noon Sun.) has 2004 Mitsubishi Lancers, 2005 Suzuki Lianas (US$82/day, US$492/week), and 2006 Toyota Corollas (US$97/day, US$571/week).

Internet

Power Plus Computers (Shop #6, Rexo Plaza, Main St., tel. 876/795-4664, powerpluscomputers@yahoo.com, 9:30 A.M.–5:30 P.M. Mon.–Fri., Sat. till 3 P.M.) sells and repairs computers and basic accessories and offers Internet access at eight computer terminals, one with a webcam and microphone. Power Plus charges the Jamaican equivalent of about US$2.25 per hour for Internet access.

Computer Wizz (Shop #11, Island Plaza, Main St., tel. 876/974-5844, 8:30 A.M.–7:30 P.M., Mon.–Sat.) sells computers, accessories, service, and repairs and offers Internet access with almost a dozen desktops in use and Wi-Fi access for those who bring their own machine (US$2/half hour, US$3/hour, and J$100/half hour, J$150/hour if paying in local currency).

Jerkin' @ Taj Internet Cafe (Taj Mahal Centre, tel. 876/795-0862, 9 A.M.–5 P.M. Mon.–Sat.) has access for US$8 per hour. The restaurant section (10 A.M.–7 P.M.) serves decent jerk; a quarter chicken is US$15.

Banks

NCB Bank is at 40 Main Street next to Island Plaza/BK and across from the craft market (tel. 876/974-2522).

Scotia Bank also has a branch on Main Street, three buildings west of NCB (tel. 876/974-2311).

Nancy's Cambio (Taj Mahal, 4 Main St., tel. 876/974-2414; 50 Main St., tel. 876/795-4285; St. Ann's Bay, tel. 876/972-8842, 9 A.M.–5 P.M. Mon.–Sat.) offers slightly better exchange rates than the banks. Travelers' checks are accepted with two forms of ID. Money transfers are also possible at the St. Ann's Bay Moneygram outlet.

Healthcare and Pharmacies

Kulkarni Medical Clinic (16 Rennie Rd., tel. 876/974-3357, cell tel. 876/990-7726) has a well-respected private practice used by many of the area's better hotels. It's located between RBTT bank and Jamaica National.

St. Ann's Bay Hospital (Seville Road, tel. 876/972-2272) is the most important in the region, with people coming from kilometers around. Better service can be obtained at private health centers in Ocho Rios, however.

Ocho Rios Pharmacy is in Ocean Village Shopping Centre (Shop #67-A, tel. 876/974-2398, 8 A.M.–8 P.M. daily).

Pinegrove Pharmacy is east of the clock tower on Main Street (Shop #5, Ocho Rios Mall, tel. 876/974-5586, 9 A.M.–8 P.M. Mon.–Sat., 10 A.M.–3 P.M. Sun.).

Photo

Quick Shots Imaging Labs (4 DaCosta Dr., tel. 876/974-8498 or 876/974-8498, 9 A.M.–6 P.M. Mon.–Sat.) offers one-hour processing and sells film and memory cards.

Bailey's Photo Studio & Colour Lab (2 Rennie Rd., tel. 876/974-2711) offers photo processing and sells a limited range of digital camera products.

Laundry

Carib Laundro-Mat (Shop #6, Carib Arcade opposite of 112 Main St., tel. 876/974-7631, 7 A.M.–6:30 P.M. Mon.–Sat.) and **Express Laundromat** (18–20 Pineapple Place, Main St., tel. 876/795-0720 or 876/795-0721, 7 A.M.–7 P.M. Mon.–Sat., 9 A.M.–4 P.M. Sun.) both offer laundry services.

Communications and Media

DHL is at Ocean Village Plaza (Shop #3, tel. 876/974-8001, 9 A.M.–5 P.M. Mon.–Sat.).

Studio Tokyo (Coconut Grove, cell tel. 876/864-3640) offers music recording, mastering, and video production services in a modest studio near Irie FM.

GETTING THERE

Route taxis and buses leave for Kingston and points east and west along the coast from the lot just south of the clock tower in downtown Ocho Rios. Buses go between Ochi and Downtown Kingston (US$4) as well as to Montego Bay (US$4), while route taxis ply every other route imaginable: to Brown's Town (US$3), Moneague (US$1), and east and west along the coast to Oracabessa (US$2) and St. Ann's Bay (US$1.50).

Flights into the Oracabessa Aerodrome, renamed Ian Fleming International Airport in 2010, 15 minutes east of Ochi, can be booked with any of the island's charter operators from Kingston, Montego Bay, Negril, or Port Antonio. All the fixed-wing operators are based in Montego Bay and offer better rates when departing from there.

International Airlink (tel. 876/940-6660, res@intlairlink.com, www.intlairlink.com) offers service from Montego Bay (US$302 one-way paid in cash for two persons), Kingston (US$1,324), and Port Antonio (US$1,575). Airlink passes on bank charges of an additional 5 percent when paying with a credit card.

TimAir (tel. 876/952-2516, timair@usa. net, www.timair.net) also offers service from Montego Bay (US$316 for up to four persons plus tax), Kingston (US$579), Port Antonio (US$549), and Negril (US$566).

Captain John's Island Hoppers (tel. 876/974-1285, helicopter@mail.infochan. com, www.jamaicahelicopterservices.com, 8 A.M.–5 P.M. daily) offers helicopter airport transfers for up to four passengers from Montego Bay to Ochi (US$970), from Kingston (US$811), and to and from virtually any other points on the island, as well as tours for sightseeing. The company has two Bell Jetranger aircraft.

GETTING AROUND

Route taxis are the most economical way of getting around if you don't mind squeezing in with several other people. Taxis leave from the rank by the clock tower and can also be flagged down by the roadside if there is any room. Route taxis display their destination and origin in painted letters on the side of the cars and are typically white Toyota Corollas. Overcrowding has been somewhat reduced in recent years with increased oversight from the authorities. It is impossible to walk the streets of Ocho Rios without being offered a chartered taxi; bear in mind that these drivers will quote any figure that comes to mind. Haggling is very much a part of hiring a local charter, and be sure not to pay the total in advance if you hope to see your driver stick around.

West of Ocho Rios

As you head west from Ocho Rios, the North Coast Highway hugs the waterfront passing Dolphin Cove, Dunn's River Falls, and Laughing Waters before reaching a cluster of villas and resorts that front Mammee Bay. Just past the entrance to the resorts, an Epping gas station marks the junction where Scotchie's Jerk Centre occupies one corner across the highway from the Drax Hall Polo Club.

Continuing west, the next community is St. Ann's Bay, a busy town with one of the better hospitals on the North Coast and a few attractions worth stopping for, including Seville Great House and Heritage Park and the Marcus Garvey Statue by the Parish Library.

Still farther west, the small community of Priory sits along a dusty stretch of highway with few passersby stopping there, except on Sundays when the community's public beach comes alive for dance parties.

From Priory westward the highway passes Richmond Estate, used as a venue for several annual events, a few subdivisions in various stages of construction, and Chukka Cove. The next community of any size is Runaway Bay, where several hotels straddle the highway and waterfront. From Runaway Bay the highway continues westward to Discovery Bay, the last settlement of any size before the Trelawny border. Discovery Bay is one of Jamaica's most exclusive villa communities, the eastern side

OCHO RIOS

of the bay dotted with luxury villas. In the center of the bay a bauxite wharf feeds ships from an immense domed storage facility made famous as Dr. No's lair in Ian Fleming's first James Bond film.

SIGHTS

Rainforest Bobsled Jamaica at Mystic Mountain (tel. 876/974-3990, reservations. jam@rfat.com, www.rainforestrams.com/jamicaintro.html, 9 A.M.–5 P.M. daily) is the latest tourism development to hit Ocho Rios, located on 100 acres of forest west of town, just before Dunn's River Falls and Dolphin Cove. The site is Rainforest Aerial Tram's fifth such attraction in the region, with similar ecotourism theme parks in Costa Rica, Dominica, and St. Lucia. The tours include a 15-minute ride up to the peak of Mystic Mountain on the Sky Explorer, a chair lift similar to what you'd find at ski resorts. The ride and summit afford stunning views over Ocho Rios, and once at the peak, there's a photo and memorabilia exhibit covering Jamaican history and culture, a gift shop, and a bar and restaurant housed in a wooden replica of an old Jamaican train station. There's a water slide and infinity pool in front of the building overlooking the sea. The Bobsled Jamaica ride consists of a two-seater bobsled-like tram that travels through the forest along suspended rails. It's an exhilarating five-minute blast of adrenaline, but only as gut-wrenching as the person in front controlling the brakes decides. The canopy tour (US$104) consists of a ride on a zipline through the forest along five different segments. The Sky Explorer costs US$42 per person or can be packaged with the Bobsled ride (US$62) or canopy tour (US$104), with a complete package including all three rides costing US$124 per person. Additional Bobsled runs cost US$20 each, while a family pack sold for US$40 gives you five rides. There is no additional charge for the pool and water slide.

© OLIVER HILL

Presentation is not lost on the chefs at Mystic Dining, who prepare some of the best food in Ocho Rios.

OCHO RIOS

■ Mystic Dining offers a Saturday night (6–10 P.M.) prix fixe three-course dinner (US$33.50 per person including lift, gratuity, and taxes) in what is perhaps the most affordable way to experience Mystic Mountain, albeit without sun, and eat some of the best food served in Ocho Rios. There's a surcharge on lobster and steak, and beverages are sold at an extra cost.

Dolphin Cove (tel. 876/974-5335, info@dolphincovejamaica.com, www.dolphincovejamaica.com, 8:30 A.M.–5:30 P.M. daily, reservations required for encounters) is located just around the corner from Dunn's River Falls and offers a variety of programs where visitors interact with dolphins to a varying degree of intimacy, depending on the price—starting with a Touch Encounter (US$67), where you get to touch the dolphins' snout in knee-high water, to the Swim Encounter (US$129), where you get to touch the dolphins while swimming in an enclosed area of the ocean, to Swim with Dolphins (US$195), where visitors actually do a dorsal pull and a foot push with two dolphins.

In the shark program (US$119), there is a feeding show and petting and snorkeling session with six nurse sharks, ranging from 0.6 meter to up to three meters long.

The basic admission (US$45) includes kayaking, snorkeling, mini motor-boat rides, and glass-bottomed boat tours. Listed prices reflect direct booking through Dolphin Cove.

Dunn's River Falls

Dunn's River Falls (tel. 876/974-4767 or 876/974-5944, www.dunnsriverfallsja.com, 8:30 A.M.–4 P.M. daily, US$15 adult, US$12 children 2–11) is the most highly visited tourist attraction in Jamaica, if not the Caribbean. The site is owned by the Urban Development Corporation (UDC) and receives over 300,000 visitors a year who come to climb the steps up the falls. There is a small beach by the mouth of the river and two restaurants serving local dishes and beer. Patricia Parkins manages the attraction.

Dunn's River Falls is best visited on days when there are no cruise ships in Ocho Rios, which is easy to determine by taking a look at the pier. Every all-inclusive resort offers tour packages to the falls, however, so it's hard to avoid the crowds on any day. While it's a worthwhile attraction, there are several other falls in the area that see fewer visitors and offer a more serene experience, even if they aren't as spectacular for their size.

Dunn's River is located a few minutes' drive west of Ocho Rios. Route taxis pass by the falls on their way to St. Ann's Bay and will stop at Dunn's River by request. A private taxi charter from Ocho Rios shouldn't cost more than US$10, though the hard-hustling Ochi cabbies will likely start at a much higher price. Don't be afraid to haggle and remind the driver it's only a few kilometers.

Drax Hall Polo Club

Located across the highway from Scotchie's and the Epping gas station just west of Riu, Drax Hall Polo Club has one of the oldest polo fields in the world, and certainly in the Caribbean. Home to the St. Ann Polo Club (Contact Shane Chin, tel. 876/952-4370 or cell tel. 876/383-5586, chinrcpolo@yahoo.com; or Lesley Masterton-Fong Yee, cell tel. 876/681-4660), the fields have been in continual use since 1905. Polo has been in Jamaica since 1800 when it was introduced by the British army. The game is played strictly on an amateur level in Jamaica, with approximately 40 playing members spread over two clubs: the Drax Hall Polo Club in St. Ann and the Kingston Polo Club. There are three other privately owned fields on the island.

The St. Ann Polo Club originated in Orange Hall in 1882 and today has a casual ambience where members hang out to enjoy English tea or a beer after matches. In addition to the polo grounds, the facilities at the club include a full-size dressage ring and jumping ring, stable, turn-out paddocks, and, of course, the Polo Bar. The polo season at Drax Hall starts in late January with practice matches on Thursday afternoons and

OCHO RIOS

matches on Saturdays at 4 P.M. The club is host to many international players and riders from the United States, Colombia, Costa Rica, England, Guatemala, Scotland, India, Barbados, and Argentina. The players on the island are handicapped international from -2 to 4 goals. The Association can host tournaments from 1-goal to 14-goal polo. The Jamaica Polo Tournament is played at the St. Ann Polo Club and starts in March and goes through the end of May.

Fire River

Fire River is found in a park area a few hundred meters off the highway about 1.5 kilometers before the main junction to turn off into St. Ann's Bay. The river is so named thanks to flammable gas that rises from a pool in the river and can be lit in a curious mixing of the elements. While locals will tell legends of the history and significance of the spot, a large housing subdivision just through the trees prompts the question of whether the gas is actually methane derived from the area's septic systems. Still, claims are made that the phenomenon predates the bordering urbanization. The attraction is not managed and can be reached by turning off the highway by the easternmost entrance to St. Ann's Bay and taking an immediate left after the dog clinic, off the road along a dirt track leading to the river.

MAMMEE BAY AND OLD FORT BAY

Mammee Bay, located a few minutes' drive west of Dunn's River Falls, is home to Riu Ocho Rios and a complex of small hotels just to the east in Old Fort Bay.

Accommodations

Cannon Villas (tel. 876/754-1623, saanu10@yahoo.com, cannonvillasja.com) in Old Fort Bay is an assortment of old Jamaican cottage-style villas, four three-bedroom units and one four-bedroom, complete with lattice box windows, cushioned wicker furniture, and attractive interior decor. Villas have air-conditioning in the bedrooms, DSL, Wi-Fi, cable TV, a fully equipped kitchen, and a housekeeper. It's just steps from a fine white sand beach.

ST. ANN'S BAY

The parish capital, St. Ann's Bay is a small bustling town at the base of the hills that lead into the interior along rough potholed roads. Originally called Santa Gloria by Columbus, St. Ann's Bay was the site for the earliest Spanish settlement of Sevilla La Nueva, or New Seville, which became the colony's first capital. Santa Ana, as the area was named by the Spanish, was where they formed a cultural mix with the native Taino population and imported enslaved Africans. From the Spanish arrival straight through to the emancipation of slaves, the area was an epicenter of conflict between the violent anti-missionary Colonial Church Union and the Baptist abolitionists. It was these struggles for liberation that inspired St. Ann's most renowned son, pan-Africanist Marcus Garvey.

Sights

A **Marcus Garvey statue** stands in the yard in front of the St. Ann parish library (tel. 876/972-2660, 9:30 A.M.–5:30 P.M. Mon.–Fri., 9:30 A.M.–3 P.M. Sat.) just above the center of town. Garvey's bust stands in remembrance of a man whose ideas were suppressed by the powers of his day, but whose teachings nonetheless made serious ripples around the globe, inspiring black power movements the world over. The library has several computers free to use for half-hour intervals.

Marking the spot where the first Spanish capital of Jamaica was established, **Seville Great House** (tel. 876/972-2191 or 876/972-0665, seville@anbell.net, 9 A.M.–5 P.M. daily, US$5 adults, US$2 children) stands atop a hill commanding a panoramic view of the North Coast at the center of rolling lawns. The great house contains a museum where visitors are offered an historical tour highlighting the area's history and a selection of artifacts on display.

MARCUS MOSIAH GARVEY: BLACK POWER PROPHET

Marcus Mosiah Garvey was born in St. Ann's Bay in 1887 to humble but educated parents. After completing elementary school, he moved to Kingston, where he worked in a print shop and became increasingly interested and engaged in organized movements aimed at improving conditions for black Jamaicans. Black Jamaicans, while free from the bonds of slavery since 1838, were far from equal to their white counterparts and denied suffrage, among other basic rights. In 1907 Garvey was elected vice president of the Kingston Union, a charge that would cost him his job at the printer when he became involved in a strike. At the age of 23 Garvey left the island to work in Central America, as many Jamaicans in search of opportunity did at the time. His travels around the region gave Garvey an awareness of the common plight faced by the black race, seeding in him what would become a lifelong struggle to unite Africans of all nations under one common aim. In 1912 Garvey traveled to England, where he became engaged with black Africans and further broadened his vision of seeing black people take control of their destiny across the globe. In 1914 Garvey returned to Jamaica and founded the first chapter of the United Negro Improvement Association (UNIA) whose motto, "One God! One Aim! One Destiny!" summed up the broad goal of the organization to improve the lot of black people through solidarity and self-determination.

While Garvey's message was well received by his followers in Jamaica, it was in the midst of the Harlem Renaissance in New York City that he was first lauded as a prophet. Garvey is credited as the father of the Black Power movement, which would take Harlem, and ultimately the entire United States, by storm and eventually lead to the Civil Rights Movement of the 1960s. Garvey sought to enfranchise black people by generating black-owned businesses that would be linked on an international level. To facilitate this project he established the Black Star Line, an international shipping company that was to promote commerce. Garvey's following numbered four million members worldwide in 1920, a movement large enough to catch the attention of both the U.S. and British governments. When Garvey began to sell the notion of a mass return to Africa, however, he met resistance at the highest level of government. Garvey was convicted of mail fraud and imprisoned for a five-year term on what his followers considered trumped-up charges. After two years, he was released on an executive pardon and deported back to Jamaica. Local authorities were none too happy to see Garvey continue agitating for increased rights by forming the People's Political Party (PPP) in an effort to bring reform to Jamaica's colonial system. Garvey ran for a seat in Parliament and lost; later he won a seat on the Kingston and St. Andrew Corporation (the local government) from a jail cell, where he'd been placed for contempt of court. At the time, suffrage was limited to landowners, a class to which many of Garvey's followers did not belong, and his political support was accordingly stifled. Frustrated by the slow pace of change in Kingston, Garvey returned to London in 1935, where he would remain until his death in 1940. In 1964 Garvey was declared a national hero in Jamaica, and his remains were reinterred at Heroes Memorial in Kingston.

Garvey's legacy has been mixed in Jamaica, to say the least. Perhaps the greatest disservice to his teachings lies in the fact that his pleas for universal education have never been answered at an institutional level. At the same time, there is no doubting the impact he has made in certain circles. Rastafarians claim Garvey repeatedly iterated the call, "Look to the east for the crowning of a black king." It was one of Garvey's followers, Leonard Howell, who first cited the crowning of Ethiopian Emperor Haile Selassie on November 2, 1930, as a fulfillment of that prophecy, leading to the birth of the Rastafarian movement. Even today, it is the Rastafarian community both in Jamaica and abroad that has embraced Garvey's teachings to the greatest extent, often comparing him to John the Baptist.

OCHO RIOS

© OLIVER HILL

Seville Great House marks the spot where the first Spanish capital was established in Jamaica.

A large water wheel located along the driveway below the great house stands as a reminder of the sugar works.

Hooves (Seville Heritage Park, tel. 876/972-0905, hooves@cwjamaica.com, www.hooves-jamaica.com) offers 2.5-hour horseback rides (9 A.M. and 2 P.M. daily) from Seville Great House to the beach (US$65/person; with transport, US$70/person from Ochi, US$75/person from Runaway). The beach ride can be upgraded to a private ride for US$196 per couple for two horses.

Accommodations

High Hope Estate (Priory, tel. 876/972-2277, reservations@highhopeestate.com, www.highhopeestate.com, US$95–165) is a lovely B&B-style accommodation. Lunch and dinner are served, but the kitchen is closed on Sundays. Rooms have ceiling fans, a nice breeze to keep things cool, coffee pots, mini refrigerators, a radio and CD player, and cable in many of the rooms, with TVs on request. The property has beautiful gardens and a large swimming

pool. Dennis Donald is the on-site owner/manager.

Seacrest Beach Hotel (Richmond Cove, Priory, tel. 876/972-1594 or 876/972-1547, cell tel. 876/880-3130, seacrestresort@cwjamaica.com, www.seacrestresorts.com, from US$80) is a 35-room property with standard rooms that have air-conditioning, private baths with hot water, cable TV, and private balcony with sea view. There is also a pool and juice bar on property. Honeymoon suites and one- and two-bedroom cottages are a bit more spacious and separate from the main building.

Seascape Hotel (tel. 876/972-2753 or cell tel. 876/335-5195, seascape@seascapejamaica.com, www.seascapejamaica.com, US$45–50) has 10 basic rooms in three separate cottages centered on a common living area run under a hostel concept. Amenities include hot water, fans, air-conditioning, and a common kitchen facility available for guest use. Seascape caters to budget travelers, offering dorm room accommodations (US$25/person). The seafront property has 6.5 hectares. Lloyd Chen is the owner/manager. Cell phone rentals are also offered for a nominal charge (US$10). The property has a swimming pool and access to a craggy beach.

Priory

Just east of the stoplight in Priory, a turnoff leads down to **Priory Beach,** where an inflatable water slide is set up on Sundays and a sound system blasts dancehall, with selectors from Bass Odyssey entertaining the locals. There are several small cook shops, pan chicken vendors, a pudding shop, and a billiard hall along the stretch of highway running through Priory.

Cranbrook Flower Forest and River Head Adventure Trail (tel. 876/770-8071, www.cranbrookff.com, 9 A.M.–5 P.M. daily, US$10 adults, US$5 children 12 and under) is one of Jamaica's best-maintained and most highly acclaimed gardens. The nature trail follows the Little River to its source. The park is located 29 kilometers west of Ocho Rios and 6.5 kilometers east of Runaway Bay. A large sign 1.5 kilometers west of Chukka Cove indicates where to turn inland off the main road.

RUNAWAY BAY

Runaway Bay is lined with a strip of fine sand with all-inclusive resorts like SuperClubs' Breezes and Hedonism commanding the choice properties at the center and eastern tip of the Bay, respectively. The center of the Runaway Bay community consists of a few strips of buildings that include hole-in-the-wall restaurants, grocery stores, and a multitude of small dive bars decorated with strands of colored Christmas lights.

While many would suggest the bay was named after the flight of Don Cristobal Arnaldo de Ysassi, Spanish Governor of Jamaica at the time of the British takeover, Ysassi actually fled from Christopher's Point in St. Mary, and the more likely story involves the flight of runaway slaves to Cuba to seek their freedom.

Sights

Runaway Bay Public Beach has Flavours Grill, which serves fried chicken and beer and is a popular hangout that attracts throngs on weekends with loud music. The beach itself has clean, fine sand with a reef just offshore.

Green Grotto Caves (tel. 876/973-2841 or 876/973-3217, 9 A.M.–4 P.M. daily) is Jamaica's most commercially successful cave attraction, located on a 26-hectare property between Runaway and Discovery bays. While tamer than the experiences you can have in the heart of Trelawny's Cockpit Country a bit farther west, Green Grotto, also known as Runaway Cave or Hopewell Cave, is nonetheless a well-conceived organized tour, especially considering it is owned and operated by Jamaica's Urban Development Corporation. During the 45-minute tour that descends to an underground lake, well-rehearsed guides give a history of the caves, their formations, and their importance to the Taino and Spanish. A drink is included in the price of admission (US$20 adults, US$10 children). Green Grotto is located on the eastern edge of Discovery Bay.

Swallow Hole Fisherman's Beach (tel. 876/870-7331), located about one kilometer west of Breezes Runaway Bay, is a nice chill-out spot shaded by sea grapes. Women can be found in the mornings scaling the day's catch, which they'll readily sell, as children play in the water. The beach itself does not have fine sand.

Shopping

Stop & Shop (Salem, tel. 876/973-7168, 9 A.M.–8 P.M.) has a good selection of supplies and groceries, as does H&H Wholesale, also along the main strip.

Rasta's World (tel. 876/781-5820, 6 A.M.–1 A.M. daily) is a fruit stand and Rasta gear shop run by Doug Johnson, selling colorful hats and other knitted items, T-shirts, Haile Selassie patches, and other accessories.

Earth Kloz & Tingz (adjacent to Hedonism

OCHO RIOS

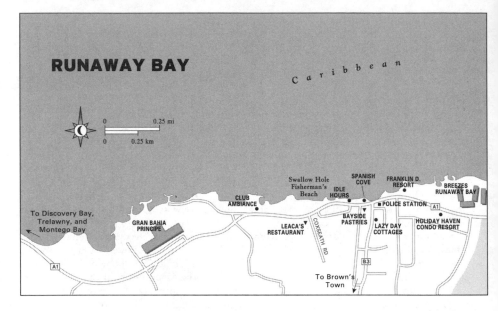

RUNAWAY BAY

Caribbean

0   0.25 mi
0   0.25 km

Swallow Hole
Fisherman's
Beach

SPANISH
COVE

IDLE
HOURS

FRANKLIN D.
RESORT

BREEZES
RUNAWAY BAY

CLUB
AMBIANCE

POLICE STATION

A1

To Discovery Bay,
Trelawny, and
Montego Bay

GRAN BAHIA
PRINCIPE

LEACA'S
RESTAURANT

COXSEATH RD

BAYSIDE
PASTRIES

LAZY DAY
COTTAGES

HOLIDAY HAVEN
CONDO RESORT

A1

B3

To Brown's
Town

III and the Baptist church, contact Worknesh, cell tel. 876/880-5859) sells Afro-centric clothing, tie-dye, and African fabrics.

Sports and Recreation

Breezes Golf Club (Runaway Bay, tel. 876/973-7319, greens fees US$80 or US$25 JGA members, US$16 for caddy, US$35 for cart, US$20–30 clubs) has an 18-hole championship course. The course recommends gratuity of US$10 or more per person. Golfing on consecutive days drops the rate, down to US$40 on the third day and thereafter. Guests at Breezes Runaway Bay have greens fees waived, and Hedonism guests get reduced rates.

Entertainment and Nightlife

Runaway Bay has not been known historically as a nightlife haven outside the hotel clubs at Hedonism, Breezes, and Club Ambiance.

Seven Stars, located on the left just past the stoplight as you enter town from the east, hosts occasional street party sessions in an open-air compound.

Club Jamaica Jamaica (Lot #20-B, Cardiff Hall, tel. 876/973-5815, info@club-jamaicajamaica.com, www.club-jamaicajamaica.com) is at times one of the hottest venues on the North Coast. The venue has four floors, with bars on each and plush white-cushioned furniture on the upper levels. A bar on the first floor is painted with pictures of some of Jamaica's legendary reggae artists.

Accommodations

Lazy Day Cottages (turn left at stoplight toward Brown's Town and left down a narrow lane just before Save a Dollar variety store, tel. 876/973-4318, cell tel. 876/776-3372, US$–30) has basic rooms with double beds, fans, and cold water in private bathrooms. One room has a kitchenette, while one two-bedroom cottage separate from the rest, known as the Bob Marley Cottage, is more tasteful, in a rustic sense, with simple wood construction and a lovers' loft. Lazy Day Cottages rooms are frequently used in three-hour intervals but also get their share of foreign guests on a shoestring budget. You may see the owner, Marlene Taylor, who is often off working abroad. Security at Lazy Day is dubious, with

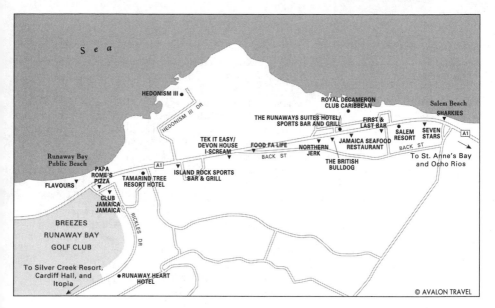

threats and break-ins having been reported by management.

The Runaways Suites Hotel (tel. 876/408-2101, runaways001@yahoo.com, US$70) has basic rooms with tiled floors, air-conditioning, and hot water. While it is not the most charming accommodations, rates are reasonable and the hotel is situated centrally along the highway with food upstairs and the beach five minutes away.

Salem Resort (Salem, tel. 876/973-4256, salemresort@yahoo.com, www.salemresort.com, US$40–80) offers basic accommodation with rooms ranging from basic with a standing fan to suites with ceiling fans, air-conditioning, and kitchenettes.

Runaway Heart Hotel (tel. 876/973-6671, runaway.heart@cwjamaica.com, www.runawayheart.com.jm, US$83/90 low/high season) is a hotel run by Jamaica's HEART training institute in close proximity to the golf course. The hotel has 56 rooms, which are well maintained with tiled floors and floral bed-covers on one king-size or two double beds, balconies overlooking the bay, TV, air-conditioning, and private baths with hot water. A computer in the office is available for guests to browse the Web and is included in the rate. There is a pool and small fitness center at the hotel as well.

Club Ambiance (tel. 876/973-6167, 876/973-4605, or 876/973-4606, toll free tel. 800/822-3274, info@clubambiencejamaica.com, www.clubambience.com, US$95/105 low/high season) is a 90-room property billed as an alternative to the mega resorts. Rooms have king-size beds, air-conditioning, hot water, and TV, with basic wooden furniture and tiled floors. Decor is definitely early 1990s, with loud colored bedspreads and kitschy art on the walls. There is one villa on property with a private pool that can accommodate up to six people (US$570/630 low/high season). The hotel has a lively activities schedule. Guests must be 18 or over.

Idle Hours villa (www.vrbo.com, Ingrid Fitt, sfittja@hotmail.com, www.vrbo.com, tel. 876/361-3488, US$2,800/3,300 weekly low/high season) is a three-bedroom, three-bath villa on one of Jamaica's finest strips of private beach in the heart of Runaway Bay. Amenities include a private pool overlooking the beach, a well-manicured lawn, and Wi-Fi, with full-time housekeeper, chef, and security. Rooms have king-size beds, ceiling fans, and air-conditioning.

Itopia (Cardiff Hall, tel. 876/965-3000, toll-free from the U.S. tel. 800/OUTPOST (800/688-7678), US$495/night) is a lovely country home owned by the Henzells, the family whose late patriarch, Perry, brought the world *The Harder They Come,* the film that helped to catapult a young Jimmy Cliff to international superstardom in the early 1970s. Built in 1660 as the overseer's house at Cardiff Hall estate, the cutstone three-bedroom home is cozy and charming, in a preserved colonial state enhanced by the design genius of Sally Henzell and appointed with colonial era furnishings and funky family memorabilia. A fourth bedroom and entertainment room are located around back in a separate building. To get there, head inland at the gas station on the edge of the Breezes Runaway Bay Golf Course, and take the second left after

Runaway Heart Hotel on Poinciana Road. Stay to the left when the road splits, pass a Water Commission pump station and then Cardiff Hall Great House on the left, and then take the second left and the first right. It's about a 15-minute drive to Runaway Bay. Euphemia, the cook and housekeeper, prepares delicious meals.

Last Lick (Black Ants Corner, Runaway Bay, contact Adina Parchment, villa manager at Jakes, tel. 876/965-3000 or 876/844-9803, jakesvillas@cwjamaica.com, jakes@cwjamaica.com, US$95/115 low/high) was a piece of land given as a 40th birthday gift from the late director Perry Henzell (*The Harder They Come*) to his wife Sally. Right away Sally painted a watercolor of the house she wanted to build there, and in 1981 a Robinson Crusoe–like two-story cottage was erected amid a garden of flowering shrubs and trees true to her artistic vision.

Built on a cake slice–shaped piece of land with the sea on two sides of the triangle, the two-bedroom stone cottage has a little

Once the overseer's residence at Cardiff Hall estate, Itopia has been transformed by artistic designer extraordinaire Sally Henzell into a psychadelic, one-of-a-kind villa, with a homely charm that transcends the ages.

© LANCE WATSON

OCHO RIOS

sitting room with a kitchen in one corner on the ground floor, a bathroom with a tub that doubles as a powder room and leads into a bedroom with three French windows opening to the sea. Another door leads to the outside patio, which serves as the dining room and hangout area. A sandpit for sunbathing and a shower for washing off separate the cottage from the sea, where a ladder descends to the water, shallow enough to stand, and good for snorkeling around the coral heads. Other steps lead down to a shallower part of the sea, which has mineral water flowing in from a stream, known as "the healing baum." The spring is prized for its regenerative powers and the sea is crystal clear. An upstairs bedroom and bathroom has French windows opening out to a sea view and is accessible by using the outside stairs or a ladder from the ground level. Housekeeping is included, with meals prepared for an additional US$25 per day per person.

Holiday Haven Condo Resort (Opposite Breezes Runaway Bay, tel. 876/973-4893, www.holidayhaven.biz, www.holidayhaven@cwjamaica.com, US$88–260) is a condo complex offering standard rooms as well as one- and two-bedroom suites with kitchen and living and dining areas. The complex is located across the road from the coast, a short walk to the fishermen's beach.

ALL-INCLUSIVE RESORTS

Franklyn D. Resort (FDR) (tel. 876/973-4591, reservations@fdrholidays.com, www.fdrholidays.com, US$250/375 per person low/high season) is a family-oriented all-inclusive that differentiates itself by offering each family a dedicated nanny (US$4/hour).

Royal DeCameron Club Caribbean (tel. 876/973-4802, ventas.jam@decameron.com, US$94/110 per person low/high season) is the second hotel of the DeCameron group in Jamaica. There are 183 pleasant rooms, some in a main block; others are either beachfront or garden cottages with king-size beds, air-conditioning, TV, and hot water. The property has two pools and a private beach. The

property offers guests bicycles, which can be quite useful for those interested in moving about, as Runaway Bay is a configured in a spread-out strip.

Hedonism III (tel. 876/973-4100 or U.S. tel. 877/GO-SUPER (877/467-8737), www.superclubs.com) is the second such establishment on the island, after Negril's Hedonism II. The resort bills itself as a place to escape inhibitions and worries and focus on guilty pleasures. All the features of SuperClubs all-inclusive resorts are present, from the trapeze on the beach to swim-up bars. Of course Hedonism sets itself apart with whirlpool tubs in every room, mirrors over the bed, and nude beaches outside. With the exception of sex out in the open, everything else goes. Several organized events are held throughout the year to market vacation packages, and porn stars like Devin Lane have been invited guests in the past to help cement the resort's risqué reputation.

Breezes Runaway Bay (tel. 876/973-4820 or 876/973-6099, www.superclubs.com) was closed for six months in 2006, during which time the resort underwent a massive refurbishment that gave the entire property a facelift. The renovations have left the flagship Breezes Resort with five restaurants, including the SuperClubs signature Japanese-inspired Munasan and culturally inspired Reggae Café, plus three swimming pools, 40 suites with private plunge pools, and a total of 266 rooms. A new three-story block on the western beach has 30 oceanfront rooms and suites, 14 of which have private plunge pools. In the eastern courtyard, 30 garden-view rooms were converted into veranda suites, also with private plunge pools. Rooms at Breezes are spacious with complete amenities.

Gran Bahia Principe (Salt Coppers Villa, tel. 876/973-7000, U.S. toll-free 866/282-2442) is a monstrous, 680-room resort quite obviously built in a hurry. The hotel features junior suites facing the sea or the pool area, buffet and a la carte dining, and Jamaica's longest lazy river. Rooms have one king or two queen beds, local cable and satellite TV with en suite bathrooms.

This is one of the least expensive all-inclusive hotels on the island, with the value of the experience corresponding to the cost.

Food

Sharkies (Salem Beach, cell tel. 876/881-5760, 8 A.M.–10 P.M. daily) is a seafood restaurant serving items like fried, roasted, and steamed fish (US$7–10), conch (fritters, stewed, or curried, US$5–7), and lobster (US$15).

The Runaways Sports Bar and Grill (tel. 876/408-2101, 11 A.M.–2 A.M. Mon.–Fri., 10 A.M.–2 A.M. Sat.–Sun., US$9–36) is a cool spot on top of a four-story building in the easternmost of Runaway Bay's little shopping plazas in Salem district. The roof has a small swimming pool, a billiards table, and flat-screen TVs linked with satellite feed for major sports broadcasts. The bar serves domestic beers and mixed drinks, with the kitchen serving items like fried chicken, crab backs, and tacos, with sides of fried plantain. Fresh juices are also served (US$2).

Northern Jerk (tel. 876/973-7365, 10 A.M.–midnight daily), in Northern Shopping complex next to Northern Bar, has good food and maintains a clean kitchen. Fried and baked chicken are served, in addition to jerk (US$2–5.25), plus ice cream, cakes, and pastries.

Food Fa Life (contact Lantie Minto, cell tel. 876/388-5322, 6 A.M.–9 P.M. Mon.–Sat.), located in a container near the Devon House ice cream shop, opened in 2007 serving veggie dishes like veggie chunks, mince, ackee (US$3–4.50) and natural juices like June plum, cherry, beet, lemonade, and ginger (US$2–3.50).

Devon House I Scream has a shop next to Tek It Easy.

Flavours (tel. 876/973-5457, 10 A.M.–10 P.M. daily), located on Runaway Bay's public beach, is a popular local hangout specializing in seafood, burgers, and local dishes (US$5–40).

Papa Rome's Pizza & Family Restaurant (beside Shell Station, tel. 876/973-4435, cell tel. 876/438-1428, or 876/581-5893, noon–9:30 P.M. Mon.–Thurs., noon–10 P.M. Fri.–Sun., cash only) serves small (US$6.75), medium (US$10), and large pizzas (US$14.50) with a variety of topping choices.

Bayside Pastries (2-A Main St., tel. 876/973-5807, 8 A.M.–6 P.M. Mon.–Sat.) sells rum and fruit cake, potato pudding, and Jamaican staples (US$2.50–4.25), soups (US$.70–2.25), and patties (US$.80).

Island Rock Sports Bar and Grill (Main St., Salem, tel. 876/973-6661, 10 A.M.–midnight daily, US$3–22), located across from the road leading to Hedonism III, is a laid-back restaurant and bar serving a variety of local dishes.

At **Jamaica Seafood Restaurant** (Main St., tel. 876/398-2838, 8:30 A.M.–10 P.M. daily) chef Noel serves typical Jamaican dishes, fish, and conch soup.

Leaca's Restaurant (Main St., tel. 876/434-5466, 8 A.M.–9 P.M. Mon.–Sat.) serves Jamaican breakfast and lunch and dinner staples like ackee and saltfish, fried chicken, curry goat, and oxtail accompanied by rice and peas.

The British Bulldog (Main St. Salem, tel. 876/540-4662, 10 A.M.–11 P.M. daily) claims the title of the only British-owned pub in Jamaica. Karaoke is staged every Sunday (8:30 P.M.–late), and there's a pool table for the slower nights. Little differentiates this from other bars where the beverage offering is concerned.

DISCOVERY BAY

Originally named Puerto Seco (Dry Harbor) by Christopher Columbus, Discovery Bay was renamed to reflect the debated assertion that this was the first point in Jamaica where the explorer made landfall. Many experts believe that the actual first point of entry was in Rio Bueno, a few kilometers farther west, where Columbus could have sought freshwater. Irrespective of this disputed historical detail, Discovery Bay has played an important role in Jamaica's more recent history, first as a bustling export port where barrels of sugar and rum departed for Europe, and then from the early part of the 20th century as a bauxite port. It remains one of the few active bauxite facilities in Jamaica following the global economic downturn of 2009, when half the island's alumina and bauxite operations went idle. The industrious port is the curious backdrop for perhaps Jamaica's staunchest enclave of old Jamaican money, with several of the country's wealthiest families owning beachfront villas facing the bay.

Sights

Puerto Seco Beach (tel. 876/973-2660 or 876/973-2944, cell tel. 876/325-7520 or 876/450-8529, 9 A.M.–5 P.M. daily, US$3.50 adults, US$2 children 7–12, US$1.50 children under 7), pronounced "SEE-ko," can be accessed by turning in across from the Texaco station in Discovery Bay. The public beach has some of the cleanest bathrooms at any public beach in Jamaica, Jupsy's Snack Bar, and Puerto Seco Beach Bar. Isolyn Walters is the friendly property manager.

Just west of the public beach in Discovery Bay, around the bend from the gas station, is Old Folly, a district covering the narrow valley containing the bauxite plant and terminal, overlooking the stretch of sand on the opposite side of the bay that is home to some of Jamaica's most luxurious villas.

Quadrant Wharf is the old sugar terminal where an old winch lies rusting. A plaque on the wall facing the road tells of the importance of the location, from Columbus' landing to the export of sugar, arms, and bauxite.

Just around the bend from the bauxite terminal in Old Folly, **Columbus Park** (free) hugs the steep slope rising from the western side of the bay. The park consists of an open-air museum wedged between the highway and the slope descending to the water, with a mural depicting the arrival of Italian explorer Christopher Columbus and several relics from the colonial period scattered about.

Accommodations

Many of Jamaica's wealthiest families have weekend homes on Discovery Bay, making it one of the island's most exclusive villa enclaves. Many of these homes rent through agents, while some rent directly through the owners, but usually the pricing is the same either way and renting through an agent can afford some accountability and recourse should you have any problems. A dependable agent for villas throughout Jamaica, including in Discovery Bay is SunVillas (contact Alan, tel. 888/625-6007, or locally contact Latoya, tel. 876/544-9497, info@sunvillas. com, www.sunvillas.com). For direct bookings, Vacation Rentals by Owner (www.vrbo. com) is a good bet.

A smattering of low-key budget accommodations can also be found in Discovery Bay, with little in between the budget and luxury extremes.

Discovery Bay Villa (tel. 876/973-2836 or 876/973-2663) is a convenient and affordable accommodation a three-minute walk from Puerto Seco Beach across the highway. The spacious two-story house has a downstairs bedroom with queen-size bed, TV, and fan (US$40), as well as two rooms upstairs: one with queen-size bed, air-conditioning, and TV (US$55), the other with a king-size bed, air-conditioning, TV, and a whirlpool tub in the bathroom (US$60).

Paradise Place (54 Bridgewater Garden, Poinciana Drive at the corner of and Sunflower Dr., contact owner Paul Shaw, tel. 876/973-9495, or cell tel. 876/862-2095, in the UK 44/(0)876973-9495, shawtop@aol. com, www.paradiseplace54.com) is set back from the highway in a quiet subdivision, run by a returning resident who offers a total of six rooms, four in two two-bedroom apartments (US$80) and two additional stand-alone rooms (US$60), all of them with pine furniture, air-conditioning, microwave, and fridge. There's a front and back veranda accessible to all guests with sea views from the back, with a hot tub in a gazebo in the yard also for common use.

Sugar Bay (Peter McConnell, tel. 876/903-6125, pmcconnell@worthy-parkestate.com, www.jamaicavillas.com, US$11,900/14,400 weekly low/high season) is a deluxe five-bedroom, 5.5-bath villa, with private beach and exquisite decor.

Amanoka (contact Denise McConnell, tel. 876/361-4008, denmcc2@gmail.com, www.amanoka.com, US$18,000/21,000 weekly low/high season for up to 14 people) is one of the most luxurious villas in Jamaica, if not the most over-the-top, catering to the pinnacle of the high-end market. Amenities include a spa, tennis courts, private beach, infinity pool, and a large hot tub.

Whispering Waters (Fortlands Rd., contact Mark McConnell, tel. 876/361-4005 or 876/708-2155, nicolab@cwjamaica.com, www.whisperingwatersjamaica.com, US$13,950/17,950 per week low/high) is a 9,000-square-foot ultra luxurious villa with seven bedrooms, each having en suite bathrooms, air-conditioning, and flat panel TVs with cable and DVD players. Other features include a business center, private beach with kayaks, a large pool and Jacuzzi, lighted tennis courts, and a state-of-the-art gym.

Fortlands Point (rents through SunVillas, contact Alan, tel. 888/625-6007, or locally contact Latoya, tel. 876/544-9497, info@sunvillas.com, www.sunvillas.com) is a seven-bedroom villa with three private beaches affectionately known as The Fort. Amenities include a squash court and full gymnasium. The whole of the living and entertainment areas are on the north side of the property, with a 180-degree view and absolutely great privacy.

Food

(Ultimate Jerk Center (10 minutes west of Breezes approaching Discovery Bay, tel. 876/973-2054, 10 A.M.–10 P.M. daily, US$1–5) does stewed chicken and pork, curry goat, stewed conch, potato, festival, bammy, fritters, rice and peas, and french fries. The bar serves a variety of liquor, and every last Saturday of the month an oldies party is held. Ultimate is a popular spot for locals to congregate to take in a cricket match, eat jerk, and vibe out. The jerk is the best in the area and doesn't linger on the grill thanks to a steady flow of traffic.

Coconut Tree Restaurant & Bar (Dairy Pen, tel. 876/973-9781, 8 A.M.–8 P.M. daily) serves typical Jamaican fare, jerk, and patties.

(Grill 3000 (Main Street, 0.25 mile west of Green Grotto Cave, by Auto Towing and Repossession Enterprises, contact proprietor Lindel Lawrence, tel. 876/973-3000, 9 A.M. until the last person leaves, US$1–3.50) serves steamed fish and fish soup accompanied by cornmeal dumplings, as well as cappuccino to wash it down. Grill 3000 is little more than a roadside BBQ pit, but the bargain-priced steamed fish is some of the best available on the island, incredibly prepared by a man who spends most of the day towing vehicles.

PSSL Supermarket (Philmore Mall, tel. 876/670-0327) is a good bet for groceries and supplies.

Ebony Restaurant and Natural Juice Bar (Main St., tel. 876/578-3317, US$1.50–2.25) serves typical local and vegetarian cuisine and natural juices. **Pizza King,** at the same location, serves pizza by the slice (US$2) or whole (9-inch or 11-inch, US$10–12).

Seafood Restaurant (next to bauxite wharf, Tanesha, tel. 876/870-5411, or contact Ardale Harvey, tel. 876/357-6637, 7 A.M.–midnight, daily, US$3–8) serves lobster, chicken, fish, and conch.

Baywatch Bar & Restaurant (Old Folly, across from bauxite terminal, tel. 876/578-7706, noon–11 P.M. Mon.–Sat., US$3–4.50) serves typical Jamaican fare in a local atmosphere overlooking the bay.

Hot & Spicy Tavern is a cook shop run by Morton "Beaks" Willis (tel. 876/853-0103) located inside the ruins of the old warehouse at Quadrant Wharf. Beaks also runs the bar on the property.

Coconut Lagoon Bar and Restaurant (Queen's Highway, contact Alvin Spencer, tel. 876/899-1245, 8 A.M.–9:30 P.M. daily), located on the sea side of the road as you round a bend approaching Rio Bueno from Discovery Bay, opposite derelict Bay Vista resort, is a popular pit stop serving typical Jamaican fare and fish dishes (US$5–12).

Inland from Ocho Rios

From Ocho Rios, Milford Road (A2) heads south from the main intersection by Turtle Park and uphill along the steep, winding route through Fern Gully. A few roadside vendors sell crafts in the cool shade of the wider corners. The road exits in Colgate and continues on to Bromley, Walkerswood, and then Moneague before reaching Faith Pen just before the border with St. Catherine. From the main intersection in Moneague, the A1 heads to St. Ann's Bay, passing through Claremont. A left at the intersection in Claremont leads to Nine Mile. Staying on the A1 past Claremont will take you through Green Park, where the road splits. By taking a left at the Y intersection you reach Brown's Town, where the road meets the B3, which runs from May Pen through Cave Valley, Alexandria, and from Brown's Town to Runaway Bay on the North Coast. The region is known as the Dry Harbour Mountains. Brown's Town is the closest town of any size to the Bob Marley Mausoleum in Nine Mile and is famous for its bustling market. Cave Valley is a small community along the Clarendon border, which has a bustling Saturday market where livestock is sold.

WALKERSWOOD

Walkerswood (located between Fern Gully and Moneague just past Bromley Great House heading south, contact Denise Perkins, cell tel. 876/379-4749 or 876/917-2318, www.walkerswood.com) makes some of the finest and most successful barbecue sauces, marinades, curry seasonings, and fruit pickles exported from Jamaica. A factory tour has been offered in years past but ceased when the company was sold in 2008. Once the company is back on its feet under the new ownership, tours are expected to resume, according to the new management.

Accommodations and Food

Bromley (contact Johnathan or Alex Edwards,

© OLIVER HILL

Bromley sits atop a hill in Walkerswood, commanding the best views around of the St. Ann interior.

OCHO RIOS

cell tel. 876/857-2960, alexandra.sale@gmail.com, www.bromleyjamaica.com, US$80 per night) is a stately great house owned by the founding family of Walkerswood jerk sauces. A quaint cottage, Lignum Vitae, located next to the great house operates as a bed-and-breakfast, with a large bedroom suite containing a queen-size bed plus an additional twin bedroom with a veranda. Bromley is set in the cool hills of Walkerswood, a 15-minute drive above the resort town of Ocho Rios. Miss Mineta, the caretaker, cooks breakfasts of fresh fruits, homemade granola, eggs, and Blue Mountain coffee, with other meals prepared to order at US$25 per day plus the cost of food. Views of the St. Ann interior are remarkable, and a host of birds thrive in the lush gardens. The property is suitable for retreats, with a yoga deck and small immersion pool in the yard. Wi-Fi is complimentary.

Lyming at Walkerswood (tel. 876/917-2812 or cell tel. 876/364-3407, US$5–10) makes a great pit stop for authentic jerk chicken, pork, and sausage, accompanied by breadfruit and festival.

MONEAGUE

Moneague is a small community along the main road between Spanish Town and the North Coast notable for the Moneague Teacher Training College, the Jamaica Defense Force Training Camp, the mysterious rising lake, and Café Aubergine, one of the most charming restaurants on the island.

Food

C Café Aubergine (tel. 876/973-0527, noon–9 P.M. Sat.–Sun., US$15–30) had the first tavern license to sell booze to the carriage men taking the two-day journey over the mountains to the North Coast from Kingston and Spanish Town. Today it is a well-recognized local favorite with Old World charm, serving a mix of Caribbean and Mediterranean cuisine. Owner Neville Anderson carries on the tradition begun in partnership with the late Rudolf Gschloessl, bringing European haute cuisine to a Caribbean sensibility with starters

that include French onion soup, escargot provençales, conch in lemon vinaigrette, and pâté de la maison. Main courses include pork tenderloin medallions in sherry mushroom sauce, grilled lamb chops, grilled filet mignon, and lobster in tarragon wine sauce. Top it off with an apple pie à la mode or chocolate mousse and you're good to go.

Faith's Pen, a few kilometers south of Moneague, has a famous rest stop lined with shacks dishing out jerk and conch soup at the best local prices. Fruit stands also appear sporadically along the road north and south of Faith's Pen.

BROWN'S TOWN

A large inland town named after Hamilton Brown, who represented the parish for 22 years, Brown's Town was a center of the Baptist-fueled abolitionist movement before the Colonial Church Union destroyed the Baptist chapel following the Christmas Rebellion. Brown was a colonel in the militia who saw the chapel torn to the ground. If you're heading to Nine Mile via route taxi, Brown's town is the connection point from St. Ann's Bay.

NINE MILE
C Bob Marley Mausoleum

The Bob Marley Mausoleum (call mausoleum manager Harry Shivnani for booking at cell tel. 876/843-0498 or US tel. 305/665-5379, harry.reggaeking@yahoo.com, bobmarleymovement.com, 9 A.M.–5 P.M. daily, admission US$15) was built next to the humble country house where the world's foremost reggae superstar was born. Today it's part of a complex that draws fans from around the world to experience the humble beginnings of a man many consider prophetic. Arriving at the hillside hamlet of Nine Mile, the Cedella Marley basic school looms up in its full red, gold, and green splendor just before reaching the Marley family home. In a large parking area, countless Rastas offer guide services and other paraphernalia, all of which will require compensation at the end of the tour. The tour (US$15) starts at the gift shop, where visitors

BOB MARLEY: KING OF REGGAE

If you mention reggae, Jamaica, Rastafari, or marijuana, chances are the first thought that comes to most peoples' minds is Bob Marley. The man has become synonymous with all things good about Jamaica and its people, carrying the country's cultural torch decades after his death in 1981. There's no way to measure the goodwill this man has brought the country. Even in times of global economic crisis, Jamaica is among the top tourism destinations in the Americas, ranked tenth in the Western Hemisphere in terms of visitor volume, and third in the Caribbean after Barbados and Puerto Rico. The goodwill Bob Marley has brought the world at large through his intoxicating music, full of uplifting messages, is also hard to quantify.

Born Robert Nesta Marley on February 6, 1945, in Nine Mile, St. Ann, to Cedella Malcolm Marley Booker and Norval Sinclair Marley, Bob grew up a country boy in the small agricultural community before moving with his mother to Trench Town, a ghetto of Downtown Kingston. His father, a white English naval officer and plantation overseer, had a scarce presence throughout Bob's childhood, and died in 1955 at the age of 60. Bob's racial mix set him apart from his peers as a boy, often the target of jeering and name calling, but this same heritage afforded him the distance to approach issues of race and justice from an unbiased perspective, and infused his music with a universal appeal.

While his late mother, Cedella, has said in documentaries that Bob could frequently be heard singing as a youth, it wasn't until he reached Trench Town that he teamed up with Peter McIntosh and Bunny Livingston to form the Wailin' Wailers. Trench Town in the 1960s was the creative epicenter of Jamaican music, where fledgling composers and musicians listened attentively to radio broadcasts of American music and reinterpreted classics on their ramshackle

instruments, sparking a swing away from traditional Jamaican music, like mento, that led to the birth of ska, rocksteady and reggae. Bob's early career spanned the development and evolution of these three genres, but it was reggae that became the vehicle for his message at the international level.

While Bob's talent was clearly apparent in the early days of the Wailers to producers like Leslie Kong, who recorded his first two singles "Judge Not" and "One Cup of Coffee," and Clement Dodd who later produced "It Hurts to be Alone," and "I'm Still Waiting," it wasn't until Bob traveled to London and recorded his first full album, *Catch a Fire*, on Chris Blackwell's fledgling label Island Records that he gained international recognition. Blackwell nurtured the Wailers and helped create a sound that had wide international appeal, without watering down the message.

After recording several albums on the Island Records label, Bob established his own label, Tuff Gong, using the pet name he was known by on the street. Tuff Gong remains a symbol of artistic independence, a departure from the days when musicians were paid measly sums to play on studio recordings while the producers reaped the rewards. Bob's larger-than-life persona outgrew the Wailin' Wailers, creating resentment among fellow founders Bunny Livingston, known as Bunny Wailer, and Peter McIntosh, or Peter Tosh, both of whom left the group to pursue successful solo careers. Following the departure of his former band mates, he renamed his band Bob Marley and the Wailers and went on to tour the world, filling stadiums and concert halls, up to his untimely death at the age of 36. Bob's popularity has only grown since his passing, with his posthumous *Legend* album going platinum several times over. Countless up-and-coming artists aspire to carry on his work, crowning him with immortality.

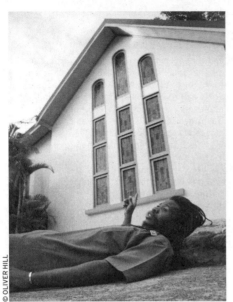

© OLIVER HILL

A guide at the Bob Marley Mausoleum rests his head on the rock pillow mentioned in "Talkin' Blues."

pay an entry fee and from there are led up to the mausoleum and Bob's small house. In and around the house are countless details the Rasta guides make note of as inspiration for a multitude of songs from Marley's discography, including the single bed and the rock pillow from "Talkin' Blues." Below the mausoleum a clubhouse-style building with contemporary, sleek Rasta styling has a restaurant and lounge on the second floor and great views from the balcony over the quiet hills of the St. Ann interior. A bus requiring a day's advance reservation departs Mama Marley's (tel. 876/795-4803), Cedella Marley's restaurant on Main Street in Ocho Rios, usually around 10 A.M. daily, contingent upon adequate bookings (US$55 including entry, transport, and lunch).

Claremont

Home of an annual kite festival held on the Saturday before Easter, this small hilltop village draws thousands of people who come out for the competitive event and an evening stage show.

St. Mary

One of the most under-visited corners of Jamaica, St. Mary is considered by many the most attractive parish for its proximity to Kingston, Ocho Rios, and Portland; for its vast wilderness areas; and for its people, who don't exhibit the same hustler mentality rampant in more touristy urbanized areas. St. Mary is one of the best places in Jamaica for birding and farm tours, with Green Castle Estate standing out clearly among the large plantations of the area that are still active in agricultural production.

The White River has figured prominently in the history of the North Coast; the first Spanish road from Spanish Town followed its banks. The Spanish Bridge, which still stands at its upper reaches, is the oldest on the island. Near its mouth, anglers bring in their catch and people wash cars under the highway overpass. To get down to the banks, take a right immediately

after the Texaco station across from Jamaica Inn when heading east out of town, and then take the first left. A few bars and fish spots make for a decent hangout. To reach Irie Beach, the Prospect Plantation Great House, and Chukka Caribbean, take a right after leaving the main road at the Texaco gas station and follow the river upstream.

TOWER ISLE AND BOSCOBEL

Now suburban outskirts of Ocho Rios, the area between Tower Isle and Boscobel is dotted with cottages and villas on the sea side of the road, with several housing developments inland that are home to many commuters working in Ocho Rios. Boscobel has the only airstrip in the area at the **Ian Fleming International Airport**, which underwent an expansion in 2010 to accommodate larger aircraft.

OCHO RIOS

Shopping

Jamma Design by Marie Smith (Huddersfield, Boscobel, tel. 876/431-8122, caryl_smith2005@yahoo.com) is a funky home apparel shop specializing in handmade African-inspired rootsy designs, with excellent children's clothes and stylish dresses (from US$25). Marie Smith won the Singer sewing festival competition in 2005.

Accommodations

UNDER US$100

Heaven's Wynter Lodge (Tower Isle, tel. 876/975-5886, 7:30 A.M.–11:P.M.) serves typical Jamaican dishes like curry goat and fried chicken (US$3.50–6), and a vegetarian restaurant on the premises serves tofu chunks, vegetables, and sip (US$4). The all-you-can-eat dinner buffet every Friday (6 P.M.–10 P.M., US$7) serves shrimp, fish, jerk pork, jerk chicken, and fried chicken. Rooms (US$43) on the premises have air-conditioning, ceiling fans, TV, and private bath, with a recently opened swimming pool free of charge.

Saki (contact Oliver Magnus, cell tel. 876/368-1036, olivermagnusja@hotmail.com, US$50/person per night) is a two-bedroom villa, each room with a king-size bed and private bath. There's a full kitchen for guest use, and a six-person hot tub on the deck overlooks the sea.

Contentment Jungle Resort (also owned and managed by Oliver Magnus, cell tel. 876/368-1036, olivermagnusja@hotmail.com) is located in Mason Hall, inland from Oracabessa, with seven basic rooms (US$25–50) furnished with four double beds and three queen-size beds. The setting is rustic and vibesy, with functional bathrooms and kitchen but few creature comforts.

US$100-250

Tranquility Cove (tel. 876/999-3147, US toll-free tel. 888/790-5264, UK toll-free tel. +0/800-7297-2900, res@tranquilitycoveresort.com, www.tranquilitycoveresort.com) is located across the road from Harmony Hall in Tower Isle with 26 units containing one-, two-, and three-bedroom suites (US$180–600), inclusive of a housekeeper/cook. A clubhouse has

an infinity pool out front overlooking the sea. There are laundry facilities on the property. Reggae Beach, the closest piece of fine sand, can be reached in about 10 minutes by foot.

Sea Palms Resort (contact Robert Cartade, tel. 876/926-4000, cartade@cwjamaica.com, www.seapalmsjamaica.com), located next door, is a seafront property with a handful of buildings containing condo-style rooms and suites (from US$105/145 low/high season), each with balconies, kitchens, air-conditioning, washer and dryer, and TV. A beach has been created on the waterfront with levies that create a small protective cove. Next to the beach is a clubhouse and pool.

Villa Viento (tel. 876/975-4395, US$125 per night per room, US$4,800/6,800 weekly low/high season for the whole house) has seven bedrooms in a large seaside ranch-style house two minutes down the road from Reggae Beach. This is one of the few villas that will rent out individual rooms.

Moxons Beach Club (tel. 876/975-7023, www.moxonsbeachclub.com, US$85–225) is a boutique property perched atop the cliffs in Stewart Town, between Tower Isle and Boscobel about 12 kilometers east of Ocho Rios. The four-level property descends to a private beach. Rooms face the sea or a courtyard and have queen- or king-size beds and en suite bathrooms. Wi-Fi is complimentary. A restaurant serves a mix of Jamaican and international dishes (US$8–28).

Beaches Boscobel (tel. 876/975-7777, US$420/night for double in high season) dominates the waterfront just west of the airfield, and with 323 rooms it's easily the largest hotel on the North Coast east of Ocho Rios. Like all Beaches resorts, Boscobel is a family-oriented all-inclusive getaway.

OVER US$250

Castles on the Sea (contact Henri or Joyce Verne, tel. 561/793-7257, exotica@webtv.net, www.chateauonthesea.com, US$745/845 nightly low/high season for up to six guests, US$45 nightly for each additional person) is a luxurious villa perched on the coral cliffs

CHRIS BLACKWELL AND ISLAND RECORDS

One of the world's foremost music producers and founder of Island Records, London-born Chris Blackwell is credited with having introduced reggae music to the world. He built his early career first by selling record imports to the Jamaican market and then by bringing international attention to the budding careers of artists like Millie Small, whose "My Boy Lollipop" topped the charts in England in 1964, giving Island its first hit. Blackwell signed a slew of early English rock artists like Jethro Tull, King Crimson, Robert Palmer, and Cat Stevens. Then came Bob Marley, whose 1973 *Catch a Fire* album would be the first of many for Bob on the Island label. The deal was a huge hit and brought world recognition to a genre that was gaining popularity in Jamaica but unheard of elsewhere.

While Blackwell was scoping the world for new talent, Jamaica was never far from his mind, and he cultivated his love for the country by buying some of the island's most beautiful properties, including Strawberry Hill and Goldeneye, eventually forming Island Outpost to market them to discerning travelers seeking luxury without hype. His grand vision has set in motion a transformation in Oracabessa with the new villa development on a private island next to Ian Fleming's Goldeneye. The development was designed as an exclusive community where those lucky enough to get their hands on a piece of Goldeneye have access to all the amenities and services the resort offers, with a private villa they can call home.

Blackwell was inducted into the Rock and Roll Hall of Fame in 2001 for his contribution to the world music industry. Blackwell sold Island Records to PolyGram UK Group in 1989, staying on at the head of the Island division. Blackwell left the company in 1997, just before PolyGram was acquired by Seagram and merged into Universal Music Group. A year later Blackwell established Palm Pictures, a film production and distribution company based in New York. Palm sources films from across the world and produced the touring film festival RESFEST for a decade. Palm Pictures was by no means Blackwell's first foray into film however. He first entered the film industry by backing Perry Henzell's cult hit *The Harder They Come* in 1971, which brought fame to Jimmy Cliff, before going on to produce other Jamaican classics like *Country Man*, as well as successful Hollywood films.

In Jamaica Chris Blackwell receives a mix of admiration from his peers and disciples and resentment from those who jealously allege he made his millions on the back of Bob Marley. Some who are bitter refer to him as "Whitewell." What is indisputable is that his business acumen and eye for talent and opportunity have made Blackwell one of the world's most creative and successful businessmen. Beyond Island Outpost, Blackwell maintains other business interests that include Island Village in Ocho Rios and recording studios.

overlooking the sea in Boscobel just east of the aerodrome. There are a total of six queen-size beds and two king-size beds, with air-conditioning in four bedrooms with en-suite baths, mini refrigerators, and balconies. The villa is staffed with a chef, housekeeper, and gardener. A hot tub and large pool overlook the sea, with a staircase leading down to the water.

ORACABESSA

Oracabessa is yet another bastardized Spanish name, whose derivative, Oro Cabeza, translates as "gold head." A half hour's drive east of Ocho Rios, Oracabessa is a secluded enclave of high-end tourism where Ian Fleming's Goldeneye has become the benchmark for sophisticated, hip luxury tourism in Jamaica. Oracabessa has fostered a number of artists whose crafts show more originality while being far less expensive than what is offered in the markets of Ochi, Montego Bay, or Negril. The small community offers some decent beaches and picturesque countryside for those looking to get off the beaten track.

Oracabessa experienced a brief boom as an important banana port in the early 1900s. Today the community is experiencing a different kind of boom, with entrepreneur Chris Blackwell building a luxury villa development at Goldeneye that will cement the area's reputation for exclusivity.

The area from Oracabessa to Port Maria has one of the nicest stretches of coast in all of Jamaica, where cliff-side villas were built by the likes of Ian Fleming, Noel Coward, and in more recent times, record magnate Chris Blackwell. The districts of Race Course, Galina, and Little Bay have small, quiet communities where discreet tourism accommodations blend so well with the surrounding landscape that they're easy to miss.

◖ James Bond Beach

James Bond Beach (US$5) is a private beach park in Oracabessa that holds several annual events, including **Follow Di Arrow,** a popular stage show in February, and **Beach J'ouvert,** held Easter weekend. Other events include **Fully Loaded** (third week in August) and **Pepsi Teen Splash** (Boxing Day, December 26). Fully loaded unites a long list of top-ranking dancehall, reggae, and hip-hop artists from Jamaica and abroad, backed by virtually all the best selectors. Pepsi Teen Splash is an annual dancehall stage show geared toward a youthful crowd. The park extends from the roundabout at the junction of the main road and Jack's River Road to the edge of Goldeneye. Events are held on the beach park jutting out into the sea, as well as at a venue closer to the main road. There is a restaurant and bar, as well as beach chairs.

Stingray City (tel. 876/726-1630, www.stingraycityjamaica.com, 9 A.M.–5 P.M. daily) is the main attraction, where visitors swim with the pet fish (US$55 adult, US$25 children; locals pay US$25 adults, US$8.50 children) on James Bond Beach when there isn't an event being held.

The entrance to James Bond Beach is located right by the roundabout on the western end of Oracabessa.

Other Sights

Sun Valley Plantation (cell tel. 876/995-3075 or 876/446-2026, sunvalleyjamaica@yahoo.com, 9 A.M.–2 P.M. daily, US$12) offers an excellent guided farm tour that includes a welcome drink, and a drink and snack at end of the tour. The educational stroll about the farm familiarizes visitors with native crops like sugarcane and banana that have played important roles in Jamaica's economy and in the history of the area. Sun Valley is owned by Lorna and Nolly Binns, who live on the property with their son Bryan. Nolly's father bought the property in 1966 to grow bananas for export. Today the farm produces mainly coconuts for the local market. To get to Sun Valley, head inland at the roundabout in Oracabessa, passing through Jack's River, and stay straight rather than left at the Epping gas station for about 1.5 kilometers farther.

Brimmer Hall (tel. 876/994-2309, 9 A.M.–4 P.M. Mon.–Fri.) offers tractor-drawn jitney tours around the plantation, where there's also a pool for swimming and a lunch area. Guides teach visitors about the fruit trees and give a bit of history of the estate. Brimmer Hall great house dates to the 1700s, when the farm was a slave plantation owned by Zachary Bailey. The house is full of period furnishings and antiques. To get to Brimmer Hall, head east from Port Maria and turn right three kilometers past Trinity on the road toward Bailey Town, continuing about 1.5 kilometers past there.

Asset Recording Studio (Race Course, tel. 876/726-2362) run by Lawrence Londal "Jah Vibes" Oliver (cell tel. 876/990-0378) and Kenya (cell tel. 876/440-4087) is owned by Germany-based Papa Curvin (cell tel. 876/389-0508, papacurvin@gmx.d), who runs back and forth between Europe and Jamaica. The studio has digital audio mixing, dub cutting, and live recording facilities. Asset Recording recently put out an album: *Asset Vol. 1,* with 13 tracks on their Wan-T Wan-T rhythm. This is a cool spot to stop.

Entertainment and Food

In the center of Oracabessa there is a covered

open-air produce market as well as a super-market. Across from the police station there is also a produce stand, and up a lane by the school a bit farther east there's a shop that sells the basics like eggs, bread, and jam that opens around 7 A.M.

Chicken Hut (Center of Oracabessa, cell tel. 876/485-8217), operated by Kerri and Yhan Chin-loy, is the best spot for a quick bite to go, with the house specialty being Chinese-style fried chicken, of course with the requisite rice and peas.

Tropical Hut (Race Course, cell tel. 876/818-8376 or 876/434-5155, US$2.50–5) is a very mellow local bar, restaurant, and jerk center owned by Ciyon Gray with chef Clinton Clarke making excellent local dishes.

Dor's Fish Pot (Race Course, US$4.50–8.50) is a local favorite for all manner of fish from steamed to fried.

The **Galina Sports Bar** (Galina, US$5) sells local dishes like fried chicken with rice and peas.

Feeling Night Club (Wharf Road, tel. 876/726-1499) has music on weekends.

Concious Corner Bar, located in Rio Nuevo, is a popular hangout for locals and bikers associated with the St. Mary Off-Road Biking Association and run by Norval (tel. 876/458-1430).

Shopping

Exotic Jewelry by Jasazii (Jasazii and Maji McKenzie, cell tel. 876/726-0013 or 876/909-8403, jasazii@gmail.com, www.exoticjewelry-byjasazii.com) is based in Gibraltar Heights, where Jasazii and Maji have their Sacred Healing Artz Sanctuary.

Wilderness House of Art (Idlewhile Rd., between Galina and Race Course districts, across from a yellow house, cell tel. 876/462-8849 or 876/994-0578, babaireko@yahoo.com) is the home and studio of Ireko "Baba" Baker, who is a member of A Yard We Deh artist collective together with Tukula N'Tama and Orah El. Ireko does excellent screen-printing work and gourd art and has several good value items of practical art for sale. Ireko

takes his work to various crafts fairs, on occasion to Harmony Hall in Ocho Rios or to the Grosvener Gallery in Manor Park, Kingston. Ireko's work can also be seen displayed in the foyer and rooms at Couples Negril.

Accommodations

Sagaree (Race Course, between Dor's Fish Hut and Tropical Hut), run by Walton Gordon, a.k.a. "Sparrow" (cell tel. 876/379-6089), is a seafront property with three permanent tents (US$45) set on raised wooden platforms that have use of common bathrooms. Sparrow lives on property with his family in true Ital style. Rates include breakfast.

 High View Cottages (Gibraltar Heights, tel. 876/975-3210, cell tel. 876/831-1975, U.S. tel. 718/878-5351, fax 876/726-4199, kee-lie07@hotmail.com, US$60) is owned by the amiable Colleen Pottinger, who lives in the main house on the property. There are two one-bedroom self-contained cottages with kitchens, private bathrooms with hot water, access to the swimming pool, and wireless Internet. There is one queen-size bed in one cottage, and two twin beds in the second cottage. There are also inflatable mattresses for extra persons. The nightly rate includes breakfast, and additional meals can be arranged. The personal attention of its owner and the quiet location on the lush Gibraltar hillside make High View a favorite home away from home for budget-minded travelers.

Tamarind Great House (cell tel. 876/995-3252, tamarindgreathouse@yahoo.com, US$75–105 d) on Crescent Estate was destroyed by fire in 1987, and then rebuilt and restored to a 10-bedroom colonial-style great house by English couple Gillian and Barry Chambers, who live on the property with their son Gary. Nine attractive rooms have fans and private baths with hot water. Some rooms have private balconies. The house was completely rebuilt on the foundation of the original, while furnishings and decor reflect the colonial period. To get to Tamarind House, head inland at the roundabout in Oracabessa along Jack's River Road, keeping straight ahead at the Epping gas station;

continue for about 0.8 kilometer past Sun Valley Plantation, keeping left at the broken bridge and continuing up the hill.

VILLAS

Goldenfoot (Gibraltar Heights, tel. 876/842-1237 or U.S. tel. 650/941-1760, agoldenfoot. villa@yahoo.com, www.agoldenfootvilla.com, US$600) is a spectacular two-bedroom villa owned by Joel Goldfus. You won't find a place with more privacy, and caretaker Godfrey is a phone call away to ensure every need is attended to.

The villa features a master bedroom with a canopy queen-size bed, and across the living room/dining room the second bedroom has two twin beds. The ceiling of the living room is detailed with bamboo work to match the bamboo construction throughout the property. Wicker furniture sits on a large veranda overlooking the pool (which is imprinted with golden feet along its edges), Oracabessa, and out to sea.

Goldeneye (tel. 876/975-3354, Kingston office tel. 876/960-8134, goldeneye@cwjamaica. com, www.islandoutpost.com/goldeneye) the former home of James Bond series author Ian Fleming, is today the most exclusive resort in Jamaica. From the moment the gates swing open off the main road, you know you have arrived at a place unlike any other. No large sign announces the property's presence from the road, a reflection of the understated grandeur that lies within.

Ian Fleming's villa boasts enormous bamboo-framed canopy beds, which beg to be slept on, but there is too much competition to stay there long. Deluxe indoor master bathrooms are complemented by an outdoor bath area that resembles paradise, surrounded by a wooden fence to ensure privacy. The villa lacks nothing, from its spacious living area to the pool outside, to the lawns overlooking Fleming's private beach. Adjacent to the pool, an enclosed lounge features a projection screen and bar.

On the opposite side of the vast property, Royal Palm sits on the tranquil lagoon surrounding a private island. It's the kind of place that makes you grateful to be alive. Downstairs,

a living area with windows on all sides opens out to the front veranda, where you can step into the lagoon.

Meals are offered in a casual setting in a centrally located gazebo overlooking the water. The food is delicious and generally features the best local cuisine. It is also possible to arrange meals in your villa.

If you can drag yourself away from your villa, Nico is ready to take you on a Jet Skiing adventure to remote waterfalls for a hike and swim. Otherwise, there's always windsurfing, kayaking, or simply lazing on the beach of your private island.

Goldeneye has evolved in recent years into Jamaica's most exclusive resort community with several villas owned independently. Phase 1 of a transformational expansion completed in October 2010 adds two-bedroom and a one-bedroom satellite cottages to the grounds of Fleming House, 11 one- and two-bedroom cottages facing Low Cay Beach complemented by a restaurant and bar, and six one-bedroom villas facing the island at the edge of the lagoon. The new villas rent as part of the Goldeneye pool. A spa is also in the works.

This is not a resort for those with shallow pockets. Nightly rates vary based on the villa, but you can expect to pay in excess of US$1,000 per couple. The service is accordingly top-notch.

GALINA AND LITTLE BAY
◖ Firefly

Firefly (Goldeneye manages the property, tel. 876/975-3677, or contact caretaker Victor cell tel. 876/420-5544, US$10 admission includes guided tour and refreshment, 9 A.M.–5 P.M., closed Fri. and Sun.) is easily one of Jamaica's most beautiful properties, with the most magnificent view of the St. Mary and Portland coast. The property has had a glamorous past, first as the home of the pirate Henry Morgan, and centuries later as a playground for playwright Noel Coward, both of whom were captivated by the stunning view that graces the small plateau. Henry Morgan's house, which

© OLIVER HILL

Noel Coward sits immortalized in bronze on the lawn at Firefly, perpetually relishing one of the best views in Jamaica over Port Maria and up the northeast coast.

dates from the 17th century, has been rebuilt and is now used as the visitors center and has a small bar and several tables. Across the lawn, Noel Coward's house remains preserved as a museum essentially as he left it. Downstairs in his studio an incomplete painting stands on the easel as if Coward was interrupted mid-stroke. His famous "room with a view" was inspiration for several works completed in there, and the piano where he entertained his famous Hollywood guests remains the centerpiece in the study. On the lawn outside, a statue of Coward immortalizes his fascination with the view as he holds his cigarette and ponders the northeast coastline. Coward's tomb is in a corner of the lawn.

At the time of Coward's death the property was left to Graham Payne, who in turn gave it to the Jamaican government, which today leases it to Chris Blackwell, whose Island Outpost manages the attraction. Up to 120 people visit Firefly daily in the high season, while the visits can drop to a trickle during the slower months.

Kokomo Beach

Kokomo Beach is a decent free public beach across the road from Casa Maria frequented mostly by locals. The beach is small and not particularly noteworthy, but good enough for a dip to cool off.

Accommodations

Little Bay Inn (Little Bay, tel. 876/994-2721, US$20–25) opened in 2005 as a basic and clean guesthouse overlooking Little Bay just west of Port Maria. Nine bedroom suites have private baths with hot water, fans, double beds, and simple furnishings. The more expensive rooms have TV. A small jerk center in the yard serves food and beverages on occasion. Downstairs in the same building is Cribs Disco, where music at times blasts into the wee hours.

Casa Maria Hotel (Castle Gardens, tel. 876/725-0156, fax 876/725-0157, emaxwell@ cwjamaica.com, www.nwas.com/casamaria, US$50 standard, US$75 suites) is a massive concrete hotel with 18 rooms, which range from standard ocean view with double bed and shared bathroom to suites with private bath, private balconies with ocean views, king beds, and cable TV. A restaurant (7 A.M.–10 P.M. daily) and bar on the premises are open to nonguests.

Galina Breeze (Galina, tel. 876/994-0537, office@galinabreeze.com, www.galinabreeze.com, US$75) is a small property of 14 rooms in a basic concrete structure overlooking the pool and an excellent view of the northeastern coast; there's also one stand-alone villa. Standard rooms (single or double occupancy) have air-conditioning, king-size beds, cable TV, and hot water. The property is geared toward accommodating special-interest groups, and the management helps in engaging guests with the community, whether for educational, church, or outreach programs.

◖ **Dowling House** (Galina, call Nancy or Steven Sicher, tel. 876/725-1004 or U.S. tel. 309/693-2830, ssicher@comcast.net, www.dowlinghouse.com, generally not available Oct., Nov., Jan., and Feb.) is a three-bedroom seafront cottage (US$1,000/1,200 per week low/high season) with king-size beds in two rooms, and two twins in the third. The cottage can accommodate up to six people (US$1,400/ week), comes with a caretaker and cook, and is tastefully decorated with a pool and large lawn overlooking Blue Harbour and Port Maria. A land line, an iPod docking station, a gas stove, hot water, DSL, and a washer/dryer make up for the lack of TV.

Bolt House (book through Marco Fila, marco.fila@gmail.com, bookings@bolthousejamaica.com, www.bolthousejamaica.com, with Island Outpost, www.islandoutpost.com, or SunVillas, www.sunvillas.com, US$1,800/2,200 daily low/high, four-day minimum) is a spectacular 50-acre hilltop property owned by the family that founded Fila sportswear. It overlooks Port Maria's stunning infinity pool, Blue Harbour, and has a three-bedroom villa. The property was built and occupied by Blanche Blackwell, mother of Island Records founder Chris Blackwell, whose boutique hotel group now manages the property and affords Bolt House guests a one-bedroom cottage, Spanish Elm, along with beach access at Goldeneye. Bolt House was refurbished in 2009, with an impeccable mix of modern and colonial styling, which, together with unparalleled views and grounds, place it at the top of the high-end villa market.

The master bedroom has a king bed, as does the second bedroom with two double beds. An annex has two additional cozy bedrooms appointed with rustic touches. The house is fully equipped with Apple TV, Wi-Fi, and a surround sound system. A yoga deck, wet and dry saunas, and a hot tub round out the luxurious amenities. The property has a rich history, having hosted many a soirée with luminaries including Sean Connery, Audrey Hepburn, Elizabeth Taylor, Charlie Chaplin, Noel Coward, Ian Fleming, and the Queen of England. Food runs US$60 per person daily, not including alcoholic beverages.

PORT MARIA

One of the most picturesque towns in Jamaica, Port Maria has a large protected harbor with the small Cabarita Island, also known as Treasure Island, in the center. Originally inhabited by the Tainos and later by the Spanish, the island was vulnerable to pirate attacks and warring colonial powers and fell into the hands of the pirate Henry Morgan until he lost it in a gamble. By the late 1700s a village began to take shape on the harbor shores, on land owned by Zachary Bailey. The parish vestry acquired land for the growing village from Bailey's nephew in 1816, and by 1821 public buildings including the parish council offices and the courthouse were built. Port Maria boomed with exports that included sugar, rum, indigo, pimento, tropical hardwoods, and coffee. Port Maria has long since passed its prime. Nevertheless, it still has a strong fishing community and is a commercial center for the people of the surrounding rural districts. Several infrastructure improvements associated with the North Coast Highway project have recently given the town a bit of a face-lift. The Outram River forms the eastern border of town, beyond which begins a vast wilderness area wrapping around the hilly coastline all the way to Robin's Bay.

Sights

St. Mary Craft Market (Port Maria Civic Center, by appointment cell tel. 876/373-7575) is one of the island's most eclectic, featuring work exclusively from artists residing in the parish. If you're planning a stop to check out the old Court House and Anglican Church, call in advance to arrange to see the crafts.

Pagee Beach is where Port Maria's anglers keep their boats and bring in their catch. Outings to Cabarita Island, a great place to explore in true Robinson Crusoe fashion, can be arranged from here by negotiating with the fishermen (US$10 per person is a reasonable round-trip fare). Pagee is not an ideal place for swimming.

Fort Haldane, or sparse and scattered remains of it, are located on a road that cuts across the point jutting into the sea, forming the western flank of Port Maria's harbor. The road runs between the Anglican Church and the middle of the bend on the other side of the hill on Little Bay. Two cannons overgrown with bush aim out to sea just past the oldest structure on the premises, a low brick building sitting alongside discarded car parts. The Fort was built in 1759 for coastal defense during the Seven Years' War and named after then-governor George Haldane. The property was later a home for the elderly, called Gray's Charity, but has since fallen into disuse. The gates to this seldom-visited historical site are typically left ajar and are otherwise unlocked.

The old **courthouse** and **police station** (across from the Anglican church on east side of town), originally built in 1821 is one of the nicest examples of Georgian architecture in Port Maria after its recent restoration. Much of the original building was destroyed by fire in 1988 and then marked for restoration by the Urban Development Commission in 2000. The partial restoration was completed in 2002 with funds from the Jamaican and Venezuelan governments, and the building is now in use as the Port Maria Civic Center. A plaque by the main entrance dedicates the premises to labor

Cabarita Island sits at the center of Port Maria protective harbor.

OCHO RIOS

TACKY'S WAR

On the morning after Easter Sunday in 1760, a slave known as Tacky led a revolt in St. Mary that would reverberate around northeastern Jamaica until September of that year. The uprising became known as Tacky's Rebellion or Tacky's War.

Tacky was an overseer on Frontier Plantation outside Port Maria, giving him the limited freedom necessary to strategize and organize the rebellion at both Frontier and bordering Trinity plantations. A former chief in his homeland of Ghana, Tacky had the confidence and clout to amass wide support for what was meant to be an island-wide overthrow of the British colonial masters.

Tacky and about 50 of his followers awoke before dawn that morning and easily killed the master of Frontier Plantation before raiding the armory at nearby Fort Haldane, where they killed the storekeeper and took guns and ammunition. The owner of Trinity Plantation escaped on horseback to warn the surrounding estates. But with newfound artillery, the ranks of the rebel army began to swell, and they quickly took nearby Haywood and Esher plantations and began to celebrate their early success. A slave from Esher plantation, however, slipped away to call in the authorities, and before long a militia of soldiers from Spanish Town and Maroons from Scott's Hall were sent to quell the uprising.

The rebels' confidence had been bolstered by Obeah men (witch doctors) among their ranks who spread incantations and claimed the army would be protected and that Obeah men could not be killed. This confidence took a blow when the militia, learning of these claims, captured and killed one of the Obeah men. Nonetheless, the fighting would last months and take the lives of some 60 whites and 300 rebels before it was diffused. Tacky himself was captured and beheaded by the Maroons from Scott's Hall, who took his head to Spanish Town on a pole to be displayed as dissuasion for any further resistance.

The legend of Tacky spread across the island, giving inspiration to other resistance movements that would come in the later years of slavery and after emancipation. Many of Tacky's followers committed suicide rather than surrendering, while those who were captured were either executed or sold and shipped off the island. Ringleaders were either burned alive or starved in cages in the Parade in Kingston. It was during Tacky's War that the British authorities first learned of the role African religion played behind the scenes in these uprisings, and Obeah thus became part of the official record with a 1770 law passed to punish its practitioners by death or transportation, at the court's discretion.

---

leader and Jamaica Labour Party (JLP) founder Alexander Bustamante; a second plaque recognizes former Prime Minister P. J. Patterson, who attended the official opening in 2002.

St. Mary Parish Church was built in 1861 and has an adjoining cemetery with an epitaph dedicated to the Jamaicans who fought in World War I. The **Tacky Memorial** is also located in the church cemetery.

Practicalities

(Almond Tree Club Restaurant (56 Warner St., tel. 876/994-2379, 9 A.M.–11 P.M. daily, US$2–6) is the best bet in Port Maria, serving typical Jamaican dishes like curry goat, fried chicken, oxtail, stew peas, and stew

pork. Other dishes like chicken chop suey and shrimp fried rice are cooked to order. This Almond Tree claims to be the original, predating the one in Ocho Rios. Dawn Gibbs is the friendly and helpful manager.

Uncle B's Miracle Jerk Center on the road east of out town has great jerk and an irie roadside atmosphere.

Most country folk arriving in Port Maria come for the market, to stock up at the **Hi-Lo** supermarket (7–11 Stennett St., tel. 876/994-9878), or do their banking at **NCB** (8 Main St., tel. 876/994-2219) or **Scotiabank** (57 Warner St., tel. 876/994-2265).

Port Maria is serviced by regular route taxis from Ocho Rios (US$3), Oracabessa

(US$1.50), and Annotto Bay (US$1.50) that leave the square as they fill up.

The **Port Maria police station** (tel. 876/994-2223) is located at the plaza by the bus park.

Islington

Islington is a small community 20 minutes east of Port Maria, which sits atop a hill and offers great views eastward along the coast toward Buff Bay and Port Antonio from some of its lookout points along the road. Islington is of little importance as a tourist destination, but it is the proud hometown of dancehall deejay Capleton, who organizes an annual festival called A St. Mary Mi Come From. The agricultural community is also known for its pimento (allspice) crop, as well as for growing some of Jamaica's most potent illicit weed.

ROBIN'S BAY

One of the most laid-back and picturesque corners of Jamaica, Robin's Bay is entirely apart from what is marketed on JTB posters.

Robin's Bay is the Treasure Beach of yesteryear, remaining a quiet fishing and subsistence agricultural community with a few accommodation options catering to those looking for an easygoing retreat or the experience of enjoying intimacy with nature. Beginning with Green Castle Estate, a working farm that commands a large swath of land fronting the bay, the area has a delectable, charming pace found nowhere else on the island.

Green Castle Estate

Green Castle Estate (contact property manager Angie Dickson for reservations, cell tel. 876/881-6293, or U.S. tel. 612/986-4709, angie@gcjamaica.com, www.gcjamaica.com or www.greencastletropicalstudycenter.org) is a 650-hectare farm producing a mix of fruit and—above all in terms of revenue—orchids, which today fill four large shade houses. Named after the Irish holdings of one of its earlier owners, several archaeological finds on the property indicate it has been continuously lived on since the time of the Tainos.

Horses graze in the shadows of windmill ruins at Green Castle Estate.

© OLIVER HILL

OCHO RIOS

Early English settlement at Green Castle left the iconic windmill that still stands today. Land use has changed from cassava cultivation under the Tainos and Spanish to orange, cotton, pimento, cacao, indigo, sugarcane, and then bananas. For centuries the estate was connected with the rest of Jamaica only by sea. After years of British and then American ownership fraught with frequent mortgage defaults and border disputes, the property ended up in the hands of one of the world's foremost agricultural families and majority-share owners of Cargill, still the largest private company in the United States. Since the 1950s the farm has grown an increasingly diverse mix of fruit crops; it more recently went into organic fruit production and became one of Jamaica's foremost orchid farms, now supplying a large portion of domestic demand. Current ownership is with an English developer who intends to add ecotourism into Green Castle's mix. Historical sites on the expansive estate include excavated Taino middens (1300), a militia barracks (1834), and the signature coral stone windmill tower (1700).

A variety of tours are offered on Green Castle Estate, all of them excellent values. Children always pay half-price. The **Estate Tour** (US$20) introduces visitors to some of the 120 hectares of certified-organic tree crops planted on the farm. No other farm in Jamaica has more certified organic hectares under cultivation, and the organic coconut oil operation is one of the farm's more important products and a central focus of the tour. Visitors also learn about the roughly 2,000 organic pimento (allspice) trees and cocoa trees organically grown on the farm. Pedigree beef production is also a major activity, with hundreds of head of cattle roaming around the rolling grassy hills. The tour concludes with a visit to the orchid propagation shade houses, where visitors are dazzled with 50,000 orchid plants of several varieties and taught the basics of one of the island's most important orchid operations.

The **Green Castle Garden Tour and Tea** (US$40) is highly recommended, not least for the great company of one Mrs. Susan Crum

Ewing, who has impeccable knowledge of the history and plantlife of the farm. The tour starts in the orchid shade houses before continuing on to the grounds of the great house, planted with gorgeous flower specimens, which are visited throughout the day by countless birds. The tour ends with high tea, where guests sample delectable finger sandwiches, cake, and, of course, tea. You'll also get to sample some of the best seasonal juices in Jamaica, made from fruit grown on the property. Mrs. Crum Ewing and her husband, who manages the beef operations, have lived on the farm for decades and share a wealth of knowledge on its history, as well as having an enlightened perspective on Jamaica's socioeconomic development since independence.

Another option offered, best for more dedicated birding and exploring, is a **Day at Green Castle** (self-guided tour is US$10 for half day and $15 for full day; guided is $30 half day and $50 full day), where visitors are allowed to roam the vast estate to count bird species, visit the orchid houses, or just relax and enjoy nature along the many hiking trails and coastline. The birds that frequent Green Castle Estate are as spectacular as the orchids and include 20 of the country's 28 endemic species: the chestnut-bellied cuckoo, Jamaican owl, yellow-billed parrot, red-billed streamertail, Jamaican mango, Jamaican tody, Jamaican woodpecker, rufous-tailed flycatcher, sad flycatcher, Jamaican becard, Jamaican elania, Jamaican pewee, Jamaican crow, white-chinned thrush, Jamaican vireo, Jamaican euphonia, orangequit, yellow-shouldered grassquit, and the Jamaican stripe-headed tanager. In total 120 species have been sighted at Green Castle Estate, including the native and visiting birds.

Jacks Bay Beach

Jacks Bay Beach (US$3 adults, US$1 children) has a bar and restaurant serving fish and Jamaican fare. Jacks Bay is located on the main road from the North Coast highway going into Robin's Bay. It is part of Green Castle Estate but managed independently by Gary Smith and Melicia Clarke (cell tel. 876/394-4982 or 876/360-6341, jacksbayvillage@yahoo.com). Jacks Bay is open daily and is happy to accommodate large groups or special occasions. Stop in for excellent food and drinks (US$8–10) or give Gary a call to make special arrangements for groups.

Sunrise Lawn

Sunrise Lawn (contact the proprietor Sanchez Swaby, cell tel. 876/436-1223, noon–last customer leaves, daily) is one of the coolest chill-out spots in Robin's Bay, with its picket-fenced east-facing lawn overlooking the sea. There are benches for enjoying the view on the lawn, and a cook shop prepares steamed and fried fish and conch soup, based on demand throughout the day (US$5–15). A bar serves white and red rums and beer, with stacks of speakers perpetually warming up for the next session. Try the house drink, "Smooth Sunrise," made with Guinness, Supligen, and Wray & Nephew white rum. It allegedly improves

stamina and enhances libido, according to its creator, Sanchez. Gold Label is on special on Thursday nights with DJs spinning dancehall, reggae, R&B, and all sorts of classics.

Accommodations and Food

Robin's Bay Village and Beach Resort (tel. 876/968-3031 or cell tel. 876/361-2144, www. robinsbayvillageresort.com, US$75–135) has 43 rooms designed mainly for retreats or romantic getaways. The lower-priced rooms have mountain views with ceiling fans; the more expensive rooms have sea views and air-conditioning. All rooms have private bathrooms and hot water. There is a pool on the roof as well as a restaurant serving Jamaican dishes open to nonguests (US$6.50–21).

(Strawberry Fields Together Beachfront Cottages and Adventure Tours (tel. 876/610-8658, cell tel. 876/999-7169 or 876/337-6127, kim@strawberryfieldstogether.com, www.strawberryfieldstogether.com, US$90–220) sits on a seven-hectare property with six cottages ranging

Strawberry Fields Together is a quiet retreat with an assortment of cottages along the waterfront.

OCHO RIOS

© OLIVER HILL

in comfort level from rustic Hibiscus to seaside honeymoon lavishness in Moonlight Magic. Two small private beaches with fine white sand line idyllic crystalline coves protected by coral reefs. An outdoor dining area has a wood deck, bar, pizza oven, and jerk center for eating and entertainment under the heavens.

Nature excursions based at Strawberry Fields include five-hour ATV tours (US$125 per person) through the bush to waterfalls, mountain biking to a volcanic black-sand beach (US$75), guided hikes to the same black-sand beach and Kwamen Falls (US$20), and snorkeling on Long Reef (US$50). Jeep tours with Everton in one of his many Land Rovers can also be arranged. Picnic lunches can be arranged for any of the tours at US$12 per person.

River Lodge (tel. 876/995-3003, river-lodge@cwjamaica.com, www.river-lodge.com, US$32–50 per person including breakfast and dinner) is located on the site of a refurbished 400-year-old Spanish fort owned by Brigitta Fuchslocher. Rooms inside the fort complement a pair of cottages. From River Lodge there are hectares and hectares of unspoiled wilderness reaching almost all the way along the coast to Port Maria, where waterfalls and black-sand beaches are best reached by boat with the local fishermen.

Green Castle Estate Great House (contact property manager Angie Dickson for reservations, cell tel. 876/881-6293, U.S. tel. 612/986-4709, angie@gcjamaica.com, US$3,200/3,600 weekly low/high season, for up to four people, inclusive of meals, or US$3,600/4,200 low/high season for up to six with meals) is the fanciest accommodation you're likely to find between Port Maria and Port Antonio. While a weekly rental is preferred, it is also possible to rent a room at the Estate House for as little as three nights (US$260 d nightly). For those who enjoy nature and an alternative idea of tourism but don't want to sacrifice elegant comfort and old-time Jamaican pace, there's probably no better accommodation option around. The great house has classy colonial furnishings

in three spacious bedrooms with private baths, and a fourth room with two twin beds. The swimming pool overlooks gardens with a spectacular view of the coast and Blue Mountains from almost every window and veranda. You're guaranteed to see several species of hummingbird buzzing about, including the red-billed streamertail, the country's national bird. Tennis courts are well maintained. All estate tours are included with the great house rental. Opportunities for farm volunteer work and outreach in the neighboring community of Robin's Bay can be pursued with Angie.

Getting There and Around

The best way to reach Robin's Bay is by route taxi (US$0.75) or private taxi charter (US$7) from Annotto Bay. Getting around in Robin's Bay often requires long waits before a car passes, but the road is only a few kilometers long before it becomes a dirt track and disappears in the wilderness to the west.

ANNOTTO BAY

At one time an important port town for export of the area's annatto crop, from whence it got its name, Annotto Bay is today bustling only by the busy taxi stand in the center of town. Otherwise, sleepy is a good description. Two notable attractions are the unique **Baptist Chapel** on the main road through town, and the **Human Service Station** (Emmannuel "Irie" Johnson, cell tel. 876/843-1640), an excellent pit stop on the east side of town that serves great fresh seafood and some of the best fish tea and conch soup in Jamaica.

JP Tropical Foods (Annotto Bay, tel. 876/996-2401) one of Jamaica's largest fruit and food groups, offers Banana Walk Tours (US$7/person), a farm tour that covers the production cycle from plantation to packed box on the St. Mary Banana Estate. Tours are scheduled by appointment.

Accommodations

River Edge (contact Cavelle Chuck, cell tel. 876/385-4943, or Shermaine Hyatt, cell tel. 876/862-8412, riveredge99@hotmail.com,

OCHO RIOS

reservation required) is a camping facility nestled on the banks of the Pencar River in Fort George, about five kilometers inland from Annotto Bay. In addition to campsites there are furnished dorms (US$20 per person) and two self-contained units (US$45) with kitchenettes and private bathrooms. Tents are also available to rent (US$15). A kitchen is available for campers' use and a cook can also be available (US$10), with meals prepared by arrangement. The owner can facilitate transfers as well as overnights in Kingston. The river is excellent for swimming and cooling off. River Edge also allows entry of nonguests during the day (US$3). Call for directions from Annotto Bay.

Services
Annotto Bay Hospital (tel. 876/996-2742 or 876/996-9004) is the largest and best-equipped medical facility in St. Mary.

Getting There and Around
Annotto Bay is a major transfer point for route taxis and minibuses. The major destinations serviced from Annotto Bay include Constant Spring (US$3) in Kingston, Port Maria (US$1.50) to the east along the coast, Buff Bay (US$1.50) across the border in Portland, and Port Antonio (US$3) farther east into Portland. Route taxis also go to Islington and Robin's Bay (US$0.75), but at times it will take a while before the car fills up. To charter a route taxi in the Annotto Bay area, call Aldene "Ansel" Fairclough (cell tel. 876/477-0544), who can take you up to Fort George or Robin's Bay (US$7) or to any other destination for a negotiable price.

ST. MARY INTERIOR
Castleton Botanical Gardens (Castleton, tel. 876/942-0717, free) along the main Kingston-to-Annotto Bay road (A3) just over the border from St. Andrew, is still one of the nicest parks in Jamaica, despite having suffered years of neglect and recurring hurricane damage. Castleton was established in the 1860s and planted with 400 species from Kew Gardens in England. It remained an important

introduction point for ornamental and economically important species, including scores of palms as well as poincianas and the large Bombay mango variety. One of the most interesting specimens in the gardens is the Scew Palm (*Pandanus tectorius*), which sends down aerial, or stilt, roots, and another notable tree is the Poor Man's Orchid (not a true orchid), which has become ubiquitous around the island. Other economically important tree species still growing at the gardens are the Burma teak and West Indian mahogany.

Scott's Hall is one of the less-known but every bit as strong communities of the Windward Maroons, presided over by Colonel Noel Prehay (cell tel. 876/533-5325). Prehay is St. Mary's top Maroon representative.

Clonmel Potters (Arthur's Ridge, east of Highgate on the B2, tel. 876/992-4495, clonmelpotters@hotmail.com, www.theclonmelpotters.com, call to arrange a visit 9 A.M.–5 P.M. Mon.–Sat.), established by Donald and Belva Johnson in 1976, work in a variety of local media from porcelain to terra cotta. Like many of his fellow Jamaicans, Donald's favorite subject is the female nude, which is countered by his wife's concentration in organic forms. Works are thrown on the wheel and made from rolled slab, and they include both artistic pieces as well as practical vessels. Both Donald and Belva are graduates of Edna Manley School of Visual Arts, Jamaica's foremost art college, located in Kingston.

Accommodations and Food
Tapioca Village (6.5 kilometers north of Castleton, tel. 876/924-0091 or 876/472-5255, tapioca_retreat@yahoo.com, US$50 room only, US$60 includes breakfast for two, US$75 for three-meal package for two), just over the border from St. Andrew in Devon Pen, St. Mary, has simple, respectable rooms, a large lawn in a lush river valley, and a nice swimming pool. Bunks for the frugal go for US$7. Breakfast, lunch, and dinner are cooked to order (US$3–5). A popular Sunday Jamaican brunch costs US$30 per couple or US$20 single, ages 6–12 US$12, under age 6 complimentary.

MONTEGO BAY AND THE NORTHWEST

Montego Bay is the capital of St. James parish. Commonly referred to by locals as "Mobay," it's a place buzzing with cruise ships and international flights brimming with tourists. Many of these tourists spend barely a day on land before climbing aboard to depart for the next port. Others stay with their families in private villas for months of the year. Mobay's bustling service economy serves a large middle class, many of who spend much of the year abroad. This contrasts with large squatter settlements and an urban squalor that permeates the downtown area. On the quiet peninsula of Freeport, the city has an active yacht club, whose members partake in exciting events throughout the year; world-class golf courses lie east and west of the city. It's little wonder that many hotels register high occupancy throughout much of the year. Yet because the economy is overwhelmingly dependent on tourism, there arises at times a tangible resentment between the local population, a proud lot with fiery roots steeped in a not-so-distant, brutal history, and the endless flow of transient visitors, often perceived as cogs in the local economic machinery. But the congested angst of downtown Mobay quickly dissipates beyond the city limits, where the landscape of rural St. James quickly transforms into forested hills traversed by the occasional river.

The bordering parish to the east along the North Coast is Trelawny, seemingly still reminiscing over a glorious but languished past when Falmouth, its ornate capital, had money and class. As sugar lost importance

© OLIVER HILL

MONTEGO BAY

HIGHLIGHTS

◖ Richmond Hill: With the best view over Mobay – and a hotel, bar, and restaurant rich in history and ambience – this is a choice spot for a sunset cocktail (page 221).

◖ Gallery of West Indian Art: Not only does it have an excellent collection of Jamaican work, but there are Cuban and Haitian paintings as well (page 222).

◖ Rose Hall Great House: There's perhaps no great house as ominous and grand, and the spirit of White Witch Annie Palmer can still be felt (page 224).

◖ Greenwood Great House: One of the most beautiful and true-to-its-day estate

houses in Jamaica, it played a central role in the island's sugar history (page 224).

◖ Doctors Cave Beach: Center stage on Mobay's Hip Strip, this is the best spot to see and be seen on weekends. It's also the site of monthly full-moon parties (page 226).

◖ Falmouth: Considered one of the world's best examples of a Georgian town, it's changed little from its boom years at the height of the island's sugar trade (page 245).

◖ Queen of Spain Valley: Home to a 810-hectare citrus plantation, ceramics studio, and luxury retreat, it's worth every bit of bad road covered on the way (page 253).

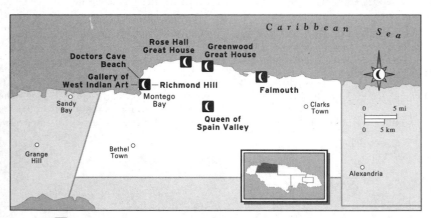

LOOK FOR ◖ TO FIND RECOMMENDED SIGHTS, ACTIVITIES, DINING, AND LODGING.

in the island's economy in the late 1800s, Falmouth faded from preeminent port to sleepy backwater. Today the parish is slowly showing signs of rejuvenation as the world begins to acknowledge its architectural treasures, with international funding being successfully sourced and funneled by local NGO Falmouth Heritage Renewal. Trelawny boomed during the years of the sugar trade but was an important strategic area even before the time of parishes—going back to

when the Spaniards used the Martha Brae River as a thoroughfare to traverse the island from the South to North Coasts. Their first major settlement of Melilla is said to have been near the mouth of the river. Before the Spaniards, the Martha Brae was the lifeblood for the area's Taino population, whose surviving legends are evidence of the river's importance to them.

Cockpit Country occupies the interior between the North and South Coasts, covering

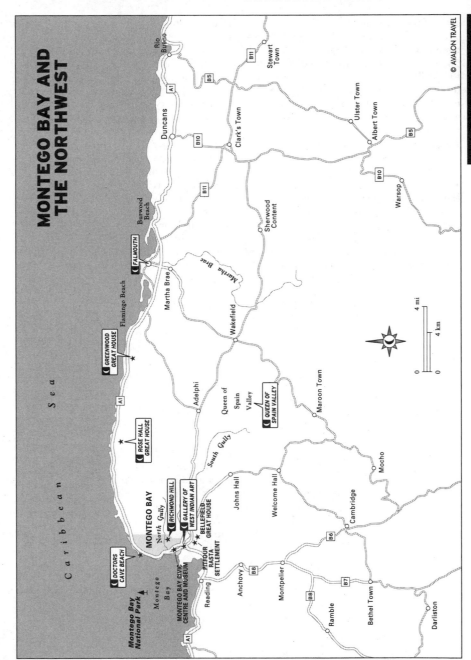

MONTEGO BAY

MONTEGO BAY AND THE NORTHWEST

© AVALON TRAVEL

Caribbean Sea

Montego Bay National Park

MONTEGO BAY

Montego Bay

DOCTORS CAVE BEACH

GREENWOOD GREAT HOUSE

ROSE HALL GREAT HOUSE

RICHMOND HILL

GALLERY OF WEST INDIAN ART

BELLEFIELD GREAT HOUSE

PITFOUR RASTA SETTLEMENT

MONTEGO BAY CIVIC CENTRE AND MUSEUM

North Gully

South Gully

Flamingo Beach

Burwood Beach

FALMOUTH

Rio Bueno

Stewart Town

Duncans

Clark's Town

Ulster Town

Albert Town

Sherwood Content

Warsop

Martha Brae

Martha Brae

Wakefield

Adelphi

Queen of Spain Valley

QUEEN OF SPAIN VALLEY

Maroon Town

Mocho

Johns Hall

Welcome Hall

Cambridge

Reading

Anchovy

Montpelier

Ramble

Bethel Town

Dariston

A1

B5

B11

B10

B11

B5

B10

A1

A1

B6

B8

B8

B7

0   4 mi

0   4 km

some of the most rugged terrain in the world, where limestone sinkholes, craggy hillocks, countless caves, and underground rivers made pursuit of Jamaica's Maroons a difficult task for the British colonists attempting to establish order and dominion. Together with the island's mountainous northeast, Trelawny gave respite to the indomitable Maroons; the parish remains a Maroon stronghold and adventurers' paradise. At the same time, the parish has the most peaceful and romantic farmlands in Jamaica, the Queen of Spain Valley being a particularly beautiful crown jewel amidst rough, rounded hilltops, where a citrus plantation today stands on the sugar estate of yesteryear. Cruising on horseback through this part of Jamaica is exhilarating and timelessly romantic, with orange and coconut groves and picturesque misty hills making for breathtaking scenery. This parish is rarely explored by tourists beyond the coastal areas of Falmouth, the Luminous Lagoon, and the Martha Brae River. As remote as Trelawny may seem when deep inside a cave or otherwise immersed in the bush, you are never more than a couple hours from civilization, or some semblance of it, in Montego Bay.

PLANNING YOUR TIME

Given the proximity of Negril, Jamaica's most developed beach town, as well as the mountains of the Dolphin Head range in Hanover, the interior and South Coast of neighboring Westmoreland, and Cockpit Country in St. James and Trelawny, there are plenty of opportunities for recreation and relaxation from a base in Montego Bay without being on the road for more than a couple hours. Closer to town there are several estate great house tours and plantation tours that make excellent half-day outings. Should you wish to hit the beach, there are plenty of options right

in town, while Trelawny also has its share of good beaches.

Mobay makes a convenient base thanks to Sangster International Airport on the eastern side of town. As a point of entry, Mobay is probably the best option, and a night or two in the city, especially if you arrive on the weekend, can be a good way to catch the Jamaican vibe before heading off to a more tranquil corner of the island. But Mobay shouldn't be the only area you visit on a trip to Jamaica. Ideally the area deserves around five days, splitting your time between the beach or another natural attraction, and a visit to a historical site, with some fine dining around the city.

Historical places of interest include Sam Sharpe Square in downtown Mobay, Bellefield, Rose Hall and Greenwood great houses—at least one of which should be seen on a trip to Jamaica—and the Georgian town of Falmouth. All of these make good half-day visits, while Falmouth can easily consume the better part of an unhurried day. Natural attractions in the region include the Martha Brae River, Cockpit Country caves, Mayfield Falls, the Great River, and a handful of working plantations that offer tours. Organized tour operators on the western side of Jamaica usually include transportation to and from Montego Bay or Negril hotels. A few decent beaches along the Hip Strip, on Dead End Road, and at the resorts farther east along the coast make Mobay a good place to hang out and catch some sun, but the city is by no means the place to go for secluded stretches of sand or unspoiled wilderness.

A few times a year, Mobay comes alive for music festivals that are, for many people, reason enough to travel to Jamaica. These include the island's premier music festival, Reggae Sumfest, held in July, and Jazz and Blues Festival (www.jamaicajazzandblues.com), held each January.

Montego Bay

Jamaica's "vibes city," Mobay has been the principal hub of the island's tourism industry since the 1950s, with the country's most well-heeled duty-free shops and beaches. The close proximity of the area's hotels to the Montego Bay airport makes it a convenient destination for long-weekenders visiting from the United States and those looking to take advantage of the proximity of destinations on the western side of the island. Sangster International Airport receives most of Jamaica's three million annual tourists, and the surrounding region offers plenty of activities for day trips out of town, making the Mobay area the most popular place for visitors to Jamaica to find lodging. But the picture is not entirely pretty, and plenty of strife plagues the city, not least of which derives from growing squatter communities in and around town. Many visitors find in Montegonians, also known as "bawn a bays," a hard-edged, matter-of-fact idiosyncrasy that reflects the dual worlds coexisting in the energetic city. Perhaps a tumultuous history kept fresh by perpetuating injustices leads the city's inhabitants to despise the subservience inherent in a tourism-based economy out of pride, even if it is tourism that sustains the town. Montego Bay has been at the center of the island's economic picture since the days of the Spanish, and it is not lost on the local population that the city remains an economic powerhouse with its booming service economy.

Old timers recall the golden years of 1960s Mobay, when clubs like the Yellow Bird on Church Street, Club 35 on Union Street, and Cats Corner were brimming with tourists and locals alike. Taxis would carry guests from the hotels to the city center, where they would await patrons into the early morning hours to emerge from smoky cabarets bursting with live music. The Michael Manley era, which began in 1972, ushered in a socialism scare that destabilized Jamaica, affecting the tourism market directly with travel advisories warning would-be visitors to stay away. Nowhere was

the impact more severe than in Montego Bay, which was the most-developed resort destination in Jamaica at the time. It was during the 1970s that all-inclusive tourism became a phenomenon, and gated resorts became the norm. The overwhelming dominance of all-inclusive hotels in recent years has led fewer visitors to leave the hotel compounds to explore the city, stifling business for restaurants and bars, the more successful of which cater as much to the local market as to tourists. Today Mobay comes alive on certain nights of the week and gets especially lively for several notable annual festivals, like Jazz and Blues Festival and Reggae Sumfest.

Commercially Montego Bay is organized like many U.S. cities. Large shopping centers dot the urban landscape, with KFC and Burger King dominating two strong poles of the quasi-modern city—only quasi-modern because Mobay contains in a small space some of Jamaica's roughest areas (there have been weeks in recent memory that saw several police-inflicted killings in some of Mobay's worse districts). But along Mobay's Hip Strip in the vicinity of Doctors Cave, Cornwall, and Dead End Beaches, the mood is as outwardly genteel as during the early British colonial period.

Mobay has been crucial to the island since the arrival of the Spanish conquistadores. The name Montego is said to have its origin in the Spanish word *manteca* (lard), referring to the use of the bay as an export center for wild hog products, namely lard. The city was previously named Golfo de Buen Tiempo (Bay of Good Weather) by Christopher Columbus.

Orientation

Montego Bay has distinct tourist zones, well separated from the bustling and raucous downtown area. The main tourist area is the **Hip Strip** along Gloucester Avenue, where most of the bars, restaurants, and hotels catering to tourists are located. Extending off the strip is **Kent Avenue,** a.k.a. Dead End Road, which

MONTEGO BAY

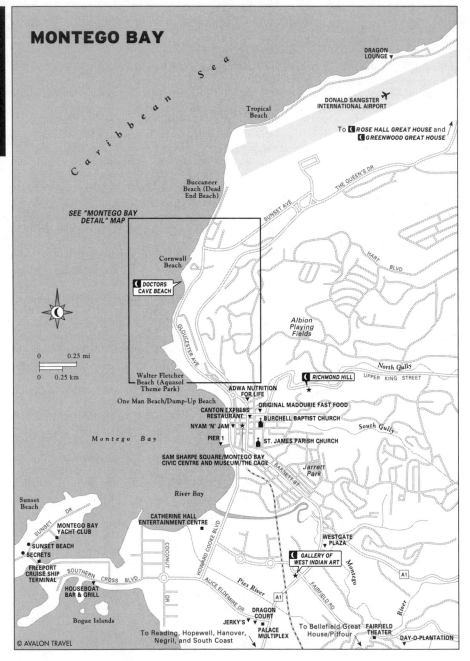

MONTEGO BAY

Caribbean Sea

DRAGON LOUNGE ▼

DONALD SANGSTER INTERNATIONAL AIRPORT ✈

Tropical Beach

To **C** *ROSE HALL GREAT HOUSE* and **C** *GREENWOOD GREAT HOUSE* →

THE QUEEN'S DR

Buccaneer Beach (Dead End Beach)

SUNSET AVE

HART BLVD

SEE "MONTEGO BAY DETAIL" MAP

Cornwall Beach

C *DOCTORS CAVE BEACH*

Albion Playing Fields

GLOUCESTER AVE

North Gully

UPPER KING STREET

0   0.25 mi
0   0.25 km

C *RICHMOND HILL* ★

Walter Fletcher Beach (Aquasol Theme Park)

ADWA NUTRITION FOR LIFE

One Man Beach/Dump-Up Beach

CANTON EXPRESS RESTAURANT ▼

ORIGINAL MADOURIE FAST FOOD

South Gully

NYAM 'N' JAM ▼ ★

BURCHELL BAPTIST CHURCH

Montego Bay

PIER 1

ST. JAMES PARISH CHURCH

SAM SHARPE SQUARE/MONTEGO BAY CIVIC CENTRE AND MUSEUM/THE CAGE

BARNETT ST

Jarrett Park

River Bay

Sunset Beach

CATHERINE HALL ENTERTAINMENT CENTRE

SUNSET DR

MONTEGO BAY YACHT CLUB

HOWARD COOKE BLVD

COCONUT DR

WESTGATE PLAZA

● SUNSET BEACH
● SECRETS

FREEPORT CRUISE SHIP TERMINAL

SOUTHERN CROSS BLVD

C *GALLERY OF WEST INDIAN ART* ★

Montego River

A1

HOUSEBOAT BAR & GRILL

ALICE ELDEMIRE DR

Pies River

FAIRFIELD RD

A1

Bogue Islands

JERKY'S ▼

DRAGON COURT ■

PALACE MULTIPLEX

To Bellefield Great House/Pitfour

FAIRFIELD THEATER

River

To Reading, Hopewell, Hanover, Negril, and South Coast

DAY-O-PLANTATION

© AVALON TRAVEL

terminates at the end of the airport runway. **Queens Drive** passes along the hill above the Hip Strip with several budget hotels, many of them frequented by locals seeking privacy with their special someone.

Downtown Montego Bay is centered on **Sam Sharpe Square,** where a statue of the slave rebellion leader stands in one corner. The peninsula of **Freeport** sticks out into the Bogue Lagoon and the Montego Bay Marine Park just west of downtown, with the cruise ship terminal, the yacht club, Sunset Beach and Secrets resorts located there.

East of the airport, Ironshore is a middle class area that covers a large swath of hill in subdivisions and oversized concrete houses. East of Ironshore, Spring Garden is the most exclusive residential neighborhood in Mobay, bordering Rose Hall Estate where many of the area's all-inclusive resorts are wedged between the main road and the sea. Half Moon Resort, the Ritz Carlton, and Palmyra are the most luxurious of Mobay's accommodation options. Also nearby is Rose Hall Resort (a Hilton hotel), Sea Castles, a former resort now rented as apartment units, and three Iberostar hotels in a large complex a few kilometers further to the east down the coast.

SIGHTS
◖ Richmond Hill
Whether or not you choose to stay at this gorgeous hilltop property, a sunset cocktail from the beautiful poolside terrace will remain a romantic memory indefinitely.

The hotel has an illustrious history. Columbus apparently stayed here for a year while he was stranded in Jamaica, and it was once part of Annie Palmer's Rose Hall Estate. Later, in 1838, the property was acquired and built into a palatial abode by the Dewar family of Scotch whisky fame. Today the hotel is owned and operated with charm by Stefanie Chin and daughters Gracie and Gale, Austrian expatriates in Jamaica since 1968.

Montego Bay Marine Park
Montego Bay Marine Park (tel. 876/952-5619, contact@mbmp.org, www.mbmp.org) consists

of the entire bay from high-tide mark on land to 100-meter depth from Reading on Mobay's western edge, to just east of the airport on the eastern side. The marine park encompasses diverse ecosystems that include mangrove forests, islands, beaches, estuaries, sea-grass beds, and corals. The best way to see the marine park is with a licensed tour operator for a snorkeling trip or with a glass-bottomed boat tour. Tropical Beach and Aquasol both operate glass-bottomed boat tours, with the former including snorkeling.

Pitfour Rasta Settlement
Pitfour (contact Sister Norma, cell tel. 876/882-6376) is a Rastafarian settlement in the Granville district in the hills above Montego Bay. A Nyabinghi ceremony lasting more than a week begins every November 1 to celebrate the coronation of His Imperial Majesty Haile Selassie I, revered by Rastafarians as their God. On Good Friday of every year, a Nyabinghi vigil known as the Coral Gardens Groundation is held to commemorate the murder of Rastafarians by the Jamaican authorities in the early years of the

movement. When events are held, Rastas come from across Jamaica to participate. Otherwise the settlement is very sleepy, with little happening beyond perhaps a reasoning between *bredren* over a burning chalice. To get to Pitfour head inland from Catherine Hall along Fairfield Road, taking a right after the Fairfield Theatre, passing Day-O Plantation. Take the first right after the police station in the square, then continue straight, and then take the first left in Granville. By the gate to Pitfour you will see Bongo Manny and Daughter Norma Ital food shop.

Montego Bay Civic Centre and Museum

Mobay's Civic Center (Sam Sharpe Square, tel. 876/971-9417, 9 A.M.–5 P.M. Mon.–Fri., US$2 adults, US$0.75 children) houses a museum featuring a history of St. James. The small collection of artifacts spans the Taino period to the present day. The museum is under the management of the Institute of Jamaica, with assistant curator Leanne Rodney offering 30-minute tours throughout the day. Arrangements can be made for the museum to be open on weekends for 10 or more visitors by calling during the week to make a request.

The Cage, also in Sam Sharpe Square, was once used to lock up misbehaving slaves and sailors.

St. James Parish Church (Church St., tel. 876/971-2564) is one of the most attractive buildings in town. It's set amongst large grounds that house a small cemetery.

Burchell Baptist Church (Market St., tel. 876/971-9141) is a more humble church where Sam Sharpe used to preach. His remains are interred there.

◖ Gallery of West Indian Art

The Gallery of West Indian Art (11 Fairfield Rd., Catherine Hall, tel. 876/952-4547, nikola@cwjamaica.com, www.galleryofwestindianart.com) is one of the most diverse galleries in Jamaica—as far as carrying both Jamaican art and pieces from neighboring islands, especially Haiti and Cuba. The gallery is owned and operated by Nicki and Steffan, who make

Locals take cover from a light rain outside the Montego Bay Civic Centre in Sam Sharpe Square.

© OLIVER HILL

SAM SHARPE, NATIONAL HERO

Sam Sharpe was the central figure of the Christmas Rebellion of 1831-1832, which many point to as the beginning of the end of slavery in Jamaica (officially granted in 1838). Sharpe was a Baptist deacon, well respected across the deep societal divides. Despite this, Sharpe was executed in a public hanging on May 23, 1832, in what is now Sam Sharpe Square in the heart of Montego Bay. Over 300 slaves were also executed for their role in the rebellion. Sharpe had originally envisioned and promoted a peaceful rebellion of passive resistance, whereby the slaves would stage a sit-down strike until the planters agreed to pay them for their labor, in accordance with what was perceived as a royal decree from England being withheld in Jamaica. The rebelling slaves were swept up in the excitement of the hour, however, as Sharpe's lieutenants swept across the western parishes to the sound of war drums belting out from the slave villages. Only 16 white people were killed during the rebellion, but around 20 large estates were torched, and the rebellion struck fear into the heart of the "plantocracy." Sharpe took responsibility for the rebellion, relieving the white missionaries of the blame that was focused on them by the established powers of the day, including the Anglican Church (which with few isolated and notable exceptions backed the landed elite, even organizing terror squads to target the Baptist missionaries who had made it their charge to foment discontent among the slaves). The Christmas Rebellion was consequently also known as the Baptist War.

quality pieces accessible with very reasonable pricing. Look out for work by Jamaican artists Delores Anglin and Gene Pearson, a sculptor specializing in bronze heads.

Mount Zion

Mount Zion is a quaint community that overlooks Rose Hall, with excellent panoramic views of the coast northeast of Mobay. A small church forms the centerpiece of the village, where views over Cinnamon Hill Golf Course and along the coast of Iron Shore and Rose Hall are unmatched. To get to Mount Zion, turn inland on an uncommonly well-paved road (no name) just past the small bridge that crosses Little River heading east from the Ritz-Carlton. The road heads up a steep hill toward the community of Cornwall. As the hill tapers off toward the top, a right turn leads farther up to the community of Zion Hill. Heading straight at the junction leads to Cornwall.

ESTATE GREAT HOUSES

Each of the area's estate great houses is worth visiting and quite distinct from the others. A visit to one or all of these historic properties is like traveling back in time—a great way to catch a glimpse of the island's glorious and tumultuous past.

Bellefield Great House

Bellefield Great House (tel. 876/952-2382, www.bellefieldgreathouse.com), five minutes from Mobay at Barnett Estate, offers a lunch tour Wednesdays and Thursdays (10:30 A.M.–2 P.M., US$40). It consists of a 45-minute visit through the great house and gardens, and a one-hour lunch serving well-prepared Jamaican dishes. The tour can be arranged on any day of the week for parties of 10 people or more. A basic tour, without the delicious lunch, is also offered (US$20). Bellefield belongs to the Kerr-Jarretts, a family that at one point controlled much of the land in and around Mobay as part of Fairfield Estate. The tour is operated by Nicky and David Farquharson, who are also behind the production of the exquisite meal. To get to Bellefield, take Fairfield Road from Catherine Hall, staying right where the road splits on to Chambers Drive until you reach the Granville Police Station. Take a right on Bellefield Road at the police station and go until you see the great house on the left.

Rose Hall Great House

Rose Hall Great House (tel. 876/953-2323, greathouse@rosehall.com, www.rosehall.com, US$20 adults, US$10 children) is the former home of Annie Palmer, remembered as the White Witch of Rose Hall in Herbert De Lisser's novel of the same name. It's the most formidable and foreboding estate great house on the island today, with a bone-chilling history behind its grandeur. The tour through the impeccably refurbished mansion is excellent. Rose Hall was built in 1770 by John Palmer, who ruled the estate with his wife, Rosa. The property passed through many hands before ending up in possession of John Rose Palmer, who married the infamous Annie in 1820. A slight woman not more than five feet tall, Annie is said to have practiced voodoo, or black magic, and would eventually kill several husbands and lovers, starting with Mr. John Rose. Annie ruled the plantation brutally and was much feared by the estate's slaves. She would ultimately taste her own medicine, as she was killed during the Christmas Rebellion of 1831 (which pushed England one step closer to the abolition of slavery).

Rose Hall was virtually abandoned with the decline in the sugar economy until an American rags-to-riches businessman, John Rollins, bought the estate in the 1960s and restored the great house to its old grandeur. Today the estate is governed by Mrs. Rollins, who has upheld the ambitious development ethic of her late husband. Rose Hall Great House forms the historic centerpiece of the vast Rose Hall Estate, which encompasses three 18-hole golf courses, the Ritz-Carlton, Half Moon and Rose Hall resorts, and the most desirable residential district of Montego Bay, Spring Farms. Also on the Rose Hall Estate, Cinnamon Hill Great House was the home of the late Johnny Cash. Cinnamon Hill is not currently open to the public except for special events.

Greenwood Great House

Greenwood Great House (tel. 876/953-1077, greenwoodgreathouse@cwjamaica.com, www.

greenwoodgreathouse.com, 9 A.M.–5 P.M. daily, US$14) is the best example of a great house kept alive by the owners, Bob and Ann Betton, who live on property and manage the low-key tour operation. Built in the late 1600s by one of the wealthiest families of the British colonial period, the Barretts first landed in Jamaica on Cromwell's voyage of conquest, when the island was captured from the Spanish in 1655. Land grants immediately made the family a major landholder, and its plantations grew over the next 179 years to amass 2,000 slaves on seven estates by the time of emancipation. Greenwood Great House boasted the best stretch of road in Jamaica as its driveway. Little upkeep has been performed over the past four centuries, apparently, and today the 1.5-kilometer-long road requires slow going, but the panoramic view from the house and grounds are still as good as ever.

Interesting relics like hand-pump fire carts and old wagon wheels adorn the outside of the building. Inside the house is the best collection of colonial-era antiques in Jamaica, including obscure musical instruments, Flemish thrones, and desks with secret compartments from the 17th century. An inlaid rosewood piano belonged to King Edward VII, and a portrait of poet Elizabeth Barrett Browning's cousin hangs on the wall. Another historical treasure at the great house is the will of Reverend Thomas Burchell, who was arrested for his alleged role in the Christmas Rebellion.

Farther inland from Greenwood lie the ruins of Barrett Hall, the family's primary residence.

Bob Marley School of the Arts Institute (Flamingo Beach, Ras Astor Black, cell tel. 876/327-9991, tel. 876/861-5233, or 847/571-5804, astor@bobartsinstitute.com, www.bobartsinstitute.edu), located in Greenwood on a hill above the highway marked by waving Rasta-colored flags, is a bold project dreamed up by Ras Astor Black to draw Jamaica's youth into a technologically focused education in the arts, with music and production courses. As an annex to the school, the vision includes a **Reggae Walk of Fame,** where artists deemed

MONTEGO BAY

© OLIVER HILL

Wagon wheels and a variety of other colonial-era knick-knacks decorate the courtyard veranda of Greenwood Great House.

honorable will be inducted once per month. Black lives up on a hill between Falmouth and Greenwood, where he has created the Reggae Village. He intends to host regular live concerts to appeal to the masses of tourists who arrive expecting to see more in the way of live reggae music, like they are accustomed to seeing in the United States and Europe.

Plantation Tours

Several plantations in the area offer visitors a chance to learn about Jamaica's principal agricultural products—from those that were important historically to crops adapted to the modern economy. These include Croydon, John's Hall, and Mountain Valley Rafting, which offers a basic banana plantation tour.

Croydon Plantation (contact Tony Henry, tel. 876/979-8267, tlhenry20@hotmail.com, www.croydonplantation.com, open Tues., Thurs., and Fri., as well as other days when cruise ships are in port) is a pineapple and coffee plantation located at the base of the Catadupa Mountains and was the birthplace

of slave rebellion leader and national hero Sam Sharpe. The walking tour takes visitors through a working section of the plantation with an accompanying narrative, with three refreshment stops allowing visitors to sample some of the 12 different kinds of pineapple grown on the estate, in addition to other crops like jackfruit, sugarcane, and Otaheite apple, depending on what's in season. The tour includes a typical Jamaican country lunch. Total tour time from pickup to return is six hours, and the cost (US$65 per person) includes transportation, refreshments, and lunch. Croydon Plantation has the only privately owned forest reserve in the country. The 53-hectare estate is owned by Dalkeith Hanna, with Tony Henry, a partner in the tour operation.

John's Hall Adventure Tour (tel. 876/971-7776, relax.resort@cwjamaica.com, www.johnshalladventuretour.com) offers a plantation tour (US$70 per person inclusive of jerk lunch and fruits) with a historical and contextual commentary by the guides. Stops along the way include the Parish Church, Sam

Sharpe Square, and Mt. Olive Basic School. John's Hall Adventure Tour also operates the **Jamaica Rhythm Tour** (6–9 P.M. Wed. and Sun., US$80 inclusive of dinner), a musical show held at John's Hall featuring old-time heritage (from Maypole dancing and limbo to mento). Both tours include transportation from Mobay area hotels.

BEACHES

Walter Fletcher Beach is the location of **Aquasol Theme Park,** where go-carts, bumper boats, water sports, and two tennis courts heighten the entertainment inherent in the small strip of sand facing Mobay's harbor. The beach is located on the Hip Strip across from The Pork Pit.

Cornwall Beach (US$5, 8 A.M.–6 P.M. daily, tel. 876/979-0102) is wedged between the beaches for what was Breezes Montego Bay and DeCameron. The beach is owned by the St. James Parish Council and managed by David Chung. It was renovated in 2009 with clean restrooms, changing rooms, and showers, and there's a restaurant and beach bar. "Irie Mon" beach parties including a lunch buffet and open bar (US$80/person), with live music and entertainment are held on Wednesdays 11:30 A.M.–3:30 P.M. when a Carnival cruise ship delivers partygoers.

Tropical Beach is a decent, narrow strip of sand on the far side of the airport with the best windsurfing and Jet Ski rental outfit in Mobay. The beach isn't a bad spot for a dip, but it's not a destination for spending the whole day unless you're there for the water sports. To get to Tropical Beach turn left after the airport, heading east toward Ironshore and Rose Hall.

Sunset Beach (10 A.M.–6 P.M., US$60 adult, US$40 children for all-inclusive day pass) is the private beach for Sunset Beach Resort (tel. 876/979-8800 or U.S. tel 800/234-1707, www.sunsetbeachresort.com), which occupies the tip of the peninsula known as Freeport. The resort has a small water park with large pools and slides, as well as excellent tennis facilities. The day pass includes

food and drink at the main buffet-style restaurant and several bars scattered throughout the property. To get to Sunset Beach continue past the cruise ship terminal on Southern Cross Boulevard.

Dead End Beach is the best free public beach in close proximity to the Hip Strip at the heart of Mobay's tourism scene. Sandals Carlyle faces the beach, which borders the end of the runway at Donald Sangster International Airport. The beach is located on Kent Avenue, better known as Dead End Road.

One Man Beach and **Dump-Up Beach,** located across from KFC and Mobay's central roundabout, are venues for occasional events and horse grazing. The beach here is no good for swimming however, as the city's effluent emerges from a neighboring gulley.

Old Steamer Beach is located 100 yards past the Shell gas station heading west out of Hopewell, Hanover. An embankment leads down to the skeleton of the U.S.S. *Caribou,* a steamer dating from 1887 that washed off its mooring from Mobay. You can hang your towel on the skeleton ship and take a swim at one of the nicest beaches around, which only gets busy on weekends when locals come down in droves to stir the crystal clear waters.

◖ Doctors Cave Beach

Doctors Cave Beach (US$5) is the see-and-be-seen Hip Strip beach that is always happening. The beach is a favorite for the area's uptown youth on weekends, and a popular venue for full moon parties and other events and activities. The Groovy Grouper, situated to one side of the beach near the entrance, is a dependable spot for seafood and continental fare.

ENTERTAINMENT AND EVENTS
Bars and Clubs

For an early evening drink, the **Montego Bay Yacht Club** (10 A.M.–10 P.M. daily) is a popular spot among the uptown crowd, especially on Fridays. The **HouseBoat Bar** is also a popular early evening spot, while **Mobay Proper** (44 Fort St., tel. 876/940-1233, noon–2 A.M. daily) has the most consistently happening local scene every night of the week.

Hilites Cafe, Bar and Gift Shop (19 Queens Dr., tel. 876/979-9157, jamaica_flamingo_ltd@hotmail.com, 8:30 A.M.–6 P.M. daily) has a great view over the harbor and airport and is another great spot for an early evening drink or to watch the planes take off and land from Sangster Airport.

Margaritaville (Gloucester Ave., tel. 876/952-4777, 11 A.M.–you say when daily, US$10) is a wildly popular restaurant and bar with a water slide dropping off into the sea and giant trampoline inner tubes just offshore for use by customers. The restaurant serves dishes like cheeseburgers, jerk chicken and pork, and lobster (US$9–28), while almost every night of the week has a different theme: Tuesday is Caribbean night, which shifts each week to a different cultural theme—Latin, soca, etc.; Wild Wednesdays features wet T-shirt contests and Jell-O wrestling; Thursday is ladies' night, where women enter free till midnight; on Fridays there is a rotating guest selector or featured artist; and Saturday is World Beat Night with a sound system.

Margaritaville is the brainchild of a Jamaican partnership between Ian Dear and Brian Jardim, who struck a deal with Jimmy Buffet to carry his franchise in the Caribbean. In 10 years the pair has grown a business venture that is today a fixture in the three major tourism hubs: Ocho Rios, Negril, and Mobay, now with a branch at Sangster Airport as well.

Blue Beat (Gloucester Ave., tel. 876/952-4777, 6 P.M.–2 A.M. daily, free entry) is Margaritaville's more sophisticated and upscale cousin, located at the same property under the same ownership. The laid-back club features a resident DJ every night and live jazz Wednesday, Thursday, and Sunday 10 P.M.–2 A.M.

Jamaican Bobsled Cafe (69 Gloucester Ave., tel. 876/940-7009) is a popular bar serving bar food and pizza, and it offers delivery. The bar is at the center of the action on the Hip Strip.

Royal Stocks (Half Moon Shopping Village, tel. 876/953-9770) is an English pub-style bar and restaurant, serving pricey international cuisine. The air-conditioned bar is a great place to go when missing the cool of England, though the beer selection is not the same as back home: Guinness, Red Stripe, and Heineken are the only brews on offer.

The Keg (across from the fire station, no phone) is a local dive bar and a good place to soak up the local scene and listen to oldies.

Billiards

Mobay Proper (44 Fort St., tel. 876/940-1233, noon–2 A.M. daily) is the best place to grab a beer (US$2) and play some billiards (US$1 per game).

Rehab Pool Bar & Lounge (contact proprietor Gary Rose, cell tel. 876/409-1130, 6 P.M.–2 A.M. daily), located across from Lover's Park, next door to China House Restaurant, offers billiards (US$5/45 minutes or US$1 per game in the more spacious room with a/c at seven tables; this place opened in February 2009.

Live Music

Unfortunately, live music in Mobay is hard to come by—in sharp contrast to decades past when there was an active regular music scene. Today, the all-inclusive resorts have house bands that entertain the hotel guests, who are often discouraged from leaving the compound. Nevertheless, there is often live jazz at Day-O Plantation, as well as at Blue Beat, and Margaritaville. Of course if you want world-class music the best time to visit is during Reggae Sumfest (July) or the Jazz and Blues Festival (January). Catherine Hall Entertainment Center, the main venue for Sumfest, also holds occasional stage show concerts throughout the year.

Festivals and Events

Several annual festivals draw thousands from around the island and abroad, chief among them being **Jamaica Jazz and Blues** (www.airjamaicajazzandblues.com) and **Reggae**

Sumfest (www.reggaesumfest.com). The Montego Bay Yacht Club (tel. 876/979-8038, fax 876/979-8262, mbyc@cwjamaica.com, www.mobayyachtclub.com) has its share of events, including annual and biannual yacht races and a **Marlin Festival.** In Albert Town, Trelawny, the highlight of the year is the **Yam Festival** (www.stea.net/yam.htm), which is a family fun day centered on one of the island's most important staple foods, with tugs of war, beauty competitions, and, of course, music. Jamaica's **Carnival** season also brings at least one night of events to Mobay, with a free concert at Dump-Up Beach.

In the hills above Mobay, the Rastafarian community of Pitfour hosts annual **Nyabinghi sessions,** lasting for days to commemorate the coronation of the late Ethiopian Emperor Haile Selassie I, as well as to commemorate the Coral Gardens Massacre on Good Friday. Sadly, the area has fallen into disrepute over the last few years due to crime and violence. Visitors to Pitfour should proceed with caution.

Art and Theater

Alpha Arts (tel. 876/979-3479, cell tel. 876/605-9130, alphaarts@hotmail.com, www. alphaarts.com), adjacent to Sahara de la Mar resort in Reading, produces and sells on-site a variety of colorful ceramics.

Fairfield Theatre (Fairfield Rd., tel. 876/952-0182, US$10) is the only venue in the Mobay area for small, amateur theatrical productions that strive to uphold professional standards. Performances are generally held on weekends. Fairfield Theatre was originally founded as Montego Bay Little Theatre Movement in 1975 by Paul Methuen and Henry and Greta Fowler. The theatrical company was named after the Little Theatre Movement in Kingston, which was formed by Jamaican cultural icons like Louise Bennett. Contact theater chairman Douglas Prout (cell tel. 876/909-9364, dprout@globeins.com, d_freezing@hotmail.com) for more information or call the theater directly for performance schedules.

Mostly contemporary works from the best Jamaican and Caribbean writers are performed at the Fairfield Theatre, but the company produces works from a wide range of playwrights from Shakespeare to Noel Coward, Peter Schaeffer, Lorraine Hansbury, and Neil Simon. Caribbean writers such as Derek Walcott, Errol Hill, and Douglas Archibald have been produced to critical acclaim, but greater audience appeal has been found with the current crop of Jamaican playwrights that include Basil Dawkins, Trevor Rhone, Patrick Brown, and David Heron.

Palace Multiplex (Eldemire Dr., next to Jerky's, tel. 876/971-5550, movie times tel. 876/979-8624) is a cinema showing standard Hollywood films.

SHOPPING

Montego Bay is full of duty-free stores and gift shops.

Klass Traders (Fort St., tel. 876/952-5782) produces attractive handmade leather sandals from a workshop adjacent to Mobay Proper. Leroy Thompson (cell tel. 876/546-8657) is the head craftsman.

Rastafari Art (42 Hart St., tel. 876/885-7674 or 876/771-7533) has a variety of red, gold, and green items, including flags, belts, T-shirts, bags, and friendship bands that make inexpensive, authentic, and lightweight gifts and souvenirs.

For clothes, try **Lloyd's** (26 St. James St., tel. 876/952-3172), which has a great selection of trendy urban and roots wear and carries the CY Evolution brand.

Craft centers abound in Mobay, from Harbour Street to Kent Avenue to Charles Gordon Market and Montego Bay Craft Market. A discriminating eye is required at all these markets to sift out the junk from the quality Jamaica-produced crafts.

Freeport Cruise Ship Terminal has several shops, most of which carry overpriced souvenirs and mass-produced crafts items of little inherent value.

Duty-free shops are found anywhere you glance in Mobay, concentrated around City Centre Complex, the Hip Strip, and at the Half Moon Shopping Village east of town. The new Rose Hall Shopping Complex also has its share of duty-free items.

Bookland (34 Union St., 876/940-6185, bookland-mobay@cwjamaica.com, Mon.–Fri. 9 A.M.–6 P.M., Sat. 10 A.M.–5 P.M.) has the best selection of Caribbean books, as well as local and international magazines.

Sangster's Bookstore is at 2 St. James Street (tel. 876/952-0319).

Habanos Gift Shop (Shop #1, Casa Blanca Building, Gloucester Ave., tel. 876/940-4139, cell tel. 876/884-8656, habanoscigars1492@ yahoo.com), run by Raj Jeswani, sells Cuban and Jamaican cigars out of a walk-in humidor, plus rum, spices, coffee, and a full array of "Jamaica no problem mon" T-shirts, trinkets, and souvenirs.

Tad's International Records (retail outlet in the departure lounge at Sangster International Airport) has an extensive catalog of reggae.

Great River Studios (contact Paul Taylor, cell tel. 876/609-6266) is a recording studio operated by the owners of Spyglass Hill and located on the same estate as the villa. The studio rents for US$30–50 per hour with Pro Tools, voicing and live band rooms, and a two-inch analog tape. Led by studio musician, Palma Taylor, it's based just outside Hopewell.

SPORTS AND RECREATION

Tropical Beach Fitness (tel. 876/952-6510, tropicalfitness@hotmail.com, Mon.–Thurs., 6 A.M.–10 P.M., Fri. 6 A.M.–9 P.M., Sat. 9 A.M.–4 P.M., Sun. 9 A.M.–2 P.M.) is a decent beachfront gym with free weights, treadmills, bicycles, stair steppers, and weight benches. Membership is offered by the day (US$5) and month (US$30). The club has about 200 local members, with two trainers available for an extra fee.

Water Sports

The **Montego Bay Yacht Club** (tel. 876/979-8038, fax 876/979-8262, mbyc@cwjamaica. com, www.mobayyachtclub.com) was refurbished in 2006 with a new building, landscaped grounds, and a small swimming pool. The club is a warm and friendly family environment with a great bar and restaurant, making it the place in western Jamaica for sailing, fishing, or just to hang out and make friends. Entertainment at the club is facilitated by pool tables, foosball, and table tennis. Every Friday, the club hosts a buffet dinner. Social and sailing membership is available by the day (US$5) or by the year (US$150). The annual fee grants members access to the Royal Jamaica Yacht Club in Kingston as well.

The Mobay Yacht Club is the final destination of the famous **Pineapple Cup Race** (www.montegobayrace.com), which covers 1,305 kilometers of water from its starting point in Fort Lauderdale. This classic race—a beat, a reach, and a run—is held in February of every odd year. Other events include the annual J-22 International Regatta held every December, and the Great Yacht Race, which precedes every Easter Regatta, a fun-filled, friendly, and competitive multi-class regatta. The International Marlin Fishing Tournament is held every fall. Sailing camps for children are held during the summer and courses offered to adults based on demand.

If you arrive in Jamaica on a private vessel, the Mobay Yacht Club has some of the lowest docking fees anywhere (US$0.87 per foot 1–7 days), which are reduced even further for longer stays (US$0.50 per foot for 8–30 days). Utilities are metered and charged accordingly, while boats at anchor can use the club facilities for the regular daily membership fee (US$5 per person). Mobay's mangrove areas in the Bogue Lagoon are often used as a hurricane hole for small vessels. All charges carry 16.50 percent tax.

Aquasol Theme Park (Gloucester Ave., tel. 876/979-9447 or 876/940-1344, 9 A.M.–6 P.M. Mon.–Thurs., till 10 P.M. Fri.–Sun., US$5 adults, US$3 children under 12) is a small theme park located on Walter Fletcher Beach, with go carts (US$3 single-seated, US$7 double), two tennis courts (operated by Steve Nolan, cell tel. 876/364-9293, 6:30 A.M.–10 P.M. daily, US$6/hr.), billiard tables (US$.50 per game), a video games room, glass-bottomed boat excursions to the coral reef (US$25 per person for a 30-min. tour), and personal watercraft like Jet Skis ($75 for 30 min.). There's also a sports bar with satellite TV and the Voyage restaurant (US$5–10), serving fried chicken, fried fish, and jerk. A gym on property, Mighty Moves (tel. 876/952-8608, 7 A.M.–8 P.M. daily, US$8), has free weights, weight machines, and aerobics classes included with the day pass.

Tropical Beach Water Sports (tel. 876/940-0836, 9 A.M.–5 P.M. daily) is run by Chaka Brown with professional-quality equipment, including windsurfing sailboards (US$45/hour) and Jet Skis (US$75/half-hour, US$130/hour). Bogue Lagoon excursions are also offered (US$220/hour for up to six people).

Ezee Fishing (Denise Taylor, cell tel. 876/381-3229 or 876/995-2912, chokey@reggaefemi.com, dptgonefishing@hotmail.com, www.montego-bay-jamaica.com/ajal/noproblem, US$450 half day, US$890 full day) operates a 39-foot Phoenix Sport Fisher for deep-sea expeditions, offering a good chance of catching big game like wahoo, blue marlin, or dorado (depending on time of year). Ezee also offers sailing charters (www.jamaicawatersports.com) on catamaran Suncat and trimaran Freestyle vessels (US$400 for two-hour sails for up to 10 people).

Rapsody Tours, Cruises & Charters operates the **Dreamer Catamaran Cruises** (contact Donna Lee, tel. 876/979-0102, reservations@dreamercatamarans.com, 10 A.M.–1 P.M. and 3 P.M.–6 P.M. Mon.–Sat., US$65 per person, reservations required) with two daily three-hour cruises on its two 53-foot catamarans and one 65-foot catamaran. The catamarans depart from Cornwall Beach for morning and afternoon cruises at 10 A.M. and 3 P.M., and an evening cruise on Thursdays and Saturdays leaves from Doctors Cave Beach a 5 P.M. The excursion includes an open bar and use of snorkeling gear.

Two-hour **Calico Sunset Cruises** (5–7 P.M. Tues.–Sun., US$40 adults, US$20 children 3–11) are offered on the same Calico sailboat, with an optional dinner package (US$65) that includes a four-course meal at the Town Voyage Restaurant following the sail.

Lark Cruises by Barrett Adventures (contact Captain Carolyn Barrett, Barrett Adventures, cell tel. 876/382-6384, info@barrettadventures.com, www.barrettadventures.

com) operates half-day (US$400) and full-day (US$600) cruises out of Mobay for up to three passengers, with snorkeling and a Jamaican lunch included (US$100 for each additional person up to 10). Weekly charters are also offered (US$3,000 for up to six, plus provisions), inclusive of captain and cook. Charter cruise options include excursions to Negril, Port Antonio, or even Cuba, contingent upon favorable weather conditions.

Golf

Montego Bay is the best base for golfing in Jamaica, with the highest concentration of courses on a nice variety of terrains, some with gorgeous rolling hills, others seaside, all within the immediate vicinity.

White Witch Golf Course (Rose Hall, tel. 876/953-2800 or 876/518-0174, www.rosehall.com, 6:30 A.M.–9 P.M. daily) is the most spectacular course in Jamaica, for its views and rolling greens. The course has a special for Ritz guests (US$180 per person includes greens fees, cart, and caddy, not including US$20 recommended gratuity per player). The course is also open to nonguests (US$200 includes cart caddy and 18 holes, but not gratuity). White Witch offers a Twilight Golf Special (US$99 per person, inclusive of cart, caddy, and greens fee, after 2:30 P.M.). The last tee time is at 4:30 P.M.

A gorgeous clubhouse features beautiful views and the **White Witch Restaurant** (noon–9 P.M.), open to nongolfers as well, and a pro shop. The restaurant serves sandwiches, soups, and salads for lunch and fish and steak for dinner.

Cinnamon Hill Golf Course (Rose Hall, tel. 876/953-2650) is operated by Rose Hall Resort and offers special rates to in-house guests (US$141, inclusive of cart, caddy, and greens fees—extended to Half Moon and Sandals guests). The club also offers a Twilight Special (US$99 after 1:30 P.M.), in addition to the standard rack rate (US$160 inclusive of cart, caddy, and greens fees) with club rental an additional charge (US$40–50). Recommended caddy tip is US$10–15 per player. Cinnamon Hill is the only course in Jamaica that's on the coast. Holes five and six are directly at the water's edge. There is a gorgeous waterfall at the foot of Cinnamon Hill great house, which was owned by Johnny Cash until his death.

Half Moon Golf Course (Rose Hall, tel. 876/953-2560, www.halfmoongolf.com) is a Robert Trent Jones Jr.–designed course, with reduced rates for Half Moon Guests (US$75 for nine holes, US$105 for 18 holes). Rates for nonguests are US$90/150 for 9/18 holes, US$12/20 for caddy, US$40/50 for club rental, and US$25/35 for cart. Half Moon is a walkable course.

SuperClubs Golf Course at Iron Shore (tel. 876/953-3682) is a very respectable 18-hole course, with regular greens fees (US$50) waived for SuperClubs hotel guests. Caddy (US$11/16 for 9/18 holes) and cart (US$17/35 for 9/18 holes) fees are the lowest in Mobay; many prefer the course, in spite of it never having hosted a PGA tournament. Shelly Clifford is the friendly golf course manager.

Horseback Riding

Half Moon Equestrian Centre (Half Moon Resort, tel. 876/953-2286, r.delisser@cw-jamaica.com, www.horsebackridingjamaica.com) has the most impressive stables open to the public in Jamaica, for beginning to experienced riders. The center offers a pony ride for children under 6 for US$20 and a 40-minute beginner ride for US$60 (suitable for children over 6), a beach ride for US$80 that includes a horseback swim (for riders over age 8), and 30-minute private lessons for any experience level that can include basic dressage, jumping, and polo.

Chukka Caribbean (www.chukkacaribbean.com) offers a Ride 'N Swim tour in Sandy Bay, Hanover, about a half-hour drive west of Mobay.

ACCOMMODATIONS

Accommodation options vary widely from cheap dives and inexpensive guesthouses to luxury villas and world-class hotels. In the center of town, on Queens Drive (Top Road), and to the west in Reading there are several low-cost options, while the mid-range hotels are concentrated around the Hip Strip along Gloucester Avenue (Bottom Road) and just east of the airport. Rose Hall is the area's most glamorous address, both for its private villas and mansions surrounding the White Witch Golf Course, and for the Ritz-Carlton and neighboring Half Moon, the most exclusive resorts in town. Also on the eastern side of town is Sandals Royal Caribbean, easily the chain's most luxurious property, complete with a private island.

Along the Hip Strip several mid-range hotels provide direct access to Mobay's nightlife, a mix of bars and a few clubs, and guesthouses farther afield offer great rates.

Mobay is the principal entry point for most tourists arriving on the island, many of whom stay at one of the multitude of hotels in the immediate vicinity. The old Ironshore and Rose Hall estates east along the coast are covered in luxury and mid-range hotels.

Under US$100

⟨ Altamont West (tel. 876/620-4540, www.altamontwesthotel.com, altamontwesthotel@yahoo.com, US$90 d) is the latest boutique hotel to crop up along the Hip Strip in Montego Bay. The Altamont West marks the first foray into Western Jamaica for the Jarrett family, which has run the Altamont Court hotel in Kingston for years. Rooms at the Altamont West are cozy and well appointed, with flat panel TVs, Internet, air-conditioning, and private baths with hot water. Linens are soft and clean. The hotel is ideally situated across from Walter Fletcher Beach, a short walk to bars and restaurants along Gloucestershire Avenue, as well as Doctor's Cave and Cornwall beaches.

Palm Bay Guest House (Reading Rd., Bogue, tel. 876/952-2274) has decent, basic rooms (US$48) with air-conditioning and hot water in private bathrooms. While not the most glamorous location in town, opposite Mobay's biggest government housing project—Bogue Village, built to formalize the squatters of Canterbury—Palm Bay is quiet and safe and appreciably well removed from the hustle and bustle along the Hip Strip.

Big Apple Rooms (18 Queens Dr., tel. 876/952-7240, bigapplehotel1@yahoo.com, www.bigapplejamaica.com, US$65) is a no-frills hotel perched on the hill above the airport. The basic rooms have private baths with hot water, air-conditioning, and cable TV. There is a pool deck with a view of the ocean.

Satori Resort & Spa (tel. 876/952-6133, www.satorijamaica.com, US$65/85 low/high season) has 21 basic, no-frills, waterfront rooms with air-conditioning, cable TV, and hot water in private bathrooms. The hotel faces Mobay's lagoon from its location west of town in Reading.

Sahara de la Mar (Reading, tel. 876/952-2366, sahara.hotels@yahoo.com, www.saharahotels.com, US$60) is a 24-room oceanfront property nicely designed to hug the coast and provide a central protected swimming area. Amenities include hot water in private bathrooms, fans, air-conditioning, and TV. Food is prepared to order in the restaurant on the ground level.

Calabash Resorts (5 Queens Dr., tel. 876/952-3900 or 876/952-3999, www.calabashresorts.com, US$77–87 low season, US$105–115 high season) has a variety of basic rooms and studios with air-conditioning and hot water in en suite bathrooms. Some rooms command a view of the bay, and the pool has a great view over the city and bay.

(Hartley House (contact Sandra Kennedy, tel. 876/956-7101, cell tel. 876/371-3693, sandravkennedy@yahoo.com, US$50/ night per person including breakfast) is a lovely B&B located on a two-acre property at Tamarind Hill by the Great River, on the border of Hanover and St. James about 20 minutes from Sangster International Airport. Four rooms in the villa are rented, with the innkeepers living on property. Rooms are appointed in traditional colonial style with four-poster queen-size beds, or two twins in one room, and have sitting areas, ceiling fans and private baths. The stone-cut villa

was designed by architect Robert Hartley as a satellite property to Round Hill in 1965. Guests have access to a common area with a library and TV room. Meals can be prepared to order (US$8–12). Wi-Fi, tea, and coffee are complimentary all day long. Guests have a choice of low-calorie, continental, Jamaican, or English breakfast.

Villa Nia (cell tel. 876/382-6384, info@barrettadventures.com, www.carolynscaribbeancottages.com/VillaNia/indexnia.htm, US$85–95 per room) is a four-bedroom duplex property owned by Ron Hagler, located right on the water adjacent to Sandals Montego Bay on the opposite side of the airport from the Hip Strip. The rooms rent independently and feature either queen-size or king-size beds with sitting areas, small kitchens, and balconies. Each room has a private bath with hot water.

US$100-250

(Richmond Hill (tel. 876/952-3859, info@richmond-hill-inn.com, www.richmond-hill-inn.com, US$70/115 low/high season) is located at the highest point in the vicinity of downtown Mobay, with what is easily the best view in town from a large terraced swimming pool area and open-air dining room. While the accommodations fall short of luxurious, the sheets are clean, the restaurant is excellent, and the pool area's unmatched view and free wireless Internet access make Richmond Hill one of the best values in town.

Gloustershire Hotel (Gloucester Ave., tel. 876/952-4420 or U.S. tel. 877/574-8497, res@gloustershire.com, www.gloustershire.com, US$100/120 low/high season) is well situated across from Doctor's Cave Beach on the Hip Strip. It has a total of 88 rooms, many with balconies with a view of the bay. Other amenities include 27-inch TVs, hot water, and air-conditioning.

El Greco Resort (Queens Dr., tel. 876/940-6116 or U.S. tel. 888/354-7326, elgreco4@cwjamaica.com, www.elgrecojamaica.com, US$125/134 low/high season) is a large complex of suites overlooking the bay with a long stairway down to Doctors Cave Beach across Gloucester Avenue. Suites feature living areas with ceiling fans, air-conditioning in the bedrooms, and private baths with hot water. Many of the suites have balconies with sea views.

At the **Wexford Hotel** (39 Gloucester Ave., tel. 876/952-2854, wexford@cwjamaica.com, www.thewexfordhotel.com, US$144/177 low/high season), most rooms have two double beds, all with private baths and full amenities. Two rooms have king-size beds that can be requested. The hotel has a restaurant, The Rosella restaurant (7 A.M.–11 P.M. daily) that does an excellent Sunday Jamaican brunch buffet (US$10), well attended by locals and tourists alike.

Casa Blanca Beach Hotel (Gloucester Ave., tel. 876/952-0720, info@casablanca-jamaica.com, www.casablancajamaica.com, US$148, cash only) was, in its heyday, one of Mobay's most glamorous hotels. Only around 20 of the hotel's 72-rooms have been in operation over the past years, however, with a construction effort brought under way more recently. The rooms all overlook the water along the prime strip of Gloucester Avenue adjacent to Doctors Cave Beach. Unfortunately, poor maintenance and signs of neglect abound. Nonetheless the hotel sits on the best location in town for bars and nightlife. Norman Pushell is owner/manager. Amenities include private bath with hot water, air-conditioning, waterfront balconies, and cable TV. Guests get free entry to Doctors Cave Beach.

Doctors Cave Beach Hotel (Gloucester Ave., tel. 876/952-4355, info@doctorscave. com, www.doctorscave.com, from US$140/190 low/high season) is a no-frills hotel catering to those looking for direct, easy access to Doctors Cave Bathing Club across the street. Amenities include cable TV, air-conditioning, and hot water. Rooms are spacious with either a garden or poolside view. The cozy den-like bar has a Rum Punch Party happy hour with free rum punch 6–7 P.M. Tuesday and Saturday, and two-for-one rum punch thereafter.

Over US$250

Coyaba Beach Resort (Rose Hall, tel. 876/953-9150, www.coyabaresortjamaica. com, US$240/320 low/high season) is one of the most professionally run hotels in Mobay, with impeccably clean and well-appointed rooms with all the amenities of home and pleasantly unobtrusive decor. The hotel grounds are also attractive, with a pool and private beach area. The only drawback to the property is its proximity to the airport and the occasional roar of a departing flight. On the other hand, the proximity is also an advantage for the majority of guests, who tend to be weekend getaway visitors to Jamaica who stay three or four nights on average. Coyaba is located 10 minutes east of the airport and 15 minutes from Mobay's Hip Strip.

Ritz-Carlton Rose Hall (Rose Hall, tel. 876/953-2800 or U.S. tel. 800/241-3333, rc.mbjrz.concierge@ritzcarlton.com, www. ritzcarlton.com, US$189/499 low/high season room-only, US$429/899 low/high season all-inclusive) is a 427-room, AAA Five-Diamond golf and spa resort with the Rose Hall Estate Great House as its historical centerpiece. Rose Hall is easily one of the nicest Ritz properties in the world, with a private beach and two world-class golf courses right next door. A 1,003-square-meter ballroom and meeting space for up to 700 people make the Ritz one of the most popular corporate retreat destinations in the Caribbean, with on-site spa facilities and Jamaican touches to help ease any work-related tension. The property also boasts a state-of-the-art fitness center. The rooms at the Ritz uphold the highest standards of the brand, with attractive art depicting Jamaican flora and fauna throughout.

Half Moon Resort (Rose Hall, tel. 876/953-2211, reservations@halfmoonclub.com, www. halfmoon.com, US$250–400 low season, US$1250–1,800 high season) is one of the most upscale resorts in Jamaica, comprising an assortment of rooms, cottages, and villas. Most of the cottages and all the villas have private pools. Set on a 400-acre estate, the resort has 33 staffed villas with 3–7 bedrooms, 152 suites,

MONTEGO BAY

© OLIVER HILL

Fern Tree Spa at Half Moon Resort sets a high bar for luxurious pampering.

and 46 rooms. The cottages are tastefully furnished and cozier than the villas, which can feel cavernous due to their immense size and vary considerably in decor based on the taste of their individual owners.

Half Moon attracts golfers to its championship, par-72 Robert Trent Jones Sr. course; it is also a favorite for tennis players with 13 lighted courts. A range of water sports are on offer, and Half Moon is the only resort in Jamaica to have its own dolphin lagoon, operated by Dolphin Cove exclusively for Half Moon guests. Food at the estate's six restaurants is top-notch, with a number of snack bars dotting the property for quick bites. Also on the resort is the recently renovated **Fern Tree Spa,** among the best in the Caribbean, and a shopping complex. The crescent-shaped Half Moon Beach is one of the finest private beaches in the Mobay area.

All-Inclusive Resorts

Sunset Beach (tel. 876/979-8800, US tel. 800/234-1707, reservations@sunset-mobay.com, www.sunsetbeachresort.com, US$280/320 low/high season) occupies the choice property on the Freeport peninsula, which is also home to the Yacht Club and the cruise ship terminal. Sunset Beach is a 430-room mass-tourism venture and part of the Sunset Resorts group. It is very comparable to the group's property in Ocho Rios in catering to everyone with its motto, "Always for Everyone, Uniquely Jamaican," but especially popular among families on a budget. The rooms are divided between a main building and smaller structures on the other side of a large pool area. Rooms either face out to sea or toward downtown Montego Bay. The hotel has excellent tennis facilities, a popular water park with slides, a great beach, and spa facilities. Food is mass-market American fare with large buffet spreads at Banana Walk, complemented by Italian Botticelli, and pan-Asian Silk Road. Several bars dot the property offering unlimited bottom-shelf product. This is a convenient place to stay for Reggae Sumfest, with a hotel shuttle to the Catherine Hall Entertainment Center a few minutes away. It is not centrally located for walking the Hip Strip, but still within 10 minutes by cab.

Royal DeCameron Montego Beach (2 Gloucester Ave., tel. 876/952-4340 or 876/952-4346, ventas.jam@decameron.com, www.decameron.com, US$116/240 per person low/high season) is a budget-minded all-inclusive recently opened as the chain's second property in Jamaica. At times it can be hard to get through for a reservation, but otherwise the property could be a good value when compared to the other all-inclusive prices.

Holiday Inn Sunspree (Rose Hall, tel. 876/953-2485, www.montegobayjam.sunspreeresorts.com, US$315/535 low/high season) has the most decidedly mass-market ambience of all the all-inclusive resorts.

Secrets St. James and **Secrets Wild Orchid** (tel. 876/953-6600, reservations.sesmb@secretsresorts.com, www.secretsresorts.com, US$188/326 low/high), located next to one another on the southwestern tip of the Freeport peninsula, opened in March 2010. All 700 suites at the two properties have essentially the same layout, with whirlpool tubs and either a balcony or patio. The food is above average for all-inclusive hotels, with an excellent breakfast buffet spread and fine dining restaurants specializing in French, Italian, and Japanese cuisine.

Sandals Carlyle Montego Bay (Kent Ave., a.k.a. Dead End Rd., tel. 876/952-4141 or 888/sandals (888/726-3257), chbrown@grp.sandals.com, www.sandals.com, starting at US$334 d all-inclusive), formerly Sandals Inn, is a 52-room property that has been undergoing a transformation over the past few years as its renovations move forward little by little. Located along Dead End Road, steps from Mobay's Hip Strip, this is the most proximate Sandals property to the city's buzzing bars and nightlife, with the popular Dead End Beach located across the street. Rooms have balconies looking over the central pool area and out to sea. Tennis and beach volleyball courts are found at the far end of the property. A mix of standard rooms and suites have king-size beds and private baths, all with air-conditioning and cable TV.

Sandals Montego Bay (tel. 800/726-3257, www.sandals.com, US$970–4,050) was the first Sandals property and remains the group's flagship resort. Located near the end of the runway, guests are encouraged to wave to the planes as they fly overhead. The property boasts the largest private beach in Jamaica with 251 rooms, a Red Lane Spa, a butler service in the highest suite category, four pools and four whirlpool tubs, private villa cottages, and a private wedding chapel. The resort has a series of gazebos along the beach, as well as canopy beach beds to rent for an additional charge. Sandals imposes a minimum stay of three nights at all its properties. Promotions are ongoing throughout the year, slashing rates by as much as 65 percent.

Sandals Royal Caribbean (Mahoe Bay, Ironshore, tel. 876/953-2231, srjmail@grp.sandals.com, starting at US$473 d with a minimum three-night stay) is the most opulent Sandals hotel in Montego Bay, with 197 rooms and suites well deserving of the

a beach bed at Sandals Montego Bay

© OLIVER HILL

chain's "Luxury Included" motto. The suites are over-the-top with wood paneling, large flat-panel TVs, and tiled baths with standing showers and tubs. Balconies look over the courtyard and out to sea, with steps off ground floor suites leading directly into a large pool. The private island at Sandals Royal Caribbean is the trademark feature, where boats shuttle guests out for dinner or to laze away the days on the fine-sand beach. Gazebos are spaced across the property at the end of piers, favorite locations for wedding vows.

Riu Montego Bay (tel. 876/940-8010, www.riu.com, US$115/160) is a 680-room all-inclusive resort with standard double and suite rooms and an immense swimming pool. Suites have hydro-massage tubs and lounge areas. All rooms have a mini-bar, satellite TV, air-conditioning, balconies, and en suite baths. The resort offers a host of activities, including water sports and tennis on two hard-surface courts. The gym has a weight room, sauna, and Jacuzzi. The resort is located in Ironshore, near the end of the runway for Donald Sangster International Airport, next door to Sandals Royal Caribbean.

C Rose Hall Resort & Spa (Rose Hall, tel. 876/953-2650 or U.S. toll-free 866/799-3661, rosehallroomscontrol@luxuryresorts.com, www.rosehallresort.com, starting at US$149–199 d low season, US$169–219 d high season for room only, US$289–339 d low season, US$309–359 all-inclusive high season), a Hilton Resort, is a 489-room, seven-floor property built in 1974. The hotel underwent a US$40 million renovation in 2008 after being bought by Hilton and boasts a sleek South Beach design. Food is excellent, with indoor and outdoor seating in buffet and à la carte formats, and a seaside bar and grill by the Olympic-size pool directly in front of the hotel. The Sugar Mill Falls Water Park on property boasts a 280-foot water slide for a thrilling ride on tubes, spilling into a freeform pool with a swim-up bar, lazy river, waterfalls, and hot tubs

in a lush garden setting. The beach, located below the main pool and grill area, has fine white sand along a respectable stretch of coast.

Iberostar (tel. 876/680-0000, or US tel. 305/774-9225, reservations@iberostar-hotel.com, www.iberostar.com) completed a massive resort complex in 2007, with three all-inclusive hotels representing three distinct price categories. Guests staying at the more expensive hotels can use the restaurants and facilities of the lower categories, but guests of the lower-category hotels are not permitted on the more expensive properties. The quality of the food varies considerably by the price point, as you'd expect.

The **Iberostar Rose Hall Beach** (starting at US$190/309 per person low/high season) is a 424-room property that caters to the lower end of the Iberostar spectrum. Standard rooms have either one or two beds, and overlook the gardens with junior suites having either ocean view or garden view rooms.

Iberostar Rose Hall Suites (starting at US$235/363 per person low/high season) has 319 rooms, two pools with swim-up bars, and a lazy river meandering across the lawn. All rooms have a suite format with living rooms and mini-bars, with full tubs in the bathrooms of the higher category rooms and either ocean or garden view.

Iberostar Grand Rose Hall (starting at US$336/472 per person low/high season) has 295 rooms, all with living areas, day beds, verandas, bathtubs, and mini-bars. The property has two pools, each with a swim-up bar. The food at Iberostar Grand is excellent and has buffet and à la carte options with top-of-the-line dishes like lobster and steaks.

Villas

Hammerstein Highland House (up Long Hill from Reading in Content, U.S. tel. 805/258-2767, keressapage@yahoo.com, www.highlandhousejamaica.com, US$7,500/9,500 low/high season with four-night minimum for entire property) is a stunning six-bedroom

MONTEGO BAY

villa on a lush 17-acre property overlooking Montego Bay in the community of Content. Smaller groups can opt to rent a minimum of four bedrooms (US$6,500/8,500 low/high season). There are two king-size beds, one queen-size bed, two rooms with two twin beds, and the last room has a double bed. The two twin rooms can be converted to king-size beds. Amenities include complimentary Wi-Fi, a large pool, and beach club membership at Round Hill. All rooms have air-conditioning and satellite TV. A screened-in yoga pavilion with ceiling fans that accommodates up to 12 adults makes the property a favorite for yoga retreats. The staff includes a housekeeper, butler, cook, laundress, gardener, and farmer. The two-acre organic farm on property supplies much of the food for the villa and is linked with the Anchovy school breakfast program and an orphanage up the road, as part of the villa's support for the One Love Learning Foundation.

Spyglass Hill (contact Paul Taylor tel. 876/601-6456, or cell tel. 876/871-8454, spyglass@cwjamaica.com, www.spyglasshilljamaica.com, 1–4 br US$5,000/5,950; 5–6 br US$7,000/8,950; 7–8 br US$9,300/11,500) is an eight-bedroom, 6,500-square-foot former plantation house set on 10 acres of lush lawns and gardens and named for its breathtaking view over the St. James and Hanover coastline. The property can accommodate up to 18 guests and boasts a 20- by 40-foot pool, as well as a 24-inch wading pool for children. No amenities are left out, with a component stereo system and DVD player in the living room and TVs in all eight bedrooms, seven of which have air-conditioning. DSL Internet and fax are available for guests. The staff includes a cook, butler, housekeepers, laundress, pool maintenance person, gardeners, night watchman, and driver. A gazebo with a stunning oceanview backdrop makes the property a favorite for weddings. Rooms have en suite bathrooms and comfortable furnishings with king-size or queen-size beds, spread across the main house and three outlying buildings located a across the lawn: Tree House, Garden Room, and the two-bedroom River House, the latter with a 10- by 13-foot plunge pool.

SunVillas (contact Alan Marlor, SunVillas, U.S. tel. 888/625-6007, alan@sunvillas.com, www.sunvillas.com) rents a nice assortment of villas across Jamaica, varying considerably in price while all having much more than the basic amenities. Highlights in the Mobay area include the four-bedroom Afimi property on the Bogue Lagoon in Freeport, the glamorous 10-bedroom Silent Waters villa on the Great River along the St. James–Hanover border, and the six-bedroom Endless Summer and Greatview properties in the auspicious Spring Farm neighborhood, as well as several of the most luxurious villas at Round Hill and Tryall Club.

FOOD
Jamaican
Original Madourie Fast Food (80 Barnett St., contact owner Valtona Madourie, cell tel.

Original Madourie Fast Food is a popular local joint for Jamaican staples.

876/852-1041, 7 A.M.–midnight Mon.–Sat., US$2.50–4) has been a local favorite for staple Jamaican fare since it was founded in 1976. Specialties include fry chicken, curry goat, oxtail, and brown stew fish. Madourie's is always packed with a clientele that's almost exclusively Jamaican, a testimony to the good food that's reasonably priced.

Musiq (72 Gloucester Ave., 5 P.M.–1 A.M. daily) was opened in July 2009 by Pork Pit owner Uhma Williams as a musically focused bar located next door to her original establishment. The bar features an in-house DJ from Thursday to Sunday playing R&B, hip-hop, reggae, and dancehall. A chic setting with musical motif lends itself to chilling out and watching passersby along the Hip Strip. The bar food is very reasonably priced compared to other establishments along the Strip, with 10 chicken wings going for US$8, a slew of burgers with a variety of seasonings for US$8–12, and soups (US$3) and salads (US$6–9).

Dragon Lounge (Whitehouse, tel. 876/952-1578, 7 A.M.–11 P.M. daily, US$8.50–14), run by Sebil and Peter Tebert, serves excellent seafood dishes, including shrimp, conch, and lobster, in a gritty and rootsy Jamaican bar environment with a dining room out back by the kitchen.

(Adwa Nutrition for Life is the best place in town for natural food. It has three locations, including one full-service, sit-down restaurant (Shops #158–160, City Center, tel. 876/940-7618) and two stores (Shop #7, West F&S Complex, 29–31 Union St., tel. 876/952-2161; and Shop #2, West Gate Plaza, tel. 876/952-6554) with imported and domestic products and delis serving freshly made foods and juice blends. Dishes (US$1–4.50) include curried tofu, peppered veggie steak, and red pea sip, with beverages like cane juice, fruit smoothies, and carrot juice also served.

Ruby Restaurant (Shop #3, Westgate Shopping Centre, tel. 876/952-3199, 8 A.M.–8:30 P.M. Mon.–Sat., US$3.50–11) has Jamaican breakfast dishes like callaloo and codfish, ackee and saltfish, kidney and onion, and brown stew chicken, as well as more international standards like eggs and bacon, French toast, and ham and bacon omelettes. The lunch menu ranges from curry goat to escovitch fish. More expensive dishes include shrimp plates and steamed fish. Sui mein, foo yong, and chow mein are also available.

(Mobay Proper (44 Fort St., tel. 876/940-1233, noon–2 A.M. daily, US$3.50–14) is the in spot for Mobay's party-hearty youth and fashionable businesspeople alike. The food is excellent and a great value, with dishes like fried or jerk chicken, fish done to order, curry goat, roast beef, and steamed, escovitch, or brown stew fish. This is the best place to get a beer (US$2) and play some billiards (US$1 per game).

The Pelican (Gloucester Ave., tel. 876/952-3171, 7 A.M.–11 P.M. daily, US$10–40) serves a mix of local and international dishes at international prices. Jamaican favorites like stewed peas (US$8), curry goat (US$12), steamed or brown stew fish (US$11), and lobster (US$40) complement international staples like cordon bleu (US$17) and hamburgers (US$9).

The **Montego Bay Yacht Club** (Freeport, tel. 876/979-8038, 10 A.M.–10 P.M. daily, US$6–25) has a good menu with burgers, sandwiches, salads, and entrées like lobster and shrimp thermidor, snapper, lamb chops, seafood pasta, coconut curry chicken, and zucchini pasta in a pleasant waterfront setting. A popular buffet dinner (US$14) with a rotating menu is served on Fridays.

Jerk

(Scotchie's (Carol Gardens, tel. 876/953-3301, 11 A.M.–11 P.M. daily, US$4–11) is easily the best jerk in Jamaica, serving pork, chicken, and steamed fish. Sides include breadfruit, festival, and yam. Scotchie's was forced to move back from the expanded highway and took the opportunity to redesign the dining area, adding a nice bar in the open-air courtyard. Scotchie's founder Tony

Rerrie used to have parties where he would bring a master jerk chef from Boston Bay in Portland, where locals claim jerk originated, and patrons would beg him to make the jerk offering a regular thing. He started his first jerk center on the roadside in Montego Bay with a few cinder blocks, some bamboo poles, and a few sheets of zinc roofing.

The Pork Pit (27 Gloucester Ave., tel. 876/940-3008, US$5–11) has jerk by the pound: pork, chicken, ribs, and shrimp.

Jerky's (29 Alice Eldemire Dr., tel. 876/684-9101 or 876/684-9102, 11 A.M.–midnight Sun.–Fri., open later on Sat. for karaoke, US$3–10) has jerk chicken, steamed fish, escovitch fish, ribs, conch, shrimp, and fried fish. There is a large bar where a beer costs US$1.75.

Nyam 'n' Jam (17 Harbour St., tel. 876/952-1922, 7 A.M.–11 P.M. daily, US$3–4.50) has a variety of Jamaican staples like fried chicken, curry goat, and oxtail. Breakfast items include ackee and saltfish, calaloo and saltfish, brown stew chicken, yam, boiled bananas, and fried dumpling.

Nyam 'n' Jam Jerk Centre (just before descending the hill into Mobay from "top road," a.k.a. Queens Dr., tel. 876/952-1713, 7 A.M.–11 P.M.) has local dishes as well as decent jerk under the same ownership. The jerk center offers delivery in addition to having a small dining area.

Palm Bay Guest House (Bogue Main Rd., 7 A.M.–10 P.M., US$4–6.50) has a small restaurant serving local dishes like curry goat, stew pork, fried chicken, and oxtail, as well as an outdoor jerk center (noon–midnight daily) that serves decent Boston-style jerk.

Pimento's (Reading Rd., cell tel. 876/446-2125, 10 A.M.–7 P.M. Mon.–Sat., US$3–9) is a new jerk and Jamaican food joint just past Bogue in Reading, heading west out of town. Original Jamaican dishes include curry goat, steamed fish, fried chicken, stewed peas with pig tail, fish, and shrimp.

International

Dragon Court (Fairview Shopping Center, Alice Eldemire Dr., Bogue, tel. 876/979-8822 or 876/979-8824, fax 876/979-8825, 11:30 A.M.–10 P.M. Mon.–Sat., US$5–18) has good dim sum every day. The shrimp dumplings are a favorite.

Canton Express Restaurant (43 St. James St., tel. 876/952-6173, 10:30 A.M.–7 P.M. Mon.–Sat., US$3.50–7.50) has roast chicken, oxtail, shrimp, chicken chow mein, and shrimp fried rice.

China House Restaurant (32 Gloucester Ave., tel. 876/979-0056, 10 A.M.–10 P.M. daily, US$2.25–22.50) serves Chinese, Mongolian, Thai, and Jamaican cuisine, as does its neighbor, **Golden Dynasty Chinese Restaurant** (39 Gloucester Ave., tel. 876/971-0459, 11 A.M.–10 P.M. Mon.–Sat., noon–10 P.M. Sun., US$2–20). China House serves dim sum on Sundays.

Chilitos (Shops #1 and #2, Doctors Cave Beach Hotel, Gloucester Ave., tel. 876/952-4615, 11 A.M.–10 P.M. Mon.–Sat., 1–10 P.M. Sun.) serves Jamexican specialties like quesadillas, tacos, and burritos, as well as mixed drinks and of course tequila, with a happy hour 5–7 P.M. on weekdays.

Akbar and Thai Cuisine (tel. 876/953-8240, Half Moon Shopping Village, noon–3:30 P.M. and 6–10:30 P.M. daily, US$10–24) is a decent, dependable Thai restaurant sharing a venue with a North Indian place. Staples like chicken or shrimp pad Thai on the Thai side complement items like chicken tikka masala and lobster bhuna from the Indian kitchen. This is Mobay's branch of the same restaurant found on Holborn Avenue in Kingston.

Fine Dining

The HouseBoat Grill (Southern Cross Blvd., Freeport, tel. 876/979-8845, houseboat@cwjamaica.com, www.montego-bay-jamaica.com/houseboat/index.html, 6–11 P.M. Tues.–Sun., bar open from 4:30 P.M., happy hour 5:30–7 P.M., US$12–26) on Montego Bay's Marine Park is an unparalleled setting for a romantic dinner, and the food is excellent. Dishes include chicken, fish, and lobster.

MONTEGO BAY

© OLIVER HILL

You won't find a more picturesque setting for a romantic sunset dinner than at The HouseBoat Grill, which sits on Bogue Lagoon.

The HouseBoat Grill is run by Scott Stanley, and reservations are recommended.

(The Groovy Grouper Bar & Grill (Doctors Cave Beach, tel. 876/952-8287, fax 876/940-3784, groovynews@islandentertainmentbrands.com, margaritavillecaribbean.com, 9:30 A.M.–10 P.M. daily, US$10–24) serves excellent food ranging from fish tea to steamed fish and bammy to steak and lobster tail. The setting on Doctors Cave Beach is unbeatable in Montego Bay and is popular with locals and tourists alike. The restaurant holds regular events like its seafood buffet every Friday (7–10 P.M., US$25) and full-moon party every three months (on select Saturdays).

The Twisted Kilt (tel. 876/952-9488, 11 A.M.–2 A.M. daily, US$8–25) is a sports bar that opened in 2008, offering "pub & grub." The pub has several big-screen TVs, free Wi-Fi, and a bar menu with wings, fries, fish and conch shamrocks, soups, salads, sandwiches, burgers, and entrées like fish and chips, steaks, pasta, and sautéed tofu. On Fridays, 2-for-1 martinis are on offer for the ladies 6–9 P.M. The bar

serves specialty drinks like the twisted mojito, Mackeson Stout, and Olde English Cider in addition to the typical bottled beers found widely in Jamaica.

(The Native Restaurant (29 Gloucester Ave., tel. 876/979-2769, US$9–12) is easily one of Mobay's best, with an extensive menu including items like smoked marlin appetizer or Caesar salad with spicy shrimp and entrées like Yard Man steamed or escovitch fish or gingered plantain–stuffed chicken. Vegetarian options include garlic char-grilled vegetables and green vegetable coconut curry. The Boonoonoonos Native sampler platter is a good way to get a taste for a variety of Jamaican dishes in a single sitting. Other creations bring an international flair to traditional cuisine with dishes like ackee and saltfish quesadillas and lobster roll-ups. The restaurant's in-house band performs smooth, live dinner music Tuesday–Saturday. Dinner is served starting at 5:30 P.M., with the last order taken at 10:30 P.M. Families are always welcome, and reservations are strongly suggested. Free door-to-door transport is provided to many hotels and villas in the area.

Marguerite's (Gloucester Ave., adjacent to Margaritaville, tel. 876/952-4777, 6–10:30 P.M. daily, US$20–50) is the fine dining wing of Mobay's popular Margaritaville, serving dishes ranging from the Caribbean-style chicken to seafood penne and sugarcane-seared drunken lobster tail.

Ⓒ Day-O Plantation (Fairfield Rd., tel. 876/952-1825, cell tel. 876/877-1884, dayorest@yahoo.com, www.dayorestaurant.com, US$16–35) was formerly part of the Fairfield Estate, which at one time encompassed much of Mobay. It is perhaps the most laid-back and classy place to enjoy a delicious dinner. Entrées range from typical chicken dishes to lobster. A beer costs US$3–5. Day-O is a favorite for weddings and other events that require the finest setting around a gorgeous pool. Owners Jennifer and Paul Hurlock are the most gracious hosts, and on a good day Paul will bring out his guitar and bless diners with his talent. Other professional musicians who have played at the restaurant's dinner shows include guitar legend Ernest Ranglin, jazz artist Martin Hand, and steel pan artist Othello Molineaux.

Pier 1 Restaurant and Marina (tel. 876/952-2452, 9 A.M.–11 P.M. daily, later on weekends) is an excellent restaurant and entertainment venue. The Sunday seafood buffet starting at 3 P.M. is a must. Pier 1 hosts a Pier Pressure party on Fridays, a fashion and talent show on Wednesdays, and occasional large events. The grounds just outside the restaurant are a venue for a few nights of Reggae Sumfest. Appetizers include crunchy conch (US$4.50), chicken wings (US$6.25), and shrimp cocktail (US$7.50), while entrées include chicken and mushrooms (US$10), bracelet steak (US$18), whole snapper (US$16/lb.), and lobster (US$28).

The Sugar Mill Restaurant (across the highway from Half Moon Shopping Village, tel. 876/953-2314 or 876/953-2228, 6–10 P.M. daily) is one of the area's high-end establishments, specializing in Caribbean fusion cuisine with openers like pumpkin or conch soup

(US$7.50), spring rolls, smoked marlin or conch in fritters, salad, or jerked (US$13–15). Entrées range from coconut-crusted or escovitch fish to lobster tail (US$35–50).

Norma's (Altamont West, tel. 876/620-4540, US$15–35) specializes in Caribbean fusion cuisine. Its founder, Norma Shirley, manages several restaurants under her name around the island. The food is on the pricey side and includes entrées like stuffed chicken breast, oxtail, curried goat with the chef's own mango chutney, lamb chops and lobster. Appetizers include ackee with salt fish, marlin salad, and crab back.

Sweets and Ice Cream

Calypso Gelato (Lot 9, Spring Garden Main Rd., Reading, tel. 876/979-9381, 8 A.M.–6 P.M. Mon.–Fri., 9 A.M.–6 P.M. Sat., 10 A.M.–6 P.M. Sun.) is the only producer of Italian gelato in Jamaica, with a small retail shop at its factory west of Montego Bay in Reading, just past the turnoff up Long Hill, next door to Ramson Wholesale. Calypso boasts more than 50 flavors of gelato, either milk or water-based, using local fruits. A cone or cup with two scoops costs US$2, medium cups are US$3.50, and large cups are US$5.

Tortuga (www.tortugarumcakes.com) located on the same compound, produces the Caribbean's most commercially successful rum cake and retails the cakes from the same shop.

Devon House I Scream (Bay West Center, tel. 876/940-4060) is open 11 A.M.–11 P.M. daily and has some of the best ice cream around.

INFORMATION AND SERVICES
Organized Tours

Most of the major organized tours to attractions across the island run out of Montego Bay and/or Negril, with transportation included as part of a package with entry fees and sometimes a meal. These include Mayfield Falls, Chukka Cove, Rhodes Hall, and Caliche White River Rafting. The farm and plantation tours operate similarly, including transport and food.

The best and most versatile tour operator running, with transport to even the most remote and unheard-of interesting corners of Jamaica, is **Barrett Adventures** (contact Carolyn Barrett, cell tel. 876/382-6384, info@barrettadventures.com, www.barrettadventures.com). With personalized service, Barrett Adventures tailors an excursion or even an entire vacation precisely to your interests and likings. Whether it's climbing Blue Mountain Peak, more humbly climbing Reach Falls in Portland, tubing down the YS River, or getting a historical tour of Falmouth, veteran adventurer Carolyn Barrett will get you there and ensure that anything you could want to do gets done in the allotted time-frame—which, if you're lucky, won't be less than a week.

Banks and Money

As elsewhere in Jamaica, the easiest way to get funds is from an ATM with your regular bankcard. Nevertheless, you can get slightly better rates in the cambios, or currency trading houses, that can be found all over town.

NCB has locations at 93 Barnett Street (tel. 876/952-6539), 41 St. James Street (tel. 876/952-6540), and Harbour Street (tel. 876/952-0077), with ATMs at Sangster Airport and at the junction of 92 Kent and Gloucester Avenues.

Scotiabank is at 6–7 Sam Sharpe Square (tel. 876/952-4440), 51 Barnett Street (tel. 876/952-5539), and Westgate shopping plaza (tel. 876/952-5545).

FX Trader is a an exchange house that gives the best rates around. FX has locations at Hometown FSC (19 Church), Medi Mart (Shop #1, St. James Place, Gloucester Ave.) and at Hometown Overton (Shop #9, Overton Plaza, Union St.).

Government Offices

Jamaica Tourist Board (18 Queens Drive, tel. 876/952-4425) has information about attractions in the region.

Internet Access

The best place in Mobay to get online if you have a laptop is **Richmond Hill,** where there is no charge to use the Wi-Fi, which reaches from the open-air lounge across the veranda and pool area. Richmond Hill has the best view of Mobay's harbor in town. Buy a drink from the bar or a snack in appreciation for the service. Otherwise the **Parish Library** (Fort St., tel. 876/952-4185, 9 A.M.–5 P.M. Mon.–Sat.) offers Internet access as well (US$1.50/hour.)

Computer World (13 Strand St., tel. 876/952-3464, fax 876/952-3464, cell tel. 876/538-9519, computerworld@cwjamaica.com or earljoel@yahoo.com, 10 A.M.–6:30 P.M. Mon.–Fri., 10 A.M.–7 P.M. Sat.) offers Internet, copies, and printing as well as making CD compilations. Internet rates run US$1.10 per half hour.

Medical Services

Mobay Hope Medical Center (Half Moon, Rose Hall, tel. 876/953-3981) is considered by many the best private hospital in Jamaica.

Soe-Htwe Medicare (14 Market St., tel. 876/979-3444) is the best private clinic in town.

Supermarkets

Adwa (West Gate Plaza) has a wide array of natural foodstuffs like imported organic grains as well as cosmetics products by Tom's of Maine.

Little Jack Horner Health Food Store (2 Barnett St., tel. 876/952-4952) has nice baked goods and pastries.

Parcel Services

Both **DHL** (34 Queens Dr., tel. 888/225-5345) and **FedEx** (Queens Dr., tel. 888/GO-FEDEX or 888/463-3339) have operations near the airport. Domestic carrier AirPak Express (tel. 876/952-8647) is located at the domestic airport terminal.

GETTING THERE AND AROUND
By Air

Donald Sangster International Airport (Jamaica Tourist Board information desk, tel. 876/952-2462, airport managers MBJ Ltd., tel. 876/952-3133) is the primary point of entry for most tourists visiting Jamaica. The airport is located by Flankers district a few minutes east of the Hip Strip and about 10 minutes from Downtown or from Rose Hall.

Beyond the national airline, Air Jamaica, Sangster airport is served by many North American and European carriers including US Airways, Delta, United, Air Canada, Northwest, American, Spirit, Continental, Cayman Airways, and Virgin. The domestic airline industry has been challenging historically, with little continuity of service among carriers and a slew of different domestic airlines coming and going over the years.

The domestic terminal is located separately from the international terminal. To get to the domestic terminal turn left from the main entrance just after coming off the roundabout, before reaching the gas station.

Skylan Airways (tel. 876/932-7102, reservations@skylanjamaica.com, www.skylanjamaica.com, office hours 8:30 A.M.–4:30 P.M. Mon.–Fri.) operates out of Norman Manley International Airport in Kingston with six weekly flights between the capital and Montego Bay (morning and afternoon departures Mon., Wed., Fri.). The morning flights depart Kingston at 7:30 A.M., with the return departing Mobay at 8:30 A.M.; afternoon flights depart Kingston at 4 P.M. with the return departing Montego Bay at 5 P.M. The trip lasts about half an hour and costs US$70 each leg. Skylan also offers charters when its aircraft is not in use on regularly scheduled flights. It operates a Jetstream 32 19-seater aircraft with a pressurized cabin.

Jamaica Air Shuttle (tel. 876/906-9025, 876/906-9026, or 876/906-9027, www.jamaicaairshuttle.com) is an affiliate of air cargo and courier companies Airways International and Airpak Express. It began offering regular flights between Kingston and Montego Bay in late 2009, departing from Tinson Pen Aerodrome with three Beach 99 Turbo Props seating 12 and one Queen Air with a five-person capacity. The carrier has 62 flights between Kingston and Mobay weekly Monday–Saturday (US$120 each way) and also offers charters.

International AirLink (tel. 876/940-6660, tel. 876/971-4601, or from U.S. tel. 954/241-3864, intlairlink01@gmail.com, res@intlairlink.com, www.intlairlink.com) offers charter service from Mobay to Kingston (US$134), Negril (US$134 for two persons), Boscobel, and Port Antonio ($1,575). Airlink passes on bank charges of an additional five percent when paying with a credit card.

Buses and Route Taxis

Buses and route taxis run between Mobay and virtually every other major town in the neighboring parishes, most notably Sav-la-Mar in Westmoreland, Hopewell in Hanover, Falmouth in Trelawny, and Runaway Bay in St. Ann. The bus terminal on Market Street is a dusty and bustling place where it pays to keep your sensibilities about you. Buses to any point on the island, including Kingston, never exceed US$7. Time schedules are not adhered to but you can generally count on a bus moving out to the main destinations at least every 45 minutes.

Real Deal Taxi Service and Tours (Curtis cell tel. 876/436-5727 or 876/971-8212) will take you wherever you want to go in a comfortable van holding up to eight passengers.

Car Rentals

Island Car Rentals (tel. 876/952-7225, icar@cwjamaica.com, 8:30 A.M.–10:00 P.M. daily) is Jamaica's largest and most dependable rental-car agency, aligned with Alamo, Enterprise, and National. It has an outlet in the international terminal at Donald Sangster International Airport. Island offers Toyota, Mitsubishi, Nissan, and Suzuki vehicles, with sedans, SUVs, and vans at competitive rates.

Central Rent-A-Car (Gloucester Ave., tel. 876/952-3347, or Sunset Ave., tel. 876/952-7485, toll-free tel. 800/486-2738) rents Mazda, Toyota, Nissan, and Honda sedans, plus Toyota and Mazda minibuses (US$90–115 daily).

Dhana Car Rental & Tours (4 Holiday Village Shopping Centre, tel. 876/953-9555) has vehicles ranging from Toyota Starlets to Toyota Noah minivans and gives heavy discounts on the walk-in weekly rates for reserving a month (US$75) or week (US$50) in advance.

Sunsational Car Rental & Tours (Suite #206, Chatwick Centre, 10 Queens Dr., tel. 876/952-1212, fax 876/952-5555, sensational@cwjamaica.com, www.sensationalcarrentals.com) is located across from the airport and has decent rates on a variety of Japanese cars (from US$40/55 per day low/high season for a Corolla). The company also offers free cell phones with a minimum two-day rental. The minimum age is 21, with a young driver surcharge until age 25. Maximum age for drivers is 68.

Alex's Car Rental (1 Claude Clarke Ave., Karen Fletcher, tel. 876/940-6260 alexrental@hotmail.com, www.alexrental.com) has 2001–2005 Corollas, Nissan Xtrail, Suzuki Vitara, and Honda CR-Vs (US$40/50 per day low/high season plus tax and insurance).

Thrifty Car Rental (28 Queens Dr., tel. 876/952-1126, 7 A.M.–9 P.M. daily) has 2003 and 2004 Toyota Corollas (US$92 per day including insurance and tax).

Prospective Car Rentals (2 Federal Ave. at Hotel Montego, across from the airport, tel. 876/952-3524, fax 876/952-0112, reservations@jamaicacar.com, 8 A.M.–5 P.M. Mon.–Fri., till 4 P.M. Sat.) rents a 2004 Toyota Yaris, Nissan Sunny, Toyota Corolla, and RAV4 (US$45–85 per day plus tax and insurance).

ST. JAMES INTERIOR

The St. James Interior extends from the coast inland as far as the Trelawny border, where Cockpit Country begins. The interior can be accessed from Montego Bay along three main thoroughfares: One extends up Long Hill from Reading west of Mobay; the next heads inland from Catherine Hall along the continuation of Fairfield Road, ultimately skirting the western end of Cockpit Country leading into St. Elizabeth; and the third road heads inland due east into Trelawny along the northern flanks of Cockpit Country. This last road (B15) is an alternate scenic route leading to Windsor Caves, even if it does take a few extra hours due to the road's poor quality.

From the western side of town, Long Hill

extends from Reading up along the Great River to where it meets the Westmoreland border. Developed tourist attractions in this area consist mainly of a few low-key river rafting operations, Rocklands Bird Sanctuary, and a few plantation tours.

Sights and Recreation

Caliche Rainforest Whitewater Rafting

(tel. 876/940-1745 or 876/940-0163, calicheadventuretours@yahoo.com, www.whitewaterraftingmontegobay.com) is the only true whitewater-river rafting tour in Jamaica, based on the upper reaches of the Great River, which runs along the St. James–Hanover parish border. Rafting excursions (1.5–2 hrs.) depart daily at 10 A.M. and 1 P.M. (US$90 per person with transport from Negril or Mobay included). For those with their own transportation (deduct US$10), park at the Caliche office (first building on left above the post office at the base of Long Hill in Reading) and ride up with the group that was picked up from hotels in Mobay or Negril. Caliche also operates on the Rio Bueno in Trelawny. The location in Trelawny affords Class III rapids even during the dry season (Feb.–Apr.) when it's no longer possible to navigate the upper reaches of the Great River. A slower, Class I–II rafting ride (US$80 adults, US$60 children under 12) is geared toward children as well as adrenaline-shy adults. Caliche is an Arawak word meaning "river in the mountain."

Mountain Valley Rafting (Lethe, tel. 876/956-4920 or 876/956-4947, 8:30 A.M.–4:30 P.M. daily, US$45 per raft) operates bamboo pole rafts along the Great River for a meandering rather than thrilling ride. To reach the launch site, go up Long Hill, take the second right turn at Cross Roads at the small Les Supermarket, and continue nearly five kilometers from the intersection until you cross the bridge into Hanover. Pickups from hotels in Montego Bay are offered (US$20 per person), as is a tractor-drawn banana plantation tour (US$15).

Great River Rafting (US$20) is offered on long bamboo rafts along the lower reaches of the Great River and out onto the tranquil bay where it exits into the sea. Immediately after crossing the Great River, turn inland and back to the river's edge, where several rafts are tied up under the bridge. Ask for Hugh.

Rocklands Bird Sanctuary and Feeding Station (Anchovy, tel. 876/952-2009, noon–5:30 P.M. daily, US$10 per person) was created by the late Lisa Sammons, popularly known as "the bird lady," who died in 2000 at age 96. Sammons had a way with birds, to say the least, summoning them to daily feeding sessions even after going partially blind during the last years of her life. Since her death, the feeding sessions have been upheld and the sanctuary maintained by Fritz, his wife Cynthia, and their son Damian. Visitors are instructed to sit on the patio and hold hummingbird feeders, which entice the birds to come perch on their fingers. There is also a nature trail where the property's 17 species can be sighted. To get to Rocklands, head up Long Hill from Reading and turn left off the main road as indicated by a big green Rocklands Bird Sanctuary sign. Follow one abominable road to the top of the mountain and down the other side, about 100 meters, turning right at the first driveway on the downhill.

Rocklands Cottage (US$150–200 for up to six people) is a cute three-bedroom on the property that has one king-size bed, one queen-size bed, two twin beds, two bathrooms, and a kitchen with a big living and dining room. The cottage has air-conditioning and hot water.

Northern Cockpit Country

East of Montego Bay proper, Ironshore and Rose Hall cover the coast with hotels and housing developments that range from middle-class to super-luxury before reaching Greenwood, a small community once part of the Barrett estate that sits beside the sea, bordering the parish of Trelawny. The Trelawny coast has a smattering of tourism development concentrated in the area just east of Falmouth along the bay, while the inhabited parts of Trelawny's interior are covered in farming country, where yam, sugarcane, and citrus fruit are major crops. The early morning mist that rises from dew-covered cane fields makes a trip through the interior from Rock, Trelawny, to St. Ann a magical alternative to the coastal route at this time of day.

◖ FALMOUTH

Trelawny's capital, Falmouth, is today a run-down shadow of its short-lived former Georgian prime. Nevertheless, noble and much-appreciated efforts are under way to dust off years of neglect and shine favor on the town's glorious past by restoring its architectural gems. Falmouth was formed in 1790 when the port of the former capital Martha Brae silted up and shippers needed an export base. The town was laid out in a well-organized grid and named after Falmouth, England, birthplace of then-governor William Trelawny, who lent his name to the parish. The land for the town was acquired from Edward Barrett, who owned Greenwood Estate a few kilometers west. For the town's first 40 years during the height of Jamaica's sugar production, Falmouth experienced a housing boom and was fashionable amongst the island's planter class. But as the sugar industry faded in importance, so too did Falmouth, leaving a virtual ghost town by the late 1800s.

Today, with somewhat decent roads and its close proximity to resort areas in Montego Bay, the town is attracting a growing population once more. Thanks to the efforts of a nongovernmental organization (NGO) known as **Falmouth Heritage Renewal** (4 Lower Harbour St., tel. 876/617-1060, jmparrent@yahoo.com, www.falmouth-jamaica. org), the town has become a laboratory for architectural restoration. Falmouth Heritage Renewal, directed by James Parrent, has been working for several years to revitalize the architectural heritage of Jamaica's most impressive Georgian town by training local youth in restoration work. The Georgian Society in Kingston (tel. 876/754-5261) has a wealth of information on Falmouth.

Falmouth is famous for its **Bend Down Market,** held every Wednesday since the town's founding.

Sights

The **Baptist Manse** (Market St., cell tel. 876/617-1060) was originally constructed as the town's Masonic Temple in 1780. The building was sold in 1832 to the Baptist Missionary Society, which had lost many buildings in raids of terror and reprisal following the slave rebellion of 1831, in response to the Baptists' fiery abolitionist rhetoric. The building was home to several Baptist missionaries before it was destroyed by fire in the 1950s, to be reconstructed as the William Knibb School in 1961. Today the building serves as headquarters for the Falmouth Heritage Renewal.

Falmouth Courthouse was built in 1815 in classic Georgian style, destroyed by fire, and rebuilt in 1926. The building stands prominently on a little square facing the water just off the main square at the center of town.

Trelawny Parish Church of St. Peter the Apostle (Duke St.) is one of the most impressive Anglican structures in Jamaica, built in typical Georgian style. It was constructed in 1795 on land donated by rich estate owner Edward Barrett, whose descendent, Elizabeth Barrett Browning, would go on to become a well-recognized feminist poet of the Romantic movement. The parish church is the oldest public building in town and the oldest house of worship in the parish.

Other historic churches in Falmouth include the **Knibb Memorial Baptist Church** (King and George Sts.) named after abolitionist missionary William Knibb, who came to Jamaica in 1825 and established his first chapel on the site of the existing structure, which was erected in 1926, and the **Falmouth**

The restored Baptist Manse operates as headquarters for Falmouth Heritage Renewal, an NGO dedicated to the restoration of the town's architectural treasures.

Presbyterian Church (Rodney and Princess Sts.), which was built by the Scots of the parish in 1832. Knibb's first chapel was destroyed by the nonconformist militia after the Baptist War, a.k.a. Christmas Rebellion of 1831–832. Later structures were destroyed by hurricanes. A sculpture relief inside Knibb Memorial depicts a scene (repeated at several Baptist churches across the island) of a congregation of slaves awaiting the dawn that granted full freedom in 1838.

Falmouth All Age School sits on the waterfront in a historic building and makes a good destination for a stroll down Queens Street from the square.

Shopping

Falmouth is by no means a shopping destination. Nevertheless, there is a small mall on Water Square with a few crafts shops to poke around.

For more original crafts, call **Isha Tafara** (cell tel. 876/610-3292 or 876/377-0505), an artist and craft producer who lives in Wakefield near Falmouth, farther inland from Martha Brae. Tafara makes red, green, and gold crocheted hats, Egyptian-style crafts, handbags, belts, and jewelry with a lot of crochet and fabric-based items. Tafara works from home, which can be visited by appointment, and supplies Things Jamaican, among other retailers.

Services

Club Nazz Bar & Restaurant (23 Market St., tel. 876/617-5175, 7 A.M.–11:30 P.M. daily) offers customers free Wi-Fi.

For groceries and supplies, try **T&W Supermarket** by the Texaco station.

Next to the courthouse there's a **Scotiabank** branch built in replica Georgian style, with an ATM.

FX Trader (tel. 888/398-7233) has a branch at Big J's Supermarket on Lower Harbour Street (8:30 A.M.–4:30 P.M. Mon.–Wed. and Fri.–Sat., 8:30 A.M.–12:30 P.M. Thurs.).

Trelawny Parish Library (Rodney St., with entrance on Pitt St., tel. 876/954-3306, 9 A.M.–6 P.M. Mon.–Fri., till 4 P.M. Sat.) offers free DSL Internet.

The **Falmouth Police** are based along the waterfront on Rodney Street (tel. 876/954-5700).

MARTHA BRAE

The town of Martha Brae was Trelawny's first parish capital, before the mouth of the river silted up and forced the relocation of the port from Rock to Falmouth. Along with several other locations in Jamaica, Martha Brae is thought to have been the location of the first Spanish settlement of Melilla. Until 1790 when the first bridge was constructed across the river, a ferry was in service. Today, with the North Coast Highway, it's possible to speed past without noticing the river at all. Martha Brae is a literal backwater, with little to distract tourists as they pass through on their way to start the rafting trip or to Good Hope Plantation in the Queen of Spain Valley.

The **Martha Brae River** is one of Jamaica's longest rivers and is navigable for much of its 32 kilometers, extending to the deep interior of Trelawny, from where it wells up out of the earth at Windsor Cave. The river's name is an awkward derivation of Para Matar Tiburon Rio, which translates literally as "to kill shark river." Legends surround the Martha Brae, likely owing to its important role in the early colonial years, when the Spanish used the river to reach the North Coast from their major settlement of Oristan, around present-day Bluefields. The first commercial rafting tour began in 1970.

Just east of Martha Brae, straight inland from Falmouth, the **Greenfield Stadium** was built for the Caribbean's hosting of Cricket World Cup in 2007. The stadium is now used for sporting events and entertainment, becoming the venue for Jamaica Jazz and Blues Festival in 2010.

Martha Brae Rafting

Martha Brae Rafting (tel. 876/940-6398 or 876/940-7018 or 876/952-0889, info@jamaicarafting.com, www.jamaicarafting.com, 9 A.M.–4 P.M. daily) is the most developed bamboo rafting attraction in western Jamaica.

Rafts hold two passengers in addition to the raft man, who guides the vessel down the lazy Martha Brae. The tour (US$55) includes a welcome drink; round-trip transport can be arranged from Mobay (US$15 per person). To reach the departure point on the Martha Brae River, exit left off the highway ramp after passing the first turnoff for Falmouth heading east. Turn inland (right) through the underpass, continuing into the small village of Martha Brae. At the intersection in the town, turn left and then right after the second bridge. The five-kilometer raft ride takes about 90 minutes. The excursion will not get the adrenaline pumping, but it's a relaxing and romantic experience.

The Luminous Lagoon

The Luminous Lagoon is one of Jamaica's favorite natural phenomena, created from a unicellular dinoflagellate less than $1/500$th of an inch in diameter, *Pyridium bahamense,* which glows when the water is agitated. The organism photosynthesizes sunlight using chlorophyll during the day and then emits the energy at night. Tours of the Luminous Lagoon are offered at **Glistening Waters Restaurant & Marina** (tel. 876/954-3229, info@glisteningwaters.com, www.glisteningwaters.com) and **Fisherman's Inn** (tel. 876/954-4078 or 876/954-3427, fishermansinn@cwjamaica.com). The Glistening Waters tour (US$17/person) lasts half an hour, with boats leaving the marina every half hour 7–9 P.M. nightly. Fisherman's Inn organizes virtually identical outings (US$15/person) every evening at 7 P.M.

Glistening Waters also offers fishing charters from the Marina (US$600) on a 46-foot sport fisher with a capacity of eight people. A smaller, 32-foot boat (US$400/four hours) carries five people. Two complimentary drinks per person are included on fishing excursions. The marina also welcomes visiting yachts (US$1/foot/day) and can accommodate boats of up to 86 feet. Boaters should call ahead for special instructions on entering the lagoon. Longer stays can be negotiated.

Montego Bay Jamaica Fishing Charter and **Luminous Lagoon Tours** (contact captain David Muschett, cell tel. 876/995-9885, awahoo2@yahoo.com), based at Fisherman's Inn on the Luminous Lagoon, is a one-stop-shop for deep-sea fishing, night excursions on the lagoon, and a variety of water sports activities from parasailing to scuba diving, water skiing, and snorkeling aboard a 38-foot Bertram with an eight-person capacity. Fishing trips chase marlin, kingfish, barracuda, sailfish, wahoo, and a host of other species. Rates range from US$550 for a half day with up to four passengers to US$1,000 for eight hours with up to four passengers, including bait and tackle. Add US$35 per extra person. Paintball and ATV tours are also offered by David Muschett in the Martha Brae vicinity.

Accommodations

Queen of Spain Villa (Irwin Towers Estate, Martha Brae, contact Michele Lawrence, cell tel. 876/877-6959, michelelawrence1@yahoo.com, US$40–60 per night) has a total of five rooms available for rent in an owner-managed villa along the Martha Brae River. Three rooms have queen-size beds, and one has two single beds, with a king-size bed in the master room. Wi-Fi and continental breakfast are complimentary. There's a pool on the one-acre property and the river is also suitable for swimming.

Fisherman's Inn (tel. 876/954-4078 or 876/954-3427, fishermansinn@cwjamaica.com, from US$75) is a hotel and restaurant on the Luminous Lagoon with clean, spacious rooms overlooking the lagoon and a small marina with private baths and hot water, TV, and either fans or air-conditioning. Jean Lewis is the very helpful and accommodating manager.

The inn organizes outings every evening (US$15 per person) at 7 P.M. on the lagoon to see the phosphorescent microbes light up the agitated water.

Time 'N' Place (adjacent to Pebbles, call owner Tony Moncrieffe, tel. 876/954-4371, cell tel. 876/843-3625, timenplace@cwjamaica.com, www.mytimenplace.com) is the quintessential laid-back rustic beach spot with an open-air seafood restaurant and beach bar and four cottages planted in the sand (US$80–100). The spot has been a local favorite since it opened in 1988. The cottages are comfortably rustic, with front porches, basic foam queen-size beds, fans or air-conditioning, Jamaican art on the walls, and private bathrooms sectioned off with hot water. Tony offers coffee, fruit, and toast for breakfast. The restaurant (8 A.M.–8 P.M. daily) prepares excellent seafood and Jamaican favorites including jerk chicken, coconut shrimp, and grilled lobster, as well as burgers and fries. Wi-Fi covers the entire property.

FDR Pebbles (next to Time 'N' Place along the old main road, tel. 876/973-5657 or 876/617-2500, US$250) bills itself as an ecofriendly, family-oriented resort. The hotel is by no means exemplary in the environmental department, however, with clear signs of dumping of gray water into the bay and a generally untidy backyard. Pebbles, along with its sister property in Runaway Bay, has created the family-friendly niche by proving nannies for guests. Pebbles' private beach has been sectioned off from the expanse with a pair of stone piers. Nevertheless, guests often hop the fence to get a taste for the authentic Jamaica vibe found next door at Time 'N' Place. All rooms at Pebbles have air-conditioning, ceiling fans, and hot water.

Excellence Resorts (www.excellence-resorts.com) is building a 450-room, adults-only, luxury all-inclusive resort on five kilometers of beach adjacent to Time 'N' Place. Construction began in 2007 but completion was delayed when the global economy fell into recession in 2009.

Food

(Club Nazz Bar & Restaurant (23 Market St., tel. 876/617-5175, or contact manager Carlton Cole, cell tel. 876/475-7125, 7 A.M.–11:30 P.M. daily, US$4–25) serves good seafood and Jamaican staple dishes and offers customers free Wi-Fi. The food is excellent and a good value. The Upa Level Culture Bar & Grill on the third floor serves food from the same kitchen with a view over town.

Located on the second level, **Club Nazz** opens Tuesdays–Sundays, from 6 P.M. until you say when, playing mostly reggae, dancehall, R&B, and hip-hop. A jazz bar and lounge is located downstairs in the basement.

In the center of Falmouth on the square there is a small Juici Patties kiosk, as well as **Spicy Nice** (Water Square, tel. 876/954-3197), a bakery that sells patties, breads, pastries, and other baked goods.

Three roads lead off the North Coast Highway into Falmouth, one from the east, where the old highway used to run, the other, Market Street, a straight shot to Martha Brae, and the third, Rodney Street or Foreshore Road, to the west toward Mobay. Along the easternmost road, two restaurants sit adjacent to one another on the Luminous Lagoon in Rock district.

Fisherman's Inn (tel. 876/954-4078, fishermansinn@cwjamaica.com) is a hotel and restaurant facing the lagoon. The restaurant serves items like callaloo-stuffed chicken breast, stuffed jerk chicken, lobster, and surf and turf (US$13–30).

Glistening Waters Restaurant & Marina (tel. 876/954-3229, info@glisteningwaters.com, www.glisteningwaters.com) has food ranging from oyster bay seafood chowder (US$4) to the Falmouth Seafood Platter (US$35), which comes with grilled lobster, shrimp, and snapper.

(Aunt Gloria's (Rock district, cell tel. 876/353-1301, 6 A.M.–8:30 P.M. Mon.–Sat., US$3–4.50) serves brown stew fish, fried chicken, curry goat, and brown stew pork. Gloria opens her jerk center on Fridays and sometimes on Saturdays for the best jerk pork and chicken in town. Breakfast items include ackee and saltfish, kidney, dumpling, yam, and banana.

Along the same road toward Falmouth, a jerk center keeps irregular hours, mostly opening on weekends.

Culture Restaurant (Foreshore Road, contact proprietor Pablo Plummer, cell tel. 876/362-4495, 8 A.M.–8 P.M. daily, US$4–8) offers a decidedly Rasta experience and takes the cake for original roots value. It's a small restaurant and cultural center where Ital food and juices are served in an atmosphere brimming with black pride and Rastafarian symbolism. Owner Pablo Plummer is as conscious as they come and also incidentally runs independent PADI diving courses with full equipment provided, after spending years as a dive instructor at a number of resorts along the North Coast.

EAST OF FALMOUTH
Sights

Outameni Experience (Coopers Pen opposite Breezes Trelawny, tel. 876/954-4035, cell tel. 876/836-6725 or 876/409-6108, info@outameni.com, www.outameni.com, US$36 adults, US$18 children under 12) is a cultural attraction that takes visitors through Jamaica's history into modern times, from the Taino to Rastafarians. The 90-minute tour, set on a five-acre property, touches on Jamaica's art, music, theater, and dance traditions. A fun

village offers children games and a water slide at an additional cost of US$3.

Duncans

A small community on a hillside overlooking the sea, Duncans has little to interest visitors in the town itself. Just below the population center, however, the coast is lined with fine, white sand, split between two spectacular beaches: Jacob Taylor Public Bathing Beach, and **Silver Sands Beach** along the waterfront at the gated community of Silver Sands, comprising cottages and villas. Silver Sands charges US$15 per person for day use of the beach and facilities. There's a restaurant and bar and small grocery store, the Villa Mart, at the complex. It's necessary to call ahead (tel. 876/954-2518) to gain access to Silver Sands so they expect you at the gate.

About a kilometer east of Silver Sands, a private estate house lies in ruins facing a small beach, also with fine white sand and crystal waters. To get there, turn off the main road down to Silver Sands through a green gate and

Sea grapes grow along Harmony Cove, a pristine beach near Duncans destined for a major hotel and casino development.

© OLIVER HILL

drive along a rough, sandy road pocked with coral through the scrub forest until reaching the coast again.

A 20-minute walk farther east along low coral bluffs leads to **Mango Point,** where one of Jamaica's few remaining virgin beaches is found. Known as **Harmony Cove,** the area is to be the site of a massive resort development planned for the coming years, with several hotels and casinos envisaged, pending a change in Jamaica's law to allow gambling of this sort. Harmony Cove can also be reached by turning off the North Coast Highway next to a cell phone tower coming from the east; from there, drive toward the coast along a dirt road and turn off along a sandy track that disintegrates at the water's edge. Park and rejoin the road on the other side of the fence, walking the remaining distance. It's about 20 minutes' walk from the east as well. Contact Harmonisation (876/954-2518) for more information on the status of the resort development.

Silver Sands

Silver Sands (www.mysilversands.com) is a gated community of 44 rental cottages and villas that range considerably in their level of price and comfort, from rustic to opulent. Even at the higher end of the price range, Silver Sands villas are among the best value for your money to be found in Jamaica, on what is considered by many the island's finest beach.

Queen's Cottage (US$275/325 nightly, US$1925/2275 weekly low/high season) is named after the cottage's most illustrious guest, Queen Elizabeth II, who stayed there on a trip to Jamaica, and located directly on the waterfront. It is a three-bedroom villa with a king-size bed in the master, one queen-size bed in the second bedroom and two twins in the third, making it ideal for families or a small group of friends. Bedrooms have ceiling fans, air-conditioning, and private bathrooms. A large wood deck overlooks the sea a few steps off the beach. The villa boasts a large Jacuzzi and is the closest of any at Silver Sands to the water's edge.

Windjammer (tel. 876/929-2378 or 876/926-0931, dianas@cwjamaica.com or

© OLIVER HILL

Silver Sands is a small villa community on the Trelawny coast ideal for family getaways.

bookings@windjammerjamaica.com, www. windjammerjamaica.com, US$457/557 nightly, US$3,200/3,900 weekly low/high season) is an impeccably furnished four-bedroom luxury villa with a private pool, DSL Internet, a large veranda with sea view, and a built-in barbecue. Two bedrooms have king-size beds, one has a queen, and the fourth has two twins.

Jacob Taylor Bathing Beach

Located across the compound walls from the gated community at Silver Sands, Jacob Taylor Bathing Beach is a local hot spot where low-key craft vendors sell their goods and anglers park their canoes to while away the days playing dominoes in the shade. The beach itself extends for a few kilometers to the west, and while not immaculately swept and maintained daily like Silver Sands, the sand is fine, the water's clear, and there's no entry fee. You can't miss the entrance to Jacob Taylor Bathing Beach, marked by a large sign by the road that leads downhill toward the sea to the left of the gated entrance to Silver Sands.

Accommodations

The Sober Robin Inn (tel. 876/954-2202, soberrobin@gmail.com, US$35 d) is a no-frills accommodation opened in 1979 that rents nine rooms, each with one double or two single beds, air-conditioning, and cable TV. The inn was under expansion in 2010, with additional rooms under construction for a projected total of 23. The inn was once owned by the grandparents of Harry Belafonte, who is said to have spent his childhood there. It is located just past the Silver Sands turnoff heading west out of Duncans, or on the right just after leaving the highway on your way into Duncans from the west.

Sea Rhythm (Jacob Taylor Bathing Beach, contact caretaker Cardella Gilzine, cell tel. 876/857-0119, US$200) is a three-bedroom cottage a few steps from the shore. The master bedroom has a king-size bed and air-conditioning, with a double bed and fan in the second room and two twins in the third. Each room has a private bath with hot water, and there's a fully equipped kitchen. Meals are prepared to order.

Food

Leroy's (cell tel. 876/447-2896, US$3–12) is a local bar and restaurant, located seaside at Jacob Taylor Fisherman's Beach that serves fish and Jamaican staples. Leroy can usually be found in the kitchen, and his step daughter, Cameika "Chin" Wallace, works the bar. The Silver Lights Band performs live reggae on Saturdays starting at 8 P.M. late into the night. The no-frills restaurant and bar is notable for its relaxing atmosphere that draws a healthy mix of locals and tourists, appreciably devoid of hustlers to interrupt the quiet seaside landscape.

GREENWOOD

Natural Vibes Gift Shop Bar & Restaurant (Long Bay, Greenwood, tel. 876/953-1833, 8 A.M.–10:30 P.M. daily) has a mix of seafood and Jamaican favorites like curry lobster (US$25), curry shrimp (US$20), escovitch fish (US$15), jerk chicken (US$10), and jerk pork (US$12–13). The waterfront property is a favorite chill-out spot for Montegonians and tourists alike.

Father Bull Bar, Jerk Centre and Restaurant (Greenwood, cell tel. 876/422-3011, 8 A.M. until you say when daily) specializes in jerk chicken and pork, roast fish, seafood, and Jamaican staples, accompanied by breadfruit.

Far Out Fish Hut and Beer Joint (Greenwood, contact owner Ian Dalley, cell tel. 876/954-7155 or 876/816-6376, 10 A.M.–10:30 P.M.) serves steamed and roast fish, conch, octopus, and escovitch grilled conch, accompanied by bammy or bread.

Johnnie Reid's Paradise Grill & Restaurant (contact Johnnie Reid, cell tel. 876/863-4659, 10 A.M.–close), located in Salt Marsh between Greenwood and Martha Brae, serves Jamaican staples, seafood, and conch (US$5–8), as well as fish and lobster priced according to weight.

COCKPIT COUNTRY

Some of the most gorgeous and unexplored countryside in Jamaica lies in the interior of Trelawny, where Cockpit Country, with its myriad caves, sinkholes, and springs, stretches from the St. James border in the west to St. Ann at the heart of the island. Hiking and exploring in this region is unparalleled, but adequate supplies and a good guide are essential. Meanwhile, the Queen of Spain Valley, only a few minutes' drive inland, is one of the most lush and picturesque farming zones in Jamaica, where the morning mist lifts to reveal stunning countryside of magical, lush pitted hills.

Cockpit Country has some of the most unusual landscape on earth, where porous limestone geology created what is known as Karst topography, molded by water and the weathering of time. Cockpit Country extends all the way to Accompong, St. Elizabeth, to the south and Albert Town, Trelawny, to the east. Similar topography continues over the inhospitable interior as far as Cave Valley, St. Ann, even farther east.

There are three principal routes leading into Trelawny's interior and providing access to the northern border of the impassible Cockpit Country. The first few routes lead inland from Martha Brae. To get to Good Hope Plantation, bypass the town of Martha Brae to the right when heading inland from the highway, and take a left less than 1.5 kilometers past the town, following well-marked signs. Continuing on the road past the turnoff to Good Hope ultimately leads to Wakefield, where the B15 heads back west to Montego Bay.

By taking a left at the stop sign in Martha Brae, and then a right after crossing the river, the road leads inland past Perth, Reserve, and Sherwood Content, to where it ultimately peters out near Windsor Caves.

Queen of Spain Valley

Good Hope Plantation (cell tel. 876/469-3443, goodhope1@cwjamaica.com, www.goodhopejamaica.com) located in the Queen of Spain Valley, is one of the most picturesque working estates on the island. Citrus has today replaced the cane of the past, while the plantation's great house and a collection of its historic buildings have been converted into the

© OLIVER HILL

the Great House at Good Hope Plantation in the Queen of Spain Valley

most luxurious countryside villas, with a total of 10 bedrooms between the main house, the carriage house, and the river cottage (rates starting at US$3,500/4,400 weekly low/high season for 3BR River Cottage). Good Hope features old-world luxury that sets itself apart from any other accommodation option on the island, with authentic antique furniture decorating every room, while not skipping the modern luxuries like iPods and air-conditioning. The villas are fully staffed with the most professional chefs, housekeepers, and gardeners to be found anywhere.

Good Hope is the ideal place for family retreats, birding, hiking, and mountain biking. There is no better place for horseback riding, which is still the best means of exploring the surrounding countryside. Of course, the inviting swimming pools and a brimming river make relaxation a favorite pastime for guests as well. Good Hope is rented through the owners.

David Pinto's Ceramic Studio (8 km north of Falmouth, cell tel. 876/886-2866, dpinto@cwjamaica.com, www.jamaicaclay.com, 8 A.M.–4 P.M. Mon.–Fri. or by appointment) is run by a Jamaican-born potter who studied ceramics during high school in the United Kingdom and later at Rhode Island School of Design before practicing in New York City. He returned to Jamaica in 1992 to establish his present studio in the Queen of Spain Valley on Good Hope Plantation, where he runs retreats led by internationally acclaimed guest master potters. Pinto's work includes both functional and decorative pieces and is on display in the permanent collection at the National Gallery in Kingston. A stop by Pinto's bustling studio with its five kilns is a great excuse to visit the spectacular grounds of Good Hope, a working citrus plantation.

Albert Town

A small hamlet at the edge of Cockpit Country, Albert Town is the center of Trelawny's yam-growing region, which celebrates the crop each year with the **Trelawny**

Yam Festival. Albert Town is the base for the **South Trelawny Environmental Agency (STEA)** (tel. 876/610-0818, www.stea.net), which organizes the yam festival and also offers guided excursions with its **Cockpit Country Adventure Tours** outfit in the surrounding area. They offer four different tours that cover caving and hiking. STEA is one of the best-organized environmental advocacy organizations in the country.

Windsor

Located at the farthest accessible point into Cockpit Country, Windsor is a small community. **Windsor Great Caves** is its main draw. Franklyn (Dango) Taylor is the sanctioned warden for the Jamaica Conservation and Development Trust (JCDT) and the official guide for Windsor Great Caves. The caves are best visited with Dango (US$20), though experienced cavers may prefer to go it alone. All visitors should check in with Dango, and sign the guestbook at the very least, which serves to both monitor efforts and provide some degree of accountability in the case of emergencies. Dango runs a little shop selling drinks and snacks. The source of the Martha Brae River is located nearby, affording a great spot to cool off.

The Windsor Caves are rich in both geological history and animal life, with up to 11 bat species emerging to feed in the evenings in large swarms. The geological formations should not be touched inside the caves, and a minimal-impact policy should be generally observed, which starts with visitors staying on the established path. Shining flashlights on the ceiling is also not advisable, since it disturbs the resting bats. Michael Schwartz, of Windsor Great House located nearby, warns of a chronic respiratory ailment caused by a fungus that grows on bat dung, afflicting cavers.

For more in-depth spelunking of lesser-known attractions, **Jamaica Caves Organization (JCO)** (info@jamaicancaves.org, www.jamaicancaves.org) is a useful group that knows Cockpit Country literally inside and out. It can arrange guides for hiking as well as caving. There is also a good circuit mapped out on its website to take a driving tour of Cockpit Country for those not interested in exercise. For those with a serious interest in hiking, the **Troy Trail** is one of the most interesting and arduous hikes in western Jamaica, traversing Cockpit Country from Windsor to Troy. Again, the JCO can provide guides and maps for a reasonable fee that goes toward helping to maintain the organization.

Accommodations

The Last Resort (Ivor Conolley tel. 876/931-6070, cell tel. 876/700-7128, iscapc@cwjamaica.com) is the most remote accommodation option in Cockpit Country. It's the headquarters for Jamaica Caves Organization, led by chairman Stefan Stewart. The facilities were recently renovated but remain rustic with 20 bunk beds (US$15 per person) and a common bath. One private room has a queen-size bed. Expect intimacy with the surrounding environment—bug repellent is an essential item.

Windsor Great House (cell tel. 876/997-3832, windsor@cwjamaica.com, www.cockpitcountry.com) was built by John Tharp in 1795 to oversee his vast cattle estate, which included most of the land bordering the Martha Brae River. Today the great house is operated by Michael Schwartz and Susan Koenig, who offer rustic accommodation and a weekly "Meet the Scientists" dinner (US$25 for the dinner).

Getting There

To get to Windsor, head inland from Falmouth to Martha Brae, crossing the bridge to the east and turning right to follow the valley south into the hills. On the way, the road passes through the small farming communities of Perth Town and Reserve. Once the road leaves the riverbanks, it heads to Sherwood Content, Coxheath, and finally Windsor. To get to Last Resort, turn right at Dango's shop, continuing for about 1.6

kilometers; a left at Dango's shop leads to Windsor Great House. A vehicle with good clearance is recommended, but the route is traveled frequently by vehicles with low clearance, driven with caution.

BURWOOD BEACH

The small community neighboring SuperClubs Breezes Trelawny has the spectacular Burwood Beach in Bounty Bay, which is also called Mutiny Bay. It's the best spot in Jamaica for **windsurfing** and **kite surfing** thanks to its gradual slope and lack of reefs that make these sports perilous in most other areas of the island. Brian Schurton runs **Brian's Windsurfing and Kitesurfing** (cell tel. 876/586-0900 or 541/490-2047, bws@gorge.net) with an informal windsurfing and kite-surfing school and rental outfit on the beach. With essential equipment like harnesses lacking in most of the all-inclusive resorts, windsurfers will find more professional gear at Brian's. Rates run US$160 for a 2.5-hour kitesurfing lesson. Windsurfing is US$60/day for gear, US$70 for a two-hour lesson. To get there, turn off the highway toward the sea about 1.5 kilometers east of Breezes Trelawny next to a sign for Bounty Bay.

Accommodations

Breezes Trelawny (Coopers Pen, Falmouth on Burwood Beach, tel. 876/954-2450 or U.S. tel. 800/GO-SUPER (800/467-8737), www.superclubs.com, US$99/139 per person low/high season) is the place to go if you love water slides, video gaming, trapeze acrobatics, and water sports. Rooms come with a stocked fridge, TV, air-conditioning, and CD player, but with all the activities in store, you won't be there much. Starfish is the SuperClubs brand's most budget-friendly and family-oriented property.

Breezes Rio Bueno (tel. 876/954-0000 or U.S. tel. 800/GO-SUPER (800/467-8737), glbreservations@superclubs.com, www.superclubs.com, US$224/349 per person low/high season) is the second all-inclusive in Jamaica, centered on a re-created and much-tamer-than-typical Jamaican village courtyard area, where dinners are served under the stars. Rooms are luxurious by American standards, with spacious suites that have balconies and large sitting areas. All the amenities of home are there, and the fridge is stocked daily with beer and soft drinks. Breezes has a decent beach and large swimming pool areas with the best food of the SuperClubs properties and premium liquors. The hotel sits on a 34-hectare estate. Horseback riding and tennis are some of the more popular activities at the resort, while water sports like scuba, snorkeling, and sailing are also offered.

Braco Stables (tel. 876/954-0185, bracostables@cwjamaica.com, www.bracostables.com, US$70 with transportation from Mobay or Runaway Bay, US$60 without transport) offers very tame horseback riding tours where riders traverse the Braco estate in single file. Experienced riders may be disappointed, as there is little freedom to roam about and leaving the group is not an option.

RIO BUENO

The first community in Trelawny across the border from St. Ann, Rio Bueno is considered by many experts to have been the actual landing point for Christopher Columbus on his second voyage, while that claim is also made for Discovery Bay. The port at Rio Bueno was an important export point, as can still be seen by the dilapidated warehouses and wharves along the waterfront beside the community's only accommodation, the **Rio Bueno Hotel.**

The small village is today undergoing somewhat of a renewal, with the new North Coast Highway bypassing the town entirely, which could ultimately enhance its picturesque appeal even while the busy Rio Braco rest stop will be less relevant.

The riverbank along the Rio Bueno is great for a stroll; visitors can see ruins of the **Baptist**

Theological College. The college was the first of its kind in the hemisphere. Other ruins in town include those of **Fort Dundas** behind the school. The **Rio Bueno Baptist Church** was originally built in 1832 before being destroyed by the Colonial Church Union, whose mostly Anglican members organized militias to terrorize the abolitionist Baptists, who were upsetting the status quo. The church was quickly rebuilt twice as large in 1834, and the present structure was built in 1901. While the roof is largely missing, services are still held downstairs.

The **Rio Bueno Anglican Chuch** was built at the water's edge in 1833 and remains there today. The church was petitioned by the community after years of attending service in a rented space.

The extensive **Gallery Joe James,** on the grounds of the Lobster Bowl and Rio Bueno Hotel, displays artwork by proprietor Joe James, among other selected Jamaican artists. The gallery extends throughout the restaurant, bar, and hotel and makes for a surreal waterfront setting. The restaurant itself is enormous, with outside seating extending out on a dock along the waterfront, as well as inside a large dining hall.

The Rio Bueno Primary School up the road is sometimes used for entertainment and events.

Accommodations and Food

Rio Bueno Hotel (tel. 876/954-0048, galleryjoejames40@hotmail.com, US$100) is a 20-room rustic accommodation with balconies overlooking the sea, ceiling fans, TV, and hot water in private baths. The ground floor rooms are larger and geared toward families, with three double beds.

The Lobster Bowl Restaurant (tel. 876/954-0048, 8 A.M.–10 P.M. daily, US$18–40) serves excellent shrimp, chicken, fish, and lobster. The restaurant was founded by Joe James and his wife, Joyce Burke James, over 40 years ago.

NEGRIL AND THE WEST

Hanover and Westmoreland are Jamaica's westernmost parishes. Hanover wraps around from Montego Bay on its northeastern border to where Negril's large hotel strip overflows from Westmoreland at its western reaches. It's a picturesque parish with small mountains tapering down to the coast with rivers, lush valleys, and deep, navigable coves. Caves dot the landscape of some of Jamaica's most biologically diverse ecosystems, in the shadow of the Dolphin Head mountain range.

Negril, which straddles the Hanover–Westmoreland border, has become a mass-market destination popular among Jamaicans and foreign visitors alike. The Kingstonian phenomenon of a weekend escape to "country" often implies a trip west to kick back and adopt the beach life, which necessarily involves taking in spectacular sunsets and the enviable slow pace evoked in Tyrone Taylor's 1983 hit, "Cottage in Negril." A constant stream of new visitors also gives hustlers a chance to do their thing, and Negril has gained a reputation as a mecca for sinful indulgence as a result.

While Negril is the region's most well-known draw, there are several low-key communities farther east that are just as easily accessible from Montego Bay's international airport and worthy coastal destinations in themselves, namely Little Bay, Bluefields, Belmont, and Whitehouse. The Westmoreland interior consists of vast alluvial plains on either side of Cabarita River, still some of Jamaica's most productive sugarcane territory. The plains extend from the base of the Orange Hill, just east of Negril, to where the Roaring River rises

HIGHLIGHTS

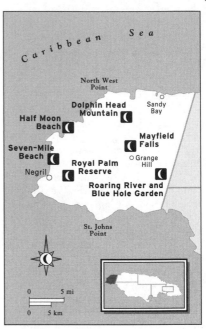

🌙 **Seven-Mile Beach:** Seven-Mile Beach is great for long walks into the sunset (page 261).

🌙 **Royal Palm Reserve:** Home to the Morass species of palm, found nowhere else, the reserve is also an important habitat for a slew of domestic and migratory birds (page 262).

🌙 **Dolphin Head Mountain:** The small mountain range near Lucea claims some of Jamaica's highest rates of biodiversity and endemic species (page 290).

🌙 **Half Moon Beach:** A languid horseshoe-shaped beach 15 minutes' drive east of Negril has fine sand and undeveloped coastline, reef, and islands (page 291).

🌙 **Roaring River and Blue Hole Garden:** One of Jamaica's most picturesque blue holes sits in a lush garden near the source of Roaring River (page 293).

🌙 **Mayfield Falls:** The best waterfalls attraction in Westmoreland, Mayfield is easily accessible and a good day's fun (page 293).

LOOK FOR 🌙 TO FIND RECOMMENDED SIGHTS, ACTIVITIES, DINING, AND LODGING.

out of the earth from its underground source in the hills above Blue Hole Garden.

PLANNING YOUR TIME

Negril is the ultimate place to kick back on the beach and forget what day of the week it is. The general area has other worthwhile sights, however, which can help avoid sunburn and provide a glimpse of the "true" Jamaica—with all the allure of its countryside lifestyle and lush scenery. Most visitors to Negril come specifically to laze on the beach in the dead of winter, but there are special events throughout the year to be considered if you're planning a trip with some flexibility.

Negril is invaded each year March–April by American college kids on all-inclusive spring break vacation packages. The spring breakers come from different institutions over the course of the month, but mostly during the first and second weeks of March. Recent years have been disappointing from an economic standpoint, with fewer visitors than years past. Still, you will want to keep this in mind when planning your trip to Negril—to either avoid the spring break crowd or coincide with it, depending on what you hope to get out of your beach vacation.

HISTORY

Negril's natural beauty has been appreciated for centuries, first by the Tainos, Jamaica's

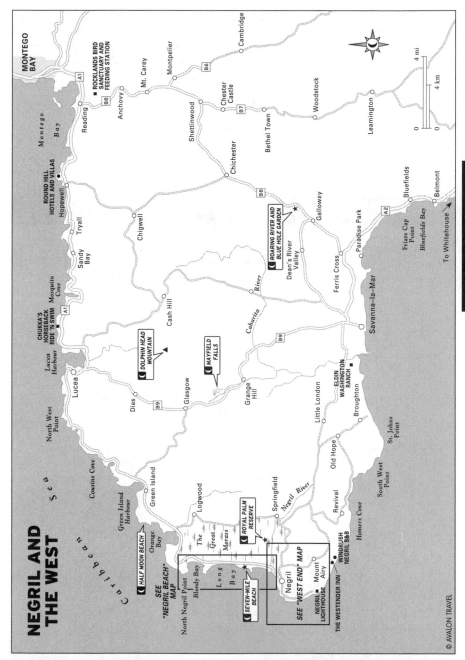

NEGRIL AND THE WEST

MONTEGO BAY

Montego Bay

Caribbean Sea

© AVALON TRAVEL

NEGRIL

◄ HALF MOON BEACH

SEE "NEGRIL BEACH" MAP

◄ SEVEN-MILE BEACH

SEE "WEST END" MAP

NEGRIL LIGHTHOUSE

THE WESTENDER INN

◄ ROYAL PALM RESERVE

WINDRUSH NEGRIL B&B

◄ DOLPHIN HEAD MOUNTAIN

◄ MAYFIELD FALLS

CHUKKA'S HORSEBACK RIDE 'N SWIM

ROUND HILL HOTELS AND VILLAS

ROCKLANDS BIRD SANCTUARY AND FEEDING STATION

◄ ROARING RIVER AND BLUE HOLE GARDEN

ELDIN WASHINGTON RANCH

North West Point

Cousins Cove

Green Island Harbour

Orange Bay

Green Island

North Negril Point

Bloody Bay

Long Bay

Negril

Mount Airy

Logwood

The Great Morass

Springfield

Negril River

Revival

Old Hope

Little London

Broughton

Homers Cove

South West Point

St. Johns Point

Savanna-la-Mar

Paradise Park

Friars Cap Point

Bluefields Bay

Bluefields

Belmont

To Whitehouse

A2

Ferris Cross

Galloway

Dean's River Valley

Cabarita River

B9

Grange Hill

Glasgow

Dias

Lucea

B9

Lucea Harbour

Mosquito Cove

Sandy Bay

Tryall

Chigwell

Cash Hill

Chichester

Shettinwood

Chichester

B8

Bethel Town

Woodstock

Leamington

Chester Castle

B7

Cambridge

B6

Montpelier

Mt. Carey

Anchovy

Reading

Hopewell

A1

A1

B8

0   4 mi

0   4 km

c a r i b b e a n   S e a

first inhabitants; later by pirates and fishermen; and, finally, after a road was built connecting Negril to Green Island in 1959, by the rest of Jamaica and the world at large. Negril Harbor, or Bloody Bay as it is more commonly known, got its name from the whales slaughtered there, whose blood turned the water red. Today the water is crystal clear. The bay was a favorite hangout for the pirate Calico Jack Rackham and his consort piratesses Mary Read and Anne Bonney, all of whom were captured drunk and partying in Bloody Bay.

Calico Jack was hanged in Kingston, while his female counterparts were pardoned. Bloody Bay was also a regular departure point for ships heading to Europe, which would go in fleets to ensure their survival on the high seas. The Bay also provided a hiding place from which ambushes were launched on Spanish ships. It was also the departure point for the British naval mission, which saw 50 British ships launch a failed attempt to capture Louisiana, culminating in the Battle of New Orleans during the American War of Independence.

NEGRIL

Negril

Negril has become Jamaica's foremost beach town, evolving over the past decade along with the changing nature of the tourists who come to bask in the sun and adopt the island's pace. Today, world-class restaurants and lodging provide an alternative to the low-key guesthouses and seafood stalls that became the norm during Negril's transition from fishing village to tourist boomtown in the 1970s. What was once Jamaica's secret paradise is today the heart of the island's diversified tourist economy.

Orientation

Life in Negril is focused on the west-facing coastline, which is divided between Seven-Mile Beach and the West End, or the Cliffs. Seven-Mile Beach runs from Bloody Bay in Hanover on its northern end to the mouth of the Negril River in Westmoreland, on the southern end of Long Bay. There are three principal roads that meet at the roundabout in the center of Negril: Norman Manley Boulevard, which turns into the A1 as it leaves town heading northeast toward Mobay; West End Road, which continues along the coast from the roundabout hugging the cliffs well past the lighthouse, until it eventually turns inland, rejoining the main south coast road (A2) in the community of Negril Spot; and Whitehall Road, which extends inland

from the roundabout toward the golf course, becoming the A2 at some point, with no warning before continuing on toward Sav-la-Mar.

Saftey

Due to its status as Jamaica's foremost tourism mecca, Negril tends to attract some of the island's most aggressive hustlers. Many will feign friendship and generosity only to demand, often with aggression and intimidation, exorbitant compensation for whatever good or service is on offer, whether it's a CD of one of the countless "up-and-coming artists," a marijuana spliff handed to you as someone extends their hand in greeting, or a piece of jewelry. As a rule, do not accept anything you don't actually want, and clarify the expected compensation if you do want it before allowing anyone to put something in your hand or mouth. It is not uncommon for these kinds of hustlers to draw a knife to intimidate you, and there is generally little fear of repercussions from the police, who tend to be slow-moving if responsive at all. The police are unlikely to be sympathetic, especially if a quarrel or skirmish involves drugs, even if the mix-up was unprovoked. Do your best to stay in well-populated areas, and try to avoid unsolicited approaches from strangers offering something you don't want.

SIGHTS
Bloody Bay

Bloody Bay is located just north of the piece of land jutting out toward Booby Cay that is home to Hedonism II, Point Village, and Breezes Grand Negril. Bloody Bay is currently dominated by all-inclusive hotels, including two relatively new Riu hotels, SuperClub's flagship Breezes Grand Negril, Couples Negril, and the private beach for Sunset at the Palms, located across the road. The beach on Bloody Bay is accessible to nonguests at several points along the road, most easily at the **Office of Nature** (contact PR agent Joseph Reid, cell tel. 876/369-0395), which is just past the fenced-off private beach of Sunset at the Palms. Here you can chill out and get lobster and fish (11 A.M.–sunset, US$10–30) from the outdoor grill manned by Robert, Symore, and Binghi. Next door, Johnny P's Jamaican Kitchen (cell tel. 876/999-6325, US$2–3) serves up staples like chicken with rice and peas. On the same little stretch of beach, Ackee (Roydel Reid, cell tel. 876/868-7312) and Andy (Conrad Getten, cell tel. 876/894-3042) take visitors out for snorkeling excursions (1.5 hrs, US$20/person with two-person minimum) and glass-bottomed boat tours. The fish and lobster vendors at the Office of Nature tend to be quite aggressive in soliciting business, to the point of discomfort, and sadly the lobster and fish they extract from the sea get smaller and smaller with each passing year, throwing into question the ethical merit of supporting their business from an environmental standpoint.

🌐 Seven-Mile Beach

Jamaica's longest beach is no longer the undisturbed keep of fishermen, as it was in the 1960s, but there are plenty of benefits that have come as a result of the virtually uncurbed development of the last 30 years. The sand remains a beautiful golden color, and the waters, while increasingly over-fished, remain crystal clear. A bar is never more than an arm's length away, and every kind of water sport is available. Expect advances from all manner of

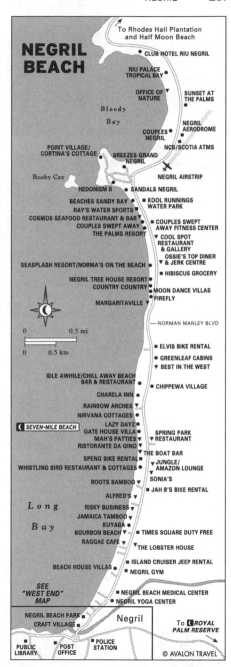

NEGRIL

Seven-Mile Beach is what put Negril on the map as a favorite subdued hideaway for roving hippies in the 1970s.

peddler and hustler until your face becomes known and your reaction time to these calls for attention slows. The northern end of the beach is cordoned off by security in front of the all-inclusive resorts, while at the southern end the Negril River forms a natural border by the fishermen's village and crafts market. Also on the southern end is Negril's community park, where dances and daytime events are sometimes held.

【 Royal Palm Reserve

Managed by the Negril Area Environmental Protection Trust (NEPT) and located 1.5 kilometers into the middle of the Great Morass from Sheffield, the 121-hectare Royal Palm Reserve (cell tel. 876/364-7407, nept_negril@yahoo, www.nept.wordpress.com, 9 A.M.–6 P.M. daily, US$15) is home to 114 plant species, including the endemic morass royal palms found only in western Jamaica. It's also home to over 300 animal species, including insects, reptiles (including two species of American crocodile), and birds.

The 26 resident bird species, which include the Jamaican woodpecker, Jamaican oriole, Jamaican euphonia, Jamaican parakeet, and the endemic endangered West Indian whistling duck, are joined by 16 migratory species that arrive at different times of the year. Admission includes a guided tour around 0.75 kilometers of boardwalk, and the ponds are open for sportfishing (US$5 with your own gear); you are almost guaranteed to catch African perch, tilapia, or tarpon. Shuttle service can be arranged (US$20 per person) from Negril. Royal Palm Reserve was leased by NEPT from the Petroleum Corporation of Jamaica (PCJ) as an alternative to a peat-mining project that had been planned. In the environmental impact study, it was found the project would have destroyed the beach and reef ecosystems. The present facilities were completed in 1989. Bird-watchers should make reservations with the NEPT office (tel. 876/957-3736) to get in earlier than normal opening hours. There is a nice bar area overlooking the water where drinks are served.

Other Sights

Whitehall Great House is yet another great house in ruins, located on the old Whitehall Estate on the ascent to Mount Airy. To get there, take a right immediately before the Texaco Station on Good Hope Road heading east from the Negril roundabout toward Savla-Mar. The ruins are about a mile up the hill on the left and command an excellent view of Negril Beach and the morass. One of the largest cotton trees in Jamaica stands on the property.

Bongo's Farm (tel. 876/880-7500, fanette@mail.infochan.com), owned by Bongo and Fanette Johnson, hosts visitors for hikes over gorgeous terrain with great views of Negril's coastline. This is the best place within 10 minutes of the beach to kick back and unwind in a truly Jamaican rural setting; the lush vegetation and laid-back company make for a great attraction. Jelly coconuts are served fresh from the tree, and visitors are shown a variety of botanical specimens cultivated on the farm.

Negril Lighthouse is located near the westernmost point of Jamaica on West End Road just past The Caves. The lighthouse dates from 1894 and stands 30 meters above the sea.

ENTERTAINMENT

The great thing about Negril is the fact that no matter the season, you can forget what day of the week it is in a hurry. While weekends remain "going-out nights," and important acts that draw large Jamaican audiences will perform generally on a Friday or Saturday, big artists also perform on Monday, Wednesday, and Thursday nights. Because Negril is so small, the handful of clubs that monopolize the regular live entertainment market have made a tacit pact whereby each takes a night, or two, of the week. This way, the

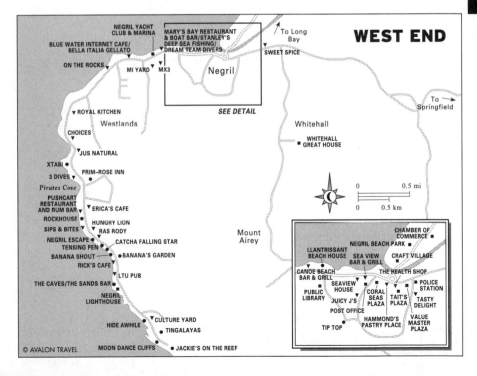

NEGRIL

NEGRIL WEEKLY NIGHTLIFE SCHEDULE

Note that ranges in cover fees indicate the charges for a regular night with a local group versus a big-name act.

MONDAY
Live Reggae at Bourbon Beach (US$5-10)

TUESDAY
Live Reggae Beach Party at Alfred's (US$4)

WEDNESDAY
Live Music at Roots Bamboo (from US$5)

THURSDAY
Live Reggae at Bourbon Beach (US$5-10)

Ladies Night at The Jungle (US$7-9)

FRIDAY
Live Reggae Beach Party at Alfred's (US$4)

SATURDAY
Live Reggae at Bourbon Beach (US$5-10)
Party Night at The Jungle (US$7-9)
Saturday Night Live buffet at Seastar Inn (US$15)

SUNDAY
Jazz at Roots Bamboo (free)
Live Reggae Beach Party at Alfred's (US$4)

main clubs are guaranteed a weekly following, and Negril's transient crowd can somewhat keep tabs on where to go on any particular evening.

Bars and Clubs

Negril has an overwhelming number of bars and grills. This section covers establishments that are recommended more as nightlife draws, rather than for their food.

The Jungle (tel. 876/954-4005 or 876/954-4819, info@junglenegril.com, www.junglenegril.com) is Negril's only off-the-water club, located in an old bank toward the middle of the beach on the morass side of Norman Manley Boulevard. It has regular theme nights throughout the week, as well as special events, normally held on weekends. Ladies' Night on Thursdays gets packed, and Saturdays generally see a good crowd dancing well into the morning. The Amazon Lounge at Jungle is open daily (4 P.M. to midnight).

Margaritaville (tel. 876/957-4467) has been headquarters for spring break activities for a number of years and is one of the most successful bar chains on the island. Villa Negril, as the Negril branch is called, is a more laid-back version of the Jimmy Buffet franchise than its Mobay or Ochi counterparts.

When it isn't peak party season, it's mostly known for its giveaways and beach parties on Tuesdays and Wednesdays in the early evening. Margaritaville is one of the venues frequently used for the Absolute Temptation Isle (ATI) events around Emancipation weekend.

Risky Business (tel. 876/957-3008) has live reggae three nights a week and is a bar and grill daily. Monday is Appleton's Ladies' Night, on Thursdays all local liquor is US$2. Saturday it's a bottomless mug 8 P.M.–1 A.M. (US$12).

Roots Bamboo Beach Resort (tel. 876/957-4479, rootsbamboobeach@hotmail.com) is run by the congenial Ted Plumber. It's been in business since 1979, when Ted bought the property and constructed bamboo bungalows. Ted was inspired by camping communities he saw along lakes in Canada. When Hurricane Gilbert destroyed the bungalows in 1988, he built the current concrete-and-wood houses. Care should be taken to secure your belongings, should you stay at Roots Bamboo. Security has been an issue in the past, as the bar hosts live music a few nights per week and nonguests take over the property. Roots Bamboo has been an entertainment venue since 1985 and recently started free live jazz 6–10 P.M. on Sundays, in addition to its long-standing live performances on Wednesdays.

© OLIVER HILL

The Jungle is Negril's longstanding club, with a busy schedule of guest selectors, parties, and performances througout the year.

Bourbon Beach (tel. 876/957-4405, www. bourbonbeachnegril.com, www.negrilreggae. com) took over from Debuss and is owned by four brothers and two sisters and managed by Jimmy Morrell. Monday Reggae Magic features internationally known acts like Gregory Isaacs, John Holt, and Yellowman, who are all regulars. Bourbon Thursdays features young and up-and-coming reggae acts and some of the more obscure local acts, and Saturdays Live on the Beach are usually reserved for a live local act, like Vybz Kartel or vintage artist like Ken Booth and The Mighty Diamonds. Bourbon Beach serves the best jerk on the beach from a pit on one side of the venue from mid-morning late into the night.

Alfred's Ocean Palace (tel. 876/957-4669, info@alfreds.com, www.alfreds.com) has been in operation since 1982. Jamaican and international cuisine with chicken, shrimp, and fish dishes (US$10–15) is served 8 A.M.– 10:30 P.M. daily in high season; the kitchen closes at 9 P.M. in the low season. Alfred's also has eight double- and triple-occupancy rooms

(US$40–50). Sundays, Tuesdays, and Fridays are Live Reggae Beach Party nights, which typically feature local acts (US$4) with occasional big-name international acts like Toots and Capleton (US$10–15).

Jamaica Tamboo (tel. 876/957-4282,) is perhaps best known as the location for some of the parties during ATI weekend around Independence Day. Occasional events are held at other times throughout the year as well, while it functions day-to-day as a restaurant and sports bar. The beachfront property has basic rooms and wireless Internet at a good value (US$60).

MX3 (contact Clive "Kubba" Pringle, cell tel. 876/851-8831, actionparknegril@gmail. com) has been functioning as a party lawn since 1990 where occasional plays, stage shows and boxing matches are held. Email or call to find out what's upcoming. In 2010 Spiritz Nightclub opened at the lawn.

Sexy Rexy Sunset Cliff (between Rick's Cafe and The Caves, www.sexyrexynegril.com, cell tel. 876/445-3740, 10 A.M.–6 A.M. daily)

serves Jamaican and vegetarian dishes with a cliff-side bar ideal for taking in sunsets. Rexy Tomlinson established the joint in 1978. **Wavz** (cell tel. 876/881-9289, www.wavzevents.com) is a seasonal venue and promotions company that hosts occasional parties throughout the year.

Negril Beach Park hosts Flava Sundays, drawing the biggest crowd in Negril on any given week with a nice mix of tourists, expats, and locals for dancehall sessions featuring top sound systems from Jamaica and abroad. Contact the park manager Clive "Kubba" Pringle (cell tel. 876/851-8831, actionparknegril@gmail.com) for more information.

On The Rocks (noon–midnight daily) is an interesting bar with what looks like a drive-in movie theater in its parking lot. Movies are played nightly (free admission), and popcorn and ice cream are served. Inexpensive drinks in a vibesy setting close to the water's edge make this a good place to down a mid-evening drink before hitting the clubs.

Festivals and Events

The weekends around Emancipation Day (August 1, 1838) and Independence Day (August 6, 1962) are filled with parties in Negril as **Absolute Temptation Isle** (www.ati-weekend.com) and competing event **Appleton Treasure Island** (contact Appleton's Kingston office, tel. 876/923-6141, appleton@infochan.com) try to outdo each other by throwing the hottest and most frequent parties. Big-time promoters from Kingston and Miami draw Jamaica's party youth from across the globe, who arrive to indulge in booze, ganja, general debauchery, and a few stage shows. ATI Weekend is well worthwhile as a more genuinely Jamaican party scene and it's the only

NEGRIL'S EMANCIPATION-INDEPENDENCE PARTIES

Every summer at the end of July, masses of Jamaican youth descend on Negril and book virtually every room in town for what's known as ATI Weekend (www.atiweekend.com), or simply ATI. All-inclusive parties go virtually non-stop for three or four days straight. ATI stands for Absolute Temptation Isle, but in 2006, Appleton's Rum, a sponsor in previous years, formed its own competing ATI the following weekend – adopting the same acronym, which in this case stands for Appleton Treasure Island.

The original ATI, organized by Alex Chin, promoter and founder of Absolute Entertainment, began in Negril in 2000 as Stages, bringing to Jamaica a regular party held in Miami a few times per year. The idea was to replicate the mood of Trinidad's or Brazil's Carnival, with crowds moving from party to party for days on end. The event has grown steadily with several promoters coming together each year to organize different parties at venues around Negril that include Wavz, Tamboo, Margaritaville, and Chances, each with a different theme – from foam parties to stage shows. A host of selectors are brought in, as well as many of Jamaica's most popular contemporary dancehall artists. Selectors often include Black Chiney from Miami, Xcaliber from Trinidad, Jamaica's top sound, Renaissance, and DJ Chrome from Zip FM. There is no better week to be in Negril for those seeking an overwhelming dose of booze, flesh, and sound.

Even though Appleton's pulled its sponsorship of the original ATI, other sponsors stepped in readily. The Jamaica Tourist Board also endorsed the event for the first time in 2006. Appleton's competing event now bookends the festivities held to coincide with Jamaica's Emancipation and Independence celebrations. Spring break pales in comparison.

All-inclusive parties in Jamaica have been around since the early 1990s, when the famous Frenchman's Parties, organized by Ian Wong as Jamaica's most exclusive regular all-inclusive soiree, began. Frenchman's parties are held a few times annually, the main "sell-off" events being staged for New Year's and Heroes Weekend.

time of year when Negril is decidedly taken over by Jamaicans, making spring break look like child's play. The **Reggae Marathon, Half Marathon, and 10K** (contact director Alfred "Frano" Francis, tel. 876/922-8677, racedirector@ reggaemarathon.com, or marketing director Diane Ellis, frandan@cwjamaica.com, www. reggaemarathon.com) held at the beginning of December, is a popular event drawing locals, expats, and runners from abroad for a race on a mostly flat, IAAF-certified route starting at Long Bay Beach Park on Seven-Mile Beach, going into the town of Negril, and heading north toward the town of Green Island before looping to the finish line back at Long Bay Beach Park. Events start on Friday with registration, a pasta party, and village bash. Races start at the crack of dawn on Saturday, with a ceremony later in the day where winners compete for a total purse of over US$10,000 in prize money. You must be 18 years old to run the marathon, and at least age 10 for the 10K.

Fees are US$85 per person for the marathon and US$60 for the 10K on or before July 31, US$95 for marathon and US$70 for 10K after August 1.

The **Negril Jerk Festival** (contact 3 Dives Jerk Centre owner Lyndon Myrie, a.k.a. Lloydie, tel. 876/957-0845 or 876/782-9990) is held on the last Sunday of November, where different jerk vendors from across the island are invited to set up stalls by 3 Dives Jerk Centre on the West End.

Miami Linkup (contact Robert "Dozer" Williams, cell tel. 954/479-0202 or 876/815-2198, rebeltsound@gmail.com, www.rebeltsound.com), an event promotions group, hosts an annual Spring Break party that draws large crowds to a stage show brimming with the hottest of Jamaica's dancehall and reggae artists around the second weekend in March.

Western Consciousness (contact promoter Worrel King, cell tel. 876/383-7717 or 876/849-8426, kingofkingspro@hotmail.com, www.westernconsciousness.com) is a not-to-be-

NEGRIL

© OLIVER HILL

Branzo stands in front of One Stop Branzo Wood Sculptures, where he carves away the days beachside.

NEGRIL

missed reggae show for fans of conscious roots music put on by King of Kings Promotions in late April or May each year at Paradise Park on the outskirts of Savanna-la-Mar.

SHOPPING

Natural Vibes Souvenir Shop (between Jamaica Tamboo and Risky Business, tel. 876/352-5849, naturalvibesjamaica@gmail.com, 8 A.M.–7 P.M. daily) has been run by Haresh "Hassle Free Harry" Pahilwani since 2004 and is known for hassle-free shopping for Cuban cigars, Jamaica T-shirts and sweats, sandals, sunglasses, Rasta hats, and smoking paraphernalia.

Bongo Johnson (tel. 876/486-0006) makes beautiful art sculptures, which can be seen by special arrangement. Johnson's delicate lignum vitae sculptures are on exhibit at the National Gallery in Kingston. He could be convinced to sell a piece if the price is right.

Abdel, a.k.a. Branzo (cell tel. 876/867-4246), can be found in his **One Stop Branzo Wood Sculptures** shop on the beachfront at Wavz Entertainment Centre (8 A.M.–8 P.M. daily). Branzo is one of the most talented wood carvers around and also sells the work of several other woodworkers in his little shop.

Errol Allen (cell tel. 876/385-5399) is a talented local artist who makes unique silhouette sculptures and oil paintings. Allen's sculptures can be seen on the grounds of Whistling Bird.

CY Clothing, the best in Jamaican roots wear, can be found at **Tesori's** and **Joy's Boutique.**

Mary Wonson's Flower Hill Oil and Soap Company produces natural products like lip balms, soaps, rejuvenating oils, and restorative hair oil from extra virgin coconut oil. Contact Nordia Hill (cell tel. 876/358-9732) to see which retailers in the area are currently carrying the products or to place a direct order.

Chances Gift Shop and Cigar Hut (on beach next to Chances, tel. 876/957-3177) has all the Cubans you could smuggle home in your suitcase (or—less risky—enjoy while in Jamaica). Manager Martin is a pleasant chap and not overly pushy. The air-conditioning and smell of fresh tobacco is a good reason to stop in and browse.

Negril Crafts Market (between the Negril Beach Park and the river) has a wide variety of crafts, some better and more authentic than others. Sadly, an increasing proportion of the products on sale are made in China rather than locally produced.

Rutland Point Craft Centre is located next to the aerodrome just before the Petcom gas station, heading northeast toward Mobay.

A Fi Wi Plaza, next to Scotia Bank by the roundabout, has crafts and T-shirts from Sun Island.

Time Square Mall Plaza (tel. 876/957-9263, 9–7 P.M. daily, duty-free closed on Sun.) is located on Norman Manley Boulevard across from Bourbon Beach. The duty-free shopping center has several shops selling jewelry, Cuban cigars, crafts, liquor, watches, and trinkets.

Kosmic Gift Shop & Boutique (located next to Cosmos on the beach, Norman Manley Blvd., tel. 876/957-3940) has a mix of Rasta knit hats and "Jamaica, No problem" T-shirts.

SPORTS AND RECREATION

Opportunities for outdoor recreation are everywhere in Negril, from hiking to windsurfing and scuba diving.

Motor Bikes and Car Rentals

Speng Bike Rental (across from Jungle next to Westlea Cabins, tel. 876/414-5189) rents scooters (US$40) and dirt bikes (US$50), negotiable for multiple-day rental. Proprietor Tony Hilton also does airport transfers (US$60), as well as private tours.

Elvis Bike Rental (in front of Coco la Palm, tel. 876/848-9081) rents scooters (US$30/day, $140/week), a Honda shadow 600cc (US$50/day US$280/week), dirt bikes (US$40/day, US $210/week) as well as a Toyota Corolla (US$60/day, US$250/week).

Jah B's Bike Rentals (tel. 876/957-4235 or 876/353-9533, 8 A.M.–6 P.M. daily) rents 125cc Honda and Suzuki Scooters (US$35) and a 60cc Honda Shadow (US$50). The sign on the road says JB Bike Rental.

Tykes Bike Rental (West End Rd. across

from Tensing Pen, just before Rick's Cafe, tel. 876/957-0388, tonyvassell@yahoo.com, 8 A.M.–6 P.M. daily) rents 125cc scooters (US$45) and 175cc dirt bikes (US$50).

Island Cruiser Rentals (contact Patrick Marzouca, tel. 876/618-1277, cell tel. 876/422-2831 or 876/298-5400, info@islandcruiserjamaica.com, www.islandcruiserjamaica.com) rents a selection of brightly colored cruising vehicles for US$50 per day or US$325 per week.

Water Sports

Negril is overflowing with water sports opportunities. From excursions in glass-bottomed boats to parasailing, riding personal watercraft, windsurfing, scuba, snorkeling, and catamaran cruises, there is something for every level of enthusiasm and interest.

Dream Team Divers (Mary's Bay, tel. 876/957-0054 or 876/831-0435, info@dreamteamdiversjamaica.com, www.dreamteamdiversjamaica.com, 8 A.M.–4 P.M. daily) has English, German, Italian, and French-speaking dive instructors. Dive master Ken Brown has run every dive shop in town since he landed in Negril in 1991 and finally opened his own shop in October 2008. Dream Team offers free pickup and drop-off for clients from any accommodation in Negril. The outfit sets itself apart by visiting dolphin dive sites and locations not visited by any others. Rates range from the Discover Scuba intro course (US$80) to the dive master certification (US$600).

Negril Scuba Centre (neg.scuba.centre@cwjamaica.com, www.negrilscuba.com) has three locations, Negril Escape (tel. 876/957-4425), Mariner's (876/957-4425), and Negril Beach Village (tel. 876/957-0392) on Bloody Bay Beach across Norman Manley Boulevard from Sunset at The Palms. The scuba center offers dive packages that include accommodations at Negril Escape and Spa, where the center is based, or at other participating hotels. Popular dive sites include Booby Cay Island, The Arches, Ballard's Reef, a Deep Plane, Gallery, King Fish Point, the Throne Room and Blue Castle Ship Wreck, among several others. PADI courses range from a beginner three-hour Discover

Diving session (US$80) to Advanced Open Water (US$300), Rescue Diver (US$350), and Scuba Master (US$600) courses. Those already certified can rent tanks (US$40) and shortie wetsuits (US$6/day). Several other water sports activities are offered besides.

Ray's Water Sports (tel. 876/957-5349, info@rayswatersportsnegril.com, www.raywatersportsnegril.com) is one of the more successful outfits on the beach, impossible to miss with the parasail chutes plastered with his name.

Negril Treehouse has a water sports center managed by Ron Mirey, which offers parasailing (US$40), Jet Skis (US$50/half hour) and fishing trips (US$150 up to four people).

Aqua Nova Water Sports (Mariners Beach Club, tel. 876/957-4323 or 876/957-4754) offers Jet Skis (by Coral Seas) and parasailing (US$50/person or US$80/couple) from its office at Mariners Negril Beach Club. Aqua Nova also runs regular three-hour catamaran and trimaran cruises, one leaving at 10:30 A.M. (US$60 includes lunch and open bar), the other at 3:30 P.M. (US$50 includes snack and open bar). Boats pick up guests from hotels along the beach. Private charters are also offered for US$250 for three hours.

Kool Runnings (tel. 876/957-5400, info@koolrunnings.com, 11 A.M.–6 P.M. Wed., Sat., and Sun. in low season, 9 A.M.–5 P.M. daily in high season, US$28 adults/over four feet, US$19 children under four feet tall, two years and under free) is a water park with several slides and a lazy river for gentle tubing. It's located across from Beaches Sandy Bay. There is food and a bar on the property, as well as a juice bar and coffee shop. With a 2,500-person capacity, the water park regularly hosts events, including wild parties during Emancipation-Independence celebrations in early August. A stage provides live entertainment, with reggae pumping throughout the day.

Kool Runnings' Kool Kanoe Swamp Adventure Tour takes visitors on a guided tour of the Great Morass, Jamaica's largest wetland area, located in the water park's back yard. Visitors ride on an inflatable "kanoe" to paddle along a guided tour through the canals of the morass to see some of the plants and animals in their natural habitat. Those favoring a more independent experience can use kayaks to guide themselves through the morass. You are likely to encounter yellow snakes, land crabs, mongoose, turtles, and birds. The water park holds a Soldier Crab Derby, allowing visitors to bet on the winners.

Three restaurants on property serve Jamaican dishes, while the Kool Blendz juice bar serves natural smoothies.

Golf

Negril Hills Golf Club (Sheffield, east of the roundabout on the A2, tel. 876/957-4638, www.negrilhillsgolfclub.com, 7:30 A.M.–3 P.M.) has reasonable rates for nonmembers. For 9 holes: greens fee (US$28.75), cart (US$17.25), caddy (US$7); for 18 holes: greens fee (US$57.50), cart (US$34.50), caddy (US$14). Clubs can also be rented (US$18 for older, US$25 for newer, and US$40 for top-of-the-line and Hybrid clubs (e.g. Taylor Made and Cobras).

Horseback Riding

Wild Crocodile Adventures & Tours (contact Paul Washington, cell tel. 876/881-6917, wildcrocodile@hotmail.com, www.wildcrocodileadventures.com, US$60 per adult, US$45 children under 10, including transportation from Negril) based at Eldin Washington Ranch on the main road from Negril to Savanna-la-Mar, features horseback riding on a 900-acre farm populated by a variety of animals from peacocks to ostriches, donkeys, and goats. There are three riding times daily: 9 A.M., noon, and 3 P.M. There's no minimum group size. The 2.5-hour ride ends on a one-mile stretch of private beach.

Paradise Park (tel. 876/955-2675, paradise1@cwjamaica.com, US$40 per person) is one of the best places in Jamaica for down-to-earth small-group rides on an expansive seaside ranch a few kilometers east of Savanna-la-Mar in Ferris Cross. Groups of up to 10 riders are led through beautiful countryside to a river park and private beach for a 1.5-hour ride. The cost of the ride includes a complimentary soft drink. Lunch can be arranged for groups of at least six with a 24-hour reservation (additional US$12 per person).

Chukka's Horseback Ride 'N Swim (tel. 876/953-5619, montegobay@chukkacaribbean.com, US$73) offers 2.5-hour rides through forest and along the shoreline before swimming on horseback. Remember to bring a change of clothes, and a waterproof camera if you don't want to buy photos from Chukka. The tour is located between Negril and Mobay, about a half hour to Negril and 40 minutes to Mobay in the fishing village of Sandy Bay. Chukka offers a two-hour dune buggy excursion for people over 18 ($76) and two-hour ATV tours ($75). Canopy ziplines, tubing, and kayaking are staged from the Montpelier Chukka location.

Rhodes Hall Plantation (tel. 876/431-6322 or 876/957-6422, rhodesresort@comcast.net, www.rhodesresort.com) also has good horseback riding with an expansive seaside property five minutes northeast of Negril heading toward Montego Bay.

Fishing

The waters just off Negril's shoreline are severely over-fished, with very low counts found in surveys conducted by the Negril Area Environmental Protection Trust. Nevertheless, a bit farther offshore in deeper waters it's possible to catch plenty of wahoo and even marlin.

Stanley's Deep Sea Fishing (www.stanleysdeepseafishing.com, tel. 876/957-6341) is the most professional outfit in Negril. It's run by Captain Stanley Carvalho and offers a good mix of options from half-day (US$500) to three-quarter day (US$750) to full-day trips (US$1000) for up to four people. Additional persons can be added, up to eight passengers (additional person US$50/75/100 for the different length excursions). Stanley's also offers the option of charter sharing, where individuals can team up with others to fill up the boat (US$100) rather than charter exclusively.

Fitness Centers

Couples Swept Away (7:30 A.M.–9 P.M. daily)

has the best sports complex in Negril and offers a day pass (US$20/per person), which includes access to tennis, squash, and racquetball courts, a sauna, steam room, whirlpool tub, and a lap pool. Rackets are available for rent (US$10 each). Yoga and Pilates classes are offered daily at no extra charge. Tennis clinics are also included (Mon.–Fri.), but private lessons incur an additional charge.

Negril Fitness Centre (US$5/day, US$25/week, US$45/month) next to the Café Taino, has basic equipment like dumbbells, Stairmasters, and treadmills and serves a mostly Jamaican clientele.

Yoga and Massage

Fanette Johnson (cell tel. 876/897-9492, fanette@mail.infochan.com) leads Iyengar-style yoga sessions at Tensing Pen and Rockhouse and will also do private sessions. She has 20 years' experience teaching yoga around the globe.

Oya Oezcan (cell tel. 876/440-7071) offers therapeutic body massage.

Jackie's on the Reef (tel. 876/957-4997 or 718/469-2785, jackiesonthereef@rcn.com, www.jackiesonthereef.com) accepts nonguests for daily yoga sessions.

ACCOMMODATIONS
Seven-Mile Beach

Negril definitely has something for everyone when it comes to finding the ideal place to stay. From couples-only, all-inclusive resorts, to hip, inexpensive independent cottages by the sea and exclusive villas, there's an option for every taste and budget. Low-season and high-season rates apply here as much as, if not more than, the other tourism centers on the island. Some establishments increase rates in the middle of the low season for special events like Independence weekend at the beginning of August, when Jamaicans from "yard" and "abroad" flock for a torrent of nonstop parties that last for days on end.

Accommodations and food have been divided geographically by Negril's roundabout, which is used to distinguish between the properties on either side of Norman Manley Boulevard from those on the either side of West End Road. Within each price category, the accommodations are organized from north to south.

Seven-Mile Beach starts at the mouth of Negril River and stretches the length of Long Bay as well as Bloody Bay farther north. Long Bay is fronted by a multitude of small hotels as well as large all-inclusive resorts on its northern end.

UNDER US$100

☾ Cortina's Cottage (cell tel. 876/382-6384, www.carolynscaribbeancottages.com, US$75) is actually a studio apartment located in the Point Village complex at the end of Seven-Mile Beach. It's a good option for those looking for all the amenities normally associated with a large resort at an affordable price. Swimming pool access, a private beach reserved for Point Village, make Cortina's an excellent option on the beach. The apartment is tastefully decorated with plenty of curtains.

Chippewa Village (tel. 876/957-4676, cell 876/885-7676, toll-free from US and Canada, 877-670-8426 or tel. 213/291-8382, chippewavillage@hotmail.com, www.chippewavillageresort.com) is a comfortable assortment of seven cottages on the morass side of Norman Manley Boulevard tastefully decorated with a Sioux motif. Owner John Babcook is a leather designer whose great-grandfather Red Shirt was chief of the Dakota Sioux and represented his nation at the 1906 World's Fair. Trails cut a quarter mile into the morass lead to a 16-foot viewing platform that affords an incredible 360-degree view of Negril, the morass, and the surrounding hills. In mid-2010 an open-air home theater was built under a canvass teepee in keeping with John's modernistic interpretation of Chippewa style.

Greenleaf Cabins (next to Chippewa Village on the morass side of Norman Manley Blvd., contact Marni, cell tel. 617/448-5180, info@indikanegril.com, www.indikanegril.com) has a spacious four-bedroom main building called Devon House, which sleeps up to seven people, and a next large structure with three bedrooms called Dolton House, which also sleeps seven (US$150 each building). Also on the property is a self-contained cottage with a full kitchen and two beds (US$60), as well as two rustic cabins (US$35), each with two beds, a small fridge, shower, and floor fan. The Dolton House bedrooms all have exterior entrances and can rent separately (US$50) and share the kitchen and living area. Airport transfers are offered with Devon (US$110 round-trip).

Firefly (tel. 876/9574358, tel. 8769579325, firefly@jamaicalink.com, www.jamaicalink.com, US$60–96 d) offers a range of accommodations from studio apartments to beachfront penthouse suites, in a garden setting with an assortment of cottages and rooms in a multi-story building.

Negril Yoga Centre (tel. 876/957-4397, negrilyoga@cwjamaica.com, www.negrilyoga.com, US$30–75), also known as The Little Oasis, has simple, clean, and nicely decorated rooms with single and double beds. The center is tasteful and secure, with a very good restaurant that specializes in vegetarian curries and Thai food cooked to order. The property boasts, "There is no bar, no pool, and no dance club at the Centre which keeps our prices low, and our ambience low-key."

Westport Cottages and Youth Hostel (tel. 876/957-4736, www.negrilwestportcottages.com, US$20–45) is a favorite budget accommodation, centrally located along Norman Manley Boulevard across from the beach, run by Joseph Matthews and Sister. The rustic wooden cottages have not increased their rates in decades, with simple double beds, standing fans, and use of the common kitchen, while the newer concrete buildings have virtually the same amenities at the higher rate. Joseph does airport pickups at reasonable cost.

US$100-250

⟨ Kuyaba (tel. 876/957-4318 or 876/957-9815, kuyaba@cwjamaica.com, www.kuyaba.com) is one of the longest-standing rental options on the beach and has developed into a handful of tasteful cottages. The more rustic cottages

© OLIVER HILL

the view from a raised thatch-roofed dining cabana at Kuyaba

(US$56–64 low, US$70–77 high season) hold true to Negril's original rustic hippie vibe, while newer, more elegant cottages (US$77–85 low, US$97–106 high season) have been added in recent years to round out the mix. All cottages have ceiling fans, air-conditioning, and private baths with hot water. A restaurant on the property has good food.

Rooms Negril (tel. 876/957-3500, toll-free from U.S. or Jamaica 877/467-8737, info@superclubs.com, www.superclubs.com, US$115–143 d) has basic garden view and oceanfront rooms with air-conditioning, cable TV, phones, and either one king-size or two double beds. Rates include continental breakfast.

Charela Inn (tel. 876/957-4277, fax 876/957-4414, info@charela.com, www.charela.com, US$126–183 d low season, US$189–194 d high season) is a medium-size hacienda-style property with deluxe suites facing the beach, as well as more humble garden-view rooms. Charela is one of the more tasteful large properties on Seven-Mile Beach, with well-designed and lushly planted grounds.

Seasplash Resort (tel. 876/957-4041, seasplash@cwjamaica.com, www.seasplash.com, US$96/146 low/high season) is a large concrete structure with little to distinguish it from many other similar hotels that crowd Seven-Mile Beach. The suites are nonetheless spacious, clean, and well appointed with complete amenities. It's also home to Norma's on the Beach.

⦅ Whistling Bird Restaurant & Cottages (tel. 876/957-4403, or from the U.S. toll-free 800/276-8054, whistlingbird@negriljamaica.com, www.whistlingbird.com, from US$98/140 low/high season) has been operated by proprietor Jim Boydston since 1978, when Negril's tourism boom was in its infancy. The property consists of 12 cottages with a total of 20 rooms spread over lush tropical gardens. The rainforest-like setting attracts many birds, including Jamaica's national bird, the red-billed streamertail. The cottages have simple, tasteful rooms with an open layout, the larger ones villa-sized at 4–6 rooms. Half the rooms have air-conditioning, with TV available on request. Whistling Bird has an excellent restaurant that prides itself on its "fancy Jamaican" cooking, offering five-course gourmet dinners (US$35). A variety of packages are available, with a significant proportion of guests opting for the all-inclusive option at US$125–189 per person daily. Whistling Bird is a popular setting for weddings, retreats, and corporate meetings.

The Palms Resort (tel. 876/957-4375, info@thepalmsnegril.com, www.thepalmsnegril.com, US$113/120 low/high season) previously Paradise View, has been undergoing a process of complete transformation under the new ownership of the Nelson family. Wooden furniture, louvered windows, and sleek styling throughout have added a modern, classy mood to the once-tired complex. Kristyl's restaurant on the beach is set poolside on a wooden deck with plush furniture. Wireless Internet reaches the rooms and pool/bar area, and guests are provided a computer in the office. Rooms have queen- or king-size beds, private baths with hot water, private balconies, and cable TV. Most of the rooms are garden view, with a few seaview deluxe rooms (US$210/237 low/high season).

⦅ Country Country (tel. 876/957-4273, countrynegril@gmail.com, www.countryjamaica.com, US$140–155 low season, US$170–190 high season) has 17 cottages on the beach side of Norman Manley Boulevard, and three self-contained apartments on the morass side. Built in 2000, the cottages are well laid out in a lush garden setting that promotes quiet and privacy. Rooms have the same amenities throughout, namely air-conditioning, flat panel TVs with cable, spacious private baths with hot water, and porches. The superior and premium categories relate to the proximity to the beach. An expansion into the adjacent lot for a total of 50 units is in the works. Rates include breakfast, and Wi-Fi is available in the communal lounge by the office.

Negril Tree House Resort (tel. 876/957-4287, info@negril-treehouse.com, www.negril-treehouse.com, US$100–200 low, US$145–340 high season) has reasonable rates that vary depending on the size of the room and the view out the window (garden or sea). Manager Gail Jackson and her husband Jimmy Jackson had the first two buildings built in 1982 and have expanded the property successively to its current 70 units. Most rooms have king-size beds or two twins. Wireless Internet is available in the lobby and beach areas. There is also a water sports shop on the property. Jimmy Jackson runs Negril Spot Farm, which provides all the meat served at Negril Tree House. He was named farmer of the year in 2005 and 2006. Negril Tree House is moving toward 100 percent solar-powered hot water, with 25 percent of the hot-water systems already converted to solar.

Our Pastime Villas (tel. 876/957-5422 or U.S. tel. 636/448-8185, info@ourpasttimenegril.com, www.ourpasttimenegril.com) offers unpretentious deluxe rooms, studios, and two-bedroom apartments (US$60–250).

OVER US$250

⦅ Idle Awhile Resort (tel. 876/957-3303, U.S tel. 877/243-5352, fax 876/957-9567, stay@idleawhile.com, www.idleawhile.com, from US$130–200 low season, US$210–270 high season) opened in 1999, immediately

NEGRIL

establishing itself as one of the finest properties on Seven-Mile Beach. The rooms are beautifully decorated with louvered windows, minimalist designs, wooden furniture, ceiling fans, and air-conditioning. Idle Awhile guest have access to Negril's best sports complex at Couples Swept Away. Wireless Internet is included. An excellent restaurant, Chill Awhile, faces the beach, serving Jamaican and continental cuisine and fresh juices.

Aqua Negril Resort (tel. 876/957-9037 or cell tel. 876/417-1237, aquanegril@gmail. com, www.aquanegril.com, US$250–425) is a five-room high-end boutique resort with luxurious amenities run by Trini-Jamaican couple Ken and Liz Sealey. Rooms have king beds, air-conditioning, en suite baths, minifridges, flat panel TVs, and iPod docks. Wi-Fi is complimentary in the common area on the ground floor, and a computer terminal is available for those not carrying laptops. Prices include a complete breakfast. A Jacuzzi on the deck upstairs overlooks the sea and beach bar. The bar is open to the public and offers over 70 types of rum and countless cocktail concoctions.

Beach House Villas (tel. 876/957-4731, U.S. tel. 801/363-3529, contact@negriljamaicavillas.com, www.negril-hotels.com, from US$200/250 low/high season) has an assortment of self-contained units, which are well maintained and clean and command good views of the sea. All rooms have air-conditioning, TV, and hot water. The property has a total of 21 bedrooms for a maximum of 62 guests. An Internet connection is available in the common living area.

VILLAS
Gate House Villa (call Ali Provines to book, U.S. tel. 435/615-7474 or 888/595-1579, info@gatehousevilla.com, www.gatehousevilla.com) is a comfortable and stylish house with four rooms and a fully equipped kitchen. This is an ideal place for a medium-size group of up to eight people. The rooms, each with one king-size or two twin beds, rent individually for rates ranging US$89–109 in low season, and US$139–159 in high season. (The most-expensive room is the large upstairs suite, which has a veranda overlooking the sea and a large open shower.) There is a bar, Tony's Hut, on the property, right on the beach. The whole property can also be rented (US$400/550 low/high season) and can sleep up to 10 people.

Moon Dance Villas (U.S. tel. 800/621-1120, info@moondancevillas.com) has an assortment of one- to five-bedroom villas (US$600–1,500 low season, US$700–1,900 high season) and is centrally located, with 300 feet of private sand on Seven-Mile Beach. Moon Dance rates include a chef, bartender, housekeeper, security, Internet, private pool and Jacuzzi, and airport transfer, with an unlimited food option (add US$115 per person daily). Moon Dance is an ideal accommodation option for families and small groups. A four-night minimum stay is required.

ALL-INCLUSIVE RESORTS
❰ Sunset at the Palms (resort tel. 876/957-5350, reservations tel. 876/979-8870, or U.S. tel. 800/234-1707, www.sunsetatthepalms .com) is the most alluring of the Sunset Resorts' all-inclusive properties. It features small one-bedroom bungalows spread out across lush, well-manicured grounds. The food, with a mix of buffet style and à la carte meals, is markedly better than at the other Sunset properties, as is the level of service; prices are accordingly higher: US$350/545 low/high season per couple for a deluxe bungalow (US$75 extra per child), and US$540/742 low/high season for the one-bedroom suite.

Inside the bungalow-style cottages, a pleasant natural design with wooden furniture, Bali-esque detailing, and plush bedding are overwhelmingly inviting. The bathrooms are sleek and modern, with shower fixtures suitable for two.

Sunset at the Palms is set back from the beach across Norman Manley Boulevard, with a private beach right in the middle of Bloody Bay, a two-minute walk from the lobby. There's a bar and grill on the beach and water sports equipment. A tennis court and weight room are located across the road, as is a beautiful whirlpool tub and pool with a swim-up bar. Internet is available off the lobby.

Breezes Grand Negril (www.superclubs. com, US$224/389 low/high season), formerly Grand Lido Negril, is the flagship SuperClubs resort. One of the first SuperClubs properties, Breezes Negril has a dramatic entrance corridor surrounded by fountains and reflecting pools that lead into the lobby and dining areas. Breezes Negril has 210 junior and full suites, each equipped with full amenities including air-conditioning, satellite TV, direct-dial telephones, and CD player.

Several restaurants on the property give guests a lot of options. Piacere serves Nouvelle French–inspired cuisine in an elegant candlelit setting that requires formal attire (jackets, slacks, and shoes for men). Cafe Lido serves continental cuisine and is a bit more toned down on the dress-code, with a no-shorts rule. La Pasta is a more casual, Italian-inspired pasta bar open 3–10 P.M. daily. Breakfast and lunch are served at Gran Terraza, the open-air buffet area between the beach and the lobby; dinner is also served there 7:30–10 P.M. on Monday and Friday evenings. RASTAurant serves Jamaican favorites like jerk chicken and roti. Munasan is the newest restaurant on the property, serving authentic sushi and teppanyaki. The specialty restaurants are open 6:30–9:30 P.M. except Monday and Friday, and reservations may be required. Guests from other hotels may purchase a pass in order to dine at the restaurants (day pass US$79 per person, evening pass US$99 per person).

Breezes occupies the choice property on Bloody Bay, where calm inviting waters gently lap the shore. There is an *au natural* beach on one end of the property, with the main expanse of beach open to those who can keep their bathing suit on. The highlight of the nine-hectare gardens is a centuries-old cotton tree that stands between the 24-hour bar and the spa.

◖ Couples has two properties in Negril: Couples Negril (tel. 876/957-5960, U.S. tel.

800/COUPLES, US$408/590 low/high season per couple per night), which is actually just across the border into Hanover, and Couples Swept Away (tel. 876/957-4061, US$413/602 low/high season per couple per night), at the north end of Long Bay. For proximity to off-site activities and an easy walk to Negril's nightlife, Couples Swept Away has clear advantages. On the other hand, for couples looking to get away from it all, including adjacent public beaches and other reminders of the existence of outside civilization, Couples Negril could be a better option.

Couples Swept Away is an exceptional all-inclusive with a new wing on the south end of the compound that has a wet bar, grill, and beautiful lounge tastefully decorated by Jane Issa, wife of Couples owner Lee Issa. Mr. Issa can often be found around the property, checking in with his guests and making sure everything is running smoothly. The gym facilities and tennis courts at Couples are top-notch. Day passes, offered for eight-hour periods (US$75), entitle pass-holders complete access to everything on the property.

Hedonism II (tel. 876/957-5200, www. superclubs.com, US$135–215 low season, US$175–285 high season) is the original and notorious all-inclusive resort where anything goes. Situated at the northern end of Negril's Long Bay, Hedonism II has 280 rooms and 15 suites, all with tiled floors, air-conditioning, TV, and, of course, mirrored ceilings. Many of the suites have private whirlpool tubs right on the beach. It's a great place for couples and singles looking to unwind and let go, and potentially do things they would never do at home—or alternatively, do exactly what's done at home whenever, wherever, and with whomever they see fit. Repeat guests don't keep going back for the food, but for the sexually charged atmosphere.

Two private beaches (one nude, one not) offer plenty of activities from water sports to volleyball to acrobatics. The main terrace dining area is complemented by Italian-inspired Pastafari, Japanese-inspired Munasan, and Reggae Cafe, as well as beach grills. Many premium-brand liquors are served at several bars throughout the property, which also has excellent spa, fitness, and tennis court facilities. There is also an underwater disco where "nuff tings a gwaan."

It's important to be aware of any special theme weeks being held at Hedo when booking, lest you should arrive and be expected to swap spouses with one of your fellow guests during Swingers' Week.

Sandals Negril (Long Bay, www.sandals. com, US$818–2,454 per night) is a 222-room resort on Negril's famed Seven-Mile Beach. The resort offers exclusive butler service in its top room category, a Red Lane Spa, two-story loft suites with spiral staircases, a pro sports complex offering racketball, squash and tennis, two pools, two whirlpool tubs, and a scuba certification pool. Swim-up river suites have stairs descending from the veranda doors into a lazy river with views out to sea, and plantation suites have private plunge pools, outdoor showers, and private balconies. Rooms have complete amenities, from cable TV to air-conditioning and en suite baths.

Sandals imposes a minimum stay of three nights at all its properties. Promotions are ongoing throughout the year, slashing rates by as much as 65 percent based on length of stay.

Club Hotel Riu Negril (tel. 876/957-5700, www.riu.com, US$228 and up) is a 420-room all-inclusive resort on Bloody Bay with a large main building and four two-story annexes. The resort has a gym, Jacuzzi, and sauna reserved for guests over 18. Rooms have mini-bars, king or two double beds, and a balcony or terrace. Four restaurants offer a la carte and buffet dining options, with bars spread across the property. The resort has two hard-surface tennis courts, table tennis, volleyball, and a variety of water sports. The hotel has a computer room available at an additional charge, with a free Wi-Fi zone for guests with laptops. The Renova Spa offers a variety of massages and treatments at an additional charge.

Riu Palace Tropical Bay (tel. 876/957-5900, www.riu.com) is a 416-room all-inclusive resort, also located on Bloody Bay, with double rooms, junior suites, and suite categories. Renovated completely in 2008, rooms have mini-bars, cable TV, air-conditioning, lounge areas in junior suites, and en suite baths with verandas or balconies. The resort features several buffet and a la carte options, formal dress required in the fine dining restaurants for evening dinners. The hotel features 24-hour room service, a free Wi-Fi zone, and several bars and pool bars scattered throughout the property.

West End
UNDER US$100

Tip Top (turn inland on Red Ground Rd. at Scotia Bank, cell tel. 876/360-4857 or 876/435-7222) sits at the top of a hill in an area known as Red Ground. It's a popular spot for budget travelers from Europe, as well as for long-term stays. Rates start at US$25 for simple rooms with private bath and fan. For US$35 you get a kitchenette. Clean sheets and towels are provided. Marva Mathe manages the guesthouse, which has been in business for 30 years.

Khus Khus Negril (tel. 876/957-4263, reservations@khuskhusnegril.com, www. khuskhusnegril.com, US$87–117) is an affordable option that puts comfort first—with an appreciable departure from the floral bed covers so typical of run-of-the-mill hotels across Jamaica. Blue Mountain Aromatics toiletries, iPod docking stations, and complimentary Wi-Fi complement the soothing linens to make Khus Khus a pleasurable retreat. Khus Khus has a total of 27 rooms, with room categories like "satisfy my soul," which has two double beds, "one love a queen," with one standard bed, the premium "garden peace suites," and "cease and settle" suites with a queen bed and pull-out couch. All rooms have a mini-fridge and iPod docks, comfortable lighting, and a sleek atmosphere. Several units surround a small pool in the back courtyard, while a restaurant and bar are in a second courtyard closer to the office and parking area.

Xtabi (tel. 876/957-0121, fax 876/957-0827, xtabiresort@cwjamaica.com, www.xtabi-negril.

com) is one of the most accommodating properties in Negril in terms of the price range for the rooms on offer and value for your money. From economy rooms (US$49/65 low/high season) with fans to spacious suites (US$59/90 low/high season) with air-conditioning and TV to stylish cliff-top cottages (US$120/210 low/high season), there is something for every budget. The restaurant and bar, also on the cliffs, serve up some of the best lobster (US$25) in Negril, and the conch burger is highly acclaimed. Xtabi is the most unpretentious, well-situated hotel on the West End. The name Xtabi is Greek for "meeting place of the gods."

Prim-Rose Inn (tel. 876/771-0069 or 876/640-2029, US$20/35 low/high season) is a real shoestring joint run by Gasnel Hylton. It has five basic rooms featuring fans, hot water, and hammocks on a porch. The inn is set back on the bush side of West End Road. The driveway is marked by a sign for Haciender Inn; Prim-Rose is about 100 meters from the main road on the left.

US$100-250

Negril Escape and Spa (tel. 876/957-0392, info@negrilescape.com, www.negrilescape.com, US$90/180 low/high season) offers a variety of themed accommodations: the Oriental Express, Passage to India, Romancing the Kasba, Back to Africa, Atlantis, Negril Cottage, and Coconut Grove. Some of these are more tasteful than others, but the fact that a variety of options are offered is well appreciated by its returning guests, who found the recent renovations a welcome infusion of color. Rooms come with all the basic amenities including hot water, air-conditioning, cable TV, clean sheets and towels, and Internet in the main office. If diving is on your agenda, it's a great base.

Negril Escape has earned a well-deserved reputation as a nightlife hotspot on Negril's West End. On Tuesday nights the hotel hosts some of Jamaica's top billing reggae and dancehall artists in its beautiful oceanfront setting. Acts have included Queen Ifrica, Taurus Riley, Jah Cure, Shaggy, and Wayne Wonder, among many others.

Catch a Falling Star (tel. 876/957-0390, stay@catchajamaica.com, www.catchajamaica.com, US$95–175 low season, US$120–250 high season) has five one-bedroom cottages, two two-bedroom cottages, and a recently completed thatch-roofed building on the cliffs with six units. With its cliff-top grounds well maintained with neat walkways and verdant gardens, this is one of the choice properties on the West End.

C Banana Shout (tel. 876/957-0384, cell tel. 876/350-7272, reservations@bananashoutresort.com, www.bananashoutresort.com, US$80–100 low season, US$150–200 high season) is owned by Milo Gallico, named after the Mark Conklin novel of the same name about Jamaica. It's a beautifully decorated property on one of the West End's most gorgeous stretches of cliffs. Four one- and two-bedroom cottages adorn the cliffs with cozy furniture and an artsy vibe. A live band performs classic reggae covers every evening from Rick's Cafe next door, for an earful of music to set the mood for sunset.

Banana's Garden (across West End Road from Rick's Cafe, tel. 876/957-0909, cell tel. 876/353-0007, bananasgarden@gmail.com, www.bananasgarden.com, US$85–135 low season, US$100–165 high season), owned and operated by Nicole Larson, is a tasteful retreat with five quaint, self-contained cottages surrounded by lush vegetation. Each cottage has unique, hand-carved wood trim detailing, ceiling fans, louvered windows, hot water, and kitchenettes, making the property ideal for those looking for independence and the modest, back-to-basics vibe that put Negril on the map. The pool is beautiful. The property operates as a B&B, with rates including a continental or Jamaican breakfast. Banana's Garden is ideal for small groups looking to book the entire property, for which discounts can be negotiated. The Solar Wellness Spa on property offers massage and treatments.

OVER US$250

Rockhouse (tel. 876/957-4373, fax. 876/957-0557, info@rockhousehotel.com, www.rockhousehotel.com) is a favorite for hip New York

NEGRIL

© OLIVER HILL

Widely regarded as the best boutique all-inclusive resort in Jamaica, The Caves pampers its guests in cliffside bliss.

weekenders looking to get away in style. The hotel is always booked, testament to good marketing, quality service, well-maintained grounds, and competent management. The beautiful villas (US$295–350 low, US$355–425 high season) are perched on the cliffs with views out to sea. A total of 34 rooms include standards (US$125/160 low/high season) and studios (US$150/185 low/high season). The restaurant has a nice evening ambience—and the coconut-battered shrimp are a must. The pool is also notable for its assimilation with the cliffs. An eight-room spa offering massages, wraps, scrubs and holistic treatments using all-natural local ingredients is a recent addition to the property and includes two cliff-side treatment cabanas.

Rockhouse took over Pirates Cave Restaurant located next door in early 2009, renaming it Pushcart Restaurant to promote a rootsy Jamaican vibe, referencing the traditional handcart commonplace at the country's open-air markets.

C The Caves (tel. 876/957-0270, fax 876/957-4930, thecaves@cwjamaica.com, www.islandoutpost.com) is Negril's most vibesy upscale hotel. Thatch-roofed, contoured cottages are seamlessly integrated with the cliffs. The property is perfectly conducive to spiritual relaxation, with its sophisticated African motif, soft music floating on the breeze, and hot tubs carved into the cliffs like they belong there. At the same time, you're never far from the greatest adrenaline rush of your life, thanks to the many cliff-tops from which to vault into the crystal-clear waters—as much as 18 meters below. Everywhere you turn there are platforms for sunbathing or for diving. At night, a large grotto just above water level is strewn with flowers and set up as the most romantic dining room imaginable, lit with hundreds of candles.

Bertram and the late Greer-Ann Saulter teamed up with former Island Records boss Chris Blackwell to create their idea of paradise at The Caves. The rooms are all unique with king-size beds, African batik pillow covers, classic louvered windows, and well-appointed baths. Cozy wooden ceilings and whitewashed walls create a soothing ambience, and love seats are nestled into the surroundings wherever they fit. The cottages are decorated with an assortment of Jamaican carvings and paintings. Every detail at The Caves is consciously designed to set guests in a relaxed mode—to the point of entrancement. Open bars (some manned, some self-serve) dot the property, and a snack bar has gourmet food ready whenever you're hungry.

Rooms range from one-bedroom suites (US$615/800 low/high season) to two-bedroom cottages (US$720/915 low/high season). Perhaps the nicest two-bedroom cottage, Moon Shadow, is separated from the rest by The Sands bar, which is open to the public for sunset and features a balcony overlooking the lighthouse and an azure cove below. All suites have king-size beds, while the two-bedroom cottages have queen-size beds downstairs.

◖ Tensing Pen (tel. 876/957-0387, fax 876/957-0161, tensingpen@cwjamaica.com, www.tensingpen.com) is the West End's crown gem. Luxurious, thatch-roofed, bungalow-style cottages adorn the cliffs above lapping turquoise waters. The absence of TVs in the cottages is deliberate, as is every other meticulous detail that makes Tensing Pen so hard to leave. The staff at Tensing Pen exhibit the epitome of Jamaican warmth. They all conspire to make guests feel a deep sense of belonging. They treat guests with the utmost attentiveness and the highest regard for those minute details that create the most pleasant and relaxing environment on earth, from the hibiscus flowers on your pillow to cool water at the bedside. An infinity-edge 16-by 30-foot saltwater pool was recently installed in front of the dining area and is fed by a rock fountain.

◖ Moon Dance Cliffs (www.moon-danceresorts.com, from US$225/275 low/high season) is a sleek, modern property completed in 2008, located on the West End about a mile past the lighthouse and offering a combination of rooms in the main building and villas. The resort offers all-inclusive and European plan packages. Villas come with a personal butler who attends to every need, from morning to night. Moon Dance Cliffs villas lack nothing, with stereos, computers, and phones in the living area with plush couches and a bar, outdoor patios with breakfast tables and lounge chairs overlooking the sea, and private whirlpool tubs in the yard just outside the master bedrooms.

Jackie's on the Reef (tel. 876/957-4997 or 718/469-2785, jackiesonthereef@rcn.com, www.jackiesonthereef.com, US$125/150 d low/high season) is the place to go for a nature, yoga, or tai chi retreat. The rates include morning activity sessions and are a great value. The hotel is one of the farthest out along West End Road, where there's less development and it's easy to meditate undisturbed.

The Westender Inn (tel. 876/957-4991, from US toll-free 800/223-3786, cell tel. 876/473-8172, westenderinn@yahoo.com, www.westenderinn.com, US$90–199) is a low-key accommodation a bit farther out from Jackie's, deep on the West End. Rooms are comfortable with polyester bed covers on a variety of bed sizes, and layouts from studios to one-bedrooms to oceanside suites. The hotel has a raised pool and deck with a restaurant and bar by the main parking area where nonguests are welcome.

Windrush Negril Bed & Breakfast (Orange Hill, tel. 876/425-5621 or 876/412-0794, from the U.S. tel. 508/873-1158 or 508/667-1257, windrushnegril@gmail.com, www.windrushnegril.com, US$175–225/day or US$1,400/week d, add US$25 per person nightly for extras) accommodates up to six guests between the bamboo house, a private cottage with a king-size bed, and a twin cot in an adjacent room, and Blue Snapper, a room on the ground level of the main house with a separate entrance, also with a king-size bed and a twin. There are two pools on the property, one fed by the lapping waves carved out of the low, coral cliffs at the seaside, and a freshwater pool by the main house. A boccie ball court makes the place singular in Negril.

Meals are prepared to order in an idyllic open-air kitchen (not included in room rate). Windrush prioritizes the private, exclusive experience. To get to Windrush, keep straight where the main turns left up to Good Hope.

COTTAGES AND VILLAS

Llantrisant Beach House (tel. 876/957-4259, cell tel. 305/467-0331, U.S. tel. 305/668-9877, info@beachcliff.com www. beachcliff.com), owned by Dr. and Mrs. Travis, is a unique property in that it is extremely proximate to everything in Negril. Llantrisant sits out on a point just west of the roundabout with a perfect view over Long Bay and Seven-Mile Beach. Rates are reasonable, given the luxury of having a tennis court and two private beaches (ranging US$320/400 low/high season for two persons to US$530/660 low/high season for up to the maximum occupancy of 11). Three meals per day cost an extra US$30 per person. A friendly and committed staff include two housekeepers, a groundskeeper, and night watchmen.

Hide Awhile (three-minute drive west of the lighthouse, tel. 876/957-9079, www.jamaicajane.com, www.idleawhile.com) is Negril's most exclusive and luxurious private villa complex. Best for those looking for independence away from the hustle and bustle, the three villas feature a duplex layout with a spacious master bedroom upstairs. Amenities include all the details expected in a top-end property, from flat-panel televisions to a fully equipped kitchen, plush bedding, and a porch that puts all worries to rest. The property is ideally suited for those with a car and provides guests with a remote control to open the gate, giving the feel of a 007 retreat. Wireless Internet is available. Chisty (cell tel. 876/841-5696) is the Rastafarian caretaker who serves up excellent cooking.

Tingalayas (tel. 876/957-0126, reservations@tingalayasretreat.com) is named after a donkey, Tingalaya, that lives on the property. It has two independent cottages plus five rooms in two bigger cottages with a big communal kitchen. Owned by David

Rosenstein, Tingalayas is a good place for a group or family, with accommodations for up to 14 people. Amenities include ceiling fans, hot water, wireless Internet, and a combination of queen-size and bunk beds. Breakfast is included and resident Rasta cook Jubey does excellent lobster, jerk chicken, and rice and peas to order.

FOOD
Seven-Mile Beach
JAMAICAN

Best in the West is Negril's favorite jerk chicken spot; it's located directly across the road from Idle Awhile.

Rainbow Arches (Joy James, tel. 876/957-4745) has excellent curry shrimp and curry goat to order. The James family is one of oldest Jamaican families in Negril.

Niah's Patties (10 A.M.–8 P.M. daily Dec. 15–May 15) at Wavz Entertainment Centre, has been making the best patties in Negril, and perhaps all of Jamaica, since

Niah takes the prize for best patty in Negril, if not all of Jamaica.

2005. Patty fillings include Italian, fish, red bean, potato, chicken, vegetable, and lobster (US$3.50–7).

Spring Park Restaurant (across from Mariposa, cell tel. 876/373-8060 or 876/401-5162, 8 A.M.–10 P.M. daily, US$5–10), is run by Henry Gardener, a pig farmer who makes the best roast pork around, as well as fried and grilled chicken. Henry also does Jamaican breakfast every day.

Ossie's Jerk Centre (opposite The Palms, tel. 876868-5858, 10 A.M.–10 P.M. daily, US$5–10, cash only), serves the best steamed fish and jerk on the beach. A beer costs about US$2.

Sonia's (across from Roots Bamboo, 8 A.M.–9 P.M. daily, US$5–10) is well recognized for her delicious Jamaican cuisine and homemade patties.

(Sweet Spice (Whitehall Rd., tel. 876/957-4621, 8:30 A.M.–10:30 P.M. daily, US$5–25) is the best place along the main road heading toward Sav for typical Jamaican fare at local prices. Sweet Spice is the most popular restaurant with locals for good reason, offering refreshing real-world value in a town where prices are more regularly on par with U.S. cities. Dishes like fried chicken, coconut curry, or escoveitch fish, conch, and lobster are representative of Jamaica's traditional cuisine.

Peppa Pot (Whitehall Rd., tel. 876/957-3388, 9 A.M.–8 P.M. Mon.–Sat., US$4–10) is located a bit farther down Whitehall Road heading east out of Negril. It's a popular local joint for jerk, as well as steamed fish with the requisite sides of breadfruit and festival.

Ackee Tree Restaurant (Whitehall Road, across from the Texaco station, cell tel. 876/871-2524, 8 A.M.–10 P.M. daily, US$5–8) serves the best Ital stew and local dishes and is frequented by popular artists in the know. Noel "Wall" Masters runs the joint.

Tasty Delight (Fire Station Rd., no phone) is the favorite restaurant of local taxi drivers, with typical Jamaican dishes at local rates.

Beach Road SeaFood Restaurant (across from Roots Bamboo, cell tel. 876/371-9643, 8 A.M.–9 P.M. Mon.–Sat., free delivery) serves fish, lobster, soursop fish, conch, and shrimp.

Devon "Tiger" Reid is the shop owner. **Late Night Hot Spot Bar** is located next door.

Rankcle Stankcle fish shop, run by Owen Keith Oliver "Taurus" Morgan (cell tel. 876/401-2503), operates out of a riverside corner of the Negril Fishing Cooperative.

The Black Star Line is an Ital restaurant located at Bongo's Farm in Sheffield, serving natural foods out of calabash bowls, natural juices, and jelly coconut water. The eatery is open by reservation only.

FINE DINING AND INTERNATIONAL

Charela Inn (tel. 876/957-4277, 7:30 A.M.–9:30 P.M. daily) serves vegetarian, chicken, fish, steak, lobster, and shrimp dinner entrées (US$20–48) and has good Jamaican and international dishes with a large selection of wines.

(Kuyaba (tel. 876/957-4318, 7 A.M.–11 P.M. daily, US$12–27) has consistently decent, but pricey, international and Jamaican fusion cuisine, including pork kebab, brown stew conch, peppered steak, and seafood linguine lobster for main courses.

Whistling Bird Private Club for Fine Dining (at Whistling Bird villas, tel. 876/957-4403, 7 A.M.–7 P.M., by reservation only) specializes in gourmet five-course meals (US$35) that offer a choice of dishes that include "Grandma's Favourite" pepperpot soup, pineapple chicken, escovitch fish, stuffed grouper, and bourbon rock lobster.

The Lobster House (at Sunrise Club, beside Coral Seas Garden, tel. 876/957-4293, noon–11 P.M. daily) serves Italian and Jamaican food: Dishes range from pasta with tomato sauce (US$8) to gnocchi (US$12), pizza baked in a wood-fired brick oven (US$10–16), and grilled lobster (US$26). Wines are about US$24–26, and great coffee is served.

The Boat Bar (between Rondel Village and Mariposa, tel. 876/957-4746, 8 A.M.–10 P.M. daily, US$10–30) is a favorite that has been serving chicken, fish, shrimp, goat, pork, and steak since 1983. The garlic lobster gets rave reviews. Bunny and Angie are the proprietors. A webcam is set up on Fridays, viewable at www.realnegril.com, to allow fans to keep in touch.

Ristorante da Gino (at Mariposa Hideaway, tel. 876/957-4918, 7 A.M.–11 P.M. daily) is a good Italian restaurant managed by Vivian Reid, the wife of the late Gino. He was killed in 2005, allegedly by Italian thugs. The menu includes mixed salad (US$5), spaghetti alioli (US$10), linguine lobster (US$20), grilled lobster (US$25), and mixed grilled fish (US$30). A complete breakfast (US$10) comes with eggs and bacon, toast, fruit, juice, and coffee. Gino's also has a decent selection of Italian wines.

Marley's by the Sea does breakfast (8 A.M.–10 P.M.), lunch by the beach grill, and dinner with a rotating menu including items like shrimp linguini (US$15) or pan-fried pork and mozzarella (US$18).

Pancake House at Firefly (tel. 876/957-4358, 7 A.M.–10 P.M.) serves breakfast all day, with pancakes, eggs, French toast, and breakfast sandwiches. Cheapest Red Stripe on the beach (US$1.50) is here.

❰ Cosmos Seafood Restaurant and Bar (next door to Beaches Negril, tel. 876/957-4330, 9 A.M.–10 P.M. daily, US$5–43) serves excellent Jamaican seafood dishes, including conch soup, shrimp, and fried fish—in addition to other local dishes like curry goat, stewed pork, fried chicken, and oxtail. The beach out front is wide and good for swimming. A mix of Jamaican, expat, and tourist clientele, perhaps even weighted toward the local crowd, is testament to the reasonable prices and tasty Jamaican home-style cooking.

Chill Awhile (at Idle Awhile Resort, tel. 876/957-3303, 7 A.M.–9 P.M. daily) offers free lounge chairs and wireless Internet for its customers. The charming beachfront deck restaurant serves a variety of light food items for lunch including club sandwiches, burgers, fish and chips (US$6–8), and jerk chicken (US$10). For dinner, international and Jamaican-style entrées range from grilled chicken breast with peanut or Jamaican sauce (US$8.50) and coconut-breaded snapper with tartar sauce (US$12.50) to lobster thermidor (US$23.50) or a seafood platter with grilled lobster and

coconut shrimp (US$25). There is also a full bar next to the restaurant.

Norma's on the Beach (at Sea Splash Resort, tel. 876/957-4041, 7:30 A.M.–10 P.M. daily) is owned by the legendary Jamaican culinary dynamo Norma Shirley, who has contributed recipes and menus at numerous fine dining restaurants in Jamaica, starting with her flagship Norma's on the Terrace in Kingston. Her pioneering Jamaican and Caribbean fusion dishes attracted wide acclaim, even if it would seem on occasion that her reputation and pricing have outgrown the cuisine. A third restaurant under Norma's tutelage is based at the Errol Flynn Marina in Port Antonio.

West End

Hammond's Pastry Place (at the roundabout, tel. 876/957-4734, 8 A.M.–6 P.M. Mon.–Sat.) serves patties, cakes, and deli sandwiches.

Juicy J's (behind Scotiabank , tel. 876/957-4213, 7 A.M.–10 P.M. daily, US$4–15) is a popular local joint serving typical Jamaican dishes at low cost.

❰ Sea View Bar & Grill (West End Rd., around the bend from Scotia Bank, tel. 876/957-9191, 4 P.M.–2:30 A.M. daily), run by Tony Montana, does the best steam roast conch (US$2) around, as well as steam roast fish (US$4–11), conch soup (US$1/US$1.50) and jerk chicken (US$4).

Seaview House Chinese Restaurant (Cotton Tree Place, between Vendors' Plaza and the Post Office, tel. 876/957-4925, 10 A.M.–10 P.M. daily) has decent Chinese food. It serves vegetable dishes (US$7–10), chicken (US$10), seafood (US$18), and roast duck and lobster variations (US$27).

Mi Yard (located across from the Houseboat, tel. 876/957-4442, www.miyard.com) serves snack items like fish, egg, cheese, or ham and cheese sandwiches, as well as Jamaica's favorite starchy food snacks or accompaniments like plantain, festival, breadfruit, and bammy. Meals are done to order and include items like cabbage and carrot cooked down, curry chicken, brown stew chicken, and fish (US$3–4). Eight computers are available for Internet browsing by purchasing a card (US$3.50 per hour). It is a 24-hour restaurant and an especially convenient and popular spot for a late-night bite.

Canoe Beach Bar & Grill (across from MX3, tel. 876/957-4814, or Kirby's cell tel. 876/878-5893, canoebeachbar@gmail.com) serves Jamaican favorites at reasonable prices.

◖ Mary's Bay Restaurant & Boat Bar (tel. 876/957-0981 or 876/819-3005, 10 A.M.–10 P.M. daily, US$3–25) serves a variety of seafood like grouper, mahimahi, tuna, and snapper. It is also the home of "the serious burger," a double patty layered with mushrooms and bacon. Scottish couple Janet and Alan Young took over in May 2009, infusing the seaside setting with a relaxing ambiance true to the original laidback vibe that put Negril on the map. They serve a great mix of Jamaican favorites and international dishes at competitive prices.

◖ Blue Water Internet Cafe (One Love Drive, tel. 876/957-0125, or contact proprietor Randy cell tel. 876/884-6030, randysbluewater@yahoo.com, www.bluewaterinternetnegril.com, 8 A.M.–11 P.M. daily, US$2 per 20 minutes) serves Jamaica's best gelato, Calypso Gelato. The Internet café has the best equipment in Negril with CD burning, fax, webcam, and inexpensive VoIP telephony. Pizza is made from scratch daily (US$2 per slice, US$19 for a large pie) and is some of the best in Negril. Internet costs US$5 on his computer or for Wi-Fi.

Jus Natural Restaurant Seafood and Vegetarian (next to Xtabi, across from La Kaiser, tel. 876/957-0235, 8 A.M.–9 P.M. daily, closed on Sundays in low season, US$6–30) serves breakfast, lunch, and dinner with items like calalloo or ackee omelettes and fresh juices. Vegetarian dishes and seafood items are served for lunch and dinner. The phone line can get waterlogged but comes back when it dries out, so clients are advised to simply "set out an' reach," or show up assuming it's open during normal business hours.

3 Dives Jerk Centre (contact owner Lyndon Myrie, a.k.a. Lloydie, tel. 876957-0845

or 876/782-9990, noon–midnight daily) offers a quarter chicken with bread (US$3.50) or with rice and peas and vegetables (US$4.50), half chicken with rice and peas and veggies (US$8), steamed or curried shrimp (US$17), and grilled lobster (US$34). This is *the* place to get jerk on the West End. Located right on the cliffs, the open-air restaurant has a nice outdoor barbecue vibe. The 3 Dives hosts the Negril Jerk Festival every November.

Pushcart Restaurant and Rum Bar (tel. 876/957-4373, www.rockhousehotel.com/pushcart.php, 3–10 P.M. daily, US$9–16) serves entrées including peppered shrimp, homemade jerk sausage, curry goat, and oxtail. Opened in early 2009, Pushcart brings a Jamaican street food experience to one of the West End's most exclusive accommodations enclaves. The name is derived from the pushcarts used by Jamaican street vendors across the island in open-air markets, whether for selling produce or cooked food. The pushcart provides the inspiration for the menu, which is inspired by street food from Jamaica and throughout the Caribbean. A lively local mento band provides nightly live entertainment. Pushcart offers casual dining in a breathtaking cliff-side setting made famous as a location in the films *20,000 Leagues Under the Sea* and the Steve McQueen classic, *Papillon*.

Ras Rody (across from Tensing Pen, 10 A.M.–6 P.M.) is an Ital food shop that specializes in soups, normally red pea soup (US$8–10) and other vegetarian specialties of the day.

The Health Shop (Tait's Plaza, tel. 876/957-4274, cell tel. 876/427-1253, 10 A.M.–6 P.M. Mon.–Thurs., 10 A.M.–4:30 P.M. Fri.) sells whole-wheat vegetarian patties, hearty juice blends, and other natural foods at local prices.

◖ The Hungry Lion (West End, tel. 876/957-4486, 4–10:30 P.M. daily, closed in Oct., US$8–24), under the ownership of Bertram Saulter, who also owns The Caves, is an excellent dinner spot with healthy-sized entrées. The lobster burritos are delicious. A pleasant atmosphere is created with irie music, carved faces, and mellow tones covering the walls. The Hungry Lion is good value for the money, and the drink special—the Lion Heart, made with mango, ginger, and rum—shouldn't be missed.

Royal Kitchen (Chef Errold Chambers, cell tel. 876/287-0549, 8 A.M.–11 P.M. daily, US$3–5) is one of the best spots in Negril for Ital vegetarian food, prepared Rasta style with excellent fresh juices to accompany the meal.

Erica's Cafe (cell tel. 876/889-3109, 5–10 P.M. daily) has excellent Jamaican staples. Many locals consider Erica's the best stewed chicken (US$5) on the island.

Sips & Bites (adjacent to Rock House, tel. 876/957-0188, 7 A.M.–10:30 P.M. Sun.–Thurs., 7 A.M.–5:30 P.M. Fri., closed Sat., US$5–10) is a good spot for breakfast and has good Jamaican dishes like fried chicken, curry goat, and oxtail.

Choices (across from Samsara, tel. 876/957-4841, 7 A.M.–11 P.M., US$4–7) is an earthy restaurant on the West End serving Jamaican fare like ackee and saltfish and steamed calalloo for breakfast, plus curry goat and fried chicken at moderate prices.

LTU Pub & Restaurant (tel. 876/957-0382, 7 A.M.–11 P.M. daily, US$10–30) has good Jamaican and international food in a laid-back setting perched on the cliffs. Specialties include crab quesadilla, stuffed jalapeño, and crab ball appetizers, plus schnitzel, surf and turf, pasta, chicken, and seafood dishes like grilled salmon and the snapper papaya boat. The name of the place is taken from the Germany-based airline Lufthansa Transport United, of which founder Walter Bigge was a shareholder. Bigge was killed in 1992 and the restaurant closed for a spell before being taken over by the present owner, Bill Williams, who bought the place around 2000. Wi-Fi is available free for customers.

Rick's Cafe (tel. 876/957-0380, noon–10 P.M. daily, US$18–28) is a moneymaker that has other business owners in Negril envious. It's worth stopping by for a look at the immense

© OLIVER HILL

Boutique resort Banana Shout, left, neighbors Rick's Cafe, the most popular sunset venue in Negril, where cliff jumping is the favored activity.

crowd that is bussed in each evening, making it one of Negril's most successful commercial ventures. The property was renovated in the recent past after a large chunk of cliff fell into the sea during a hurricane. A huge boom was erected for a rope swing, and there are plenty of platforms to jump off for all levels of adrenaline junkies. A diver in a Speedo climbs to the top of a tree for the highest dive of all, waiting for enough tips to be collected by his cohort before tucking into a cannonball for the 25-meter drop. Meanwhile, a live band belts out reggae classics throughout the evening, some of them coming across more true to the originals than others. Food and beer at Rick's is mediocre and outrageously expensive, but nobody seems to mind. Choices include chicken, shrimp, fish, and lobster with rice and peas, french fries, or sweet potato sides; a beer costs US$5. If you don't want to pay the cover (US$5) to get in at Rick's but still want to partake in the action, you can enjoy the same scene with a more local perspective from the outcropping next door behind an artist's shack, Jah Creation, where kids beg US$2 from the tourists to jump off the cliffs. There are plenty of better, more tranquil, and less hyped spots for cliff-jumping, including Pushcart Restaurant and The Sands, both of which are recommended.

The Sands is the best place to experience the West End's cliffs away from the gawking crowds that convene at Rick's each evening. It is a great bar, right next to the nicest and most secluded villa at Negril's top resort, and therefore a great way to experience The Caves' vibe if you can't stay there. There is a challenging-enough spot to jump into the water approximately 12 meters below—with the best view of Negril's lighthouse right next door. Professional jumpers come show off on Wednesday and Saturday, when jerk is served.

INFORMATION AND SERVICES

Negril has a very active online community (www.negril.com) where message boards, news, and events are posted, as well as advertising for hotels in Negril and beyond. Other relevant organizations include the Negril Resort Association (www.negriljamaica.com), which has special offers at select hotels.

Banking can be done at **NCB** (at Sunshine Village, tel. 876/957-4117; ATMs at Plaza Negril and Petcom) or **Scotiabank** (Negril Square, across from Burger King near the roundabout, tel. 876/957-4236; ATM at the Petcom next to the airstrip across from Breezes).

FX Trader (888/398-7233) has a branch at Hi-Lo supermarket in Sunshine Village Plaza by the roundabout (9 A.M.–5 P.M. Mon.–Thurs., 9 A.M.–5:30 P.M. Fri.–Sat.).

The Negril **police station** (tel. 876/957-4268, emergency dial 119) is located just beyond the roundabout on Nompriel Road. Negril police officer Dwayne advises travelers to stay away from dark, secluded areas at night, as people have had bags grabbed. Don't leave valuables on the beach while swimming, and take care not to get robbed by prostitutes. Prostitution is illegal but common and not prosecuted, the penalty being nominal in court.

The Negril **post office** (tel. 876/957-9654, 8 A.M.–5 P.M. Mon.–Fri.) is located on West End Road between Cotton Tree Hotel and Samuel's Hardware just past Vendor's Plaza.

The **Negril Chamber of Commerce** (Vendors Plaza, West End Rd., tel. 876/957-4067, www.negrilchamberofcommerce.com) has tourist information, including a regularly updated brochure full of ads for hotels and attractions.

Long Bay Medical & Wellness Centre (Norman Manley Blvd., tel. 876/957-9028) is run by Dr. David Stair.

Omega Medical Centre (White Swan Plaza and Sunshine Plaza, tel. 876/957-9307 or 876/957-4697) has two branches run by husband-and-wife team Dr. King and Dr. Foster.

Dr. Grant (Sunshine Plaza, West End, tel. 876/957-3770) runs a private clinic.

Negril Nightscape Tours (cell tel. 876/407-8414 or 876/407-8489, info@negrilnightscape-tours.com, www.negrilnightscapetours.com) is a nightlife tour-company run by two young expats, Angela Eastwick and Danielle Velez, which offers an all-inclusive service that includes a driver, admission to the hotspot of the night, and drink specials.

Roge Croll (cell tel. 876/468-5001, rogecroll@yahoo.com) and his team offer photography and videography services for weddings or any other event you want to remember.

Internet Access

Complimentary Wi-Fi is found at most of the more modern hotels and restaurants in Negril, from Chill Awhile and Kristyl's Restaurant on the Beach to Canoe Bar & Grill and LTU Pub & Restaurant on the West End. For those traveling without a laptop, try **Sue's Easy Rock Internet Cafe** (tel. 876/957-0816 or cell tel. 876/424-5481, www.easyrockinternetcafe.com, US$2 for 30 minutes) which offers phone calls, fax, and breakfast all day at Mary's Bay, or **Lynks Internet Café & Gift Shop** (US$2 for 20 minutes), located beside Sips and Bites. Mi Yard (tel. 876/957-4442, www.miyard.com) offers Internet access for US$3.50/hour.

Blue Water Internet Café (One Love Drive, tel. 876/957-0125, or contact proprietor Randy, cell tel. 876/884-6030, randysbluewater@yahoo.com, www.bluewaterinternetnegril. com, 8 A.M.–11 P.M. daily) offers access on several desktops for US$2 per 20-minute interval, or US$5 per hour, with the best equipment in town for CD burning, fax, webcam, and inexpensive VoIP telephony. Wi-Fi is also available at the same rates if you bring your laptop.

GETTING THERE

Air

Negril's Aerodrome can accommodate small private aircraft and charters. The only operator in Jamaica currently offering charter flights to Negril is Jamaica Air Shuttle, which will take passengers in from Kingston and Montego Bay. Contact marketing manager Derrick Dwyer (tel. 876/923-0371, 876/923-0372, 876/923-0373, or 876/901-5196, ddwyer@jamaicaairshuttle.com) to schedule service. Charter fares run US$2,000 per hour, with any single flight around the island not lasting more than an

hour, and as little as 15 minutes, depending on point of origin and destination.

Ground

Negril can be reached by several means, depending on your budget and comfort requirements. Most accommodations offer airport transfers at additional cost, and a host of private taxi operators generally charge around US$60 per couple, with an additional US$20 for extra passengers.

The best option for budget-minded travelers is booking an airport pickup or drop-off through the Jamaica Union of Travelers Association (JUTA) in cars, vans, and coaches of up to 45-person capacity. JUTA's Negril Chapter (Norman Manley Blvd., tel. 876/957-4620 or 876/957-9197, info@jutatoursnegrilltd.com, www.jutatoursnegrilltd.com) offers transfers for US$20 per person from the beach and US$25 from the cliffs, by far the most affordable way to get between Negril and Montego Bay's Sangster International Airport. Reservations made by email receive a US$2 discount. JUTA also takes tourists on excursions to popular attractions across the island.

For more personalized taxi and tour services, try **Alfred's Taxi and Tour Company** (tel. 876/854-8016 or 876/527-0050, or from U.S. tel. 646/289 4285, alfredstaxi@aol.com and negriltracy@aol.com, US$50 for two). Proprietor Alfred Barrett recently acquired a 15-seat bus, upping capacity and expanding on "Irie Airport Rides and Vibes" in his standard tinted Toyota Corolla station wagon.

For those with less money and more time, there are buses from Mobay to Savanna-la-Mar (US$2) and then from Sav to Negril (US$2), mainly serviced by route taxis. It is also possible to take a route taxi from Mobay to Hopewell (US$2), then another from Hopewell to Lucea (US$2), and then a third from Lucea to Negril US$2), but these cars leave when full and won't have much room for luggage.

Negril has two main taxi stands: one next to Scotiabank in Negril Square, where taxis depart for points along the West End following the cliffs; the other in the main park next to the police station on Whitehall Road, where taxis and buses depart for points along Norman Manley Boulevard and east toward Sav-la-Mar.

GETTING AROUND

Route taxis run up and down the coast from the Beach to the West End, generally using the plaza across from Burger King by the round-about as a connection point. Some negotiating will generally be required, as the route taxis always try to get a higher fare from tourists, especially at night when everyone is charged extra. From anywhere on the West End to the round-about should never be more than US$1.50 during the day, and as much as double at night. From there to the beach should also not cost more than US$1.50. Excursions beyond the beach and the West End can be arranged with private taxi and tour operators.

Hanover

Hanover is Jamaica's third-smallest parish after Kingston and St. Andrew, with roughly 451 square kilometers of land. It has six major rivers, two of which flow into Lucea Harbour. The Great River, along the border with St. James, has Jamaica's most heart-thumping navigable rapids in the hills of the interior, as well as serene bamboo rafting where it lazily meets the sea.

Lucea, Hanover's capital, sits on an idyllic horseshoe-shaped harbor a few kilometers from **Dolphin Head Mountain.** Dolphin Head is a small limestone peak at 545 meters, which overlooks some of the most biologically diverse forestland in Jamaica, with the island's highest concentration of endemic species. A few kilometers away, **Birch Hill**—at 552 meters—is the highest point in the parish. Together the small

© OLIVER HILL

Lucea's famous clock tower

range protects Lucea harbor from the dominant easterly winds. Both Lucea and Mosquito Cove are well-regarded hurricane holes for small yachts. Hanover is the only parish without a KFC.

HISTORY

Hanover exists as a parish since it was portioned off from Westmoreland in 1723 and given the name of English monarch George I of the House of Hanover. The Spanish first settled the area when New Seville was abandoned in 1534 and the capital moved to Spanish Town. Lucea became prosperous, with a busier port than Montego Bay in its heyday, which served 16 large sugar estates in the area. Remnants of many estate great houses dot the landscape to the east and west of Lucea, their abandoned ruins showing evidence of having been torched and destroyed during slave riots. Kennilworth, Barbican, and Tryall are a few of the old estates that have visible ruins; although they have been declared national heritage sites, they are not maintained.

HOPEWELL TO TRYALL

Just west of Montego Bay, the Great River marks the border of St. James and Hanover, which represents Jamaica's high-end tourism. Before arriving at Round Hill, one of Jamaica's most exclusive club hotels, Tamarind Hill and its surrounding coastline are strewn with luxurious villas, most of which fetch upwards of US$10,000 per week during the high season.

The town of Hopewell is not especially remarkable beyond its present status as a somewhat active fishing community. There's a Scotiabank ATM, a small grocery store, and a few hole-in-the-wall restaurants for typical Jamaican fare in the heart of town. There is generally a sound system slowing traffic through town on Friday evenings, which precedes a busy market day on Saturday; if you're staying in the vicinity, it's worth a stop.

A few kilometers farther west of Round Hill and Hopewell is Tryall, a former sugarcane plantation destroyed during the Christmas Rebellion of 1831–1832. The old water wheel,

fed by an aqueduct from the Flint River, can be seen as you round the bend approaching Tryall from the east, but little else remains as a reminder of its past as a sugar estate. Today the hotel and villa complex, which fans out from the historic great house, sits on one of the Caribbean's premier golf courses; its winter residents include boxing champion Lennox Lewis.

Bordering Tryall to the west is a burgeoning bedroom community, Sandy Bay, where new housing developments are rapidly springing up. Still farther west, the highway wraps around Mosquito Cove, where sailboats create a flotilla to party the night away before Easter weekend in preparation for a morning race back to Mobay every year.

Accommodations

◖ **Round Hill Hotel and Villas** (tel. 876/956-7050, fax 876/956-7505, reservations@roundhilljamaica.com, www.roundhilljamaica.com, suites US$419–843 nightly low season, US$631–1,261 high season), just over the Great River, is an exclusive hotel and club on meticulously manicured grounds. The hotel's main Pineapple Suites, featuring plush lounge furniture, were designed by Ralph Lauren and boast an atmosphere of stately, oceanfront elegance. A host of returning guest luminaries has sealed Round Hill's well-deserved reputation for excellence.

In the Pineapple Suites, a series of hinged louvered windows open to overlook an infinity pool and the sea beyond, perfectly aligned for dreamy sunsets. The bathrooms feature rainwater showerheads above glass enclosures and large bathtubs. Just above the hotel suites, villas are strewn across the hillside, each surrounded by a maze of shrubs and flowers, ensuring the utmost privacy. Next to the small, calm beach there's a charming library with a huge TV (to make up for their absence in the suites) and an open-air dining area; a short walk down the coast leads to the spa, based in a renovated plantation great house. Villas at Round Hill (US$875–2,875 nightly low season, US$1,250–4,100 high) can be booked

COURTESY OF ROUND HILL/DAVID MASSEY

Round Hill Hotel and Villas is Jamaica's premiere waterfront resort.

fees are US$125 daily plus tax, carts are US$30 plus tax, and a caddy is US$30, plus a customary US$20 tip). Tryall guests pay substantially less (greens fees US$70/100 plus tax low/high season). There are nine tennis courts, two with lights. The cushioned courts are less slippery than the faux clay. Courts are for members and guests only and included in the stay. Related fees include US$23/hour for hitting partner, US$48 to play with a club pro, and US$7 per hour for a ball boy. At night, courts cost US$20 per hour for the lights.

The food at Tryall is an excellent value, while far from inexpensive, with Master Chef Herbert Baur demonstrating his wealth of experience in overseeing day-to-day operations. Meals are kept interesting with the Jamaican barbecue dinner on Wednesday, seafood buffet dinner on the beach on Friday, and open-air à la carte dining on the veranda of the main house on other evenings (7–9:30 P.M.). Tryall sources 95 percent of the produce it serves locally, as well as 100 percent of the chicken and pork.

NEGRIL

through the hotel office. Round Hill rents a total of 27 villas.

Tryall Club (tel. 876/956-5660, U.S. tel. 800/238-5290, reservation@tryallclub.com, www.tryallclub.com, one-bedroom suites from US$395/550 low/high season) has private suites adjoining the main house, as well as villas scattered throughout the property that are pooled and rented through the club reservation office.

Tryall Villas rent for US$630–785 low season, US$1,185/1,570 high, for superior or deluxe category, respectively. They come fully staffed with excellent cooks who prepare delectable Jamaican favorites and are adept at international cuisine. Most suites and villas have a one-week minimum stay during the high season, reduced to three or four days during the low season. Given the villas are privately owned, certain owners establish their own low and high season dates and discounts, so these can vary.

Tryall has one of the top golf courses in the Caribbean; it sits on an 890-hectare estate that extends deep into the Hanover interior. Tennis and golf are offered to nonmembers (greens

Food

Charis Restaurant (just before the entrance to Round Hill heading west, tel. 876/956-7530, or cell. 876/441-9992, Mon-Sat 9 A.M.–6 P.M., US$5–10) serves jerk chicken and pork, curry chicken and goat, a variety of pasta dishes including alfredo sauce, shrimp and chicken, or Rasta pasta with ackee, in season. Steamed, grilled, or fried fish is done to order. The restaurant reopened in January 2009 under the new ownership of two local couples, Geoffrey and Jackry Harris, and Marcine and Oniel Brown.

Sea Shells (cell tel. 876/436-9175, 9 A.M.–9 P.M. daily, US$7–21), just west of Hopewell, is run by Lorna Williams and serves chicken, pork, fish, and lobster dishes. The restaurant has a rootsy vibe, with the dining area right next to the water and a bar by the roadside.

Dervy's Lobster Trap (cell tel. 876/783-5046, open by reservation daily, US$18–30), owned by the charismatic Dervent Wright, and operated by the whole family, including his wife Gem, daughter Tiffany, and son, Junior. Dervy's has some of the island's best lobster, plus a great view of Round Hill from its vantage point on the waterfront. Be sure to call ahead to make reservations. Reach it by taking the second right in Hopewell, heading west down Sawyer's Road to the sea's edge. A sign for Lobster Trap indicates the turnoff from the main road.

LUCEA TO GREEN ISLAND

Hanover's capital, Lucea is a quiet town that occasionally comes alive for special events like Independence Day, when the town hosts a talent show. Lucea's **Fort Charlotte,** which sits at the mouth of the harbor, was never used. The town was busier than Montego Bay at the height of the colonial period following emancipation and would become important for the export of molasses, bananas, and yams. The large Lucea yam, exported to Jamaican laborers in Cuba and Panama during the construction of railroads and the canal, is still an important product from the area today. The clock tower atop the historic 19th-century courthouse was originally destined for St. Lucia, but the town's residents liked it so much they refused to give it up in favor of the less ornate version they had commissioned by the same manufacturer in Great Britain.

Sights
Fort Charlotte, located on the point of Lucea Harbor, is the most intact fort in western Jamaica, with three cannons in good condition sitting on the battlements. It was built by the British in 1756, with 23 cannon openings to defend their colony from any challenge from the sea. Originally named Fort Lucea, it was renamed during the reign of King George III after his Queen Charlotte. The **Barracks,** a large rectangular Georgian building next to the fort, was built in 1843 to house soldiers stationed at Fort Charlotte. It was given to the people of Jamaica in 1862 by the English War Office; it became the town's education center and is now part of the high school complex.

Hanover Historical Museum (US$1.50 adults, US$0.50 children) is housed in the old police barracks and *gaol* (jail). It opened in 1989 and was at one point expanded to include

artifacts from excavated Arawak middens (refuse piles) found in Hanover. The community museum has displays covering the history of Hanover from the Tainos to the present.

Kenilworth is one of Jamaica's most impressive great houses, located on the former Maggoty Estate. Currently the property is home to the HEART Academy, a training skills institute. To get there, pass Tryall and then Sandy Bay, then Chukka Blue; turn right after crossing a bridge over the Maggoty River in the community of Barbican and look for the sign for HEART Trust NTA Kenilworth on the left. Turn in and look for the ruins behind the institute, which is painted blue and white.

📖 Dolphin Head Mountain
Dolphin Head Mountain and the Dolphin Head Forest Reserve contain some of Jamaica's few remaining pockets of biodiversity and high endemism. A **Nature Trail** and **Living Botanical Museum** were developed over the past several years and are currently maintained by Jamaica's Forestry Department (contact regional manager Ian Wallace, iwallace@forestry.gov.jm, abromfield@forestry.gov.jm).

To reach the Dolphin Head Nature Trail and Live Botanical Museum, take the B9 inland from Lucea toward Glasgow. The trail starts in Riverside on the east side of the road a few kilometers before reaching Glagow. The trail was opened in February 2007 and leads along Retirement and Rugland mountains on the western flank of the Dolphin Head range. A second trail starts from Kingsvale leading into the forest reserve.

Accommodations and Food
The **Fiesta Group,** a Spain-based hotel chain, opened the 2,000-room Fiesta Paladium Palace (tel. 876/620-0000, www.fiestahotelgroup.com), a massive all-inclusive hotel just west of Lucea on Molasses beach in 2008.

Tapa Top Food Hut is located on the south side of the main road just east of the town center, with **Vital Ital** (contact Ray "Bongo Ray" Gonsalves, tel. 876/956-2218 or cell tel. 876/379-3423, 10 A.M.–10 P.M., Mon.–Sat.), on the harbor side of the road a few meters farther east. They serve a strictly vegan ital menu with dishes like tofu, stew, brown rice, veggie soup, and natural juices (US$2–5). Likewise, you can always count on a patty from **Juici Beef** (Mid Town Mall, tel. 876/956-3657) in the heart of Lucea on the west-bound circuit.

Services
NCB bank has a branch (tel. 876/956-2204) as well as an ATM location at Haughton Court.
    Scotiabank (tel. 876/956-2235) has a branch on Willie Delisser Boulevard facing the main intersection by the courthouse on the western side of town.
    Lailian Wholesale Supermarket is at Shop #14, Mid Town Mall (tel. 876/956-9712).
    Family Care Pharmacy is at Shop #1, Mid Town Mall (tel. 876/956-2685).
    Shoppers' Choice Supermarket is located in Green Island (tel. 876/955-2369).

BLENHEIM
Just before the one-way circuit around Lucea reaches the courthouse heading west, the B9 leads inland through Middlesex to Dias, where a right-hand turn leads back toward the coast and Davis Cove. About five kilometers west of Dias is Blenheim, the birthplace of Jamaica Labour Party founder William Alexander Clarke, who later took the name Bustamante after traveling and living in several Latin American countries. Blenheim is a quiet village with a simple museum devoted to the national hero popularly known as "Busta." The museum is located inside a re-created house, built by the National Heritage Trust after Busta's original house was destroyed by fire. More of a thatch-roofed hut, the house's interior has newspaper clippings and pictures of Sir Alexander adorning the walls.

GREEN ISLAND TO NEGRIL
Mandela Green Entertainment Centre
Established over a decade ago, Mandela Green is an entertainment lawn inside a walled compound, its interior walls painted with portraits of Jamaican artists and heroes in typical Rasta style. It's used for parties, stage shows, theatrical performances, and other private and public functions. The entertainment center was revitalized over the past couple of years, opening a restaurant and bar (11 A.M.–11 P.M. daily) serving Jamaican dishes and seafood (US$5–10) in mid-2009. Contact Paul Taylor (cell tel. 876/871-8454, grentertainment1@gmail.com) for info and bookings.
    According to Palma Taylor, Paul's father, who controls the property, the venue has given several up-and-coming Jamaican singers a *buss,* or career break, over the years.

(Half Moon Beach
Orange Bay, just west of Green Island, is a quiet little community with the idyllic **Half Moon Beach,** managed by Tania and Andrew Bauwen (cell tel. 876/827-1558 or 876/531-4508, halfmoonbeach1@hotmail.com, www.abingdonestate.com) just east of Rhodes Hall Plantation. Half Moon is a great place to come for a more low-key alternative to Negril's often-crowded Seven-Mile Beach.
    Half Moon Beach Bar & Grill (7 A.M.–10 P.M. or until the last person leaves the bar) serves breakfast, lunch, and dinner in a laid-back beach shack setting, with typical Jamaican favorites as well as creative international fusion like shrimp with pineapple, sweet pepper kabob, seafood crepes, and lobster on the menu (US$5–18).
    Accommodation is offered at Half Moon Beach in a number of cabins (cash only). Coconut Cabin (US$65) is a one-bedroom with a bathroom, ceiling fan, and mini fridge. Blue Moon Cabin (US$75) has two bedrooms that share a bathroom, sleeping up to four, plus ceiling fans and mini fridge. Seagrape I (US$65) and Seagrape II (US$65) each have one bed and bath with ceiling fans; they share a balcony. Half Moon Beach is one of the few places in Jamaica ideal for camping for those with their own tent (US$15).
    Half Moon Beach is a great location for weddings, and the reefs offshore make for great snorkeling.
    Rhodes Hall Plantation (tel. 876/957-6883

or 876/957-6422, rhodesresort@comcast.net, www.rhodesresort.com, US$95–340) sits on a 223-hectare estate adjacent to Orange Bay. Far enough removed from the hustle and bustle of Negril to feel neither the bass thumping at night nor the harassment during the day, Rhodes Hall has enough outdoor activities to not feel like you're missing anything either. The most recent addition to the list is the Rhino Safari on inflatable speedboats that will take you to cruise Seven-Mile Beach in no time. Other activities include horseback riding, hiking, and birding. A variety of modern, comfortable rooms, suites, and villas all have verandas with views out to sea. Satellite TV, air-conditioning, cell phones, queen-size beds, and hot water are standard. Ignore the floral bedcovers and focus on the woodwork and bamboo detailing, much of which was handcrafted from materials sourced on the property. Rates vary depending on size and amenities, which include three bathrooms, full kitchen, dining room, and whirlpool tub in the largest villa.

Savanna-la-Mar and Vicinity

Along the route from Negril to Savanna-la-Mar, the hills open up a few kilometers east from the beach to vast alluvial plains along Cabarita River that sustain Jamaica's largest sugarcane crop, processed at Frome. Small communities like Negril Spot and Little London dot the route and offer little excuse to stop. A turn off the main road in Little London leads to Little Bay, one of Jamaica's most laid-back beach towns, which is predominantly the keep of small-scale fishermen.

LITTLE BAY AND HOMER'S COVE

About 1.5 kilometers farther east from Homer's Cove is Little Bay, another rootsy fishing village relatively untouched by the outside world. Little Bay was a cherished retreat for Bob Marley, who would come to escape the pressures of Kingston and his burgeoning career.

Accommodations

Purple Rain Guest House (call Cug, pronounced "Cudge," cell tel. 876/425-5386, or book through Donna Gill Colestock at U.S. tel. 508/816-6923, greenbiscuit03@hotmail.com) is a small cottage set back from the beach owned by Livingston "Cug" Drummond. It's a basic cottage with two rooms in the downstairs and a loft with ceiling fans and lukewarm water. Rates are US$60 per person or US$400 per week, which includes two meals a day.

◖ Tansobak Seaside Cottage (U.S. tel. 608/873-9391 or 608/873-8195, mmoushey55@aol.com, www.littlebaycottages.com) is a tastefully appointed accommodation a few meters from the water's edge in Little Bay. It has simple but comfortable decor, louvered windows, tiled floors, and hot water. Air-conditioning is available by request. Denis and Michelle Dale have owned the property since the mid-1990s. Rates run US$665 per person per week, which includes two meals a day. There is a minimum three-night stay for double occupancy.

Coral Cove Resort & Spa (2 Old Hope Road, U.S. tel. 217/649-0619, cell tel. 876/457-7594, cclbayj@yahoo.com, www.coralcovejamaica.com, US$250–330 d all-inclusive) is a lovely five-acre property with a quarter mile of ocean frontage and 16 well-appointed rooms that have en suite bathrooms and wooden furniture. Beds are mostly king-size with a few queen and twin setups available. The property does a lot of wedding business and places an emphasis on fine cuisine. The family members who run the hotel go back and forth between Jamaica and their home in Illinois. Steven Zindars bought the land and started building in 1997 and opened the rental business in 1999, later buying an adjacent piece of land to expand toward Homer's Cove in 2004.

Food

Tiki's Guinep Tree Restaurant & Bar (in front of Uncle Sam's, tel. 876/438-3496, 10 A.M.–9 P.M., US$3.50–5), run by Vernon "Tiki" Johnson, is a favorite with locals. It serves dishes like stewed conch, fried fish, fried chicken, and jerk pork, accompanied with rice and peas or french fries.

Uncle Sam's Garden Park (next to sea, tel. 876/867-2897, US$1–3), run by Tiki's uncle, Samuel "Uncle Sam" Clayton, serves fried chicken, fried fish, and conch soup.

BROUGHTON BEACH

Broughton Beach is a secluded eight-kilometer-long beach reached by taking a right at the gas station in Little London, followed by a left at the T junction. Keep left at the Y junction and you will come to the parking lot of the Lost Beach Hotel on Brighton Beach. It is principally a fishing beach, but it has nice, fine white sand and an open expanse free of peddlers and hustlers.

Blue Hole Mineral Spring (Brighton, cell tel. 876/860-8805, www.blueholeinjamaica.com, 9 A.M.– 11 P.M. Mon.–Thurs., 9 A.M.–2 A.M. Fri.–Sun.) is a sink hole mineral spring located along the coast in Brighton suitable for jumping and swimming. A manmade swimming pool is fed with mineral water from the spring, and a bar keeps visitors cool, even if they're not inclined to jump into either pools.

SAVANNA-LA-MAR

Savanna-la-Mar, or simply Sav, as it is commonly referred to by locals, is one of the most subdued parish capitals in Jamaica in terms of attractions, with a few notable exceptions—namely the annual Curry Festival held in July behind Manning's School, and Western Consciousness, held in April at Paradise Park on the eastern outskirts of town. A free concert and symposium are also held in Sav every year in October to commemorate the life of the late Peter Tosh, who was born a few kilometers away in Grange Hill.

Sights

Manning's School, the most architecturally appealing building in town, is one of Jamaica's oldest schools, established in 1738 after local proprietor Thomas Manning left 13 slaves with land and what it could offer as the endowment for a free school. Now serving as a high school, the attractive wooden structure (built in late-colonial style in 1910 on the site of the original school) is backed by newer, less stylish concrete buildings set around a large field.

◖ Roaring River and Blue Hole Garden

Ten minutes from Savanna-la-Mar off of the B8, Roaring River and Blue Hole Garden (tel. 876/446-1997, 8 A.M.–5 P.M. daily) make for a good day trip from Negril or Bluefields. The Roaring River cave guided tour costs US$5 per person. Expect to be aggressively approached as soon as you near the main building for the site. Tipping the guide is also expected.

If you are headed for the Blue Hole, the real highlight of the park, continue farther up the road to the Lover's Cafe and guest cottages provide access to Blue Hole Garden (US$7). The Blue Hole is one of Jamaica's most spectacular subterranean springs, welling up in a refreshing turquoise pool.

◖ Mayfield Falls

The Original Mayfield Falls (tel. 876/610-8612 or cell tel. 876/457-0759, info@mayfieldfalls.com, www.mayfieldfalls.com) operates a four- to five-hour tour costing US$85 per person, inclusive of roundtrip transportation from Mobay, entry fee with a guided hike up the river, and lunch afterward. The entry fee is significantly lower (US$15) for those with their own transportation, inclusive of guide. Lunch may be purchased separately (US$10–22). Located in Flower

NEGRIL

© OLIVER HILL

The current at Mayfield Falls can send you scampering for the banks.

Hill near the Hanover border, Mayfield Falls is one of the best waterfall attractions in Jamaica, having been developed with minimal impact to the natural surroundings. It's a great place to spend an afternoon cooling off in the river and walking upstream along a series of gentle cascades and pools. Run by Sarah Willis, the guided tour begins and ends at a group of buildings that house a gift shop and restaurant. Rubber Crocs shoes are rented for US$6 for those without their own waterproof footwear.

Mayfield Falls can be reached from either the North or South Coasts. From the North Coast, turn inland before crossing the bridge at Flint River on the eastern side of Tryall Estate and follow Original Mayfield signs. From the South Coast, turn inland in Sav, keeping straight ahead at the stoplight by the gas station on the east side of town rather than turning right toward Ferris Cross, and head straight toward the communities of Strathbougie, then take a left off Petersfield main road toward Hertford at the four-way

intersection. From Hertford, head toward Williamsfield and then to Grange, before making a right in the square to continue on for about 10 minutes to the settlement of Mayfield. You'll see a sign on the right indicating the entrance to Mayfield Falls. The road from the north passes through Flower Hill before you see the Original Mayfield sign on the left.

Paradise Park

Paradise Park (tel. 876/955-2675, paradise1@cwjamaica.com, US$40) is one of the best places in Jamaica for down-to-earth small-group rides on an expansive seaside cattle ranch located a few kilometers east of Savanna-la-Mar in Ferris Cross. Tours are offered for a maximum of 10 riders. The 1.5-hour ride covers diverse scenery, and the price includes complimentary soft drink, while lunch can be prepared for groups of six or more (US$12 per person). For those not interested in horseback riding, the park features a lovely picnic area with a barbecue

NEGRIL

© OLIVER HILL

The beach at Paradise Park is among the few pristine stretches of white sand left in Jamaica.

grill, bathrooms, and a gentle river suitable for a refreshing dip (US$5).

Accommodations and Food

Blue Hole Garden (contact property manager cell tel. 876/401-5312) has a handful of basic cottages (US$40–50), the nicest of which, Lover's Nest, sits right over Roaring River. There is also a large house (US$80) up on the hill, which has a full kitchen and TV.

The Ranch Jerk Centre cooks up Boston-style jerk on the western side of Sav.

Sweet Spice (Barracks Rd., beside new bus park, tel. 876/955-3232, US$4.50–7.50) serves fried chicken, curry goat, oxtail, and fish fillet.

Devon House I Scream is at 104 Great George Street, across from the post office (tel. 876/918-1287, daily 11 A.M.–9 P.M. Mon.–Thurs., 11 A.M.–11 P.M. Fri.–Sun.).

Hammond's Pastry Place (18 Great George St., tel. 876/955-2870, 8 A.M.–6:30 P.M. Mon.–Fri., closing at 8:30 P.M. on Saturday) serves patties, cakes, and deli sandwiches.

Hot Spot Restaurant (23 Lewis St., contact manager Elaine Jagdath, cell tel. 848-6335, 7 A.M.–8 P.M. Mon.–Sat., US$2.25–4.50) serves local dishes like fried chicken and curry goat. It is perhaps more mediocre than hot, but good enough to fill your belly in a crunch.

One Blood Illusion Night Club, on the outskirts of town heading toward Ferris Cross and Cave, may be the most happening nightspot in Sav, typically open on weekend nights.

Services

Shopper's Choice Wholesales & Retail has three locations in Sav (Queen St., tel. 876/955-2702 or 876/955-9645; 12 Brooks Plaza, tel. 876/955-2936; and Llandilo Rd., tel. 876/918-0620 or 876/918-1482).

Del-Mar Laundromat is at 2 Queen Street (tel. 876/918-2105).

Carlene (tel. 876/955-8078, cell tel. 876/872-9080 or 876/378-7853) runs a spa at her home and is trained in deep tissue and Swedish massage and reflexology (US$60/

WESTERN CONSCIOUSNESS

Conscious Reggae is back in the limelight after nearly 20 years in the backseat – thanks to steadfast artists and promoters like Worrel King who have stood by the principles established by the genre's early pioneers. Starting around the time of Bob Marley's death in 1981, the reggae industry was taken over by dancehall artists like Shabba Ranks and Yellowman. The style of these artists' lyrics signified a departure from roots reggae, with its messages of truth and progress, to an often violent and sexually explicit form of music that became known as "slackness." When Peter Tosh was killed six years later in 1987, dancehall had taken over, and conscious reggae music was like yesterday's news. It was around that time that Worrel King founded King of Kings Promotions to try to rescue the truth from the mire.

King of Kings hit the ground running in 1988, organizing a very successful event at Titchfield High School in Port Antonio dubbed Eastern Consciousness, which showcased several artists, all of whom displayed some conscious leaning. "It was to attract people who needed to be uplifted, rather than just wasting away gyrating," King says. After a second successful Eastern Consciousness the following year, King took the event to Westmoreland, the parish of his birth, where he says the people were yearning for it. King describes his work as being guided by the hand of the Most High Jah, but says it has not been an easy road as consciousness is not something that sells easily. Nevertheless, the success of these early conscious stage shows has been mirrored in a multitude of other annual events inspired directly or indirectly by Eastern Consciousness. These include East Fest, held in Morant Bay and organized by Morgan Heritage,

and Rebel Salute, held at the Port Kaiser sports ground in Saint Elizabeth and organized by Tony Rebel. Both events have a decidedly "conscious" theme rarely challenged by the invited performers. "I look at artists that have been depicting consciousness," King says, "I don't look only at the hardcore consciousness, but at those who have the repertoire of conscious songs – even Beenie Man has a good 40-minute set that depicts consciousness – he performed at Western Consciousness as Ras Moses – it's not just those artists that are hardcore roots."

In 2006, King succeeded in bringing producer/performer extraordinaire Lee Scratch Perry back to Jamaica to perform for the first time in decades. King says he was termed a madman when he first suggested bringing Scratch home to perform, not any less given that many consider Scratch himself mad. After meeting with Scratch and his manager wife however, King said, "If he was mad that was the kind of madness I wanted to work with."

King has also created other concert events, including Tribute, dedicated to Peter Tosh. The free event held yearly in Sav's Independence Park is meant to showcase reggae sanity. In addition to the concert there is a Peter Tosh Symposium at the University of Westmoreland, which looks at the intellectual side of Peter Tosh and also highlights the work of other artists such as Burning Spear and Lee Scratch Perry. The event has drawn attendees from the highest levels, including finance minister Omar Davies, a self-proclaimed Tosh scholar. The Tribute concert is held on the Saturday closest to Peter Tosh's October 19 birthday, with the symposium held the previous Saturday.

hour). She can also be convinced to come to you if you're staying in the area.

WESTMORELAND INTERIOR

Beyond Mayfield Falls, which has grown into a favorite ecotourism attraction, the interior of Westmoreland sees few visitors. Nevertheless, there are a few notable cultural

and agricultural attractions, namely Seaford Town, reached via the South Coast from Ferris Cross.

Border Jerk (11 A.M.–10 P.M. daily, US$5–12), located in Mackfield, Westmoreland at the Hanover border along the B8 heading toward Montego Bay from Ferris Cross, is a notable jerk pit owned by Clive McFarlane (cell tel.

876/542-1852), who opened the business in 2004. It serves jerk chicken, pork, festival, and breadfruit. There's also a bar on-site.

Sights

Seaford Town is a cultural anomaly deep in the hills of Westmoreland. Founded in 1835 under a township act aimed at populating Jamaica's interior with Europeans, Seaford Town became the isolated home for 249 individuals transplanted from Germany. Jamaica's landed elite had feared the country's interior would be captured or settled by slaves, who were to be given full freedom in 1838. Baron Seaford thus allocated 202 hectares of his Montpelier Mountain Estate to the cause, and Jamaica's first German township was soon founded. The immigrants didn't find in Jamaica exactly what they had expected, however, and many died within the first weeks due to food shortages and their vulnerability to tropical diseases. The majority survived, however, adopting Jamaican food and customs and all but losing their connection to their homeland.

To this day many residents in Seaford Town have a light complexion, Catholicism is still an important religion, and some residents can still recall a few words of German. A small museum in the center of town features the area's unique history. The African Caribbean Institute recently launched a project called The Seaford Town Community History Project with support from the German Embassy to produce a comprehensive history of the community from 1835 to the present, including an audio documentation as part of the Jamaica Memory Bank (JMB).

To get to Seaford Town, head east in Mackfield toward Struie, continuing straight through Lambs River.

Bluefields and Belmont

This stretch of Westmoreland coast is as laidback and "country" as Jamaica gets, with excellent accommodation options and plenty of seafood. Bluefields public beach has more locals on it than tourists, with shacks selling fried fish, beer, and the ubiquitous herb. The windfall of jobs and revenue that Butch Stewart and the Jamaican government were to bring to the area from the opening of another monstrous all-inclusive resort, Sandals Whitehouse, has hardly materialized, as the guests are not encouraged to venture off the compound and rarely do so.

History

The stretch of coast around Bluefields has a rich history. One of the three earliest Spanish settlements, named Oristan, which was initially based in Parottee, St. Elizabeth, and later moved to present-day Bluefields. Oristan was connected by road to Sevilla la Nueva, the Spanish capital just west of present-day St. Ann's Bay, as well as to Santiago de la Vega, in present-day Spanish Town. The area was favored by the Spanish under early colonial rule, and later, the pirate Henry Morgan departed from Bluefields Bay to sack Panama in 1670. Still later, it was the spot Captain Bligh landed after finally successfully completing his charge of bringing breadfruit to the island from Tahiti. What is said to be the original breadfruit tree in Jamaica was taken down by Hurricane Ivan in 2004 and sits in a pile of cut-up pieces on one side of the lawn at **Bluefields Great House.** Pimento, or allspice as it's known in many places, was an important cash crop in the area, at some point having been replaced by marijuana in importance for the local economy.

SIGHTS

Bluefields Beach is a popular local hangout and sees very few tourists. It has fine white sand and is lined with vendors. Music is often blasted on weekends when the beach fills up.

Bluefields Great House, located about 0.4 kilometer inland from the police station, on the road to Brighton, was the home of many of the area's most distinguished temporary inhabitants, including Philip Henry Goss, an English ornithologist who resided in Jamaica 1844–1846, subsequently completing the work *Birds of Jamaica, a Naturalist's Sojourn in Jamaica.*

The **Peter Tosh Memorial Garden,** where the remains of this original Wailer lie, is worth a quick stop, if only to pause amid the ganja seedlings to remember one of the world's greatest reggae artists. An entrance fee is assessed (US$5) when there's someone around to collect it. Otherwise the gate is unlocked and a quick visit usually goes unnoticed. In mango season the yard is full of locals fighting over the heavily laden branches. Peter Tosh was born in nearby Grange Hill before making his way to Kingston, where he became one of the original three Wailers along with Bob Marley and Bunny Livingston. His mother still lives in Belmont.

RECREATION

The Bluefields area is the perfect place for activities like hiking, swimming, snorkeling, and relaxing. Nobody is touting parasailing or Jet Skis, and the most activity you will see on the water are catamarans crossing Parker's Bay off the Culloden shoreline from Sandals Whitehouse. There's a good horseback riding operation within a 15-minute drive at the expansive beachside **Paradise Park** estate (tel. 876/955-2675, paradise1@cwjamaica.com, US$40 per person) to the west in Ferris Cross.

ACCOMMODATIONS
Under US$100

Brian Wedderburn has a **Roots Cottage** (cell tel. 876/384-6610, US$30) at his yard in

Bluefields Beach is the most utilized public beach on the South Coast, where residents of Belmont and Bluefields spend many a Sunday.

© OLIVER HILL

Belmont with a little fridge, fan, and bathroom with cold water.

Belmont Garden Cottages (contact Damian "Juicy" Forrester, cell tel. 876/425-2387 or tel. 876/955-8143, US$30) has six cottages, with private baths, one with hot water. All have standing fans, TV, stove, fridge, and microwave.

(Rainbow Villas (tel. 876/955-8078, cell tel. 876/872-9080 or 876/378-7853, info@rainbowvillas-jamaica.com or rainbowvillas@cwjamaica.com, www.rainbowvillas-jamaica.com, US$25 s, US$45 d), owned and managed by the stunning Carlene and her German husband Ralph, is located across the road from the water along a little lane adjacent to Sunset Paradise Bar & Grill. The spacious and clean rooms have ceiling fans and kitchenettes, hot water, and air-conditioning. Carlene has a spa on property specializing in deep tissue and Swedish massage and reflexology (US$60/hour).

US$100-250

Shafston Great House (contact Frank Lohmann, cell tel. 876/869-9212, mail@shafston.com, www.shafston.com) is one of the few plantation great houses that you can actually stay in. Set on a hill overlooking Bluefields Bay, Shaftson has a large pool and rooms that range from basic with shared bath (US$140 d) in the side building, to suites in the Great House with hot water in private baths (US$180 d). Rates include meals and drinks. Frank also offers transfers from the airport in Mobay (US$75).

(Horizon Cottages (cell tel. 876/382-6384, info@barrettadventures.com, www.carolynscaribbeancottages.com, US$110, three-night minimum stay, fourth night is free) define rustic elegance, with two perfectly situated wooden cottages on Bluefields Bay. Each cottage is tastefully decorated with local artwork and has classic wooden louvered windows, queen-size beds, soft linens, attached bath with private outdoor showers, and cute, functional kitchens. The porch steps of **Sea Ranch** descend onto the small and beautiful private white-sand beach, and a pier off

the manicured lawn makes the perfect dining room and cocktail bar. **Rasta Ranch** is a slightly larger cottage set farther back in the yard. Kayaks and snorkeling gear are on-hand for excursions to the reef just offshore. Property manager Carolyn Barrett is a seasoned tour operator who runs Barrett Adventures, one of the island's best outfits, and can accommodate the interests of every kind of adventure seeker. Horizon's main house was the first built on the waterfront in the area. Wireless Internet, hot water, and gentle lapping waves make Horizon a very hard place to leave. The property owners also control Blue Hole Garden on Roaring River, 20 minutes to the west.

Over US$250

Bluefields Villas (tel. 202/232-4010, fax 703/549-6517, vacations@bluefieldsvillas.com, www.bluefieldsvillas.com) are easily the area's most luxurious accommodation option, and among the most scrupulously maintained villas in Jamaica. If you've ever had the desire to feel like royalty, there is no better place than **The Hermitage** (US$5,600/8,400 weekly low/high season). Antique furniture and four-poster beds, seamlessly integrated with the classic design of the spacious villa, seem to have been specially created for a neocolonialist emperor. A large sundeck off the dining room looks over the sea, while the next dining room door opens over a tiled pool. The "silent butler" is never far off to deliver anything you might require, and delicious food is served at mealtimes with the utmost attention to presentation and form.

San Michele (a Bluefields Villas property), 1.5 kilometers down the coast, is another gorgeous villa from the set. It has a small island perfect for enjoying the area's spectacular sunsets with cocktail in hand, connected to the lawn by a narrow bridge.

FOOD

Judge Beer Joint (just west of Kd's, tel. 876/385-5184), run by Eugene "Judge"

© OLIVER HILL

The Hermitage is among the finest villas in Jamaica, with impeccable service and unparalleled sea vistas.

Stephenson, serves steamed or roast fish (US$6–7/lb.), and fish tea (US$1 per cup).

Sunset Paradise Bar & Grill (across from Kd's, tel. 876/955-8164) is owned by Quashi and serves drinks around a nice rustic bar, as well as Jamaican staples like stewed chicken (US$3). Quashi's cousin Patrice can usually be found behind the bar.

Kd's Fish Pot (on the water 50 meters east of the Peter Tosh Memorial Garden) has been in business since 1973. Opening hours are not regular. Kd died in 2008, but his girlfriend still runs the place and cooks in the afternoons, depending on supply of fish and demand from customers. A small stage setup on the waterfront is sometimes used for events.

Fresh Touch Restaurant (Bluefields Beach Park, contact owner Otis Wright, cell tel. 876/870-6303, or manager Pearl Stephenson, cell tel. 876/357-0875, 6:30 A.M.–10 P.M. daily) serves steamed, roasted, and fried fish, as well as other coastal staples like fish tea, lobster, fried chicken, and curry goat, all served with a side of rice and peas. On Sundays and holidays Bluefields Beach Park is the most happening scene on the South Coast.

WHITEHOUSE

A quiet seaside community, Whitehouse has developed into a favored community for Jamaicans returning after years of working abroad, thanks to a few developers who've built subdivisions and sold off lots and homes. The nicest beach in the area, Whitehouse Beach, was cordoned off and annexed by the last Sandals to be built in Jamaica.

Recreation

Brian "Bush Doctor" Wedderburn (cell tel. 876/384-6610), also known locally as Rasta Brian, leads **hiking excursions** (US$10 per person) into the hills to learn about local flora and fauna.

Fishing excursions can be organized by Lagga or Trevor, who can be contacted through Carolyn Barrett, manager of Horizon Cottages and owner of Barrett Adventures (tel. 876/382-6384, info@barrettadventures.com).

Reliable Adventures Jamaica (tel. 876/955-8834, cell tel. 876/421-7449, wolde99@yahoo.com, www.jamaicabirding.com) organizes community tours as well as birding, hiking, and marine excursions with local fisherman, led by Wolde Kristos. One-day bird tours run US$85 per person including lunch.

Accommodations

Natania's (tel. 876/963-5349, cell tel. 876/883-3009, nataniasjamaica@yahoo.com, www.nataniasjamaica.com, US$80–100) is run B&B-style with eight double-occupancy rooms, some facing inland, the others out to sea. Rooms have either two single beds or one king-size. Owner Veronica Probst took the name Natania from the names of her two daughters, Natalie and Tania. Veronica has run the place since 1983. The property sits on the waterfront overlooking Parker's Bay. Food is prepared to order. Amenities include direct TV, a pool, and sandy ocean access with a seaside gazebo.

Culloden by the Sea is a large subdivision development just west of Whitehouse. Several repatriated Jamaicans have built houses there to retire to and a few of them rent as nice, low-key guesthouses. **Sierra-la-Mar Villa** (Lot #150, Culloden-by-the-Sea, contact Garth Lee at tel. 876/963-5922, cell tel. 876/841-2299, garthlee1@cwjamaica.com, www.sierralamar.com, US$1,790 weekly for up to 12 people or US$900 weekly for exclusive rental of the entire house for two guests) is a nice six-bedroom villa perched high on the hill overlooking Whitehouse. Sierra-la-Mar has a three-day minimum year-round. Amenities include satellite TV, washer/dryer, fully equipped kitchen, air-conditioning in bedrooms, private pool and deck with a beautiful view, and Wi-Fi.

FantaSea (Culloden by the Sea, contact manager Marcia Laird, cell tel. 876/383-5347, or owner Rudy Miller, U.S. tel. 973/214-1423, www.fantaseavilla.com, US$1,600 weekly for up to four adults) is a five-bedroom, four-bath hilltop villa with a little swimming pool, a wrap-around kitchen bar/counter, and verandas that take full advantage of the breathtaking

---

PEDRO BANK AND PEDRO CAYS

Nearly 100 kilometers offshore south of Bluefields Bay, the Pedro Cays form the surface of the Pedro Bank, one of Jamaica's few remaining unspoiled marine ecosystems. The Pedro Bank is a submerged mass about three quarters the size of mainland Jamaica, one of the largest banks in the Caribbean Basin, and provides a habitat for queen conch, which has historically been one of Jamaica's most important exports. Increased fishing is threatening the bank however, and an international conservation effort is underway to protect the unique marine habitat. Fishermen leave from points all along the South Coast for extended periods on the cays, usually returning with a lucrative catch to bring to market.

---

views. The villa can sleep a maximum of 12 people with a US$100 per week surcharge added for each additional adult. Bedrooms have air-conditiong, and the villa has internet and offers unlimited calls to the U.S. and Canada.

Ocean Air Guest House (84 South Sea Park Drive, contact owner/manager Marcia Palmer, tel. 876/389-9155, oceanairguesthouse@yahoo.com, US$43–71) has eight standard rooms and a suite with four queen-size beds. Rooms have queen-size beds, air-conditioning, and local TV. The pool overlooks the waterfront, and there is a small beach below the house. Meals can be arranged to order (US$5–20/person).

South Sea View Guest House (tel. 876/963-5172, run by Norman Forrester, cell tel. 876/404-6040, southseaview@yahoo.com, www.southseaviewjamaica.com, US$75–85) is a seaside guest house with king-size beds, air-conditioning, TV, and private bath. Much of the food served in the restaurant is grown on Norman's organic farm.

Sandals Whitehouse (U.S. tel. 800/726-3257, starting at US$790) took about 15 years to complete at a total cost of around US$110 million—among the most expensive hotels ever built and nearly double the initial budget estimates. At the high end of Sandals' many properties island-wide, the four-star Sandals Whitehouse features premium drinks, a variety of dining options, and a beautiful cabaret bar. Rooms have all the amenities you could ask for. The property is stunningly grand, designed like a European village with a large central courtyard and enormous pool with a wet bar. The beach is one of the best in the area. Day passes (US$85, good until 6 P.M.) and evening passes (US$80, 6 P.M.–2 A.M.) are also available, and the hotel also offers a full-day pass (US$130, 10 A.M.–2 A.M.). There's a two-night minimum stay.

C **Culloden Cove** (contact Andy McLean, tel. 876/472-4608, info@jamaica-holidayvilla.com, www.jamaicaholidayvilla.com, US$2,660–3,100 weekly low season, US$2,975–3,745 high season), located at the former home of the Culloden Café, received a complete refurbishment under new ownership in 2008, leaving the property in the immaculate condition of a top-notch villa. The property sleeps up to 10, six in the villa and four in a separate cottage. An infinity pool is located seaside, at the bottom of a sloping lawn extending from the main house, with a gazebo at the water's edge.

FOOD
C **Box Video Rental and Cook Shop** (Whitehouse Square, cell tel. 876/363-0091, 9 A.M.–3 P.M. daily, rent videos until 8 P.M.; food US$2–4) is a great food joint run out of a shipping container by enterprising Raquel "Keisha" Smith. Chicken and pork dishes come in three sizes. Fish is also cooked when it's available.

Ruby's 24/7 (Whitehouse Square, tel. 876/453-0003) serves typical Jamaican dishes around the clock, in a box to go or to stay.

Becky's (8:30 A.M.–11 P.M. Mon.–Sat., US$3–6), located about 100 meters farther west, serves typical Jamaican dishes like oxtail, fish, pork, curry goat, and fried chicken, as well as burgers and fries.

Jimmyz Restaurant and Bar (tel. 876/390-3477, Mon.–Sat. 6 A.M.–7 P.M., US$3.50–11) located at the local fishing beach and run by George "Jimmy" Williams, serves Jamaican breakfast items like ackee and saltfish accompanied by yam and boiled banana, with lunch and dinner dishes that include chicken and seafood staples. Fresh juices are also served.

Getting There and Around
Route taxis ply the coast all day long from Sav-la-Mar (US$2) and Black River (US$2) to Whitehouse. Karl (cell tel. 876/368-0508) is a JUTA-licensed driver based in the area who offers tours and taxi service.

MANDEVILLE AND THE SOUTH COAST

The parishes of Clarendon, Manchester, and St. Elizabeth make up the south-central part of Jamaica. It's *the* place to get away from the tourist hubs and see some of the country's farmland and less-frequented coastline. Locals in these parishes are less dependent on tourism and accordingly less pushy in soliciting business. While the region doesn't boast grandiose or glitzy resorts, the accommodations often make up for it with their rootsy charm, and there's still plenty of comfortable lodging options, especially in Treasure Beach, where villas and cottages range from rustic to unpretentious luxury. Languid fishing villages dot the St. Elizabeth coast, the most popular of which are found in Treasure Beach, and farther east in Alligator Pond, which straddles the St. Elizabeth–Manchester border. High above the plains, the cool air of Mandeville has been a draw in the heat of summer for centuries and is often referred to as the "retirement capital of Jamaica" for the number of repatriating Jamaicans who settle here. Over the past 50 years the bauxite industry gave Mandeville a strong economic base, while the 1970s saw the flight of many of the town's gentry during the Manley administration, when the prime minister's socialist lean drove fear into the wealthy class. The old moneyed families in Mandeville were somewhat replaced by an influx of nouveau riche, some allegedly owing to drug money, who have arrived over the past few decades to fill uptown neighborhoods with conspicuous concrete mansions. A lull in Jamaica's bauxite industry hit Mandeville especially hard after half the country's production ceased in early 2009. As the global economy recuperates and the world

© OLIVER HILL

HIGHLIGHTS

◖ **Lower Black River Morass:** As one of Jamaica's largest wetlands, this mangrove and swamp is home to a variety of unique animals and plantlife (page 307).

◖ **Pelican Bar:** Located on a sandbar about 1.5 kilometers offshore, this is the best place to spend an afternoon snorkeling and eating fresh fish (page 308).

◖ **Font Hill Beach Park and Wildlife Sanctuary:** An excellent beach park with a small, coral-lined, fine-sand beach and picnic facilities bordering miles of unspoiled coast (page 313).

◖ **Y.S. Falls:** The best-managed waterfall attraction in Jamaica offers swimming, tubing, and a heart-thumping zipline (page 314).

◖ **Bamboo Avenue:** A strip of road planted with giant bamboo groves shades jelly coconut and peanut vendors, making this a fantastic refreshment stop (page 315).

◖ **Appleton Estate:** Jamaica's most popular rum tour features the country's most important and timeless export at the distillery of its most recognized brand (page 317).

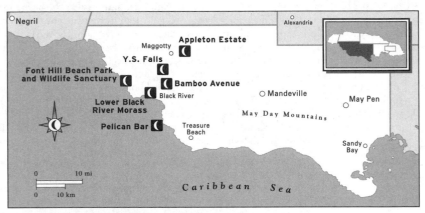

LOOK FOR ◖ TO FIND RECOMMENDED SIGHTS, ACTIVITIES, DINING, AND LODGING.

market price of aluminum rebounds, so too will Mandeville's economy. Independent of cash-flow considerations, the town's temperate climate and relatively well-developed infrastructure make it easy to forget you're in Jamaica. Mandeville boasts several noteworthy restaurants, making it a worthwhile place to stop for a bite on trips between Kingston and the South Coast. Other than that, it's not a place that keeps many tourists for any length of time, which makes it an attraction in itself for those seeking the "normal" Jamaican experience, not found so readily in Negril or Ochi where tourism dominates the economy.

PLANNING YOUR TIME

If your goal is to hit the main sights and take in a bit of the South Coast culture, a night or two in Black River, a few days in Treasure Beach, and a night in Mandeville is probably sufficient. Treasure Beach is one of those places where a certain type of person falls into the groove immediately and finds it very difficult to leave. Others find that the area is too popularly off-the-beaten path and prefer seafront communities that are even more sedate, like Black River, a few kilometers away, or Belmont and Little Bay in Westmoreland,

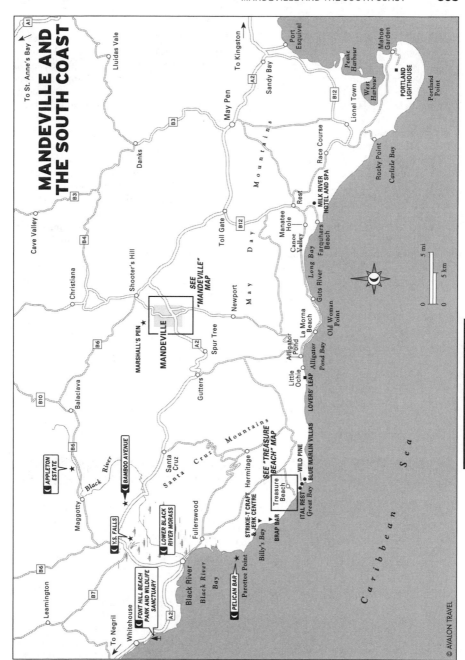

MANDEVILLE AND THE SOUTH COAST

MANDEVILLE

What is certain is that Treasure Beach has a unique feel with a land and people unto itself and the length of time visitors deem sufficient depends on how easy they are entertained by the rough-edged natural beauty that gives the area its charm. The immediate surroundings of Treasure Beach lend themselves to long walks, hiking in the Santa Cruz Mountains, boat rides, and cautious swimming.

Most people visiting the South Coast choose Treasure Beach as a base, making easy day trips to surrounding attractions. This is probably the best option with the most varied accommodation options, a hip-cum-chic vibe, and several beaches and unique scenery to enjoy. Decent accommodation options are also available in Black River farther west, but it's not a magnetic destination for most. Mandeville also has a smattering of decent hotels, and for those set on getting as much curative power as possible from the hot baths at Milk River, the hotel on-site has basic affordable rooms. Clarendon's capital, May Pen, also has a few decent hotels, but there is little here that draws visitors.

Both Treasure Beach and Black River make convenient bases for exploring the interior with attractions like Accompong Town, Appleton Estate, and Y.S. Falls all within about an hour's drive. Apart from laying low with the alligators and hanging out at Pelican Bar, there's little to keep visitors long in Black River.

SAFETY

Thankfully, Jamaica's South Coast is a welcome respite from the hustling that goes on in virtually every other area of the island that participates in the tourism industry. The most important dangers and annoyances in the region are accordingly more nature-oriented than human-related. Beaches along the South Coast are commonly deserted, and swimming alone is therefore not the safest activity, especially in Treasure Beach, where every year the list of drowned anglers seems to grow. The current and undertow in all the bays of Treasure Beach can be quite dangerous, and it's wise to ask the locals about conditions before getting too comfortable in the water.

Also related to the sea, there are times when jackfish contains high levels of toxins. It is better to avoid this fish altogether to be safe. Lobster is widely available on the South Coast and is the specialty at Little Ochie restaurant. Nevertheless, spiny lobster has a designated closed season (Apr.–June), established to protect the species from over-harvesting. The ban on lobster fishing during this time should be acknowledged and supported first and foremost by visitors to discourage any potential breach of the seasonal ban by fishermen—who ultimately are more prone to respond to the market rather than government regulations. It is illegal to land lobsters smaller than 76.2 millimeters, the established minimum size for a mature female.

Black River to Parottee

An important economic center in years past, especially for the export of logwood and mahogany, Black River is today a quiet literal and littoral backwater parish capital, with the main tourist attraction being the river at the heart of town that serves as the entry point into the Great Morass. There are a few popular tourism attractions within a half-hour's drive and plenty of forlorn stretches of mediocre beach just east of town along the coast toward Parottee. A few minutes west, Font Hill offers great swimming on a beautiful small tract of sand surrounded by coral reef. A few interesting buildings around town are worth a look, most notably Invercauld Great House.

SIGHTS

Invercauld Great House along the waterfront between town and the hospital is the most striking structure in Black River, with well-preserved Georgian architecture. The great house was built in 1894 by Patrick Leydon. It was for many years a hotel but has fallen out of use and sits idle within its gated compound.

© OLIVER HILL

Fishing boats idle on the Black River next to Irie Safari, where excursions depart into the morass for fishing and sightseeing.

Luana Orchid Farm (contact Dr. Bennett, cell tel. 876/361-3252, admission US$5) offers formal tours by appointment only to check out the 150,000-odd local and foreign orchid plants at the 1.5-acre farm. Dr. Bennett has bred several new varieties himself. The farm is located on the northern outskirts of Black River along the road between Black River and Middle Quarters, opposite Luana Sports Club and quarry.

Lower Black River Morass

The Lower Black River Morass is one of Jamaica's largest wetlands, with 142 square kilometers of mangrove and swamp providing a rich habitat for a variety of animal and plantlife. Turtles and crocodiles are still abundant, while manatees, once relatively common around the mouth of the river, are gone today. It's the largest remaining undisturbed wetland in the English-speaking Caribbean at 7,285 hectares. The Black River Morass has 113 species of plants and 98 species of animals. The Anchovy Pear *(Grias cauliflora)* of the Brazil

Nut family *(Lecythidaceae)* grows in the morass. Sawgrass, or razor grass *(Cladium jamaicensis)*, first described by botanists in Jamaica and thus given the Latin name *jamaicensis,* covers about 60 percent of the wetlands area. Sable palm *(Sabal jamaicensis)*, or thatch palm, is another wetland plant abundant in the reserve that was first described in Jamaica.

The crocodiles along the Black River are quite accustomed to being around people, to the point where many tourists think the ones sitting on the river's edge next to the restaurant are tame. While it's not recommended, some people swim in the same water as the crocs, which, according to one seasoned adventurer, are more afraid of us than we are of them. It's best to respect their space, however, and not give them the chance to prove they are anything but friendly.

The Black River and the Lower Black River Morass are best accessed by taking one of the river safari tours that start in the town of Black River, where three tours are offered from the river banks on pontoon boats.

MANDEVILLE

Black River Safaris

Charles Swaby's **Black River Safari** (tel. 876/965-2513 or 876/965-2086, jcsafari@ hotmail.com, www.jamaica-southcoast.com/ blackriver, US$16.50 adult, US$8.25 children), run by parent company South Coast Safari, has a pontoon boat tour up the Black River for 75 minutes with a commentary by the captain. Tours run daily at 9 A.M., 11 A.M., 12:30 P.M., 2 P.M., and 3:30 P.M. Swaby started the tour in 1987. Lunch is served at the Bridge House Inn and at Riverside Dock.

St. Elizabeth Safari (tel. 876/965-2374 or 876/361-3252, donovan.bennett07@yahoo. com, US$16 adults, US$8 children under 12) runs on the opposite side of the river, with local businessman Dr. Bennett operating a virtually identical 75-minute tour up the Black River.

Irie Safari (12 High St., tel. 876/965-2211, lintonirie@hotmail.com, 8:30 A.M.–5 P.M. Mon.–Sat., 9 A.M.–4 P.M. Sun.) offers a narrated tour on pontoon boats lasting 75 minutes (US$17 per person, minimum charge of US$40 per boat with two people). Proprietor Lloyd Linton is a wetland biologist who leads many of the tours himself. Irie is the smallest of the three tours, which can help avoid the long wait sometimes found at the competitors, which get more large groups. Irie Safari also offers sportfishing for tarpon and snook. The tour was established in 1993.

Lost River Kayak Adventures (www. lostriverkayak.com), also run by Lloyd Linton from the Irie Safari location, has two three-seater, four two-seater, and two single-seat kayaks. Tours venture into the upper reaches of the Black River, where there are blue holes suitable for swimming, birds that wouldn't be seen from a motorized craft, and no crocodiles, thanks to the fresh water. The tour lasts about two hours at US$40 per person.

◖ Pelican Bar

One of the most exceptional attractions in all of Jamaica, Pelican Bar is a ramshackle structure less than 1.5 kilometers offshore on a sandbar off Parotee Point. Run by the charismatic Denever Forbes, known by everybody as Floyde (cell tel. 876/354-4218), Pelican Bar serves drinks and cooks up excellent plates of fish (US$10) and lobster (US$15) accompanied by rice, bammy, or festival. The sandbar is an excellent spot to spend the day relaxing and snorkeling. The best way to reach the bar is by calling Daniel McLenon, known as Dee (cell tel. 876/860-7277), who offers round-trip shuttle service in his fishing boat (US$10 per person) from Parotee. Dee leaves from near his yard past Basil's, just after some houses with blue roofs. Turn right and park along a little lane that leads to the beach. Call Floyde before heading out to make sure he's around. Generally he keeps hours starting at 9 A.M. until the last customers are ready to leave in the evening. The bar is closed when bad weather requires. The only land tour operator servicing Pelican Bar on a regular basis is **Barrett Adventures** (contact Carolyn Barrett, cell tel. 876/382-6384), which offers transport from Mobay or Negril and can also arrange snorkeling equipment.

ENTERTAINMENT AND EVENTS

Calabash Literary Festival (www.calabashfestival.org) is a fun, free event held the last weekend in May at Jake's in Treasure Beach (tel. 876/965-0635, 800/OUTPOST (800/688-7678), jakes@cwjamaica.com, www. islandoutpost.com/jakes) that draws writers and attendees from across the Caribbean and African diaspora, as well as featuring some of Jamaica's own lyricists and authors.

Jake's Jamaican Off-Road Triathlon and Sunset Run (contact Tamesha Dyght, tel. 876/965-0748 or cell tel. 876/564-6319), organized by BREDs, sponsored by Jake's, and held the last weekend in April, consists of a 500-meter swim, a 15-kilometer mountain bike ride, and a seven-kilometer cross-country run. It draws Jamaicans from across the island as well as international competitors. The winner typically receives a weekend for two at a sponsoring hotel.

BREDS (Kingfisher Plaza, Calabash Bay, contact Sean Chedda, assistant project manager,

REBEL SALUTE

Rebel Salute is the most popular annual music event held in St. Elizabeth. It started out to commemorate the January 15 birthday of reggae icon Tony Rebel, who shares the same birthday as Martin Luther King Jr., as he's quick to point out. The first show was staged in 1994 in Mandeville, Manchester, and featured the late, great Garnett Silk, among a host of other artists. The successful annual event was moved to the Port Kaiser Sports Club in St. Elizabeth in 2000.

Rebel demands adherence to a strict no-alcohol, no-meat, no-degrading lyrics policy for the event, but patrons burn herb freely throughout the night, raising lighters to the air when their favorite artists "buss" a big tune. The show typically starts in the evening and lasts well past sunrise, with veteran concert-goers pitching tents to rest once in a while.

Among the more memorable acts was a two-hour performance in 2005 by Jimmy Cliff, during which "nobody moved, nobody got hurt" says Rebel of the crowd's fixation with the reggae all-star's performance. Burning Spear's Winston Rodney delivered a captivating performance the following year, with other notables to bless the stage including Beres Hammond, Barrington Levy, Sizzla Kalonji, Junior Gong, Taurus Riley, and Etana. In 2004, Junior Byles made a comeback performance after a long spell of mental illness, a miraculous recuperation Rebel attributes to the positive vibe of the show.

The mission, says Rebel, is to keep and preserve the healthy aspects of reggae music and to support community tourism along the South Coast, an undeveloped area people from all over the world should experience for its one-of-a-kind vibe.

Contact Tony Rebel (tony_rebel@hotmail.com, www.tonyrebel.com, www.flamesproductions.com) for more information and to purchase tickets. The annual event, held the closest Saturday to January 15, draws thousands of reggae fans from Jamaica and abroad, and typically features the more conscious artists of the genre.

Capleton performs at Rebel Salute, a highlight of the annual reggae event calendar, drawing thousands to the Port Kaiser Sports Club.

© OLIVER HILL

MANDEVILLE

tel. 876/965-0748, info@breds.org, www.breds. org, 9 A.M.–5 P.M. Mon.–Fri., 9 A.M.–1 P.M. Sat.) is a community-based organization engaged in community betterment activities and staging events. The nongovernmental organization (NGO) is currently involved in bringing a couple of benchmarking organizations to test for environmental integrity to keep the community green and sustainable. It is also working to have lifeguards posted along the beaches. The group has already trained lifeguards who are posted at Frenchman's Beach, one of the area's most notorious, which has claimed the lives of many locals. There is no reef protection at Frenchman's Beach, and thus the currents tend to be very strong. Jason Henzell, of Jake's, is the BREDS chairman.

BREDS also organizes the **Hook 'n' Line Canoe Tournament** held at the Calabash Bay Beach on Heroes weekend in October (second weekend of the month). The popular event starts on Saturday and goes into Sunday, when all the boats come in by noon to weigh in their catch. Whoever gets the largest fish (by weight) wins. Any kind of fish is fair game. Tourists may participate by renting boats. The entry fee is kept low (around US$7 per boat) to ensure that the event remains decidedly local. The top prize ranges from an inflatable boat with an engine (2006) to other fishing-related equipment in past years. Contact the BREDS office (tel. 876/965-0748) for details.

Little Ochie Seafood Festival (tel. 876/961-4618, thelkar@cwjamaica.com), held in August, is a definite must and worth traveling from the other side of the island for the lobster, fish, oysters, and cultural activities that range from traditional dance to popular reggae acts.

ACCOMMODATIONS
Black River
The options for staying in Black River are not highly varied. Most visitors come to town just for the day from either nearby Treasure Beach or Negril.

Waterloo Guest House (44 High St., tel.

876/965-2278, US$29–47) is really the only option in town. Once the home of English racehorse breeder John Leyden, who made the Waterloo the first building to have electricity in 1893, the amenities seem to have changed little since then. Basic rooms have ceiling fans, double beds or two single beds, and private bath. There are also rooms with queen-size beds, TV, and air-conditioning; some rooms have a small fridge and coffeemaker. The guesthouse has a popular restaurant and bar (7 A.M.–11 P.M. daily, US$2.50–7) serving chicken, pork, oxtail, fish, and fried rice.

East Toward Parottee Point
South Shore Guest House Bar & Restaurant (Crane Rd., tel. 876/965-2172) is wedged between the road and the beach with decent basic rooms facing the water (US$21 with fan, no hot water or TV; US$28 with TV, fan, and hot water; US$46 for two double beds, hot water, TV, and air-conditioning). South Shore is owned by Rose Williams.

Bridge House Inn (14 Crane Rd., tel. 876/965-2361, US$21–26) has 13 basic rooms with either fan or air-conditioning. Private bathrooms have hot water. A restaurant on the property (8 A.M.–10 P.M. daily) serves chicken, beef, pork chop, curry goat, and fish (US$3.50–6).

Port of Call Hotel (136 Crane Rd., tel. 876/965-2360, US$31–36) has a variety of rooms, some with one double bed, others with one double and one single. All rooms have private bathroom with hot water and air-conditioning.

Parottee Beach Resort (Crane Rd., tel. 876/383-3980) is a no-frills property toward the end of Parottee Point with four two-level buildings that have combinations of two rooms with two single beds or one king-size and two single beds (US$95). One half of the duplex suites can also be rented alone (US$50).

■ Idlers' Rest Beach Hotel (Crane Rd., tel. 876/965-9000, US$100 d), owned by attorney Courtney Hamilton, has spacious and well-decorated rooms with king-size beds and all the amenities (air-conditioning, ceiling fans, cable TV, mosquito nets) on a pleasant and quiet beachfront stretch along the road to Parottee Point.

Ocean View Restaurant and Resort Cottages (74 Crane Rd., tel. 876/634-4602, U.S. tel. 404/402-3257, njgravity@yahoo.com) owned by Neville Jackson, has a restaurant serving fish tea, vegetable soup, steam/escovitch/brown stew/fried fish, shrimp, conch, lobster, chicken, curry goat, and chow mien. Cottages are small and basic (US$50).

North Toward Middle Quarters
Ashton Great House & Hotel (tel. 876/965-2036, US$75), located just outside Black River along Central Road in Luana, has 22 rooms with hot water and air-conditioning. Meals are cooked to order for guests. The only negative is the dated linoleum floors in baths. Otherwise there are wood floors throughout, gorgeous views, and a sizable pool near a spacious covered area used for parties and functions. The house was built in the late 1600s by a sea captain, Earle from England, who married a Jamaican woman and raised hogs and cattle.

West Toward Whitehouse
Font Hill Villas Guest House (contact guesthouse manager Ian Blair, tel. 876/462-9011, US$40) has comfortable and well-appointed rooms, all of which have hot water, air-conditioning, and a kitchenette. Some have ceiling fans. This is a great place to get away from it all on the grounds of the expansive Font Hill Estate, with ample room for walking and hiking. The Font Hill Beach Park is just minutes away. The guesthouse was temporarily closed in 2009 and no reopening date is yet on the horizon.

FOOD
Northside Jerk Centre (5 North St., tel. 876/965-9855, 8 A.M.–7 P.M. daily, US$2.50–5) a.k.a. Alvin's Fish & Jerk Pork Center, serves fried curry, stew, jerk chicken, stew jerk pork, curry goat, and steamed, brown stew, and escovitch fish.

Tasty Foods (2 Market St., tel. 876/634-4027, 8 A.M.–9 P.M. Mon.–Sat., US$2.50–7) serves ackee and saltfish, salt mackerel, chicken (stew, fried, baked, and curry), cabbage, callaloo, oxtail, sliced brown stew fish, whole fish, garlic or curry shrimp, and fries. Eulalee Bennett runs the restaurant.

Tern's Cafe (tel. 876/965-2685 or 876/634-0084, 7 A.M.–11 P.M. daily, US$2–4.50) serves Jamaican dishes like escovitch fish, fried and baked chicken, curry goat, and pork and beans right along the waterfront in the heart of town. Tern's also sells Devon House and Nestle ice cream.

Bayside Restaurant and Pastry (19 North St., tel. 876/634-3663, 7 A.M.–9 P.M. daily, US$3.50) serves curry goat, stew pork, and fried chicken. Cakes are also served by the slice (US$1.25) or whole (from US$10). Dahlia is the helpful supervisor.

The Fish Pot Bistro and **Indies Irie Pizza** franchise (riverside on the Black River, adjacent to Riverside Dock, tel. 876/965-2211 or contact Lloyd Linton, cell tel. 876/472-4644; 9:30 A.M.–5 P.M. Mon.–Sat., US$6–15) predominantly serves fish: escovitch, steamed, and brown stew—fried and cooked back down in a sauce accompanied by rice, festival, or bammy. It also has curried or garlic shrimp, as well as jerk chicken at times, and lobster in season. Pizza is also served at the same establishment (US$6–20). Toppings include pepperoni, ham, ground beef, and pineapple.

Basil's Seafood Restaurant (cell tel. 876/369-2565, 7 A.M.–midnight daily, US$6.50–13) in nearby Parottee has good seafood. The restaurant serves excellent fish, conch, and lobster. Basil Bennett is the congenial proprietor.

Yellowtail Restaurant (1 Brigade St., tel. 876/634-1319, tel. 876/887-5160, 8 A.M.–11 P.M. Mon.–Sat., noon–9 P.M. Sun., US$3–15) serves good Jamaican fare with a menu that includes curry goat, cow foot, fried or curried chicken, stew beef, brown stew, and steamed fish and shrimp.

Cloggy's on the Beach (22 Crane Rd., tel. 876/634-2424, www.cloggys.com,

US$3–11) is the quintessential beachfront bar and restaurant, serving a range of dishes from chicken to steamed fish, brown fish stew, fried fish, and lobster. This is a great place to kick back and unwind, even if the beach along this stretch out to Parotee Point is a bit muddied by the mouth of the Black River.

Las Vegas Café (70 Crane Rd. 504-2396/373-1028, 11 A.M.–midnight, or until last person leaves) serves seafood including conch, shrimp, and lobster and typical Jamaican dishes to order (US$4.50–9).

Pelican Bar is the most interesting restaurant around, but it requires a boat ride to reach. It's offshore on a sandbar off Parotee Point. Run by Denever Forbes, known as Floyde (cell tel. 876/354-4218), Pelican Bar serves drinks and cooks up excellent plates of fish (US$10) and lobster (US$15) accompanied by rice, bammy, or festival.

The Barn Jerk Centre & Grill (107 Main St., thebarnjg@gmail.com, 11 A.M.–11 P.M. daily, US$4–20) is housed in a barn-like structure—keeping with its name—on the north side of the main road through Whitehouse. Jeffrey Jameison (cell tel. 876/583-9787 or 876/298-6599) opened the place in April 2009. The jerk center serves jerk chicken and pork, grilled shrimp and lobster, steamed and roasted conch and fish, conch soup, spare ribs, BBQ ribs, and jerk sausage.

Queen Diamond Sports Bar & Club has a pool table and TV. Peter Tennent keeps the joint open from 3 P.M. till you say when Thursday–Sunday, and on select Mondays. A shop next door to the sports bar sells Devon House Ice Cream out of a freezer.

Duke's Mile Post 99 (Main St., contact Boris "Duke" Samuels, cell tel. 876/584-0210, 2 A.M.–midnight daily, US$10–20) sits next to the road on a little rise unmistakably plastered with green Heineken branding. Founded in December 2006, it has a club license so it can go all night and usually goes till around 4 A.M. on Friday, Saturday, and Sunday nights, when selectors are brought in from the greater area to play mostly dancehall. A restaurant specializes in seafood dishes like lobster, shrimp, conch, octopus, and fish.

The bar makes for a good pit stop, as Duke welcomes passersby to come in, use the bathroom, and spend some money.

INFORMATION AND SERVICES

The **post office** (35 High St., tel. 876/634-3769) is open 8 A.M.–5 P.M. Monday–Friday. **DHL** is at 17 High Street (tel. 876/965-2651, 9 A.M.–5 P.M. Mon.–Sat.).

The Internet Shop (13 North St., tel. 876/965-2534, 10 A.M.–6 P.M., US$2.25/hour) has DSL Internet access. **Surf D Net** (12 High St., tel. 876/634-4535, 9:30 A.M.–6 P.M. Mon.–Fri., 10 A.M.–6:30 P.M. Sat.) also offers Internet access. The **St. Elizabeth Parish Library** (64 High St., 8:45 A.M.–5:15 P.M. Mon.–Fri., 8:45 A.M.–3 P.M. Sat.) also offers Internet service (US$1.50/hour).

The Globe Store (17 High St., tel. 876/965-2161) sells souvenirs and computer parts.

Both **NCB** (13 High St., tel. 876/965-2207) and **Scotiabank** (6 High St., tel. 876/965-2251) have branches with ATMs.

GETTING THERE AND AROUND

Black River is easily reached by route taxi from Sav-la-Mar in Westmoreland (US$3) or from Santa Cruz in St. Elizabeth (US$2). If you're driving, there's a dodgy but interesting road along the coast to Treasure Beach that's much shorter and not too much more potholed than the long way around. To take the coastal route, head over the bridge east of Black River along Crane Road and turn off the main road toward the water after passing the communications tower east of Parottee. A left turn at a Y intersection leads along the coast to Treasure Beach.

WEST OF BLACK RIVER
Scott's Cove

One of the best road stops along the South Coast, Scott's Cove on the Westmoreland–St. Elizabeth border has several stands with friendly competition between vendors of fried escovitch fish, conch soup, shrimp, and lobster. Check Ras Collie-Bud for an excellent cup of

conch soup or any of the vendors for escov-
eitch-style fried fish and bammy.

❰ Font Hill Beach Park and Wildlife Sanctuary

Owned and operated by the Petroleum
Corporation of Jamaica (PCJ), Font Hill has
a beautiful little coral-lined sandy beach (Ian
cell tel. 876/462-9011, 9 A.M.–5 P.M. daily, visitors can stay later, but no one is admitted after
5 P.M. and lifeguards are not on duty, US$5
adults, US$3 children) with picnic tables,
grills, and bathroom facilities. The beach attracts a predominantly local crowd and is busy
on weekends. Across the road, the Font Hill
estate extends deep inland.

The nature reserve is not officially open to the
public and the PCJ makes clear that those who
enter do so at their own risk. In addition to the
healthy birdlife found in the sanctuary, there's
quite a crocodile population. Not long ago, a sci-
entist member of a research team, with years of
observing the area's crocodiles under his belt, inadvertently stepped on one and received severe
gashes to his leg. Crocodiles are not generally aggressive, but avoid stepping on them at all costs.

Newmarket

Straddling the Westmoreland–St. Elizabeth border and best accessed by turning inland along
the road just east of Whitehouse and just west of
the South Sea Park subdivision, Newmarket has
the best weekly market in the area, generally held
on Mondays. When the incline levels out, turn
right to reach Newmarket, passing the striking
Carmel Moravian church sitting on a hill. It's
well worth stopping to have a look around. The
church is in a good state of repair with an impressive organ in its modest interior.

EAST OF BLACK RIVER

Middle Quarters is a favorite motorist stop,
where women line the road selling "pepper
swimps" (shrimp), and **Howie's HQ** (contact Howie Salmon, cell tel. 876/860-5733 or
876/860-5396, open 24/7) roadside restaurant
serves up typical Jamaican dishes out of huge
pots to motorists.

© OLIVER HILL

The escoveitch fish at Scott's Cove is a great reason to stop when passing through.

MANDEVILLE

Marcia Williams' Rasta-Colored Roadside Shop (tel. 876/363-7242, 10 A.M.–7 P.M. daily) is an excellent choice for fresh-out-the-pot swimps. Ms. Williams also serves beer at her shop and has a good fruit and vegetable stand out front.

Bubbling Spring (contact proprietor Lincoln Fagan, cell tel. 876/850-1606, 9 A.M.–6 P.M. daily, admission US$15) is a natural mineral spring impossible to miss thanks to the bright rainbow colors painted on the compound's outer walls, located along the main road on the western side of Middle Quarters. Patrons can take a dip in a small spring-fed pool of water said to have healthful properties, hang out, and sample food and drinks at the restaurant and bar. Visited predominantly by locals, Bubbling Spring hosts an annual "Swimps" festival in mid-October.

【 Y.S. Falls

Y.S. Falls (ysfalls@cwjamaica.com, www.ysfalls.com, 9:30 A.M.–3:30 P.M. Tues.–Sun., US$15 adults, US$7.50 children 3–15 years) on the Y.S. Estate is by far the best conceived and organized waterfalls destination in Jamaica. It's been operated by Simon Browne since 1991. The Y.S. River changes with weather—crystal clear blue normally, and swelling after rain in the mountains to make the perfect venue for tubing (US$6). There is a bar and grill on the property, as well as gift shops with an excellent array of books, crafts, and Jamaica-inspired clothing. There is also a swimming pool just below the falls.

A series of ziplines traverse over the falls (US$42) and is operated by Chukka Caribbean Adventures. It is a rush, to say the least, and perhaps the most exhilarating of Chukka's three canopy tours in Jamaica.

The origin of the name "Y.S." is somewhat disputed: one version is that it comes from the Gaelic word "wyess," meaning winding and twisting. The second version is that it comes from the last names of the two men who ran the estate in 1684, John Yates and Richard Scott, who branded the cattle and hogshead of sugar with "Y.S." The 3,238-hectare property was bought out of bankruptcy from the list of Encumbered Estates in London by

Howie's HQ is a favorite pit stop for Jamaican staples in Middle Quarters.

© OLIVER HILL

Simon's great uncle, John Browne, in 1887 for £4,000—without Browne ever having seen the estate. Some of the land was sold, leaving 809 hectares today where champion thoroughbred racehorses are bred and Pedigree Red Poll cattle graze the Guango tree–lined fields. Sugarcane production was discontinued in the 1960s.

The Y.S. River originates in Cockpit Country and is fed by many springs on its course to where it meets the Black River. A spring on the estate is the original source of water for the town of Black River, 13 kilometers downstream.

◖ Bamboo Avenue

One of the most beautiful four-kilometer stretches of road in Jamaica, running from Middle Quarters to West Lacovia, Bamboo Avenue is also known as Holland Bamboo. The stretch is lined with Jamaica's largest bamboo species, the common bamboo *(Bambusa vulgaris)*, brought from Haiti by the owners of the neighboring 1,780-hectare Holland sugar estate, which once belonged to John Gladstone (1764–1851). Gladstone went on to father 19th-century British prime minister William Gladstone. Bamboo Avenue provides shade for several jelly coconut and peanut vendors. On the eastern side of Bamboo Avenue is **Bamboo Ville,** a vibesy jerk center with big pots on open fires.

Lacovia

Just about all that's noteworthy about Lacovia, other than being the turnoff for Maggoty, Accompong, and Appleton Estate, are a few restaurants and a gas station.

Kingmon's Restaurant (tel. 876/966-6705 or cell tel. 876/425-6721, US$3.50–5.50), run by Kingsley and Monica, serves natural juices and Jamaican staples like baked and fried chicken, cow foot, curry chicken, and curry goat.

Tropical Jerk Center (contact proprietor Neville Douglas, tel. 876/845-3814, 9 A.M.– 10 P.M. daily) serves jerk chicken and pork, food, soup, and jerk and steamed fish next to the Texaco station.

© OLIVER HILL

Lined with bamboo to shade travelers, Bamboo Avenue is one of Jamaica's prettiest stretches of road.

Southern Cockpit Country

The interior of St. James, St. Elizabeth, Manchester, and Clarendon parishes is rugged terrain, much of it forming part of Cockpit Country, which blankets pitted limestone hills full of caves and underground rivers. As the impassible interior descends to the sea, ridged hills taper down around lush valleys, which have proved some of the most fertile in Jamaica. The Y.S. and Appleton estates remain prized lands. The **Nassau Valley,** where Appleton Estate is located, is still heavily planted in sugarcane to feed the healthy rum business.

From Maggoty the main road (B6) heads east, skirting a large wetland area fed by the upper reaches of the Black River before rejoining the main south coast "highway" (A2) just east of Santa Cruz. From Balaclava, a turn to the north (B10) leads deep into the interior to Troy and then Warsop, passing by Ramgoat Cave before hitting Clarks Town, Trelawny. North of Clarks Town the road emerges on the coast in Duncans. For extreme adventure-seekers, the **Troy Trail** is a challenging traverse of the most rugged part of Cockpit Country. The trail is best accessed with the help of a guide, which can be set up through the **Jamaica Caves Organization** (info@jamaicancaves. org, www.jamaicancaves.org).

Hiking excursions in the vicinity of Accompong can be arranged by contacting Maroon Colonel Ferron Williams (cell tel. 876/850-9567).

MAGGOTY

Apple Valley Park (contact Lucille Lee, cell tel. 876/487-4521 or 876/963-950, or Andrea, cell tel. 876/449-7718, www.applevaleypark. com, 10:30 A.M.–5 P.M. daily, reservations are imperative as the park is closed when none have been made) is one of those places where even locals aren't entirely sure whether it's open or not. Nonetheless, pedal-boating around a man-made pond, swimming pools, a cold-water whirlpool tub, rope swing, and picnic area make it a potentially entertaining affair. The

park offers a tractor tour and meals. Admission is US$8.50 adults, US$7 children under 12 with a jerk or fried chicken lunch included or US$5 adult, US$3.50 children for admission alone. Visitors may bring their own food. Four cabins on the property (US$14) offer basic accommodation for up to three persons with private baths and cold water.

Apple Valley Guest House (contact Lucille Lee, cell tel. 876/487-4521 or 876/963-9508) has slightly less basic double-occupancy rooms (US$36) than those at the park, with hot water in private baths and air-conditioning or fans available by request.

ACCOMPONG

Home of the Leeward or Trelawny Maroons, Accompong (derived from Achumpun, or Acheumpun, from the Twi language of Ghana) was named after a brother of the famous leader Cudjoe (Kojo) who signed a peace treaty with Great Britain that granted his people autonomy from the crown on March 1, 1738. In exchange for their sovereignty, granted 100 years before emancipation, and freedom for the rest of the black population, the Maroons were called on repeatedly by the British to assist in the suppression of slave rebellions and to help capture runaways. Accompong falls within the borders of St. Elizabeth Parish, but it's really outside the confines of any parish— the land occupied by the Maroons predates the establishment of parishes by the British. Today Accompong is led by Colonel Ferron Williams (cell tel. 876/850-9567), a police inspector with the Jamaica Constabulary Force elected for his first five-year term in 2009. It's best to check in with the colonel so he can anticipate your arrival, as he'll help with the logistics and ensure fair treatment by representatives of the community.

The best time to visit is for the annual **Accompong Maroon Festival** (Jan. 5–6), when the village comes alive with traditional

ACCOMPONG MAROONS

Jamaica's Maroons date back to the Spanish settlement of the island, when it came to be accepted that a fraction of the blacks brought from Africa as slaves would not succumb to live in perpetual subordination and would instead resist perpetually until granted their freedom. These so-called "runaway slaves" were termed "Cimarrones" by the Spaniards, a name later translated into English as Maroon. To name these warriors "runaway slaves" is to diminish the fact that not only did they flee the plantation, but they also beat into the most remote and mountainous regions of the island to claim land and hold it against assault. The Spaniards ultimately gave up in their attempt at putting down the Maroons, many of whom it is said descended from the warrior Ashanti people of West Africa. The British would also eventually sign a peace treaty with the Maroons in 1738, the legacy of which has left the Maroons with their sovereignty to this day. The Maroon treaty was signed by Cudjoe (Kojo), whose repeated defeat of British forces led to granting the Maroons privilege to large swaths of Jamaica's highlands. Large Maroon settlements grew in Accompong, St. Elizabeth, as well as in Moore Town in the Rio Grande River Valley, and above Buff Bay in Charles Town, Portland, and in Scott's Hall, St. Mary. Today the Maroons are still a force to be courted by those representatives of government who have Maroon lands within their constituencies. While the communities themselves have been largely diluted since emancipation, the warrior spirit of the Maroons has permeated Jamaican society at large, influencing social movements like the Rastafarians, who draw on their experience as rebels against the status quo to present an alternate worldview based on principles that can be traced through the Maroon heritage to Africa.

Maroon music and dance as well as stage shows more typical of the rest of Jamaica. During the rest of the year it's a great destination for getting some fresh air and spectacular views of a seldom-visited corner of St. Elizabeth. Guides from the community are available to take visitors to the cave (US$10/person) where the famous treaty was signed, as well to a few other important sights in the community, like a burial ground and the church where English names were given to the Maroons after emancipation.

◖ APPLETON ESTATE

Appleton Estate (tel. 876/963-9215 or 876/963-9217, fax 876/963-9218, appleton@ infochan.com, www.appletonrum.com, tour hours 9 A.M.–3 P.M. Mon.–Sat., US$22 admission includes a miniature bottle of rum) in Nassau Valley is one of the most popular tours in Jamaica and well worth a visit, both to sample the several grades of rum and to experience the most lush corner of St. Elizabeth and its impressive topography.

The distillery at Appleton Estate is run by Wray and Nephew, which makes Appleton's, Jamaica's best-known rum. To get there, turn inland off the A2 toward Maggoty in West Lacovia after passing through Bamboo Avenue from the west or Lacovia from the east. Where the road splits keep right, following well-marked signs for Appleton Estate.

SANTA CRUZ

A bustling transportation hub more than a destination of any note, Santa Cruz can get congested during the day; if you're just passing through there is a very useful bypass around the town center that saves a lot of time. Arriving from the east, veer right off the main road at the Y where the road splits at the Total gas station before getting to town. Take the third left to rejoin the main at the stoplight on the western edge of town. Arriving from the west, follow the reverse route: a left at the first stoplight, and then a right until the road meets the main at the Total station on the eastern edge of town. The dusty bus terminal parking lot in the heart of Santa Cruz is a good place to catch a route taxi for Treasure Beach, Black River, or Mandeville.

Entertainment and Shopping

Toxic Night Club (no phone, Thurs.–Sat.) in Leddister's Plaza is the best spot in town to get your groove on at night should you be stranded in Santa Cruz.

Record Mart (right before Singer in Santa plaza, tel. 876/966-2564) sells both domestic records and imports with plenty of reggae, R&B, and hip-hop.

Accommodations

Chariots Hotel (Leeds, tel. 876/966-3860, US$40–75) has a pool, restaurant, and bar. Heading west through Santa Cruz, turn left at the stoplight onto Coke Drive, pass RBTT bank and then NCB, four kilometers from Santa Cruz on the road to Malvern. The restaurant serves typical Jamaican dishes (US$4–8.50). All rooms have private bath, cable TV, air-conditioning, and floral-print bedcovers on either two double beds or one king-size bed. It's a decent, well-kept place. The more expensive rooms have hot water.

Kool Rooms Guest House (just west of the last stoplight in Santa Cruz, cell tel. 876/312-8735, tel. 876/387-9417, vernonbourne@yahoo.com, US$50) has four rooms with two queen-size or two double beds in each room with air-conditioning, cable TV, and en suite bathrooms with tub and shower. Run by roots rock reggae singer Vernon Bourne, a.k.a. Singing Vernon, the guesthouse is a good place for young travelers looking to unwind and kick back in rural St. Elizabeth. You're likely to "buck up" other popular reggae artists during your stay.

Food

Grills & Frills (39 Main St., across from Rapid True Value, tel. 876/966-3515, Mon.–Sat. 10 A.M.–10 P.M., US$3–4.50) serves Boston-style jerk chicken and pork and roast fish, as well as other Jamaican staples.

Miguel's Cafe (5 Jewel Close, tel. 876/966-4304, 8 A.M.–9:30 P.M. Mon.–Sat., until 10 P.M. Fri. and Sat., US$2.50–3.75) in the heart of town just below KFC has fried chicken, baked chicken, curry goat, stewed peas, and pork chops.

Hinds Restaurant & Bakery (Santa Cruz Plaza, tel. 876/966-2234, 7:30 A.M.–5 P.M. Mon.–Thurs., until 7 P.M. Fri. and Sat., US$4–6) has decent Jamaican dishes liked fried, stewed, and baked chicken, as well as oxtail, curry goat, stew pork, and escovitch fish.

Services

G-Link World Internet Cafe is at Shop #21, Jake's Plaza (tel. 876/966-4497).

NCB (7 Coke Drive, tel. 876/966-2204) and **Scotiabank** (77 Main St., tel. 876/966-2230) have small branches with ATMs.

Treasure Beach

Isolated from the rest of the island by the Santa Cruz mountains, which create the area's distinct coastal desert environment by capturing the westbound rainfall, Treasure Beach is a catch-all name for a series of bays and fishing villages that extend from Fort Charles at the greater community's western edge, to Billy's Bay, Frenchman's Bay, and Great Bay on the eastern edge of the community. Treasure Beach prides itself on offering a different kind of tourism than that found in Jamaica's more built-up tourist centers. Local ownership of the guesthouses and restaurants is more the rule than the exception, and it's impossible not to interact with Jamaicans in a more substantial context than being served your cocktail.

The earth in St. Elizabeth is a deep red, and the people, thanks to a mix of Scottish and African blood, also have a reddish complexion, often with striking blue or green eyes. These Jamaicans are commonly referred to as "red" by the rest of the island's population, with typical disregard for innuendos or connotations outsiders might deem politically incorrect. In spite of St. Elizabeth receiving the least rainfall on the island, the parish is known as Jamaica's "breadbasket," not for any grain produced there per se, but mainly for vast quantities of vegetables it sends across the island.

Many of the bays have decent swimming areas, but it's best to inquire with locals about the safety of jumping in the water at any particular point until you get accustomed to the area. Remain vigilant of rip tides and strong currents.

History

The light complexion generally seen in Treasure Beach and St. Elizabeth is said to owe to Scots who had unsuccessfully settled in Darion Point, Panama, and were forced to flee. It is said that William III sent word that the Scots were not to come into any port, so they beached their ships at Treasure Beach. Treasure Beach started to become an offbeat destination in the 1970s, and fortunately developed at a slow pace, giving the area a chance to define for itself an alternate approach that has been far more equitable for the community than other tourist destinations around Jamaica.

SIGHTS

As an off-the-beaten-track destination, the main appeal of Treasure Beach is the community itself and the infectious sleepy pace that permeates the area. Despite their laid-back nature, residents of St. Elizabeth pride themselves on being extremely hardworking, from the fishermen who spend days out at sea to the farmers who take great care in mulching and watering their crops to fight the perpetual drought. Despite the lack of differentiable sights of interest along the Treasure Beach coast itself, there are several worthwhile excursions within an hour's drive, many of which are around Black River. East of Treasure Beach along the coast there are also a few notable natural attractions.

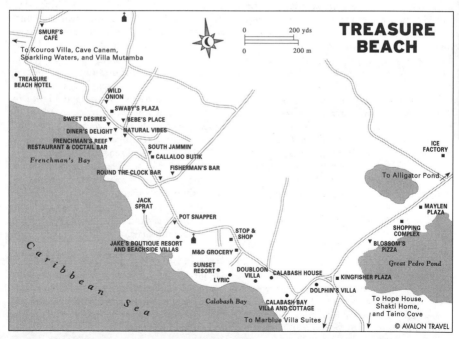

Lovers' Leap (Southfield, 9 A.M.–9 P.M. daily, closing later on Sun.) is a 480-meter drop to the sea less than 16 kilometers east of Treasure Beach along the coast. According to legend, a slave couple leapt to their deaths to avoid forced separation by their master, who was lusting after the girl. As the legend has it, an old woman who witnessed their leap said the moon caught them up in a golden net and they were last seen holding hands standing on the moon as it sank over the horizon. A lighthouse was built on the point in 1979 and can be seen from 35 kilometers out at sea. Admission is US$3, or support the bar and restaurant in lieu of admission.

Lovers' Leap Guest House (Southfield, tel. 876/965-6004, US$36 upstairs, US$50 poolside) has decent, basic rooms with double beds and private bath, hot water, air-conditioning, and ceiling fans.

ENTERTAINMENT AND EVENTS

If you're looking for wild all-night parties, Treasure Beach is probably not the best destination. Romantic sunsets and quiet nights are more the norm than live music. Nonetheless, a few venues see regular activity on weekends. Most of these venues operate as restaurants as much as nightspots.

Treasure Beach comes alive for annual events like Calabash Literary Festival and the Hook 'n' Line Fishing Tournament, with bonfires on the beach and roots reggae pumping from sound systems well into the night. Rebel Salute, a massive reggae concert held annually in mid-February in nearby Port Kaiser, is another exception to the rule of calm and quiet nights along the South Coast.

C South Jammin' (contact owner/manager Joe Isaacs, cell tel. 876/291-5364; open daily from 7 A.M. until the last person leaves, US$3–13) is a centrally located restaurant serving as a local hangout and nightspot with darts, billiards, and dominoes. Satellite TV and live music every weekend on Saturday and Sunday (9 P.M.–2 A.M.) are strong draws. Ladies' night on Friday (7–10 P.M.) avails two-for-one drinks for women.

Fisherman's Bar (cell tel. 876/379-9780) is a club open nightly with dancehall and roots reggae booming. A pool table and domino area around back are popular with locals, while the restaurant out front serves typical Jamaican fare at reasonable prices. The venue occasionally hosts live music.

Wild Onion (contact business manager Lurline Rhodes, tel. 876/965-3619, 3 P.M.–2 A.M. Tues.–Sun., US$4–7) is a bar and restaurant serving Jamaican lunch and dinner items like rice and fish, curry goat, vegetable pasta, pork, and chicken. As a nightspot Wild Onion contracts a selector on Friday, Saturday, and Sunday nights. In the high season the venue hosts live music once a month.

Brap Bar (Billy's Bay, 8:30 A.M.–midnight daily) comes alive in the evenings for poker and dominoes; enter the fray if you dare.

SHOPPING

Treasure Hunt Craft Shop (Old Wharf Road, tel. 876/965-3878, 9 A.M.–3 P.M. Mon.–Fri., 9 A.M.–1 P.M. Sat.), run by the **Treasure Beach Women's Group,** makes handcrafted items out of calabash and other local materials. The parent organization holds regular meetings and provides a forum for addressing issues affecting the community's matriarchs. Baskets, gourds, post cards, and the signature Star Light candle holders are other nice gift items sold at the shop. The group hosts a variety of events, from summer camps to bingo to fashion shows.

Callaloo Butik (Frenchman's district, cell tel. 876/390-3949, 9 A.M.–6 P.M. daily, www.callaloo-jam.com) is an upscale craft and souvenir shop run by Sophie Eyssautier, selling clothing, bags, jewelry, beach wraps, baby items, ceramics, and home decor, 100 percent of it made in Jamaica.

SPORTS AND RECREATION

People come to Treasure Beach to avoid or escape the busy tourist hubs of Ocho Rios, Negril, and Montego Bay. Swimming, fishing, long walks, and yoga may be the most popular recreational activities.

Captain Dennis Adventure, run by Dennis Abrahams (cell tel. 876/435-3779 or tel. 876/965-3084, dennisabrahams@yahoo.com), offers excursions and fishing trips to get to Black River Safari (US$120), Pelican Bar (US$75 for two), or to a white-sand beach called Gallon Beach in Malcolm Bay just past Black River. Dennis also offers fishing (US$60/hour) and excursions to Little Ochie (US$120). Additional passengers can be added for an extra fee (US$45 per person).

Andy Nembhard (cell tel. 876/438-1311, andytours@yahoo.com) rents Trek, Raleigh, and Cannondale mountain bikes (US$25 per day), operates two-hour sea kayak tours (US$60 per person), and rents single-person kayaks (US$45 per day). Andy also runs 2–3-hour hiking and biking tours (US$60 per person) to Great Bay, Fort Charles, and Lover's Leap. Snorkeling excursions are also offered for US$65 per person, including equipment and transportation to Font Hill Beach Park near Whitehouse, where the reefs are more colorful and waters calmer than in Treasure Beach.

Beaches

Wherever you go in the water in Treasure Beach, it's best to have a companion and to inquire with locals to ensure it is safe. Treasure Beach maintains a growing list of locals who have fallen victim to the hungry sea, which can have strong currents and undertows. While Treasure Beach is not sought after specifically for the quality of its beaches (which aren't as suitable for Jamaica Tourist Board posters as those in other parts of the island), the beaches it has are picturesque in an entirely different way and romantic all the same.

Frenchman's Beach is a great beach for body surfing when the sea is a little rough. There is coral aplenty toward the edges of this beach, even in shallow waters. The safest spot to swim is directly in front of Golden Sands Guest House.

Calabash Bay Beach is a fishing beach with a large, clear, sandy area good for swimming. The safest spot to swim is in front of Calabash House before you reach the boats. **Great Bay** also has a decent beach for a dip.

ACCOMMODATIONS

The popularity of Treasure Beach as an off-the-beaten-track destination has led to a blossoming in the accommodations market. Most of the guesthouses are remarkably affordable when compared with other tourist areas, with comfortable accommodations for two starting around US$30 per night. Even villas rent for considerably less than in other areas of Jamaica, with rates starting at around US$1,200–2,600 per week for 2–8 people.

The only time of year it becomes hard to find a room is during Calabash Literary Festival, when those who haven't booked well in advance happily settle for whatever's available, even staying in Black River, Junction, or as far away as Mandeville if necessary. Rebecca Wiersma has over the past decade created a great online presence with her **Treasure Tours** website (tel. 876/965-0126, treasuretours@cwjamaica.com, www.treasuretoursjamaica.com), subscribed to by most of the accommodations in the area with prices and amenities listed (www.treasurebeach.net). Unless otherwise noted, all the accommodations listed can be booked through Treasure Tours.

Under US$100

Bebe's Place (www.treasuretours.com, US$50–75) has three cottages, dubbed Yellow House, Blue House, and Brown House, with single and queen-size beds and fans. Occasional dance parties are held next door at Wild Onion.

Ashanti Village (Frenchman's Bay area, contact Alieda Ebanks, cell tel. 876/433-1593 or 876/387-4887) is a great budget option with a one-bedroom (US$45) and a two-bedroom (US$65) seaview cottage and four additional rooms (US$35) in the main house. The rooms come with a private bath, small fridge, fan, and electric kettles, with screens on the windows. The cottages have equipped kitchens and verandas with sea views. Meals are prepared by request. There's lots of garden space and a play area great for kids. Ashanti is well situated in a very quiet location still within an easy stroll to most restaurants and bars and Frenchman's Beach.

((Ital Rest (contact Frankie and Jean, tel. 876/863-3481, US$40/night, US$250/week) is about as roots as you can get. The property has limited electricity supplied by solar panels to the smart wood cabins, which are an easy walk from several sandy coves. Mosquito nets cover the beds to keep the bugs out at night. No fans or air-conditioning, and a kitchen on the property is available for guest use. Vegetarian food can also be prepared by request.

Nuestra Casa (Billy's Bay, tel. 876/965-0152, roger@billybay.com, www.billysbay.com, US$45/50 low/high season) is a villa-style guesthouse run by Lillian Chamberlain and her son Roger. It rents three rooms, two with a double bed, and a third with two twin beds. One room has a private bath, while the other two share a bathroom. Amenities include ceiling and standing fans and hot water. Dinner is prepared by request. Anika Elliott is the housekeeper.

Wild Pines (www.treasuretoursjamaica.com, US$65) is a two-bedroom, two-bath wooden cottage near Great Pond set in a charming garden. The two-story building has a bedroom on each floor with a queen-size and a single bed, and a common kitchen at the ground level.

Dolphin's Villa (US$50 per room, US$70 with air-conditioning, or US$290 for entire house) is a spacious five-bedroom, five-bath villa with en suite bathrooms with hot water, screened windows in rooms with fans, satellite TV and stereo in the common living area, and spacious verandas. The house rents through Treasure Tours.

US$100–250

((Villa Mutamba (tel. 876/920-8194, cell tel. 876/868-4658, mutabarukax@hotmail.com, www.villamutamba.com, US$150) is a physical embodiment of the minimalist philosophy of dub poet Mutabaruka, who owns the property. African relics adorn the entrance after one of the longest staircases, dubbed the "stairway to heaven." Inside, simple and tasteful bamboo furnishings complement the funky master bathroom, which has a small window looking out to sea from the colorfully tiled tub.

Calabash House (Calabash Bay, tel. 876/965-0126, US$75/85 low/high season per room or US$200/US$250 low/high season for house) is a four-bedroom villa right on Calabash Bay, one of the best spots for swimming in Treasure Beach. Bedrooms have air-conditioning, with hot water in the bathrooms. A housekeeper tidies up during the day while a cook can be arranged to prepare breakfast and dinner (additional US$25 daily for four persons). Two cute mini-cottages were recently added to the yard, where there's also a hammock for lazing the days away and watching the fishermen bring in their catch. Owner Elizabeth Seltzer is an artist who brings a creative vibe to the house and its ambience.

((Shakti Home (books through Treasure Tours, tel. 876/965-0126, treasuretours@cwjamaica.com, www.shaktihomeja.com, US$1,750/1,950 weekly low/high season) "your Om away from home" as its owner, Jamaica's number one yoga proponent, Sharon McConnell puts it, is an airy, well-appointed, and tastefully decorated beach house with mosquito nets and fans in two bedrooms. The house sits beachfront, overlooking Old Wharf and includes a great cook and caretaker/gardener. The chef specializes in vegetarian cuisine in addition to traditional Jamaican food. Shakti Home has a beautiful yoga deck overlooking the sea that comfortably fits six people, with yoga mats provided.

Sunset Resort Hotel (Calabash Bay, tel. 876/965-0143, srv@sunsetresort.com, www.sunsetresort.com, US$90–115 garden view, US$135 oceanview, US$150 honeymoon suites) basically defines "Butu," the Jamaican equivalent of kitsch, with its Jamaican nouveau-riche exaggerated decor. Floral bedcovers with matching curtains and plastic flower arrangements seem to be transplanted straight from the home of a Kingston drug don. Nonetheless, it's hard to overlook the charm and care taken to make everything match so carefully, even if it is sorely lacking in taste.

Perhaps the best deal at Sunset Resort Hotel

are the small villas adjacent to the main building, which rent for less (from US$97) and have more basic amenities—with appreciably less gaud strewn about.

Treasure Beach Hotel (Frenchman's Bay, tel. 876/965-0110, US$107/$119 low/high season) is the closest thing you'll find to Sandals in Treasure Beach—with split-system air-conditioning in the tile-floor rooms, private balconies, and floral bedcovers matching the drapes. Rooms have either two singles or one king-size bed.

Taino Cove (tel. 876/965.3893, cell tel. 876/845-6103, frontdesk@tainocove.com, www.tainocove.com, US$100–150) is an eight-bedroom boutique hotel located at the far eastern corner of Treasure Beach. Bedrooms have queen-size or double beds, overlook the sea and pool area, and have tile flooring, comfortable linens, and wooden ceilings in the suites. Owned by Winnie Hylton, the large property features a common area on the ground floor of the main building and a pool with an adjacent bar and restaurant. Meals are prepared to order.

Marblue Villa Suites (tel. 876/965-3408, info@marblue.com, www.marblue.com, US$129-285) is an attractive seafront property located on a quiet, windswept stretch of beach along Calabash Bay offering junior, villa, and honeymoon categories. The well-appointed suites have air-conditioning, CD players, fans, attractive decor, and full, king-size, or queen-size beds. Nice sitting areas with day beds overlook one of two pools on the property from the veranda or pool deck.

Andrea's Seaside Restaurant and Steakhouse is a popular upscale restaurant on property, where fellow hotelier Axel Wichterich whips up creative dishes borrowing from Jamaican and international culinary traditions.

Lyric (www.treasuretoursjamaica.com, US$1,100/1,350 weekly low/high season) is a beautiful, cut-stone, four-bedroom, two-bath house; a stone patio and pool overlooking the beach on Calabash Bay is its distinguishing feature. Two rooms have king-size beds and the others have single beds, making the property ideal for families or small groups.

La Sirena (www.treasuretoursjamaica.com, US$1,200 weekly for two, add US$120 per additional person) is a beautiful, airy, three-bedroom villa with queen-size beds in two rooms and two single beds in last room; all bedrooms have private bath, air-conditioning, and ceiling fans. The villa features a private pool on the sun deck and a stairway leading to Billy's Bay Beach. Amenities include a stereo, Internet, and TV/DVD.

Over US$250
Jake's Boutique Resort and Beachside Villas (tel. 876/965-0635 or 800/OUTPOST (800/688-7678), jakes@cwjamaica.com, www.islandoutpost.com/jakes, US$113–385 low, US$136–468 high season) has taken rustic chic to a new level, pouring on the kind of details sought out by those members of the jet set always on the prowl for the next "in" spot. To call Jake's rustic is to ignore the posh bedding and elaborate detailing reminiscent of an Arabian love lair. The honeymoon suites have outdoor showers and sunbathing decks on the roof. The most unpretentiously hip accommodation at Jake's is the two-bedroom Jack Sprat (US$177/230 low/high season), located right next to Frenchman's Beach with its iconic buttonwood tree.

The bold and classy architectural style at Jake's owes to the creativity of Sally Henzell, wife of the late Perry Henzell, who became Jamaica's biggest film icon after directing the cult classic *The Harder They Come* in the early 1970s. Sally Henzell has an aesthetic that blends the old colonial charm found in the island's historic buildings with a windswept rustic edge one might associate more with the Maine coast of New England.

Sometimes described as "shabby shacks," the cottages at Jake's don't neglect the modern essentials, with hot water provided in all the rooms with solar heaters. The Henzells bought the property in 1991 and opened and developed the rooms and cottages little by little. Jake was a pet parrot of the Henzells', but Jake is also a generic term used to call out to a white person.

MANDEVILLE

© OLIVER HILL

Jake's Boutique Resort and Beachside Villas

Calabash Bay Villa and Cottage is a spectacular property with a four-bedroom villa and adjacent two-bedroom cottage managed by Jake's. The villa has an industrial kitchen, a beautiful pool, and a lounge area outside with direct access to the beach on Calabash Bay.

Hope House, also managed by Jake's and a bit farther to the east, is a new two-story house exquisitely laid out and appointed with aged wood detailing, sleek interiors, and a veranda and plunge pool to die for.

Cave Canem is a four-bedroom property, also rented through Jake's, built in a Mediterranean style reminiscent of Morocco or southern Spain, with whitewashed walls and curvy architecture. Several balconies and terraces help make the most of the serene sea views, while an infinity pool graces the front of the property overhanging the beach. Amenities include four-poster king-size beds, flat-panel TVs, Wi-Fi, a fully equipped kitchen, and housekeeper.

⟨ Doubloon Villa (tel. +44 (0) 1543 480612, judy@doubloonvilla.com, www.doubloonvilla.com, or book through Treasure Tours, www.treasuretoursjamaica.com) is a comfortable four-bedroom villa with a small pool and deck overlooking the beach on Calabash Bay. One of the area's premier properties, Doubloon amenities include private baths, a well-equipped kitchen, air-conditioning, complimentary Wi-Fi and three full-time staff members.

Blue Marlin Villas (contact Sandy Tatham, tel. 876/965-3311, cell tel. 876/855-1122, bluemarlinvillas@cwjamaica.com, www.bluemarlinvillas.com) comprises two villas, Blue Marlin and Coquina, located on a 2.5-acre beachfront property at the western side of the beach in Great Pedro Bay. The villas can be rented together or separately. Wi-Fi covers the property. **Blue Marlin** (US$1,700 for 1–4 guests, US$2,000 for 5–8 guests low season, US$1,900/2,500 high season) is a four-bedroom, three bathroom, single-story villa with air-conditioning and ceiling fans in the bedrooms. **Coquina** (US$1,700 for 1–4 guests, US$1,900 for 5–8 guests low season, US$1,900/2,300 high season) is a three-bedroom, three-bathroom two-story villa with ceiling fans. Staff for both villas includes a cook/housekeeper, housemaid, and gardener.

Kouros Villa (US$2,500/week for up to four people, minimum three-night stay) is a four-bedroom villa built adjacent to and in a similar style as Cave Canem, with a whitewashed finish and a pool area overlooking the sea. Kouros books through Treasure Tours (www.treasuretoursjamaica.com).

⟨ Sparkling Waters (Billy's Bay, tel. 876/927-8020, reservations@sparklingwatersvilla.com, www.sparklingwatersvilla.com, US$250 for up to four people) is an exquisitely decorated collection of three modern, two-bedroom duplex villas: Villa de la Sable, Villa de l'Ocean, and Villa du Soleil (US$200 per night 1–2 guests, US$1,575 weekly 1–2 guests, US$1,750 weekly 3–4 guests). The three villas share the grounds, which contain a pool, whirlpool tub, and a gorgeous private beach. The villas have comfortable and inviting bathrooms with hot water, plus satellite TV, stereos, and air-conditioning in the bedrooms. Spacious and comfortable living and dining rooms are found downstairs along with the kitchen. The bedrooms are on the second floor at the top of a spiral staircase. Wi-Fi is included.

Great Escape (Fort Charles, tel. 574/707-0132 or 269/641-5451, greatescape@jamaicavilla.com, www.jamaicavilla.com, from US$1,800/2,000 low/high season) is a three-bedroom house well removed from the languid center of Treasure Beach, with queen-size beds in each room. A large pool overlooks the water with a clubhouse area. Great Escape is a good spot for families, with a small private beach and plenty of space to roam about.

FOOD

Thanks to Treasure Beach's popularity as Jamaica's number one off-the-beaten-track destination, a wide variety of restaurants have popped up. They cater to both a local and tourist market, serving a mix of cautious international dishes and local favorites. Few of these restaurants have landlines, and addresses in Treasure Beach are somewhat relative.

⟨ Jack Sprat (adjacent to Jake's, tel. 876/965-3583, 10 A.M.–10 P.M.) is a favorite for fried fish, conch soup, pizza, and Devon House ice cream.

Sweet Desires (10 A.M.–7 P.M. daily) serves homemade ice cream and has an Internet café.

Hearts of Love Café serves fresh baked goods like pineapple upside-down cake, banana bread, baguettes, and chocolate cake, as well as breakfast items like callaloo, cheese omelettes, and fresh juices.

Frenchman's Reef Restaurant & Cocktail Bar (tel. 876/965-3049, Owen's cell tel. 876/428-5048 or Elizabeth's cell tel. 876/861-4917, jeclarke@live.co.uk, 7–11 P.M. daily) serves seafood and pizza, as well as burgers and Chinese and Jamaican staples. Natural juices and local and international-style breakfasts are also served. Frenchman's delivers, accepts credit cards, and offers patrons complimentary Wi-Fi.

Smurf's Cafe (cell tel. 876/483-7523) is named after proprietor Kevin "Smurf" Mills, but his wife Dawn is the cook at this reputable establishment serving Jamaican breakfast and lunch and dinner staples. The roast coffee is excellent.

Pardy's Coffee Shop (Calabash Bay, cell tel. 876/326-9008, 7 A.M.–7 P.M. Mon.–Sat., US$5–20) serves Jamaican breakfast with items like ackee and saltfish, callaloo and saltfish, and continental favorites like a Spanish omelette, callaloo omelette, or any other kind of eggs done to order. Lunch and dinner are prepared to order, with items like fish, lobster, and curry goat. Pardy's serves High Mountain coffee and freshly squeezed OJ in season, and you can also grab a beer anytime.

Diner's Delight (across from Swaby's Plaza next to Golden Sands Resort, contact Andrea Wright, tel. 876/839-2586, 9 A.M.–10 P.M., US$3.50–13) serves typical Jamaican dishes including curry goat, peppered steak, brown stew chicken, shrimp, fish, and lobster at reasonable prices. Diner's Delight is a favorite among locals. Takeout is also available.

Natural Vibes (no phone) is a restaurant, bar, and souvenir shop in one serving local Jamaican dishes on an outdoor patio or for takeout. It's open for breakfast, lunch, and dinner.

The Gold Coast Restaurant (Kingfisher Plaza, cell tel. 876/391-2458) serves Jamaican fare like fried chicken, curry goat, and steamed fish. It's open for lunch only.

Oliver's Dutch Pot Restaurant (Lazza Plaza, cell tel. 876/375-5217, 10 A.M.–11 P.M. daily, US$3–12) serves up Jamaican staples like fried, jerk, and sweet and sour chicken, curry goat, cow foot, oxtail, fish, shrimp, and lobster.

Andrea's Seaside Restaurant and Steakhouse (Calabash Bay, tel. 876/965-3408, US$20–50) is an open-air restaurant at Marblue, where Andrea's award-winning chef husband, Axel Wichterich, creates dishes of local and international inspiration.

Jake's Place (tel. 876/965-3000) is the restaurant at the hipper-than-hip accommodation, Jake's, serving Jamaican and international cuisine for breakfast, lunch, and dinner daily.

Shantz Eating Place (toward Billy's Bay, no phone, open for lunch) serves quality, cheap eats with a rotating menu including items like fried chicken, pork, and fish—plus curry goat on Saturdays—out of a little shack-like restaurant. The food is served for takeout in Styrofoam boxes.

Pot Snapper is a small restaurant located next to the entrance to Jack Sprat. It prepares excellent fish, Jamaican dishes, and decent pizza at reasonable prices (US$5–15).

Sunset Resort (tel. 876/965-0143) serves Jamaican and American fare from steamed fish to pizza, with an all-you-can-eat buffet nights.

M&D Grocery (tel. 876/965-0070, 7 A.M.–8 P.M. Mon.–Fri., 4 A.M.–until you say when Sat.), named after proprietors Maureen and Delvin Powell, is a small grocery shop and bar good for basic supplies. Jerk chicken and pork as well as conch and mutton soup are prepared on Fridays and Saturdays.

New Dimension Supermarket and Scoop-A-Licious (Linda's Plaza, tel. 876/965-3875, 6:30 A.M.–7:30 P.M. Mon.–Sat., 6:30–10 A.M. and 4–8 P.M. Sun.) sells Devon House ice cream (US$2–2.25 cones, US$2–9 container) and basic groceries.

Round the Clock Bar (Frenchman's Bay, contact owner Charmaine Moxam, cell tel. 876/378-6690, open 24/7) is a small grocery

shop and bar good for basic supplies and drinks, located next to Jake's.

Strikie-T Craft & Jerk Centre (Billy's Bay, tel. 876/289-9555, 7 A.M.–10 P.M. Mon.–Sat.) is run by Christopher Bennett, a.k.a. Strikie-T, with help from Tanice (tel. 876/899-6436). It serves peanut, banana, or hominy porridge until noon, when jerk chicken and pork start coming off the grill.

INFORMATION AND SERVICES

The Calabash Bay **post office** (five minutes east of Southern Supplies on foot, 10:30 A.M.–4:30 P.M. Mon.–Fri., closed for lunch 1–2 P.M.) often lacks stamps.

Kingfisher Plaza is a small shopping center and home to **The Bird's Nest Bar,** which has a billiards table, a grocery shop, and a supermarket.

Treasure Beach Meat Mart & Grocery (Kingfisher Plaza, cell tel. 876/489-3641, 9 A.M.–5 P.M. Mon.–Sat.), run by Marjorie Henry-Somers, sells fresh fruit, vegetables, ground provisions, and frozen fish and meat.

Southern Supplies (eight minutes north of Kingfisher Plaza on foot, just before the ice factory) is the largest supermarket in Treasure Beach, selling among other essentials international phone cards, gift items, and music. The store also has an Internet café.

Global Camera Technology (cell tel. 876/384-8197 or 876/965-0657, global-camtech.videopro@gmail.com), based in nearby Watchwell, offers videography and editing services for weddings, funerals, parties, business events, documentaries, and music videos.

L. H. Malahoo & Nephews Fishing Tackles (Kingfisher Plaza, cell tel. 876/409-7305, 10:30 A.M.–2 P.M. Mon. and Wed., 10:30 A.M.–1:30 P.M. Fri.) is your best bet in the area for fishing gear, but Mr. Malahoo doesn't keep regular hours so it's best to call ahead.

Massage

Shirley's Steam Bath (tel. 876/965-3820 or cell tel. 876/827-2447, smgenus@hotmail.com, open daily by appointment) run by Great Bay native herbalist Shirley Genus, is a local institution offering 15-minute herbal steam baths along with 30- or 60-minute massage sessions (US$70–90).

Joshua's Massage & Bodywork (tel. 876/965-0583, cell tel. 876/389-3698, doctorlee85@hotmail.com, US$70–100), run by Joshua Lee Stein, offers deep and light pressure, gentle movement, and sensitive touch massage therapy on location by appointment.

Jake's Driftwood Spa (Calabash Bay, tel. 876/965-3000, jakes@cwjamaica.com, www.islandoutpost.com, US$75–135) offers a mélange of techniques and philosophies from around the world, with treatments that include Swedish, aromatherapy, and T'ai Chi energy massages; coffee, wild ginger, and mint scrubs; mocha rum, wild ginger, and lemongrass wraps; and Jake's signature facials.

GETTING THERE AND AROUND

Treasure Beach is serviced by frequent route taxis from Santa Cruz, direct, and via Watchwell (US$2) and from Junction (US$2). If you're driving, there are three routes to get there. From Black River there is a short, direct road along the coast that is a bit iffy in places, but still passable with a two-wheel-drive vehicle. Turn off the main toward the sea on a road just east of the communications tower east of Parottee. To get to Treasure Beach from Mandeville, take a left at the base of Spur Tree Hill, following signs for Little Ochie, and take a right at the first four-way intersection following signs for Alumina Partners. At the first junction take a left and pass the bauxite and alumina plant, followed by a right at the stop sign to continue up the hill, passing straight through Junction. From Santa Cruz, turn south toward the sea about 1.5 kilometers west of the stoplight on the west side of town. The turnoff is marked by a sign for Jack Sprat.

EAST OF TREASURE BEACH
Junction

A busy stopover point on the way over the Santa Cruz Mountains, Junction is the closest outpost of civilization to Treasure Beach with supermarkets and banks. Junction Guest House offers basic accommodations, and a few restaurants are worth stopping for.

Pine's Plaza has a few bars that can heat up on weekend nights, namely **Cheatah's Sports Bar & Lounge** (Shop #34-A) and **The Gazebo Lounge and Rushours Night Club.**

⟨ Atlantis Seafood (Main Rd. just before reaching Junction, next to Lunie's Hot Spot, which is plastered with Heineken posters, contact Shay tel. 876/409-3373 or Ms. Lunie tel. 876/436-1057) serves the best seafood in Junction, with fish, lobster, conch, and shrimp (US$700–1700/pound) on the menu.

Hot Pot Restaurant (Shop #8, cell tel. 464-0356, 7:15 A.M.–5 P.M. Mon.–Sat., from US$4) serves Jamaican staples.

Top Hill Chinese Restaurant (Shops #5 and 6, Roye's Plaza, tel. 876/458-1738 or 876/578-1634, 11 A.M.–10 P.M. Mon.–Sat., 1–10 P.M. Sun., from US$4) serves strictly Chinese dishes with chicken, pork, beef, and seafood.

Althea's Bar (Dunder Hill, tel. 876/340-1460) does great outdoor cookouts with advance notice. Althea prepares excellent curry goat and fish dishes.

Heavy's Bar & Grill (on the way from Junction to Bull Savannah) is the hottest club in the area.

Junction Guest House (tel. 876/965-8668, simplepunkie@yahoo.com, US$25–100) has basic rooms with fan, private bath, TV, and air-conditioning. There's also a suite with a kitchen and veranda.

Devon House I Scream is sold at the Texaco station.

The **Shopper's Fair** and **Intown Super Save Supermarket** are the best options for groceries.

NCB (tel. 876/965-8611) and **Scotiabank** (Shop #1, Tony Rowe Plaza, tel. 876/965-8257) have branches with ATMs, as does Jamaica National.

Alligator Pond

One of the busiest fishing villages on the South

Coast, Alligator Pond has as its central attraction the seafood restaurant Little Ochie, and the nearby Manatee Hole.

Oswald's, located on the main fishing beach in Alligator Pond, serves excellent seafood in a setting a few notches up on the rustic pole from Little Ochie just down the beach.

To get to Alligator Pond, turn south at the bottom of Spur Tree Hill (a left coming from Mandeville, a right from Santa Cruz) and keep straight until you reach the coast.

Little Ochie

◖ Little Ochie (cell tel. 876/382-3375, tel. 876/610-6567 or 876/610-6568, littleochie@cwjamaica.com, www.littleochie.com, 9 A.M. until you say when daily, US$10–30) is a seafood paradise, serving a wide range of dishes like jerk and garlic crab, fish, and lobster. Over 75 seafood recipes are utilized on a daily basis, with lobster cooked 15 different ways, the best of which could very well be the garlic lobster. Everald Christian, a.k.a. "Blacky," is the founder who built the place in 1989 in

a rustic style reminiscent of the good old days in Ocho Rios on the North Coast. At the inception of Jamaica's tourism economy, before it became dangerously over-developed, Ocho Rios (known locally as Ochi or Ochie) had similar rustic thatch huts on the beach as the ones used today as the restaurant's boat-shaped dining areas. Little Ochie has become wildly popular with uptown Jamaicans, who will drive from Kingston or Mobay just for the spectacular cuisine.

The first or second Sunday in July, Little Ochie hosts the annual Little Ochie Seafood Festival, which draws a good crowd for cultural shows and even more seafood than normal.

CANOE VALLEY WETLAND

Canoe Valley Protected Area (contact rangers Devon Douglas, cell tel. 876/578-9456, or Ucal Whyte, cell tel. 876/874-1422) is a coastal wetlands area managed by Jamaica's National Environment and Planning Agency (NEPA) full of diverse plant and animal life. The manatees that live in semi-captivity

Everald Christian runs one of Jamaica's best seaside restaurants, Little Ochie.

© OLIVER HILL

along the river in the park are the highlight. **Rowboat excursions** (US$10/person) to spot the manatees and snorkel in the surreal crystal blue waters are offered from the ranger station, a few kilometers south of Milk River. The rangers at the station also offer hikes to remote Taino Caves (rates negotiable). Turtles and alligators also share the waters; swimmers are advised to keep their eyes peeled.

About five kilometers west of the Canoe Valley Protected Area, or 16 km east along the coast into Manchester from Alligator Pond, the **Guts River** creates a small pool as it emerges from the rocks with cool, crystal-clear waters said to have medicinal qualities. The deserted beach nearby is great for a stroll. Getting to Guts River requires chartering a taxi if you don't have your own vehicle, or hiring a boat from Treasure Beach if that's where you're based.

Mandeville

Manchester is Jamaica's sixth-largest parish, much of its land located at relatively high altitudes with three mountain ranges: the May Day Mountains, the Don Figuerero Mountains, and the Carpenters Mountains, where the highest peak in the parish stands at 844 meters. Any approach to Mandeville, the parish capital, entails steep climbs, which fortunately feature some of Jamaica's most well-maintained roads.

Manchester has been at the center of Jamaica's bauxite industry, led by Jamalco (Alcoa-Jamaican government joint venture), which has massive mines around Mandeville. It also has processing facilities across the border in Clarendon, as well as in St. Elizabeth, where Port Kaiser along the coast west of Little Ochie is an important export terminal.

The parish was named by the Duke of Manchester, who served as Governor General 1813–1821, after his eldest son, William de Mandeville. The small city of Mandeville was at one time a British enclave where colonial government officials preferred to spend their summers in the high altitude's relatively cool climate.

The 1970s destroyed Mandeville as the gentry left when Manley came into power (they were scared off by his socialist lean). Bauxite has benefited the local economy and has created an income for skilled workers since the industry was established in the 1950s. The bauxite industry has trained and paid many Jamaicans while the lucky were educated at the Belair School, which remains one of Jamaica's best preparatory institutions.

SIGHTS

Mandeville's historic sights are concentrated around the town square, known as Cecil Charlton Park. These include the **Mandeville Courthouse,** which was built of limestone using slave labor and finished in 1820. The courthouse housed the town's first school on its ground floor. The **Mandeville Jail and Workhouse,** also among the first public buildings in town, is now in use as the police station. Adjacent to the courthouse, the **Mandeville Rectory** is the oldest house of worship and the original Anglican rectory in Mandeville, having once also served as a tavern and guesthouse, to the dismay of many parishioners.

Marshall's Pen

Marshall's Pen (contact owner Ann Sutton, tel. 876/904-5454, asutton@cwjamaica.com) has been a popular spot for serious birding for many years. Birders come especially to see the Jamaican owl, which can often be seen in its favorite easily accessible tree. Of Jamaica's 28 endemic birds, 23 have been spotted at Marshall's Pen, with a total of 110 species recorded on the property over the years.

At this point tourism is not the main business at Marshall's Pen. Only experienced birdwatchers should attempt to visit.

Marshall's Pen was built in 1795 at the latest,

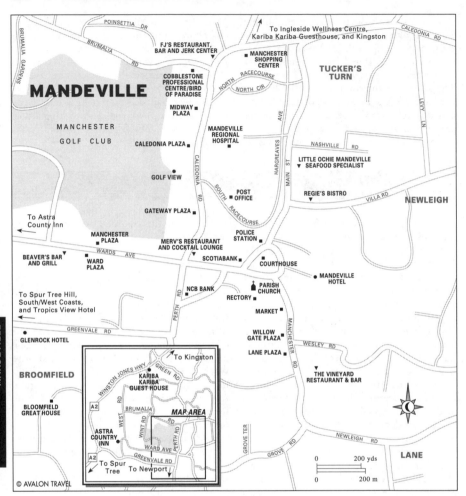

© AVALON TRAVEL

the exact date being something of a mystery. Originally the estate was about 809 hectares, whereas today is has dwindled to a still-respectable 121 hectares.

The origin of its name is a bit ambiguous, but it seems it does not refer to an identifiable previous owner. The present owner is Dr. Ann Sutton, widow of the late Robert Sutton, one of Jamaica's foremost ornithologists, who created an audio catalog of Jamaican bird songs that was released by Cornell University's ornithology department. Robert Sutton also co-authored *Birds of Jamaica,* the island's best bird guide. Dr. Ann Sutton is also an ornithologist, as well as being a conservationist and secretary of the Society for Conservation and Study of Caribbean Birds.

Marshall's Pen welcomes serious birders, who find warm hospitality and even accommodation sometimes. It is also possible to tour the great house and extensive gardens (US$10/ person, minimum six persons) by appointment;

visitors can find orchids, anthuriums, ferns, and other indigenous plantlife. It's not a place to show up unannounced; call ahead to arrange a visit and for directions.

ENTERTAINMENT

Beaver's Bar and Grill (contact owner Wayne Wiltshire, tel. 876/469-4922, 4 P.M.–close Tues.–Sun.) is the most happening bar/club in Mandeville with a series of weekly theme nights: Seafood Tuesday, Retro Wednesday, Thursday is low key, College Friday (for university students), Beaver's Saturday (a big club night), Classic Sunday (with a live band, attracts an older crowd). Beaver's sometimes charges a US$6 cover. There's a bar menu serving mozzarella sticks, stamp and go fritters, chicken fingers, burgers, and fish (US$2–10).

Odeon Cineplex (5½ Caledonia Rd., tel. 876/962-1354) is the local movie theater and often the most entertaining venue in town for a night out. Movies are typically shown at 5 P.M. and 8 P.M. daily.

Upper Level (Upper Level Plaza, Caledonia Rd.) is Mandeville's regular nightspot with pool tables.

Shockwave HQ Sports Bar (Willow Gate Plaza, contact owner Mark Haughton, cell tel. 876/866-6216, 10 A.M. till you say when daily) is a bar with a few billiard tables and dancehall music blasting in the speakers. The bar turns on the strobe lights as it heats up into the night.

SPORTS AND RECREATION

Manchester Club (Caledonia Rd., contact Janice Wright, tel. 876/962-2403, manchester_club@hotmail.com) is the oldest golf course in the Western Hemisphere, dating to 1865. It remains the least expensive course in Jamaica (US$30 greens fees, US$12 clubs, US$14 caddy per round), and perhaps in the hemisphere. The nine-hole course is well maintained, even if it is not the bright green of more popular courses on the island. For those staying in the area for a length of time, membership brings the fees down significantly. Beyond golf, the club also offers tennis on three hard courts,

the only squash court on the south coast, table tennis, a swimming pool, and the only billiard table with over a hundred years in use. The club also hosts barbecues and luncheons. A golf tournament is held every month where golfers from across the island participate. The All Jamaica Hard Court Tennis Championship is held each summer, attracting over 200 children and adults over a one-week period. There's a resident tennis coach and a golf professional.

Ingleside Wellness & Recreation Centre (Ingleside Dr., tel. 876/961-3632) has tennis courts, badminton, table tennis, weight lifting equipment, and a bar that no longer keeps regular hours. Day membership is available for use of the facilities. Call manager Janice Robinson for more details. Ingleside is the base for the Manchester Table Tennis Association.

ACCOMMODATIONS
Under US$100

Golf View (5½ Caledonia Rd., tel. 876/962-4471, 876/962-4472, or 876/962-4473, gviewrosi@hotmail.com, www.thegolfviewhotel.com, US$94) is a 62-room hotel near the center of town with basic rooms that have a ceiling fan and private bathrooms with hot water. A deluxe room (US$118) and a one-bedroom suite (US$130) have air-conditioning, while the sole two-bedroom suite (US$148) does not. The central location is probably the best feature of this hotel. The hotel claims the same address as the Odeon Cineplex but is actually not adjacent, sitting a bit farther down Caledonia Road at the top of Golf View Plaza bordering the golf course.

Glenrock Hotel (3-A Greenvale Rd., tel. 876/961-3278 or 876/961-3279, glenrockhotel@yahoo.com) has a total of 24 rooms, with additional rooms and features in the works. Standard rooms (US$28) have double beds, standing fans, cable TV, and private baths with hot water. Deluxe rooms (US$39) have queen-size beds, and a junior suite (US$50) has a king-size bed, air-conditioning, a small fridge, microwave, and a couch. The family suite (US$56) also has a small fridge, king-size bed, and microwave.

Astra Country Inn (62 Ward Ave., tel. 876/962-7758, or cell tel. 876/585-8600 or 876/488-7207, skype: diamite1, countrystyle@mail.infochan.com or countrystyletourism@yahoo.com, www.countrystylejamaica.com, US$50–60) offers rooms in a homestay setting. The 10 rooms have cable TV, fans, private bathrooms with hot water, and either two double beds or one king-size bed. The Astra is home to Country Style Tourism, run by Diana McIntyre-Pike, which places visitors in homestays around the island and offers community village tours all over the island. Diana markets the Mandeville Hotel, run by her family, as an alternative to the community tour experience. Wi-Fi is offered free to Astra guests, and there's also a small business center with a computer and office equipment available.

Kariba Kariba Guest House (tel. 876/962-8006, kariba@cwjamaica.com, US$50) was built about halfway in 1997 and has operated since 1998 without any real appearance or sense of completion inside or out. Dobson the caretaker is friendly enough nonetheless, and the four rooms in operation have TV and ceiling fans with double or queen-size beds and private baths with hot water. Rooms, while not immaculately maintained, are a decent value and come with continental breakfast. Derrick O'Connor is the owner.

US$100-250

Mandeville Hotel (4 Hotel St., tel. 876/962-2460, reservations@themandevillehotel.com, mandevillehoteljamaica.com, US$77–242) is the oldest hotel operating in Mandeville. It recently underwent a restoration that left it with nice parquet floors and soothing color schemes in many of the rooms, while it seems details in the bathrooms were overlooked. Clean sheets, ceiling fans, air-conditioning, a fridge, cable TV, and hot water round out this comfortable yet quite basic hotel in the heart of town. Bring your own soap and shampoo. Rooms have full-size, queen-size, and king-size beds. There are also junior suites and one-, two-, and three-bedroom apartments.

Tropics View Hotel (Wardville District, off Winston Jones Hwy., tel. 876/625-2452, tropicsview@cwjamaica.com, www.tropicsview-whoteljamaica.com, US$70–98) hotel offers wireless Internet in the lobby. Standard rooms have queen-size beds and private baths with hot water. Two-bedroom suites are also available for US$158, where one room has a king-size and the other a queen-size bed. There is a restaurant and bar on the property by the front gate open 7 A.M.–10 P.M. daily. Rooms have ceiling fans rather than air-conditioning, but it rarely gets hot in Mandeville.

FOOD
Jerk, Jamaican, and Fast Food

FJ's Restaurant, Bar and Jerk Center (23 Caledonia Rd., tel. 876/961-4380 or 876/360-2082, 10 A.M.–11 P.M. Mon.–Sat.) serves seafood and jerk dishes (US$4–6). Faith Joan Miller, from whence the initials are derived, is the proprietor.

Merv's Restaurant and Cocktail Lounge (4-A Caledonia Rd., behind Juici Beef Plaza, tel. 876/961-0742, 8 A.M.–9 P.M. Mon.–Sat., until 6 P.M. Mon. and Wed., US$3–4) serves cabbage and stewed, baked, and rotisserie chicken. Merv's has a second branch at Midway Mall (tel. 876/961-6378, 8 A.M.–6 P.M. Mon.–Sat.).

Cake, Coffee and Ice Cream (59 Main St., tel. 876/962-6636, 8 A.M.–10 P.M. daily) is the local Devon House franchise, owned and operated by Christopher Bird.

Foodz to Go (Shop #8, Elethe Mall, tel. 876/961-8646, 8 A.M.–8 P.M., US$4–6) cooks food for takeout and delivery with dishes like curry, fried, or fricassee chicken, oxtail, brown stew fish, curry goat, and stew peas. Breakfast is served in the mornings with stew chicken, ackee and saltfish, and mackerel rundown.

Sandra's Restaurant (Lane Plaza, tel. 876/625-4149, 7 A.M.–midnight daily) serves a changing menu of Jamaican dishes like fried chicken, curry goat, and oxtail (US$4–8).

D'Palms Sports Bar & Grill (just past the roundabout heading out of town toward Spur Tree Hill, tel. 876/622-0490, 11 A.M.–you say when Mon.–Sat., 3 P.M.–4 A.M. Sun.) is a jerk center and bar located by the roundabout on the western end of town heading up toward Spur Tree Hill. Occasional stage shows are held in the parking lot. The bar has a billiards table and Wi-Fi. Retro Thursdays features old hits, Appleton Special Fridays offers 2-for-1 deals on small flask-size bottles of Appleton Special rum, and Wednesday night brings karaoke. Menu items include appetizers like mozzarella sticks, quesadillas, and wings; calamari and shrimp tempura, soups, salads, and sandwiches; and seafood, pasta, beef, pork, lamb and jerk dishes (US$4.50–18.50).

Fine Dining

Regie's Bistro (37 Main St., entrance on Villa Road, tel. 876/285-6605, 11:30 A.M.– 10:30 P.M. Mon.–Sat., US$3.50–40), run by Patrick Adizua, who runs his private medical practice on the ground level, serves creative Jamaican and Caribbean dishes in a cozy second-floor dining room and bar. The top level has a beautiful outdoor bar area suitable for large groups and parties. The menu includes starters like jerk chicken drumsticks, buffalo wings, shrimp bruschetta, seafood chowder, cream of chick pea, and garden or Greek salad. Sumptuous entrées range from prime aged steaks, chops, and ribs to lobster thermidor and coconut shrimp beignets with pepper jelly dipping sauce. Named after Patrick's mother and daughter, both named Regina, Regie's also has one of the area's best wine lists, which includes French, Spanish, Chilean, Argentine, and North American brands, among them ice wine from Canada.

Bird of Paradise (1 Brumalia Rd., tel. 876/962-7251, 7 A.M.–10 P.M. Mon.–Sat., 10 A.M.–3:30 P.M. Sun. for brunch, 5–10 P.M. Sun. for dinner, US$10–50) is an upscale restaurant with marble tables and a sleek bar. It serves a mix of vegetarian and meat dishes with appetizers like calamari al aioli, shrimp margarita, and spring rolls. Entrées range from snapper cutlet pan fried in caper butter to duckling breast. Bird of Paradise is located in Cobblestone Professional Centre, the first set of buildings on Brumalia Road on the left coming up from Caledonia Road.

The Vineyard Restaurant & Bar (61 Manchester Rd., tel. 876/625-6113, 2–10:30 P.M. Mon.–Fri., noon–10:30 P.M. Sat., 5–8 P.M. Sun., US$6–12) opened in 2003. It has Jamaican and international cuisine, with dishes including fish, chicken, ribs, shrimp, and lamb chops.

Bloomfield Great House (tel. 876/962-7130 or 876/383-7130 bloomfield.g.h@cw-jamaica.com, noon–10 P.M. Mon.–Sat.) is one of the most beautiful colonial-era houses in Mandeville. Bloomfield opened for business in 1997 following a two-year restoration by Aussie Ralph Pearce and his wife, Pamela Grant, whose father became the first Jamaican to own the property when he bought it in the 1960s. The panoramic view over Mandeville is spectacular, and food is excellent, albeit a bit pricey. A good bet is the local snapper, which is prepared in typical Jamaican fashion with onions, pepper, and okra. Bloomfield is a great spot for an evening cocktail and smoked marlin appetizer. There are tentative plans to build rooms off the back.

Chinese

Bamboo Garden Restaurant (35 Ward Ave., tel. 876/962-4515, noon–10 P.M. Mon.–Sat., 1–10 P.M. Sun., US$7–30) serves Chinese food ranging from sweet and sour chicken to butterfly shrimp to lobster with butter and cola. The restaurant is located upstairs from Cash & Carry Supermarket.

International Chinese (117 Manchester Rd., opposite Guardsman, tel. 876/962-0527, noon–9 P.M. Mon.–Thurs., till 9:30 Fri. and Sat., noon–8 P.M. Sun., US$6–14) serves items like Cantonese-style lobster, cashew shrimp, and chicken with mushrooms.

Lucky Dragon Restaurant (Shops #9-10, 5½ Caledonia Rd., tel. 876/961-6544 or 876/867-6720, 11 A.M.–10 P.M. Mon.–Sat., noon–10 P.M. Sun., US$2–8) offers dine-in, takeout, and delivery of standard Chinese fare.

Seafood

Little Ochie Mandeville Seafood Specialist (beside Nashville Plaza, cell tel.

876/625-3279, 11 A.M.–11 P.M. Mon.–Thurs., 11 A.M.–until you say when Fri.–Sun.) serves fish, conch, and lobster tail (US$7–20) in an urban outpost of the original **Little Ochie** in Alligator Pond. It's the best place in town for seafood, answering the call locals were making for years for Blacky to bring Little Ochie to them instead of having to make the trek down Spur Tree Hill to the St. Elizabeth coast. Next door a vendor sells roasted breadfruit, a favorite accompaniment for the seafood.

Gran's Seafood and Bar (tel. 876/603-4254, noon–midnight daily) is located in the Hopeton district between Kingsland and Hatfield going up Spur Tree Hill from Mandeville. Gran's is the best spot on the hill for seafood items including steamed, escovitch, or fried fish, shrimp, and lobster (US$7–17).

Spur Tree Hill

The main road west from Mandeville (A2) rises over Spur Tree Hill, famous for being a dangerous stretch to drive as the road plunges from more than 2,000 feet to near sea level in the span of just a few kilometers, and just as famous for a couple of sumptuous roadside jerk pits and a noteworthy curry goat hut.

From atop Spur Tree Hill, the view of Manchester's lowlands, St. Elizabeth and Westmoreland is spectacular, even if it is dotted with the scarred red earth and smoke stacks of the massive Alumina Partners bauxite processing plant. To the west, the Santa Cruz Mountains can be seen tapering down to the sea.

⬛ Claudette's Top Class (Spur Tree Hill, tel. 876/964-6452, 8 A.M.–4 P.M. daily) is a favorite local spot to get curry goat. The little sit-in restaurant is across the highway from Hood Daniel Well Company.

⬛ All Seasons Restaurant Bar and Jerk Centre (tel. 876/965-4030, 8 A.M.–11 P.M. daily) is considered by many to be the best jerk spot in Manchester, with other typical Jamaican dishes served as well. Perched on the steep slopes of Spur Tree Hill, All Seasons commands an impressive view of southern Manchester and St. Elizabeth, down to where the sky meets the sea.

Hill View Jerk Centre is farther down Spur Tree Hill, but it still has a decent view. Hill View also serves jerk, while not as highly rated as its cousin farther up the hill.

INFORMATION AND SERVICES

Diana McIntyre-Pike heads up **Countrystyle Jamaica** (Astra Inn, 62 Ward Ave., cell tel. 876/488-7207, tel. 876/962-7758, diana@countrystylejamaica.com, www.countrystylejamaica.com), a community tourism outfit that sells "the real Jamaica," organizing community visits and homestays across the island.

The Real Thing Health Food (Shop #33, Mandeville Shopping Center, tel. 876/962-5664 or 876/625-7703, 9 A.M.–5 P.M. Mon.–Sat.) sells healthful groceries.

Bookland (Shop 23 Manchester Shopping Centre, 876/926-9051, bookland-mandeville@cwjamaica.com, Mon.–Fri. 9 A.M.–6 P.M., Sat 10 A.M.–5 P.M.) has the best selection of Caribbean books, as well as local and international magazines.

SuperPlus has four locations in Mandeville (17 Caledonia Rd., tel. 876/961-1624; 16 Manchester Rd., tel. 876/625-2310; 12 Ward Way, tel. 876/961-5702; and 2 Park Crescent, tel. 876/625-0842).

Shoppers Fair supermarket is located at 5 Caledonia Road (tel. 876/962-6217).

Scotia DBG pays an honest exchange rate at its branch on 6 Park Crescent (tel. 876/962-6000 or 876/962-6001).

FX Trader also observes fair rates at its Heaven's Texaco location at 2 Manchester Road. It has another location in S&V Cambio at 16 Ward Avenue.

Finishing Touches (Shop #2, Midway Mall, tel. 876/961-3217) family grooming center is a convenient place to stop for a haircut.

Express Laundromat is located at 30 Hargreaves Avenue (tel. 876/962-6701).

DHL is at Perth Road, Brumalia Town Mall (tel. 876/961-0744, 9 A.M.–5 P.M. Mon.–Fri.).

Gaia Day Spa (1 Brumalia Road, tel. 876/962-1756, 9 A.M.–6 P.M. Mon.–Sat.) is located at

Cobblestone Professional Centre, offering facials, manicures and pedicures, and massage.

Medical

Hargreaves Memorial Hospital (Caledonia Ave., tel. 876/961-1589) is a private clinic, with many of its staff also working at Mandeville Regional.

Mandeville Regional Hospital (32 Hargreaves, tel. 876/962-2067) is the largest hospital for kilometers around, with a good reputation.

Dr. Patrick Adizua (tel. 876/383-4353) runs a private medical practice in the same building as his Bistro on Villa Road.

Fontana Pharmacy has outlets at Mandeville Shopping Centre (tel. 876/962-3129) and SuperPlus (tel. 876/961-3007).

Money

Both **NCB** (9 Manchester Rd., tel. 876/962-2083; Mandeville Plaza, tel. 876/962-2618) and **Scotiabank** (1-A Caledonia Rd., tel. 876/962-2035) have bank branches with ATMs in Mandeville.

Internet

Manchester Parish Library (34 Hargreaves Ave., tel. 876/962-2972, manparlib@cwjamica.com, 9:30 A.M.–5:30 P.M. Mon.–Fri., until 4 P.M. Sat.) offers free Internet access.

Manchester Shopping Centre has an Internet café, along with a food court with a lot of hole-in-the-wall restaurants.

GETTING THERE AND AROUND

Mandeville is served by regular buses from Kingston and May Pen and regular route taxis departing from the square for surrounding destinations including May Pen, Christiana, and Santa Cruz (US$2).

One of Jamaica's best thoroughfares is a stretch of toll road known as Highway 2000, or Usain Bolt Highway, as it was renamed in 2009 in post-IAAF World Championship fervor, begins in Portmore and leads west to rejoin the A2 in Free Town at the Clarendon border. From May Pen the A2 climbs to the upper reaches of Manchester, passing Mandeville along the bypass before descending to the South Coast and extending as far west as Negril. To get between Mandeville and the North Coast, the most direct route can be found by following signs for Christiana heading east towards Kingston, and then toward Spaldings, Cave Valley, Alexandria, and Brown's Town, before hitting the coast in Runaway Bay.

From Mandeville, the drive to Kingston takes about 1.5 hours along the toll road from May Pen, with Treasure Beach within 1.5 hours in the opposite direction. Negril, Mobay, and Ocho Rios are all about a 2-hour drive, and Port Antonio is another 1.5 hours east of Ocho Rios along the North Coast.

CHRISTIANA

A small community near the highest reaches of Manchester Parish, Christiana is a quiet town with one main drag and a single guest house. The most popular attraction in town is **Christiana Bottom,** a gorge located within walking distance from the center of the small village. **Gourie State Park** (contact Trevor Anderson for guiding services, tel. 876/964-5088, cell tel. 876/771-4222 or 876/292-4631, trevormanderson@hotmail.com, US$20 per person) is a recreational area on government land managed by Jamaica's Forestry Department, located between Christiana and Colleyville, about two miles past Christiana. Immediately after passing Bryce United Church, take the first left turn and then the first right until reaching the unmanned Forestry Department station and picnic area. **Gourie Cave,** the highlight of the park, is not actually inside the park but rather about a quarter mile down the hill to the left of the park entrance. By the cave entrance there's a picnic and camping area with a hut and tables and benches. There is one main trail through the park that leads to the community of Ticky Ticky, with excellent views along the way of the Santa Cruz Mountains, Spur Tree Hill, and the historic Bethany Moravian Church.

Gourie Cave was a hideout for runaway slaves. The cave follows the channels of an underground river about three to four feet deep, depending on how much rain has fallen. If you go north from the entrance and upstream against the current, you end up on the other side of Colleyville Mountain. A different route leads downstream along the underground river, deep into the earth where there are several caverns along the way. If you're going to be exploring in the cave, you should monitor the weather and be aware of any fronts on the horizon. It's not wise to venture into the cave alone. Contact Trevor Anderson for his guide services.

In Christiana Bottom, there's a Blue Hole fed from underground streams with two waterfalls dumping into the pool. There's another waterfall at William Hole farther downstream. To get to Christiana Bottom coming from Mandeville, turn right immediately after the NCB bank on Moravia Road, then take the first left around a blind corner, and then the first right, which leads to Christiana Bottom. Continue past the first left that leads to Tyme Town and park at the entrance to the second left, a wide path that leads down to the river. Ask for Mr. Jones for a guided tour (US$20) of Blue Hole and William Hole and his farm, where he grows ginger, yam, potato, pineapple, bananas, and sugarcane.

Sights

The **Pickapeppa Factory** (at base of Shooter's Hill beside Windalco plant, call in advance to arrange a visit, tel. 876/603-3441, fax 876/603-3440, pickapeppa@cwjamaica.com, www.pickapeppajamaica.com, US$3 adults, US$1.50 children) offers a half-hour educational tour (8:30 A.M.–3:30 P.M. Mon.–Thurs.) led by Diana Tomlinson or Noel Miller, which covers the company's founding in 1921 and the process involved in the manufacture of its world-famous sauces. The factory is closed for the first two weeks in August and between Christmas and New Year's, but at any other time of year a sampling of the Pickapeppa sauces is included in the tour. The sauces are made with all-natural ingredients, and include mango chutney, jerk seasoning, and mango sauces in hot, spicy, and gingery varieties. The only preservative agents used in Pickapeppa sauces are vinegar and pepper.

Scott's Pass (between Toll Gate and Porus) is the headquarters for the Nyabinghi house of Rastafari in Jamaica, with the House of Elders based there. The land was bought by Bob Marley and given to the Binghi for that specific purpose. The community members are for the most part welcoming of visitors, but you may get some evil eyes if you fail to recognize their customs for the Binghi celebrations: women must wear skirts or dresses (no pants) and cover their heads, while men must not cover their heads. To arrange a visit or learn about the birthday celebrations or other Nyabinghi events around the island contact the Rasta in Charge, Paul Reid, known as Iyatolah (cell tel. 876/850-3469) or Charlena McKenzie, known as Daughter Dunan (cell tel. 876/843-3227). Arts and crafts are sold throughout the year at Scott's Pass.

Roy "Ras Carver" Bent (cell tel. 876/866-7745, rascarver@yahoo.com) is a Nyabinghi elder and master drum maker associated with the Scott's Pass order of Rastafari who lives in nearby May Pen. Ras Carver fashions, tunes, repairs, and sells the full line of drums used at Nyabinghi ceremonies.

Other important **Binghi celebrations** throughout the year include Ethiopian Christmas (January 7), one during Black History Month (a couple of days in February), commemoration of His Majesty's 1966 visit to Jamaica (April 21), All African Liberation Day (May 25), Marcus Garvey's birthday (three nights around August 19), Ethiopian New Year's (3–7 days starting September 11) and Haile Selassie's coronation (November 2).

To get to Scott's Pass, take the first left heading west of the train line in Clarendon Park where the Juici Patties plant is located. Look out for a small bridge crossing the Milk River before reaching Porus.

Accommodations

Villa Bella (tel. 876/964-2243, villabella@cw-jamaica.com, www.jamaica-southcoast.com/villabella US$65-80) is billed as "Jamaica's original country inn." Located in a cool setting at 914 meters above sea level, you won't find a more comfortably temperate climate on the island. The hotel has a lot of old-world charm in a gorgeous setting. Its allure as an accommodation is somewhat lessened by the tired state of its rooms. Owner Sherryl White-McDowell has initiated efforts to refurbish the property, which will be ongoing. The restaurant serves Jamaican dishes like ackee and saltfish, roast and jerk chicken, and steamed fish (US$6–12).

Clarendon

The second most-populous parish, Clarendon is a major agricultural region with a lively market (Mon.–Sat.) by the square (or triangle) in its capital, May Pen. The parish, like all others in Jamaica, was originally settled by the Tainos, who were later pushed out by Spaniards who favored the area for cattle farming on their *hatos* or haciendas. Cotton and indigo became important crops during the early British period, before sugar took over later into the British colonial period. The parish developed as British troops settled on land granted to them as rewards for service by Charles II in the 17th century. Cudjoe, the Maroon leader, is said to have been the son of a slave on Sutton Plantation in Clarendon, the site of Jamaica's slave rebellion of 1690. Following emancipation, large numbers of Indian indentured laborers were brought in, forming the basis of a distinct cultural enclave that still exists today.

Visitors to May Pen will find virtually no tourism infrastructure, as the parish has little developed coastline and scarce attractions to excite the imagination of the short-term visitor. The undeveloped coastline can, on the other hand, be an attraction in and of itself, for the adventurous, and it is known to be dotted with caves in the vicinity of Portland Point. The brush-filled landscape in this same area is a favorite place for hunters to shoot birds in season for about five weeks starting in mid-August. The protected areas along the coast are the last place in Jamaica you have a good chance of seeing a manatee—native to the country's waters but severely endangered. The famous bathhouse in the parish, Milk River, warrants a visit if you're an old-school spa buff; if you're into hanging with the locals and taking a dip, try Salt River, where a spring wells up from the earth and sound systems blast music to bathers' delight.

MAY PEN

Jamaica's second-largest inland town after Spanish Town, May Pen is strictly Jamaican—receiving few foreign visitors compared with other major population centers on the island.

May Pen is the parish capital, with several heritage sites in its vicinity, including Halse Hall Great House, and the birthplace of acclaimed writer and poet Claude McKay, who went on to contribute to the Harlem Renaissance movement after moving to the United States.

May Pen was established on the banks of the Rio Minho and grew thanks to the river, which hampered travelers who took rest in the inns that were established on its banks. In the 1880s a railway station was built, further fueling the town's growth. Clarendon has a disproportionately large population of East Indian descent and is the location for **Hosay,** a traditional Indian festival that has been Jamaicanized.

The town gets its name from the Reverend William May, who owned the estate that predates the settlement. May served as rector in Kingston, and his son went on to become custos of Clarendon and Vere. The second important annual event held in May Pen is the **Denbeigh Agricultural Show,** which is a fantastic display of the region's farming prowess.

MANDEVILLE

Sights

Halse Hall Great House (halsehallgreathouse@ hotmail.com, http://halsehall.tripod.com) has been owned since 1969 by aluminum mining giant Alcoa. The property was named Hato de Buena Vista (Ranch with a Nice View) by the Spaniards who laid the foundation on which the present structure stands. Major Thomas Halse arrived with the British forces in 1655 and was given the property as a land grant following the British takeover. Halse built the present structure in the fortified style of the time to defend against potential reprisals from the Spanish and their Maroon allies. A second story was added by his heirs in the 1740s. Perhaps the most distinguished owner of the property was Thomas Henry de la Beche, an English geologist who founded the geological survey of Great Britain Royal School of Mines and Mining Record Office and wrote *Remarks on the Geology of Jamaica*. Ownership passed from the hands of the family in the 1830s to settle debt. Visitors are welcome to pass through to tour the house and grounds with prior notice and approval. Call Vanecia Harris tel. 876/986-2561, extension 4210, to request a visit.

Clarendon Park Garden (managed by Alfred Gayle) is a well-maintained park right across the street from Alcojuice and next to the Juici Patties factory. This is a good place for a picnic and break from the road.

Practicalities

Sweet and Juicy (Swanzey district at the end of Bustamante Highway, contact Jamie Levy tel. 876/359-6158, 7 A.M.–9 P.M. daily, US$3–4.50) serves staples like fried and curried chicken, and curry goat.

Murray's Fish and Jerk Hut (Toll Gate, tel. 876/987-1111 or 876/987-1684, 8 A.M.–10 P.M. daily, US$5–10) is a roadside hut serving roast tilapia caught on the Murray family farm, as well as jerk chicken and pork.

Alcojuice Restaurant & Bar (Clarendon

HOSAY

A traditional Shia Muslim festival that arrived with the indentured Indians brought to Jamaica in the years following emancipation, Hosay (oft-pronounced Hussay) used to be held in communities of significant East Indian populations across the island, including Kingston, Spanish Town, Sav-la-Mar, and Port Maria. Known as Moharram in other countries where the festival is observed, Hosay is today held only in Clarendon, with a procession from Lionel Town to the banks of the Rio Minho taking place every August.

Traditionally, Mahorram participants mourn the Prophet Mohammed's martyr grandsons Hosain and Hasan by whipping themselves and praying as they follow the Tazia or Tadjah, a giant bamboo and paper replica of the slain Hosain, with dancing and stick fighting until the figure is set on the river or sea to float away.

In the Caribbean, the festival has been creolized, starting with its name change, which derives from the chanting of Hosain during the festivities – interpreted as Hosay. The original dates of the festival were also changed from the first 10 days of the lunar cycle in January–February to August-September, when there was less work on the sugar estates and more time to allow for the personal pursuits of the workers. To a large extent the festival lost its religious connotations in Jamaica even while it was observed by non-Muslims in India as well. It has been suggested that the festival today represents an affirmation and remembrance of the struggle of the participants' ancestors as they left the lives they knew to come toil on the sugar estates. The festival is also observed in Suriname, Guyana, and Trinidad, also former sugar colonies where Indians were brought as cheap labor. Contact the **Museum of Ethnography** at the IOJ in Kingston for more information (tel. 876/922-0620, ioj. jam@mail.infochan.com, www.instituteofjamaica.org.jm).

Park, tel. 876/987-1029, alcojuice@netcomm-ja.com, 6:45 A.M.–8 P.M. daily, until 9 P.M. on weekends), managed by Madge Bowen (cell tel. 876/876-6250), across from the Juici Patties factory, has excellent juices and typical Jamaican dishes (US$2.50–6.50). Soups are also served (US$0.75–2.50).

Daily Delicious Restaurant & Sports Bar (28 Main St., next door to Island Grill, a Jamaican fast-food joint, tel. 876/986-9842, 8 A.M.–9:30 P.M. Mon.–Sat., weekends till 11 P.M., US$2.50–6) serves cow foot, cow head, oxtail, fish, pork, curry goat, and baked, stew, curry, and fried chicken.

Juici Patties (tel. 876/904-2618) has its factory and an adjacent outlet and drive-through in Clarendon Park.

Versalles Hotel (42 Longbridge Ave., tel. 876/986-2775) is reached by taking the second left from Mineral Lights Roundabouts. Suites with air-conditioning and hot water, cable TV, and king-size bed or two double beds run US$56.

Bridge Palm Hotel (Toll Gate, tel. 876/987-1052, cell tel. 876/819-4332, U.S. tel. 905/963-3251, bridgepalmhotel@yahoo.com, www.bridgepalm.com, US$50–67) has rooms with mini refrigerator, air-conditioning, and ceiling fans. Some rooms have balconies and overlook the swimming pool.

Fyah Side Jerk (Toll Gate, contact David Tapper, tel. 876/384-6703, 10 A.M.–midnight Mon.–Sat., 10 A.M.–11 P.M. Sun.) serves jerk roadside just past the Bridge Palm Hotel.

NCB (876/986-2343) has a branch and ATM located at 41 Main Street, with a **Scotiabank** (tel. 876/986-2212) branch at 36 Main Street.

Clarendon Parish Library (Main St., tel. 876/902-6294 claparlib@cwjamaica.com) offers DSL Internet access (US$1.50/hour).

SOUTH OF MAY PEN

The area south of May Pen is the prime agricultural land celebrated in the Denbeigh Agricultural Show each year. The area is dominated by cane production at the Moneymusk Sugar Estate. Few visitors to Jamaica make it to this remote side of Clarendon, and the few who do typically visit the somewhat run-down Milk River Baths. More interesting is the coastal region of Portland, where the Portland Lighthouse stands on the farthest point south on the island, which juts out into the sea. You will need to charter or rent a vehicle to properly explore this remote area.

Alley was the capital of the former parish of Vere and remains the sugarcane-producing heartland of Clarendon. The area was once dominated by the Moneymusk Estate and is still largely covered in cane fields that feed the factory, now located closer to **Lionel Town.**

Lionel Town is the largest and most bustling community in the region and the starting point during Hosay, which celebrates Jamaica's East Indian heritage with a procession all the way to May Pen.

Jackson Bay has some of Jamaica's deepest coastal caves, where legend has it the pirate Morgan stashed booty. The little-explored coastline around Jackson Bay is dotted with such caves, while the beach is a popular spot with locals on weekends and holidays. A four-wheel-drive vehicle is very helpful for heavy exploring along this stretch of coast.

At **Salt River**, 10 minutes east of Lionel Town near the coast, there is a public mineral spring that is a favorite among locals. Dances are held on weekends for what they call **Early Sundays.** This is a far more popular bath spot than Milk River, although it's seldom visited by tourists. Unfortunately the lack of tourists also means upkeep is substandard, as the locals don't seem to mind the rubbish that litters the place. Nevertheless, it's a great spot to soak up the up the scene and eat some fried fish and festival. To get to Salt River, take the left turn before reaching Lionel Town heading south, or a left at the T junction after passing through Lionel Town. When the road splits in a Y about a kilometer from the junction, keep left, and then keep left at the following junction. Salt River will be on your right.

Sights
St. Peter's Church is one of the oldest churches

MANDEVILLE

in Jamaica. It was founded in 1671 as the parish church of the former parish of Vere. The present building was erected around 1715 on the foundation of the original. The church bell weighs a quarter ton and was commissioned by the same company that created Big Ben, London's most distinguishing landmark.

The original Moneymusk Sugar Estate windmill in nearby Amity Hall is an interesting octagonal brick structure that now houses a branch of the **parish library** (tel. 876/986-3128, 11 A.M.–5 P.M. Mon.–Fri.); Maxine Reid is the branch assistant. Internet service is offered (US$1.50/hour) on one terminal. The Moneymusk windmill was the only one in Jamaica to be constructed of brick, which raises the question of why the owners went through the trouble of importing such heavy materials from England when other estates were building the structures of locally quarried limestone.

Accommodations

Milk River Hotel and Spa (tel. 876/902-4657, milkriverhotel@yahoo.com) has three types of rooms. There are rooms with two twin beds and either shared bath (US$110) or private bath (US$117), both of which include breakfast, dinner, and bath access. The third room category has either a king-size or queen-size bed with private bath (US$137) and breakfast, dinner, and bath access. These can also be rented with just bath access included (US$48 shared bath, US$55 private bath, US$75 private bath and queen-size bed). One suite has a king-size and a twin bed (triple occupancy, US$112 room and bath alone, US$206 with bath, breakfast, and dinner). Most rooms have air-conditioning and TV. Rooms without air-conditioning have standing fans.

The **Milk River Baths** (7 A.M.–9 P.M. daily, US$4 per 15 minutes for adults, US$2 children 10 and under), located at the hotel, are spring fed with lukewarm water. A bath can be enjoyed whether or not you're staying at the hotel. For curative purposes, a minimum of three baths is recommended, but it is not advisable to stay in the water for longer than an hour because the water is highly radioactive—more so even than the springs at Vichy in France. To get to Milk River, turn south at the roundabout in Toll Gate before reaching Clarendon Park, heading west from May Pen. Continue straight from Toll Gate without turning off until reaching the hotel on the right. Keep heading south in Rest, instead of turning east along the B12 toward Alligator Pond in St. Elizabeth.

Getting There and Around

Route taxis and buses serve May Pen from Kingston and Mandeville. May Pen is located at the western end of Highway 2000, one of Jamaica's best toll roads, making it a quick 45-minute drive from Kingston. From the taxi stand in the square in May Pen, route taxis for points south (like Milk River) leave sporadically as they fill up.

BACKGROUND

The Land

Jamaica enjoys widely varied topography for its small size, ranging from tropical montane regions in the Blue and John Crow Mountains to temperate areas at the higher elevations of Manchester, to lush tropical coastline along much of the coast to near-desert conditions south of the Santa Cruz Mountains in St. Elizabeth. The variety of climatic conditions is what bestows on Jamaica its singularity. Not every island in the Caribbean can boast natural features and attractions in such abundance and close proximity. The most expansive wetlands area in the Caribbean, the Lower Black River Morass, for example, is a popular wintering ground for birds from across the continent, while Jamaica's various mountain ranges create distinct ecosystems that support high levels of endemism.

Land use in Jamaica was historically framed in the context of the colonial plantation economy, where overseers would control vast tracts of land on behalf of absentee landowners and slaves would not be granted title. The plains were coveted for growing cane, while the more mountainous regions produced timber and spices. The birth of the banana industry in the Northeast opened up large new areas to plantation agriculture, before plague virtually wiped out the crop.

After the abolition of slavery, migration

made towns into cities, and a cultural aversion to agriculture and rural life persists today. As you drive across the island you still see vast cane fields in many parishes, with banana and citrus plantations in others. However, it's clear that, just as in many other parts of the world, farming as a way of life has fallen out of fashion, and much agricultural land is left unfarmed.

When the Jamaica Labour Party came to power in 2008 after being in the opposition for 18 years, a renewed emphasis was placed on agriculture by minister Christopher Tufton, who correctly recognizes the vital importance of the sector for country's growth and development. Nonetheless, Jamaica has struggled to bring its land-use policies into the modern era to encourage productive use of land, and squatting continues to be a problem throughout Jamaica. In the greater Kingston area, subdivisions are claiming old cane fields as the urban sprawl continues to fan outward from bedroom communities like Old Harbour, Spanish Town, and Portmore.

GEOGRAPHY

Jamaica is a relatively small island: 235 kilometers miles long and 93 kilometers miles at its widest point, covering an area of 10,992 square kilometers (slightly smaller than the state of Connecticut in the United States). Distances in Jamaica can seem much greater than they really are thanks to mountainous terrain and poor roads.

CLIMATE

Jamaica has a tropical climate along the coast and lowlands, with average annual temperatures of 26–32°C. In the mountains, temperatures can drop down near freezing at night at the highest elevations. Jamaica has two loose rainy seasons: between May and June and then later, with heavier, more sustained rains and coinciding with hurricane season from September to November.

Flora and Fauna

In terms of native biodiversity, Jamaica is surpassed in the Caribbean only by Cuba, a country many times its size. What's more, Jamaica has an extremely high rate of endemism, both in plant and animal life. Perhaps most noticeable are the endemic birds, some of the most striking of which are hard to miss. The national bird is the red-billed streamertail hummingbird (also called the doctor bird), ubiquitous across the island. Other endemic birds, like the Jamaican tody, are more rare—requiring excursions into remote areas to see.

FLORA

While agriculture has diminished in importance as bauxite and tourism have taken over as Jamaica's chief earners, the country still depends heavily on subsistence farming outside the largest cities and towns, where even still many houses have mango and ackee trees in the yard. Coffee remains an important export crop, the Blue Mountains varieties fetching some of the highest (if not *the* highest) prices per pound in the world. In recent years, a growing number of entrepreneurs have begun developing cottage industries based on key agricultural crops. The market for Jamaica's niche products is strong both domestically and abroad. It helps that prices within the country are buoyed by heavy reliance on imported foodstuffs, which, while posing a challenge for consumers, means producers can get a fair price for their goods at home. Some of the most notable of these cottage industries based on natural products of Jamaica are Walkerswood, Starfish Oils, Pickapeppa, and Belcour Preserves. Look out for these in crafts shops and specialty supermarkets across the island. Many of these enterprises offer tours of their production facilities.

Jamaica's flora consists of a diverse mix of tropical and subtropical vegetation. Along the dry South Coast, the landscape resembles a

© OLIVER HILL

Ackee is the key ingredient in Jamaica's national dish, ackee and saltfish.

desert, while mangrove wetlands near Black River provide a sharp contrast within relatively close proximity. In the highlands of Manchester, temperate crops like potato, known as Irish, and carrots thrive.

Fruits and Plants

Ugli fruit is a hybrid between grapefruit *(Citrus paradisi)* and tangerine *(Citrus reticulata)* developed at Trout Hall, St. Catherine. It has a brainy-textured thick skin that is easily removed to reveal the juicy, orange-like fruit inside. A few large citrus estates, most notably Good Hope in Trelawny, make this an important export.

Ackee *(Blighia sapida)* is a small to mid-size tree native to West Africa, its introduction to Jamaica having been recorded in 1778 when some plants were purchased from a slave ship captain. It is said to have been present earlier, however, owing to a slave who wouldn't relinquish his grasp of the fruit across the Middle Passage. Ackee is Jamaica's national fruit.

Anatto *(Bixa orellana)* is an important dye and food coloring, and was at one point an important Jamaican export, likely lending its name to Annotto Bay in St. Mary, which was a center of production and export.

Jimbalin is the Jamaican name for what is known as passion fruit in the United States. **Passion fruit** *(P. edulis flavicarpa)* has one of the world's most beautiful flowers and a delicious fruit not commonly seen fresh in northern countries.

Antidote cacoon *(Fevillea cordiflora)*, known as sabo, segra-seed, and nhandiroba, is a perennial climbing vine whose fruit has been used for its medicinal and purgative qualities.

Agave *(Agave sabolifera)* is a succulent, its broad leaves edged with prickles, notable for its tremendous 5- to 10-meter flower shoot February–April. Bulbils fall from the shoots to develop into independent plants.

Arrowroot *(Maranta arundinacea)* was brought from South America by pre-Columbian populations and used medicinally. Later it was grown on plantations and used as a starch substitute and thickener.

Apple in Jamaica is a generic term that could

refer to any number of fruits, starting with the delicious Otaheite apple. Other apples include star apple, custard apple (sweet sop, sour sop), mammee apple *(Mammea americana)*, crab apple (also known as coolie plum), golden apple *(Passiflora laurifolia)*, velvet apple *(Diospyros discolor)*—also known as the Philippine persimmon, and rose apple *(Syzyguim jambos)*, used as a windbreak and for erosion control. The imported American or English apple, the common apple of the United States, has been slowly and unfortunately taking over from the more exotic varieties on fruit stands in recent years due to its exotic appeal.

Avocado *(Persea americana)* is known commonly in Jamaica as "pear." Avocado is a native of Mexico, from where it was taken by the Spaniards throughout the Americas and much of the world. The Spanish name, *aguacate,* is a substitute for the Aztec name, *ahucatl.* Avocados are in season in Jamaica from August to December with a few varieties ripening into February. Alligator, Simmonds, Lulu, Collinson, and Winslowson are some of the varieties grown on the island.

Banana *(Musa acuminata* x *balbisiana)* is the world's largest herb (non-woody plant); it became an important Jamaican export in the post-Emancipation period of 1876–1927. Jamaica was the world's foremost producer of the fruit during the period, with Gros Michel and later Cavendish varieties. The banana trade gave rise to Caribbean tourism when increasingly wealthy shippers began to offer passage on their empty boats returning to Jamaica from New England, where much of the produce was destined. In this way Portland, an important banana-growing region, became the Caribbean's first tourism destination with the Titchfield Hotel, built by a banana baron, exemplifying the relationship between the fruit and the tourism economy that would come to replace it in importance. Several varieties of banana are still grown in Jamaica, including plantain, an important starch; boiled bananas are a necessary accompaniment in the typical Jamaican Sunday breakfast of ackee and saltfish, callaloo, and dumpling.

Barringtonia *(Barrintonia asiatica)* is a large evergreen with its center of origin in Asia. Its large coconut-like fruit will float for up to two years and root on the shore where it lands. Known locally as the duppy coconut, the tree has been naturalized in Portland and 220-year-old trees grow at Bath Gardens in St. Thomas.

Wild basil *(Ocimum micranthum)* is a wild bush used in folk medicine and in cooking, popularly called barsley or baazli.

Bauhinia *(Bauhinia spp.),* known locally as "poor man's orchid," is a favorite of the streamertail hummingbird, or doctor bird, which visits the orchid-like flowers. It grows as a shrub or mid-sized tree with pinkish flowers.

Madam Fate *(Hippobroma longiflora)* is a poisonous perennial herb with a five-petaled, star-shaped flower used in Obeah and folk medicine. Found along pastures or on riverbanks, it's commonly called star flower or horse poison.

Trees and Flowers

Kingston buttercup *(Tribulus cistoides)* is a low, spreading plant with bright yellow flowers. It's known commonly as "Kill Backra" because it was thought to have caused yellow fever, which killed many European settlers. It's also called "police macca" because of its thorns, and turkey blossom.

Blue mahoe *(Hibiscus elatus)* is a quality hardwood of the Malvaceae family. It grows native in the Blue Mountains and is the national tree.

Ironwood *(Lignum vitae)* is an extremely dense tropical hardwood that produces Jamaica's national flower.

Mahogany *(Swietenia mahagoni)* was and still is highly valued for its timber and has accordingly been unsustainably harvested since the Spanish colonial period, resulting in dwindling numbers today. Mahogany can still be seen growing, albeit sparsely, along the banks of the Black River, which was originally called the Mahogany River by the Spanish, or Rio Caobana.

Sorrel *(Rumex acetosa)* is a cousin of the hibiscus whose flowers are boiled to make a drink popular around Christmas time.

FAUNA
Mammals

The **coney** or Jamaican hutia *(Geocapromys brownii)* is Jamaica's only surviving indigenous land-dwelling mammal, the only other being bats. Conies are nocturnal and thus seldom seen. The animal is basically a large rodent with cousins inhabiting other Caribbean islands like Hispaniola. Its meat was prized by the Taino centuries ago, while it is still a delicacy for the mongoose today, which is blamed for pushing it towards extinction. Another threat is loss of habitat, owing to encroaching urbanization of its principal habitats in the Hellshire Hills and Worthy Park of St. Catherine. It is also found in the John Crow Mountains in Portland and St. Thomas.

Mongooses are today a common animal seen scurrying across the road. Widely regarded as pests, it is said that all mongooses in the Western Hemisphere are descendants of four males and five females introduced to Jamaica from India in 1872 to control the rat population on the sugar estate of one William Bancroft Espeut. They soon went on to outgrow their function, eventually being held responsible for killing off five endemic vertebrates and bringing Jamaica's iguanas to the verge of extinction.

Bats

In Jamaica, the term bat typically refers to moths. Jamaica has 23 species of bat, known locally as rat bats, bats being used for moths. Many species of the Bombacaceae family are bat-pollinated, including the baobab, cottonwood, cannonball, and night cactus trees. Bats also go for other pulpy fruits like sweet sop, banana, naseberry, and mango. *Noctilio leporinus,* a fish-eating bat, can be seen swooping low over harbors and inlets at twilight.

Birds

Of the 280 species of birds that have been recorded in Jamaica, 30 species and 19 subspecies are endemic (found nowhere else). Of these 30, two are considered extinct. There are 116 species that use Jamaica as a breeding ground, while around 80 species spend the northern winter months on the island. The Jamaican tody, the ubiquitous "doctor bird" (Jamaica's national bird, properly called the red-billed

A male doctor bird perches for a meal of hibiscus nectar.

streamertail), and the Jamaican mango hummingbird are especially colorful species to look out for.

Reptiles

Jamaica has 26 species of lizards, including the island's largest, the iguana, now protected in the Helshire Hills and in slow recovery after near extinction due to slaughter by farmers and mongooses. The *Anolis* genus includes seven of the most common species, often seen in hotel rooms and on verandas, their showy throat fan extending to attract females. The largest *Anolis* is the garmani, which prefers large trees to human dwellings. All Jamaica's lizards are harmless.

Six of Jamaica's seven snake species are endemic, and all of them are harmless. Mostly found in remote areas like Cockpit Country, snakes have fallen victim to the fear of country folk, who generally kill them on sight, and to the introduced mongoose, famous for its ability to win a fight with the cobras of its native India. The island's largest snake is the yellow

© OLIVER HILL

A Jamaican yellow boa peers out from a dark crevasse.

snake, with yellow and black patterns across its back. The snake is a boa constrictor, known locally as nanka, which can grow up to 3.5 meters in length. The nanka is seldom seen, as it is only active at night when it emerges from hiding to feed on bats and rats. Other less impressive snakes include three species of grass snake of the *Arrhyton* genus and the two-headed or worm snake *(Typhlops jamaicensis),* which burrows below ground with its tail end virtually indistinguishable from its head. The black snake is considered an extinct victim of the mongoose.

Crocodiles are Jamaica's biggest reptiles, and are often referred to on the island as alligators. The American crocodile *(Crocodylus acutus)* is found across the island in swampy mangrove areas like Font Hill Wildlife Sanctuary and the Lower Black River Morass. This is the same species of croc found in Florida and other coastal wetlands of the Caribbean. Crocodiles have a long tapering snout, whereas alligators have a short, flat head.

SEALIFE
Marine Mammals
Jamaica has no large native mammals on land. The largest mammals are instead marine-based, namely dolphins and manatees, the latter being known locally as sea cows. Manatees are endangered and now protected under wildlife laws after having seen their population dwindle due to hunting.

Turtles
Of the six sea turtle species known worldwide, four were once common, and now less so, in Jamaican waters: the green turtle *(Chelonia midas),* the hawksbill *(Eretmochelys imbricata),* the leatherback *(Dermochelys coriacea),* and the loggerhead *(Caretta caretta).* Turtle meat formed an important part of the diet of the Tainos and was later adopted as a delicacy by the colonial settlers. In keeping with Taino practice, they kept green turtles in large coastal pens known as turtle crawles, to be killed and eaten at will.

ENDANGERED FISHERIES

The spiny lobster is one of Jamaica's most prized culinary delicacies, often prepared either grilled, with garlic sauce, or with a curry sauce. Lobsters fetch a high price, usually somewhere between US$10 and US$20 per pound at local grills and restaurants, and as high as US$40 per plate in many tourist establishments. The sustainability of lobster harvesting depends on allowing the creatures a safe period for reproduction, which has been acknowledged in Jamaica by the Fisheries Division in the Ministry of Agriculture and Land with a ban on harvesting between April 1 and June 30. It is crucial that visitors to the island respect this ban and in so doing support efforts to ensure that lobster populations are kept at a sustainable level so the delicacy can continue to be enjoyed in the future. Some establishments serve what is said to be frozen lobster during the closed season. Regardless, it's best to avoid ordering it during this period to be on the safe side and avoid adding incentive to any potential shortfall of integrity on the part of restaurateurs and anglers. The Fishing Industry Act of 1975 makes it illegal to catch lobster during closed season and also puts a general ban on landing undersized lobster (under 76.2 mm, or 3 inches) and those bearing eggs, throughout the year. As the Fisheries department has struggled in recent years under financial constraints, it's imperative to be supportive in the effort to curb illegal harvesting. Conch *(Strombus gigas)* is also protected from over-fishing and has a closed season from July 1 through October 31.

Jamaican waters are also becoming severely over harvested where finned fish are concerned. It's best to avoid buying fresh fish smaller than six inches unless it's a type of fish that doesn't grow to a larger size. The median size of the catch brought in from traditional line fishing and spear fishing in waters close to Jamaica's shores has decreased noticeably over the past decade. The situation becomes clear when snorkeling along Jamaica's coastal reefs as few large fish can be seen today, and snapper, once common, are increasingly scarce near to the shoreline.

Responsible Tourism

The most important thing to remember in any visit to a foreign country is that your dollar is your most substantive demonstration of support. Jamaica is an expensive place to live by any measure, and foreign currency is the chief economic driver. The benefit, or lack thereof, that tourism brings to the island is dependent on where the incoming dollars end up. Though rock-bottom all-inclusive packages are an easy way to control your vacation spending, it should be noted that the money that flows to these groups is not widely distributed and typically ends up lining the pockets of a few individuals. What's more, large resorts often pay their workers a pittance.

Jamaica has gone through several different eras of tourism development dating back to the booming banana trade in the late 1800s. Up until the 1960s Jamaica remained a niche destination for the early yacht set, which later became the jet set. In the late 1960s and early 1970s the hippie movement discovered Jamaica, and large groups would tour around on motorbikes, reveling in the laid-back lifestyle and plentiful herb. Montego Bay was the upscale destination on the island, with Port Antonio the playground of movie stars and Negril a newly discovered fishing beach only just connected by road to the rest of Hanover parish. In those days the numbers of visitors were low and, outside Montego Bay, the environmental impact of tourism was negligible. Then came the all-inclusive resorts, the largest of which, Sunset Jamaica Grande, had 750 rooms by 2006. Since 2006, several new hotels have been built along the North Coast with over 1,000 rooms. The water resources required by these facilities puts a huge strain on the environment, as does wastewater, which is often poorly or minimally treated before being dumped into the sea. The enormous demand for food at these establishments generally is insufficiently met by local producers. These hotels cite inconsistency in the local market as a factor in their heavy reliance on imported goods.

Perhaps the best way to make a positive impact with a visit to Jamaica is by promoting "community tourism" by staying in smaller, locally run establishments and eating at a variety of restaurants rather than heeding the fear tactics that keep so many tourists inside gated hotels. Treasure Beach in St. Elizabeth parish is a mecca for community tourism, where the few mid-size hotels are far outnumbered by boutique guesthouses and villas, many of which are locally owned.

ENVIRONMENTAL ISSUES

In the past 10 years the Jamaican government has opened the country to an incursion from multinational hotel groups that are some of the most blatant culprits of environmental destruction. Ever-larger all-inclusive resorts are covering what were a few years ago Jamaica's remaining untouched stretches of coastline. The absence of beaches has not inhibited developers from making their own, at incalculable environmental cost to the protective coral reefs and marinelife they support along much of the coast. When scuba diving and snorkeling along Jamaica's reefs, make your impact minimal by not touching the coral.

Bauxite Mining

The bauxite industry is an important foreign exchange earner for Jamaica but the environmental costs are clear. The Ewarton Aluminum Plant in St. Ann is noticeable by its stench for kilometers around, and from the heights of Mandeville several bauxite facilities scar the landscape. Discovery Bay and Ocho Rios have important export terminals, as does Port Kaiser in St. Elizabeth with another bauxite port, and Rocky Point in Clarendon and Port Esquivel in St. Catherine.

Litter

Environmental education in Jamaica is seriously lacking. Environmental awareness has only recently been directly linked to the island's tourist economy by some of the more responsible tourism groups. The difference in sanitation and upkeep between the leisure destinations frequented principally by Jamaicans rather than foreign tourists is marked. Choice spots like Salt River in Clarendon are littered with trash, while other popular local spots like Bluefields Beach Park in Westmoreland make greater efforts to clean up after their patrons. Regardless of how senseless it may seem to take a green stance when it comes to litter in the face of gross negligence on the part of Jamaicans themselves, it's important to be aware of the fact that Jamaicans watch visitors very carefully: Make a point of not trashing the country, even if you seem to be up against insurmountable odds.

Water Table Salination

Several coastal areas suffer salination of the water table when water is extracted more rapidly than it is replenished. While Jamaica is blessed with high rainfall in the east and abundant hydrology generally, there will likely be an increasing problem in drier northwest coast areas where new all-inclusive resorts are being built. Wherever you end up staying, the best way to lessen your impact on finite water resources is by not taking long showers and by heeding the requests made at many of the more responsible and proactive hotels to reuse towels during your stay rather than throwing them on the floor after a single use for housekeeping personnel to deal with.

Deforestation

Despite the known harm it causes and the ensuing potential for erosion, slash-and-burn agriculture remains the predominant means of smallholder cultivation in rural areas. While significant portions of land have been designated as protected areas across Jamaica, pressure on the environment, especially around tourism boom towns like Ocho Rios, where little planning preceded the influx of workers from other parishes, is leaving the water supply under threat and causing erosion where forestlands on steep inclines are cut for ramshackle housing settlements.

History

EARLY INHABITANTS AND SPANISH DISCOVERY

Jamaica was first inhabited by the Tainos, sometimes referred to as Arawaks, who arrived from the northern coast of South America in dugout canoes around A.D. 900. The Tainos practiced subsistence agriculture to complement hunting, fishing, and foraging activities, forming mostly seaside settlements from where travel by dugout canoe remained an important mode of transport.

Upon his arrival on the island in 1494, Italian explorer Christopher Columbus claimed the island on behalf of his financiers, King Ferdinand and Queen Isabella of Spain—in spite of the presence of a large Taino population with whom the Europeans engaged in an easily-won battle. The exact point of his arrival is contested; it is likely the explorer landed in Rio Bueno, on the border of present-day St. Ann and Trelawny, where there is freshwater,

rather than in Discovery Bay, which he named Puerto Seco, or Dry Harbour, because it lacked freshwater—something historical observers say would have influenced where explorers chose to make landfall.

Jamaica was not deemed of much import to the Spanish Crown due to its relatively rugged terrain, and more importantly its lack of gold. Spain was more concerned with exploits in Mexico and Central and South America. Neighboring Hispaniola had more gold and was thus deemed more worthwhile, while Cuba, 145 kilometers to the north, was also more important to the Crown as it was easily settled with vast arable flat lands and a strategic position as the key to the Gulf of Mexico. While Cuba became increasingly important as a transshipment point for gold and other goods from the New World to Europe, Jamaica remained a backwater left largely under the control of

© OLIVER HILL

indigenous Taino paintings at Mountain River Cave

Columbus' heirs. Within 50 years of "discovery," the indigenous Taino population, estimated at as much as one million inhabitants at time of contact, was virtually annihilated through forced labor and, more importantly, European diseases to which the natives had no immunological defenses.

Four early Spanish settlements are known to have been established at Melilla, somewhere on the North Coast, at Oristan, near present-day Bluefields, Westmoreland, at Spanish Town, which grew into the principal city of Santiago de la Vega, and in Yallahs, near the border of St. Andrew and St. Thomas today. These settlements were mainly focused on cattle ranching, while horse breeding was also an important endeavor. Jamaica became a regular provisions stop for Spanish galleons heading to Colombia, among other important gold coasts. While a few inland routes were carved out of the tropical jungle, transportation around the island remained almost entirely sea-based with the long and navigable Martha Brae River becoming an important route between the North and South Coasts. The lack of a centralized strategy for settlement and defense left Jamaica extremely vulnerable to attack from other early colonial powers, ultimately leading to an easy takeover by Britain's naval forces led by Cromwell. While it was the Spanish who first brought many of plants that would become key to the island's economy in subsequent centuries, including banana, sugarcane, and indigo, it was the British who created an organized plantation system—key to effectively exploit the land and establish lucrative trade with Europe.

THE ENGLISH TAKEOVER

In 1655 English naval forces, led by Oliver Cromwell, invaded Jamaica and easily captured Spanish Town, the colonial rival's capital. The Spanish colony had virtually no defense strategy in place, a fact known and exploited by Cromwell, who distributed vast tracts of land to his fellow officers as a reward for their service. These land grants would form the first plantation estates of the British Colony. The former Spanish rulers were loath to abandon the island, waging guerilla warfare and reprisal attacks on the British with the help of loyal Maroons, led by Ysassi. The Spanish fled to the North Coast or left the island altogether for Hispaniola or Cuba.

Soon after Cromwell's forces seized Jamaica, the British began a policy of legitimizing the activity of pirates—in effect gaining their allegiance in exchange for allowing them to continue their raids on mostly Spanish ships as privateers instead of buccaneers. The alliance made Port Royal at the tip of the Palisadoes in Kingston harbor into a boomtown, fueled by bustling trade in slaves and rum in addition to commerce in luxury goods, some imported from England and beyond, others plundered from victim ships.

While the slave trade had been established on the island under Spanish rule, it wasn't until the British set up vast, well-organized sugarcane plantations that slave labor was imported en masse from Africa. Jamaica became the Caribbean's primary transshipment point for slaves to other parts of the New World, including the United States.

PLANTATION CULTURE AND THE SLAVE TRADE

As an incentive to see Jamaica reach its full potential as a plantation colony, the British offered land not only to those who had been involved in the successful takeover, but also to Britons from England and other British colonies, most notably Barbados. Vast estates covered thousands of acres, with many absentee landowners installing overseers to take care of business on the island while reaping the benefits from quiet England. The cultivation of sugar expanded during the 1700s to the point where Jamaica was the world's foremost producer and England's prized colony. But the economic boom was far from equitable, relying heavily on a slave trade set up first by the Portuguese and later by the Dutch and English along the Gold Coast of Ghana and Slave Coast of Nigeria. Slavery was not a new phenomenon in Africa, but with the arrival of

European traders it was formalized, and raids into the interior began to supplement the prisoners of war who were first exported as slaves. The slaves brought to Jamaica were a mix of different ethnicities, including Coromantee, Ibo, Mandingo, Yoruba, and Congo. Slaves of different ethnic backgrounds and tongues were intentionally put together to complicate any potential resistance.

Slaves were not only used in the fields on the plantations, but also as domestic workers, carpenters, masons, and coopers. The tendency for women around the plantation to give birth to children of lighter complexion helped loosen the hold of the slave system as the moral high ground assumed by the British as the boundaries of race became increasingly blurred.

RUMORS AND REBELLION

The 1700s saw Jamaica rise to be the world's greatest producer of sugar and rum, with large estates worked by thousands of slaves covering the island's arable land. The runaway slaves, or Maroons, consolidated their autonomy in the country's rugged highland interior, while overseers managed the large estates for their mostly absentee masters.

But the plantation system could not be taken for granted by the British, with a series of slave uprisings stirring the foundations of their booming economy. The rumors of freedom began with Tacky's War in 1760, in which a Coromantee chief known as Tacky, a driver on Frontier Estate in St. Mary, orchestrated an uprising that spread to neighboring estates, and had as its objective the overthrow of the colonial masters throughout the island. Even while the Maroons maintained, and still maintain, aloofness when it came to how they viewed enslaved Africans who accepted their lot, their parallel existence in free communities served as a constant reminder on the plantation that slavery was not unshakable. Free people of color, meanwhile, helped maintain the status quo, breeding a culture of superiority related to complexion, which remains as a historical retention in Jamaican society to this day.

With fellow slaves in North America earning or buying their freedom in increasing numbers following the War of Independence, the nonconformists in Jamaica took added encouragement. In 1783 one such freed slave, the Baptist reverend George Liele, arrived in Jamaica to establish a ministry in Kingston that would give birth to the Baptist nonconformist movement on the island as he proceeded to baptize slaves by in scores. These early Baptists, like nonconformist Methodists, Moravians, and Congregationalists, struck a chord with the masses with their anti-slavery stance. One follower, Liele, baptized those who would seek patronage from the Baptist Ministry Society of Great Britain, which responded by sending the first British Baptist Missionary in 1814. For the next twenty years, anti-slavery rumblings grew until Sam Sharpe's rebellion, known as The Baptist War, broke from its intent of carrying out a peaceful strike with several plantations burned to the ground. While the uprising was suppressed by the plantocracy's militia and a British garrison, the British Parliament held inquiries that would lead to abolition two years later.

EMANCIPATION, APPRENTICESHIP, AND THE FALL OF COLONIAL RULE

The abolition of slavery in 1834 preceded a four-year period of "apprenticeship" designed to integrate newly freed slaves into more "sophisticated" jobs, and more importantly, allow the plantation economy to adapt to a labor force that required compensation.

Following the apprenticeship period, however, the plantation owners soon found it difficult to secure workers, as many left the countryside for town in search of alternative livelihoods far from the memory of chains. Soon after emancipation, Jamaica's plantocracy, along with cane growers in places like Trinidad, Guyana, and Suriname, resorted to the importation of indentured Indian and Chinese laborers to work their fields beginning in 1845 through to 1921. The period following emancipation was the cradle for the modern identity of the Jamaican people. It was by no means an easy time, as Jamaica continued to be wrought with oppression and injustice, as evidenced by the Morant Bay Rebellion of 1865. Continued repression and oppression in Jamaica led many ambitious and frustrated young men to seek their fortunes overseas, whether in Panama, where the canal would be built between the late 1800s and the early 1900s, thanks in part to Jamaican labor, or to the U.S., where a similar cultural identity was being formed as uprooted Africans became African Americans. Many of these fortune seekers, among them Marcus Garvey, George Stiebel, and Alexander Bustamante, returned with wealth, which afforded them a voice in society they used to advance the cause of the worker, and ultimately, an independent Jamaica. Suffrage was tied to land ownership until it was universally declared in 1944, one of the many reasons for ongoing struggle throughout the post-emancipation period, and Jamaica's dark history of forced labor was a natural hotbed of resistance leading to the rise of the country's vibrant labor movement.

"INDEPENDENT" JAMAICA

Jamaica's road to independence was trod with baby steps. In 1938, Norman Manley founded the People's National Party, and Alexander Bustamante formed the Jamaica Labour Party five years later. The first elections with universal suffrage were held in 1944. World War II had a significant impact on Jamaica, with widespread shortages adding to the urgency of rising social and political movements. The 1950s saw waves of emigrants leave Jamaica for England, with the tendency for emigrants to head for the United States increasing when Britain restricted immigration following independence. Many old folks in Jamaica still bemoan the country's independence, recalling the good old days when schools were better and society more proper under the British. The past several decades have been characterized, however, by a young nation, still under the commonwealth system, experiencing growing pains, still dependent as ever, albeit on different external forces. The flow of remittances from Jamaicans abroad, health of the global economy, approving nod of multilateral financial institutions, maintenance of bilateral trade agreements, and uninterrupted receipt of royalty payments from foreign mining companies are all vital for the government's economic welfare and that of the Jamaican people today more than ever. Until Jamaica becomes a net exporter of goods and services, it will have a difficult time claiming true independence, as today it relies little on its own productivity for survival.

Government and Economy

The Jamaican central government is organized as a constitutional monarchy and member of the British Commonwealth with Queen Elizabeth II as its official head of state. On the island, the Queen is represented by the governor general, who is a signatory on all legislation passed by the bicameral Jamaican Parliament. The bicameral government comprises a Senate and a House of Representatives, known as the Upper and Lower Houses, respectively. Representatives are elected for five-year terms, one from each of the island's 60 constituencies. Of Jamaica's 50 senators, 21 are appointed by the governor general, 13 on the advice of the prime minister, and eight by the opposition leader. The cabinet consists of the prime minister and a minimum of 13 other ministers, including the minister of finance, who must also be an elected representative in the house, with not more than four cabinet ministers selected from the members of the senate.

Beyond the national government, Jamaica has been organized into parishes of ecclesiastical origin since the arrival of the British, who installed the Church of England as their watchdog and pacifier. The Church of England later became the Anglican Church, whose rectories are still some of the most impressive buildings in the more rural areas across the island. The 60 federal constituencies are subdivided into 275 electoral units, each of which has a parish councillor in the local government. The Corporate Area, as metropolitan Kingston is known, combines the parishes of Kingston and St. Andrew into one local government entity known as the Kingston and St. Andrew Corporation.

Local representation dates to 1662, when the Vestry system was installed to manage local affairs across the island. The Vestry was composed of clergy members and lay magistrates of each parish and was in effect indistinguishable from the Church of England insomuch as governance and policy were concerned, as it operated almost exclusively for the benefit of the landed elite. The amalgamated ruling class of the planters, clergy, and magistrates became known as the plantocracy. After 200 years of the Vestry system, it was abandoned in favor of a system of Municipal and Road Boards following the Morant Bay Rebellion in 1866. During the period when Jamaica was ruled by the Vestry system, the number of parishes increased from seven at the outset to 22 by the time it was abandoned. In 1867, the number of parishes was reduced to the 14 recognized today. In 1886, a new representational system of local government was installed consisting of Parochial Boards, which merged the operations of the Municipal and Road Boards into one entity. A general decentralization occurred during the intermittent period before the Parochial Boards were established, leaving local governments in charge of public health, markets, fire services, and water supply. Following implementation of the Parochial Board system, the oversight of building regulations, public beaches, sanitation, slaughterhouses, and streetlights was also assigned to the local government bodies.

Jamaica's political system is notoriously bureaucratic and corrupt, with little to suggest this will ever change—regardless of which party comes to power. Many say this is a legacy of British rule, but the fact that money is the chief motivator behind decision-making at Gordon House is generally acknowledged.

POLITICAL PARTIES AND ELECTIONS

Jamaica's two political parties, the People's National Party (PNP) and the Jamaica Labour Party (JLP) were founded by cousins Norman Manley and Alexander Bustamante. Bustamante was a labor leader who came to some degree of wealth through his travels around Latin America before exploiting the anti-colonial sentiment of the day to push for greater worker rights and ultimately Jamaican independence. The PNP held on to power since the 1980s, instating Portia Simpson-Miler in 2007 before the JLP's Bruce Golding toppled her in 2008.

Election time tends to be tense and tumultuous in Jamaica, when memories of the political violence in the 1970s become fresh again. Kingston's poor neighborhoods bear the brunt of the tension and are often barricaded during elections to prevent opposition loyalists from entering with their vehicles to stage drive-by shootings.

ECONOMY

Jamaica's economy is supported by agriculture, bauxite, tourism, and remittances (in order of increasing importance). The financial sector is closely tied to other English-speaking Caribbean countries, namely Trinidad and Tobago, with large regional banks and insurance companies dominating the market. Jamaica has a serious balance of payments problem owing to high external debt dating back several decades. Austerity measures imposed by IMF restructuring packages during the political reign of Edward Seaga left little money for education and social programs, a situation which persists today. A new IMF arrangement was brokered in 2009–2010, which will impose a heavy burden on the country, with a two-year public sector wage freeze likely to be accompanied by large governmental job cuts. Universal education, a promise made by the JLP prior to coming to power, has inched nearer with the removal of school fees, but the quality of schools varies widely from district to district, and many old timers claim education was better under British rule. Failure to guarantee universal education is a serious shortfall of both political parties and has directly impacted productivity. The flip side of the coin sees the country's best educated leaving for higher-paid jobs overseas.

Agriculture

Agriculture remains an important part of Jamaica's economy, if not in sheer numbers then for its role in providing sustenance. The cultivation of provision grounds established during slavery persists to some degree in rural areas today, where most households grow some kind of crop, even if it is limited to a few mango and ackee trees.

Sugar production is still ongoing on a handful of large estates across the country, some of them private, others government-owned, but the end of preferential pricing for Jamaican sugar in England has affected the crop's viability just as it dampened the prospects for Jamaica's banana industry. Apart from sugar, important export crops include coffee, the Blue Mountain variety fetching some of the highest prices in the world, and citrus including oranges and ugli fruit.

Mining

Bauxite mining and processing in Jamaica is dominated by foreign entities like Russia's United Company RUSAL, Norway's Norsk Hydro, and U.S.-based Alcoa. Bauxite is mined across the island, where gaping red holes in the earth are the telltale sign. Bauxite is converted into alumina before being

Quandrant Wharf frames historical and present mainstays of the Jamaican economy with a sugar pier overshadowed by the St. Ann bauxite wharf.

smelted into aluminum, both processes requiring huge amounts of energy. Jamaica has a serious energy problem in that it is overwhelmingly dependent on imported oil for electricity generation. High global energy prices combined with global recession and low aluminum prices paralyzed the bauxite and alumina industry in early 2009, eliminating a large royalty revenue stream earning foreign exchange for the government. Jamaica remains one of the most important bauxite sources in the world, once ranked third in production of bauxite ore and fourth in alumina production globally, but it requires high aluminum prices and low energy prices to be viable. At its peak, the bauxite industry accounted for 75 percent of the country's export earnings. Other less important mineral resources found in Jamaica include gypsum, limestone, marble, silica sand, clay peat, lignite, titanium, copper, lead, and zinc. The export of crushed limestone, or aggregates, and limestone derivatives, is an important growth industry with several players across the island.

Tourism

Tourism continues to be the primary driver of economic growth in Jamaica. Tourism development in recent years has taken the form of mega-projects that employ large numbers at low wages and keep foreign exchange and profits offshore. There seems to be little interest in seeing tourism dollars more evenly distributed among the population at large, with the government apparently happy to collect its general consumption tax for each guest that passes through the mass-market all-inclusive resorts. Despite the government's lack of effort to see tourism revenue more widely distributed, entrepreneurial Jamaicans see great benefits from tourism, with a slew of niche attractions having been created and developed to serve this market.

Remittances

As a percentage of GDP contributed by remittances, Jamaica is ranked seventh in the world and fourth in the Caribbean—after the Dominican Republic—with nearly US$2 billion entering the country each year for the past several years. The "Jamaican Dream," pursued by many who are able, consists of leaving the country to pursue a career abroad for however long it takes to make it, and then returning to Jamaica to flex pretty. Sometimes the required time lasts generations, especially when those they left back home weigh heavily on conscience and wallet alike. In tough economic times, Jamaica is more dependent than ever on expatriates, with large concentrations living in Toronto, New York, Florida, and London.

DISTRIBUTION OF WEALTH

Some say there are two Jamaicas, made up of the haves and the have nots. In fact, there are many more Jamaicas. You don't need a whole lot of money to have a high quality of life when the hot sun is shining; mangos, ackee, and breadfruit are ripe on the trees; and the rivers are pleasantly cool for bathing. So in a sense how you live is based on how close you are to the natural resources that make this a tropical paradise.

However, land isn't free, fruit goes out of season, and some days it rains. More importantly, there is a serious cash-flow problem in Jamaica, and as they say, what little there is goes like water. The reality is that many Jamaicans don't find the time, let alone the resources, to travel around and enjoy tourism centers in the focused and intensive way foreigners tend to on their two-week vacations. With nearly half of the island's population living in the Corporate Area and nearby Spanish Town, there gets to be competition for things that might otherwise be picked from the tree. But more overwhelming than the price of local produce from the market are imports, which basically covers everything else. With jobs hard to come by for underqualified youth, and even for qualified youth, there is a desperate situation for many, especially as prices for groceries and other basic goods keep rising. Add in the fact that it is not uncommon for a man to have several children from more than one woman, and the role of what's termed "social capital" becomes clear. If it weren't for the way Jamaicans help each other out—whether by raising children belonging to a niece or nephew, or employing a man around the house who really doesn't do much gardening but clearly has no better prospects—Jamaica would find itself in a far worse state. But it is this cycle of too many mouths to feed with too little to go around that maintains a steep class divide on the island. Education costs money, for school fees, books, and uniforms, and with competing interests vying for the limited resources in many cash-strapped homes, school can take the back seat. Without a proper education, the youth become stuck doing menial jobs or nothing at all, and to "breed one gyal" (a common, albeit crass, way to say "get a girl pregnant") may be the most rosy thing going for them.

People and Culture

Jamaica's national motto, "Out of many, one people," reflects the tolerance and appreciation for diversity promulgated from an institutional level. Meanwhile individuals and communities comprising Jamaica's myriad ethnic groups keep old prejudices and stereotypes very much alive, usually without the slightest hint of malice but still with names that are considered derogatory in other parts of the world. "Coolie" is the term generally used to refer to East Indians, or those of Indian descent, "Chiney" for those of East Asian descent, and "Syrian" for anyone of Middle Eastern descent. If you find yourself the victim of this kind of stereotyping, try not to be offended. Ethnic divisions and cultural prejudices in Jamaica are a result of a history steeped in confrontation and oppression. Rarely, if ever, do these prejudices lead to conflict or violence. While racism is still very much a baffling reality in a country with such an overwhelming black majority, Jamaica's African heritage is celebrated in popular music enjoyed across social and economic classes.

RACE AND CLASS

Race in Jamaican society is and has been of utmost importance in maintaining the strict class structure historically, while in contemporary society everything boils down to money. Nonetheless, complexion and ethnic background still often form the basis of an individual's perception of self and place in society. While the island has an overwhelming black majority, other minority groups play an important, even dominant role in the local economy. Chinese and Indians who were brought to the island as indentured labor following the abolition of slavery became and remain prominent members of society as shopkeepers and traders, even in the smaller communities. Lebanese-Jamaicans have also played a significant role in business as well as in national politics. White Jamaicans still own some of the most beautiful and expansive estates. The British established the precedent of "complexionism" by putting lighter-skinned, or "brown," Jamaicans—often their own errant progeny—in managerial positions, a self-perpetuating phenomenon that continues today in the nepotism that pervades the political and economic elite. The Maroons, who initially put up fierce resistance to the British colonial government and forced a treaty giving them autonomy and freedom from slavery long before abolition, have been an important source of pride for Jamaicans, even while the issue of their collaboration with the British in suppressing slave rebellions remains something of a cultural taboo.

RELIGION

Jamaica holds the Guinness Book World Record for most churches per capita. Virtually every religion and denomination on earth is represented on the island, with churches everywhere you turn. A common sight on weekends is large tents set up across the countryside for the open-air services preferred by the evangelical denominations. Only those churches that are unique to Jamaica or have played an important role in the country's history have been described, with listings in the destination chapters for those of historical or architectural significance.

Revival

Born as a distinctly Jamaican fusion between Christian and African beliefs during the Great Revival of 1860–1861, Revival today is composed of two different branches: Pukkumina (Pocomania or Poco) and Revival Zion, the former being further toward the African end of the merged spectrum, the latter incorporating more obviously Christian beliefs and practices. Revivalists wear colorful robes and turbans during energetic ceremonies, during which trance-like states are reached with drumming, singing, and a wheeling dance that is said to induce possession by spirits. Revival has its roots in the Native Baptist and Myal movements that lie at the margins of Jamaica's more prominent Anglican and Baptist churches. Baptist churches were early venues for the emergence of what would become known as the Revival faith. Morant Bay rebellion leader Paul Bogle's church in Stony Gut was one such Native Baptist church, where elements of African worship were incorporated into more typical Baptist practice. Today Revival is closely associated with the Pentecostal denomination and practitioners will generally attend one of the established churches in addition to observing Revival practices.

Core to Revival philosophy is the inseparability of the spirit and physical worlds. It is based on this belief that Revivalists can be possessed and influenced by ancestral spirits. Revivalists reinterpreted the Christian theme of the Father, the Son, and the Holy Spirit, placing emphasis on the last, which manifests as the "Messenger" attending services and possessing believers.

Baptist Church

Significant in Jamaica for its role in fomenting abolitionist sentiment and fueling revolt, the Baptist church was first brought to the island by a freed American slave, Reverend George Liele, in 1738. Liele was baptized in Savannah, Georgia, before receiving a preacher's license and being ordained a minister. He brought his ministerial prowess to Jamaica, where he attracted large numbers of converts with his abolitionist sentiment that would prove indispensable in firstly attracting followers and ultimately in bringing about emancipation with the help of the British Baptist Mission, which arrived on the island in 1814. After emancipation the Baptist Church was instrumental in organizing the free villages that allowed the former slaves a new start after leaving the plantation and the church was also important in promoting education among the former slaves. Three of Jamaica's seven national heroes were Baptists, including rebellion leaders Sam Sharpe and Paul Bogle. Today Baptists remain one of Jamaica's strongest religious groups following their separation from the British Baptists in 1842.

Hinduism

Brought to the island by indentured Indians, Hinduism is still practiced but maintains an extremely low profile within tight-knit and economically stable Indian communities. There is a temple on Maxfield Avenue in Kingston that holds regular service on Sundays.

Judaism

The first Jews arrived in Jamaica early in the colonial period during the Spanish inquisition, when they were expelled by King Ferdinand and Queen Isabella and found refuge in Jamaica—in spite of not being officially allowed in the Spanish colonies. Many of these Jews outwardly converted to Catholicism while continuing to practice their own religion in secret. When the British arrived in 1655 to capture the island from the Spanish, they were aided by the Jews, who were subsequently free to practice their religion openly after the conquest. Sephardic Jews of Spanish, Portuguese, and North African descent were the first arrivals, followed in the 1770s by Ashkenazi who left Germany and Eastern Europe.

Ethiopian Orthodox Church

Brought to Jamaica in 1972, the Ethiopian Orthodox Church was the official state church of Ethiopia. Following Haile Selassie's visit to the island in 1966, he instructed the establishment of a church in Kingston in an attempt to legitimize the Rastafarians with a bona fide institution. Many Rastafarians were drawn to the church, even while it does not recognize Selassie as a divine person beyond his own affiliation with the church and the divinity that would convey.

Obeah

Essentially the Jamaican version of Voodoo, Obeah plays an important role in Jamaica, evoking fear even among those who don't believe in it. The mysticism and use of natural concoctions that help bridge the physical and spiritual worlds has similar African roots as the Santeria or Voodoo found in neighboring Cuba and Haiti. While there are few who practice Obeah as priests or worshippers, its casual practice is a widespread phenomenon evidenced by markings and charms strewn about many Jamaican homes.

Rastafari

The name of Ethiopian Emperor Haile Selassie I prior to his coronation was Ras Tafari, Ras meaning Prince, and Tafari Makonnen his given name at birth. When Leonard Howell, a Jamaican follower of Marcus Garvey, saw Ras Tafari Makonnen crowned His Imperial Majesty Emperor Haile Selassie I on November 2, 1930, he viewed the coronation as the fulfillment of biblical prophecy, more so given the emperor's title, King of Kings, Lord of Lords, Conquering Lion of Tribe of Judah. The original prophecy that foretold of a black man rising in the East is attributed to black nationalist and Jamaican national hero Marcus Garvey, who had written a play performed in support of his movement in the United States, from which the now-famous line, "look to the East for the crowning of a black king" was supposedly gleaned. It is interesting to note that Garvey never viewed Selassie as a god or claimed his coronation a fulfillment of prophecy at any point during his turbulent life, but this did not stop Leonard Howell from making the proclamation, which fell upon eager ears among his own followers in rural Jamaica and sparked a global movement that continues to grow today.

Leonard Howell chose an opportune time to proclaim Selassie's divinity. Disillusionment by the masses of blacks descended from slaves was high in the 1920s and 1930s, fueling Jamaica's labor movement and the establishment of the two political parties. The Harlem Renaissance of the 1920s gave blacks in the United States a confidence that was exported to the Caribbean in the form of bold ideas that came to a people that never really forgot Africa. Thanks to the important role Jamaica's Maroons played in preserving African belief systems, and the persistence of Revivalist

© OLIVER HILL

Rastas will tell you ganja is not a drug, and many people, including music mogul Chris Blackwell, are calling for its decriminalization in Jamaica.

and Obeah religious practices even within the many Christian denominations that were established on the island, select segments of the Jamaican population were well primed for the proposition that the divine had manifested in an African king. Nevertheless, these select segments were predominantly poor blacks, essentially social outcasts seen as the dregs of society. Dreadlocks, as the hairstyle became known to the chagrin of many adherents who scorn the fear and criminality the term "dread" implies, predates the Rasta movement and was effectively a natural occurrence for those who neglected to use a comb. With the conversion to the Rastafarian philosophy among many up-and-coming reggae musicians during the 1960s and 1970s, the faith gained traction in Jamaica, and as the island's music became an increasingly important export, Rasta soon became almost synonymous with reggae, and the philosophy spread around the world.

The Rastafarian movement can be traced directly to the recognition of the divinity of Selassie upon his coronation in 1930, but most Rastafarians assert their faith is far more ancient, going back at least to the Nazarenes mentioned in the Old Testament from whence they derive their aversion to razors and scissors, as well as to the eating of flesh. King Selassie has become the head of the movement by default as the most recent manifestation of divinity on earth, despite his own disagreement with being viewed as a god. But the line is traced straight back to the divine theocracy of the Old Testament, Selassie himself said to be the 225th descendant of King Solomon and the Queen of Sheba. Rastafarians essentially claim the Hebrew lineage as their own and have reinterpreted the Old Testament by identifying Africans as the Israelites of modern times, having been enslaved just like the Jews in Babylon. In effect, Rastafarians espouse a natural lifestyle free of the contamination and corruption of modern society. Repatriation to Africa, whether spiritual or physical, forms a central theme.

Along the movement's course of development, charismatic leaders carved out the many "houses," or denominations, that can be found today across the island, including the Nyabinghi, Bobo Ashanti, and the Twelve Tribes of Israel.

The Nyabinghi invoke the warrior spirit of the African empress Iyabinghi; drum ceremonies that last for days around important dates are a central feature.

The Bobo Ashanti, or Bobo Shanti, is a group based at Bobo Hill in Nine Mile just east of Kingston along the coast. The Bobo live a ritualized lifestyle away from society, putting emphasis on the teaching of Marcus Garvey and founder Prince Emmanuel. Themes of self-reliance and self-confidence are central to the Bobo philosophy. The group has gained as converts many contemporary dancehall reggae musicians including Sizzla and Capleton.

Perhaps the most international house of Rastafari is the Twelve Tribes of Israel, founded by the late Vernon Carrington, known by his brethren as Brother Gad. Members of the Twelve Tribes are found across the world with the denomination having crossed social and economic barriers more than other houses, perhaps due to its Christian lean. The Twelve Tribes of Israel embraces Christianity and views Haile Selassie I as representing the spirit of Christ.

Another important force within the Rastafarian movement has been that of Abuna, or Rasta priest Ascento Fox, who has made strong inroads in society by establishing churches in Kingston, London, and New York. These churches are used as a base for maintaining a presence in the community and providing an alternative for convicts in the prison systems, where the group does a lot of work.

Rastafarians in Jamaica and "in foreign" (abroad) are viewed with a combination of respect and fear to this day. Many Rasta colloquialisms have become everyday parlance in Jamaican society as reggae music grew to a global force recognized and appreciated far beyond the Caribbean, with phrases like "one love," "blessed," and "irie" used commonly even by those who don't claim the faith as their own. Use of marijuana, or ganja, has been legitimized to some degree in society at large thanks to the important role it plays for Rastas as a sacrament, even while the ubiquitous herb remains officially prohibited.

LANGUAGE

In Jamaica, free speech is held as one of the foremost tenets of society. Nevertheless, using the wrong language in the wrong place can cause scorn, embarrassment, or even murder, and knowing how to speak under given circumstances defines a Jamaican's identity and the reveals the layers of a highly classist society. Language use ranges from thick patois to the most eloquent of the Queen's English and generally suggests to which tier of society the speaker belongs. Nevertheless, those raised in Jamaica to speak an impeccable form of English will often flip in mid-conversation to outwardly unintelligible patois. The rich flavor of Jamaica's language is the most apparent expression of feverish pride based on a 400-year struggle that spanned the country's anti-slavery, black power, and independence movements. The rise of the island as a cultural hotspot owes not disparagingly to the influence of Indians, Lebanese, Syrians, Jews, and Chinese, and a remaining smattering of the old white plantocracy.

SEXUAL RELATIONSHIPS AND FAMILY LIFE

Uncommitted sexual relationships are commonplace in Jamaica, for both men and women, and particularly among those at the lower end of the economic spectrum. It takes little more than a visit to a nightclub to understand that women and men are quite comfortable flirting and flaunting their sexuality in a lighthearted game played out on a daily basis. The exchange of money is very common in relationships, where a man will often support or "mind" his mistress by giving her money and buying her things. This regular occurrence offers no disincentive for a woman to keep a number of such suitors, just as it relieves the man of any need to keep the fact that he's married with kids a secret from his mistresses.

Prostitution, although it is illegal, is widespread in Jamaica and most conspicuous in tourist areas. In Negril especially, and to a lesser extent in Ocho Rios, prostitution is heavily solicited to tourists. It is quite common for Jamaican men and women to maintain a handful of steady relationships with repeat visitors who live abroad and support their romantic interest by sending regular money wires.

The Arts

MUSICAL HERITAGE

Music has been an integral element of Jamaican society for centuries—from use of song on the plantation to mitigate the torturous work, to funeral rituals that combine Christian and African elements in the traditional nine nights. Most of the instruments used in Jamaica have been borrowed or adapted from either European or African traditions, while some Taino influence surely occurred before their cultural annihilation.

Today music remains as important and central to Jamaican culture as ever. From the beach resorts to the rural hills, sound systems blare out on weekends into the early dawn hours, with a wide variety of genres appreciated on the airwaves.

Jonkunnu

Pronounced "John Canoe," Jonkunnu is a traditional music and skit-like dance performed primarily at Christmas. The Jonkunnu rhythm is played in 2/2 or 4/4 time on the fife, a rattling drum with sticks, bass, and grater. Dancers wear costumes and masks representing characters like Pitchy Patchy, King, Queen,

Horse-head, Cow-head, and Belly Woman that act out skits and dance.

The origin of Jonkunnu is revealed in the word's etymology: Jonkunnu is an adaptation of the Ghanaian words *dzon'ko* (sorcerer) *nu* (man), derived from secret societies found on the African mainland. Among the costumes found in Jonkunnu are pieced-together sacks similar to those seen in the Abakua, a secret society in neighboring Cuba that also uses dance and drumming.

In Jamaica, Jonkunnu became associated with Christmas time likely because it was the only real holiday for the slaves in the whole year, during which they would tour the plantation with their music, dance, and skits, typically with headgear consisting of ox horns. At the height of the British colonial period, plantation owners actively encouraged Jonkunnu and it took on European elements, including satire of the masters, and Morris dance jigs and polka steps. The importance of Jonkunnu declined as it was replaced by the emergence of "set girls" who would dance about to display their beauty and sexual rivalry. Later, following emancipation, nonconformist missionaries suppressed Jonkunnu and the mayor of Kingston banned the Jonkunnu parade in 1841, leading to riots. In the years leading up to Jamaican independence, as the country's cultural identity was being explored, Jonkunnu gained the support of the government, which still sponsors the folk form in annual carnival and Jamaica Cultural Development Commission events.

Kumina

The most distinctly African of Jamaica's musical forms, Kumina was brought to Jamaica after emancipation by indentured laborers from Congo and remains a strong tradition in Portland and St. Thomas. Kumina ceremonies are often held for wakes and burials, as well as for births and anniversaries, and involve drumming and dancing.

Mento

Jamaica's original folk music, mento is a fusion of African and European musical elements played with a variety of instruments that were borrowed from plantation owners and fashioned by the slaves themselves as the genre developed. A variety of instruments have a place in mento, from stick and hand drums to stringed instruments, flutes, and brass. Mento was one of the most important foundations for ska, which gave birth to reggae.

Ska and Rocksteady

The origins of ska date to the early 1950s, when Jamaicans began to catch on to popular music from the United States that reached the island via the radio and U.S. military personnel stationed here following World War II. Popular American tunes were played by mobile disc jockeys, the predecessors of today's sound systems, before being adopted and adapted by Jamaican musicians. The emphasis on the infectious upbeat was carried over from mento and calypso, with the trademark walking baseline sound borrowed from jazz and rhythm and blues. The birth and popularity of ska coincided with an upbeat mood in Jamaica at the time of independence, and the lyrics of many ska classics celebrate the country's separation from England. Spearheaded by pioneering producers like Prince Buster, Duke Reid, and Clement "Sir Coxone" Dodd, the genre became a hit, especially among Jamaica's masses of working-class people. The genre was popularized and taken international by bands like Byron Lee and the Dragonaires, Derrick Morgan, and Desmond Decker.

As ska's popularity began to wane by the late 1960s, the rhythm was slowed down, making way for the syncopated base lines and more sensual tone of rocksteady. A series of hits representative of the genre brought artists like Alton Ellis and Hopeton Lewis to fame with songs like "Girl I've Got a Date" and "Tek it Easy." Made for dancing, rocksteady continued to adapt popular American hits, with rude boy culture and love dominating the lyrics.

CRUCIAL REGGAE

The following selections are not intended as an exhaustive list of reggae releases but are a few essentials for any reggae fan's collection and some of the author's favorites.

In the United States, the best source for reggae albums is Ernie B's, which has an excellent online catalog of full albums and singles (www.ebreggae.com).

ROOTS

Abyssinians	Satta Massagana
Augustus Pablo	King Tubbys Meets Rockers Uptown
Beres Hammond	Can't Stop A Man Ultimate Collection
Black Uhuru	Ironstorm
Bunny Wailer	Blackheart Man
Burning Spear	Marcus Garvey, Live in Paris
Cocoa Tea	One Cup
The Congos	Heart of the Congos
Culture	Two Sevens Clash
Dennis Brown	Revolution, Milk and Honey
Desmond Decker	Israelites
Ernest Ranglin	Below The Baseline
Ethiopians	All the Hits
Freddie McGregor	Bobby Babylon
George Nooks	Tribal War
Gladiators	Dreadlocks, The Time Is Now
Gregory Isaacs	Night Nurse
Half Pint	Half Pint
I Jah Man	Marcus Hero
Israel Vibration	Power of the Trinity
Jimmy Cliff	Wonderful World Beautiful People, The Harder They Come (various artists)
John Holt	Stealin'/Ali Baba
Junior Murvin	Police and Thieves
Ken Boothe	Everthing I Own, Best

	of Ken Boothe
Lee Scratch Perry	Roast Fish Collie Weed & Corn Bread
Leroy Sibbles	It's Not Over
Max Romeo and	War Ina Babylon
Maxi Priest	Best of Me
Melodians	Swing and Dine
Morgan Heritage	Family & Friends, Protect Us Jah
Paragons	Best of
Peter Tosh	Legalize It, Equal Rights
Rita Marley	Who Feels It Knows It
Sugar Minott	Inna Reggae Dancehall
Third World	96° in the Shade
Tony Rebel	If Jah
Toots and the Maytals	Pressure Drop
Wailers	Exodus, Burnin, Natty Dread, Songs of Freedom

ONE DROP

Buju Banton	Till Shiloh
Bushman	Higher Ground
Capleton	More Fire, Still Blazin
Chuck Fenda	The Living Flame
Damian Marley	Half Way Tree, Welcome to Jamrock
Fanton Mojah	Haile H.I.M.
Garnett Silk	Gold
Gentleman	Confidence, Intoxication
Gramps Morgan	Two Sides of My Heart
Gyptian	My Name is Gyptian
I-Wayne	Lava Ground
Jah Cure	Freedom Blues
Jah Mason	Wheat & Tears
Junior Kelly	Love So Nice, Tough Life
Luciano	Messenger
Lutan Fyah	Phantom War
Perfect	Bobbylon Bwoy

Richie Spice	*In the Streets to Africa*	Busy Signal	*Step Out*
Sanchez	*One In A Million*	Lady G	*God Daughter*
Sizzla	*Praise Ye Jah, Da Real Thing*	Lady Saw	*Strip Tease*
		Macka Diamond	*Money-O*
Tanya Stephens	*Gangsta Blues, Rebelution*	Movado	*Gangsta For Life*
		Mr. Vegas	*Heads High, Hot Wuk,*
Turbulence	*Notorious*		*"Galis"* (single)
VC	*By His Deeds* (single)	Ms. Thing	*Miss Jamaica*
Warrior King	*Virtuous Woman*	Red Rat	*Oh No It's Red Rat*
		Sean Paul	*The Trinity*

EARLY DANCEHALL

Shabba Ranks	*As Raw as Ever*	Shaggy	*Mr. Lover Lover*
Yellowman	*King Yellowman*	T.O.K.	*Unknown Language*
		Tanto Metro and Devonte	*Musically Inclined*

CONTEMPORARY DANCEHALL

Beenie Man	*From Kingston to King, Undisputed*	Tony Matterhorn	*"Dutty Whine"* (single)
		Voicemail	*Hey*
Bounty Killer	*Nah No Mercy: The Warlord Scrolls*	Vybz Kartel	*Up 2 Di Time*

Buju Banton perfoms as day breaks at Sumfest.

ANNUAL EVENTS

JANUARY

- **Accompong Maroon Festival:** (Jan. 5 and 6), Accompong, St. Elizabeth

- **Rebel Salute:** (second Sat. in Jan.), Port Kaiser Sports Park, St. Elizabeth

- **Bacchanal J'ouvert:** (launch second Fri. in Jan., each subsequent Fri. till Easter), Mas Camp, Kingston

- **Jamaica Jazz & Blues:** (last week in January) Venues change throughout the week from Kingston to Montego Bay and the Greenwood Stadium, Trelawny

FEBRUARY

- **Bob Marley Birthday Celebrations:** (Feb. 6-12), Bob Marley Museum, Kingston and Nine Mile, St. Ann

- **Miss Jamaica Universe Competiton:** (first week in Feb.), Pulse Entertainment, Kingston

- **Fatta Tyre Festival:** (Feb. 8-11), Ocho Rios, St. Ann, and St. Mary

- **Fi Wi Sinting:** (third Sun. in Feb.), Somerset Falls, Portland

- **Follow Di Arrow:** (last Sat. in Feb.), James Bond Beach, Oracabessa, St. Mary

MARCH

- **Portland All Fest:** (Sun. in mid-March), Somerset Falls, Hope Bay, Portland

- **Spring Orchid Show:** (last weekend in March), Assembly Hall, UWI Mona, Kingston

- **Bacchanal Beach J'ouvert:** (March 22), James Bond Beach, Oracabessa, St. Mary

- **Bacchanal J'ouvert:** (last Fri. of March), Mas Camp, Kingston

- **Jamaica Boys and Girls Championships (Champs):** (late March) annual track and field event, National Stadium, Kingston

APRIL

- **Luau:** (first Sat. in April), Reggae Beach, Tower Isle, St. Mary

- **J'ouvert:** (first or second Sun. in April), Chukka Cove, St. Ann

- **Trelawny Yam Festival:** (mid-April), Albert Town, Trelawny

- **Kite Festival:** (Easter Monday), Seville Heritage Park, St Ann's Bay, St. Ann

- **Claremont Kite Festival:** (Easter Saturday), Claremont, St. Ann

- **Bacchanal Road March:** (Sunday following Easter), Oxford Road, Kingston

- **Jake's Annual Triathlon:** (second weekend in April), Treasure Beach, St. Elizabeth

- **Western Consiousness:** (last Saturday in April), Paradise Park, east of Sav, Westmoreland

- **Strawberry Hill High Stakes Backgammon Tournament:** (one weekend in April) in Irish Town, St. Andrew

MAY

- **Belmont Crab Fest:** (last Sunday in May), Belmont Marina, Belmont, Westmoreland

- **Take Me Away:** (last Sunday in May), National Indoor Arena, Kingston

- **Calabash Literary Festival:** (last weekend in May), Jake's, Treasure Beach, St. Elizabeth

- **Style Week:** (last week in May), Kingston

- **Jamaica Observer Food Awards:** (last Thursday in May), Kingston

JUNE

- **Caribbean Fashion Week:** (second weekend in June), National Stadium, Kingston

- **Ocho Rios Jazz Festival:** (second week in June), Ocho Rios, St. Ann

JULY

- **International Reggae Day:** (July 1), Kingston
- **Portland Jerk Festival:** (first Sun. in July), Folly Oval, Port Antonio, Portland
- **Bling Dawg Summer Jam, Portland:** (mid-July), Somerset Falls, Hope Bay, Portland
- **Reggae Sumfest:** (third week in July), Montego Bay, St. James
- **Breadfruit Festival:** Bath, St. Thomas
- **Emancipation Jubilee:** (July 31), Seville Heritage Park, St Ann's Bay, St. Ann
- **Denbigh Agricultural Show:** (third weekend in July), May Pen, Clarendon
- **Little Ochie Seafood Festival:** (mid-July), Alligator Pond, St. Elizabeth

AUGUST

- **Emancipation Day:** (Aug. 1), island-wide, festivities most pronounced in Negril and Kingston
- **Independence Day:** (Aug. 6), island-wide, festivities most pronounced in Negril and Kingston
- **St. Mary Mi Come From:** (first Sat. in Aug.), St. Mary
- **Cure Fest:** (Aug. 24-26), Kingston and North Coast
- **Fully Loaded:** (third week in Aug.), James Bond Beach, Oracabessa, St. Mary
- **Miss Jamaica World Competition:** (third Sat. in Aug.), Kingston
- **Jamaica Cultural Development Competitions:** (all month), Kingston
- **Caribbean Model Search:** Hilton, Kingston

SEPTEMBER

- **Freshers Fete** (second weekend in Sept.) UWI Mona, Kingston

OCTOBER

- **Best of Jamaica Heritage Festival:** (first week in Oct.) Breezes Rio Bueno, Trelawny
- **Port Royal Seafood Festival:** (second weekend in Oct.), Port Royal, St. Andrew
- **Treasure Beach Hook 'n' Line Canoe Tournament:** (second weekend in Oct.) Treasure Beach, St. Elizabeth
- **Old Harbour Fish & Bammy Festival:** (second Sun. in Oct.), JPSCO Sports Club, Old Harbour, St. Catherine
- **World Championship of Dominoes:** (third weekend in Oct.), Holiday Inn Sunspree, Rose Hall, Montego Bay
- **International Marlin Tournament:** (third Saturday in Oct.), Port Antonio, Portland

NOVEMBER

- **Season of Dance:** (all month), Movements Dance Company, Kingston
- **Kingston Restaurant Week:** (mid-Nov.), Kingston and select restaurants farther afield

DECEMBER

- **Reggae Marathon:** (first Sun. in Dec.), Negril, Westmoreland
- **East Fest:** (Dec. 26), Goodyear Oval, Morant Bay, St. Thomas
- **Pepsi Teen Splash:** (Dec. 26), James Bond Beach, Oracabessa, St. Mary
- **Sting:** (Dec. 26), Jam World, Portmore, St. Catherine

Reggae

Most people know Jamaica by its legendary king, Bob Marley. Marley brought international attention to the island, now popularly known as Jam Rock thanks to the Grammy-winning album of his youngest son Damian, or "Junior Gong." Yet apart from Marley, Jamaica's music has had limited impact beyond the country's expatriate communities in London, Toronto, New York, and Miami. Only recently has dancehall reggae become mainstream internationally, thanks in part to crossover artists like Shaggy and Sean Paul, who took hip-hop charts by storm with his hit, "Gimme the Light." The genre has its roots in ska and rocksteady of the 1950s and 1960s, when radio brought American popular music to Jamaican shores and the country's creative musicians began to adapt American tunes to an indigenous swing.

After a decade of slackness in reggae during the late 1980s and early 1990s, several talented artists have managed to capitalize on a resurgence of conscious music by launching successful careers as "cultural" reggae artists in the one-drop sub-genre, sometimes using original musical tracks, sometimes singing on one of the more popular rhythms of the day or the past. These include I-Wayne, who came out with a huge hit critiquing the prostitution lifestyle with "Can't Satisfy Her" and the conscious tune, "Living in Love" on his 2005 breakout album *Lava Ground*. Richie Spice pays tribute to his ghetto roots with "Youth Dem Cold," an immensely popular hit. Chuck Fenda's "Gash Dem and Light Dem," released in 2005 and banned on the radio in Jamaica, is still reverberating years later. Luciano, Capleton, Sizzla, and Buju Banton top the pack of contemporary conscious reggae artists, while roots artists like Jimmy Cliff, Toots and the Maytals, Burning Spear, Israel Vibration, Third World, and Freddie McGregor continue to perform and produce the occasional album. In 2006, Joseph Hill of the seminal reggae group Culture passed away while on tour in Germany, leaving the masses to mourn back home in Jamaica. Another artist of note is Tanya Stephens, whose eloquent lyrics are being appreciated around the globe following the success of her 2006 *Rebelution* release. More recently, Flames artist Queen Ifrica has taken the conscious reggae world by storm with the release of her album, *Montego Bay*, and Gramps Morgan, of the seminal reggae band Morgan Heritage, attracted critical acclaim with the release of *Two Sides of My Heart Vol. 1*.

Dub, a form of remixed reggae that drops out much of the lyrics, was an offshoot of roots reggae pioneered by King Tubby and others, that led to the dub poetry genre, whose best-known artists include Mutabaruka and Linton Kwesi Johnson. The most accomplished new artist of the dub-poetry genre is DYCR, whose 2005 hit, "Chop Bush," won fans everywhere.

Dancehall

Clearly the most popular genre of music in Jamaica today, dancehall refers to the venue in which it is enjoyed. Dancehall music is born of the street, with themes typically reflecting struggle, defiance, girls, and more girls. Bounty Killer, Assasin, Voicemail, Busy Signal, Movado, Vybz Kartel, Tony Matterhorn, Elephant Man, and Mr. Vegas have led the pack in popularity and influence in modern dancehall, while Beenie Man is still regarded as the "King of Dancehall." Lady G and Macka Diamond are popular female artists of the genre whose clever and sometimes raunchy lyrics have garnered fans, while veteran peer Lady Saw maintains her top ranking as Jamaica's favorite female performer.

FINE ART

The Jamaican art world can be classified broadly into folk artists, schooled artists, and self-taught or intuitive artists. Folk art has been around throughout Jamaica's history, as far back as the Tainos, whose cave paintings can still be seen in a few locations on the island. European and African arrivals brought a new mix, with the planter class often commissioning works from visiting European portrait painters, while enslaved Africans carried on a wide range of traditions from their homeland, which included wood carving, fashioning musical instruments, and creating decorative masks and costumes for traditional celebrations like Jonkunnu. The annual Hosay celebrations, which date to the mid-1800s in Jamaica, as well as Maroon ceremonies, are considered living art. Folk art had a formative influence on Jamaica's intuitive artists.

The century after full emancipation in 1938 saw deep structural changes and growing pains for Jamaica, first as a colony struggling to maintain order and then more tumultuous years leading up to independence. Jamaican art as a concerted discipline arose in the late 1800s, and culminated with the establishment of formal training in 1940. In the early years, sculpture and painting reflected the mood of a country nursing fresh wounds of slavery, with progressive, renegade leaders and indigenous Revival and then Rastafari movements giving substance to the work of self-taught artists.

Edna Manley, wife of Jamaica's first prime minister, Norman Manley, is credited with formally establishing a homegrown Jamaican art scene. An accomplished artist herself, Edna Manley was born in England in 1900 to a Jamaican mother and English father and schooled at English art schools. On arrival in Jamaica, Manley was influenced by Jamaica's early intuitive sculptors like David Miller Sr. and David Miller Jr., Alvin Marriot, and Mallica Reynolds, a revival bishop better known as "Kapo." Edna Manley's 1935 sculpture *Negro Aroused* captured the mood of an era characterized by cultural nationalization, where Afro-centric imagery and the establishment and tribulations of a black working class were often the focus. Manley began teaching formal classes in 1940 at the Junior Center of the Institute of Jamaica, giving the structure necessary for the emergence of a slew of Jamaican painters including Albert Huie, David Pottinger, Ralph Campbell, and Henry Daley. Her school later developed into the Jamaica School of Art and Crafts, which was ultimately absorbed by Edna Manley College. Several other artists, who did not come out of Edna Manley's school, gained prominence in the early period, including Carl Abrahams, Gloria Escofferey, and John Dunkley. Dunkley's works consistently use somber shades and clean lines with dark symbolism reflective of serious times, making them immediately recognizable.

Jamaican fine arts exploded in the fervent post-independence years along with the country's music industry, fueling the expansion of both the National Gallery as well as a slew of commercial galleries, many of which still exist in Kingston today. The post-independence period counts among its well-recognized artists Osmond Watson, Milton George, George Rodney, Alexander Cooper, and David Boxer. Black Nationalism and the exploration of a national identity remained important topics for artists like Omari Ra and Stanford Watson, while many other artists like the ubiquitous Ras Dizzy or Ken Abendana Spencer gained recognition during the period for the sheer abundance of their work, much of which celebrated Jamaica's rural landscape. In the late 1970s, the National Gallery launched an exhibition series called The Intuitive Eye, which brought mainstream recognition to Jamaica's self-taught artists as key contributors to the development of Jamaican art. Some of the artists to gain exposure and wider recognition thanks to The Intuitive Eye series include William "Woody" Joseph, Gason Tabois, Sydney McLaren, Leonard Daley, John "Doc" Williamson, William Rhule, Errol McKenzie, and Allan "Zion" Johnson.

The Institute of Jamaica together with its various divisions continues to bring new exhibition space into use, notably opening a gallery in late 2006 on the top floor of the Natural History building, where a very successful photo exhibit on the 1907 earthquake that ravaged Kingston was staged.

Sports

The sporting arena has provided many achievements that have been etched in the hearts of Jamaicans and become a part of the country's national identity. Jamaica has come to embody the sporting adage of "punching above one's weight," echoed in the local expression, "we likkle but we tallawa" (we're little but we're strong), and this has been shown most emphatically on the sprinting track in recent times, but also historically on the cricket ovals, football (soccer) fields, boxing arenas, and, to add a bit of pizzazz to the diverse accomplishments, with bobsledders and aerial skiers competing in the Winter Olympics.

Athletics

In an island nation with modest sporting infrastructure, track and field events have always been a mainstay in schools and communities with participants in organized events being as young as primary school age. In fact, arguably the biggest and best attended annual sporting event in the island's calendar would be the Boys & Girls Championships held at the National Stadium for the various high schools, known popularly as Champs. It is from this background that the likes of Arthur Wint, Herb McKinley and Donald Quarrie enjoy legendary status for running towards Olympic gold wearing Jamaican colors in the 1940s, '50s and '70s, respectively. Up to the present time, the little island that has come to be called the "sprint factory" has produced the likes of Merlene Ottey, Juliet Cuthbert, Veronica Campbell-Brown, Shelly-ann Fraser, Asafa Powell, and, of course, the inimitable Usain Bolt. Many gold-medalists who have run for other nations were also born and raised in Jamaica, including Linford Christie, Ben Johnson, and Donovan Bailey. No one can deny that Jamaicans have every right to consider themselves the powerhouse team on the short track.

Cricket

A nostalgic remnant of British colonialism, cricket is also a ubiquitous sporting activity on any level field throughout the island. Jamaican cricketers play on the regionally federated West Indies Cricket Team (affectionately called "the Windies"), which joins the other island nations of the Caribbean sharing a British colonial past. Though the fortunes of the Windies have drastically fallen in the past decade, there was a time when they were the unmistakable rulers of the sports. West Indies cricket did not lose a single international Test series for 15 years from the mid-1970s to early '90s. It was a particular joy whenever the beloved Windies would defeat the team from England. Notable Jamaican cricketers include former Windies captains Michael Holding, Jimmy Adams and Courtney Walsh, as well as current captain Chris Gayle.

Soccer

Though lacking in the historical exploits of the cricketers, Jamaican soccer players enjoy every bit of the adoration of the population. The highest achievement of the "Reggae Boyz" undoubtedly came when they qualified for the FIFA World Cup in 1998, which was held in France. Several Jamaicans, or players of Jamaican parentage, have plied their trade for clubs in the English Premier League, including the legendary John Barnes (who actually represented England as a player but was one-time coach of the Jamaican national team), and more recent players such as Deon Burton, Ricardo Gardner, Marlon King and Ricardo Fuller.

Boxing

Champion boxers who have raised the Jamaican flag include Mike McCallum, Trevor Berbick, and Glen Johnson, while noted boxers Lennox Lewis and Frank Bruno, although representing Great Britain, speak fondly of their Jamaican roots.

ESSENTIALS

Getting There and Around

ARRIVING BY AIR

Regular airlines from the United States and Canada into Kingston's **Norman Manley International Airport** include Air Jamaica, Spirit Airlines, JetBlue Airways, Air Canada, American, Delta, and US Airways.

Virgin Atlantic and British Airways offer service from London to Montego Bay and Kingston.

Within the Caribbean, Caribbean Airlines offers service to St. Kitts, Barbados, Trinidad and Tobago, and St. Lucia, while Cayman Airways offers service between Jamaica and Grand Cayman. Copa is the only option direct from Latin America, with service connecting through Panama City from most countries in the region.

Sangster International Airport in Montego Bay is the most popular entry point for visitors to Jamaica.

Most accommodations can provide transportation from either airport, and the more remote hotels and villas often make an extra effort to help provide transportation to guests.

ARRANGING TRANSPORTATION

Public transportation is readily available and very affordable for those who are patient and adventurous. Buses run between major cities

© OLIVER HILL

and towns, and route taxis run between even the smallest villages and their closest transport hubs. The inevitable drawbacks include blaring music, long waits, ripe body odor, and reckless drivers. Car rentals, JUTA charters, and internal flights are expensive, but well worth it under the right circumstances. Nothing compares with the freedom of a rental car, and for two or more people looking to explore the island, it can be reasonably affordable and indispensable. Many visitors are thrown off by the fact that traffic circulates on the left, and if that weren't confusing enough to pose a challenge, abundant, deep potholes and dodging the ubiquitous white route taxis careening around every corner leave little time to enjoy the scenery.

Chartering a car is also very expensive; the standard rate of US$60 for the one-hour trip between Montego Bay and Negril is a good indication of typical charges island-wide. A comfortable and affordable coach service, the Knutsford Express, runs twice daily between Kingston and Montego Bay with one-way fare around US$20. Apart from the multiple internal flights that service the route for at least three times the price (US$70), the Knutsford Express is the best option. Public buses and route taxis are the mass transport option used by most Jamaicans who don't have their own vehicle.

PUBLIC TRANSPORTATION

It can be challenging to get around Jamaica via public transportation, and you will likely arrive at your destination a bit frazzled by the congested route taxis and buses, dangerously fast driving, and the inevitably loud R&B or dancehall blasting from the speakers. It's important to keep reminding yourself that this is all part of Jamaica's charm.

In and around Kingston, the public bus system is quite functional—with bus stops along all the main roads and the fare under US$1. The two hubs in Kingston are the Half Way Tree Transport Centre and a similar transport center south of Coronation Market downtown.

Route Taxis

Arriving with luggage or backpacks to hike up to the road and hail down a route taxi is perfectly feasible in Jamaica, even if it does make the locals laugh at you. Most taxis will want to give you a charter, however, when you are carrying luggage, and others won't stop. This makes getting a licensed taxi a good idea.

Route taxis are typically white Toyota Corolla station wagons with the origin and destination painted in small letters on the side by the front doors. These cars can be flagged down from the side of the road anywhere along their route and when not operating as route taxis will generally offer private charters at greatly inflated rates. Haggling is a must when chartering a car, while routes have fixed rates that are not typically inflated for tourists except in highly touristy areas like Negril or Ocho Rios, or at night, when fares are increased.

Internal Flights

A few airlines operate internal flights around the island that are an affordable option between Kingston and Montego Bay if time is of concern (US$70 one-way). Routes to smaller, less trafficked destinations are significantly higher priced, but for an extended stay with a small group, a charter from Negril to Port Antonio can make sense.

RENTING A CAR

For those who can afford it and have the confidence and experience, a rental car is by far the best way to get around the island for several reasons, the most important being independence. However, rentals are expensive by international standards and you should expect to pay no less than US$60 per day for a compact car, plus insurance and fuel. Options for different car rental agencies are included in the destination chapters.

Visas and Officialdom

American citizens now require a passport to reenter the United States after visiting Jamaica, as part of a campaign to bolster security. Americans and EU citizens do not require a visa to enter Jamaica and can stay for three to six months, although the actual length of stay stamped into your passport will be determined by the customs agent upon entry. For extensions, visit the immigration office in Half Way Tree (25 Constant Spring Rd., tel. 876/906-4402 or 876/906-1304).

EMBASSIES AND CONSULATES

- **Britain** 28 Trafalgar Road, Kingston 10, tel. 876/510-0700, fax 876/511-0737, bhckingston@cwjamaica.com (general), consular.kingston@fco.gov.uk (consular), ukvisas.kingston@fco.gov.uk (visa)

- **Canada** 3 West King's House Road, Kingston 10, tel. 876/926-1500 or 876/926-1507, fax 876/511-3491, kngtn@international.gc.ca

- **Cuba** 9 Trafalgar Road, tel. 876/978-0931 or 876/978-0933, fax 876/978-5372, embacubajam@cwjamaica.com

- **Dominican Republic** 4 Hacienda Way, Norbrook, tel. 876/931-0044, fax 876/925-1057, domeb@cwjamaica.com

- **European Union** Delegation of the European Commission/European Union, 8 Oliver Road, P. O. Box 463, Kingston 8, tel. 876/924-6333 or 876/924-6337, fax 876/924-6339

- **France** 13 Hillcrest Avenue, tel. 876/978-1297, 876/978-4881, or 876/978-4883, fax 876/927-4998 or 876/926-5570, frenchembassy@cwjamaica.com

- **Germany** 10 Waterloo Road, Kingston 10, tel. 876/926-6728 or 876/926-5665, fax 876/929-8282, germanemb@cwjamaica.com

- **Mexico** PCJ Building, 36 Trafalgar Road, tel. 876/926-6891 or 876/926-4242, fax 876/929-7995, embmexj@cwjamaica.com

- **Panama** 1 St. Lucia Avenue, Spanish Court, Suite 26, tel. 876/968-2928, fax 876/960-1618, panaemba@cwjamaica.com

- **Spain** 6th Floor Courtleigh Corporate Centre, 6–8 St. Lucia Avenue, tel. 876/929-5555, fax 876/929-8965, jamespa@cwjamaica.com, emb.kingston@mae.es

- **St. Kitts** 11-A Opal Avenue, Golden Acres, P.O. Box 157, Kingston 7, tel. 876/944-3861, fax 876/945-0105, clrharper@yahoo.com

- **Trinidad and Tobago** 60 Knutsford Boulevard, tel. 876/926-5730, 876/926-5739, or 876/968-0588, fax 876/926-5801, kgnhctt@cwjamaica.com

- **United States** 142 Old Hope Road, tel. 876/702-6000, consularkingst@state.gov (visa/consular), opakgn@state.gov (general)

- **Venezuela** PCJ Building, 36 Trafalgar Road, tel. 876/926-5510 or 876/926-5519, fax 876/926-7442

Accommodations

Jamaica offers a range of accommodation options to suit any budget and taste, from camping for US$10 per night to hole-in-the-wall motels to luxurious villas that go for upwards of US$20,000 per week.

CAMPING
Camping has not been developed to its full potential by any means in Jamaica, perhaps because it is not considered a good way to make money in the tourism industry. Nevertheless, decent camping facilities can be found in the Blue Mountains, and in Portland and St. Mary parishes. It is unlikely you will be bothered for setting up a tent in any remote area of the island and the safety concerns that have likely been a factor in preventing camping from becoming more popular are more hype than well-founded warnings. Nonetheless, women traveling unaccompanied by men should stick to designated camping facilities, at least until your comfort level in the specific region has been gauged. In touristy areas, camping will not be tolerated outside designated areas, and few designated areas exist.

GUESTHOUSES
Guesthouses vary in Jamaica from serious operations that register high occupancy levels throughout the year to more informal homestay arrangements like those available in the Windward Maroon stronghold of Moore Town. Guesthouses are defined by the on-site presence of the owners in either case, as opposed to hotels, which typically have different ownership and management.

HOTELS
Hotels are for the most part locally owned in Jamaica with the exception of a few foreign-owned resorts. Amenities range from shabby to world class at hotels across the island, with breakfast included at many accommodations. Many boutique hotels could be more accurately described as an assortment of cottages or villas.

In Negril and Treasure Beach certain properties have tailored their offerings to entice sophisticated travelers who swear by places like Tensing Pen, The Caves, and Jake's.

ALL-INCLUSIVE RESORTS
The all-inclusive phenomenon has, to the dismay of many, only accelerated in recent years with the arrival of several new chains including Iberostar, Secrets, Excellence Resorts, Fiesta Group, Riu, and Principe. The well-established home-grown variety include Butch Stewart's Sandals and Beaches Resorts, Lee Issa's Couples Resorts, and his cousin John Issa's SuperClubs brands Hedonism and Breezes.

All-inclusive resorts are a great way to cap your spending, even if they tend to be expensive, and if zoning out in a fantasyland with your partner is the goal, there's no better option. It's not a good way to see or get to know Jamaica, however, and you could just as well be on any other island with sun, sea, sand, and booze. While all-inclusive packages can be cut-rate and enticing, there are less expensive ways to see Jamaica without sacrificing first-world comforts. Nevertheless, there is an addictive allure to not worrying about where to eat and how much to tip the bartender. Couples stands out among the crowd as the most inviting all-inclusive chain, with great value for the discriminating vacationer, while the high-end Sandals properties, especially Royal Caribbean, are a cut above the rest in terms of opulent splendor.

Iberostar's three hotels, located next to one another just outside Montego Bay in St. James, offer a range of amenities based on the price point. Sadly the construction at the Iberostar hotels was carried out at such a fast pace that it is conspicuously sloppy, which holds true for several other Spanish hotel group resorts built over the past several years in Jamaica, namely Gran Bahia Principe and Fiesta Group's Palladium properties.

Differentiating Among the All-Inclusive Resorts

Jamaica was a pioneer in the all-inclusive formula, which has since spread the world over. While it takes little planning to spend a week or two at an all-inclusive resort, there are certainly differences among the resorts that are reflected in the quality of service, food, and, of course, the cost. Many smaller accommodation options have started offering all-inclusive packages that make sense if you're not looking to explore the different food options in the area you're visiting, and most villas offer an all-inclusive option as well. At the right place, a package deal can certainly be worth it.

Smaller all-inclusive accommodations include the Island Outpost properties, as well as some of the island's best cottages and villas. Where small properties offer an all-inclusive plan, it is indicated in the text under the accommodation listings in the chapter. All the all-inclusive resorts offer multiple pricing options within each location, which typically start at around US$150 per person per day and go up to US$400 per person for the high-end properties in the winter season.

COUPLES

Easily at the top of the all-inclusive options, Couples Resorts benefits from Lee Issa's hands-on approach and the exquisite taste of his wife Jane, who has been instrumental in ensuring tasteful decor and excellent food. Couples operates under the motto, "Couples who play together stay together," and plenty of options are offered for "play," including nude beaches at the Sans Souci and Couples Tower Isle properties. The other two properties, Couples Swept Away and Couples Negril, are within a few miles of each other, on Long Bay and Bloody Bay, respectively. Lee Issa is the son of Abe Issa, who pioneered Jamaica's tourism industry in the late 1940s and founded the first Couples Resort in 1978.

RIU

If the Spanish retained any bitterness about losing the island to the British in the 17th century, perhaps it is in the 21st century when they will have their revenge, not on the queen, but on the established all-inclusive resorts. Spanish hotel group Riu aims to undercut across the island. Its owners entered the market by setting up hotels beside Sandals properties in Ocho Rios, and virtually taking over the whole of Bloody Bay in Negril. A fourth Riu Resort was built in Montego Bay adjacent to Sandals Royal Caribbean.

Riu offers some of the most competitive all-inclusive rates in Jamaica, attracting principally cost-minded American tourists. Unfortunately the quality of food at Riu Resorts leaves something to be desired in the "fine dining" à la carte restaurants, with long lines in the morning just to reserve a table. The American-style fare in the buffet dining areas is mediocre at best. Rooms at Riu are well appointed and comfortable, though.

SUPERCLUBS

SuperClubs owner John Issa is a cousin of Lee Issa, the owner of Couples Resorts, and perhaps the more enterprising of the two when it comes to taking his hotels around the Caribbean Basin to Cuba, the Dominican Republic, Curaçao, and Brazil. SuperClubs was once a diverse holding with five different hotel brands. In 2009, however, a rebranding did away with Starfish and the two upscale Grand Lido properties, rebranding them to leave three names in the group: Breezes, Hedonism, and Rooms. SuperClubs also holds a stake in the Jamaica Pegasus in Kingston.

At all the SuperClubs properties, there is a strong emphasis on activities, although there is no pressure to partake. From volleyball and trapeze contraptions on the beach, to nude bathing at many of the properties, SuperClubs knows how to excite and entertain.

The Breezes properties are open to everyone, from families to couples to O. J. Simpson, who reportedly stayed in Runaway Bay on a recent trip to Jamaica. Breezes properties can be classified as mid-range in terms of amenities and quality of service, with good buffet-style food as well as better à la carte service for dinners served in the specialty restaurants.

Liquor is mid-range, with no premium brands offered.

The **Hedonism** properties, Hedonism II in Negril and Hedonism III in Runaway Bay, need little explanation. Nevertheless, it's worth mentioning the abundance of nude beaches, mirrored ceilings, private whirlpool tubs, and notoriously naughty guests. Hedonism also engages special-interest groups like swingers (couples who exchange partners for a bit of a change) with theme weeks interspersed throughout the year. It's therefore best to be aware of the planned happenings when booking a stay, lest you should be expected to swap spouses with the next couple.

SUNSET RESORTS

Sunset Resorts has three properties: **Sunset Jamaica Grande** in Ocho Rios, **Sunset Beach** in Montego Bay, and best of all, **Sunset at the Palms,** a boutique property across Norman Manley Boulevard from Bloody Bay in Negril. Sunset Resorts make an attempt to appeal to everybody, with its motto, "Always Jamaican, always for everyone," but the mass-market feel is palpable at the two larger properties. The rooms cover the basics nonetheless, and compared with other all-inclusive resorts the price point is attractive. The quality of food has improved, while expensive booze is not offered at the larger properties. The service is consistently good throughout the chain. The Hendrickson family, which owns Sunset Resorts, also operates the Knutsford Court and the Courtleigh hotels in Kingston. In both Ocho Rios and Montego Bay, Sunset Resorts occupy choice beachfront real estate.

SANDALS AND BEACHES

Owned by Gordon "Butch" Stewart, the Sandals chain attracts couples, and the Beaches resorts cater to families. Newly built or refurbished properties like **Sandals Whitehouse** in Westmoreland and **Sandals Royal Caribbean** in Montego Bay contrast with the more mid-range properties in Mobay, **Sandals Carlyle** and **Sandals Montego Bay.** The quality of each varies with the price point, some serving premium brand liquors and others offering a more basic package. Be sure to know what to expect, as the baseline of quality varies greatly between locations.

Royal Caribbean is easily the best Sandals property, with a small private island just offshore and easy access to Montego Bay and its attractions. Sandals Whitehouse is the newest property, but it is also the most remote, and many guests find themselves too isolated for comfort when it comes to seeing Jamaica beyond the walled compound.

VILLAS

There is no better way to experience Jamaica than by staying in a staffed villa—and with proper planning and a small group, villas can be very affordable. Typically villa employees are long-term and become like family with each other and with guests. The warm interaction you can experience at many of these villas has no parallel, and villas employ some of the best chefs on the island. Most of Jamaica's top-of-the-line villas are concentrated around Montego Bay, Discovery Bay, Ocho Rios, and Port Antonio.

Food

Jamaican food is a reason in itself to visit the island. Home-cooked meals are generally the best so it's worth seeking out an invitation whenever possible. The traditional dishes were developed during the era of slavery and typically include a generous, even overwhelming, serving of starch, and at least a token of meat or seafood protein known historically as "the watchman." In recent years pan-Caribbean fusion has caught on as a new culinary trend, with creative dishes added to the traditional staple dishes.

Ackee is a central ingredient of the national dish, ackee and saltfish. The fruit contains dangerous levels of toxic amino acid hypoglycine until the fruit pods open naturally on the tree, or "dehisce," in horticultural terminology, at which point the yellow fleshy aril surrounding the glossy, black seed is safe to eat. Ackee has the consistency and color of scrambled eggs and is generally prepared with onion and rehydrated saltfish. Dried codfish was the original ingredient, which made an important dietary contribution during slavery when it was shipped from its abundant source off Cape Cod, Massachusetts. Today cod has become scarce and very expensive when available as a result of over-fishing, and the fish is most often imported from Norway or replaced altogether with other saltfish substitutes.

Bammy is derived from the Taino word *guyami,* which was a staple for the Tainos. Bammy is made from cassava (known in many Spanish-speaking countries as *casabe*). In Jamaica, bammy is either steamed or fried and usually eaten as the starch accompaniment to fish.

Bun, or Easter Bun, is a tradition that has become popular enough to last throughout the year, so much so that by Easter there is little novelty left. Bun is typically eaten with yellow cheddar cheese.

Bulla is a heavy biscuit made with flour and molasses.

© OLIVER HILL

Jerk pork and chicken are Jamaican staples.

Callaloo is a spinach-like green often steamed and served for breakfast, either alone as a side dish or sometimes mixed with saltfish.

Curry was brought to Jamaica by indentured Indians and quickly caught on as a popular flavoring for a variety of dishes, most commonly curry goat, but also including curry chicken, conch, shrimp, crab, and lobster. Curry rivals ganja as the most popular contribution from Indian to Jamaican culture.

Dumpling is a round doughy mass that's either boiled or fried, generally to accompany breakfast. When boiled, there is little difference at the center from raw dough. **Spinners** are basically the same thing but rolled between the hands and boiled with conch or corn soup.

Fish tea is similar to mannish water except it is made with boiled fish parts.

Festival is another common starchy accompaniment to fish and jerk meals, consisting basically of fried dough shaped into a slender cylindrical sort of blob.

Food refers to any starchy tubers served to accompany a protein, also known as "ground provisions." The term has its roots in the days of slavery when provision grounds were maintained by slaves to ensure an adequate supply of food.

Jerk is a seasoning that goes back as far as Jamaica's Tainos. The most common jerk dishes are chicken and pork, optimally barbecued using pimento wood which gives the meat a delicious smoky flavor complemented by the spicy seasoning that invariable contains hot scotch bonnet pepper.

Mannish water is a popular broth with supposed aphrodisiac properties made of goat parts not suitable for other dishes (the head, testicles, legs) and cooked with green banana, spinners, and seasoned with pepper and sometimes rum.

Oxtail is a popular dish that requires little explanation.

Provisions are an inexpensive and important part of the Jamaican diet. The most commonly consumed starches include rice, yam,

cassava, breadfruit, dumpling (fried or boiled balls of flour), boiled green banana, or fried plantain.

Rice and peas is the most ubiquitous staple served with any main dish. "Peas" in Jamaica is what the rest of the English-speaking world refers to as beans and usually consist of either kidney beans sparsely distributed among the white rice, or gungo peas cooked with coconut milk and other seasoning.

Saltfish was originally codfish that was shipped from New England in large quantities, with salt used as a preservative. It became a protein staple that helped sustain the slave trade. Despite the widespread use of refrigeration today, saltfish continues to be a sought-after item, even as the stocks of cod have been depleted from the Great Banks of Massachusetts and other salted fish has been substituted in its place.

Fresh seafood is readily available throughout Jamaica, though fish, shrimp, and lobster are typically the most expensive items on any menu. Fish is generally either red snapper or parrot fish prepared steamed with okra, escovitched, or fried. **Escoveitch** fish comes from the Spanish tradition of *escaveche,* with vinegar used in the preparation. In Jamaica, scotch bonnet pepper and vinegar-infused onion is usually served with fried escoveitch fish.

The most common Jamaican lobsters are actually marine crayfish belonging to the family Palinuridae *(Palinurus argus).* Commonly known as the spiny lobster, two species are widely eaten, and, while noticeably different, are every bit as delicious as lobster caught in more northern waters.

Popular breakfast items include **hominy porridge** and **beef liver** in addition to ackee and saltfish, typically eaten on Sundays.

COFFEE

Jamaican coffee is among the most prized in the world, Blue Mountain Coffee being the most coveted variety on the island. The Blue Mountain name is itself a registered trademark, and only a select group of farmers are authorized to market their beans as such by the Coffee Board. Some of the best Blue Mountain Coffee is grown on the Twyman's Old Tavern Estate. The Mavis Bank Coffee Factory sells under the Jablum brand and is also of good quality.

Jamaica's coffee industry dates to the Haitian Revolution, when many farmers in the neighboring island fled to Jamaica out of fear for Haiti's future prospects. The cloud forests of the Blue Mountains were found to provide ideal growing conditions that allow the beans to mature slowly, giving the coffee its unique, full-bodied flavor.

RUM

Jamaica has, since the days of old when pirates stormed from port to port pillaging and plundering their way to riches, been an important consumer of rum. Rum production in Jamaica was an important component of the colonial economy under the British, and Jamaican rum is still highly regarded today. There are two varieties of Jamaican rum, white and aged. Aged rum has a reddish-brown tint and is smoother than white rum. Jamaica's high-end brand is Appleton Estate Jamaica Rum, owned by Wray & Nephew and produced in the parish of St. Elizabeth. Worthy Park Estate in St. Catherine has been attempting to rival Wray & Nephew's White Overproof Rum with its Rum Bar Rum brand in recent years.

It is said that the number of rum bars in Jamaica is matched only by the number of churches, the two classes of institution equally ubiquitous down to the smallest hamlets across the island.

SAUCES AND SPICES

Jamaica has for centuries been a great producer of spices, from pimento, known commonly as allspice, to scotch bonnet peppers and annatto. The island's historical reputation as a spice island gave birth to several successful brands sold the world over, from Pickapeppa Sauce, produced in Shooters Hill, Manchester, to Busha Browne's Jamaican sauces, jellies, chutneys, and condiments made in Kingston, to Walkerswood Jamaican Jerk Seasoning, produced in St. Ann. Belcour Blue Mountain Preserves, produced on a cottage-industry scale in the Blue Mountain foothills, continues this tradition.

Conduct and Customs

ETIQUETTE

Etiquette and manners are taken very seriously in Jamaica, although there's a lot of variation when it comes to individual concern over proper etiquette. Some people are so proper they might as well be the Queen, whereas others lack manners entirely. To a more exaggerated extent than many other places in the world where the same holds true, manners, etiquette, and speech in Jamaica are perceived as directly correlated to upbringing, socioeconomic class, and social status. Therefore it's important to be aware of the impression you make, especially with language. Cussing, for instance, is scorned by many educated Jamaicans, especially devout Christians. Meanwhile, as is the case everywhere, many people couldn't care less about the impression they make and speak quite freely and colorfully.

Photographing people in Jamaica can be touchy and should be done only after asking permission. That said, media professionals are highly respected and if you are walking with a camera, people will often ask you to take their picture regardless of whether they will ever see it. It makes a nice gesture to give people photos of themselves and is a great way to make friends. Photographing people without asking permission will often garner a request for monetary compensation. Asking permission often gets the same response. If the picture is worth it, placate your subject with whatever you think it's worth. Money is rarely turned down.

BEGGING

Begging in Jamaica is an everyday affair, from people voluntarily washing car windows at stoplights in Kingston and Mobay, to friends asking friends for money for this, that, or the other. It's important to balance altruism in providing whatever contribution you are able to offer based on your means with the practicality of perpetuating a dependence on others for monetary gifts. The truth of the matter is, underemployment is severely underreported in Jamaica and unfortunately poverty will not be eradicated anytime soon. Nevertheless, in tourist areas begging can be a nuisance, and it's best to discourage beggars by donating your money instead to a local organization or charity.

TIPPING

Tipping is common practice in Jamaica to a varying degree of formality depending on the venue, from leaving a "smalls" for the man who watched/washed your car while you were at the club, to more serious sums for the staff at your villa. It's important to help those on the receiving end differentiate between a tip and a handout, however, as Jamaica suffers from a lack of productivity in part due to handouts, whether in the form of remittances, political favors, or petty change. At the same time, it's also important to acknowledge the fact that typically those who provide a service are working on a salary and don't see the cash you are paying for the service rendered, no matter how expensive it may be.

Many of the more formal restaurants include a service charge in the bill, in which case any further tip should be discretionary based on the quality of service provided. At inexpensive eateries tipping is rare, while at the more upscale restaurants, it is expected. The amount to leave for a good meal at a mid-range to expensive restaurant follows international standards, or between 10 percent and 20 percent depending on the attention you received.

Most all-inclusive hotels have banned tipping to discourage the soliciting that makes their guests uncomfortable. Where anti-tipping policies are in place, it's best to adhere to them. At European-plan hotels, a US$5–10 tip for the bellhop is a welcome gesture.

Staffed villas usually state that guests are to leave the staff a tip equal to 10 percent of the total rental cost. This consideration should be divided equally amongst the staff who were present during your stay and given to each person individually.

Tipping is also common practice at spas, where a US$20 bill on top of the cost of treatment for the individual who provided the service will be well received.

Tour guides at attractions, even when included in the cost of the tour, greatly appreciate a token tip.

Tips for Travelers

OPPORTUNITIES FOR STUDY AND EMPLOYMENT

The University of the West Indies (UWI) has exchange programs with several regional institutions and alliances with U.S.- and U.K.-based universities.

INTERNATIONAL DEVELOPMENT AND VOLUNTEER OPPORTUNITIES

While work is often the last thing on people's minds on a trip to Jamaica, volunteering can be an immensely rewarding experience. It inevitably puts visitors in direct contact with real working people as opposed to the forced smiles associated with the tourism industry. Several church groups offer volunteer opportunities, while there are also several secular options.

Dream Jamaica (contact programs director Adrea Simmons, programs@dreamjamaica. org, or write to info@dreamjamaica.org, www. dreamjamaica.org), one of Jamaica's best volunteer programs, operates summer programs in Kingston that bring volunteer professionals from abroad and connects high school students in career-driven summer programs with the local business community. Dream Jamaica seeks local professionals who can commit four hours per month to mentoring high school students, and program coordinators and assistance from Jamaica or abroad for full-time volunteer work over the six week program each summer.

Blue Mountain Project Jamaica (contact service learning program coordinator Haley Madson, tel. 920/229-1829, slp@bluemountainproject.org, www.bluemountainproject.org) is a volunteer organization focused on the Hagley Gap community in the Blue Mountains that places visitors to Jamaica in home stays and coordinates volunteer work in any number of socioeconomic development projects it oversees, like establishing health clinics, art camps, adult education, basic infrastructure and ecological projects embodying the group's "Educating and Empowering" tag line. Volunteers pay US$79 per night for a minimum of a week, which covers lodging, meals, and transportation. Longer volunteer stints are rewarded with discounted rates.

The Peace Corps (www.peacecorps.gov) is quite active in Jamaica but generally requires an extensive application process, offering little or no opportunity for spontaneous or temporary volunteer work on the island. Nevertheless Americans looking to make a contribution to sensible development programs have found Jamaica a challenging and rewarding place to work.

ACCESS FOR TRAVELERS WITH DISABILITIES

Travelers with disabilities should not be turned off by the lack of infrastructure on the island to accommodate special needs, but it is important to inquire exhaustively about facilities available. Most of the all-inclusive resorts have special facilities to accommodate wheelchairs and the like, but outside developed tourist areas, a visit will not be without its challenges.

TRAVELING WITH CHILDREN

Despite the stereotypes associated with Jamaica (leaving many who have never visited with the impression of a hedonistic partyland or a gun-slinging Wild West), the island is a fascinating and engaging place for children. Beyond the obvious attraction of its beaches, Jamaica has a wealth of attractions that make learning fun, from jungle and mountain hikes teeming with wildlife to farm tours that offer visitors a sampling of seasonal fruits. The activities available to engage children are endless. What makes the island an especially great destination for families is the love showered on children generally in Jamaica. Nannies are readily available virtually everywhere and can be easily arranged by inquiring at any accommodation, not just at those that tout it as a unique service.

WOMEN TRAVELERS

Jamaica is a raw and aggressive society, with little regard for political correctness and little awareness or respect for what is considered sexual harassment in the United States and Europe. Flirtation is literally a way of life, and women should not be alarmed if they find they are attracting an unusual degree of attention compared with what they are used to back home. On the street, catcalls are common, even when a woman is accompanied by her boyfriend or husband; in nightclubs women are the main attraction and dancing can be very sexual. Both on the street and in the club it's important to keep your wits about you and communicate interest or disinterest as clearly as possible. It is more the exception than the norm for men to persist after women have clearly communicated disinterest.

Jamaica depends overwhelmingly on the tourist dollar, and the authorities generally make an extra effort to ensure visitor safety. Nonetheless, if you are a woman traveling alone, it's best to exercise caution and avoid uncomfortable encounters. Suitors will inevitably offer any and every kind of enticing service. Accept only what you are 100 percent comfortable with and keep in mind that local men might make romantic advances because they're motivated by financial incentives.

GAY AND LESBIAN TRAVELERS

Jamaica is notoriously and outwardly anti-gay. Many Jamaicans will defend their anti-homosexual stance with religious or biological arguments, and many reggae artists use anti-gay lyrics as an easy sell, often instigating violence against gay men (whether metaphorically or literally, it's hard to tell the difference). Some of these artists—like Buju Banton, who had a hit titled "Boom Bye Bye" which suggested killing gay people—have toned down their rhetoric following tour cancellations abroad owing to their promulgated prejudice, while others, like Sizzla, continue unabated, indifferent to the potential for promoters abroad to affect their careers.

Though on the whole Jamaica is an extremely tolerant society, it is best for gay and lesbian travelers not to display their sexual preference publicly as a precautionary measure. Many all-inclusive resorts have in recent years altered their policies to welcome gay travelers, and still other high-end resorts have a noticeably gay lean.

Health and Safety

There are no special vaccinations required to enter Jamaica.

HEAT

Jamaica is a tropical country with temperatures rising well above 38°C in the middle of summer. Sensible precautions should be taken, especially for those not accustomed to being under such hot sun. A wide-brimmed hat is advisable for days at the beach, and a high-SPF sunblock essential. Being in the water exacerbates rather than mitigates the harmful rays, creating a risk for overexposure even while swimmers may be unaware of the sun's effects—until the evening, when it becomes impossible to lay down on a burned back. While most hotels offer air-conditioning, just as many have been constructed with cooling in mind to obviate the need for air-conditioning. Louvered windows with a fresh sea breeze or ceiling fan can be just as soothing as air-conditioning, while not putting such a strain on Jamaica's antiquated and inefficient electrical grid. In the summer months, air-conditioning is a well-appreciated luxury, especially for sleeping. If you are traveling between June and September, consider spending some time in the Blue Mountains, where there's a cool breeze year-round.

SEXUALLY TRANSMITTED DISEASES

Jamaican culture celebrates love, romance, and intimacy. While not everyone is promiscuous, keeping multiple sexual partners is common, and infidelity is generally treated as an inevitable reality by both men and women. The obvious danger in this attitude is reflected in a high incidence of STDs on the island, including underreported figures on AIDS/HIV infections. If you engage in sexual activity while in Jamaica, like anywhere else, condoms are indispensable and the best preventative measure you can take apart from abstinence.

CRIME

Unfortunately, criminal acts are a daily reality for a large number of Jamaicans, from the petty crimes committed by those who find themselves marginalized from the formal economy to high-rolling politicians and drug dons who control the flow of capital, illegal substances, and arms on the island. In sharp contrast to other developing nations with high poverty rates, and perhaps contrary to what one might expect, random armed assault on individuals and muggings in Jamaica are quite rare. The crime that is most ingrained and more or less the order of the day is devious, petty thievery. Almost everybody who has stayed in Jamaica for any length of time has experienced the disappearance of personal effects, whether a wallet or a perfume or a cell phone, one of the most prized items. Stay vigilant and take every possible precaution and you will likely have no problem.

BRIBERY

Officially bribery is illegal, and people offering a bribe to an officer of the law can be arrested and tried in court. It's generally quite obvious when a police officer is seeking a pay-off. Phrases like, "do something for me nuh," "gimme a lunch money," or "buy me a drink" typically get the message across quite effectively. Do not try to bribe police when it is not solicited (or even when it is); there are officers of the law who will take offense and could even try to use this to add to the severity of the alleged offense (or required bribe).

There is a department, the **Office of Professional Responsibility** (OPR) within the Jamaican police force dedicated to routing out corruption. The office is based in Kingston (tel. 876/967-1909, 876/967-4347 or 876/924-9059) but has officers across the island. Be sure to take note of the badge number of the officer in question if you are planning to make a report.

DRUGS

Jamaica has a well-deserved reputation as a marijuana haven. Contrary to what many visitors believe, marijuana is classified by the Jamaican authorities as a drug and is illegal. Practically speaking, however, marijuana use is not criminalized and it's impossible to walk through Half Way Tree in Kingston or Sam Sharpe Square in Mobay without taking a whiff of ganja, as the herb is known locally. Nevertheless, if a police officer sees a tourist smoking, it often provides a good excuse for harassment and threats of imprisonment. These are generally not-so-subtle hints that a pay-off is in order. It's not generally a good policy to entertain bribes, but some tourists caught in this situation have found that US$20 can go a long way in preventing discomfort for all parties involved.

Beyond ganja, Jamaica has also gained a well-deserved reputation as a transshipment point for cocaine originating in Colombia. Crack addiction has been a problem in some coastal communities where cargo has inadvertently washed ashore. While marijuana use is tolerated on the island due to its widespread consumption and a Rastafarian culture that incorporates its use into religious and recreational practices as a sacrament, there is no good reason to use cocaine or any other hard drug in Jamaica, despite offers that will inevitably arise on a walk along Seven-Mile Beach in Negril.

Information and Services

MONEY

Prices throughout the book reflect a conversion to U.S. dollars as the best indication of cost. Most establishments not overwhelmingly trafficked by tourists perform most, if not all, transactions in Jamaican dollars, so U.S. dollar equivalents have been listed. In tourist hubs like Negril, Montego Bay, and Ocho Rios, as well as in establishments catering exclusively to tourists, menus will show prices in U.S. dollars. The U.S. dollar tends to be more stable and is worthwhile as a currency of reference, but most establishments will not respect the official or bank rate and set their exchange rate considerably lower as a means of skimming a bit more off the top. It usually pays to buy Jamaican dollars at a *cambio,* or currency trading house, for everyday transactions. While walking with large amounts of cash is never advisable, carrying enough for a night out does not present a considerable risk. Credit cards, accepted in most well-established businesses, typically incur heavy foreign-exchange fees that will show up on your statement as a percentage of every transaction, and can quickly add up.

The best way to access funds in Jamaica is by using an ATM with your normal NYCE, Maestro, or Cirrus bankcard. "Express kidnappings" (where victims are taken to a cash machine to withdraw the maximum on their accounts) are not especially common in Jamaica, and the little effort involved in canceling a checking account card makes the ease of 24-hour access well worth the risk of getting it lost or stolen. Travelers checks are a good back-up option and can be cashed at most hotels for a small fee. Taking large amounts of cash to Jamaica is not advisable, as it is likely to somehow disappear. Scotiabank offers Jamaican or U.S. currency from many of its ATMs, although foreign bank fees can run as high as 6 percent of the amount withdrawn. U.S. dollars are accepted pretty much anywhere in Jamaica, though restaurants and other small businesses will generally not honor current exchange rates, usually taxing about J$5 per US$1. Currency trading houses, or cambios as they are often called, typically offer a few more Jamaican dollars for each U.S. dollar exchanged, which can make a significant difference when exchanging large amounts of cash.

ELECTRICITY

Jamaica operates on 110V, the same current as in the United States. Power outages are frequent in some areas, but seldom where resorts are based. Most tourism establishments have backup generators.

COMMUNICATIONS AND MEDIA

Telephones

Fixed-line telephony in Jamaica was until recently a monopoly controlled by Cable & Wireless (C&W). As the Internet has become more widely available, voice over Internet protocol (VoIP) telephony has become increasingly important as a means of communicating with the outside world. Netstream Global began offering fixed-rate VoIP service, which compelled C&W to offer their own VoIP product; many households now enjoy this inexpensive way to keep in touch with family members in the United States, Canada, and the United Kingdom. Two new cellular providers, Megafone and MagicPhone, offer similar flat-rate calling abroad.

Cellular phones are more important than fixed lines in Jamaica due to the fact that C&W never installed lines in the more remote areas of the country before cellular obviated the need to. C&W was the first cellular provider but was soon overtaken in popularity by Digicel, which currently offers the best service island-wide in terms of reception. Both C&W and Digicel operate on GSM networks and cell prepaid SIM cards, as well as post-pay contractual service (which is more affordable in the long run, but few people use). A relatively new arrival on the scene is the third cellular carrier, MiPhone, which has established a spotty network with CDMA technology, focuses primarily on business customers who are courted by its strong data service, with coverage strongest in Kingston, Ocho Rios, and Montego Bay. The three cellular providers have roaming arrangements with select carriers in the United States, but the fees charged for roaming make buying a SIM card locally (US$5) the best option no matter your length of stay. Prepaid phone credit is sold in different increments, starting at about US$1.50.

The cellular providers penalize their customers when calling outside their own network, and many Jamaicans will carry both C&W and Digicel phones to avoid out-of-network calling. Similarly, calling landlines from cell phones is more expensive, as is calling cell phones from landlines. In order to dial a cell phone from a fixed line you must dial 1 and then the number.

The 876 country code is never used for calls within the country, and calling land lines from cell phones does not require adding the 1 before the seven-digit number.

Radio

Kingston has some of the best radio stations anywhere, and it's not just reggae you'll find on the airwaves. Reggae in fact developed with the help of a strong tradition in radio, as young musicians were inspired by American music of the 1950s and 1960s, adapting the songs with a distinct Jamaican flavor. Radio stations of note include RJR, Power 106, Irie FM (which has been referred to as the daily soundtrack of the island), Fame FM, and Zip FM. Radio West broadcasts from Montego Bay, while KLAS FM is based in Mandeville and Irie FM in Ocho Rios. Radio Mona (93 FM) broadcasts from the communications department at the University of the West Indies, Mona. Hits 92 FM is a good station in Kingston for a wide range of contemporary music, from dancehall to hip-hop and R&B.

Radio broadcasting in Jamaica dates from World War II, when an American resident, John Grinan, gave his shortwave station to the government to comply with wartime regulations. From wartime programming of one hour weekly, the station quickly expanded to four hours daily, including cultural programming. Radio would have a key impact on the development of Jamaican popular music in the 1940s and 1950s as the only means of dissemination for the new musical styles coming mainly out of the United States.

Television

Jamaica's main television stations are Television Jamaica (TVJ, www.televisionjamaica.com), formerly the Jamaica Broadcast Corporation (JBC); CVM (www.cvmtv.com); Reggae Entertainment Television (RETV); and Jamaica News Network (www.jnnntv.com). In 2006, TVJ acquired both JNN and RETV, consolidating its leadership in both news and entertainment programming on the island.

MAPS AND TOURIST INFORMATION

The map of Jamaica published by Shell (US$4.25) is the best and most easily accessible island-wide road map, with detailed inserts for major towns and cities. The city maps sold by the National Land Agency are less detailed and lack many of the road names included on the Shell map. The Land Agency does have good topographical maps on the other hand, which are sold for a hefty US$7 per sheet. Twenty sheets cover the whole island and the maps can be obtained on CD.

Handy tourism-oriented business brochures are available free of charge at the chamber of commerce offices in Ocho Rios, Montego Bay, and Negril.

WEIGHTS AND MEASURES

One of the most frustrating things in Jamaica is the lack of a consistent convention when it comes to measurements. On the road, where the majority of cars are imported from Japan and odometers read in kilometers, many of the signs are in miles, while the newer ones are in kilometers. The mixed use of metrics in weights and measurements is also a problem complicating life in Jamaica, with chains used commonly when referring to distances, liters used at the gas pump, and pounds used for weight.

TIME

Jamaica is on Greenwich Mean Time minus five hours, which coincides with Eastern Standard Time for half the year (in the northern winter) since no allowance is made for daylight saving time given the nominal difference between day length throughout the year.

RESOURCES

Glossary

Jamaican patois is a creative and ever-evolving English dialect rooted in the mélange of African and European cultures that together make up Jamaica's identity. Irish, English, and Scottish accents are clearly present, as is the influence of Spanish, with many words also of African origin. Patois carries a thick and warm twang that can be very difficult to understand for those unaccustomed to hearing it. After relaxing your ears for a few weeks however, Jamaican talk begins to make perfect sense.

Babylon used by Rastafarians to refer to any evil and oppressive system. Also used to reference the police.

bad man a thug or gangster

bad mind corrupt mentality; or a scheming person, as in, "dem bad mind, eeeh."

bakra a plantation overseer, often used to express resentment toward someone acting in an authoritarian manner

baldhead a person with little or no hair on their head. Used in a derogatory sense by Rastafarians.

bangarang when hell breaks loose

bankra basket (of West African Twi origin)

bashment a party, celebration, any form of excitement

batty backside or derriere

batty man a gay man

beah only; derived from the word "pure," as in "that boy is giving me attitude, beah attitude."

biggup used as a showing of respect; a shout-out, as in, "biggup to all mi fans."

blenda blender; a mixed-up situation rife with confusion

blessed used as a greeting, as in "blessed love!"

blood used as a greeting between close friends considered like family, as in "whaapen blood?"

blouse and skirt an exclamation, similar to "wow," that usually sounds more like "blows and skirt!"

bly a chance or opportunity; to be let off the hook

bomba claat an expletive; sometimes used without the "claat" as a less vulgar exclamation.

boopsy a man or woman who takes their mate's things; a user (as in, "boops you out")

boots condom

brawta an extra something thrown into a deal when the haggling is done

bredda brother. Used in referring to a close friend, as in "yes mi bredda!"

bredren brethren, used when referring to a close friend, as in "mi bredren dem."

brownin a light-skinned black woman

buck up meet or run into someone

buddy male genitalia

bullet bullet! an exclamation, originated by dancehall musician Bounty Killer drawing on the popular obsession with guns; the predecessor to Bounty's musical rival Beenie Man's "Breed It, Breed It!"

bruk broken or broke, meaning not having any money

bruk out to let loose and be free

bulla a heavy biscuit made with flour and molasses

buss bust, as in a career break; to bust out and make it

bway a boy

catty a girl

cha a versatile exclamation that can indicate disgust or astonishment; also written as "cho"

chalice a water pipe used to smoke ganja

clash a battle; often used in the context of a sound clash, where different sound systems or artists face off

chi chi an ant with a big behind that eats wood. Used commonly as a derogatory term for homosexual males, as in a "chi chi man."

collie marijuana

colon man a man who went off in the style of national hero Alexander Clarke, who came back from his sojourns through Latin America with a flashy style of dress, flashy gold watches, and a general cosmopolitan air

copacetic cool, nice, criss

cotch to rest or lean up against; to brace something, as in the tire of a car to keep it from rolling. Also used to say where you stay or spend the night.

craven greedy

crawle pen, likely derived from the corral where animals were kept, such as a hog crawle or turtle crawle

criss nice (crisp)

dads used as a show of respect, as in "yes mi dads"

daughta daughter, a young lady

deh pon doing, as in "mi deh pon mi homework"; or in reference to a place, as in "mi deh pon di road."

dehso there, or over there

deejay a dancehall singer

dege-dege small

don from the Italian usage, a honcho or leader

downpress to suppress

dread a derogatory term used for someone who wears locks. Also used to describe hardship, as in "the time getting dread."

duppy a ghost

eeeeh an inflection used at the end of a phrase to denote a casual query of consensus, as in "she pretty, eeeeh . . . " ("She is pretty, isn't she?")

enz a hang-out spot, as in "mi deh pon di enz."

face to demonstrate interest, as in "di gyal deh a gimme beah face."

flex to profile or show off

forward come back, as in "mi soon forward."

front female genitalia

galiss a womanizer

ginnal a con artist or hustler, either male or female

give bun (burn) to cheat (on your spouse/girlfriend)

grind pelvic gyrations central to popular dance

groundation a Nyabinghi session of drumming that can last for days; usually held around a significant date in the Rasta calendar, e.g., Selassie's birthday or Ethiopian Christmas

gwaan go on, as in "wha gwaan?" ("What's going on?")

gweh go away, as in "gweh nuh, tek weh ya self!"

gyal girl, tends to be construed as somewhat derogatory

haffi have to, must

herb marijuana

higgler a trader in the market. Also referred to small-scale importers who bring goods to sell in Jamaica from Panama.

high-grade top-quality marijuana

hush an expression of sympathy

I and I the Rastafarian substitute for "me," referring to the individual's inseparability from the divine creator

idren used like "bredren"

irie to feel nice or high

Ital natural, derived from "vital"

jacket a child born outside an established relationship that is obviously from a different father

Jah Rastafarian term for the Almighty, derived from Jehovah in the Old Testament

John Crow turkey vulture, buzzard (Cathartes aura)

juk to cut, prick, or knock; a juking stick is used to knock ackee or mangoes off a tree.

junjo a type of mushroom once used as a meat substitute

leggo let go

likkle little, as in "a likkle more" for "see you later."

lime to hang out, also used as a noun for a laid-back gathering or party

macca thorn, as in "di macca juk mi." ("The thorn cut me.")

mampi a heavy-set woman

massive the people, as in "the Kingston massive"

mawga meager, skinny, or thin

medi meditation, as in to "hold a medi"; to ponder or meditate on something

"Mi credit run out." what people will say when they place a phone call before hanging up so that the recipient will have to call back and pay for the call

natty a person who wears dreadlocks in their hair

nuff enough

nyam to eat, as in "mi a nyam some food" ("I'm going to eat"). Also used in the context of getting what you need "mi haffi go a wuk, cause me haffi nyam food." Nyam can be used to mean getting something at any cost, without regard for the consequences.

obeah Jamaican sorcery or voodoo

par hang out with

payola bribe

pickney a child or children

pop-down shabby or disheveled, referring to a place or person

posse a group of friends; a crew that hangs out regularly

pum pum female genitalia

raated an exclamation

ragamuffin a serious dude, used in referring to a true soldier, Rasta thug, or rude boy

ramp to hang out with or move with, as in "mi nah ramp wid dem people!"

ram-up packed with people

ras from Amharic, meaning "prince," as in Ras Tafari

rat-bat a bat; "bat" alone usually refers to a moth.

rass a versatile expletive

reason to converse or hold a discussion; a reasoning

red used in reference to people of a ruddy complexion, typical of the people in St. Elizabeth parish

respect a greeting or acknowledgment of appreciation

riddim rhythm

roots anything referring to something original. Roots reggae is the early form of the music considered the most traditional and authentic style.

roots tonic an herbal and root tonic consumed to uphold general health and stamina

rude boy a bad ass, as popularized by Jimmy Cliff's character in the film *The Harder They Come*

runnings the way things operate, as in "him don't understand di runnings roun' yahso."

selector a disc jockey

sell-off exclamation derived from sold out, as something in high demand. Used in the context of something that's immensely popular, as in "di dance sell-off!"

screw face an expression of bitterness

sensi, sensimilla marijuana, adapted from Spanish *sin semilla*, meaning without seeds

session party

set girls rival groups of female dancers who would sing and dance and compete in matching costumes against other such groups during the colonial period

sistren a sister, the female version of "bredren" (brethren)

skank to dance, especially to ska music

skettle a prostitute

skylark to laze away one's days rather than work or go to school

slack loose; degrading, as in "pure slackness a gwaan."

soon come used to say, "I'll be there in a bit" or "I'll be back in a bit." This is a very loose phrase, however, and could mean in a few minutes, days, or years.

sound system often referred to as simply a "sound"

spliff, skliff a marijuana cigarette or joint

stageshow a musical concert typically featuring performances by many artists

stoosh snooty, uptown

swimp shrimp

tek to take

tekeisha a female name used in jest to refer to a girl who takes a man's money

uno you (plural), "one" in the third-person sense

vex upset, angry

whine wind; gyrating, sexually suggestive pelvic motion at the heart of the bumping and grinding seen in a typical dance club

wood male genitalia

wuk work, as in "wuk mi a wuk." Also used in a sexual sense, as in "you wuk mi out."

wukless worthless

yard home, as in "mi deh pon mi yard" ("I am at home"). Also used in referring to Jamaica.

yahso here, as in "yahso mi deh." ("I am here.")

yuzimiaseh "you see what I'm saying."

Zion the holy land, as referred to by Rastafarians

Suggested Reading

HISTORY

Bryan, Patrick E. *Jamaica: The Aviation Story.* Arawak Publications, 2006. An interesting account of aviation and the role air travel has played in Jamaica's modern history.

Buckley, David. *The Right to be Proud—A Brief Guide to Jamaica Heritage Sites.* This book covers select sites from those listed by the Jamaica National Heritage trust. It is a good coffee-table book with interesting details.

De Lisser, Herbert G. *White Witch of Rosehall.* Humanity Press, 1982. A fantastic account of Annie Palmer, rooted in much historical truth. This is a great quick preparatory read for a visit to Rose Hall Great House near Montego Bay.

Goldman, Vivian. *The Book of Exodus: The Making and Meaning of Bob Marley and the Wailers' Album of the Century.* Three Rivers Press, 2006. An excellent account of the years surrounding Bob Marley's launch into international stardom with great anecdotes and lots of good context on the tumultuous 1970s.

Gottlieb, Karla. *The Mother of Us All: A History of Queen Nanny, Leader of the Windward Jamaican Maroons.* Africa World Press, 2000. The story of Nanny, Jamaica's most prominent Maroon leader and only national heroine.

Pariag, Florence. *East Indians in the Caribbean: An Illustrated History.* An illustrated look at the arrival of East Indians in the Caribbean basin—focused on Jamaica, Trinidad, and Guyana.

Price, Richard. *Maroon Societies: Rebel Slave Communities in the Americas.* The Johns Hopkins University Press, 3rd ed., 1996. An interesting look at the parallel development of Maroon societies in a number of Latin American countries.

Senior, Olive. *An Encyclopedia of Jamaican Heritage.* Twin Guinep Publishers, 2003. An A-to-Z of things, people, and places Jamaican and their historical relevance. An indispensable quick reference for scholars of Jamaica.

LANGUAGE

Adams, L. Emilie. *Understanding Jamaican Patois.* LMH Publishers, new ed., 1991. An introductory guide to Jamaican patois and phrases.

Christie, Pauline. *Language in Jamaica.* Arawak Publications, 2003. An academic examination of the significance of language in Jamaica as it relates to history, class, and prejudice.

Reynolds, Ras Dennis Jabari. *Jabari Authentic Jamaican Dictionary of the Jamic Language, Featuring Patwa and Rasta Iyaric, Pronunciation and Definitions.* Waterbury, CT: Around The Way Books, 2006.

LITERATURE

Banks, Russell. *Rule of the Bone*. Minerva, new ed., 1996. An engaging novel that traces the growth of a somewhat troubled American youth who ends up in Jamaica.

Bennett, Louise. *Anancy and Miss Lou*. Sangster's Book Stores, Ltd., 1979. A must-have among Miss Lou's many printed works. The Anancy stories are folk tales rooted in Jamaica's African heritage. Miss Lou brings them to life in a book appreciated by children and adults alike.

Figueroa, John. *Caribbean Voices: An Anthology of West Indian Poetry: Dreams and Visions*. Evans Bros., 1966. This book is a good representative of Figueroa, one of the grandfathers of Jamaican literature.

Henzell, Perry. *Cane*. 10a Publications, 2003. A novel about a white slave from Barbados who becomes a member of the planter class and owner of the largest plantation in Jamaica. While the book is fiction, it accurately portrays class dynamics and gives an excellent sense of the brutal reality that characterized the colonial period.

Kennaway, Guy. *One People*. Canongate Books, new ed., 2001. A hilarious look at the idiosyncrasy of the Jamaican people.

McKay, Claude. *Selected Poems*. Dover Publications, 1999. Many of McKay's poems are written in colorful dialect ranging in theme from clever critiques on political and economic ills to love poetry.

McKenzie, Earl. *Boy Named Ossie: A Jamaican Childhood*. Heinemann, 1991. Earl McKenzie is one of Jamaica's most respected literary figures who grew up in the years leading up to independence.

Mutabaruka. *The First Poems/The Next Poems*. Paul Issa Publications, 2005. Mutabaruka's definitive collected printed works, spanning many years of his career.

NATURE AND THE ENVIRONMENT

Fincham, Alan. *Jamaica Underground*. University Press of the West Indies, 1998. An essential guide to the sinkholes and caves of Cockpit Country. Diagram and plates of cave layouts complement anecdotal accounts and exploration logs.

Hodges, Margaret. *Guide to the Blue and John Crow Mountains*. Natural History Society of Jamaica. Ian Randle Publishers, second edition 2007. Edited by expert naturalist Margaret Hodges with chapters written by several members of Jamaica's Natural History Society, this book improves on the much-in-demand and out-of-print first edition, *Blue Mountain Guide,* published in 1993. This is an essential guide for travelers looking to get intimately acquainted with Jamaica's most spectacular national park, for which the Jamaica Conservation and Development Trust is seeking UNESCO endorsement. The book is divided into six regions, making it especially practical for devising day-trip excursions.

Iremonger, Susan. *Guide to the Plants of the Blue Mountains of Jamaica*. University Press of the West Indies, 2002. A handy guide to the flora of the Blue Mountains.

Lethbridge, John, Harvey, Guy, and Carter, David. *The Yachtman's Guide to Jamaica* Cruising Guide Publications, 1996.

BIRDING

Downer, Audrey and Robert Sutton. *Birds of Jamaica: A Photographic Field Guide*. Cambridge University Press, 1990. A good guide to Jamaica's birds.

Raffaele, Herbert, et al. *Birds of the West Indies*. Princeton University Press, 2003. This is the best bird guide for the Caribbean basin, with excellent plates.

FOOD

Burke, Virginia. *Eat Caribbean Cook Book.* Simon & Schuster, Ltd., export ed., 2005. Easily among the best Caribbean cookbooks on the market. Burke makes essential recipes easy to put together with widely available ingredients.

Quinn, Lucinda Scala. *Jamaican Cooking.* Wiley, rev ed., 2006. A selective cookbook with some excellent recipes for those seasoned in Jamaican cooking.

SPIRITUAL

Barrett, Leonard E. *The Rastafarians.* Beacon Press, 20th anniversary ed., 1997. A comprehensive study of the Rastafarian movement.

Bender, Wolfgang. *Rastafarian Art.* Ian Randle Publishers, 2004. Bender covers the contribution of Rastafarian philosophy to Jamaican contemporary art.

Bethel, Clement E. *Junkanoo.* Macmillan Caribbean, 1992. An in-depth look at Jonkunnu, a fascinating dance and music style closely associated with Jamaica's folk religions and performed for a few celebrations throughout the year, notably at Christmastime.

Chevannes, Barry. *Rastafari: Roots and Ideology.* University of West Indies Press, 1995. One of the best assessments in print of the Rastafarian movement, Chevannes is the top academic authority in Jamaica on the faith, having studied and lived amongst Rastas throughout his career.

Hausman, Gerald. *The Kebra Negast: The Lost Bible of Rastafarian Wisdom and Faith from Ethiopia and Jamaica.* St. Martin's Press, 1st ed., 1997. Considered the Rasta bible by many adherents, this is a must-have resource book for those with deep interest in the faith.

ESSENTIAL PERIODICALS

The Jamaican Magazine is an excellent periodical published by the University of Technology. Each edition highlights a different parish.

Jamaican Journal, published by the Institute of Jamaica (IOJ), is a great, easy-to-read academic publication highlighting different aspects of Jamaican culture and heritage.

Internet Resources

TRAVEL INFORMATION
Jamaica Tourist Board
www.visitjamaica.com
This is the official website of the Jamaica Tourist Board. It is smartly designed and easy to navigate. Unfortunately many of the features were left undeveloped and for practical resources beyond the tourist board offices, the site falls short.

Negril.com
www.negril.com
One of the island's most active bulletin board–style sites, with members both locally and abroad. Negril.com advertises for many tourism establishments in Negril with more and more coverage extending to other areas of Jamaica.

NEWSPAPERS
The Jamaica Gleaner
www.jamaica-gleaner.com
Jamaica's most widely circulated daily.

The Jamaica Observer
www.jamaicaobserver.com
The island's number two newspaper.

The Star
www.jamaica-star.com
Jamaica's entertainment daily is chock full of gossip and trash talk, making for good entertainment and little news.

FLIGHT INFORMATION

Norman Manley International Airport
www.nmia.aero

Norman Manley is the capital's international airport. The site has useful information, including airlines and flight schedules.

Sangster International Airport
www.mbjairport.com

Montego Bay's international airport receives the majority of the island's tourists. The airport's website provides complete travel information from arrivals and departures to shopping, and food options.

ECOTOURISM

The Jamaica Caves Organization (JCO)
www.jamaicancaves.org

The Jamaica Caves Organization is the most active scientific exploratory organization on the western side of the island, researching the caves and sinkholes of Cockpit Country on a continual basis. The JCO sells maps and offers guide services.

Jamaica Conservation and Development Trust (JCDT)
www.greenjamaica.org

The JCDT has charge of the Blue and John Crow Mountain National Park and is the go-to organization for matters related to hiking and staying at the park.

Southern Trelawny Environmental Agency (STEA)
www.stea.net

A regularly updated site dedicated to coverage of the activities of the STEA, which include the annual Yam Festival. The site also contains resources for exploring the Trelawny interior and contracting guide services.

Jamaiaca Scuba
www.jamaicascuba.com

A well-designed and useful site with some of the island's best dive sights highlighted. The site also provides an intro to Jamaica's marine life.

MUSIC AND ENTERTAINMENT

Irie FM
www.iriefm.net

Jamaica's most popular reggae station, Irie broadcasts on 107.5 and 107.9 FM as well as over the Internet.

What's On Jamaica
www.whatsonjamaica.com

A current-events website with island-wide listings.

Party Inc
www.partyinc.com

A site dedicated to Jamaican-style bashments around the globe, with listings and streaming mixes from top selectors.

Whata-Gwan
www.whata-gwan.com

A site dedicated to promoting Jamaican parties in every part of the globe, but with a strong lean toward the Kingston and Miami areas.

Whaddat
www.whaddat.com

A decidedly Jamaica-focused party site covering events from "uptown to the garrison." The site is a good resource for staying abreast of the latest talk and cultural trends.

Muzik Media
www.muzikmedia.com

A New Jersey–based website that runs the top 10 music videos of the week as well as archiving and contemporary classic videos.

Jammin Reggae Archives
www.niceup.com

A U.S.-based site with information on reggae artists and upcoming performances.

Bob Marley
www.bobmarley.com

The official Bob Marley family website, with bios on individual family members, merchandise, and news. Most of the Marley progeny have their own sites as well.

Reggae Entertainment
www.reggaeentertainment.com
A site dedicated to the reggae industry with entertainment news and downloads.

Ernie B's
www.ebreggae.com
One of the best catalogs available for purchasing reggae on vinyl, both classics and new releases. Based in California.

ART AND CULTURE
Afflicted Yard
www.afflictedyard.com
A counterculture photography site that reflects the pulse of popular Jamaican culture with enticing visuals and selected writing.

Index

List of Maps

Acknowledgments

This book would not have been possible without the support of my parents, William Blaine Hill and Maria del Pilar Abaurrea, who kindled from day one my desire to see more, learn more, and travel the world. They taught me the virtue of understanding the way other people live beyond our borders, and the joy of indulging in new cultures, hearing fresh music, and tasting new foods. Most of all, my parents taught me to make every encounter a positive interaction. Of course my brother, Antonio, and sister, Paola, helped refine this doctrine and have also been supportive in my unorthodox ventures.

I am grateful to count many of the following people not merely as professional and respectable business associates, but also as friends in a common cause. These individuals greatly facilitated the logistics behind the fifth edition of *Moon Jamaica* and generously gave their time and assistance. Chief among those who deserve recognition are Daniel Barrett, who first introduced me to the runnings of his homeland; Mary Francis and Sheldon Davis, who have been real "fam" from the beginning; Gary Codner, who opened his home and helped with the links; Lance Watson, who is both *yahso* and *dehso* anytime you need him; Robin and Mike Lumsden, who shared their piece of paradise and vision; Carolyn Barrett, who knows where and how to enjoy Jamaica better than anyone; Rebecca Wiersma, my indispensable ally on the South Coast; Jason and Laura Henzell, who were always enthusiastic aides; Helmut and Charmaine Steiner, who made me feel like visiting royalty in Port Antonio; Yvonne Blakey, who has the best links in Portland; Mary Phillips, who wrote the book on how to entertain with class; Susan McManus, whose "God Bless!" at the end of our phone conversations always smoothed over the anguish I caused her; Andria Mitzakos and Darlene Salzer for perfectly coordinating my stays with their clients; Lee and Jane Issa, who bring the highest level of professionalism and taste to Jamaica's tourism industry; Robert Anderson, who is doing things right at Tiamo and showed me one of the area's best kept secrets; Lorna Robinson at the JTB; Donahue Jarrett for making me feel presidential at the Altamont; Angie Dickson, who has revitalized Green Castle Estate magnificently; and Blaise and Tammy Hart, some of the best people in the world; Charlotte and Cary Wallace, who embellished my time in Negril; Stephanie Chin, who knows how to project the family vibe from her perch over Mobay; Tony, whose Time N Place is a much needed bastion of another; and Michelle Rollins, whose vision and perseverance continue to transform Rose Hall.

For their assistance and generous hospitality, I would also like to extend my gratitude to Jenny Wood, Linda Smith, Clinese Prendergast, Charles Burberry, Cortina Byles, David Rosenstein, David Lowe, Frank Lawrence, Gaia, Jennifer Lyn, Jeremy Jones, John Issa, Sonia Gray-Clarke, Louis Grant, Michael Fox, Barry Chevannes, Wayne Modest, David Boxer, Bernard Jankee, Andrea Davis, Michael Gleason, Carol Reid, Jonathan and Paula Surtees, Klaus Peter, Michael Hoe-Knudsen, Michelle Hussey, Nancy Mclean, Nicole Henry, Peter Frazier, Richard Bourke, Rochelle Forbes, Burchell Henry, Sharon Powell, Sherryl White-McDowell, Sigi Fahmi, Ted Ruddock, Otis and Valerie Deans, Helga Stockart, and many more who have not been mentioned.

Lastly, but certainly not least, I need to acknowledge my employers, Avalon Travel and Mergermarket. My editor, Elizabeth Hollis Hansen, and the entire team at Avalon were critical in putting the book together to the highest standards in a timely fashion. Mergermarket, and especially Charlie Welsh, was also instrumental in seeing the project to completion with his constant demand to "take the spliff out my mouth, come out from the Jacuzzi, and get back to work."

www.moon.com

DESTINATIONS | ACTIVITIES | BLOGS | MAPS | BOOKS

MOON.COM is ready to help plan your next trip! Filled with fresh trip ideas and strategies, author interviews, informative travel blogs, a detailed map library, and descriptions of all the Moon guidebooks, Moon.com is all you need to get out and explore the world—or even places in your own backyard. While at Moon.com, sign up for our monthly e-newsletter for updates on new releases, travel tips, and expert advice from our on-the-go Moon authors. As always, when you travel with Moon, expect an experience that is uncommon and truly unique.

MOON IS ON FACEBOOK—BECOME A FAN!
JOIN THE MOON PHOTO GROUP ON FLICKR

MAP SYMBOLS

▨ Expressway	◖ Highlight	✗ Airfield	⚓ Golf Course
▨ Primary Road	○ City/Town	✈ Airport	🅿 Parking Area
▨ Secondary Road	◉ State Capital	▲ Mountain	⛰ Archaeological Site
▨ Unpaved Road	⊛ National Capital	✚ Unique Natural Feature	⛪ Church
------- Trail	★ Point of Interest		⛽ Gas Station
·········· Ferry	• Accommodation	🌿 Waterfall	◌ Glacier
▬▬▬ Railroad	▼ Restaurant/Bar	▲ Park	Mangrove
▨ Pedestrian Walkway	■ Other Location	⬛ Trailhead	Reef
▨ Stairs	△ Campground	⛷ Skiing Area	Swamp

CONVERSION TABLES

°C = (°F - 32) / 1.8
°F = (°C x 1.8) + 32
1 inch = 2.54 centimeters (cm)
1 foot = 0.304 meters (m)
1 yard = 0.914 meters
1 mile = 1.6093 kilometers (km)
1 km = 0.6214 miles
1 fathom = 1.8288 m
1 chain = 20.1168 m
1 furlong = 201.168 m
1 acre = 0.4047 hectares
1 sq km = 100 hectares
1 sq mile = 2.59 square km
1 ounce = 28.35 grams
1 pound = 0.4536 kilograms
1 short ton = 0.90718 metric ton
1 short ton = 2,000 pounds
1 long ton = 1.016 metric tons
1 long ton = 2,240 pounds
1 metric ton = 1,000 kilograms
1 quart = 0.94635 liters
1 US gallon = 3.7854 liters
1 Imperial gallon = 4.5459 liters
1 nautical mile = 1.852 km

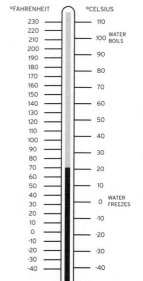

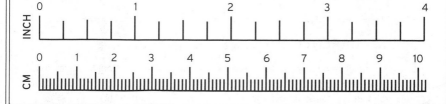

MOON JAMAICA
Avalon Travel
a member of the Perseus Books Group
1700 Fourth Street
Berkeley, CA 94710, USA
www.moon.com

Editor: Elizabeth Hollis Hansen
Series Manager: Kathryn Ettinger
Copy Editor: Valerie Sellers Blanton
Graphics Coordinator: Tabitha Lahr
Production Coordinator: Tabitha Lahr
Cover Designer: Tabitha Lahr
Map Editor: Brice Ticen
Cartographers: Chris Markiewicz, Kat Bennett
  and Allison Rawley
Indexer: Rachel Kuhn

ISBN-13: 978-1-59880-586-4
ISSN: 1088-0941

Printing History
1st Edition – 1991
6th Edition – September 2010
5 4 3 2 1

Front cover photo: Jamaican pro surfer Icah Wilmot
of Jamnesia Surf Club © Brian Nejedly/Brian Design
Photography
Title page: sunset in Bluefields Bay © Oliver Hill
Interior color section photos: © Oliver Hill
Page 4, Delroy Course bathes his horses on San
San Beach; Page 5, Hope Botanical Gardens; Page
6 icon photo, The Caves hotel in Negril; Page 7 top
left, Xaymaca Dance Theatre in Kingston; Page 7 top
right, the massage hut at Rockhouse; Page 7 bottom
left, gazebo overlooking waves at Moon Dance Cliffs
in Negril; Page 7 bottom right, a doctor bird at Green
Castle Estate in St. Mary

Printed in Canada by Friesens

KEEPING CURRENT

If you have a favorite gem you'd like to see included in the next edition, or see anything
that needs updating, clarification, or correction, please drop us a line. Send your
comments via email to feedback@moon.com, or use the address above.

FEB 1 6 2011